LEGAL OPI
CONCERNING
THE CHURCH OF ENGLAND

Ninth edition 2020

CHURCH HOUSE
PUBLISHING

Church House Publishing
Church House
Great Smith Street
London SW1P 3AZ

www.chpublishing.co.uk

ISBN 978–0–7151–1146–8

Eighth edition published 2007 by Church House Publishing

This ninth edition (comprising Recent Opinions and the full text of the eighth edition) published 2020

Typeset in 9pt Times
by RefineCatch Limited, Bungay, Suffolk
Printed and bound by CPI Group (UK) Ltd

Contents

Recent Opinions

Contents

Part 1:   Benefice and Patronage

Part 2:   Clergy

Part 3:   Parish

Part 4: Conventional Districts

Part 5:   Churchwardens

Part 6:   Parochial Church Council

Part 7:   Church Building

Part 8: Churchyards and Burial Grounds

Part 9: Burial and Cremation

Contents

Part 10: Diocese

Part 11: Faculties

Part 12: Cathedrals

Part 13: Worship

Part 14: Baptism

Contents

Preface

The Legal Advisory Commission of the General Synod, like its predecessor the Legal Board of the Church Assembly, exists to give advice on legal matters of general interest to the Church which are referred to it by the General Synod or one of its Houses, by any of the National Church Institutions, by the Church's legal officers (diocesan registrars and chancellors) and by other officers such as archdeacons and diocesan secretaries. It cannot advise on contentious matters, for that would risk turning it into a standing all-purpose legal tribunal.

Over the years it has been served by many distinguished ecclesiastical lawyers and its Opinions have established themselves as authoritative. This must in part be due to the care which the Commission takes in their preparation. A member, or more usually a small group of members, of the Commission prepares a draft, and this is then discussed by the full Commission, sometimes at a series of meetings. It is only 'starred' for publication when the text commands the general assent of the Commission.

The Seventh Edition of the collected Opinions appeared in 1994, with a Supplement some three years later. The appearance of this, the Eighth, Edition has been long awaited and its preparation proved onerous. It was not sufficient to substitute more recent Opinions for those which had been overtaken by events. The seemingly inevitable growth in the complexity of ecclesiastical law meant that many Opinions, while remaining substantially correct, needed revision on points of detail. The necessary work was initially undertaken by a sub-committee consisting of Michael Goodman, Timothy Briden and John Rees. I undertook, with the assistance of Ingrid Slaughter formerly Secretary to the Commission, further revisions in the period leading up to the submission of the final text for publication, but these changes were limited to modest updating and to matters of style. An indication is given of the dates of revisions.

David McClean
Chairman of the Commission 1996–2006

Legal Advisory Commission 2006–2011

Ex officio
The Dean of the Arches and Auditor (The Rt Worshipful Dr Sheila
  Cameron QC)
The Vicar-General of Canterbury (Chancellor Timothy Briden)
The Vicar-General of York (His Honour Judge Thomas Coningsby QC)
The Provincial Registrar of Canterbury (Canon John Rees)
The Provincial Registrar of York (Mr Lionel Lennox)
The Chief Legal Adviser to the Archbishops' Council (Mr Stephen Slack)
Standing Counsel to the General Synod (Sir Anthony Hammond QC)
The Official Solicitor to the Church Commissioners (Miss Sue Jones)

Diocesan chancellors
Chancellor Rupert Bursell
Chancellor Charles George
Chancellor Mark Hill
Chancellor David McClean
Chancellor David Turner

Diocesan registrars
Mr Peter Beesley (Ely)
Mr Owen Carew-Jones (Rochester)
Mrs Jane Lowdon (Newcastle)

Clergy
The Bishop of Guildford (The Rt Reverend Christopher Hill)
The Venerable Trevor Jones (Archdeacon of Hertford)
The Venerable Richard Seed (Archdeacon of York)
The Very Reverend Nicholas Coulton (Sub-Dean of Christ Church,
  Oxford)
The Reverend Canon David Felix (Chester)

Lay appointments
Mr Ian Garden
Ms Jacqueline Humphreys
The Rt Honourable Sir John Mummery
Mr Ted Nugee QC
Mrs Lesley Farrall (Diocesan Secretary of Bristol)

Abbreviations

APCM	annual parochial church meeting
ASB	Alternative Service Book 1980
BCP	Book of Common Prayer 1662
CCC	Council for the Care of Churches
CCEJM	Care of Churches and Ecclesiastical Jurisdiction Measure 1991
CPWM	Care of Places of Worship Measure
CRR	Church Representation Rules
DAC	diocesan advisory committee
DBF	diocesan board of finance
MA	Marriage Act 1949
MPA	The Music Publishers' Association
NSM	non-stipendiary minister
PCC	parochial church council

Table of Cases

Table of Statutes and Measures

Table of Canons

Table of Rules

Recent Opinions

The maintenance of monuments in closed churchyards

Introduction

1. The purpose of this Opinion is to provide advice upon the extent to which a local authority, taking over responsibility for the maintenance of a churchyard under Section 215 of the Local Government Act 1972, thereby becomes responsible for the safety of monuments within the churchyard.

2. Section 215 of the 1972 Act applies specifically to churchyards closed by an Order in Council. The procedure for making such Orders is contained in Section 1 of the Burial Act 1853. A churchyard may have been entirely disused for many years but it would not on that account be described as a closed churchyard, nor would a churchyard where all further burials have been prohibited by a local Act of Parliament. Where the requisite Order in Council has been made, section 215(1) provides that,

> '. . . the parochial church council shall maintain [the churchyard] by keeping it in decent order and its walls and fences in good repair.'

A PCC which is liable to maintain a closed churchyard under subsection (1) may however serve upon the appropriate local authority a request under subsection (2)

> '. . . to take over the maintenance of the churchyard'

in which event, three months after service of the request

> '. . . the maintenance of the churchyard shall be taken over by the authority on whom the request is served . . .'

Subsections (2) and (3) contain additional provisions, irrelevant for present purposes, identifying the organ of local government which is actually to assume the maintenance responsibility.

Relevant powers and duties of the parochial church council

3. The PCC is a body corporate which is entirely the creature of legislation. Its powers are derived exclusively from statute, measure or canon. They do not extend to ownership of the churchyard, the legal interest in which is vested elsewhere. Specific powers and duties in relation to the churchyard (as outlined in the following paragraphs) have however devolved upon the PCC.

4. Before the passing of the Parochial Church Councils (Powers) Measure 1921, responsibility for the maintenance of churchyards was borne by the

churchwardens pursuant to Canon 85 of 1603. In the case of closed churchyards, Section 18 of the Burial Act 1855 (now repealed, with a saving in respect of the City of London) enabled the churchwardens to recover the resultant expenses from the poor rate.

5. As from 21 July 1921, by the successive operation of Section 4(1)(ii)(c) of the Parochial Church Councils (Powers) Measure 1921 and Section 4(1) (ii)(c) of the Parochial Church Councils (Powers) Measure 1956, there were transferred to the PCC all the powers and duties of churchwardens in relation to open or closed churchyards.

6. Canon 85 of 1603, in a modernised form, became Canon F 13 of the modern Canons of the Church of England:

1. The churches and chapels in every parish shall be decently kept and from time to time, as occasion may require, shall be well and sufficiently repaired and all things therein shall be maintained in such an orderly and decent fashion as best becomes the House of God.

2. The like care shall be taken that the churchyards be duly fenced, and that the said fences be maintained at the charge of those to whom by law or custom the liability belongs, and that the churchyards be kept in such an orderly and decent manner as becomes consecrated ground.

3. . . . .

Canon F 14 reflected the transfer of the churchwardens' responsibilities to the PCC by providing that:

'The things appertaining to churches and chapels, and the obligations relating thereto, and to the care and repair of churches, chapels and churchyards referred to in the foregoing Canons shall, so far as the law may from time to time require, be provided and performed in the case of parochial churches and chapels by and at the charge of the parochial church council.'

7. The drafting of Section 215(1) of the Local Government Act 1972 is consistent with Canon F 13.2, Canon F 14, and Section 4(1)(ii)(c) of the Parochial Church Councils (Powers) Measure 1956. Whether a churchyard is open for burials, or closed by Order in Council, precisely the same duty to maintain it falls upon the PCC concerned until the obligation to maintain has been taken over pursuant to Section 215(2) of the Act. The content of the duty is expressed throughout the legislation in almost identical terms,

there being no material difference between a churchyard being kept 'in decent order' and 'in such an orderly and decent manner as becomes consecrated ground'.

The duty to maintain monuments

8. Churchyard monuments, whether ancient tombs or modern memorials, are not annexed to the freehold but remain private property. The legal complexities concerning the devolution of title to monuments are identified in the Commission's Opinion, *Churchyards: Ownership of Monuments and Trees*. The owner of the monument is the party primarily liable for maintaining it in a safe condition, and may have to satisfy a claim for damages if injury is caused by a negligent failure to keep it in good order.

9. In the case of a churchyard maintainable by the PCC under Canon F 13.2 or Section 215(1) of the Local Government Act, a liability for personal injury (secondary to that of the owner) may arise by reason of the failure of the PCC to exercise its powers in relation to a dangerous monument. These powers are also identified in the Commission's Opinion, *Churchyards: Ownership of Monuments and Trees*. They are ancillary to the duty to keep the churchyard 'in decent order' or 'in an orderly and decent manner', a concept which extends beyond its cosmetic appearance. Safety to the public is one necessary aspect of what, in the context of a place of burial, amounts to 'decency'. Thus in *The Vicar and Churchwardens of St Botolph Without Aldgate v Parishioners of the Same* [1892] P 173, the Chancellor of London held that the filling and levelling of a dilapidated vault came within the duty to keep the churchyard in a sanitary and decent order.

10. The existence of the general duty to maintain the churchyard, coupled with the power (under faculty) to make safe any dangerous monument there, constitute a sufficient degree of control for the PCC to be liable as an occupier under legislation considered at paragraph 14 of this Opinion.

Consequences when maintenance is taken over by a local authority

11. The drafting of Section 215 of the Local Government Act 1972 demonstrates that, after a request has been made for the appropriate authority to maintain a churchyard, the responsibility of the PCC will in its entirety pass to the authority leaving the PCC without any residual maintenance obligation in respect of that churchyard. So much is clear from the phrase 'the maintenance of the churchyard shall be taken over' which appears in subsection (2). The words 'taken over' themselves signify a complete transfer from one entity to another. Their meaning is reinforced by the unqualified reference to 'the maintenance of the churchyard', which relates back to the expression 'the parochial church council shall maintain'

in subsection (1). The remaining words in subsection (1), which appear after those just quoted, only serve to define the content of the statutory duty to maintain, and do not create separate self-standing duties with regard to walls or fences.

12. Where notice is properly served under Section 215, it is not open for the local authority to agree with the PCC to limit its maintenance liability or to confine it to particular areas in the churchyard whilst including liability in respect of others. The recent decision in *Lydbrook Parochial Church Council v Forest of Dean District* Council (heard in Gloucester County Court before District Judge Thomas in December 2003 and noted at (2004) 7 Ecc LJ 495), reinforces the legal position that the duty is one of substantive maintenance and not merely management of decline (see generally *R v Burial Board of Bishopwearmouth* (1879) 5 QBD 67 at 68) nor is it conditional on adequate funds being available.

13. By Section 215(2) the PCC is therefore wholly divested of its duties under subsection (1), which are also co-extensive with the duties imposed by Canons F 13.2 and F 14. The canonical obligation does not survive the transfer of function under Section 215(2) because the canon only operates 'so far as the law may from time to time require'. Thus the canon on its own terms is supplanted by the local authority's legal duty under the Act. It follows that there is nothing of a mandatory nature left for the PCC to do by way of churchyard maintenance.

14. The legal responsibility for injuries arising from the state of land, or property annexed to land, is predicated not upon ownership but occupation. The duty of care is articulated in two Occupiers' Liability Acts, that of 1957 in respect of those lawfully on the land (styled 'visitors'), and that of 1984 for trespassers. An occupier is someone who has control over the land in question. Since control may be shared (for example, as between a landlord and a tenant) two or more persons may simultaneously be occupiers. See *Wheat v E Lacon & Co Ltd* [1966] AC 552. The owner of a monument exercises control over it, and hence owes a duty of care under these statutes. Following a Section 215(2) transfer, the element of control which is the necessary foundation of an occupier's liability passes from the PCC to the local authority. Even if in particular circumstances a PCC is found voluntarily to have retained some residual control over the churchyard, it is entitled to claim an indemnity or contribution pursuant to the Civil Liability (Contribution) Act 1978 from the local authority whose breach of duty occasions injury.

15. The operation of Section 215 of the Local Government Act 1972 has no effect upon the primary liability of the owner of a monument. The secondary liability, however, is taken over by the local authority under Section 215(2) as one aspect of the duty to keep the churchyard in decent order. The local

authority thereby acquires sufficient standing to apply to the Consistory Court for a faculty empowering it to make safe dangerous monuments. See generally *Re Keynsham Cemetery* [2003] 1 WLR 66 (Bath and Wells Consistory Court), and *Re Welford Road Cemetery* (2006) *Times* 2 November (Court of Arches). Where there is an emergency involving interests of health and safety, the Consistory Court has special powers under Rule 13(10) of the Faculty Jurisdiction Rules 2000 to grant a faculty at short notice.

Employer's liability

16. The law as outlined above has further consequences for a local authority whose workforce is engaged in churchyard maintenance. The churchyard thereby becomes a 'workplace' for the purposes of the Workplace (Health, Safety and Welfare) Regulations 1992. Under Regulation 4 of those Regulations the employer has duties in relation to the safety of any workplace under his control, while parallel duties are imposed upon any other person having control of a workplace.

17. Where the workplace is a closed churchyard the maintenance of which has been taken over by a local authority, the duty to maintain it, associated with the power to seek any necessary faculty from the Consistory Court, gives rise to the requisite control under Regulation 4. If a dangerous monument constitutes a hazard to the authority's workforce (whether directly employed or not) the duties under the Regulations require the authority to take the necessary steps to obviate the hazard. In doing so the authority has to plan and conduct its operations in such a way as to comply simultaneously with the Regulations, Section 215(2) of the Local Government Act 1972, and the requirements of the faculty jurisdiction. Compliance with each of these legal regimes is mandatory.

Conclusion

18. The legal position may be summarised as follows. The primary responsibility for the safety of a monument in a churchyard closed by Order in Council rests with the owner of the monument. If the owner defaults, a secondary responsibility is imposed upon the body having the duty to maintain the closed churchyard. This may be the PCC, pursuant to Section 215(1) of the Local Government Act 1972. Where, however, a local authority has taken over the maintenance of the churchyard under Section 215(2) its maintenance obligation extends to the safety of the monuments there. In that event the PCC is discharged from further liability as from the time of transfer and, if sued for injury caused by a dangerous monument it is entitled to seek indemnity or contribution from the local authority.

(January 2007)

Revocation of presentation by patron and refusal of presentee by bishop

1. This Opinion considers the situation where the parish representatives and the bishop have consented under section 13(1)(b) of the Patronage (Benefices) Measure 1986 to the making of an offer by the patron, the offer has been made and accepted and the patron has given notice of presentation in form 38 to the bishop. New information then comes to light and:

1.1   it transpires that the presentee misrepresented certain material facts to the patron, the parish representatives or the bishop, or

1.2   although there was no misrepresentation by the presentee, had the patron been aware of the information, he would not have wished to present the priest and had the parish representatives and the bishop been aware of the information, they would not have given consent to the making of the offer.

2. Examples in the first category above (taken from actual cases) are where the presentee represented that he was happily married and that the appointment would be ideal for his wife and family, when in fact his marriage had broken down twelve months earlier and he now wished to be divorced. Or where the presentee had represented that he held various university degrees, but he did not. An example in the second category is where the bishop had taken a reference from the presentee's existing bishop and it was satisfactory, but enquiries subsequently made of the presentee's present parish revealed that the presentee and his wife had been extreme malcontents, obsessed with the alleged inadequacies of their parsonage house and there was every indication that there would be similar problems at the new parish.

3. The question is whether, in either of these circumstances, the patron can revoke the presentation prior to institution or the bishop can refuse the presentee.

4. It is stated in Halsbury's Laws paragraph 837 that presentation by a spiritual patron is complete when it is received by the bishop and it cannot afterwards be varied or revoked, but presentation by a lay person other than the Sovereign is not complete until institution or admission, and so it may be revoked.

5. Phillimore on pages 315 and 316 is somewhat equivocal, but also states the view that presentation can only be revoked by a lay patron 'and not [by] ecclesiastical persons of any kind; because they are supposed in law to be competent judges of the sufficiency of the person and do

therefore proceed by judgement and election; and whoever elects an unfit person is *ipso jure* deprived of the power of electing'. The passage quoted is referring to varying the presentation (i.e. presenting a second candidate and leaving the bishop to choose) but would appear to apply also to revocation.

6. These principles appear to be derived from some extremely old authorities, and it is suggested that they should be treated with some caution. It may have been the case in the 17th century that spiritual persons and colleges would have presented from those whom they knew personally or from amongst their own members, whereas lay patrons would rely on the recommendations of others and might never meet the presentee. But that is not the case now. Whatever the status of the patron, the process of advertising and interviewing applicants is largely the same. The fragility of the distinction is further emphasised by the dicta summarised in Phillimore that 'a patroness, though a spiritual person, as an abbess might vary her presentation, for she is no more apprised than a lay patron of the sufficiency of her clerk'. The distinction therefore seems to derive from a pragmatic assessment of the knowledge of the presentee that different categories of patron could reasonably be expected to have, rather than from any fundamental legal principles.

7. It is therefore suggested that the question should now be revisited. A sensible lay patron would take up references and invite the bishop to make appropriate episcopal enquiries, and it is normal for the patron, whether lay or spiritual, to meet the candidate in advance of offering to present them. There is now no logic for the distinction between lay and spiritual patrons.

8. Both Phillimore and Halsbury give the impression that a lay patron may revoke presentation for any reason or none and the presentee would have no redress. This seems strange and anomalous. It is suggested that in the context of the 1986 Measure and the regime that that creates, the presentation should be regarded as completed when the patron gives notice of presentation in form 38 to the bishop. The offer has been made to the presentee. The offer has been accepted and the patron has exercised his rights of presentation by completing form 38 and presenting the presentee. The patron's functions are fulfilled and, despite the earlier authorities to the contrary, there seems no justification for a lay patron revoking the presentation, at least without good grounds for doing so. This view can be reconciled with the earlier authorities on the basis that the position for a spiritual patron was the norm; an exception was made for lay patrons because they could not in the past be expected to have sufficient knowledge of potential candidates, but the justification for that exception has now gone.

9. If the foregoing proposition is accepted, it raises the question whether there are any circumstances in which the patron, lay and spiritual, can revoke the presentation. It is suggested that if the presentation has been secured by fraud or material misrepresentation, revocation may be justified. So, in the situation described in 1.1 above, if the presentee has knowingly misrepresented a material fact so that, had the patron known the true position, the offer would not have been made, the patron should be allowed to revoke the presentation. In the example of the priest who misrepresented his family situation, if the patron would not have made the offer had the true situation been known, that should be a ground for revocation.

10. The rationale for the revocation is either that the offer was induced by the misrepresentation, or that on account of deliberate deceit the presentee has shown himself to be unworthy of the post. On the same principle, the presentation could not be revoked in a case falling within 1.2 above. There has been no misrepresentation by the presentee. New information has come to light that suggests that the decision was a bad one, but the fault lies with the bishop who gave the reference and perhaps with the patron, the parish or the receiving bishop for not making other enquiries before making or giving consent to the making of the offer.

11. The position of the bishop having given consent to the making of the offer is governed by the Benefices Act 1898 and the Benefices Measure 1972. Under section 2 of the 1898 Act, the bishop may refuse to institute or admit a presentee to a benefice on the grounds of lack of experience (a ground supplemented by section 1 of the 1972 Measure), unfitness to discharge the duties of the benefice through physical or mental infirmity or incapacity, pecuniary embarrassment of a serious character, grave misconduct or neglect of a duty in ecclesiastical office, evil life, grave scandal concerning moral character since ordination or having been party to a transaction or agreement invalid under the Act. Section 3 of the Act provides a right of appeal to the Archbishop and the Dean of the Arches and Auditor where a bishop refuses to institute or admit 'on any ground included in section 3 of this Act or of unfitness or disqualification of the presentee otherwise sufficient in law, except a ground of doctrine or ritual'. The words 'or of unfitness or disqualification . . . otherwise sufficient in law' imply that there are grounds on which a bishop might lawfully refuse to institute other than those in section 2. Citing various 16th century authorities, Halsbury at paragraph 839 states that 'Any cause which would be sufficient to deprive an incumbent is a sufficient ground for refusing a presentee', but it is not stated that presentation may only be refused on such grounds, and it appears from note 10 to that paragraph that a bishop may refuse a presentee who has been guilty of ritual offences which, if he were beneficed, would be dealt with, in the first instance, not by deprivation but by monition. A refusal to institute or admit a presentee on the ground of

unfitness in respect of doctrine or ritual can be challenged by a patron in the temporal courts.

12. It is suggested that it is in principle sufficient for the bishop to refuse to present because of matters which might give rise to action under Part II of the Incumbents (Vacation of Benefices) Measure 1977 (disability cases) or an offence under the Ecclesiastical Jurisdiction Measure 1963 (whatever censure might ultimately be imposed under that Measure) or misconduct which could be the subject of proceedings under Section 8 of the Clergy Discipline Measure 2003. In any of those cases, the Bishop would be entitled to refuse to institute, but subject to the right of appeal in section 3 of the 1898 Act or an action in the temporal courts on the ground of unfitness in the case of doctrine or ritual. It would be open to the appellate tribunal to conclude that, although the bishop had grounds under section 2 of the Act to refuse to institute, the circumstances of the particular case were not such that his refusal was justified.

13. Prior to the 1986 Measure, the patron did not have to obtain the bishop's approval to the making of an offer. The patron presented and the bishop then examined the candidate. The bishop now has two bites of the cherry in that he can refuse to approve the making of an offer (subject to the patron's right to request the Archbishop to review the matter under section 13(5)), but having either approved the offer or been overruled by the Archbishop, the bishop can then refuse to present under the 1898 Act, subject to the right of appeal under section 3. It is suggested that the relevant issue for the appellate tribunal in considering any appeal under section 3, is why the bishop gave consent to the making of the offer but is now refusing to institute.

14. In the situation described in 1.1 above, the fact that the presentee's marriage had broken down is not, without more, a disciplinary offence and is not on the face of it grave misconduct, evil life or grave scandal concerning his moral character. Therefore, it does not in itself seem to be a ground for refusal under section 2 of the 1898 Act. However, the fact that a misrepresentation has been made which induced the patron to make the offer and possibly induced the bishop to approve the making of the offer could, it is suggested, be grave misconduct under section 2 of the 1898 Act and, since the misconduct was only discovered after the bishop approved the making of the offer, there is justification for his apparent volte-face. Likewise, the deceit about the university degrees may be a ground for the bishop to refuse to institute.

15. In the situation described in 1.2 above, it is suggested that the bishop would only have a ground for refusing to institute if the matters discovered after the presentation were of sufficient seriousness to come within

section 2 of the 1898 Act. In the examples given in paragraph 2, they would probably not have been.

16. Whatever the correct interpretation of the law, if a manifestly unsatisfactory incumbent is instituted to a benefice, damaging and potentially expensive pastoral difficulties are likely to follow. The Commission therefore recommends as good practice the taking up of references before parish representatives give consent to the making of the offer.

(January 2007)

The Application of the Regulatory Reform (Fire Safety) Order 2005 in relation to parish churches and the parochial use of other premises

The general effect of the Order

1. The purpose of the Regulatory Reform (Fire Safety) Order 2005 (SI 2005/1541) was to harmonise and simplify the previously existing patchwork of legislation concerning fire precautions and prevention. Its requirements are therefore expressed in broad terms which are not easily related to the legal framework of the Church of England.

2. Subject to some specific and immaterial exceptions in article 6(1), the Order applies to all non-domestic premises. Places of worship are included in its wide ambit.

3. The key provisions concerning the imposition of the duties about fire safety under Part 2 of the Order (including matters such as risk assessment, evacuation of premises and means of fire-fighting) are contained in articles 3 and 5. These duties are, by article 5, imposed upon the 'responsible person', who is defined in article 3 as follows:

> **Meaning of 'responsible person'**
> **3.** In this Order 'responsible person' means –
>
> (a) in relation to a workplace, the employer, if the workplace is to any extent under his control;
>
> (b) in relation to any premises not falling within paragraph (a) –
>
> (i) the person who has control of the premises (as occupier or otherwise) in connection with the carrying on by him of a trade, business or other undertaking (for profit or not); or
>
> (ii) the owner, where the person in control of the premises does not have control in connection with the carrying on by that person of a trade, business or other undertaking.

In addition, article 5(3) provides that any duty imposed upon the responsible person is also imposed upon every other person 'who has, to any extent, control of the premises so far as the requirements [of Part 2] relate to matters within his control'. The concept of control is further elaborated by article 5(4), which provides

'(4) Where a person has, by virtue of any contract or tenancy, an obligation of any extent in relation to –

(a) the maintenance or repair of any premises, including anything in or on premises; or

(b) the safety of any premises,

that person is to be treated, for the purposes of paragraph (3), as being a person who has control of the premises to the extent that his obligation so extends.'

4. By section 23(1) of the Interpretation Act 1978, subordinate legislation, including this Order, has to be construed in accordance with the Act. By section 5 and Schedule I, a person includes a body of persons corporate or unincorporated. Thus the expression 'responsible person' in article 3 extends both to an individual and to a body of persons. (For example, a secular employer within article 3(a) is often a partnership or a limited company.)

5. The overall scheme of articles 3 and 5 is to single out as the responsible person an employer, if there is one; in the absence of an employer, whoever is carrying on a trade, business or undertaking; and in default of either, the owner of the premises. In each of these cases some degree of control over the premises is a necessary ingredient. In addition to the responsible person, any other party who exercises control over the premises may owe a duty under article 5(3) of the Order.

6. The concept of the responsible person is not to be confused with that of the 'competent person', one or more of whom are required to discharge specific functions under Part 2 of the Order at the nomination of the responsible person.

The position of the parochial church council

7. By section 3 of the Parochial Church Councils (Powers) Measure 1956, the PCC is a body corporate and hence within the definition of a 'person' in Schedule I to the Interpretation Act 1978. Section 4(1)(ii) of the Measure vested in the PCC

'The like powers duties and liabilities as, immediately before the relevant date, the churchwardens . . . had with respect to – . . .

(a) The care maintenance preservation and insurance of the fabric of the church and the goods and ornaments thereof . . .'

8. A broad construction is given to the word 'undertaking' in the field of health and safety legislation (*R v Mara* [1987] 1 WLR 87). The powers, duties and liabilities of the PCC under the 1956 Measure collectively amount to an undertaking which will bring it within the article 3(b)(i) definition of

> 'a person who has control of the premises (as occupier or otherwise) in connection with the carrying on by him of [an] undertaking (for profit or not) . . .'

Thus the PCC in its corporate capacity is to be viewed in law as the responsible person.

9. If the PCC delegates the control of fire safety matters to a particular individual, for instance to a churchwarden, such a person is likely to become directly liable to comply with Part 2 of the Order, in addition to the PCC, by reason of article 5(3). Non-compliance with Part 2 of the Order is a criminal offence; see Part 4. It may be thought undesirable to make any arrangement which has the effect of exposing a PCC member or other parishioner to personal legal liability.

The parochial church council as employer

10. Sometimes the legal relationship of employer and employee exists between the PCC and those working as organist, verger, parish administrator and the like. In such circumstances the PCC, as employer, will be treated as the responsible person under article 3(a) instead of article 3(b). In both instances the legal consequences are the same; but if there are five or more employees, compliance with articles 9 and 10 is made more onerous in terms of record-keeping.

The minister and churchwardens

11. The minister (whether the incumbent or the holder of a licence) is by ecclesiastical law entrusted with various powers and duties in relation top the church building. Examples appear in Canons B 8 (vesture), B 20 (music), C 24 (services and sermons), F 8 (bell-ringing) and F 16 (plays, concerts and the like). Canon F 16.3, which specifically required the minister to consult appropriate authorities in respect of fire and other precautions when the church was used for plays and similar public events, supplemented section 59 (now repealed) of the Public Health Act 1936. With the introduction of the 2005 Order, Canon F 16.3 is now obsolete, at least in relation to fire precautions. It is not an aid to the construction of article 3 of the Order.

12. The minister's powers and duties are essentially spiritual and liturgical in character. They do not endow the minister with the physical control of

the church exercised by the PCC. Accordingly the minister falls outside the scope of the definition of the responsible person given in article 3(b)(i). Moreover an incumbent in whom the freehold of the church is vested is not the responsible person, as owner, under article 3(b)(ii), because the requirements of article 3(b)(i) are already fulfilled by the PCC.

13. The churchwardens, separately from the PCC, do not come within the terms of article 3(b)(i) because of the transfer of their pre-existing powers and duties to the PCC under section 4(1)(ii) of the Parochial Church Councils (Powers) Measure 1956.

Leases under the Pastoral (Amendment) Measure 2006 and licences

14. Where part of a church is the subject of a lease or licence whereby responsibilities for maintenance, repair or safety are assumed by the lessee or licensee, that party becomes the responsible person in relation to the demised or licensed part of the premises by virtue of article 5(3) and (4). Responsible persons in respect of the separate parts are, however, required by article 22 to co-operate together and to co-ordinate the measures which they adopt.

15. The identity of the responsible person is unlikely to be affected by the informal use of a church for meetings, playgroups, concerts and the like. The organisers of such events will normally have sufficient temporary control of the building to impose upon them, under article 5(3), a duty to comply with Part 2 of the Order. The article 5(3) duty is in addition to the duty resting on the responsible person.

Premises other than a church building

16. The previous paragraphs apply equally to premises other than a church building which are under the control of the PCC. Where church halls or similar premises are, however, managed by a separate body of trustees, those trustees collectively will normally be the responsible person for the purposes of the Order. If special events such as church fetes are held in premises not occupied by the PCC, it is highly desirable to establish in advance who is the responsible person for the purposes of fire safety. It should also be ensured that the responsible person has secured due compliance with Part 2 of the Order.

Sharing of Church Buildings Act 1969

17. Legal arrangements made under the Sharing of Church Buildings Act 1969 may involve the joint denominational ownership of a church building and its management by trustees upon whom section 3(5) places

'responsibility under any statutory or other legal provision'. In such a case the trustees will have the requisite control of the building to become the responsible person under article 3. Where an existing Anglican church building remains 'in the sole ownership of the Church of England' pursuant to section 5(1) and functions as a parish church, in the absence of any contrary provision in the sharing agreement the PCC will continue to fulfil the role of responsible person. Sharing agreements commonly provide for a Joint Council (on which the sharing churches are represented) overseeing a separate body charged with the management and repair of the church building. This body, often described as the 'responsible authority', will normally become the responsible person in place of the PCC. In all instances of sharing under the 1969 Act the impact of the Order will, however, depend upon the precise terms of the sharing agreement and the trusts taking effect under it.

(October 2007)

Marriage

A. Flowers

Canon B 35, paragraph 5, states in relation to Holy Matrimony:

> 'When matrimony is to be solemnized in any church, it belongs to the minister of the parish to decide . . . what furnishings or flowers should be placed in or about the church for the occasion.'

In practice, however, the choice of flowers to decorate the church is usually left to the parties to be married and, if the minister wishes to exercise his or her prerogative (for example, because of the penitential season), he or she should make it clear from the beginning. This is essential if more than one couple are being (or may be) married on the same day as it may not be possible for the flowers for the first wedding to be changed before the second ceremony. Although the parties may be able to reach an amicable agreement, that may not be possible and the minister should therefore always make it clear that any final decision will be made by him or her.

B. Timing

Canon B 35, paragraph 4, states:

> 'A marriage may not be solemnized at any unseasonable hours but only between the hours of eight in the forenoon and six in the afternoon.'

The Legal Advisory Commission has already given its opinion that the service must be completed before six in the evening: *Legal Opinions concerning the Church of England* (8th ed., 2007) at page 367. Therefore care must be taken that no marriage ceremony starts so late that either that or any subsequent marriage ceremony that day may thereby be jeopardised.

The incumbent or priest-in-charge is entitled to appoint the date and time of the marriage within the prescribed hours: Lacey, *A Handbook of Church Law* (1903) at page 236; *Anglican Marriage in England and Wales A guide to the Law for the Clergy* (1999) at paragraph 6.3. The hour, however, must not be 'unseasonable', that is, it must not be arranged at an hour which is unreasonable for the priest or the parties.

However, once the time for the ceremony has been fixed, it must be notified to the bride and bridegroom; it is then for them to ensure that the witnesses and other guests are told of the date and time.

The rubric at the commencement of The Form of Solemnization of Matrimony in the Book of Common Prayer reads:

> 'At the day and time appointed for solemnization of Matrimony, the parties to be married shall come into the body of the Church with their friends and neighbours. . . .'

Although there is no similar rubric in *Common Worship: Pastoral Services*, the BCP rubric makes it clear that it is for the parties to ensure that they are present in order to start at the appointed time.

In spite of the widespread belief that a bride is entitled to be late for her wedding, that belief runs counter to the law of the Church of England. Clearly some leeway should be granted, especially if there is heavy traffic or an accident, but the priest is not under any duty to take the service at any later hour, although in most cases he or she will no doubt endeavour to do so for pastoral reasons. More particularly the priest does not have to place in jeopardy any other important engagement or commitment (such as a burial or another wedding) later in the day.

If the minister or the PCC consider that punctuality may not be regarded as important by the couple, they will no doubt as a matter of practice warn the couple that the ceremony may not take place if they or their witnesses are late.

The fee payable towards the incumbent's stipend and to the PCC pursuant to the Table of Parochial Fees (£240 in 2007) relates to the marriage service and such fees are not due unless, and until, the ceremony actually takes place. Whether other 'fees' are payable, for example in relation to bell ringers and/or the organist and choir, will depend upon the circumstances of the particular case and the normal principles of contract law.

(October 2007)

Registration and enforcement of chancel repair liability by parochial church councils

1. This Opinion addresses the question whether there are any circumstances in which a parochial church council ('PCC') can properly:

(a)   decide not to investigate whether it is entitled to the benefit of chancel repair liability; or

(b)   having established that it is entitled to the benefit of such liability, decide not to register or enforce such liability.

Background

2. In response to the decision of the House of Lords in *PCC of Aston Cantlow v Wallbank*[1], which upheld the enforceability of chancel repair liability, the Lord Chancellor made the Land Registration Act 2002 (Transitional Provisions) (No 2) Order 2003[2], under which chancel repair liability was to continue to be an 'overriding interest' (and thus enforceable against land owners even though not registered at HM Land Registry) for ten years from the coming into force of the Land Registration Act 2003 on 13th October 2003.

3. Additionally, the 2003 Order allowed an application to be made before the end of the ten-year period, without a fee being charged, for registration of a 'caution' against first registration of unregistered land and for the entry in the register of a 'notice' in the case of registered land, in respect of chancel repair liability relating to a particular piece of land. The caution or notice will give priority to the PCC over the interest of the first registered proprietor or anyone taking from him or anyone taking from a registered proprietor. But even if the liability is not registered within the ten-year period, it will still be enforceable after the expiration of that period against the owner of the land until he or she disposes of it: it would only be his or her successor in title who would take the land freed from the liability; and it will still be possible to register a caution or notice after 12th October 2013 (albeit subject to payment of a fee) if the land subject to the liability has not changed hands.

4. In the light of this position, PCCs which believe themselves to be entitled to the benefit of chancel repair liability are encouraged to register their interest at HM Land Registry in order to be able to enforce it against subsequent purchasers from the current owner(s) of the land in question.

---

[1] [2004] 1 AC 546
[2] SI 2003/2341

The fiduciary duties of PCC members

5. As explained in the Commission's opinion *'Parochial Church Council: Legal Position of Members'*, PCCs are charities[3] and are accepted as such by the Charity Commission. Their members are in a position analogous to that of a trustee of trust property, being subject to a number of 'fiduciary' duties. One of the most basic of those duties is to act in the best interests of the PCC. That duty has a number of consequences. One is that they are under a duty to protect and preserve the PCC's assets. Another is that they are not free to give effect to obligations of a purely moral nature.[4]

6. Members of a PCC who act in breach of these fiduciary duties may be required to make good any loss which the PCC has incurred as a result of that breach, out of their own personal resources. They may also face an inquiry by the Charity Commission and, in consequence, exposure to the exercise of the Commission's protective and remedial powers (including the possibility of their removal from office).

Analysis

7. Under the Chancel Repairs Act 1932 the right to enforce chancel repair liability is vested in the PCC of the parish concerned where there is one or, if there is no PCC, in the churchwardens of the parish.[5] The right to enforce chancel repair liability therefore effectively represents an asset of the PCC.

8. *Prima facie*, the fiduciary duties referred to in paragraph 5 above accordingly require a PCC (a) to take reasonable steps to investigate whether a liability to repair exists in relation to any church within their parish and (b) if it does, to register and enforce that liability.

9. The duty to protect the assets of a charity does not require charity trustees to expend more in protecting an asset than the asset is likely to be worth: such a position would plainly be inconsistent with the underlying duty to act in the charity's best interests. Thus there is in principle scope for a PCC to argue that it need not investigate the existence of an entitlement to chancel repair liability where the costs of doing so would be disproportionate in relation to the likelihood of any liability being identified. (As noted above, there is usually no charge for registration itself.) However, in most cases it would seem doubtful whether in practice the costs of investigating the position

---

[3] See eg Lord Scott in *Aston Cantlow*, [2004] 1 AC 546 at 589.

[4] *Re Snowden* [1979] Ch 528

[5] See in particular the definition of 'responsible authority' for the purposes of that Act contained in s.4(1).

would ever be so high as to enable this argument to be advanced with any credibility: in many cases the position can be clarified relatively easily (by reference to Enclosure Acts and Awards or Records of Ascertainments). Nevertheless, there may be cases of this nature if the liability has not been enforced for a century or more and the land subject to the liability is unknown, with the consequent possibility of a multiplicity of owners.

10. There is, however, more scope for recognising that PCCs may not always be required to <u>enforce</u> chancel repair liability, again by reference to general principles of trust law.

11. In *Harries v Church Commissioners*[6] it was held that the normal duty to invest the funds of a charity in a way that produced the maximum financial return consistent with commercial prudence could be displaced in two types of situation. The first was '*when the objects of the charity are such that investments of a particular type would conflict with the aims of the charity*'. The second was '*when holdings of particular investments might hamper a charity's work either by making potential recipients of aid unwilling to be helped because of the source of the charity's money or by alienating some of those who support the charity financially*'. The latter situation was suggested to be '*comparatively rare*'; and it was said that when it arose '*the trustees will need to balance the difficulties they would encounter, or likely financial loss they would sustain, if they were to hold the investments against the risk of financial detriment if those investments were excluded from their portfolio. The greater the risk of financial detriment, the more certain the trustees should be of countervailing disadvantages to the charity before they incur that risk*'.[7]

12. Although these principles were expressed in the context of charity trustees' duties as regards investment, in principle they would seem equally applicable in the context of the duty to protect a charity's assets. But in practice the first of them would not seem to have any potential application in relation to chancel repair liability, since there appears to be no inherent incompatibility between registering or enforcing that liability and the objects of a PCC as declared in s2 of the Parochial Church Councils (Powers) Measure 1956.

13. As to the second principle referred to in the *Harries* case, there would seem, in principle, to be scope for arguing that the registration of a notice or caution, and more particularly the <u>enforcement</u> of chancel repair liability could, in the circumstances of the particular PCC concerned, hamper the

---

[6] [1993] 2 All ER 300
[7] [1993] 2 All ER 300 at 304 per Sir Donald Nicholls VC

PCC's work, either by adversely affecting its ability to pursue its object of promoting in the parish the pastoral mission of the Church[8] or by alienating potential financial support. (For example, even registering a caution[9] or notice against all the owners of houses on a newly built estate in the parish[10] could alienate people from the church and thus cause both pastoral and financial damage to its mission in the parish because the notice or caution would be a 'blot' on the owners' titles. And actually enforcing liability in those circumstances could give rise to considerable alienation.) That analysis may be supported by the statement of Lord Scott in the *Aston Cantlow* case[11] that

> 'The PCC could have decided not to enforce the repairing obligation. They could have so decided for a number of different reasons which, in particular situations, might have had weight. . . . They might have taken into account excessive hardship to Mr and Mrs Wallbank in having to find £95,000. Trustees are not always obliged to be Scrooge.'

14. In deciding to what extent the principle referred to in the preceding paragraph could apply, the PCC in question would need to carry out a balancing exercise of the kind referred to at the end of the passage quoted from the *Harries* case in paragraph 11 above; and the greater the amount of the chancel repair liability, the greater the pastoral or financial damage that would be needed for the PCC to be able to say that it was acting properly in deciding not to enforce it. Whether the party subject to the liability was an institutional body might have a bearing on the question, in that enforcement against such a body might be less likely to give rise to adverse financial or pastoral consequences. Another consideration would be the possible adverse effect that declining to enforce a right to chancel repair liability could have on the PCC's ability to fund necessary repairs or to

---

[8] Under s2 of the 1956 Measure the functions of a PCC include *'co-operation with the minister in promoting in the parish the whole mission of the Church, pastoral, evangelistic, social and ecumenical'*.

[9] Simply registering a caution against first registration where the title to the land subject to the right to chancel repair liability is not yet registered may not have any adverse impact, since it would not necessarily come to the notice of the owner of the land; but if it did come to light, the fact that it had been done without notice to the owner could in itself give rise to ill-feeling.

[10] As the law stands, the decision in *Wickhambrook Parochial Church Council v Croxford* [1935] 2 KB 417 means that chancel repair liability is enforceable jointly and severally. In *Aston Cantlow* Lord Scott expressed doubt whether the case was correctly decided and pointed out that it was open to question in the House of Lords; but that view was not endorsed by any other member of the House and Lord Hobhouse expressly dissociated himself from it.

[11] [2004] 1 AC 546 at 591. However, none of the other four Law Lords expressed support for Lord Scott's view.

obtain funding for them from other sources such as English Heritage. The date the liability had last been enforced and whether the landowner had knowledge of the liability before acquiring the land might also be relevant considerations, in so far as they might influence perceptions of the PCC's behaviour and thus the pastoral impact of a decision to register a notice of it or enforce it.

15. Having weighed these and other relevant considerations carefully, since the application of the principle described in paragraph 13 above to the facts of a particular case is not straightforward, a PCC would be well advised to seek legal advice before forming a view that it would not wish to register a notice of, or enforce, a liability to which it is entitled.

16. Additionally, the Commission strongly recommends that if a PCC considers, after careful consideration of the principle described above, that it would be contrary to its interests to enforce chancel repair liability to which it is entitled, or to register notice of it, the PCC should seek formal advice from the Charity Commission on whether not enforcing the liability would be consistent with the fiduciary duties of its members. Under s.29 Charities Act 1993 the Charity Commission has power to give the 'charity trustees' of a charity (an expression which extends to the members of a PCC whether or not it is registered as a charity) its '*opinion or advice on any matter affecting the performance of [their] duties as such*'; and charity trustees who act in accordance with such advice are deemed to have acted properly. There is therefore a simple and effective way for a PCC to obtain protection against the consequences of a decision not to enforce chancel repair liability or not to register notice of its rights, provided of course that the Charity Commission is satisfied that the PCC's decision is consistent with the fiduciary duties of its members.

Compounding chancel repair liability

17. PCCs will wish to bear in mind the possibility of 'compounding' any chancel repair liability to which they are entitled – ie of agreeing with those who are subject to the liability that it be formally extinguished in return for the payment of a capital sum.

18. Section 52 of the Ecclesiastical Dilapidations Measure 1923 contains a procedure for the formal compounding of chancel repair liability, involving the payment of a capital sum to the 'diocesan authority'[12]. That capital sum must be invested in the name of the diocesan authority and its income applied by that body, after consultation with the PCC, in insuring the

---

[12] That is, the diocesan board of finance or other body acting as trustee of diocesan property

chancel against loss or damage by fire, in maintaining and repairing the church of which the chancel forms part (and not only the chancel itself), together with its churchyard and (if there is any surplus) in forming a fund for the extraordinary repair, improvement or enlargement of the church or churchyard.

19. However, the possibility may exist in some cases of a non-statutory arrangement, in the form of a legally enforceable agreement between the PCC and those subject to the liability under which the PCC agrees <u>not to enforce</u> the liability, again in return for the payment of a capital sum. Whilst such an arrangement would not involve the formal extinguishment of the liability, the effect would in substance be the same in that it could no longer be enforced.

20. The potential difficulty with such a non-statutory arrangement is that, if liability for chancel repair is joint and several[13], so that it can be enforced against <u>any</u> of those subject to it, an agreement of the kind referred to in the previous paragraph may, in law, be of limited protection to the party who has entered into it: the PCC could in theory (in the absence of any provision to the contrary in the agreement) subsequently enforce the liability against any other parties who were also liable for chancel repair, for the full amount of the liability, and those parties could subsequently exercise their right of indemnity to recover a contribution from the party to the agreement. Thus an agreement of this kind may only be appropriate where either (a) all the parties subject to the liability join in the agreement or (b) the PCC expressly agrees that, if others who do not join in the agreement are also liable, the PCC will not seek to enforce the liability against them.

21. Subject to that important caveat, the circumstances in which a non-statutory arrangement of the kind described in paragraph 19 above may be appropriate include where the question of chancel repair liability has been raised in relation to a conveyancing transaction in the parish as a result of a search and there is doubt as to whether or not the liability exists. The cost of investigating the position fully may be beyond the fees that the purchaser is prepared to bear and an agreement not to enforce any possible, but unascertained, liability by payment to the PCC of an appropriate sum may be preferable to all parties to making a similar payment to an insurance company. Whereas an insurance policy would be good only for the sum insured and for the period of cover (generally not more than 20 years), the advantage to the purchaser of dealing direct with the PCC in such a case is that the protection would be permanent and financially unlimited.

---

[13] See footnote 10 above.

22. Even so, the obligation upon trustees to protect and preserve the PCC's property must always be borne in mind. It is therefore essential that, before any non-statutory arrangement of the kind described in paragraph 19 above is entered into, proper advice is received as to the value of the PCC's right to enforce chancel repair liability. PCCs contemplating such an arrangement should therefore seek appropriate professional advice, including as to the amount of the capital payment to be made. Prima facie that should be no less than the sum which would be payable on a formal compounding under the 1923 Measure, that is, a sum reasonably sufficient to provide for the cost of future repairs and to insure the chancel against loss or damage by fire – subject only to a possible discount if the existence of the liability has not been clearly established. However, it is unlikely that the landowners will be induced into compounding unless there is some real benefit to them. In these circumstances the PCC and diocesan authorities may feel that an informal arrangement is preferable to receiving no payment at all coupled with the continuing need to enforce the liability on future occasions.

23. Any capital sum received under a non-statutory arrangement of the kind described in paragraph 19 above would be subject to the terms of the agreement. It is most likely that a lay rector providing what may well still be a very substantial sum will effectively require the content of aspects of the 1923 Measure to be included in the agreement – namely that the capital be vested in the diocesan board of finance, with only the income being used to repair and insure the chancel and the church, but with power for resort to be had to the capital in cases of grave emergency. If the PCC is responsible for the investment of the capital sum, it will need to take appropriate advice as to how to invest it. The fund would be likely to appear in the PCC's accounts as a restricted fund.

24. In the light of these different possibilities and the fiduciary duties that lie upon members of a PCC, a PCC which proposes to enter into a non-statutory arrangement of the kind described in paragraph 19 above would be well advised before doing so to seek confirmation from the Charity Commission (in the form of an order under s.26 Charities Act 1993) that the proposed agreement is one into which the PCC can properly enter, on the basis that the terms proposed are expedient in the interests of the PCC. Only if such confirmation is received can the PCC be sure that its members will not individually be held liable to make good any loss that may afterwards be found to have been incurred.

(October 2007)

Church building: bells

Ringing of church bells: canon law and potential liability for nuisance at common law and under the environmental protection act 1990

Church bells

1. There are at present over 5200 churches in England with rings of five or more bells and there are over 3000 bells cast in medieval times that are still rung. Church bells have been ringing in England since the 7th century but change ringing was not introduced until the middle of the 17th century. Change ringing is an art (or exercise) unknown outside the Anglican Communion, where it is principally confined to England and Wales. Bells are rung to summon the faithful to worship, to celebrate weddings and festivals and to mark national thanksgivings. Muffled bells are sometimes rung at funerals and at times of local or national disaster. During times of national emergency it has always been understood that church bells would be rung as a warning of invasion. Despite the antiquity of this tradition and practice, complaints of noise nuisance sometimes arise.

Canon law

2. Canon F 8 'Of Church Bells' states that:

'1.   In every church and chapel there shall be provided at least one bell to ring the people to divine service.

2.   No bell in any church or chapel shall be rung contrary to the direction of the minister.'

3. The Commission considers this Canon imposes a composite obligation: a requirement for every church to have a bell, the purpose of the bell being to ring people to public worship, and an obligation that the bell will be rung unless the minister of the place directs that it be not rung.

4. The minister may in his/her discretion direct that the bell be not rung because for example, it may be safe to toll but unsafe to ring or for other good reason. The bell not being rung or tolled in these circumstances would not give rise to an ecclesiastical offence or found a complaint of misconduct on the part of the minister, though there would, of course, be a duty for the PCC to take all reasonable steps, as soon as practicable, to effect repairs to enable compliance in the Canon.

5. Canon B 11 also bears on the matter: '. . . Public notice shall be given in the parish, by tolling the bell or other appropriate means, of the time and

place where the prayers are to be said or sung.' Today the ringing of a bell is likely to be but one among a number of ways in which a church will communicate arrangements for public worship.

6. The canonical obligation for the bell to be rung applies to ringing before public worship only, and is limited to the tolling of at least one bell (see Canon F 8). This will embrace the most common use of bells: before the principal Sunday services in our churches (morning prayer, evening prayer and holy communion). Provision of more than one bell or the ringing of more than one bell is over and above the requirements of the Canon. Similarly ringing bells on other occasions such as for bell ringing practice, by visiting campanologists and for change ringing of a full peal are all purposes beyond the scope of the Canon.

7. It seems likely that clergy requiring the church bells – or at least one of them – to be rung in a way demanded by ecclesiastical law, namely to call the parish to public worship, will have a valid defence to an action of private nuisance. If canon law has directed a particular activity there can arguably be no liability for nuisance caused thereby. This defence is likely, however, to be limited only to what would be strictly necessary to discharge the canonical obligation.

8. Canon law however makes no reference to ringing the bell or bells on other occasions. It may be customary for church bells to be rung after a marriage in church, at festivals, to ring in the New Year, to mark national thanksgivings, to warn of invasion or national emergency, or as a mark of respect to ring muffled bells before/after funerals or at times of local or national disaster; but the minister or churchwardens would not be able to pray in aid Canon F8 as a complete defence to a complaint of nuisance. Whether in any particular case legal custom permits the ringing of church bells on these occasions, which are not preceding public worship, has not been reported in case law, and the Commission does not offer an opinion upon whether or not the long established custom of ringing on such occasions would provide a 'reasonable excuse' defence (see below) to a prosecution for statutory nuisance. This will always be a question of fact.

Nuisance at common law

9. A nuisance at common law consists of an unlawful interference with a person's use and enjoyment of his property. Making unreasonable noise is actionable as a nuisance and there are a number of earlier authorities which accept that the ringing of noisy church bells may constitute a nuisance (see *Soltau v De Held* (1851) 2 Sim NS 133, and *Martin v Nutkin* (1724) 2 P Wms 266). In the Australian case of *Haddon v Lynch* [1911] VLR 5 complaint was made of an unmelodious church bell rung in the valley of an

iron roof which served as a sounding board. The judge made an order that the bell should not be rung before 9.00 am. In *Hardman v Holbertson* [1866] WN 379, however, an injunction restraining the ringing of church bells was refused on the ground that the noise was not sufficient materially to interfere with comfort.

10. All the circumstances of a particular case are relevant and will be taken into account by the Court in deciding whether there is a nuisance. Opinions differ markedly about the acceptability of noises, but it is ultimately for the civil Court to decide (*R (on the application of the London Borough of Hackney) v Rottenberg [2007] EWHC 166 (Admin)*). It is often principally a matter of degree or place or time of day. The question for the Court will always be the effect on ordinary, reasonable people. Relevant factors and circumstances will vary from case to case but may properly include the duration of the bell ringing, the time of day the bells are rung, the purpose for which the bells are rung, and the frequency of the ringing. Of course, the volume of noise created by the bells will be a key factor (and reliable measurements should assist the Court). The Court will consider volume together with all the other relevant factors, in the light of the particular locality and context.

11. There is no prescribed or objective standard of what is, or is not, a permissible level of noise. The test the Court will apply in deciding whether the level of noise constitutes a legal nuisance is the subjective test of the Court, guided by expert evidence (if available). But such expert evidence is not determinative and all relevant factors and circumstances are to be taken into account. The Court exercises judgment as to where noise comes on a continuum between the mildly irritating and the intolerable. There is a need for an element of give and take, live and let live. But the personal vulnerability of an individual complainant(s) affected should be ignored in law (*Rottenberg*). The Court will seek to balance the competing or conflicting interests of all parties affected.

12. Those who complain about the ringing of church bells are invariably those who live close to a church. Often newcomers to the locality buy houses close to churches and then complain. This fact does not prevent such a person from proving an actionable nuisance and recovering damages or an injunction. Coming to the nuisance is not a defence. Nevertheless it is a general principle that in the case of a nuisance interfering with comfort and amenity, the local character of the neighbourhood is relevant in determining liability. A person who chooses to live near a church cannot reasonably expect the same freedom from noise as he would expect in some other place. Whether an actionable nuisance exists is not an abstract consideration; it has to be determined by reference to all the circumstances.

13. The duration of the interference is an element in assessing its actionability. Few, if any, complaints appear to have been made in respect of short periods of bell ringing prior to mid-morning or early evening service. Complaints have been made in connection with periods of week day practising where bells may be rung for an hour or so. It is not unreasonable that bell ringers should need to practise; but practising in the late evening is more likely to create a nuisance than the early evening. The test is whether the bells materially interfere with the ordinary comfort and amenity of those living in houses near the church. Each case must be determined according to its own merits. The courts are unlikely to restrain bell ringing practice except in extreme cases. The Central Council for Church Bell Ringers may assist or advise with its wealth of practical experience. It also maintains a complaints helpline.

Statutory nuisance under the Environmental Protection Act 1990

14. Section 79 of the 1990 Act defines a statutory nuisance as constituting inter alia 'noise emitted from premises so as to be prejudicial to health or a nuisance' (s79(1)(g)). Noise, which includes vibration, may fall into this category either because it is prejudicial to health or because it is a nuisance at common law, in the sense of interfering unduly with the comfort and convenience of neighbouring occupiers. The Act does not depart from the common law definitions and standards but it provides additional remedies through the magistrates' court. Where a local authority is satisfied that a statutory nuisance exists or is likely to occur or recur, it is the duty of the local authority to serve a notice requiring the abatement of the nuisance or the prohibition of its recurrence (s80(1)). Such an abatement notice may require works to be done or steps to be taken to abate the nuisance. A person who receives such an abatement notice may appeal against it to the magistrates' court (s80(3)). If there is no appeal, and if the abatement notice is not complied with, then an offence is committed. Such an offence may be prosecuted in a magistrates' court. Independent of the local authority, a person aggrieved by a statutory nuisance may make a complaint to the magistrates' court direct (s82(1)). If the magistrates are satisfied that the alleged nuisance exists they must make an order directing the nuisance to be abated and they may order the execution of the necessary works for that purpose (s82(2)).

15. The *Rottenberg* case concerned the level of noise in one half of a semi-detached house which was registered as a place of worship and had planning permission for use as a school and synagogue. As a result of complaints from the neighbour in the other half of the house the local authority served on the respondent, an Orthodox rabbi, an abatement notice in accordance with section 80 of the Environmental Protection Act 1990. The High Court decided several points on an appeal by case stated:

- The decision whether the noise constitutes a nuisance is a subjective decision of the court and the opinion of environmental health officers that the noise they heard constituted a statutory nuisance may be rejected by the court. Whether the noise on the occasions witnessed and reported by the environmental health officers was a nuisance so as to constitute a breach of the abatement order was a matter of fact for the Court to decide on the evidence.

- If on a prosecution under the 1990 Act the Court finds that the offence of a breach of an abatement order has been committed then the Court has to decide the second point of whether the nuisance is created 'without reasonable excuse'. The court in *Rottenberg* was not required finally to decide this point.

16. Some general comments may be made:

(i)   It is not for witnesses, however expert, independent or impartial, to decide whether noise complained about constitutes an actionable nuisance whether at common law or under statute (*Rottenberg* per Scott Baker LJ).

(ii)   The subjective judgment is that of the court. Parliament has not provided an objective standard to be measured by some yardstick such as the level of decibels of noise at particular times of day. The Court must take into account all the circumstances – and therefore many different factors. Technical evidence of noise readings is not required as a matter of law (*Rottenberg* per David Clarke J).

(iii) Where an offence under the 1990 Act has been found to have been committed, the Court must further decide if the nuisance was created without reasonable excuse. In that regard it is suggested the requirements of Canons F8 and B11 (if the bells were being rung prior to public worship) would be an important consideration.

(iv)   Further, the fact that the noise is created in the course of religious worship, in premises registered and with planning permission for that use, could be a relevant consideration but if, for example, a service or other activity was conducted in such a way that the court, exercising its own judgment, found a statutory nuisance exists, then the fact that the nuisance has created in such circumstances, would be unlikely in itself to amount to a defence of reasonable excuse, nor would a prosecution be disproportionate (*Rottenberg* per David Clarke J).

(v)   Cases on statutory nuisance involving church bells do not appear to have reached the Law Reports and this is no doubt due to the common sense of the ringers and local authorities concerned. However, one such case relating to St Peter Harrogate was settled by compromise, and reported in the 28 January 1977 issue of *The Ringing World*. In the compromise ringing before services was restricted to 45 minutes and a further 60 minutes per week for general ringing. Bell practice time was restricted to 90 minutes between 6.00 pm and 9.00 pm on one week day evening. There were other generous special provisions for peal attempts.

17. Part III of the 1990 Act is the statute under which a local authority will act against bell noise. Remaining sections and codes of practice under the Control of Pollution Act 1974 deal with other kinds of noise, noise from construction sites and make additional specific provision for loudspeaker noise. If, as is the case in some church towers, bell recordings are played via a loudspeaker these provisions may be relevant, but not otherwise. The Noise Act 1996 relates to 'dwellings' and provides additional powers to local authorities but seems irrelevant here.

Summary

18. Every case remains a question of fact, degree and context. Evidence of noise levels is very relevant. If the level of comfort is reduced unacceptably, the ringing of church bells even for a normal period of practice of about one and a half hours may nevertheless constitute an actionable nuisance at common law giving rise to claims for damages and/or an injunction. It could also be prosecuted in the magistrates' court as a statutory nuisance. It may therefore be wise for a parish to consider the question of abatement by ensuring that practices take place as early in the evening as possible. Consideration should also be given to the fitting of sound proof shutters to the inside of the belfry louvres which can be closed during practice periods. The ringing of bells for relatively short periods before public worship or after a wedding or at festivities is probably not actionable at the suit of those who have lived near churches for many years or of those who have bought or tenanted houses close to a church where bells are habitually rung. The tolling of bells, so long as it is not for an unreasonably long period of time, before public worship in compliance with Canon law should constitute a defence of 'reasonable excuse' to a prosecution under the 1990 Act.

19. It may be advisable for the minister and churchwardens in consultation with the PCC to establish a policy as to when and for how long the bells in the church for which they are responsible may be rung. Such a policy may be helpful in dealing with complaints or defending an action in nuisance or

establishing a 'reasonable excuse' defence on being served with an abatement notice under the 1990 Act.

20. Furthermore a bells policy should, if practicable, take into account pastoral considerations such as the particular vulnerabilities of (potential) complainants eg the position of the elderly, the very ill, night shift workers etc.

Control of church bells and bell-ringers

21. The control of the church bells and bell-ringers does not belong to the PCC but jointly to the incumbent and churchwardens. Accordingly anyone who wishes to ring the bells must comply with their requirements which could, if they thought fit, include the levying of a charge.

Who is liable

22. Clearly the persons who can give directions regarding bell ringing may be liable, usually the incumbent or churchwardens. However, the ringing of bells in a parish church which might constitute a nuisance is not actionable against the bishop of the diocese in which the church is situated (*Calvert v Gardiner and Others* (The Times 22 July 2002)).

Note: Information and advice on the conservation of church bells and bell-frames can be obtained from the Council for the Care of Churches and the Central Council for Church Bell Ringers.

(June 1992, Revised 2003, Revised 2008)

Seeking the consent of the DBF to the sale of PCC property

1. The Commission has been invited to consider the effect of section 6(3) of the Parochial Church Councils (Powers) Measure 1956, and in particular the manner in which the diocesan board of finance ('DBF') should determine whether to give or withhold its consent to the sale or other disposal of property vested in it on behalf of a parochial church council ('PCC').

2. Discussion should start with section 6(2) of the Measure, which provides for specified parochial property to be held by the DBF:

> 'Where, at or after the commencement of this Measure, a council holds or acquires an interest in land (other than a short lease as hereinafter defined) or any interest in personal property to be held on permanent trusts, such interest shall be vested in the diocesan authority subject to all trusts, debts and liabilities affecting the same, and all persons concerned shall make or concur in making such transfers (if any) as are requisite for giving effect to the provisions of this subsection.'

3. Subsection 6(3) then proceeds to establish the requirement for the consent of the DBF to be obtained before such property is sold or otherwise dealt with:

> 'Where any property is vested in the diocesan authority pursuant to subsection (2) of this section, the council shall not sell, lease, exchange, charge or take any legal proceedings with respect to the property without the consent of the authority; but save as aforesaid, nothing in this section shall affect the powers of the council in relation to the management, administration or disposition of any such property.'

4. Where property is vested in the DBF as 'diocesan authority' by virtue of these provisions the DBF is, on the face of the Measure, more than merely a 'custodian trustee', since its consent to certain dealings with the property is expressly required; but the difference may be more apparent than real.

5. The role of custodian trustee arises where a corporate body (of certain specified kinds) is appointed as such under section 4 of the Public Trustee Act 1906. In that event, trustee functions are divided between the custodian trustee and the trustee(s) otherwise responsible for managing the trust property ('the managing trustee(s)') in the way specified in section 4. The Act provides (in section 4(2)(b) and (d)) as follows:

'(b) The management of the trust property and the exercise of any power or discretion exercisable by the trustees under the trust shall remain vested in the trustees other than the custodian trustee (which trustees are hereinafter referred to as the managing trustees);

. . .

(d) The custodian trustee shall concur in and perform all acts necessary to enable the managing trustees to exercise their powers of management or any other power or discretion vested in them (including the power to pay money or securities into court), unless the matter in which he is requested to concur is a breach of trust, or involves a personal liability upon him in respect of calls or otherwise, but, unless he so concurs, the custodian trustee shall not be liable for any act or default on the part of the managing trustees or any of them;'

6. Accordingly, the position under the 1906 Act appears to differ from that under the Measure, in that the consent of a custodian trustee is not required for the sale etc of the trust property or for the taking of legal proceedings in connection with it. The DBF therefore appears to have greater powers of control than does a custodian trustee.

7. The power conferred upon the DBF as diocesan authority is a fiduciary (or trustee) power, given to it to ensure the proper administration of the trust property, and in particular to protect that property against the possibility of a decision by the PCC which is inconsistent with the duties of the PCC as trustee. The question is how far the DBF's responsibilities in this respect justify it in over-riding the views of the PCC.

8. It would seem clear that one aspect of the DBF's role as diocesan authority is to ensure that the PCC is acting within the scope of its powers in relation to the trust property, so that it should decline to give its consent to a disposition, or to legal proceedings, by the PCC which are outside those powers. In *IRC v Silverts*, [1951] Ch 521, a case of custodian trusteeship, the Court of Appeal accepted the submission of counsel for the Commissioners (at page 522), who said:

'The Crown contends that this case is governed by *British American Tobacco Co. Ltd v Inland Revenue Commissioners*, [1943]AC 335; that to find the control one must look to the character in which that bank is on the register; and that since the bank is merely a custodian trustee bound by s.4 of the Public Trustee Act, 1906, to give effect to the directions of the managing trustees, it must be regarded as being in the position of a bare trustee. That is not the correct way of looking at the position of the bank. Under s.4 the bank is bound, when it receives any directions from the managing trustees, to see that they are within its scope or powers. The relation of custodian trustee to managing trustee differs substantially from the relationship of a bare trustee and his *cestui que trust.*'

9. One particular manifestation of this principle is that if the PCC disposes of, or mortgages, its land (including a rentcharge) it has to comply with sections 36–40 of the Charities Act 1993;[1] and since it would be unlawful for it to attempt to dispose of or mortgage its land without doing so, the DBF can properly, and should, refuse consent until satisfied that the requirements of those sections have been observed.

10. Taking legal proceedings with respect to the property may involve the DBF in making a judgment as to whether there would be a breach of trust, and the DBF possibly has a more substantial role to play in such a (comparatively rare) case; but, again, so would a custodian trustee under section 4(2)(b). Charity trustees have wide powers to bring, defend and compromise legal proceedings, but those powers must (like other trust powers) be exercised prudently; and the law takes a stern approach to charity trustees bringing or defending legal proceedings irresponsibly (even when they act on legal advice in doing so: see *Re Beddoe,* [1893] 1 Ch 547). Before giving its consent to legal proceedings, therefore, a DBF would be entitled at the least to satisfy itself that the PCC was acting responsibly by asking it to justify its decision and enquiring, for example, whether the PCC had sought the advice of the Charity Commission in relation to the proceedings.

11. Beyond these cases, the right of the DBF to decline to give its consent to decisions taken by the PCC in the administration of the charity is less clear. However, it would appear that central to the interpretation of subsection 6(3) is the weight which is to be given to the saving provision at the end. This expressly states that 'nothing in this section is to affect the power of the [PCC] in relation to the management, administration or disposition of the property'. Thus the consent of the DBF should be given (even where the DBF might itself have taken a different view of the matter) unless the PCC is acting beyond the scope of its legal powers or in bad faith, has been guilty of some procedural or other irregularity (such as basing its decision on considerations which were irrelevant) or has reached

---

[1] Sections 36 and 37 require the consent of the Charity Commission for certain disposals of land held by or in trust for a charity, unless specified requirements (including obtaining and considering advice from a qualified surveyor) are met. Sections 38 and 39 require the consent of the Commission for any mortgage of land held by or in trust for a charity, unless certain conditions (including obtaining and considering proper advice) are met. Section 40 deals with rentcharges. Further advice can be found on the Charity Commission's website at http://www.charity-commission.gov.uk/publications/cc28.asp

a decision which is so far beyond the range of reasonable options that no reasonable PCC could have made it; i.e. the DBF should apply similar principles to those set out in the well known test in *Associated Provincial Picture Houses Limited v Wednesbury Corporation*, [1948] 1 KB 223.

12. It is recommended that when seeking the consent of the DBF, the PCC submits a brief written statement of its reasons for the proposed sale or other disposal together with copies of all relevant resolutions passed by the PCC. This will enable the DBF to form a view as to whether there might be reasonable grounds (of the type outlined above) to refuse to give its consent.

(March 2009)

Ordinands: Requirement of confirmation

1. The question has been asked of the Legal Advisory Commission whether the requirement of Canon C 4, paragraph 1, that a candidate for ordination must have been confirmed is met in the case of a candidate who –

(i)   has received confirmation in the Roman Catholic Church where the minister of that confirmation was a priest and not a bishop, that is, presbyteral confirmation; and/or

(ii)   has received chrismation in one of the Orthodox Churches.

Canon C4, paragraph 1, states:

'Every bishop shall take care that he admit no person into holy orders but such as he knows either by himself, or by sufficient testimony, to have been baptized and confirmed, to be sufficiently instructed in Holy Scripture and in the doctrine, discipline, and worship of the Church of England, and to be of virtuous conversation and good repute and such as to be a wholesome example and pattern to the flock of Christ.'

2. The question asked of the Commission necessarily raises the meaning of 'confirmation' in the Canons of the Church of England and for this reason it is necessary to consider the provision of Canon B 27, paragraph 1. This Canon is headed 'Of Confirmation' and states:

'The bishop of every diocese shall himself minister (or cause to be ministered by some other bishop lawfully deputed in his stead) the rite of confirmation throughout his diocese as often and in as many places as shall be convenient, laying his hands upon children and other persons who have been baptized and instructed in the Christian faith.'

It is clear that this Canon requires a confirmation in which a bishop himself lays hands upon the candidate and, indeed, this reflects the requirements both of *The Order of Confirmation in the Book of Common Prayer* ('. . . the Bishop . . . shall lay his hand upon the head of every one severally . . .') and *Common Worship: Baptism and Confirmation within a Celebration of holy Communion* ('He then lays his hand on the head of each [candidate] . . .').

3. However, under Canon B 43, paragraph 2(b)(iii), a bishop who in certain circumstances receives an invitation to take part in a service of confirmation in conjunction with another denomination may 'notwithstanding any provision of any Canon. . . in the course of that service perform any duty

assigned to him'. It is therefore clear from Canon B 43 that services of 'confirmation' conducted in a Church to which the Canon applies (which include the Roman Catholic Church in the England and Wales, the Archdiocese of Thyateira and Great Britain and the Russian Patriarchial Church of Great Britain being the Orthodox Diocese of Sourozh operating within the provinces of Canterbury and York[1]) are recognised as actual confirmation whether or not all the requisites of Canon B 27 are fulfilled. In addition, under Canon B 44, paragraph 4(i)(e) a bishop who has given his agreement to participation in a local ecumenical project may after consultation –

> 'make provision for the holding in that area of joint services with any other participating Church, including services of ... confirmation.'

4. The *Ecumenical Relations, Canons B 43 and B 44: Code of Practice*[2] sets out guidelines for such joint confirmations. Having set out that for the Church of England the minister of confirmation is 'the bishop of the diocese or some other bishop authorised by him', these guidelines state *inter alia*:

> 'Confirmation is properly administered in a locality by a commissioned representative of the wider Church. For the Church of England this must be the bishop of the diocese or some other bishop authorised by him. As Joint Confirmations are seen as admitting people to fellowship with the other participating Churches it is confusing, and therefore undesirable, for a local Church of England priest whose ministry is officially recognised by another Church to be that Church's officiating minister of confirmation; such a practice would in any case be contrary to Canon B 43 paragraph 3(a).[3]'

The *Code of Practice* then goes on to remind its readers that when the House of Bishops first agreed to permit joint confirmation the appropriate minute read:

---

[1] See *The Canons of the Church of England* (Church House Publishing, 6th ed, 2000) at 203.
[2] Original 1989 Edition with updates and amendments from the 1997 Supplement.
[3] *Code of Practice* at paragraph 112. Canon B 43, paragraph 3(a) states that a priest or deacon of the Church of England ('notwithstanding any provision of any Canon') who is invited to take part in a service (including a service of confirmation: see Canon B 43, para2(b)(iii)) may perform any duty assigned to him if 'the duty assigned to him is or is similar to a duty which he is authorized to perform in the Church of England'. Although the Canon does not strictly apply to services within local ecumenical projects the view expressed in the Code nonetheless reflects the general ecclesiastical law. What is more, Canon B 44 does not have any similar saving in relation to 'any provision of any Canon'.

'[J]oint services of Confirmation may be held, provided that the rite at least includes a form of Confirmation authorised by the Church of England and that the parish priest is satisfied that all candidates have been adequately prepared.[4]'

Having set out three broad 'schools of thought' in the Church of England on the relation of baptism to confirmation, it then continues:

'Many would not wish to polarise these views and sections 23–26 of the ASB Baptism and Confirmation Service were carefully drawn up to hold them together. Partly for this reason they have normally been used in joint services of confirmation. It is probably wise to continue this practice although a bishop might use other rites if he were satisfied that they were compatible with Church of England doctrine and practice.[5]

Nevertheless it is again clear that a joint service of confirmation, even if the rite from *Common Worship* in not used, is regarded as 'confirmation'[6].'

5. The question upon which the Commission is asked to advise arises from the fact that in the Roman Catholic Church a candidate for ordination may have received confirmation where the minister is a priest and not a bishop (that is, presbyteral confirmation)[7]. There is a related question arising from the fact that confirmation as such does not exist as a separate rite of initiation in the Orthodox Churches although candidates receive chrismation at the time of their baptism. It is therefore also necessary to refer to Canon B 28. This states:

1. Any person desiring to be received into the Church of England, who has not been baptized or the validity of whose baptism can

---

[4] *Code of Practice* at paragraph 113(a).

[5] *Code of Practice* at paragraph 113(b). The ASB service is now replaced by the service of Holy Baptism and Confirmation published in *Common Worship: Christian Initiation*: see the Approved and Commended forms of service listed in *The Canons of the Church of England* at 187. The *Code of Practice* at paragraph 113(b) suggests that it may be appropriate if at a joint confirmation the anointing of the candidate is by 'the bishop or the minister of a nother church'.

[6] It may be noted that there is no provision in relation to confirmation similar to that in relation to the 'non-celebration' of Holy Communion 'according to the use of the Church of England' notwithstanding that an authorised form of service is used: see Canon B 44, paragraph 4(3).

[7] Behrens *Confirmation Sacrament of Grace* (Gracewing) at 91, note 249, suggests that the acceptance into the Church of England of such a person without confirmation is 'uncanonical', although what the word 'uncanonical' means in this context is perhaps ambiguous.

be held in question, shall be instructed and baptized or conditionally baptized, and such baptism, or conditional baptism, shall constitute the said person's reception into the Church of England.

2. If any such person has been baptized but not episcopally confirmed and desires to be formally admitted into the Church of England he shall, after appropriate instruction, be received by the rite of confirmation, or, if he be not yet ready to be presented for confirmation, he shall be received by the parish priest with appropriate prayers.

3. If any such person has been episcopally confirmed with unction or with the laying on of hands he shall be instructed, and, with the permission of the bishop, received into the Church of England according to the Form of Reception approved by the General Synod, or with other appropriate prayers, and if any such person be a priest he shall be received into the said Church only by the bishop of the diocese or by the commissary of such bishop.

This is the only Canon that speaks specifically of 'episcopal confirmation'. Such confirmation is (at least partially) outlined by paragraph 3, namely, 'with unction or with the laying on of hands'. Therefore for the purposes of the Canons the rite of confirmation as administered by a Church other than the Church of England does not necessarily require the laying on of hands and may (at least) be by way of unction.

6. *Prima facie* a word used in one Canon should be interpreted in the same way as in other Canons. Therefore, in the light of the ecumenical Canons (but putting aside the wording of Canon B 28) the word 'confirmation' in Canon C 4 would embrace confirmation administered in another Church to which that Canon applies[8]. These Churches include those following the practices both of the Roman Catholic Church and the Orthodox Churches[9].

7. According to Canon 882 of the *Code of Canon Law* of the Roman Catholic Church:

'The ordinary minister of confirmation is the bishop; a presbyter who has this faculty by virtue of either the universal law or a special concession of competent authority also confers this sacrament validly.'

---

[8] See footnote 1 above.
[9] See paragraph 3 above.

The administration of confirmation is specified by Canon 880 of the *Code of Canon Law* which states:

> 'The sacrament of confirmation is conferred through anointing with chrism . . . The chrism must be consecrated by a bishop, even if the sacrament is administered by a presbyter.'

Moreover, as the *Commentary* on the Code commissioned by the Canon Law Society of America[10] makes clear, the bishop is 'the primary minister of confirmation as indeed he is of all the sacraments of Christian initiation'.

8. As has already been noted, the Orthodox Church has no formal rite called 'confirmation'. The rite of chrismation in nonetheless also referred to as confirmation:

> 'The sacrament of chrismation, also called confirmation, is always done in the Orthodox Church together with baptism. Just as Easter has no meaning without Pentecost, so baptism has no meaning for the Christian without chrismation. In this understanding and practice, the Orthodox Church differs from the Roman Catholic and Protestant churches where the two sacraments are often separated and given other interpretations than those found in traditional Orthodoxy. . . . It is the Eastern equivalent of confirmation in the West.[11]'

Furthermore, *The Oxford Dictionary of the Christian Church*[12] states:

> 'In the E[ast] the primitive custom of conferring 'Confirmation' in immediate relation to Baptism was retained. This was achieved by confining the bishop's part to the consecration of the oil used for the anointing. This was then conveyed to the parish priest, who performed the actual rite of Confirmation as occasion required.'

Indeed this view of chrismation was accepted by Vatican II:

> 'Regarding the minister of confirmation the practice existing in the Eastern Churches from the most ancient times is to be fully restored. Priests, therefore, using chrism blessed by a patriarch or a bishop are empowered to confer this sacrament.[13]'

---

[10] Ed Coriden, Green and Heintschel (Geoffrey Chapman).

[11] See the Orthodox Church in America website, **Chrismation**, at www.oca.org (accessed on the 6th February 2009).

[12] 3rd ed. (Oxford, 1997) at 396. See also *The Dictionary of Liturgy and Worship* (SCM Press, 1972) at 47.

[13] Quoted in *The Code of Canon Law_A Text and Commentary* at 635–635.

9. As has been noted Canon B 28 speaks of a person seeking reception into the Church of England who may not be 'episcopally confirmed'. Although the word 'episcopally' might seem at first sight to suggest that the confirmation must be directly performed by a bishop, it does not necessarily have that meaning. The legal interpretation of the Canons requires a purposive approach and that approach embraces the requirements of ecumenism as Canons B 43 and 44 indirectly emphasise. For this reason episcopal confirmation for the purposes of Canon C 4 should be interpreted so as to include confirmation under the authority of a bishop and, particularly, with a chrism consecrated or blessed by a bishop or patriarch. Therefore the answer to the question raised with the Commission is in the affirmative. Nevertheless such a person should first receive appropriate instruction and be received into the Church of England in accordance with Canon B 28, paragraph 3, before being ordained within the Church of England.

10. In addition, it is the view of the Commission that chrismation is similarly a form of confirmation for the purposes of both Canon C4 and Canons B 43 and 44.

11. This interpretation also accords both with the original draft of Canon B 28 approved by both Convocations and the understanding of the meaning of the present Canon as explained to the Convocations by Canon E. W. Kemp (as he then was)[14]. It also accords with the understanding of Canon B 28 put forward by the Council for Christian Unity Faith and Order Advisory Group and which, it is understood, has been followed in many dioceses for a number of years[15].

Summary

Presbyteral confirmation in the Roman Catholic Church and chrismation within the Orthodox Churches are both forms of episcopal confirmation within the meaning of Canon B 28, paragraph 3. They are therefore also forms of confirmation within the Canon 4, paragraph 1. A person seeking ordination in the Church of England who has been baptised and confirmed in either of these Churches should first receive appropriate instruction and be received into the Church of England in accordance with Canon B 28, paragraph 3.

(March 2009)

---

[14] See the paper LAC (08) 8B by the Bishop of Guildford.
[15] See *ibid* and LAC (08) 8A.

Wedding receptions held on church premises

1. There is a growing practice of holding wedding receptions on church premises. The Legal Advisory Commission has been asked whether, and in what circumstances, a faculty is required in order to permit such receptions taking place.

2. The faculty jurisdiction of the consistory court applies to all premises and land that has been consecrated, including buildings situated on that land. However, the faculty jurisdiction also applies to all buildings licensed by the bishop for public worship and to unconsecrated land (including buildings) which form part of the curtilage of a church within the jurisdiction of the court: see the Faculty Jurisdiction Measure 1964, s7(1); Care of Churches and Ecclesiastical Jurisdiction Measure 1991, s11. Therefore, as well as to church premises, the faculty jurisdiction applies to churchyards and to certain church halls that are adjacent to any church within the jurisdiction of the court.

Church halls outside the faculty jurisdiction

3. It follows that no issues specific to ecclesiastical law arise in respect of wedding receptions in those church halls which are entirely distinct geographically from any church within the jurisdiction of the court, although licensing, noise, hygiene, public health and safety issues arise, as with other use of such halls, and (as with other types of party) it will usually be sensible to take a deposit as security against damage.

Church halls within the faculty jurisdiction

4. It is probable that a substantial number of church halls are within the curtilage of a church, and therefore are themselves subject to the faculty jurisdiction. These are the buildings where it may be most likely that there will be requests to book the church hall for a wedding reception.

5. In some cases there will be in existence a general faculty permitting the use of the church hall for a variety of uses, including social events such as wedding receptions, subject to conditions, including conditions relating to the supply and/or sale of alcoholic liquor, as well as food hygiene, noise, public health and safety issues (though the grant of a faculty does not remove in any way the need to satisfy the requirements of the secular law in respect of these and other matters). Such a general faculty may, for example, include a condition requiring undertakings by those responsible for organising the reception in relation to the behaviour of the guests and entertainers.

6. Where there is not already a general faculty in existence, Parochial Church Councils are advised to seek such a general faculty (or possibly a variation to an existing faculty) to cover use for wedding receptions, so that it is not necessary to apply for a new faculty each time a request is made.

7. Where the holding of a wedding reception in such a hall is not the subject of a general faculty, in most cases it will be necessary to obtain a one-off faculty for the event, save in rare cases where the refreshment and entertainment is being provided by the church itself without charge, where it may be that no faculty is required. Even in such cases it is advisable to contact the diocesan registrar for confirmation that this is so. It will also be necessary to ensure that the church itself is securely locked, so that there is no overflow of unseemly activities from the hall into the church.

Churches

8. Occasionally requests are received for the wedding reception to be held within the church itself. This creates a tension between, on the one hand, the rule that by reason of consecration a building 'is dedicated thenceforth to sacred uses, and the law precludes it from being ever capable of use for ordinary secular purposes' (*Wright v Ingle* (1885) 16 QBD 400 per Bowen LJ), and, on the other hand, the increasing preparedness of chancellors to permit secondary, secular use of churches, so long as this complies with 'the principle that a church must be treated in a reverent and seemly manner consistent with its use as a place of worship' (*In re St Peter and St Paul's Church, Chingford* [2007] Fam 67 at 77, Court of Arches).

9. What has been said above in relation to general faculties in respect of church halls covered by the faculty jurisdiction applies equally to the holding of wedding receptions within churches themselves. It is unlikely that there will be applications to hold wedding receptions in churches which do not already have some kitchen facilities, and when such kitchen facilities were installed, the relevant faculty may have specified conditions relating to permitted uses.

10. Where no general faculty exists permitting wedding receptions, a one-off faculty will almost invariably be required, especially if any church furniture is to be moved other than chairs. In particular church articles of special historic, archaeological or artistic merit will require special protection. There needs to be an awareness of the risk to historic fabric and furnishing from spilled food or drink. In particular spilled wine is likely to cause damage to the floor of the church, whether or not it is carpeted, although this may be mitigated by prohibiting the use of red wine.

05/18

11. However, there is a more fundamental problem in relation to wedding receptions in churches as actions may take place during such receptions that are indeed inconsistent with the sanctity of the place, for example, bawdy speeches or rowdy behaviour or drunkenness. Moreover, whilst dancing, and the playing of accompanying music, are not necessarily impermissible in a church, their extent and regulation calls for careful consideration, which should be done through the medium of a faculty.

12. In the case of a modern church building, specifically designed for multi-purpose use, there is often a general faculty regulating the uses to which the new building can be put, and this may cover wedding receptions. But in the absence of a general faculty, a specific faculty is required even in the case of such buildings, there being no scope for assuming permission, even if the holding of events such as wedding receptions was specifically referred to at the time planning permission was sought.

Duties of churchwardens

13. The holding of wedding receptions in adjacent church halls, and particularly in churches, also requires churchwardens to give careful consideration to their duty to maintain order and decency in the church and churchyard, whether or not during divine service (see Canon E 1, para 4). Furthermore, Canon F 15, para 3, states that:

> 'If any person be guilty of riotous, violent or indecent behaviour in any church, chapel, or churchyard, *whether in any time of divine service or not*, . . . the said churchwardens or their assistants shall take care to restrain the offender and if necessary proceed against him according to law'. (Emphasis supplied)

14. Nor should any churchwarden assume that responsibility for satisfying, for example, licensing and food hygiene requirements is solely a matter for those holding the wedding reception as Canon F 15, para 2, states that the churchwardens:

> 'shall . . . take care that nothing be done [in a church or chapel] contrary to the law of the Church *or the Realm*'. (Emphasis supplied)

15. In addition to obtaining any necessary faculty, if churches are to be used for wedding receptions, it is advisable that one or more of the churchwardens or their representative is present throughout the reception to ensure that nothing inconsistent with the sanctity of the place or constituting a breach of ecclesiastical or secular law takes place and, that, if breaches do occur, they cease as soon as possible. Such considerations

may suggest that in practice the occasions when a church is likely to be able to be used for a wedding reception are likely to be limited.

Re-ordering for wider and/or community use

16. It is recommended that the issues mentioned above should be considered at an early stage when the re-ordering of a church for wider and/or community use is being considered, so that Parochial Church Councils can make proposals for the use of the re-ordered church and the chancellor can ensure that the faculty contains appropriate conditions.

(March 2011)

Administration of Holy Communion Regulations 2015

In exercise of the power conferred on it by paragraph 3 of Canon B12, the General Synod makes the following Regulations on this day, 12th July 2015.

Citation and commencement

1. (1)   These Regulations may be cited as the Administration of Holy Communion Regulations 2015.

    (2)   These Regulations come into force on 1st October 2015.

Parishes

2. (1)   The bishop of a diocese may, on an application by the incumbent or priest-in-charge of a parish in the diocese, authorise the person specified in the application to distribute the Holy Sacrament in that parish.

    (2)   The bishop may designate a suffragan or assistant bishop or an archdeacon to exercise the power under this regulation on the bishop's behalf.

3. (1)   The bishop of a diocese may give a general authority to the incumbent or priest-in-charge of a parish in the diocese under which the incumbent or priest-in-charge may authorise persons to distribute the Holy Sacrament in that parish.

    (2)   An authority under this regulation may be given so as to apply generally in relation to each parish in the diocese or only in relation to the parish or parishes specified in the authority.

4. (1)   A person may not be authorised under regulation 2, or under an authority given under regulation 3, unless the person entitled to give the authorisation is satisfied that the person is a regular communicant of the Church of England.

    (2)   The reference in paragraph (1) to a person who is a regular communicant includes a reference to a child who is neither confirmed nor ready and desirous of being confirmed but is admitted to Holy Communion in accordance with the Admission of Baptized Children to Holy Communion Regulations 2006.

    (3)   A person may not be authorised under regulation 2, or under an authority given under regulation 3, unless the person entitled to

give the authorisation has obtained the consent of the parochial church council; but this requirement does not apply if the authorisation is required only for the purpose specified in paragraph (4).

(4)   A pupil of a church school may not be so authorised to distribute the Holy Sacrament at services in the school unless the person entitled to give the authorisation has obtained the consent of the head teacher of the school.

(5)   In paragraph (4) –

'church school' has the meaning given in section 10(1) of the Diocesan Boards of Education Measure 1991, and

'head teacher' includes an acting head teacher.

(6)   A reference in this regulation to the person entitled to give an authorisation is –

(a)   in a case within regulation 2, a reference to the bishop or (where the bishop has designated a person under paragraph (2) of that regulation) the designated person;

(b)   in a case within regulation 3, a reference to the incumbent or priest-in-charge to whom authority under that regulation is given or (where regulation 8 applies) the rural dean.

5. (1)   An authorisation given under regulation 2 may specify the circumstances in which or conditions subject to which the person being authorised may act in reliance on the authorisation.

(2)   An authority given under regulation 3 may specify the circumstances in which or conditions subject to which a person being authorised under the authority may act in reliance on the authorisation.

6. An authorisation given under regulation 2, or under an authority given under regulation 3, may provide either that it has effect generally or that it has effect only for the purposes of public worship.

7. The incumbent or priest-in-charge of a parish must keep under review the authorisations given in the parish under regulation 2 or under an authority given under regulation 3.

8. In a case where the cure is vacant and no priest-in-charge is appointed –

  (a) the rural dean may make an application under regulation 2,

  (b) an authority under regulation 3 may be given to the rural dean, and

  (c) the duty under regulation 7 is to be carried out by the rural dean.

Guild churches

9. (1) The bishop of a diocese may, on an application by the vicar of a guild church in the diocese, authorise the person specified in the application to distribute the Holy Sacrament in that guild church.

  (2) The bishop may designate a suffragan or assistant bishop or an archdeacon to exercise the power under this regulation on the bishop's behalf.

10. The bishop of a diocese may give a general authority to the vicar of a guild church in the diocese under which the vicar may authorise persons to distribute the Holy Sacrament in that guild church.

11. Regulations 4 to 7 apply to authorisation under regulation 9 as they apply to authorisation under regulation 2, and they apply to an authority given under regulation 10 as they apply to an authority given under regulation 3; and for that purpose –

  (a) a reference to the incumbent or priest-in-charge of a parish is to be read as a reference to the vicar of the guild church (and a reference to the parish is to be read accordingly),

  (b) a reference to the parochial church council is to be read as a reference to the guild church council, and

  (c) regulation 4(4) and (5), and the words in regulation 4(3) from 'but this requirement' to the end, are to be ignored.

Cathedrals

12. (1) The dean of a cathedral may authorise persons to distribute the Holy Sacrament in the cathedral.

  (2) An authorisation given under this regulation may specify the circumstances in which or conditions subject to which the person being authorised may act in reliance on the authorisation.

13. Regulations 4(1) to (3), 6 and 7 apply to authorisation under regulation 12 as they apply to authorisation under an authority given under regulation 3; and for that purpose–

(a)   a reference to the person entitled to give the authorisation or to the incumbent or priest-in-charge of a parish is to be read as a reference to the dean of the cathedral (and a reference to the parish is to be read accordingly),

(b)   a reference to the parochial church council is to be read as a reference to the cathedral chapter, and

(c)   the words in regulation 4(3) from 'but this requirement' to the end are to be ignored.

Revocation

14. The Regulations on the administration of Holy Communion made by the Church Assembly in November 1969 are revoked.

(September 2011)

Liability of DACs and the church buildings council: Amendments to LAC opinion

Diocese: liability of members of diocesan advisory committee and of members of church buildings council

Diocesan Advisory Committees

1. In considering whether members of a Diocesan Advisory Committee ('DAC') may be held liable in damages to a person who suffers loss through negligent advice given by the Committee, it is necessary to begin by examining the DAC's constitution and functions.

2. The DAC of each diocese is required to have a written constitution drawn in accordance with Schedule 1 to the Care of Churches and Ecclesiastical Jurisdiction Measure 1991 (s2(2)). Every DAC has as its members a chairman appointed by the bishop, the archdeacons of the diocese, at least twelve other members appointed in accordance with the provisions of Schedule 1 and any members co-opted in accordance with those provisions.

3. The duties and functions of DACs have been enlarged and increased by the 1991 Measure and are set out in Schedule 2 to that Measure. Under the Measure a DAC is required to act as an advisory body on matters affecting places of worship in the diocese (s2(5), Sch 2, para 1(a)). It is expressly required to give advice to four broad categories of persons or bodies:

(a) office holders, individual and corporate, viz, the bishop, chancellor, archdeacons and pastoral committee of, and PCCs in, the diocese;

(b) intending applicants for faculties in the diocese;

(c) persons engaged in the planning, design or building of new places of worship in the diocese, *not* being places within the jurisdiction of the consistory court; and

(d) such other persons as the DAC may consider appropriate (Sch 2, para 2).

4. The topics on which the DAC is required to give advice, when requested to do so, to the above persons or bodies, are expressed in the 1991 Measure to be:

(a)   the grant of faculties;

(b)   the architecture, archaeology, art and history of places of worship;

(c)   the use, care, planning, design and redundancy of places of worship;

(d)   the use and care of the contents of such places; and

(e)   the use and care of churchyards and burial grounds (Sch 2, para 1(a)).

5. The following *duties* placed on a DAC may involve the giving of advice on matters other than those mentioned:

(f)   to review and assess the risks to materials or of loss to archaeological or historic remains or records arising from petitions for faculties;

(g)   to issue guidance for the storage of records relating to works to places of worship;

(h)   to publicise   methods of repair, construction, adaptation and redevelopment of places of worship and their contents; and

(i)   to perform such functions as may be requested by the bishop, chancellor or diocesan synod of the diocese (Sch 1, para 1(b), (d) (f) and (g)).

6. The advisory *functions* of a DAC under the 1991 Measure fall into three categories:

(a)   Those directly connected with the judicial functions of the chancellor and the archdeacons of the diocese when exercising the jurisdiction of the consistory court, i.e. those within a 'judicial process'. In this category the duties are to advise the chancellor and the archdeacons when any of them is considering a petition for a faculty. The only exceptions to this duty are cases before the chancellor of extreme urgency or cases involving exhumation or the reservation of grave spaces. The category also extends to the power to advise applicants for faculties who, having filed their petitions and so becoming parties to proceedings, are within the 'judicial process'.

(b)   Those connected with the special jurisdiction given to archdeacons by section 21 of the 1991 Measure, to order that articles, appertaining to a church, of artistic and other value should be removed to a place of safety. In this category a DAC has the power to make representations, no doubt couched in the form of advice, to the archdeacon who, in exercising this jurisdiction, may be said to be exercising it as an officer of the court and quasi-judicially.

(c)   All other occasions on which advice is tendered pursuant to the duties mentioned in paragraphs 3 to 5.

7. The provisions relating to the *functions* of DACs are drawn so widely in Schedule 2 to the 1991 Measure that it is difficult to envisage any advice which a DAC might give as a body which could not fairly be described as being given in pursuance of its statutory *functions* under the Measure.

8. The first question which arises in connection with potential liability for the exercise of statutory functions is whether the legislature intended to confer a right of compensation on individuals for breach. Even the fact that a particular power was intended to protect certain individuals is not of itself sufficient to confer a right of action on them (*R v Deputy Governor of Parkhurst Prison ex parte Hague* [1992] 1 AC 58 at 170; *Stovin v Wise* [1996] AC 923 at 952). Where the statutory function is a duty, it will be less likely that a right of compensation was intended than where the statutory function is merely a power. This is because, there being no obligation to exercise the power, the decision to exercise it more readily constitutes a voluntary assumption of liability for the consequences of negligently exercising that power. On most occasions that a DAC gives advice it will do so under a duty rather than a power.

9. So far as is known no DAC has been sued for damages on the ground that a claimant suffered loss through negligent advice given by the Committee. Until such a case has been heard and decided it is impossible to give confident advice on the question whether a DAC would be held to be liable in law. It is important to remember that, if the advice turns out to be wrong, it does not necessarily follow that the Committee which gave it is liable for the loss caused by its imperfection. A DAC is not under any absolute duty to be right though it *is* under a duty to exercise reasonable care and competence. Nevertheless there may be those who, applying the modern law of negligence to advice given to them by a DAC, will claim that they have suffered loss through that advice because the DAC was neither competent nor careful in giving it. For example, a PCC may allege that a new heating system commended to it by the DAC is thoroughly unsuitable and that the DAC failed to make the reasonable enquiries which would have shown it to be so. Or petitioners for a faculty may contend that

costs have been wasted because the DAC did not advise them at an early juncture that their proposal had no realistic chance of success.

10. The general rule applied by law is that anyone holding himself or herself out as possessing reasonable competence in his or her avocation and undertaking to give advice owes a duty to advise with reasonable competence and care. The duty is owed to anyone the adviser should foresee may suffer loss if the duty is breached. If, in breach of that duty, the adviser fails to exercise reasonable competence or care and as a result the person to whom the duty is owed suffers damage, the adviser is liable to compensate that person for the damage suffered: per Lord Salmon, *Saif All v Sydney Mitchell & Co* [1980] AC 198 at 230, HL. The person advised will be able to recover damages only where the claimant relied upon the advice and took some action, or refrained from taking action, in consequence of the advice. There must also be a relationship between the claimant and the DAC of sufficient 'proximity' that it imposes upon the DAC a duty to take care to avoid or prevent that loss which has in fact been sustained. Briefly stated, the questions in each case where there is potentially a right to compensation will be: was the claimant entitled to rely on the impugned advice, and was it within the reasonable contemplation of the DAC that the claimant would rely upon it? See the speech of Lord Oliver in *Murphy v Brentwood District Council* [1991] 1 AC 398, HL.

11. In the case of advice given pursuant to a statutory duty, a DAC cannot qualify its advice by stating that it is given without accepting liability. It is implicit in the statutory obligation that advice must be the best advice, that the members of the DAC, pooling their skill and knowledge, can give and that the members giving it accept responsibility for their advice. By the same token the responsibility cannot be avoided or reduced because the advice is given gratuitously and not for valuable consideration or in discharge of a contractual duty. The statutory obligation is to give gratuitous advice. But where there is only a power to advise there appears to be no reason why, in principle, a DAC cannot protect its members by making it plain that no liability is accepted.

12. As the law stands it follows that no DAC can be assured that, if it is sued for damages on the ground that the claimant has suffered loss through its advice, the claim will fail because it is not sustainable. It has to be accepted that a risk of a DAC being found liable does exist in law. The degree of risk will vary as between the categories of business referred to in paragraph 6 and (as stated above) will be greater in the relatively few cases where the advice is given pursuant to a power rather than a duty.

13. As regards the functions under the first two categories in paragraph 6, which are mainly duties:

(a) In discharging these functions DACs are exercising a function which is by statute an integral part of the judicial process of the consistory court and of the exercise of the statutory jurisdiction of the archdeacon. In exercising the faculty jurisdiction of the consistory court the chancellor and the archdeacons are bound by section 15 of the Care of Churches and Ecclesiastical Jurisdiction Measure 1991 to seek the advice of the DAC upon every petition, except in the limited classes of cases mentioned, viz, those relating to exhumation and reservation of graves and, in so far as the chancellor is concerned, cases of extreme urgency.

(b) There is a general principle that immunity from civil liability attaches to many persons who take part in proceedings before a court of justice: judges, court officials and witnesses (but not now the parties' counsel and solicitors (*Arthur J S Hall & Co v Simons* [2002] AC 615). The immunity of witnesses exists for the benefit of the public since justice would be greatly impeded if witnesses were to be in fear of disgruntled persons against whom they had given evidence subsequently involving them in litigation (*Darker v Chief Constable of the West Midlands Police* [2001] 1 AC 435). An instance of its application occurred in a case in 1981 when Drake J struck out a claim for negligence against a pathologist who was alleged to have been careless in giving advice to the police in relation to a possible prosecution against the claimant (*Evans v London Hospital Medical College (University of London)* [1981] 1 WLR 184). In *Jones v Kaney* [2011] 2 WLR 823 the Supreme Court placed a limit upon the immunity doctrine by holding that a party's own expert witness might be sued by that party for negligent acts or omissions in the course of the process of litigation.

(c) The immunity of those involved in the administration of justice for actions and words done and said in the execution of judicial office is established. The underlying principles of public policy are:

   (i) that those concerned must be free from the anxiety of possible action in discharging their office; and

   (ii) that another court with a co-ordinate level of jurisdiction should not be asked to review previous decisions by means of an allegation of negligence against the previous court.

(d) In exercising its statutory duty to advise the chancellor or an archdeacon, a DAC is assisting in a judicial function even though the decision is that of the chancellor or archdeacon and not the DAC. In this field the DAC has an obligation to give advice, and there is here an analogy with compellability of witnesses, where on the authorities the obligation to give evidence is one of the factors in granting immunity to witnesses. Also the chancellor may require the DAC to nominate a member to give evidence in court in support of any advice tendered.

(e)   It is considered therefore that the principle of immunity from suit of those concerned with the administration of justice will in principle afford a defence to a DAC alleged to have given negligent advice in the discharge of duties in the first two categories mentioned in paragraph 6. The decision in *Jones v Kaney* does not affect the position of the DAC, which has a wholly independent role not to be confused with that of an expert witness instructed by a party to litigation.

14. As regards duties under the third category in paragraph 6, the defence arising from participation in the judicial process will not be available if no proceedings in the consistory court have been commenced or are immediately contemplated. However, in cases where an intending applicant for a faculty is required by rule or practice to seek and obtain the advice of the DAC before commencing proceedings the defence may be available. In any claim for a breach of duty under this category the other defences mentioned in paragraph 15 should be considered.

15. The limits of the defence of participation in the judicial process must be borne in mind. The defence will be available to a DAC or any member of it when advising or giving evidence within a judicial process as mentioned above. But advice given to a person, e.g. to a PCC, before proceedings are begun or actually proposed (and pursuant to a power and not a duty) will not be given retrospective immunity simply because it is repeated to the chancellor, archdeacon or, by way of evidence, in court. Claims that such earlier advice has given rise to loss must be met in the light of the points mentioned in the following paragraph.

16. Even if a right to compensation exists in certain circumstances, in order to succeed in recovering damages a claimant alleging loss through reliance upon the negligent advice of a DAC would have to prove not only that in the particular case a duty of care was owed but that the duty had been broken. The fact that the advice in question was given pursuant to a statutory duty would be material in deciding the scope of the duty; what, in the circumstances, is the reasonable care required; and whether or not on the facts there had been a failure to discharge the duty. Until the facts proved in court in relation to any individual case are established it cannot

be foreseen what weight any argument or factor would carry. It might be open to the DAC to argue that the loss occasioned to the claimant was due to 'inevitable accident' or to some cause other than the negligence of the DAC. Again, the DAC might be able to establish that the effective cause of the loss was some act or omission by the claimant or that the claimant materially contributed to the loss by an act or omission (partial defence of contributory negligence). In a small category of cases the defence of voluntarily accepting the risk *(volenti non fit injuria)* might be available.

17. For convenience the previous paragraphs have discussed the liability of DACs as though there might be liability in a DAC as such. It must be borne in mind, however, that DACs are not bodies corporate; their members are appointed for limited terms. Members of a DAC are not agents for one another, as are partners in a firm. The individual members of a DAC therefore cannot be liable for negligence arising from a decision of the DAC unless the decision was that of the Committee formally arrived at and expressed in its recommendation or report. Even so, members not present when the decision was taken, or members voting against the proposal, cannot be liable. It is therefore not strictly accurate to speak of the liability of a DAC in negligence; rather, individual members, shown to be responsible for a decision, would be jointly and severally liable for it. Any action would have to be against the individual members and not the DAC as a body, and each member sued would only be liable if it were proved that that member failed to exercise the care which was to be expected, having regard to the member's own particular skill, knowledge and experience, or that the member formally adopted the negligence of another member of the DAC, e.g. by voting to support a negligent decision when a responsible member of a DAC of ordinary competence ought to have realized that it was unsafe to do so. This principle might protect non-specialist members of a DAC, if the negligent advice given was in a specialist field (such as organs or bells) and the advice given by the specialist was of such a nature that a non-specialist could not be expected to take part in giving it. However, it is considered that this argument would not assist in the majority of cases where the advice given is in areas in which all members of the DAC have competence and all members present at a meeting of the DAC concur in the advice.

18. Where an individual member of the DAC offers negligent advice on his or her own account, say on a site visit, it may be easier for a person to whom such advice is given and who relies on it to his or her detriment to establish liability.

19. In summary, it must be repeated that the circumstances certainly exist in which it is possible for members of a DAC to be held liable for negligence, but that in individual cases particular members may well be

able to show that no liability is established against them either because of the facts of the particular case or because of the legal principles. Therefore individual DACs may wish to consider taking out insurance cover against any claims which may be brought against their members for negligence.

20. Complaints are sometimes made by parishes that advice from the DAC has been unduly delayed and that this has caused loss to the parish. It is important that the advisory functions of DACs are performed with reasonable expedition to prevent potential litigation on account of excessive delay.

The Church Buildings Council

21. The Church Buildings Council ('CBC') is an unincorporated organ of the Church of England operating at national level, the functions of which are set out in Sections 55, 56 and 57 of the Dioceses, Pastoral and Mission Measure 2007. In so far as these functions involve administration, the promotion of specified policy objectives, or co-operation with other bodies, it is highly unlikely that their performance is capable of giving rise to any liability in negligence. Within its range of functions there are, however, specific areas in which the CBC is given powers or duties to advise broadly matching those of a DAC at diocesan level. They involve the provision of: –

(a) advice to the Archbishops' Council and the General Synod in matters relating to churches (Section 55(1)(a));

(b) advice to the ecclesiastical courts in relation to faculty cases or proceedings for injunctions and restoration orders (Section 55(1)(b) and Rules 15, 22 and 23 of the Faculty Jurisdiction Rules 2000);

(c) advice to persons or bodies involved in the use, care, conservation, repair, planning, design and development of church buildings or certain other places of worship (Section 55(2)).

22. In its provision of material for use in the ecclesiastical courts, whether in the form of reports, witness statements or oral evidence, the CBC enjoys precisely the same level of immunity as that of the DAC described previously. Once again, the *Jones v Kaney* exception has no bearing because the status of the CBC is independent of the parties.

23. While any claim in respect of allegedly negligent advice given to the Archbishops' Council or to the General Synod is inherently unlikely to be made, the CBC is at somewhat greater risk when giving advice outside the context of legal proceedings to persons or bodies in connection with

particular buildings (the third category in paragraph 18). In such cases the CBC has a power to advise but no duty to do so. If advice is given in such circumstances, the inclusion of a suitably worded disclaimer ought to be considered.

24. Where negligent advice is given by an individual member of the CBC on, say, a site visit, the considerations in paragraph 18 above apply.

25. Wholly exceptionally, the CBC may itself discharge the functions of a DAC in relation to a place of worship. Thus by virtue of Section 3(5) of the Care of Places of Worship Measure 1999 the CBC is to assume the responsibilities of a DAC in respect of the chapels of Lambeth Palace. In that and any similar case it will stand m exactly the same position as a DAC as regards liability m negligence.

26. The considerations relating to undue delay in paragraph 20 above apply equally to the CBC.

27. It is of course open to the CBC to take out insurance cover for its members.

(April 2012)

Collections at funerals and memorial services

1. A question has been asked of the Legal Advisory Commission as to what should happen in relation to collections taken at funerals. On some occasions relatives request that the collection should be donated to a particular charity or charities, although this may not have been notified to the minister and the funeral director may also on occasion arrive at the church with his own collection box. In some parishes the PCCs have agreed policies in relation to such collections, for example, that, if the preceding press notice of the funeral specifies a charity to which memorial donations might be made, donations placed on the collection plate in envelopes marked with the name of the charity or with other appropriate words will be forwarded to that designated charity. Some parishes have adopted a policy of a 50/50 split between a charity so nominated and parish funds of whatever collection is taken although this has caused friction with some families.

2. The opinion specifically relates to any collection (however taken and by whomsoever taken) within the church building whether before, during or after the service.

3. Again, although this opinion specifically addresses the question of collections at funerals, the same principles apply to collections taken at memorial services and services of thanksgiving for deceased persons. Moneys sent directly to an undertaker or funeral director must be forwarded directly to the specified charity.

Collections Generally:

4. In *Marson v Unmack* [1923] P 163 the Dean of the Arches said:

> 'I need hardly say that in public worship deviations from the services contained in the Prayer Book, unless authorized by or under the Acts of Uniformity, are unlawful. A collection made during Mattins or Evensong – I exclude an offertory during the Communion service because that is expressly provided for by rubric, and may therefore perhaps be regarded as a part of the service – is not provided for in the Prayer Book. It is an incident occurring during a service or interposed between different portions of it, but it is no more part of the service than a voluntary played on the organ or the action of a verger closing windows or lighting the gas while the service is in progress. Though of course varying greatly in degree of importance, they are all alike in being matters, not in themselves irreverent or unseemly, but outside the rites and ceremonies of public worship. Such a collection is an interlude entirely at the option of the minister, and has its sole justification in the sanction of long custom. It is quite

impossible to treat the action of the minister in ordering a collection to be made during morning or evening service as an ecclesiastical offence. But, if he orders such a collection, its allocation is, under the Measure of 1921, a matter for the decision of himself and the Parochial Church Council jointly. . . . Collections in church, other than those made at the offertory [at Holy Communion], may lawfully be made for objects determined by agreement between the incumbent and the Parochial Church Council. Such objects may be, and I think, having regard to the language of clause 6 (iv) of the Measure of 1921, ought to be announced to the congregation before the collection. When the objects have been so determined and announced, the resulting collections must of course be applied to those objects.'

The same reasoning would apply to collections at funeral services. At the time of the above judgment the rubric at the end of Holy Communion in the Book of Common Prayer provided:

'After the Divine Service ended, the money given at the Offertory shall be disposed of to such pious and charitable uses, as the Minister and Church-wardens shall think fit. Wherein if they disagree, it shall be disposed of as the Ordinary shall appoint.'

However, this rubric has now been superseded by Canon B 17A which overrules the rubric and states that:

'. . . moneys given or collected in church at Holy Communion shall form part of the general funds of the parochial church council and shall be disposed of by the parochial church council in accordance with the provisions of section 7(iv) of the Parochial Church Councils (Powers) Measure 1956.'

5. The provisions of the Parochial Church Council (Powers) Measure 1921, section 6(iv), were to all extents and purposes the same as section 7(iv) of the Parochial Church Council (Powers) Measure 1956, which now states:

'The council of every parish shall have the following powers in addition to any powers conferred by the Constitution or otherwise by this Measure: —
(iv) power jointly with the minister to determine the objects to which all moneys to be given or collected in church shall be allocated. . . .'

The 1921 Measure spoke of 'the Incumbent' rather than 'the minister' but the context of the 1956 Measure makes it clear that the reference is not to the minister taking the service but to the incumbent or priest-in-charge. Subsection (iv) speaks quite specifically of a 'power' to determine the objects of any collection; for this reason the final two sentences quoted above from the judgment of the Dean of the Arches should not be read as being determinative that in all cases a decision must be made jointly by minister and the parochial church council. Nevertheless, if the power is exercised, it must be exercised in favour of any charity or organisation the objects of which are such as to further any part of 'the whole mission of the church' (see *Parochial Church Council* in *Legal Opinions concerning the Church of England* (Church House Publishing, 8th ed., 2007) at pages 134–135).

6. Unless a collection is prescribed within a particular service, such as in the Holy Communion according to the Book of Common Prayer, no collection may take place without the consent of the minister taking the service. If that consent is, or has been, given two possible situations may arise: (i) where the statutory power to determine the objects of any collection has been exercised; and (ii) where the power has not been exercised in relation to the circumstances in which the collection in question is to be made. In this regard it may be noted that, although Canon B 17A assumes the statutory power will be exercised in relation to moneys collected during Holy Communion according to the Book of Common Prayer, the Measure and the Dean's judgment are both silent on the actual question who should allocate the objects of any collection not covered by an exercise of that power.

Collections at Funeral Services:

7. Neither the *Book of Common Prayer* 1662 nor *Common Worship: Pastoral Services* provide for a collection to be taken at a funeral service. However, this may take place with the consent of the minister taking the service.

8. Although a collection at a funeral service is not part of public worship, it follows from what has already been said that the parochial church council may together with the minister in charge of the parish decide for what purposes a collection is to be taken. (If there is disagreement between the minister and the parochial church council, the diocesan bishop may give directions: Parochial Church Councils (Powers) Measure 1956, s9(3).) Indeed, there is no reason why the minister and parochial church council should not agree in advance which of a number of specified charities may be the recipients of collections, for example, Cancer Research, NSPCC or Help for Heroes; these might, of course, be chosen in the light of the experience of the particular parish involved.

9. Whenever the statutory power is exercised in relation to a funeral service (whether it is exercised by the minister and the parochial church council as

a whole or by the minister and a subcommittee) it is highly desirable in order to avoid bad feeling that it is exercised well in advance; indeed, as the power may nevertheless need to be exercised quickly, it is best that its exercise has been delegated to a subcommittee. It is also good practice to ensure that continuing publicity (for example, on the church notice board) is given to any policy decided by the minister and parochial church council. The statutory power, once exercised, cannot be overridden by the wishes either of the relatives or the actions of the funeral director.

10. In relation to funerals and memorial services pastoral sensitivity is of special importance and it may therefore be felt that the statutory power should not be exercised in too prescriptive a form. For example, there is no reason why the minister and parochial church council should not determine in advance that a collection should be apportioned between, say, the parochial church council's own funds and one of several specified charities. Alternatively, if the minister and parochial church council do not wish themselves to exercise the statutory power (or only to exercise it to a limited extent), the parochial church council may specifically appoint a subcommittee to determine the charity or organisation as long as the minister agrees with any particular decision made by that subcommittee.

11. On the other hand, if (a) the minister taking the service has exercised his or her authority to permit the taking of a collection and (b) the statutory power has not been exercised, long standing custom would permit a collection at a funeral or memorial service to be distributed to such objects as the personal representatives or close relatives of the deceased may determine as long as those objects are lawful. If such objects were lawful but nonetheless inimical to the Church or Christian values, permission to take the collection should be refused. (In this regard Canon B 1, paragraph 2, Canon F15, paragraph 1, and Canon F 16, paragraph 1, reflect the wider aspect of good order within the church.) However, this latter problem may in practice often be obviated if the statutory power has been exercised in advance.

12. Whichever charity or organisation has been allocated or chosen, it is essential that (i) it is specifically named in any service sheet, card and/or envelope distributed at the church, and/or (ii) it is announced or otherwise clearly specified in church before the collection is made. Once such an announcement has been made, or a collection taken, the charity, organisation or object cannot thereafter be altered.

13. Although a collection is properly taken by the churchwardens or the sidespersons, this duty may be delegated to other proper persons or, for example, take place by means of collection bowls, plates or boxes placed in appropriate places. However, when a collection is made (in whatever form)

a trust is thereby created and whoever receives the moneys holds them as trustee for the charity or organisation specified or which has been previously determined by the parochial church council (see above).

14. A distinction needs to be made between –

(a)   a collection taken for the general purposes of the PCC;

(b)   a collection taken for a church fund raising money for specified charitable purposes where the expenditure of the money on those purposes is under the control or management of the PCC; and

(c)   a collection taken for a named charity or other organisation with the intention that the sums collected will be passed directly to that charity or organisation.

A collection within category (a) will form part of the general fund of the PCC to be applied by the PCC for any of its charitable purposes. A collection within category (b) will form a restricted fund of the PCC to be applied by the PCC only for the charitable purposes that were specified at the time the collection was taken. A collection within category (c) must simply be passed on to the named charity or organisation. Were a collection to be taken on the basis that it was to be split equally between the PCC and another, named charity (namely, the position envisaged at the end of paragraph 1 above) then 50% of the collection would come within category (a) and 50% within category (c).

15. Canon F 12, paragraph 2, provides that 'the alms or other collection and, if desired, notes of significant events' shall be recorded in the register book of services. However, although the words 'other collection' might be construed as referring to any collection whatsoever, it is the view of the Commission that they should be interpreted in a restricted sense so as to embrace only what would generally be considered as 'church' collections, that is, collections within categories (a) and (b) above.

16. As to whether money collected at a service should be included in the PCC's financial statements, *The Charities Act 1993 and the PCC* (Church House Publishing, 3rd ed. 2006) states that '[a]ll resources which become available to a PCC and which must be applied in furtherance of its charitable purposes should be included' as incoming resources in the PCC's financial statements (paragraph 6.6). A collection within categories (a) and (b) above should, accordingly, be included as incoming resources of the PCC in its financial statements; however, a collection within category (c) should not be included. Where only a proportion of a collection is within categories (a) or (b) only that proportion which is within categories (a) or

(b) should be included as an incoming resource of the PCC in its financial statements. (The PCC's accountant should advise how this money should be identified in those financial statements.)

17. In relation to any collection or part of a collection as is within category (c), it must be passed to the charity or organisation for which it was collected, although it is also good practice in such cases in order to obviate later disputes that any loose money is counted at the church and recorded in a place separate from the register book.

18. The application of the Gift Aid rules to a collection taken for a charity is explained in guidance notes issued by HM Revenue and Customs. A collection for the benefit of the church (that is, category (a)) where Gift Aid envelopes are used enables the church to make a repayment claim. If the church has set up a fund to raise money for a specified charity (category (b)) then the money collected forms part of the church's income and the church reclaims the tax and passes it on with the donations to the charity in question. Gift Aid envelopes addressed to a charity (category (c)) must only be opened by that charity which will then itself reclaim the tax. It is good practice if the number of such envelopes is first noted separately from the register of services. Further assistance from HMRC in relation to Gift Aid may be found at http://www.hmrc.gov.uk/charities.gigt_aid/rules/church-coll.htm. However, it should be noted that HMRC only permits Gift Aid to be claimed if the relevant charity is specified on the envelope filled out by the donor.

(June 2012)

Parochial Church Councils: Legal position of members

Legal status of a PCC

1. A parochial church council ('PCC') is a body corporate (see s.3 Parochial Church Council (Powers) Measure 1956).

2. The Charity Commission accepts that PCCs are charities. All PCCs were previously excepted from the obligation to register under the Charities Act 1993 (the provisions of which have now been consolidated with other provisions in the Charities Act 2011). However, since January 2009 PCCs with an income of more than £100,000 *per annum* have been required to register. (Guidance on the registration requirement and the registration process can be found on the *Parish Resources* website at http://www. parishresources.org.uk/registration.htm.)

3. The affairs of a PCC must be conducted, and the assets of a PCC must be held and applied, solely to promote the charitable purposes for which the PCC is established under the 1956 Measure, and not for other purposes (even if charitable) nor, *a fortiori*, for the private benefit of individuals, such as members of the PCC.

4. Since a PCC is a body corporate, liabilities it incurs in contract (eg under a contract of employment or for the provision of goods or services) or tort (eg by virtue of a breach of a duty of care owed to a third party) are enforceable against it rather than against its members. Thus a PCC member can only become personally liable for a debt of the PCC if he or she has voluntarily accepted legal responsibility for it (eg by giving a personal guarantee) or if the debt has arisen in circumstances involving a breach of the PCC member's fiduciary duties (as to which, see paragraph 10 below). A PCC member can also be personally liable under a contract which, whilst purportedly made on behalf of the PCC, was in fact entered into by the PCC member personally because he or she had no authority to enter into it on the PCC's behalf.

5. Similarly, statutory enforcement notices or fines imposed on a PCC will be enforceable against it, as the body corporate, rather than against its individual members. (For the position in relation to enforcement notices in relation to fire safety, see the Commission's Opinion *The application of the Regulatory Reform (Fire Safety) Order 2005 in relation to parish churches and the parochial use of other premises*.)

Fiduciary position of members of a PCC

6. The members of a PCC hold office to promote its charitable purposes. In promoting those purposes, the members of a PCC control the conduct of its affairs and the use and application of its assets.

7. The duties of a trustee in the strict sense also apply to all persons who occupy a fiduciary position analogous to that of a trustee. The duties have been held to apply, for example, to directors of a company or other body corporate in relation to the assets of the body corporate (see *Liverpool and District Hospital for Diseases of the Heart v Attorney General* [1981] Ch 193 and *Harries v Church Commissioners* [1992] 1 WLR 1241). They will accordingly apply to members of a PCC, including members aged under 18.

8. Those duties are stringent and include the following:

   (a)   the duty to protect the assets of the charity (for the implications of this duty in relation to the registration and enforcement of chancel repair liability, see the Commission's Opinion *Registration and Enforcement of Chancel Repair Liability by Parochial Church Councils* (October 2007);

   (b)   the duty to show a reasonable degree of care and skill in the administration of the charity (eg by taking appropriate professional advice before buying or selling land or investments, and avoiding imprudent or speculative investments);

   (c)   the duty not to receive a financial benefit, whether directly or indirectly, from the trust (as to which, see paragraph 14 onwards below);

   (d)   the duty not to take advantage of knowledge, information or opportunities acquired by virtue of his or her position as trustee; and

   (e)   the duty not to put him- or herself in a position where his or her duty to the trust and his or her personal interests conflict (so that, for example, the acquisition of an interest in the property of the charity, whether by way of sale or lease, can be set aside at the instance of the Attorney General, as protector of the interests of charity).

9. Those duties are based on the trustee's status, not on the nature of his or her conduct or the effect of that conduct on the trust and its assets. Thus the liability of a trustee to account to the trust for profits made in breach of duty

is not dependent in any way on proof of lack of good faith in the conduct of the trust's affairs or on the proof of any loss suffered by the trust.

10. The members of a PCC accordingly have significant legal responsibilities. Furthermore, those responsibilities can be enforced by legal proceedings brought by the PCC itself or by the Charity Commission or the Attorney General. Such proceedings could involve PCC members who had breached their fiduciary duties being required to make good to the PCC losses it had incurred as a result of the breach of duty or sums the members had received without the necessary authority.

11. However, in practice claims for breach of fiduciary duty are very rare and, even when they are made, the courts are unlikely to impose personal liability on trustees who have acted prudently, in good faith and in a way that has not benefitted themselves. PCC members should accordingly have little to fear from claims for breach of their fiduciary duties if they act with a reasonable degree of care and skill in the administration of their charity and avoid consciously applying PCC funds for unauthorised purposes.

12. If PCC members nonetheless remain concerned about the risk of personal liability for breach of fiduciary duty, there is always the possibility of exercising the power conferred by s.189 Charities Act 2011 to take out 'trustee indemnity insurance' to meet liabilities and costs arising from claims for breach of duty. In practice, many PCCs have used that procedure to extend the standard PCC insurance policy to include trustee indemnity cover. Further guidance on the use of the procedure can be found on the Charity Commission website at: www.charitycommission.gov.uk.

13. Additionally, if PCC members are concerned that pursuing a particular course of action might expose them to the risk of criticism or claims for breach of fiduciary duty, they can seek their own independent legal advice as to whether what they have in mind would be consistent with their legal responsibilities. In practice, it is unlikely that the High Court or the Charity Commission would consider them to have acted improperly if they had acted in accordance with legal advice that what they proposed to do was within their powers.

Trustee benefits

14. Prima facie, a breach of duty will occur if – without having the requisite legal authority to do so – a member of a PCC enters into any contract with a PCC under which he or she (or a connected person[1]) derives a financial

---

[1] In this opinion the expression 'connected person' means a person having a close personal or financial connection with a member of a PCC, such as a spouse, child or business partner.

benefit. Such contracts can include a contract of service (eg to provide IT related services) or a contract of employment (eg where a priest licensed to the parish is an employee of the PCC). (Note that 'financial benefit' for this purpose does not include expenses properly incurred by a PCC member: charity trustees are entitled to be reimbursed in respect of payments they have had to make personally in order to carry out their duties.)

15. If a breach of duty occurs, the PCC member who receives, or is connected to the person who receives, the benefit must account to the PCC for that benefit unless the retention of the benefit is authorised by the Charity Commission or the High Court. The charity's right to enforce the duty is an asset of the charity and, unless such authority is given, it is therefore the responsibility of the PCC members collectively (by virtue of their duties to act in the charity's best interests and protect its assets) to take steps to secure enforcement.

16. Fortunately, there are mechanisms by which potential difficulties in relation to trustee benefits can be avoided.

17. First, under s.185 Charities Act 2011, provided they meet certain conditions the charity trustees of a charity may resolve to pay one or more of their number (or a connected person falling within the definition contained in s.118 of the 2011 Act) for providing services to the charity. The conditions include that:

- there is a written agreement between the charity and the trustee or connected person concerned which sets out the amount to be paid;

- the payment is no more than is reasonable for the service provided;

- before entering into the agreement the trustees satisfy themselves that paying the trustee or connected person is in the best interests of the charity; and

- only a minority of the charity trustees must be receiving remuneration from the charity, directly or through a connected person.

18. Before entering into such an agreement the charity trustee must have to any guidance given by the Charity Commission on such agreements. They must also comply with the duty of care in the Trustee Act 2000 when deciding whether to pay remuneration. In practice, that requires them to (*inter alia*):

- act in the best interests of their charity;

- take professional or other appropriate advice when in doubt;

- be clear that payment can be justified;

- ensure conflicts of interest are properly and openly managed;

- ensure agreements are complied with, and kept on the charity's records as required by law; and

- disclose any payments in the charity's accounts.

19. Furthermore, the trustee who is to benefit (or who has the relationship with the connected person who is to benefit) must not take part in any discussion by the trustees about the making of the agreement or the services provided under it (including subsequent issues about its quality).

20. More detailed guidance on the exercise of the power conferred by the 2011 Act is available on the Charity Commission website.

21. Examples of payments for services which might be authorised under the power conferred by the 2011 Act include legal, accountancy or other professional work and building or decorating work. However, the power conferred by the 2011 Act does not extend to payment for services under a contract of employment. (For that reason, Church legislation is being brought forward to confer on PCCs a power corresponding to that conferred by the 2011 Act which <u>does</u> extend to payment of that kind; but at the date of this opinion it has not been approved by the General Synod.)

22. Whilst there is no objection to someone who is already an employee of a charity becoming one of its trustees, a trustee (or connected person) cannot become an employee without lawful authority. Such authority accordingly needs to be given by means of an Order made by the Charity Commission under s.105 of the 2011 Act.

23. To gain the Commission's consent to employment of a trustee or connected person, where the total remuneration (including all benefits) paid will be under £50,000 per year (as is likely to be the case in nearly all applications by PCCs) there is a streamlined application process using form *CSD-1381C*, details of which can be found on the Charity Commission's website. The form cannot be used where the PCC member or connected person concerned canvassed for the post or was involved in devising the job specification or advertising for the post – including by being involved in settling the terms and conditions of the employment. (In

that situation the PCC will therefore need to make out a case justifying the granting of consent.)

24. The PCC will need to show that:

- the charity has a need for the work to be carried out;

- the person to be paid has the appropriate knowledge and skills for the job;

- payment for the job is reasonable in relation to the work being carried out;

- the risks inherent in the inevitable conflict of interest have been considered and managed; and

- (usually) the job has been subject to an open and transparent selection process.

Unauthorised benefits

25. None of the procedures described above can authorise the payment of benefits after they have arisen: they are all concerned with authorising benefits before they arise.

26. As explained in paragraph 15 above, a PCC member who receives, or is connected to a person who receives, any benefit without lawful authority must account to the PCC for it unless the retention of the benefit is agreed by the Charity Commission or the High Court. It is important, therefore, that if a PCC identifies that benefits have, in error, been received by one of its members or a connected person without authority, steps are taken to put matters on a proper footing.

27. To that end the Charity Commission recommends that, where charity trustees become aware of an unauthorised trustee benefit, they should report it to the Commission, with an explanation of why the breach of trust occurred, how the trustees would prevent a similar situation occurring in the future and what benefits, if any, the charity received from the situation. On receipt of that information, the action the Commission will take will depend on the extent of the benefit and conflict of interest and the impact it has on the charity. It will also take into account other factors, such as the reason why the trustees did not obtain authority. The Commission states that it is likely to be more supportive if the trustees can show that the failure to obtain authority was an oversight.

28. Where the Commission considers the arrangements to be in the interests of the charity, it will give advice on the management of conflicts of interest and the authorisation of future benefits to trustees. However, it reserves the right formally to investigate where that is justified by the circumstances, with the consequent possibility of its using its statutory powers to protect the charity. Such cases will include those where trustees appear to have placed their personal or other interests ahead of those of the charity in order to derive significant benefit at the charity's expense, and where they have deliberately ignored the requirements of the law or of previous advice.

(January 2013)

Churchyards: Liability for personal injury accidents

General

1 Liability for personal injury accidents in churchyards can arise both in negligence and under the Occupiers' Liability Acts 1957 and 1984. Except as regards 'trespassers', the duty of care owed is similar.

Who is liable?

2 Liability rests on the 'occupier' of the churchyard. 'Occupier' denotes the person or authority that has a sufficient degree of control over the churchyard to give rise to a duty of care towards those who come lawfully into the churchyard. Depending upon the precise situation any of the following could be held to be an 'occupier':

(a) the PCC (as successor to the churchwardens – section 4(1)(ii)(c) of the Parochial Church Councils (Powers) Measure 1956);

(b) the incumbent (as owner of the freehold);

(c) in relation to a particular gravestone, the person who authorised the erection of the stone or, after his death, the heir at law of the person commemorated;

(d) in a closed churchyard where liability for maintenance has passed to the local authority, the local authority.

To whom is a duty of care owed?

Visitors

3 The term 'visitors' includes all who formerly under common law were invitees or licensees (Occupiers' Liability Act 1957, s1(2)).

Others (persons other than visitors)

4 Persons other than visitors embrace not only trespassers, but also persons using private rights of way and entrants under the Countryside and Rights of Way Act 2000.

What is the duty of care?

Visitors

5 The duty is to take such care as in all the circumstances of the case is reasonable to see that the visitor will be reasonably safe in using the

premises for the purposes for which the visitor is invited or permitted to be there (1957 Act, s2(1), (2)). Interpreting this for churchyards, it seems that the three most likely hazards are:

(a)   the condition of the paths;

(b)   the condition of the gravestones/monuments;

(c)   stonework falling from the church building on to people in the churchyard.

The following guidelines might be helpful:

Paths

6   The PCC is, under Canon F 13 and the Parochial Church Councils (Powers) Measure 1956, responsible to see that churchyards are fenced and kept in an orderly and decent manner. However, its liability to visitors under the Occupiers' Liability Acts and at common law for the state of the paths to and from the church is greater, in that it must ensure the paths are in a reasonably good condition. What this will mean will depend on the nature of the path. For instance, if there is a paved path, undue projections or holes must be avoided by regular inspection and maintenance. If it is a gravel path, it will need to be kept reasonably level so that it is safe to walk on.

Fences

7   The PCC is responsible for maintenance of fences and walls (1956 Measure; Canon F 13, para 2, and Canon F 14); thus if a boundary wall were to collapse and injure someone there would be a prima facie liability on the PCC.

Trees

8   By s6 of the Care of Churches and Ecclesiastical Jurisdiction Measure 1991, as amended by the Church of England (Miscellaneous Provisions) Measure 1995, s13, the PCC or local authority (in the case of a closed churchyard – *see* paragraph 2(d) above and *see also* **Churchyards: closed**) is responsible for the care and maintenance of churchyard trees. Such responsibility carries with it the potential liability, as occupier, for injury caused by trees. The duty of an occupier with regard to trees is to act as a prudent landowner to prevent the trees from being a danger to persons. (*See also* **Churchyards: ownership of monuments and trees for obligations of care and maintenance**.)

Gravestones/monuments

9 The PCC or (after the responsibility for a closed churchyard has been transferred to a local authority) the local authority is responsible for keeping the churchyard in decent order. Ensuring the safety of monuments is part of the general duty of keeping in decent order (re *Hutton Churchyard* [2009] PTSR 968, Court of Arches). The duty is likely to extend to all things attached to the realty, which include box tombs, war memorials and churchyard crosses. As regards monuments, however, the primary responsibility for their upkeep falls on the owners, who are the heirs of the persons commemorated (re *Welford Road Cemetery, Leicester* [2007] Fam 15, Court of Arches). This will be of little help where the heirs have died out or can no longer be traced. In those circumstances a secondary or default liability is borne by the PCC or local authority, on the footing that it has the power (albeit circumscribed by law) to intervene when a monument becomes dangerous.

10 The PCC or other authority charged with churchyard maintenance could be in breach of this secondary duty of care, and therefore negligent, if it failed to make safe monuments which it knew or ought to have known were in an unsafe condition.

11 In the event that a PCC or other authority finds that there are monuments which have become dangerous, it should act immediately to make them safe. The Diocesan Registrar should be consulted to ensure that the proposed safety measures are lawful. Sometimes a sufficient temporary response will be to display a written warning; or to place a cordon around the affected area; or to provide support, for instance with a stake. These steps will generally be viewed as minor works for which no faculty is required.

12 Consideration should be given, in appropriate cases, to the availability of the emergency faculty procedure under Rule 13(10) of the Faculty Jurisdiction Rules 2000 whereby the chancellor has power to grant an immediate faculty where there is 'an emergency that involves interests of safety or health'. A restrictive interpretation of Section 3 of the Faculty Jurisdiction Measure 1964 suggests that the chancellor has no jurisdiction to grant an emergency faculty where remedial work to a monument is proposed but the owner of the monument withholds his or her consent but is willing and able to remove it within a reasonable time. Any doubts about the extent of the chancellor's jurisdiction will, however be resolved if clause 5 of the draft Church of England (Miscellaneous Provisions) Measure, now (2013) before the General Synod, is enacted. Clause 5 will expressly empower the court to grant a faculty where urgent works to a monument are needed, without requiring the petitioner to seek the owner's consent, or to attempt to trace an unidentified owner.

Church building

13 If part of a church building falls and injures someone a prima facie case against the 'occupier' will have been made for, in the normal course of events, pieces should not fall off buildings if they are properly maintained.

Others (persons other than visitors)

14 For persons other than visitors, the 'occupier' owes a duty in respect of any injury if the occupier:

(a)   is aware of the danger or has reasonable grounds to believe it exists;

(b)   knows or has reasonable grounds to believe that the other is in the vicinity of the danger or that that other may come into the vicinity of danger; and

(c)   the risk is one against which the occupier may reasonably be expected to offer the other some protection (Occupiers' Liability Act 1984, s1(3)).

15 One needs to bear in mind that a churchyard is a public place and whilst some people may be put off by the nature of the place from visiting it, others will be attracted to it – albeit in some cases for the wrong purposes.

Warning notices

16 Warning notices are of doubtful effectiveness at law, are aesthetically undesirable and would doubtless be subject to vandalism.

Insurance

17 The standard 'Churchyard' policy from the Ecclesiastical Insurance Group indemnifies (normally incumbent, churchwardens and PCC) against any claim for public liability. This would include claims under the Occupiers' Liability Acts 1957 and 1984 or for negligence, but, of course, breach of duty of care must be proved. The policy, however, lays a duty on the insured to take all reasonable precautions, and in the event that any defect in the churchyard is discovered the insured must take immediate steps to remedy the same and cause such temporary precautions to be taken as the circumstances may require. It is important for those insured to make sure that the policy covers the churchyard. The Ecclesiastical Insurance Group states that it would automatically cover a churchyard surrounding a church, but not necessarily a detached churchyard.

(Revised 2013)

Parishes with no churchwardens or parochial church councils

1. For centuries, churchwardens have had an important place in the workings of the Church of England. Until the development of elected local councils at town and parish levels, the churchwardens and the vestry of the parish had responsibilities in local government as well as in respect of the affairs of the church.

2. Within the church, the churchwardens had responsibilities in respect of the financial affairs of the church and the maintenance of the church and churchyard. The Canons of 1571 set out their duties in these matters (see Canon 5, *Aeditui ecclesiarum et alii selecti viri* (Churchwardens and sidesmen)) but also give to the churchwardens what would now be described as a pastoral leadership role. They were, in the case of wickedness of life on the part of parishioners, to 'warn them brotherly and friendly to amend'; and they were also to 'search diligently and inquire if any of the parishioners either come not at all to church, or come later or slower at the times appointed by the laws'.

3. Many of the powers, duties and liabilities of the churchwardens and of the vestry in respect of church matters were transferred to parochial church councils on 1 July 1921 (see now the Parochial Church Councils (Powers) Measure 1956, s.4), but churchwardens continue to play an important part in the life of a parish. They are 'to be foremost in representing the laity and in co-operating with the incumbent' (Canon E1, para.4) and in practice meet frequently with the incumbent to deal with parish matters and play a leading role in the church community and in the work of the parochial church council. Where there is no incumbent or where the incumbent, having responsibility for several parishes, lives elsewhere, the churchwardens are seen even more clearly as the leaders of the local church.

4. Parochial church councils have a key role in the governance of parishes. It is the duty of the minister and the council to consult together on matters of general concern and importance to the parish, and the council is to co-operate with the minister in promoting in the parish the whole mission of the Church, pastoral, evangelistic, social and ecumenical (Parochial Church Councils (Powers) Measure 1956, s.2(1),(2)(a)).

5. Churchwardens and parochial church councils are thus key elements in the life of the parish but circumstances can arise in which the whole or a major part of the normal structure of leadership and governance in a parish ceases to exist. In an extreme case of acute pastoral breakdown or where a parish for some reason ceases to be viable, there may be no church electoral roll, no churchwardens, and no elected members of the parochial church

council. In less extreme circumstances, one or more of these normal elements of parish life may be missing. The Commission was asked to advise on the practical issues which then arise.

Action by the bishop

6. Rule 53(5) of the Church Representation Rules provides:

> 'In the case of an omission in any parish to prepare or maintain a roll or form or maintain a council or to hold the annual meeting, the rural dean upon such omission being brought to his notice shall ascertain and report to the bishop the cause thereof.'

7. It is clearly intended that the bishop will take whatever remedial action is open to him, and the provision just quoted forms part of a rule which sets out the powers the bishop may use, whether he learns of the situation from the rural dean or in some other way. The usefulness of the powers depends on there being, or being again, people willing to operate the system.

8. Rule 53 of the Rules provides in relevant part:

(1) In the carrying out of these rules in any diocese the bishop of such diocese shall have power: –

  (a) to make provision for any matter not herein provided for;

  (b) to appoint a person to do any act in respect of which there has been any neglect or default on the part of any person or body charged with any duty under these rules;

  (c) so far as may be necessary for the purpose of giving effect to the intention of these rules, to extend or alter the time for holding any meeting or election or to modify the procedure laid down by these rules in connection therewith [with certain exceptions not here material]

  (d) Subject to paragraph (1)(c) of this rule, in any case in which any difficulties arise, to give any directions which he may consider expedient for the purpose of removing the difficulties.

(2) The powers of the bishop under this rule shall not enable him: –

  (a) to validate anything that was invalid at the time when it was done;

(b)   to give any direction that is contrary to any resolution of the General Synod.

9. Under these powers, the bishop could order the revision of the parish's church electoral roll and appoint a person to carry out the duties of the electoral roll officer; could fix a date for an annual parochial church meeting; and could give directions to resolve any issues as to how many persons were to be elected. It would seem that the bishop could not deprive the incumbent of his or her right to preside at any meeting (this not being an Extraordinary Meeting within rule 23). The powers under rule 53 do not extend to the election of churchwardens, but corresponding provision is made in section 10 of the Churchwardens Measure 2001.

10. These powers are of no avail if there is nobody able and willing to operate the system. In such a case, what difficulties arise in the absence of churchwardens and/or a PCC?

Absence of one or more churchwardens

11. There are several ways in which it can come about that parishes are without churchwardens. A meeting of parishioners to elect churchwardens must be held each year (Churchwardens Measure 2001, s.4), though in certain circumstances one churchwarden may be appointed by the minister (Churchwardens Measure 2001, s.4(5)). Since no one can be forced to act as churchwarden, nor to stand for election, nor to be admitted after election, nor to remain in office longer than the rules as to resignation require, it follows that from time to time there may be either no-one elected, no-one admitted or no-one remaining in office as churchwarden of a specific parish. A vacancy as to one of the two usual posts of warden in the parish simply leaves one to do the work of two, and to bear all the legal responsibilities and duties alone, but there is no general rule applicable to the situation where there is none in post at all. In some parishes, local custom has concentrated in the hands of churchwardens tasks which could very properly be undertaken by other members of the congregation. This may both impose over-heavy demands on churchwardens and also discourage others from agreeing to serve as churchwardens.

12. Since the PCC and its officers have the general responsibilities for the management, financing and operation of the church in pursuance of its mission, it may be thought that in the absence of any holders of the post it is part of the role of the Incumbent and PCC to make working arrangements. The incumbent, having the cure of souls for the parish, should be able to rely on the support of the PCC in this. Those arrangements will mean (a) trying to find persons willing to take the practical burdens of the role until it proves possible to elect a churchwarden (either at the next annual meeting

or at special meeting called for the purpose; casual vacancy caused by the death or resignation of a churchwarden appointed by the minister may be filled by the minister (Churchwardens Measure 2001, s.4(8))), and (b) ensuring that the essential practical tasks of the churchwardens are carried out by someone until at least one of the posts can be filled.

13. There is no legal principle or provision which requires that this be an additional burden of any specific officer or of the PCC as a whole, and therefore the various responsibilities can be addressed as being susceptible of different and individual means of fulfilment, according to the available resources both personal and financial. In some parishes, there may be deputy churchwardens in post. This may occur where there are two or more churches or places of worship in a parish, the offices being created under either a scheme establishing district church councils (Church Representation Rules, r.18) or a pastoral scheme establishing a team ministry for the parish (Mission and Pastoral Measure 2011, s.34 and Sch.3 para.4). In some parishes deputy or assistant churchwardens are elected or appointed informally to assist the churchwardens in particular ways. The absence of churchwardens does not require any of these deputy churchwardens to take on the legal duties of churchwarden nor does it enlarge the powers and duties of those deputies holding office under a scheme.

A. Duties as officers of the Ordinary.

14. Canon E1, para.4, which has already been quoted in part, provides:

> 'The churchwardens when admitted are officers of the bishop. They shall discharge such duties as are by law and custom assigned to them; they shall be foremost in representing the laity and in co-operating with the incumbent; they shall use their best endeavours by example and precept to encourage the parishioners in the practice of true religion and to promote unity and peace among them. They shall also maintain order and decency in the church and churchyard, especially during the time of divine service.'

15. The meaning of the provision that on admission churchwardens are 'officers of the bishop' is not self-evident. It has long been held that the bishop or the archdeacon must admit to office a duly elected churchwarden and has no discretion in the matter as the churchwarden is 'substantially a temporal officer' (see *R v Rice* (1697) 5 Mod Rep 325; *R v Sympson* (1724) 2 Ld Raym 1379; *Phillips v Fish* (1726) 8 Mod 382) but in *R v Bishop of Sarum* [1916] 1 KB 466 Ridley J, giving the judgment of the Divisional Court, said:

> 'It would not be correct to conclude from these authorities that there are no duties in the performance of which a churchwarden acts for

the Ordinary and subject to his control. Thus, in *Fuller v Lane* (1825) 2 Add 419 at p.425) Sir John Nicholl in the Arches Court of Canterbury, in dealing with pews in a parish church, said: "The distribution of seats rests with the churchwardens, as the officers, and subject to the control, of the Ordinary." . . . There may be other such duties in the performance of which the churchwarden is not independent of the Ordinary, but we do not think that such a relationship in respect of one particular duty or of several particular duties can affect the general rule laid down in the authorities.'

16. Canon F7, para.2, reflects the law as stated in *Fuller v Lane* and declares that in allocating seats among the parishioners the churchwardens act for this purpose 'as the officers of the Ordinary and subject to his directions'. There is no similar declaration in respect of the other duties of churchwardens.

17. It is clear that part of the 'duties as are by law and custom assigned to' churchwardens and part of their role as officers of the Ordinary is the duty to ensure that the Bishop is made aware of matters of which he in his episcopal role might reasonably be expected to know so that he may address them as bishop. Under this heading the churchwardens are expected to take part in the answering of the articles of enquiry (which are specifically addressed to the Minister and churchwardens) at visitations and to be parties in any faculty matters. More directly they must see that any duties to the bishop are performed, and not participate in any action which is contrary to their office vis-à-vis the bishop. They have a general duty to report matters of factious impact on the parish, such as serious breakdowns in pastoral relationships.

18. One task that may fall to be undertaken during the absence of a churchwarden is the answering of articles of enquiry. Rather than expect the minister to deal with this alone (in the absence of churchwardens he or she will already be even busier), it is desirable that the answers be produced by someone else willing and able to bring the information together. That person would not be authorised, however, to present those answers to the Archdeacon, so the responsibility for this would remain with the Incumbent. Outside the specific context of the visitation process, the parochial church council has power to make representations to the bishop with regard to any matter affecting the welfare of the church in the parish (Parochial Church Councils (Powers) Measure 1956, s.7(v)). The archdeacon will also have the task of ensuring that the bishop is adequately informed in matters of concern where the incumbent is not able or willing to ensure this is done.

19. Canon F13, para 2 makes it the responsibility of the minister and churchwardens to ensure that faculties are obtained when needed. The minister

and churchwardens of the parish concerned are the usual petitioners in any faculty application (Faculty Jurisdiction Rules 2013, r.4.2(b)), but others having a sufficient interest in the matters may petition (Faculty Jurisdiction Rules 2013, r.4.2(d)). In the absence of churchwardens it is perfectly proper for other persons to be the named petitioners; parishes are not prevented from applying for faculties merely because they have no churchwardens or indeed are in vacancy. The usual form used in faculty matters (Form 3A in Sch.3 to the Faculty Jurisdiction Rules) is for 'proceedings started pursuant to resolution of parochial church council'; the resolution will validate the representative character of the persons petitioning on their behalf, including the case in which there are no churchwardens.

B. *Duties relating to the parish*

20. Canon E1, para.5 provides:

> 'In the churchwardens is vested the property in the plate, ornaments, and other movable goods of the church, and they shall keep an inventory thereof which they shall revise from time to time as occasion may require. On going out of office they shall duly deliver to their successors any goods of the church remaining in their hands together with the said inventory, which shall be checked by their successors.'

21. Although in one early case (*R v Rice* (1697) 1 Ld Raym 138) churchwardens were said to be a corporation, it is now clear that they are a 'quasi-corporation' for certain purposes, which purposes include the holding of property (*Withnell v Gartham* (1795) 6 Term Rep 388, 101 ER 610; *Fell v Charity Lands Official Trustee* [1898] 2 Ch 44, CA; *Kensit v Rector and Churchwardens of St Ethelburga, Bishopsgate Within* [1900] P 80). Although there is no direct authority, this implies that the property remains vested in the body of churchwardens, even if none is in office, by analogy with the position of a corporation with no current members. However, the parochial church council is responsible for the care maintenance preservation and insurance of the goods and ornaments of the church as well as of its fabric (Parochial Church Councils (Powers) Measure 1956, s.4(1)(ii)(b)). Canon F14, Of the provision of things appertaining to churches, provides further:

> 'The things appertaining to churches and chapels, and the obligations relating thereto, and to the care and repair of churches, chapels, and churchyards referred to in the foregoing Canons shall, so far as the law may from time to time require, be provided and performed in the case of parochial churches and chapels by and at the charge of the parochial church council.'

On the appointment of any new churchwardens they will acquire the property in the chattel contents of the church immediately they are admitted.

22. Many small items needed by a church (stationery, candles, drawing paper for the use of children, organ or choir music) are acquired by whoever has taken responsibility for the relevant activity with the express or implied authority of the PCC and a churchwarden is not necessarily involved. The care of the items in question is clearly a matter for the PCC, so that the absence of churchwardens will create no lacuna in that aspect of the responsibility for them.

23. Any disposal of chattels must be authorised by faculty and what has been said above about who may petition is relevant here. The petitioners in such cases need not include the churchwardens, even though title is vested in them. A sale or other disposal can be by any person whom the Court identifies for the purpose (or in special circumstances by an officer of the Court itself).

24. The more significant responsibilities are those under section 5 of the Care of Churches and Ecclesiastical Jurisdiction Measure 1991, first to compile and maintain terrier and inventory and log book in relation to the church and its contents (as to which see also Canon F17), and then to make the annual inspection and reports to the PCC. Churchwardens are required to carry out these duties 'in consultation with the minister' but the primary responsibility is that of the churchwardens.

25. It is plainly very desirable in order to safeguard the church's property that the records are up to date and that an annual process of inspection and updating is carried out. In the absence of churchwardens, the PCC should consider finding a person willing to carry out these specific functions without being a churchwarden. Strictly there would be no default by the PCC or of a person so nominated if the report were not completed, as long as some effort were made to find a means of producing the report, or the records on which it might be based. A person nominated in this way by the PCC could properly sign the statement required by s.5(5) of the 1991 Measure verifying the contents of the terrier inventory and log book but should in so doing make it clear that he or she was acting on the authority of the PCC and not as churchwarden. The same applies to the duty under Canon E1, para 5 for the checking of the inventory each year.

26. The churchwardens' canonical duty under Canon E1, para. 4 and Canon F15, para 2 of maintaining order in the church and the churchyard especially during the time of divine service is one they share with sidesmen (Canon E2, para 3). It is supported by section 2 of the Ecclesiastical Courts Jurisdiction Act 1860 which makes it an offence to be guilty of riotous,

violent, or indecent behaviour in any parish or district church or chapel of the Church of England whether during the celebration of divine service or at any other time, or in any churchyard or burial ground. Any person may take steps to report any such offence but only the churchwardens will have the statutory power of arrest under s.3 of the Act. In practice, the absence of a churchwarden may not demand special provision for this role.

27. The same applies to seating of congregations, which as has already been noted is a responsibility of the churchwardens as officers of the Ordinary (Canon F7, para. 2). Most of this work is done by sidesmen, and it rarely needs the authority of the churchwarden to achieve any required solution.

28. Processing of collections is a serious duty, and is generally regarded as something for which the churchwardens have a responsibility as part of their care for the goods of the church. It is often carried out by other members of the congregation, and particularly by PCC treasurers or sidesmen. The function in this case is what matters, and the real need is the identification of someone – even in the last resort the minister – to ensure the duty is fulfilled in any given case.

29. It is the duty of churchwardens 'with the advice and direction of the minister' to provide sufficient bread and wine for the Holy Communion. This duty again may in practice also be discharged by some other member of the congregation acting as a sacristan, and the minister will naturally be careful to ensure that proper provision is made even if there is no churchwarden.

30. Generally, the PCC's responsibility for the well-being of the parish in general should lead it to find people to carry out the duties as needed. Sometimes the carrying out of the functions has already been shared by the churchwardens with other members of the Council or even the congregation as a whole.

C. *Membership of the PCC*

31. As members of the PCC the churchwardens bear no greater legal responsibility than other PCC members, though they commonly take a leading role in its meetings. In the absence of churchwardens, others will need to take their places on the Standing Committee, and there will be extra work for the minister, so the PCC should be motivated to identify people to assist in responding to enquiries (such as the articles of enquiry at visitations), and in carrying forward through the PCC any amendment of whatever failings are discovered.

D. *Trusteeship of local or parochial trusts*

32. The position of churchwardens as trustees of specific trusts is not ecclesiastical law but trust law. There are general principles which give the Courts power to fill gaps in the legal responsibilities and a more general power still which enables the court to give directions as to how specific issues may be resolved. Proper legal advice should be taken for these purposes.

Absence of a parochial church council

33. Although it is provided in rule 53(3) of the Church Representation Rules that 'no proceedings of any body constituted under these rules shall be invalidated by any vacancy in the membership of that body or by any defect in the qualification, election or appointment of any members thereof', and an identical provision applying to PCCs is found in Appendix II to the Rules, para.17, those provisions are not adequate to deal with the case in which there is no council at all or a council consisting only of the minister, there being no elected or ex officio members.

34. In the latter case, the minister might seek to argue that he or she can hold and constitute a meeting of the PCC and take decisions in its name. In the context of company and insolvency law, it is well established that one person cannot be a 'meeting', except in the exceptional case in which a meeting of a class (e.g. of preference shareholders) is required and there is only one person in that class (see the examination of the issue, with full examination of the authorities, in *Re Altitude Scaffolding Ltd* [2006] EWHC 1401 (Ch)). The Church Representation Rules contain nothing to justify an exception to the normal meaning of 'meeting' in the parish context.

35. Section 3 of the Parochial Church Councils (Powers) Measure 1956 provides:

> 'Every council shall be a body corporate by the name of the parochial church council of the parish for which it is appointed and shall have perpetual succession.'

The position is that the council as a corporate body continues to exist, even if it has no members.

36. This situation is much more familiar in the case of the corporation sole of the incumbent, and there are numerous statutory provisions dealing with property vested in a benefice which is vacant as to the serving of notices and the taking of action on behalf of the vacant benefice. There seem to be no equivalent provisions in respect of the corporation aggregate which is

the parochial church council, no doubt because any land held or acquired by the council is vested in the diocesan authority under section 6 of the Parochial Church Councils (Powers) Measure 1956.

37. A number of practical issues could arise were there to be no council. How would the council's obligations in respect of the keeping of accounts, the maintenance and insurance of the fabric of the church building and its goods and ornaments, and the care and maintenance of the churchyard be discharged? In respect of property vested in the diocesan authority, can any dealings be entered into in the absence of a PCC? How if at all could the diocesan authority enforce its rights to indemnification under section 6(4) of the 1956 Measure? Where the council is a registered charity, how can the obligations flowing from such registration be discharged? Can any cheques be drawn on any bank account in the name of the council, or bank mandates renewed or cancelled?

38. There are provisions in the 1956 Measure which may assist. Section 9 provides in part as follows:

> '(2) If any act required by this Measure to be done by any person is not done within such time as the bishop may consider reasonable it may be done by or under the authority of the bishop.
> (3) In the event of a council and a minister being unable to agree as to any matter in which their agreement or joint action is required under the provisions of this Measure, such matter shall be dealt with or determined in such manner as the bishop may direct.'

39. Subsection (3) seems to be limited to the appointment of parish clerks and sextons, and the allocation of collection money, both under s.7 of the Measure which uses the phrase 'power jointly with the minister' in these cases. Subsection (2) appears to be much broader in scope, especially if 'person' is given its usual meaning and is therefore taken to include the PCC, a legal person. Much depends on what is covered by 'any act required by this Measure to be done'. The Measure confers a number of 'powers' on the PCC (e.g. to acquire property, to frame a budget) and describes its 'functions'; these provisions do not 'require' acts to be done. The relevant provisions which do impose duties are

> 's.4(1)(ii) as to duties previously owed by the churchwardens with respect to:
>
> (a)   The financial affairs of the church including the collection and administration of all moneys raised for church purposes and the keeping of accounts in relation to such affairs and moneys;

(b)   The care maintenance preservation and insurance of the fabric of the church and the goods and ornaments thereof;

(c)   The care and maintenance of any churchyard (open or closed). . .;

s.4(2) as to any duties under enactments imposing duties on churchwardens, vestries or church trustees; s.6(4) as to the duty to keep the diocesan authority indemnified; and

s.8(1) as to the provision of financial statements to the annual parochial church meeting.'

40. If a matter can be brought within these provisions, the bishop could give appropriate directions, but it will be seen that not all the issues raised above can be resolved in this way. Moreover, it is far from clear whether actions by the bishop would enable anyone to draw on the funds (if any) of the PCC; even if this could be implied, the diocese might well find that a bank would not release funds without some assurance that the diocesan board of finance would give an undertaking by way of indemnity.

41. A power which can be, and has been, used to rescue this type of situation is in section 80(2) of the Charities Act 2011. This provides that:

'The Commission [i.e. the Charity Commission] may by order made of its own motion appoint a person to be a charity trustee –

(a)   . . .;

(b)   if there are no charity trustees, or where by reason of vacancies in their number or the absence or incapacity of any of their number the charity cannot apply for the appointment;

(c)   if there is a single charity trustee, not being a corporation aggregate, and the Commission is of opinion that it is necessary to increase the number for the proper administration of the charity;

. . .'

42. Before exercising this power, the Commission must give notice of its intention to do so to each of the charity trustees, except any that cannot be found or has no known address in the United Kingdom; and any such notice may be given by post and, if given by post, may be addressed to the recipient's last known address in the United Kingdom (s.82). Once an order

is made, a copy is sent to the charity concerned and each charity trustee (s.86). For the purposes of these provisions, 'charity trustees' is defined (in s.177) as 'the persons having the general control and management of the administration of a charity', a definition which covers the members of a PCC. Presumably were the affairs of a parish to recover so that an election to the PCC in the normal fashion became possible, the trustees appointed by the Charity Commission would stand aside. It would be normally be desirable for the Commission's order to make provision for such an eventuality.

(February 2013)

Baptism of children: Parental responsibility and same sex couples

The Issue

1. The Legal Advisory Commission has been asked to give its opinion as to the proper completion of baptismal registers in the increasing number of cases where those bringing a child to baptism are a same sex couple. This question also raises further issues due to the great changes in parenting that have occurred over recent years.

Parochial Registers and Records Measure 1978

2. Section 1(1) of the Measure provides that a register of public and private baptisms must be provided for every parish or, if the parish has more than one parish church, such a register must be provided for each such church. Section 1(3) provides that –

> 'Such register books shall be of durable material and the heads of information required by this Measure to be entered therein shall in the case of each book provided after the commencement of this Measure be printed on every leaf thereof.'

3. Section 2(1) then provides:

> 'Where the ceremony of baptism according to the rites of the Church of England is performed –

> (a) in the parish church or, in the case of a parish having more than one such church, any parish church thereof, or

> (b) in any other place in the parish by a minister of the parish, the person by whom the ceremony was performed shall as soon as possible thereafter enter in the appropriate register book of baptism the particulars required in Form 1 in Schedule 1 to the Measure and shall sign the register in the place provided.'

4. If the ceremony has been performed in a place other than the parish church and by 'a person who is not the minister of the parish' such person must as soon as possible thereafter send to the incumbent or priest-in-charge a signed certificate certifying when and where the ceremony was provided and containing 'the other particulars required in Form 1': section 2(2). Similar provisions are laid down in relation to baptisms in extra-parochial places: section 2(3). In these circumstances the incumbent (who is given a wide definition by section 2(5)) must enter the particulars

in the register and add specified words to identify the giver of the certificate: section 2(4).

5. Form 1 has 11 columns two of which require the Father's and Mother's Christian names, two more of which require their occupations and a further column requires the names of the godparents. Moreover, Canons B 23 and 24 provide that where persons of riper years are baptised they shall have sponsors rather than godparents.

Who may initiate baptism?

The Civil Law

6. The civil law draws a distinction between parenthood and parental responsibility. However, the law is not always consistent in this distinction as 'parent' in private family law usually refers to the biological parent whereas in the context of adoption it refers to a biological parent who in law holds parental responsibility. Moreover, the 'parent' may not in fact be looking after, or bringing up, the child. A number of persons may hold parental responsibility at the same time but by section 2(7) each of them may act alone in exercising that responsibility unless there is any enactment to the contrary. 'Parental responsibility' is defined by section 3(1) of the Children Act 1989 as –

> 'all the rights, duties, powers and responsibilities and authority which by law a parent of a child has in relation to the child and his property.'

7. The presentation of a child for baptism is without doubt an exercise of parental responsibility and, if one person holding parental responsibility objects to another such person presenting the child, he or she may seek a 'specific issue order' restraining the latter from making such presentation (see also below).

8. The terms 'parent', 'mother' and 'father' are not given statutory interpretations by the Children Act 1989 or the Adoption and Children Act 2002. It is therefore necessary to glean their meaning from the contexts in which those words appear. Generally, they refer to the biological parent whether or not they hold parental responsibility. (However, only a parent with parental responsibility may give consent to an adoption: Adoption and Children Act 2002, section 52(6).)

9. Section 67(1) of the Adoption and Children Act 2002 provides that –

> 'an adopted person is to be treated in law as if born as the child of the adopters or adopter.'

The actual order may be made in favour of one person or a 'couple' (defined by section 144(4) as including civil partners and same-sex couples in a long-term relationship).

10. Similarly, sections 35–38 of the Human Fertilisation and Embryology Act 2008 give rise to the concept of a non-biological parent being 'treated' as the father when certain conditions are fulfilled. Section 38(1) states that –

> 'where a person is to be treated as the father of the child by virtue of this Act, no other person is to be treated as the father of the child.'

11. In addition, where surrogacy has occurred either here or abroad, section 54 of the Human Fertilisation and Embryology Act 2008 permits the making of a 'parental order' on the satisfaction of a number of conditions. The order may be made in favour of a single person or a couple (again including civil partners and same-sex couples in a long-term relationship). The effect of a parental order is that the child is to be treated in law as the child of the applicant or applicants.

12. If a person has acquired a new gender under the Gender Recognition Act 2004 his or her status as the father or mother of a child is nevertheless unaffected: see section 9 of the Act.

13. There are thus situations where a person who is not the biological parent is to be treated in law as a parent and the person who is the biological parent is wholly excluded in law from such parenthood.

14. In addition there are children who have been placed in care under a court order and who live in residential care or with official foster parents. A local authority who holds a care order is entitled to exercise parental responsibility to the exclusion of any other person with parental responsibility over that child. However, in practice, a local authority will not initiate presentation for baptism and, unless the care plan is for adoption, will not usually seek to prevent baptism where all those holding parental responsibility agree. If a child is subject to a special guardianship order the special guardian is similarly entitled to exercise exclusive parental responsibility.: section 14C(1)(b) of the Children Act 1989. This is called 'enhanced parental responsibility'. There are also children living with relatives who are not their parents (often referred to as 'kinship care') but such persons do not themselves hold parental responsibility unless it has been granted by the court.

15. There are also some rare occasions (for example when not all the above conditions required in law as to surrogacy have been fulfilled) where there has been no court order, no-one holds parental responsibility and a child

remains in the everyday care of a person or persons who is, or are, not his biological parents and with whom he or she has no kinship relationship. In the last situation section 2(5) of the Children Act 1989 provides that he or she may (subject to the other provisions of the Act)–

'do what is reasonable in all the circumstances of the case for the purposes of safeguarding or promoting the child's welfare.'

In effect such a person stands *in loco parentis* and within a Christian context this would seem to embrace bringing a child to baptism.

16. Unless and until superseded by a court order or by reason of any statutory provision the biological mother has parental responsibility for her child. Unless the parents are married, the biological father has in law no parental responsibility until acquired under section 4 of the Children Act 1989 (as amended). Parental responsibility may also be acquired by a second female (where that female is a parent by virtue of section 43 of the Human Fertilisation and Embryology Act 2008) or by a step-parent: see sections 4ZA and 4A of the Act.

17. A parent with parental responsibility for a child may appoint another individual to be that child's guardian in the event of his or her death and the court may in certain circumstances also appoint a guardian. Such a guardian has parental authority over the child: section 5(6) of the Children Act 1989.

The Rites

18. Although there must have been both orphans and foundlings in 1662 the original rubric preceding The Ministration of Public Baptism of Infants stated:

'Where there are children to be baptized, the Parents shall give knowledge thereof . . . And then the Godfathers and Godmothers, and the People, with the Children must be ready at the font. . . .'

Thereafter, the parents are not specifically mentioned. It is the godparents who are asked to name the children and earlier the priest is required by rubric to –

'speak unto the Godfathers and Godmothers on this wise:
    DEARLY beloved, ye have brought *this Child* here to be baptized. . . .'.

19. Today, although the body of the rite remains the same, the initial rubrics have been altered. It is no longer specified by whom notice should

be given and the minister is required to instruct the parents or guardians of the child as to their responsibilities. The final rubric before the commencement of the rite states:

> 'At the time appointed, the godfathers and godmothers and the parents or guardians with the child must be ready at the Font. . . .'

20. In The Ministration of Private Baptism of Children in Houses, once the child has thereafter been brought to church the minister is required –

> 'to examine and try whether the child be lawfully baptized, or no. In which case, if those that bring any Child to the Church do answer. . . .'

The parents are not specifically mentioned and in the final rubric mention is again made of 'they which bring the Infant to the Church'.

21. In Common Worship (Christian Initiation) Holy Baptism the parents and godparents are addressed jointly (see, for example, pages 66 and 88). Note 2 to Emergency Baptism states:

> 'Parents are responsible for requesting emergency baptism for an infant.'

Although this rubric may suggest that, if there is no person having parental responsibility present or being capable of making such a request, no emergency baptism should take place, such emergency baptisms remain valid even if administered by a lay person. (See, too, *Legal Opinions concerning the Church of England* (Church House Publishing, 8th ed., 2007) at pages 332–335). Nonetheless, no such restriction could apply to the emergency baptism of a person who has attained his or her majority.

The Canons

22. Canon B 22 does not specify by whom notice should be given nor by whom the child should be brought to church but Canon B 22, paragraph 2, implies that it will be by either the parents or guardians. This is especially so in the light of the minister's duty to instruct the parents or guardians as to their responsibilities: Canon B 22, paragraph 3.

23. Although Canon B 22, paragraph 7, is concerned with emergency baptism by a minister, it is clear from both the Book of Common Prayer and Common Worship that emergency baptisms may be performed by members of the laity and that children so baptised, if they live, must be

brought to church and received into the congregation. Registration in these circumstances is covered by the provisions of the Measure.

24. Although Canon B 22, paragraph 2, provides for the diocesan bishop to give directions concerning the baptism of infants where the minister refuses or unduly delays baptism, only the parents or guardians may apply for such directions although no doubt the minister may seek guidance.

Conclusion

25. Whatever the position may have been previously no-one without parental responsibility may now present a child for baptism unless, perhaps, that person falls within the provisions of section 2(5) of the Children Act 1989 (see above). Canon B 22 must therefore be read in this light.

Completion of the Baptismal Register

26. Adoption in England and Wales pre-dates the passing of the Parochial Registers and Records Measure 1978 and it follows that the Measure must have been passed with the knowledge of that possibility. Thus, a 'father' and/or 'mother' referred to in Form 1 must be taken, at least in some cases, to refer to adoptive parents rather than to biological parents. Similarly, the Measure was passed after the promulgation of Canon B 23 and therefore with the knowledge that those of riper years would have sponsors rather than godparents. In these circumstances the provisions of Form 1 (and therefore of the register itself) must be given a purposive interpretation. However, the columns relating to fathers and mothers are necessarily gender specific.

27. That being so and in the light of what has been said above:

(a) the columns referring to fathers and mothers must be read as relating to those currently holding parental responsibility for the child, who may or may not be a biological parent (or in exceptional circumstances to those entitled to exercise the power under section 2(5) of the Children Act 1989);

(b) where persons of the same sex share parental responsibility their names should both be inserted in the same gender specific column, namely, Father's name or Mother's name;

(c) in the case of the baptism of those of riper years the sponsors' names should be inserted in the column headed 'Godparents'. (See, too, Common Worship (Christian Initiation) at page 99, Note 6.)

The use of non-alcoholic wine and gluten free bread

1. The advice of the Legal Advisory Commission has been sought both as to whether (i) wine which has been fermented but which is 'non-alcohol' by reason of the alcohol having been removed is compliant with the provisions of Canon B 17, and (ii) whether gluten free bread or wafers may be used at a celebration of the Holy Communion. The first question arises out of the background of the reports of the Joint Implementation for the Anglican/Methodist Covenant and concerns about communicants who are alcoholic.

2. Canon B 17, paragraph 2, states:

> 'The bread, whether leavened or unleavened, shall be of the best and purest wheat flour that conveniently may be gotten, and the wine the fermented juice of the grape, good and wholesome.'

The Use of 'Non-alcoholic' wine

3. As to the wine to be used at Holy Communion it has been suggested that, if the alcohol has been removed, 'there is nothing to say that the result is not 'good and wholesome' wine in accordance with the Canon'.

4. The definition of 'wine' in the Oxford English Dictionary is:

'1   a.   The fermented juice of the grape used as a beverage. *It is essentially a dilute solution of alcohol, on the proportion of which in its composition depend its stimulating and intoxicating properties. Wines are classed as red or white, dry or sweet, still or sparkling.*

        b.   As one of the elements in the Eucharist.

2.   In wider use, usually with qualifying word: A fermented liquor made from the juice of other fruits, or from grain, flowers, the sap of various trees (e.g. birch and palm), etc.: sometimes called made wine.'

Prima facie, the term 'non-alcoholic wine' would therefore seem to be a contradiction in terms although the Legal Advisory Commission understands that such wine may in fact contain up to 0.5% alcohol.

5. Canon 20 of the Constitutions and Canons Ecclesiastical 1603 merely spoke of 'good and wholesome Wine' whereas Canon B 17, paragraph 2, spells out that the wine must be 'the fermented juice of the grape'. Putting

aside the specification of the fruit to be used, the addition of the word 'fermented' must also have been included for good reason. Fermentation is the process by which alcohol is created and therefore the Canon requires that the grape juice be turned into alcohol. By the removal of all such alcohol the required results of that fermentation are nullified and the resultant beverage then not only ceases to be 'wine' as commonly understood but also ceases to be 'the fermented juice of the grape'.

6. It follows that the provision of wine from which all the alcohol has been removed would be contrary to the Canon and its use during Holy Communion contrary to ecclesiastical law. If, however, some alcohol remains, such wine may legally be used.

The Use of Gluten Free Bread or Wafers

7. Whether gluten free bread or wafers meet the requirement of the Canon seems to depend on precisely what is meant by 'gluten-free'.

8. According to the website of Coeliac UK (http://www.coeliac.org.uk/gluten-free-diet-lifestyle/the-gluten-free-diet/communion-wafers) there are two basic types of 'gluten-free' wafers that are commercially available. One (hereafter called 'Type 1') contains specially processed wheat with the result that the level of gluten in them is very low, but the ingredients are nevertheless wheat and water only. Because of the very small amount of gluten that remains after the processing of the wheat Type 1 are apparently suitable for coeliacs. According to Coeliac UK the 'gluten-free' wafers produced by Vanpoulles and by Farris are in fact Type 1, low gluten, processed wheat wafers.

9. However, there are also wafers commercially available (hereafter called 'Type 2') that contain no wheat starch at all but are made entirely from other ingredients. For example, Type 2 wafers produced by the Gluten Free Altar Bread Company (who also produce wafers of Type 1) are described as being made of 'Rice Flour, Potato Flour, Tapioca Flour, Natural Gum, and Water'.

10. In the view of the Legal Advisory Commission Type 2 cannot be considered 'bread' within the meaning of Canon B 17, paragraph 2, as no wheat is used. On the other hand, Type 1 meets the requirement in Canon B 17 that the bread 'shall be of the best and purest wheat flour that conveniently may be gotten'. It does not cease to be 'the best and purest wheat flour' by reason of the fact that the gluten content is very low.

11. It follows that the only bread that may be used for the celebration of the Holy Communion is either (1) bread made with ordinary wheat flour, or (2)

bread made with wheat flour that has been processed to reduce the amount of gluten to a low level.

Conclusion

12. It is appreciated that the legal position outlined above may cause difficulties for those suffering from alcoholism or coeliac disease but attention is drawn to note 5 to the *Notes to the Celebration of Holy Communion at Home or in Hospital* at page 73 of *Common Worship: Pastoral Services* (see, too, note 6 at page 79. This states:

> 'Communion should normally be received in both kinds separately, but where necessary may be received in one kind, whether of bread or, where the communicant cannot receive solid food, wine.'

13. This note merely reflects the general law of legal necessity and applies equally to alcoholics and those having an allergy which makes it dangerous for them to eat anything containing wheat.

(May 2014)

Canon B 43, paragraph 3

1. The Legal Advisory Commission has been asked by the Council for Christian Unity for advice on the scope of Canon B 43, paragraph 3, in relation to the celebration of marriages by Anglican clerics in Non-Conformist chapels. Apparently Anglican clergy are being asked more frequently to celebrate such marriages using the relevant Non-Conformist rites with the Non-Conformist ministers (or those authorised to take Non-Conformist marriages) taking no actual part in the service but only registering the marriage at its conclusion. A related question arises when an Anglican deaconess, lay worker or reader is invited to take part in a Non-Conformist wedding service.

2. An Anglican cleric may only use forms of service which are authorised or allowed by Canon: see Canon C 15, paragraph 1, Declaration of Assent, and Canon B 1, paragraph 2. A similar restriction lies upon Anglican deaconesses, lay workers and readers: see, respectively, Canon D 2, paragraph 5, Canon E 8, paragraph 4, and Canon E 5, paragraph 4, each together with Canon B 1, paragraph 2. The relevant provisions in relation to ecumenical services are to be found in Canon B 43 (Of relations with other Churches) and Canon B 44 (Of local ecumenical projects). The Churches to which these provisions apply are listed in *The Canons of the Church of England* (Church House Publishing, 7th edition, 2012) at page 205. Services may not be taken in other Churches or in other circumstances.

3. Canon B 43, paragraph 3, reads:

> 'Notwithstanding any provision of any Canon, a priest or deacon of the Church of England who receives from the person authorized by a Church to which this Canon applies an invitation to take part in a service may in the course of that service perform any duty assigned to him if:
>
> (a)   the duty assigned to him is or is similar to a duty which he is authorized to perform in the Church of England, and
>
> (b)   he has before accepting the invitation obtained:
>
> (i)   the approval of the incumbent of the parish in which the service is to take place, and
>
> (ii)   in the case of an invitation to take part in the ordination or consecration of a minister of a Church to which this Canon applies or to preside at the Holy Communion,

the approval of the bishop of the diocese in which the service is to take place, and

(iii) in the case of an invitation to take part in any service on a regular basis, the approval of both the bishop of the diocese and the parochial church council of the parish in which the service is to take place.'

A similar provision is made for deaconesses, lay workers and readers by Canon B 43, paragraph 6 (omitting reference to ordination or consecration).

4. May the priest or deacon take the whole of the service in question or may he or she only take part in some of the service? In Canon B 43, paragraph 1 (which is concerned with ministers and lay persons of other Churches performing duties during Anglican services), a distinction is drawn, for example, between saying or singing Morning or Evening Prayer (*scilicet* the whole service) and assisting at baptisms or in the distribution of the holy sacrament of the Lord's Supper. However, such wording is not repeated in Canon B 43, paragraphs 3 or 6 and the *Ecumenical Relations Canons B 43 and B 44: Code of Practice* (1998 Edition) does not assist in interpreting the relevant provisions.

5. In their normal meaning the words 'take part in' convey the concept of sharing, assisting or co-operating with someone[1]. On this basis the subsequent provisions of Canon B 43, paragraph 3(a), do no more than describe the nature of the duties which the Anglican cleric may perform when taking part in a service of a church to which the Canon applies. They do not enlarge the meaning of the preceding words so as to permit the Anglican cleric to act alone. This also seems to be implicit in the words 'in the course of that service perform any duty assigned to him'.

---

[1] Chambers Dictionary, *sub verba* 'take part in': 'To share or to assist in.'

Oxford English Dictionary, *sub verbum* 'part' (meaning 23): '23.take part. a. To share, partake of or in (cf. sense 7); b.A.V.23.b To participate in (some action), to assist, co-operate (cf. 8).

1382 Wyclif Hebr. ii. 14 Therfore for children comuneden to fleisch and blood, and he also took part of the same. a 1533 Ld. Berners Huon lxxxi. 245 Such as regarded her were constrayned to take parte of her sorow. 1596 Spenser F.Q. iv. ix. 24 Each one taking part in others aide. 1875 Jowett Plato (ed. 2) IV. 19 Philebus takes no further part in the discussion.'

6. An Anglican cleric is not, therefore, permitted by Canon B 43, paragraph 3, to take the whole of a Non-Conformist marriage service even if the Non-Conformist minister (or a person authorised to take a Non-Conformist marriage) is present. Indeed, the wording of the paragraph suggests that a significant part of the service must be taken other than by the Anglican cleric.

7. The role of an Anglican deaconess, lay worker or reader is restricted to taking such part as he or she might take within an Anglican marriage service.

(October 2014)

Diocesan boards of finance: Conflicts of interest

1. A Diocesan Board of Finance ('DBF') is a company incorporated under the Companies Acts (section 1 Diocesan Boards of Finance Measure 1925 as amended). It must be registered under the Companies Act 2006, and any change in its constitution must similarly be registered. It is constituted by the Diocesan Synod, and its memorandum and articles must provide (*inter alia*) that the Bishop of the Diocese is a member, and that the majority of the members shall be lay persons. Subject to complying with the provisions of the Measure, the Diocesan Synod has considerable discretion as to the constitution of its DBF. Details of DBF constitutions seen by the Commission show a wide variety of provisions governing the membership of a DBF and the persons who, for the purposes of the Companies Act 2006, are considered to constitute the directors.

2. A DBF is also a charity. As a DBF will in practice meet the minimum requirements for registration, it must be registered under the Charities Act 2011. Once registered, a DBF must notify the Charity Commission of any change to its governing document or any of its other registered particulars (see section 35(3) Charities Act 2011). Experience suggests that in many cases changes to the memorandum and articles of association of DBFs, or to their other registered particulars, have not been registered. This is a matter to which attention should be given.

3. For the purposes of the Charities Act 2011, the persons having the general control and management of the administration of a charity are known as its 'charity trustees', even if, as in the case of a DBF, the charity is constituted as a company and not as a trust, and as such are subject to similar 'fiduciary obligations' to those of trustees in the strict sense – including the duty to act in the best interests of the charity. In the case of one form of DBF constitution seen by the Commission, where the DBF comprises all the members of the Bishop's Council, all the members of the DBF are both directors and charity trustees. In the case of the other models seen, only those members who form the board of directors, by whatever name it is known, are considered to be the charity trustees.

Functions of the DBF

4. Under the Diocesan Stipends Funds Measure 1953, one of the functions of a DBF is to keep a capital account and an income account for the diocesan stipends fund. Section 4 of the Measure provides that money standing to the credit of the capital account may be applied (*inter alia*) in the provision or improvement of parsonage houses. Section 5 of the Measure provides that moneys standing to the credit of the income account

of the diocesan stipends fund shall be applied (*inter alia*) in providing the stipends of incumbents and assistant curates in the diocese, and in meeting expenses incurred in repairing and maintaining parsonage houses. These are perhaps the matters in relation to which a member of the DBF who is a parish priest is most likely to have an interest, whether personally or on behalf of his or her parish, which may conflict with his or her duty to act in the best interests of the DBF. But the potential for conflicts of interest to arise is by no means confined to parish priests, or to the exercise of functions under the Diocesan Stipends Funds Measure.

Conflict of Interest

5. It is a general principle applicable to trustees and others in a fiduciary position that a person must not put him- or herself in a position where his or her duty to the relevant body may conflict with some personal interest (a 'conflict of interest') or some duty owed to another body (a 'conflict of loyalty'). There are clearly many decisions taken by a DBF which may affect the clergy members, and possibly other members, of the DBF, in which such a conflict of interest or conflict of loyalty may arise.

6. In the case of directors the duty to avoid conflicts of interests and conflicts of loyalty is set out in statutory form in sections 175 to 181 of the Companies Act 2006. However, section 181 contains modifications of the principle applied to other companies to meet the case of companies which are charities. With those modifications, section 175 provides as follows:

'175. The duty to avoid conflicts of interest
(1)   A director of a company must avoid a situation in which he has, or can have, a direct or indirect interest that conflicts, or possibly may conflict, with the interests of the company.

(2)   . . .

(3)   This duty does not apply in relation to a conflict of interest arising in relation to a transaction or arrangement with the company if or to the extent that the company's articles allow that duty to be so disapplied, which they may do only in relation to descriptions of transaction or arrangement specified in the company's articles.

(4)   This duty is not infringed –

(a)   if the situation cannot reasonably be regarded as likely to give rise to a conflict of interest; or

(b)   if the matter has been authorised by the directors.

(5)   Authorisation may be given by the directors where the company's constitution includes provision enabling them to authorise the matter, by the matter being proposed to and authorised by them in accordance with the constitution.

(6)   The authorisation is effective only if –

(a)   any requirement as to the quorum at the meeting at which the matter is considered is met without counting the director in question or any other interested director, and

(b)   the matter was agreed to without their voting or would have been agreed to if their votes had not been counted.'

7. Exceptions to the duty to avoid conflicts of interest can therefore be made

(a)   under subsection (3) if the DBF's articles allow the duty of its directors to be disapplied in relation to descriptions of transactions and arrangements specified in the articles; and

(b)   under subsection (5), in relation to any particular matter in which the duty would otherwise arise, if the exception to the duty has been authorised by the directors, where the DBF's articles include a provision enabling them to authorise the matter, by a decision in which those affected by the duty refrain from voting.

8. So far as company law is concerned, therefore, it is important that the articles of a DBF should include provisions which:

(a)   allow the duty to avoid a conflict of interest to be disapplied in relation to descriptions of transactions and arrangements specified in the articles, and

(b)   permit the directors to authorise the duty to be disregarded in relation to any particular matter, provided that the directors with an interest in the matter refrain from voting on the decision to give such authorisation.

9. Many (indeed perhaps most) DBFs will have had provisions in their memorandum of association for many years; and in such cases they will continue to have effect in so far as their terms are consistent with section 175(3 or (5). (Although section 175(3) of the 2006 Act refers to the company's 'articles' qualifying the normal duty to avoid conflicts of interest, provision in its memorandum of association will be equally effective for that purpose if it antedates 2009: the transitional provision contained in paragraph 1(3) of Schedule 1 to the Companies Act 2006 (Commencement No.3, Consequential Amendments, Transitional Provisions and Savings) Order 2007[1] made it clear that references in the Companies Act to a company's articles included the company's memorandum.)

10. However, DBFs will no doubt wish to satisfy themselves that their constitution contains provision having the effect described in paragraph 8 above. In that connection they may wish to note that the Charity Commission has published model articles which include an article which would give partial effect to the position described in paragraph 8(b) by authorising conflicts of loyalty in some circumstances.[2] It reads as follows:

'Conflicts of interests and conflicts of loyalties:

(1)   If a conflict of interests arises for a director because of a duty of loyalty owed to another organisation or person and the conflict is not authorised by virtue of any other provision in the articles, the unconflicted directors may authorise such a conflict of interests where the following conditions apply:

(a)   the conflicted director is absent from the part of the meeting at which there is discussion of any arrangement or transaction affecting that other organisation or person;

(b)   the conflicted director does not vote on any such matter and is not to be counted when considering whether a quorum of directors is present at the meeting; and

(c)   the unconflicted directors consider it is in the interest of the charity to authorise the conflict of interests in the circumstances applying.

---

[1] SI 2007/2194.
[2] It, and the associated note, can be found at: https://www.gov.uk/government/uploads/system/uploads/attachment_data/file/269508/gd1textc.pdf.

(2)   In this article a conflict of interests arising because of a duty of loyalty owed to another organisation or person only refers to such a conflict which does not involve a direct or indirect benefit of any nature to a director or to a connected person.'

11. The Charity Commission's note on this article is as follows:

'This article permits unconflicted directors to authorise a conflict of interests arising from a duty of loyalty owed by a director to another organisation or person provided that there is no direct or indirect benefit of any nature received by the director in question or by a connected person. Such a procedure is permitted by section 175(4) and (5) of the Companies Act 2006 (as modified for charitable companies by section 181) where provision is made for it in the articles. The Commission considers that such a procedure should be limited to conflicts arising from a duty of loyalty to another organisation or person where there is no direct or indirect benefit of whatever nature to the director or to a connected person. In other circumstances involving a situation leading to a conflict of interests on the part of a director, the Commission is able to authorise the director to act notwithstanding the conflict where it is satisfied that this would be expedient in the interests of the charity (section 105 of the Charities Act 2011).'

12. The model article could be useful if the matter under discussion involves a parish of which the director is the incumbent. It does not, however, meet the point that matters under discussion may involve conflict of interest on the part of some or all of the clergy who are directors of the DBF. This situation, which is unlikely to be so common in the case of commercial companies, can best be met by an article which disapplies the duty where the decisions of the DBF, for example relating to stipends, affect some or all of the clergy directors of the DBF generally. A suggested form of such an article is as follows:

'The duty to avoid conflicts of interest is disapplied in relation to all transactions and arrangements which apply generally throughout the Diocese or some part of the Diocese or with regard to relations between the Diocese and any other organisation or institution in the Church of England, provided that this does not extend to any transaction or arrangement which may directly or indirectly benefit an individual director differently from the other directors.'

Declaration of directors' interests

13. Section 177 of the Companies Act 2006 provides that 'If a director is in any way, directly or indirectly, interested in a proposed transaction or

arrangement with the company, he must declare the nature and extent of that interest to the other directors.' However 'a director need not declare an interest (a) if it cannot reasonably be regarded as likely to give rise to a conflict of interest, or (b) if, or to the extent that, the other directors are already aware of it (and for this purpose the other directors are treated as aware of anything of which they ought reasonably to be aware).'

14. Much of the ordinary business of a DBF or its directors may, directly or indirectly, affect the interests of its members; but that is something of which the other members are likely to be already aware; and the duty to declare an interest is therefore most likely to arise if a proposed transaction or arrangement affects an individual cleric or benefice rather than the Diocese as a whole.

15. The Charity Commission again provide a model article which might be adopted by a DBF.[3] It reads as follows:

> 'A director must declare the nature and extent of any interest, direct or indirect, which he or she has in a proposed transaction or arrangement with the charity or in any transaction or arrangement entered into by the charity which has not previously been declared. A director must absent himself or herself from any discussions of the charity directors in which it is possible that a conflict will arise between his or her duty to act solely in the interests of the charity and any personal interest (including but not limited to any personal financial interest).'

16. The Charity Commission also provides a detailed guide to handling conflicts of interest and conflicts of loyalty in its publication *Conflicts of interest: a guide for charity trustees* (CC 29): see https://www.gov.uk/government/uploads/system/uploads/attachment_data/file/343408/CC29-_PDF.pdf.

17. Not all the sections of the guidance are likely to be relevant to DBFs, but the relevant principles which apply can be readily seen, and regard should be had to those that are capable of applying to DBFs.

(June 2016)

---

[3] It can again be found at: https://www.gov.uk/government/uploads/system/uploads/attachment_data/file/269508/gd1textc.pdf.

Public rights of way over land forming part of a churchyard

1. The Commission has been asked whether it is possible for a public right of way across a churchyard to be created. The Commission is of the opinion that land forming part of a churchyard can, after 20 years use by the public as of right, be deemed to have been dedicated as a highway under section 31 of the Highways Act 1980, but that this will not always be the case.

2. The first part of this opinion (paragraphs [4] to [36]) sets out how, as a matter of law, a highway may come into existence. It is necessarily of a technical nature and is intended primarily for legal practitioners and others who are familiar with legal concepts.

3. The second part (paragraphs [37] to [44]) is concerned with the practical steps that may be available to an incumbent and parochial church council should they wish to prevent a public right of way arising.

PART 1: THE LEGAL BASIS FOR A HIGHWAY

Dedication as a highway at common law

4. As a matter of law, a highway is a way over which there exists a public right of passage. A public footpath is a highway, as is a bridleway or a way for vehicles.

5. At common law, a highway can arise in either of two ways:

(i)   express dedication by the owner of the land in question as a highway, or

(ii)   inferred dedication based on the fact of public user over a period of time (which need not be of any particular length) coupled with conduct on the part of the landowner such as to indicate that his intention was to dedicate the land in question as a highway.

6. At common law, only a fee simple owner (a person who owns land outright) can dedicate land as a highway because dedication is by nature dedication in *perpetuity;* a person with only a limited interest cannot act so as to bind land in perpetuity. So, at common law, a tenant for life could not expressly dedicate land as a highway; nor could it be inferred that he had done so.

7. Benefice and church property – including any churchyard – is vested in the incumbent in his corporate capacity. In that sense the incumbent is the 'owner' of the churchyard. But the incumbent is not an outright owner. An

incumbent's interest is less than that of a fee simple owner; the fee in respect of benefice and church property is permanently in abeyance.[1] An incumbent's position is equivalent to that of a tenant for life.[2] An incumbent, therefore, does not have the legal capacity necessary to dedicate as a highway land forming part of a churchyard and it cannot be inferred that he has done so.

8. The position at common law, therefore, is that a right of way cannot be created over a churchyard. In a 2013 Inspector's decision letter concerning a proposed addition to the Definitive Map of a footpath over a churchyard, a claim of inferred dedication at common law was rejected.[3] See, too, section 68(2) of the Mission and Pastoral Measure 2011 which provides (subject to exceptions that are not material here), 'it shall not be lawful to

---

[1] Co Lit 341a: 'the fee simple is in abeyance, as Littleton saith'. See also *Re St Gabriel's, Fenchurch Street* [1896] P 96 per Tristram Ch at 101–102: 'churchyards are by the law placed under the protection and control of the Ecclesiastical Courts and the freehold of the churchyard is in the rector, the fee being in abeyance; but the freehold is vested in him for the use (in so far as may be required) of the parishioners. Subject to that use, he is entitled to receive the profits arising from the churchyard; but he cannot by law make any appropriation of the soil of the churchyard. Such appropriation can only be made for limited purposes by a faculty issued from the Ecclesiastical Court.' See also *Re St Paul's, Covent Garden* [1974] Fam 1, 4 and *Re Tonbridge School Chapel (No. 2)* [1993] 2 All ER 339, 342.

[2] Co Lit 341a: '. . . a parson or vicar, for the benefit of the church or his successor, is in some cases esteemed in law to have fee simple qualified; but to doe any thing to the prejudice of his successor in many cases, the law adjudgeth him to have in effect but an estate for life'. In *Barker v Richardson* (1821) 4 B & Ald 579 it was held that a presumption of a grant of an easement – in that case, an easement of light – could not be made because the grant, if it had been made, would have been made by a rector who was described as 'a mere tenant for life' and who had no power to make such grant. Abbott C.J. said, at p. 582: 'Admitting that 20 years' uninterrupted possession of an easement is generally sufficient to raise a presumption of a grant, in this case, the grant, if presumed, must have been made by a tenant for life, who had no power to bind his successor; the grant, therefore, would be invalid, and consequently, the present plaintiff could derive no benefit from it, against those to whom the glebe has been sold.'

The reform of the law relating to real property brought about by the Law of Property Act 1925 has not changed the essential position in that regard. Before the 1925 Act came into force, it was possible for an interest less than a fee simple to exist as a legal estate. Under section 1 of the 1925 Act, that ceased to be the case and all estates, interests and charges in or over land other than an estate in fee simple absolute in possession, or a term of years absolute, took effect as equitable interests. The effect of the 1925 Act was to turn the incumbent's estate into an equitable interest; the Act did not have the effect of enlarging the incumbent's estate so that it became a fee simple. See *Re St Paul's, Covent Garden* [1974] Fam 1 at 4E, per Newsom Ch.

[3] *Ref: FPS/M1900/7/66/M*, 24 May 2013, para 19 (concerning the churchyard of St John the Baptist, Widford, Hertfordshire). In paras 15–18 the Inspector referred to, and purported to limit the application of, dicta contained in *In re St Mary's, Longdon* (2011) 13 Ecc LJ 370, Worcester Consistory Court.

sell, lease or otherwise dispose of . . . any consecrated land belonging to or annexed to a church . . .'.

9. It is, however, possible for a faculty to authorise the use by a highway authority of part of a churchyard as if it were a highway (or part of a highway). This, it is suggested, was the rationale for the Consistory Court of London holding in *Vicar and One of the Churchwardens of St Botolph without Aldgate v Parishioners of the Same* [1892] P 161 that that the Court had jurisdiction to authorize by faculty the appropriation of a portion of the churchyard required for a proposed widening of the adjacent street.[4] The power of the consistory court to grant a faculty 'authorising a suitable use' of land belonging to or annexed to a church is expressly preserved by section 68(15) of the Mission and Pastoral Measure 2011.

Presumed dedication under the Highways Act 1980

10. Section 31 of the Highways Act 1980 provides for dedication of land as a highway to be presumed in certain circumstances. A copy of section 31 is annexed to this Opinion.

11. The facts that have to be made out in order to establish the presumption are that 'a way over any land . . . has been actually enjoyed by the public as of right and without interruption for a full period of 20 years'. 'As of right' has its usual legal meaning – namely that the use in question has not been by force, has not been clandestine, and has not been with the permission of the owner (*nec vi, nec clam, nec precario*).[5]

12. Under section 31(1), provided the requisite facts are made out, 'the way is deemed to have been dedicated as a highway unless there is sufficient evidence that there was no intention during that period of 20 years to dedicate it.'

---

[4] Per Tristram Ch at 169, referring to an earlier decision of his: 'I therefore ordered the boundary fence of the churchyard to be placed back, and granted, by faculty, to the local authorities the use of a strip of the churchyard outside the new boundary fence for a public footpath, so long as it might be required for the public use; and in case of its not being so required, I ordered that it should revert to the use of the church.

I found, on inquiry in the registry, that my predecessor had granted one faculty of the kind; and, since the granting of the Kensington faculty, it has been the uniform practice of this Court, upon a proper case being made out by evidence, to grant by faculty to the local authorities the use of strips of the churchyard for enlarging adjoining thoroughfares upon similar terms, and this practice has been followed in several other Diocesan Courts.'
For more recent decisions see *In re St. John's, Chelsea* [1962] 1WLR 706; *In re St. Mary the Virgin, Woodkirk* [1969] 1WLR 1867.

[5] *Jones v Bates* at 245.

13. There is therefore no need to infer a dedication by an owner: the way becomes a highway by operation of law. As Scott LJ said in *Jones v Bates* [1938] 2 All ER 237 at 246, 'The change of the law brought about by statute is that, upon proof of such user for the requisite period, the conclusion of dedication follows as a presumption *juris et de jure*, instead of as an inference of fact to be drawn by the tribunal of fact. The phrase of the Act "shall be deemed to have been dedicated" is merely an historical periphrasis for saying that the way thereupon by operation of law becomes a highway.'

14. Dedication arises by virtue of the operation of the subsection: there is no requirement that the person in possession of the land in question has *power* to dedicate it. That this is the correct construction appears to be supported by a number of considerations.

Legislative history of section 31

15. First there is the legislative history of what is now section 31 of the 1980 Act. Its legislative predecessor, section 1 of the Rights of Way Act 1932, set out two bases upon which a statutory presumption of dedication would arise. The first required 20 years' uninterrupted user, with the proviso that the presumption would be defeated if '*during such period of 20 years there was not at any time any person in possession of such land capable of dedicating such a way.*' It is therefore clear that under the 1932 Act, a mere 20 years' uninterrupted user could not have resulted in a highway being established across a churchyard (or indeed over land subject to a strict settlement).

16. However, section 1 of the 1932 Act also provided a second basis whereby dedication would be deemed to have occurred. This required 40 years' uninterrupted user. If such user were made out, then a conclusive presumption of dedication arose irrespective of whether there was a person with capacity to dedicate.

17. A comparison may be made with section 2 of the Prescription Act 1832 and the two periods of user there. It was held in *Re St Martin Le Grand, York* [1990] Fam 63, that the provisions of the 1832 Act would not give rise to an easement over a churchyard. But section 2 of the 1832 Act is readily distinguishable from the relevant provisions in the 1932 and 1980 Acts. Section 2 of the 1832 Act prevents the defeat of a 'claim which may be lawfully made at the Common Law etc. to any Way or other Easement' where the requisite period of user can be shown. The restriction to a 'claim which may be lawfully made at the Common Law' would exclude an easement of way over a churchyard, as no such easement could be granted at common law. But the relevant provisions of neither the 1932 nor the 1980 Acts are restricted in this way to claims that can be made at common

law. The decision in *St Martin Le Grand* is therefore not applicable to the present question.

18. Taking the legislative history of section 1 of the Highways Act 1980 further, its predecessor, section 1 of the Rights of Way Act 1932, was amended by the National Parks and Countryside Act 1949. The second of the two bases giving rise to a presumption of dedication (i.e. 40 years' user) was entirely repealed. The first basis (20 years' user) was amended so as to remove the proviso that a way would not be deemed to have been dedicated if '*during such period of 20 years there was not at any time any person in possession of such land capable of dedicating such a way*'.

19. This followed a recommendation from the Hobson Report that the statutory machinery for establishing rights of way should be simplified. The relevant part of the report stated,

> 'We recommend that after 20 years' use of a way by the public "as of right and without interruption", that way shall be deemed in all cases to have been dedicated as a highway. This will cover entailed estates and would do away with the existing requirement that in such cases proof of 40 years' public use must be adduced.' (Cmnd 7208, para. 56).

Introducing the 1949 Act, the Minister said,

> '. . . in future there is a presumption of dedication of a right of way after 20 years user in all cases' (Hansard HC Deb, vol 463, ser 5, col 1485).

20. The result of the amendments made to section 1 of the 1932 Act was that 20 years' public user as a highway was of itself enough to give rise to the statutory presumption of dedication, irrespective of whether a fee simple owner had been in possession of the land throughout that period.

21. Section 31(1) of the Highways Act 1980 is essentially a re-enactment of section 1 of the 1932 Act as so amended. That being so, one would expect its effect to be the same as its predecessor: namely that 20 year's uninterrupted user (absent positive evidence of there being no intention to dedicate) will give rise to a statutory presumption of dedication in all cases, irrespective of the legal capacity of the person in possession.

Provision for land in possession of tenant for life

22. Secondly, the specific provision made in section 33 of the 1980 Act in relation to land in the possession of a tenant for life casts light on the

statutory intention behind section 31(1). It gives those with interests in remainder or reversion a statutory right to bring claims in trespass to prevent the acquisition of a public right of way over land as if they were in possession. Were it the case that the statutory presumption of dedication in section 31(1) only applied where there was a person with legal capacity to dedicate at common law (which a tenant for life generally lacks), then there would have been no need for section 33 (Protection of rights of reversioners).

23. The position therefore is that the (non)existence of a fee simple owner has no bearing on the question of whether section 31(1) is capable of applying. If that is so, then section 31(1) is in principle capable of applying in the case of land forming part of a churchyard vested in an incumbent (even though, at common law, he would not have the capacity to dedicate such land as a highway). In the 2013 Inspector's decision letter referred to in para 3 above, this was accepted to be the position.[6]

24. If that is so, one needs to consider whether any of the other provisions of section 31 have the effect of excluding land forming part of a churchyard from the statutory presumption of dedication after public use for 20 years.

Exclusionary provisions

25. Section 31(1) expressly excludes from its operation 'a way of such character that use of it by the public could not give rise at common law to any presumption of dedication'.

26. It is suggested in *Newsom*[7] that a path across land forming part of a churchyard would be excluded from the operation of section 31(1) by these words because, at common law, a presumption of dedication could not arise in respect of the way in question given the lack of legal capacity on the part of the owner of the land and because dedication would be inconsistent with the sacred uses on which the land was held. But it does not seem that the exclusionary words in section 31(1) do in fact have that effect.

27. In *Attorney- General v Brotherton* [1992] AC 425, the House of Lords held that the equivalent provisions of the 1932 Act are concerned with the *physical* nature of the way in question; so that, for example, the statutory presumption of dedication could not arise in respect of a navigable river. The subsection is not concerned with the legal nature of the way but with

---

[6] At para 23.
[7] GH Newsom & GL Newsom, *Faculty Jurisdiction of the Church of England*, London 1993, p. 151–2.

whether its physical character is such that use of it by the public could give rise at common law to any presumption of dedication.[8]

28. Turning to subsection (7) of section 31, it is true that it provides a definition of 'owner' for the purposes of the foregoing provisions of the section and that 'owner' is defined as 'the person who is for the time being entitled to dispose of the fee simple in the land'. An incumbent of a benefice would not, therefore, be within the meaning of 'owner' for the purposes of the earlier provisions of the section[9]; and the wording of subsection (7) suggests that the parliamentary draftsman did not have in mind the particular position of incumbents.

29. But that does not take one very far. The provision of section 31 which operates so as to turn a way into a highway – subsection (1) – makes no reference to any owner. Where the requisite period of user is established (and unless there is sufficient evidence that there was no intention during the period to dedicate it), the way is simply deemed to have been dedicated as a highway. There does not even need to be a known owner.[10] The definition of 'owner' in subsection (7) is not material for the purpose of the operation of subsection (1).

30. Finally, consideration needs to be given to subsection (8):

> 'Nothing in this section affects any incapacity of a corporation or other body or person in possession of land for public or statutory purposes to dedicate a way over that land as a highway if the existence of a highway would be incompatible with those purposes.'

As expressed in the 2013 Inspector's decision letter referred to above,

> 'subsection (8) provides a means whereby a specific class of landowner can defeat a claim for deemed dedication if they can demonstrate that the claimed right of way would be incompatible

---

[8] In his speech, Lord Oliver said, 'I cannot, for instance, think that any reader of Alfred Lord Tennyson would have regarded the Lady of Shalott, as she floated down to Camelot through the noises of the night, as exercising a right of way over the subjacent soil.'

[9] Given the absence of such an 'owner', it is not possible to use the procedure for depositing a map under section 31(6) of the Highways Act 1980 in order to negative an intention to create a right of way over a churchyard.

[10] '... the Act has got rid of all the trouble and difficulty inherent in the task of inducing the tribunal of fact to give a solemn finding of an act of dedication at some past date, which was, as a rule, wholly imaginary, and often by an imaginary owner', per Scott LJ in *Jones v Bates* at 246.

with the public or statutory purposes for which they hold the land over which it would pass'.[11]

31. An incumbent in whom a churchyard is vested is a corporation in possession of land. Given that all who are resident in a parish have a right of burial in the churchyard of that parish and, more broadly, all consecrated land is held for sacred purposes and for the benefit of the parishioners at large, there would seem to be a good case of saying that an incumbent is in possession of such land for public purposes.

32. However, even assuming that subsection (8) applies to Church of England churchyards, this will only be relevant '*if the existence of a highway would be incompatible with those public or statutory purposes*'. The test is a pragmatic one, to be applied on the facts of the particular case. As explained in the case of a railway undertaking, '. . . *a public highway could not be dedicated if at the relevant time it was reasonably foreseeable that such dedication was incompatible with the object of the statutory undertaker*'.[12]

33. Where a claimed footpath has been used by the public for more than for more than 20 years, there are likely to be (for both statutory undertakers and churches) evidential problems in proving such incompatibility, whether one looks to what was foreseeable at the start or end of the 20 year period. On the facts of the Inspector's decision letter referred to above, it was '*not convincingly demonstrated to the Inspector that the public walking along the claimed path through Widford churchyard is incompatible with the purposes for which that land is held*', so that the claim of deemed dedication under section 31 of the Highways Act 1980 was upheld.[13]

34. There could, however, be cases where continued use of the path by the public might impede further burials, or the proper functioning of the church and/or the churchyard. Even where the churchyard was closed by Order in Council, so that the public purpose of burial of bodies will have ceased and the existence of the highway could not be said to be inconsistent with future such burials, the footpath might be inconsistent with the future interment of ashes (which is permissible in a closed churchyard). The position is each case will need to be assessed on its own facts.

Conclusion

35. The conclusion therefore is that land forming part of a churchyard can after 20 years use by the public as of right be deemed to have been dedicated

---

[11] At para 27.

[12] *British Transport Commission v Westmorland County Council* [1958] AC 126, at 152 and 156.

[13] At para 33 and 46.

as a highway under section 31 of the Highways Act 1980, but that this will not always be the case: it will depend on the facts of the particular case.

Ancient paths

36. Where a public footpath or other highway existed over land before that land was consecrated as a churchyard, that highway will have continued in existence in spite of the fact that the land had become a churchyard. There may be a number of such ancient paths in existence.

PART 2: PRACTICAL GUIDANCE TO INCUMBENTS AND PCCS

The definitive map

37. If a footpath across a churchyard is already shown on the definitive map kept by the local authority under section 53 of the Wildlife and Countryside Act 1981, it is suggested that only in the rarest cases would it be sensible for the incumbent and parochial church council to challenge this. Where it is proposed to seek a modification of the definitive map, the incumbent and PCC should obtain legal advice before proceeding.

Steps incumbents and PCCs might take to prevent the deemed dedication of highways arising

38. Some parishes may understandably wish to resist the acquisition by the public of a right of passage across the churchyard.[14] Of course if the path has already become a public footpath by use for 20 or more years, there may be nothing that can now be done to safeguard the position, and the taking of steps may positively encourage users to apply for a public path to be registered.

39. There are, however, three steps which parishes should consider taking, each of which should have the effect of preventing a public right of way being acquired.

---

[14] Sub-sections (3) to (6) of the Highways Act 1980 provide means by which the owner or reversioner may take steps to prevent the accrual of public rights over land. But 'owner' bears the meaning given in subsection (7): the person who is entitled to dispose of the fee simple. In the case of a churchyard vested in an incumbent there is no such person, so that sub-sections (3), (5) and (6) have no application; nor is the incumbent's interest that of 'a tenant for a term of years, or from year to year', nor is he (or anyone else) 'a person for the time being entitled in reversion to the land', so that sub-section (4) similarly has no application (perhaps another indication that the draftsman did not have in mind the position of churches).

40. Total prevention of access for a period of time each year should have the effect of preventing a public right of way arising. That is because it would amount to bringing the public's right to use the path 'into question' for the purposes of section 31(2) of the Highways Act 1980. Where there are gates, this can readily be done by the closure of all gates once a year.[15]

41. Putting up clear notices to the effect that use of the path by the public is permitted by the incumbent and PCC, but that such permission may be withdrawn at any time, would probably suffice to make the user permissive, and thus not '*as of right*', the latter being a requirement under subsection (1) of section 31.[16]

42. Putting up of clear notices prohibiting entry (save for access to the church) would also probably negative use '*as of right*' under subsection (1)[17], although such a prohibitive notice can be expected to annoy users of the path, and could be counter-productive.

43. The effectiveness of putting up permissive or prohibitory notices to protect churchyards has not been tested in the courts.[18]

Other cases

44. Finally, there will be some parishes where the establishment of a public footpath through a churchyard is not seen as problematic. Indeed benefits may be perceived through securing highway authority funding for the maintenance of such a path.

(October 2016)

---

[15] 'Occasional closure to all comers' was instanced as a way of defeating a claim to use 'as of right' by Lord Walker in *R (Beresford) v City of Sunderland* [2003] UKHL 60; [2004] 1 AC 889, para 83. The annual closure of gates was specifically mentioned by Lord Hoffmann and Lord Neuberger in *R (Godmanchester Town Council) v Secretary of State for Environment, Food and Rural Affairs* [2007] UKHL 28; [2008] 1 AC 221 paras 37 and 89.

[16] See the observations of Lord Walker in *Beresford*, above, para 72

[17] See *Winterburn & anor v Bennett & anor* [2016] EWCA Civ 482

[18] There is a counter-argument, to the effect that since sub-sections 31(3) to (5) make express provision for owners and reversioners to post or give notice 'that the way is not dedicated as a highway', such notice cannot be given in other ways. It is considered unlikely, that such a counter-argument would succeed before an Inspector or the courts. As to sub-section (6), it is the 'owner' of land who may deposit a map and statement with the appropriate council such as to amount to sufficient evidence to negative an intention to dedicate. That sub-section is incapable of being resorted to in respect of churchyards, and it is unlikely that notice given to the appropriate council other than under sub-section (6) would be regarded as sufficiently drawn to the attention of users to prevent deemed dedication of a public footpath.

Highways Act 1980

31 Dedication of way as highway presumed after public use for 20 years

(1) Where a way over any land, other than a way of such a character that use of it by the public could not give rise at common law to any presumption of dedication, has been actually enjoyed by the public as of right and without interruption for a full period of 20 years, the way is to be deemed to have been dedicated as a highway unless there is sufficient evidence that there was no intention during that period to dedicate it.

(1A) Subsection (1) –

(a) is subject to section 66 of the Natural Environment and Rural Communities Act 2006 (dedication by virtue of use for mechanically propelled vehicles no longer possible), but

(b) applies in relation to the dedication of a restricted byway by virtue of use for non-mechanically propelled vehicles as it applies in relation to the dedication of any other description of highway which does not include a public right of way for mechanically propelled vehicles.

(2) The period of 20 years referred to in subsection (1) above is to be calculated retrospectively from the date when the right of the public to use the way is brought into question, whether by a notice such as is mentioned in subsection (3) below or otherwise.

(3) Where the owner of the land over which any such way as aforesaid passes –

(a) has erected in such manner as to be visible to persons using the way a notice inconsistent with the dedication of the way as a highway, and

(b) has maintained the notice after the 1st January 1934, or any later date on which it was erected,

the notice, in the absence of proof of a contrary intention, is sufficient evidence to negative the intention to dedicate the way as a highway.

(4) In the case of land in the possession of a tenant for a term of years, or from year to year, any person for the time being entitled in reversion to the land shall, notwithstanding the existence of the tenancy, have the right to

A116

place and maintain such a notice as is mentioned in subsection (3) above, so, however, that no injury is done thereby to the business or occupation of the tenant.

(5) Where a notice erected as mentioned in subsection (3) above is subsequently torn down or defaced, a notice given by the owner of the land to the appropriate council that the way is not dedicated as a highway is, in the absence of proof of a contrary intention, sufficient evidence to negative the intention of the owner of the land to dedicate the way as a highway.

(6) An owner of land may at any time deposit with the appropriate council –

(a)   a map of the land . . ., and

(b)   a statement indicating what ways (if any) over the land he admits to have been dedicated as highways;

and, in any case in which such a deposit has been made, . . . declarations in valid form made by that owner or by his successors in title and lodged by him or them with the appropriate council at any time –

(i)   within the relevant number of years from the date of the deposit, or

(ii)   within the relevant number of years from the date on which any previous declaration was last lodged under this section,

to the effect that no additional way (other than any specifically indicated in the declaration) over the land delineated on the said map has been dedicated as a highway since the date of the deposit, or since the date of the lodgment of such previous declaration, as the case may be, are, in the absence of proof of a contrary intention, sufficient evidence to negative the intention of the owner or his successors in title to dedicate any such additional way as a highway.

(6A) Where the land is in England –

(a)   a map deposited under subsection (6)(a) and a statement deposited under subsection (6)(b) must be in the prescribed form,

(b)   a declaration is in valid form for the purposes of subsection (6) if it is in the prescribed form, and

(c)   the relevant number of years for the purposes of sub-paragraphs (i) and (ii) of subsection (6) is 20 years.

(6B) Where the land is in Wales –

    (a)   a map deposited under subsection (6)(a) must be on a scale of not less than 6 inches to 1 mile,

    (b)   a declaration is in valid form for the purposes of subsection (6) if it is a statutory declaration, and

    (c)   the relevant number of years for the purposes of sub-paragraphs (i) and (ii) of subsection (6) is 10 years.

(6C) Where, under subsection (6), an owner of land in England deposits a map and statement or lodges a declaration, the appropriate council must take the prescribed steps in relation to the map and statement or (as the case may be) the declaration and do so in the prescribed manner and within the prescribed period (if any).

(7) For the purposes of the foregoing provisions of this section 'owner', in relation to any land, means a person who is for the time being entitled to dispose of the fee simple in the land; and for the purposes of subsections (5), (6), (6C) and (13) 'the appropriate council' means the council of the county, metropolitan district or London borough in which the way (in the case of subsection (5)) or the land (in the case of subsections (6), (6C) and (13)) is situated or, where the way or land is situated in the City, the Common Council.

(7A) Subsection (7B) applies where the matter bringing the right of the public to use a way into question is an application under section 53(5) of the Wildlife and Countryside Act 1981 for an order making modifications so as to show the right on the definitive map and statement.

(7B) The date mentioned in subsection (2) is to be treated as being the date on which the application is made in accordance with paragraph 1 of Schedule 14 to the 1981 Act.

(8) Nothing in this section affects any incapacity of a corporation or other body or person in possession of land for public or statutory purposes to dedicate a way over that land as a highway if the existence of a highway would be incompatible with those purposes.

(9) Nothing in this section operates to prevent the dedication of a way as a highway being presumed on proof of user for any less period than 20 years, or being presumed or proved in any circumstances in which it might have been presumed or proved immediately before the commencement of this Act.

(10) Nothing in this section or section 32 below affects section 56(1) of the Wildlife and Countryside Act 1981 (which provides that a definitive map and statement are conclusive evidence as to the existence of the highways shown on the map and as to certain particulars contained in the statement), . . .

(10A) Nothing in subsection (1A) affects the obligations of the highway authority, or of any other person, as respects the maintenance of a way.

(11) For the purposes of this section 'land' includes land covered with water.

(12) For the purposes of subsection (1A) 'mechanically propelled vehicle' does not include a vehicle falling within section 189(1)(c) of the Road Traffic Act 1988 (electrically assisted pedal cycle).

(13) The Secretary of State may make regulations for the purposes of the application of subsection (6) to land in England which make provision –

(a)   for a statement or declaration required for the purposes of subsection (6) to be combined with a statement required for the purposes of section 15A of the Commons Act 2006;

(b)   as to the fees payable in relation to the depositing of a map and statement or the lodging of a declaration (including provision for a fee payable under the regulations to be determined by the appropriate council).

(14) For the purposes of the application of this section to land in England 'prescribed' means prescribed in regulations made by the Secretary of State.

(15) Regulations under this section made by the Secretary of State may make –

(a)   such transitional or saving provision as the Secretary of State considers appropriate;

(b)   different provision for different purposes or areas.

Parochial church councils

1 This Opinion addresses certain specific points concerning the membership of Parochial Church Councils ('PCCs'), financial matters including loans and the giving of security, and the powers and duties of PCC committees.

Membership

2 A resolution of an Annual Parochial Church Meeting ('APCM') to make the elected members of the PCC consist of, say, six persons of each gender as a permanent arrangement would be unlawful as it would be beyond the powers conferred on the APCM by the Church Representation Rules ('CRR').

3 Vacancies occurring amongst the representatives of the laity during the year must be filled in accordance with CRR r48(1). However, the PCC would be duly constituted even if such vacancies were not filled (CRR, App. II, para. 17).

Co-options

4 A clerk in Holy Orders, or an actual lay communicant (as defined by CRR r54(1)) of sixteen years or upwards, even if not on the roll of the parish, can be co-opted as a member of the PCC by the PCC itself (CRR r14(1)(h)) even though a clerk in Holy Orders or a lay person whose name is not on the roll of the parish cannot be elected to the PCC as a representative of the laity (CRR r10(1)). The disqualification from membership under rule 14(3)(c) (which applies to those who are disqualified from being charity trustees under the Charities Act 2011 and those who are disqualified by the bishop from serving on the PCC under the Incumbents (Vacation of Benefices) Measure 1977 (as amended): CRR r 46A) applies to co-opted members in the same way as to all other members of the PCC.

5 The number of co-opted members may not exceed one-fifth of the representatives of the laity who are elected by the APCM to the PCC, or two persons, whichever is the greater (CRR r14(1)(h)). It should be noted that representatives of the laity elected to the deanery synod are not included for the purpose of this calculation.

Term of office of PCC members

6 Unless the annual meeting decides that all representatives of the laity elected to the PCC should face re-election each year, one third of those representatives retire from office in every year. The representatives to retire at each subsequent annual meeting shall be those who have been longest in

office since last elected. As between representatives elected on the same day, those to retire shall be selected by lot unless they agree otherwise among themselves (CRR, r.16).

PCC office holders

7 (a)   Although there is nothing in the CRR or the 1956 Measure to prevent one person from combining the offices of secretary and treasurer of the PCC, the arrangement is not desirable.

(b)   A PCC can appoint its officers for such term as it thinks fit. In the absence of any provision to the contrary the appointment terminates at the first meeting of the PCC held after the APCM following the officer's appointment.

(c)   Although persons who are not members of the PCC may be remunerated for acting as secretary or treasurer, members may not (CRR, App. II, para. 1(d) and (e)).

PCC agenda

8 Agenda of the meetings of the PCC are governed by CRR App II para 4. Best practice dictates:

(a)   Notices of motion should contain the words of the motion proposed to be moved, but notices fairly indicating the purport of the words may be accepted.

(b)   Matter which is defamatory, scandalous or entirely outside the functions of the PCC ought not to be put on the agenda paper.

Chairman of PCC

9 The chairmanship of the PCC is dealt with in CRR App II paras 1(a) and (h), 5 and 11. Under rule 11, in the case of an equal division of votes at a meeting of the PCC, the chairman has a second or casting vote. But the chairman's right to give a second or casting vote at meetings of a committee of the PCC depends upon any rules of procedure which the PCC itself may make. It is doubtful whether in the absence of any such rules the chairman of a committee can claim any similar right to that of the chairman of the PCC. A chairman who has a casting vote may not refrain from voting until the votes have been counted and then give his or her original vote and casting vote together.

PCC minutes

10 PCC minutes are subject to CRR App II para 12. In addition, a resolution which is not ultra vires cannot be deleted subsequently from the minutes though subsequent resolutions can express disagreement with or rescind former resolutions. Should it become apparent that a resolution of the PCC was unlawful because it was not within the PCC's powers the matter should be addressed at a subsequent meeting and dealt with in the minutes of that meeting.

Loans to a PCC

11 There is no doubt that a PCC may borrow money. Section 4 of the Parochial Church Councils (Powers) Measure 1956 confers on the PCC the powers that were formerly exercisable by the vestry with respect to the affairs of the church and the powers the churchwardens formerly had with respect to the financial affairs of the church. Both the vestry and the churchwardens had the power to borrow money: see the discussion of the position in *Re St Peter, Roydon* [1969] 1 WLR 1849, 1854–55 and the authorities cited there. Moreover, section 7 of the 1956 Measure confers a power on the PCC to frame an annual budget 'and to take such steps as they think necessary for the raising and collecting of such moneys'. The scope of that power is wide enough to include raising money by way of loan.

12 Money can be borrowed from anyone willing to lend it to the PCC and upon any terms that may be agreed, including the giving of security. The Commission considers that the view expressed by Chancellor Forbes in *Re St Peter, Roydon* that a PCC could not give security for a loan was wrong. The Chancellor only considered – presumably because that is the way the arguments of counsel were framed – the position under section 4 of the 1956 Measure (Powers vested in council as a successor to certain other bodies). No consideration was given to section 7 and the wide power it confers on the PCC to 'take such steps as they think necessary for the raising' of moneys. Nor was any consideration given to section 5. Section 5 empowers a PCC to acquire any property real or personal for any ecclesiastical purpose affecting the parish and 'to manage, administer and dispose of' any such property. A power to dispose of property includes a power to charge that property. Section 6 – which requires any land belonging to a PCC to be vested in the diocesan authority – was amended by the Ecclesiastical Property Measure 2015 and now expressly provides in subsection (3) for the PCC to charge such property provided that it obtains the consent of the diocesan authority to its doing so unless the consideration on the transaction is less than the amount specified in, or determined in accordance with, the order made by the Archbishops' Council under

subsection (4A). The giving of such a charge also requires the consent of the Charity Commission unless that requirement is disapplied by section 124(2) of the Charities Act 2011 where the advice referred to there is obtained and considered. Apart from giving security by way of a charge, a PCC can give any security it pleases by way of bond or covenant to repay a loan either in one lump sum or by instalments or otherwise and such bond or covenant would be binding on the PCC, even though its members might change, to the extent of moneys in its hands as a corporation available for the purpose for which the money was borrowed. A loan can be accepted from, amongst other sources, the diocesan board of finance if willing to lend on such terms, consistent with the duty of prudence, as may be agreed (see PAROCHIAL CHURCH COUNCIL: LEGAL POSITON OF MEMBERS). As the members of a PCC are charity trustees, an interest-bearing loan from a member of the PCC would infringe the rule against benefits to charity trustees described in the Opinion on PAROCHIAL CHURCH COUNCIL: LEGAL POSITION OF MEMBERS.

13 If a PCC has property which it can mortgage to secure its overdraft with a bank, a legal mortgage of such property can be given with the necessary authorisation (see above). In the absence of such property it is unlikely that any document executed by the PCC alone would be acceptable to a bank. Members of the PCC are under an obligation to see that the PCC's debts are duly paid. PCC members should not commit the PCC to any liabilities that they do not believe the council will be able to honour. If a particular item of expenditure is essential, and can only be funded by an overdraft, the better course would be to spread the burden of personal guarantees as widely as possible amongst the worshipping community.

Contract between PCC and member

14 As regards contracts between a PCC and any of its members, see the opinion on PAROCHIAL CHURCH COUNCIL: LEGAL POSITION OF MEMBERS.

Power to make donations to non-parochial objects

15 Whilst it should be remembered that the members of the PCC are charity trustees and have a duty to exercise their duties responsibly, in view of the PCC's widely expressed functions under the 1956 Measure (as amended) a PCC has power as a matter of law to subscribe a reasonable part of its general funds to any charity the objects of which are such as to further any part of 'the whole mission of the Church'. The 'mission of the Church' for this purpose comprises not only religious objects in the narrow sense, but also the Christian duty of relieving the poor, the sick and others in need. Provided this requirement is met, the charity need not be one which operates

within the parish or under which the parish or individual parishioners may benefit. Indeed, funds may be given to a non-charity, provided that they are to be used by it to further the 'mission of the Church' in some way. An example of this would be where funds are given to a legal entity created by a deanery synod to support the work of a youth worker employed by it. However, a PCC would be well-advised to seek advice, whether from the Diocesan Registrar or the Charity Commission, before giving funds to a non-charity. The PCC should also have regard to the advice issued by the Charity Commission 'Grant funding an organisation that isn't a charity' which is available on its website.

16 It is important that a PCC takes all reasonable steps to ensure that funds it donates to third parties are in fact applied for the intended charitable purposes. Particular care may be needed where the funds are to be applied for the support of a Christian worker who is not employed by a charity. Failure to restrict expenditure to charitable purposes could lead to the loss of tax relief on the sums misapplied and expose the members of a PCC to claims for breach of trust. Difficulties of this kind are unlikely to arise where a donation is made to a registered charity. But care is required where funds are paid to a body which is not a charity, including bodies situated outside the United Kingdom. In such cases the advice of the Legal Advisory Commission is that, as a minimum, the donation should be accompanied by a covering letter stating that the donation should only be used exclusively for the charitable purpose for which the PCC wishes it to be applied and requesting the donee's acceptance of that restriction.

Standing committee and other committees of PCC

Chairmanship of standing committee

17 The standing committee of the PCC is governed by paragraph 14 of Appendix II to the CRR. The incumbent (although the chairman of the PCC (see CRR App II para 1(a)) and thus an ex officio member of the standing committee of the PCC) is not the ex officio chairman of the standing committee, but would normally act as such. The vice-chairman of the PCC (see CRR App II para 1(b)) is not an ex officio member of the standing committee.

Powers and duties of standing committee and other committees

18 The standing committee, between the meetings of the PCC, has power to 'transact the business' of the PCC, subject to any directions which the PCC may have given it (CRR, App. II, para. 14(b)). This is a wide power which enables the standing committee to carry on the routine work

of the PCC between the meetings and to deal with most matters of real urgency.

19 But the powers of the standing committee are not as wide as those of the PCC itself. First, the committee may not act outside any directions given to it by the PCC. Secondly, it may not act in relation to matters that are outside the competence of the PCC whose business it has power to transact. Thirdly, the power to 'transact the business of the council' is not the same as a power to exercise any and every function which the PCC itself has. The import of the expression 'transact the business of the council' is that the power is concerned with taking decisions in relation to the PCC's activities, affairs and dealings and includes such matters as entering into contracts, taking decisions as to the implementation of recommendations contained in the report prepared under the Inspection of Churches Measure 1955, deciding how to address emergency situations and responding to consultation with the PCC which cannot wait until its next meeting.

20 It is not open to the standing committee to exercise functions which provisions in Acts of Parliament, Measures or Canons specifically confer on the PCC. It would not, for example, be within the powers of the standing committee to take decisions which are required to be taken at a meeting of the PCC under section 11 of the Patronage (Benefices) Measure 1986 (i.e. preparing a statement as to the conditions, needs and traditions of the parish, appointing two lay members of the council to act as representatives of the council in connection with the selection of an incumbent, etc.). Nor, for example, would it be open to the standing committee to agree to enter into a contract of employment with a member of the PCC under section 3A of the Parochial Church Councils (Powers) Measure 1956 as that section requires the council to be satisfied of certain matters before such a contract may be entered into by it. And it is not open to the standing committee to take decisions which require a resolution of the PCC, for example the delegation of functions to a district church council, the appointment of members to the standing committee, or the making of a request for an enquiry into the pastoral situation in a parish under section 1A of the Incumbents (Vacation of Benefices) Measure 1977. Because persons may be co-opted to the PCC only 'if the parochial council so decides' (CRR r14(1)(h)), the standing committee has no power to co-opt persons to be members of the PCC. Any resolution to petition for a faculty, or to apply to the archdeacon for a licence for temporary minor re-ordering, also needs to be passed by the Council itself.

21 In addition to the standing committee, the PCC may appoint other committees for the purpose of the various branches of church work in the parish (CRR, App. II, para. 15). Any committee is similarly accountable to the PCC, and may perform such functions as may be given to it by the PCC.

Membership of committees

22 The PCC is obliged to appoint members to the Standing Committee in addition those of its members who are ex officio members of that Committee (CRR App II para 14). The PCC (but not the Standing Committee or any other committee) may appoint other committees (CRR App II para 15). Under CRR App II para 14, members of the standing committee must be members of the PCC. So far as other committees are concerned persons who are not members of the council may be included (CRR, App. II, para. 15), and it is within the competence of a PCC to include as members of such committees persons who are not qualified to be on the electoral roll.

23 The incumbent is ex officio a member (but not ex officio chairman) of all committees (CRR, App. II, para. 15). The secretary of a PCC is not a member ex officio of any committee appointed by the PCC. However, it may be convenient that the secretary should attend some committees, in which case the PCC may consider it appropriate to include the secretary as a member. Churchwardens are ex officio members of the standing committee (see above), but not of any other committee unless expressly included by the PCC.

(Revised May 2003)
(Further revised October 2016)

Using Churches for Secular Purposes

1. Introduction

1.1. The Church Buildings Review Group reported in 2015. In their Summary, the Group observed:

> 'The primary purpose of churches is and should remain the worship of Almighty God, to be houses of prayer. But that can and needs to be sensitively combined with service to the community. The imaginative adaptation of church buildings for community use in many areas is breathing new life into them.'

1.2. Appendix 3 to the Report usefully summarised the legal position with regard to authorising secular use of consecrated land and/or buildings as follows:

> '1. There are currently two legal models under which rights in relation to an open church building can be conferred on a person or body. One is a contractual licence; the other is a lease. Both models involve conferring legally enforceable rights on the other party to the arrangement. The rights in question will include a right to use the building, or part of the building, for specified purposes.
>
> . . .
>
> 6. Although the incumbent (in his or her corporate capacity) will normally be the person who grants the licence or the lease, the incumbent cannot do so except under the authority of a faculty. That is for a number of reasons. First it is because although the property in the church and churchyard is vested in the incumbent in right of his or her office, it is subject to the control of the Ordinary (in the person of the chancellor as judge of the consistory court). Secondly, a consecrated church cannot lawfully be used for secular purposes except under the authority of a faculty. Thirdly, so far as leases are concerned, there are statutory provisions which require the incumbent to obtain a faculty to authorise the grant of a lease.
>
> 7. That means that before a licence or a lease can be entered into, it is necessary to submit a petition to the consistory court and to obtain a faculty. The petition will normally be accompanied by a draft of the proposed licence or lease.
>
> 8. There are no special statutory provisions which govern the exercise of the faculty jurisdiction to authorise the grant of a licence. But the court cannot grant a faculty for a licence to use a church in a way which would be inconsistent with its status as a consecrated

building as such use would be unlawful. Provided that the proposed use is consistent with the church's consecrated status, the court has a discretion whether to grant a faculty. The court will wish to be satisfied that if the licence is granted the building will continue to be a church and that the proposed use will not prevent its use as a church when it is required for that purpose – which will not merely be on Sundays but also, for example, for the occasional offices.

9. A lease of a church cannot be granted except under the relevant provisions of section 68 of the Mission and Pastoral Measure 2011. The relevant provisions were originally introduced by the Pastoral (Amendment) Measure 2006. The aim of that Measure was to facilitate alternative use of churches in cases in which parishes found that, if such use were to be possible, the intended user group needed to have a lease of the part of the church in question, rather than merely a licence. In many cases this would be because a lease was required to enable the user group to secure financial support from one or more public funding bodies (this being a common requirement of a number of such bodies). The purpose of the Measure was not to provide a mechanism for transferring responsibility for the maintenance of church buildings away from the PCC and a lease under section 68 is not an apt means for doing so. (See further below.)

10. Section 68 of the 2011 Measure empowers the consistory court, in its discretion, to grant a faculty authorising the incumbent to grant a lease. But this is subject to two overriding requirements. The lease must be of part only of a church: it is not possible to grant a lease in respect of the whole church. Moreover, the church building, taken as a whole, must continue to be used primarily as a place of worship after the lease is granted.

11. One reason for imposing these requirements was that the grant of a lease under faculty was not intended as an alternative means of effectively closing a church for regular public worship and appropriating it to other uses.

12. A further reason, of some practical importance, was that if the building as a whole ceased to be used primarily as a place of worship, it would cease to benefit from the ecclesiastical exemption from listed building control. The result of that would be that the church became subject to secular control in addition to the faculty jurisdiction.'

1.3. This Opinion sets out the relevant secular planning law on change of use and considers the implications for the Ecclesiastical Exemption of effecting such change as Ecclesiastical Law allows. The implications for rating are also considered. Other regulatory requirements are not covered in this Opinion, but will need to be considered in relevant circumstances.

For example, part of St Mary's, Ashford[1] is now a permanent performance review/arts centre with a bar which sells alcoholic drinks. Therefore, a licence is required for that part of the premises.

1.4. Nothing in this Opinion should be taken as detracting from the need for authorisation by faculty in the case of changes of use within premises covered by the faculty jurisdiction.

2. Secular Planning Law

2.1 So far as likely to be relevant to church activities, secular planning law is divided into three main areas of regulation. These are: planning control, listed building control and special controls (specifically, trees and advertisements). These three areas will be examined below, starting with listed building and conservation area control. The first and third of these matters are dealt with principally by the Town and Country Planning Act 1990 and secondary legislation made under it. The second is covered by the Listed Building and Conservation Areas Act 1990.

2.2 *Listed Building and Conservation Area Control*

2.2.1 Listed church buildings are exempt from secular listed building control by virtue of s.60 Listed Buildings Act 1990 ('LBA 1990') which provides as follows:

> '(1) The provisions mentioned in subsection (2) shall not apply to any ecclesiastical building which is for the time being used for ecclesiastical purposes.
> (2) Those provisions are sections 3, 4, 7 to 9, 47, 54 and 59.
> (3) For the purposes of subsection (1), a building used or available for use by a minister of religion wholly or mainly as a residence from which to perform the duties of his office shall be treated as not being an ecclesiastical building.
> (4) For the purposes of sections 7 to 9 a building shall be taken to be used for the time being for ecclesiastical purposes if it would be so used but for the works in question.
> (5) The Secretary of State may by order provide for restricting or excluding the operation of subsections (1) to (3) in such cases as may be specified in the order.
> (6) An order under this section may –

---

[1] Following the grant of a Faculty which was the subject of the decision of the Court of Arches in (2011) Ecc LJ 244

(a)   make provision for buildings generally, for descriptions of building or for particular buildings;

(b)   make different provision for buildings in different areas, for buildings of different religious faiths or denominations or according to the use made of the building;

(c)   make such provision in relation to a part of a building (including, in particular, an object or structure falling to be treated as part of the building by virtue of section 1(5)) as may be made in relation to a building and make different provision for different parts of the same building;

(d)   make different provision with respect to works of different descriptions or according to the extent of the works;

(e)   make such consequential adaptations or modifications of the operation of any other provision of this Act or the principal Act, or of any instrument made under either of those Acts, as appear to the Secretary of State to be appropriate.

(7) Sections 7 to 9 shall not apply to the execution of works for the demolition, in pursuance of a pastoral or redundancy scheme (within the meaning of the Pastoral Measure 1983), of a redundant building (within the meaning of that Measure) or a part of such a building.' (Emphasis added).

2.2.2   Pursuant to subsection (5) (highlighted above), the Secretary of State has made an Order[2] restricting the operation of s.60 to '*church buildings*' and defining '*church building*' as '*a building whose primary use is as a place of worship.*'

2.2.3   S.75(1) LBA 1990 similarly exempted from the requirement for Conservation Area Consent ecclesiastical buildings which are for the time being used for ecclesiastical purposes. Conservation Area Consent for demolition is now no longer applicable in England by virtue of amendments made by the Enterprise and Regulatory Reform Act 2013, meaning that demolition of unlisted churches in conservation areas is regulated – so far as secular controls are concerned[3] – by means of a

---

[2]   The Ecclesiastical Exemption (Listed Buildings and Conservation Areas) (England) Order 2010 (SI.2010/1176)

[3]   Section 17 of the Care of Churches and Ecclesiastical Jurisdiction Measure 1991 provides for faculties to be granted for the demolition of churches in the limited range of circumstances

requirement for planning permission. In Wales, the position remains as originally enacted in 1990.

2.2.4 The exclusions from the control of the LBA 1990 are colloquially referred to as the *'Ecclesiastical Exemption'*.

2.2.5 It will be noted that the exemption does not apply to clergy housing (ss.60(3), 75(1)),[4] but *'ecclesiastical purposes'* are not otherwise defined. The specific statutory exclusion of clergy housing was added in response to case law which suggested a wide interpretation both of the terms *'ecclesiastical building'* and *'ecclesiastical purposes'*: see *Phillips v Minister of Housing and Local Government* [1965] 1 QB 156 at 164, where it was said that *'Parliament never intended hard and fast lines to be drawn'* in relation to ecclesiastical buildings and, obiter, that, if necessary, *'ecclesiastical purposes'* would have been construed to include a parsonage house used by the rector as the centre of his spiritual vocation and work of the cure of souls.

2.2.6 As noted above, the Secretary of State's Order removes the Exemption in the case of church buildings which are no longer used primarily as places of worship, notwithstanding the breadth of the Act's phrase, *'ecclesiastical purposes.'*

2.2.7 In the case of a church which has been closed under the Mission and Pastoral Measure 2011, s.60(7) LBA 1990 is supplemented by the provisions of the non-statutory *'Skelmersdale Agreement'*, a convention under which the Church Commissioners seek the guidance of the Secretary of State as to the future of any closed church which they wish to demolish, after the holding of a public inquiry if the Minister deems it necessary.

2.2.8 The Ecclesiastical Exemption does not apply to planning control, which is separate from listed building control, and affects land and buildings generally.

---

set out in the section. A faculty or some other form of ecclesiastical authority (e.g. an order under section 18 of the 1991 Measure, or a scheme under Part 6 of the Mission and Pastoral Measure 2011) will be required in addition to any secular permission. Special notice of a petition for a faculty authorising demolition of listed churches and of unlisted churches in conservation areas is required to be given to Historic England, the local planning authority and relevant national amenity societies: see Part 9 and Schedule 2 to the Faculty Jurisdiction Rules 2015.

[4] Subject to the Church of England (Miscellaneous Provisions) Measure 2014 No.1, Sch.2, para 11 which provides (as amended) that the exclusion of a clergy dwelling applies *'unless it is a chapel forming part of an episcopal house of residence and is included in the list maintained by the Church Buildings Council under s.1 of the Care of Places of Worship measure 1999 or is otherwise subject to the faculty jurisdiction.'*

2.3 *Planning Control and Special Controls*

2.3.1 Broadly speaking, planning permission is required for development. *'Development'* is defined by s.55 Town and Country Planning Act 1990 ('TCPA 1990'). S.55 provides as follows (so far as relevant for the purposes of this Opinion):

'(1) Subject to the following provisions of this section, in this Act, except where the context otherwise requires, "development," means the carrying out of building, engineering, mining or other operations in, on, over or under land, or the making of any material change in the use of any buildings or other land.

(1A) For the purposes of this Act "building operations" includes –

(a) demolition of buildings;

(b) rebuilding;

(c) structural alterations of or additions to buildings; and

(d) other operations normally undertaken by a person carrying on business as a builder.

(2) The following operations or uses of land shall not be taken for the purposes of this Act to involve development of the land –

(a) the carrying out for the maintenance, improvement or other alteration of any building of works which –

(i) affect only the interior of the building, or

(ii) do not materially affect the external appearance of the building,

and are not works for making good war damage or works begun after 5th December 1968 for the alteration of a building by providing additional space in it underground;

. . .

(f) in the case of buildings or other land which are used for a purpose of any class specified in an order made by the Secretary of State under this section, the use of the buildings or other land or, subject to the provisions of the order, of any part of the buildings or the other land, for any other purpose of the same class.'

2.3.2 *'Development'* is, therefore, divided into two classes:

(a)   operational development; and

(b)   material change of use.

2.3.3 It will be appreciated that many changes to churches which require authorisation by way of Faculty do not require planning permission. If works are purely internal, no question of planning permission arises by virtue of s.55(2)(a)(i). External repairs and minor external works are unlikely to require planning permission by virtue of s.55(2)(a)(ii), though it is good practice to check that this is the case in respect of any contemplated works by speaking to an officer of the Local Planning Authority. In cases of difficulty, a binding statutory determination may be sought from the Authority under s.192 of the Act. If the matter is, for any reason, not straightforward, such that a certificate under s.192 might be appropriate, then expert planning advice should be sought.

2.3.4 Trees and advertisements are subject to specific statutory controls within the secular planning regime. In summary, if a tree is the subject of a Tree Preservation Order or is within a Conservation Area, the consent of the Local Planning Authority is required for the cutting down, topping, lopping, uprooting, wilful damage or wilful destruction of the relevant tree unless removal of the tree has been authorised under a planning permission. Notices in churchyards may require advertisement consent depending on the circumstances. The Ecclesiastical Exemption does not apply to these forms of regulation. Once more, it is always prudent to consult the Local Planning Authority when any question arises as to the possible engagement of these statutory provisions.

2.3.5 Returning to planning permission and the definition of *'development'*, it is necessary to consider the two limbs a little further. Operational development results in some physical change to land or buildings. Material change of use, on the other hand, is concerned with some change in the activities carried out on land or in buildings.[5] It is not necessary to consider operational development further for the purposes of this Opinion which is concerned with the implications of introducing secular activities into church buildings.

2.3.6 The phrase *'material change of use'* is not comprehensively defined in the legislation. It has therefore fallen to the courts to establish principles

---

[5] See Lord Denning in Parkes v Secretary of State for the Environment [1979] 1 AER 211 at 213.

to guide the determination of whether or not a change is material, subject to the overall approach which is that application of such a general concept is a matter of fact and degree for the Local Planning Authority in the first instance.

2.3.7 Of particular relevance to the question under consideration are the concepts of materiality, primary and ancillary uses and mixed uses.

2.3.8 When considering whether or not a change requires planning permission, that is, whether or not it is material, the Courts will identify what the primary use of the land in question is. Statutory provision has made this task easier in many instances by means of the Town and Country Planning (Use Classes) Order 1987, which lists and groups together certain classes of land use. Broadly speaking, changes between uses in the same groups are declared by s.55(2)(f) TCPA 1990 (set out above) not to constitute development and do not, therefore, require planning permission. Churches are included with Class D1, which groups together the following uses:

'*Any use not including a residential use –*

(a)   for the provision of any medical or health services except the use of premises attached to the residence of the consultant or practitioner,

(b)   as a crèche, day nursery or day centre,

(c)   for the provision of education,

(d)   for the display of works of art (otherwise than for sale or hire),

(e)   as a museum,

(f)   as a public library or public reading room,

(g)   as a public hall or exhibition hall,

(h)   for, or in connection with, public worship or religious instruction.'

2.3.9 Reverting to the general position, it is important to remember that, unlike planning control, listed building consent is not governed by the concept of '*development*' therefore the exception in ss.60 and 75 LBA 1990 in respect of '*any ecclesiastical building which is for the time being used for ecclesiastical purposes*' does not extend to other Class D1 uses, even though change of use of a church to, say, use as a day centre, would not require planning permission. The critical question in relation to applicability of the Ecclesiastical Exemption is, therefore, the nature of any change of use of the building *from* use for ecclesiastical purposes *to* something else. This question will need to be judged in the same way as other questions about material change of use, that is, as a matter of fact and degree and general principle. Clearly, the provisions of the Order will also be relevant and, for the benefits of the Ecclesiastical Exemption to be retained, the primary use must continue to be as a place of worship.

2.3.10 It is not every change of use which is '*material.*' A change is not material if it is de minimis (i.e. so minor in nature that the law takes no notice of it). The Courts have accepted that it is relevant to consider the possible off-site effects of a change, for example traffic or noise impacts. Of particular importance for this Opinion is the concept of primary and ancillary uses. The Courts have recognised that a primary use might encompass a range of activities. For example, in recognition that a hotel use might involve many different aspects which might otherwise be capable of being uses in their own right, it was held that a non-residents' bar was incidental to a primary hotel use, even though only 20% to 30% of its customers were hotel residents: *Emma Hotels Ltd v Secretary of State for the Environment* [1979] JPL 390; [1981] JPL 283. It is a question of judgment as to whether a use is truly ancillary; uses which start in that way may grow such that the ancillary link is lost. To choose a religious illustration of this principle, the Court considered in *Hussain v Secretary of State for the Environment* [1971] 23 P&CR 330 the planning status of use of part of retail premises for the ritual slaughter of chickens in accordance with Moslem law. Although a certain amount of preparation of articles for sale could be regarded as incidental to retail use, the Court held that the slaughtering of animals was not.

3. Ecclesiastical Law Principles

3.1 As Halsbury's Laws of England succinctly states: '*It is not possible to alienate consecrated land or buildings completely from sacred uses and to appropriate them permanently to secular uses without the authority of an Act of Parliament or a Measure of the Church Assembly or General Synod.*'[6]

3.2 As noted above, the current statutory provision which enables alienation to be authorised is the Mission and Pastoral Measure 2011. In the case of a total appropriation of a listed building to and use for non-ecclesiastical uses, then the Ecclesiastical Exemption would cease to apply, since the building in question would no longer be '*used for*

---

6 5th edn. Vol.34, para 840

ecclesiastical purposes', as set out in sections 60 and 75 LBA 1990[7]. Moreover, the provisions of the Order would operate to remove the effect of the Exemption. The special and separate position of demolitions pursuant to a scheme under the Measure are dealt with by s.60(7) LBA 1990 and the Skelmersdale Agreement.

3.3 The more usual situation and the one which has been encouraged by the Church Buildings Review Group is, however, the use of part of a church for something other than activities which would normally be regarded as use for '*ecclesiastical purposes*' and/or part time use for purposes other than worship or other church-run activities. As the Church's understanding of mission evolves, it may be that its approach to '*ecclesiastical purposes*' and '*primarily as a place of worship*' will become rather more flexible than that of the secular Local Planning Authority or Court. There is little authority on the point. The wide approach of the Court in Phillips is noted above; the proposition that any building that happened to be owned by the church might fall within the definitions was, however, rejected. That decision is now nearly fifty years old and, prior to amending legislation, concerned a building which might be thought fairly obviously to have been in use for ecclesiastical purposes. Modern secular courts faced with more innovative uses and activities in church buildings might be less deferential. On balance, though, given the caveat in s.68 Mission and Pastoral Measure 2011 that a lease may only be authorised in respect of part of a church and that the Consistory Court must ensure that the premises remaining unlet, together with the premises let are, taken as a whole, used primarily as a place of worship, we consider that any potential planning difficulties are more apparent than real in the case of leases.

3.4 Licences were not brought within the scope of the amending legislation[8] since these could already be authorised by Faculty. It nevertheless seems to

---

[7] Therefore an offence is committed if listed building consent is not obtained prior to demolition, since at the date of commission of the offence (ie. the demolition itself) the building would not be in use for ecclesiastical purposes: see *A-G ex rel. Bedfordshire County Council v Trustees of Howard United Reformed Church* [1976] AC 363. A statutory defence is available for works to a building which are urgently necessary in the interests of safety or health or the preservation of the building: see section 9(2) LBA 1990. An equivalent defence is available for the urgent demolition of an unlisted building in a conservation area: see section 196D(4) TCPA 1990. Section 18 of the Care of Churches and Ecclesiastical Jurisdiction Measure 1991 provides for the chancellor to authorise the emergency demolition of a church without a faculty in circumstances where a statutory defence would be available under LBA 1990 or TCPA 1990.

[8] The original predecessor to s.68 was contained within the Pastoral (Amendment) Measure 2006, which, as noted by the Church Buildings Group (above) was intended to enable secular use of churches by organisations which needed the security of a lease, provided such uses were not inconsistent with the primary use as a place of worship.

us that, when considering the grant of a Licence under Faculty, Chancellors should be guided by the same principle of primacy of use as a place of worship. Whether or not a material change of use has occurred as a matter of secular planning law is not determined by the precise legal nature of any occupation. Hence, loss of primacy as a matter of fact, pursuant to a licence, albeit that such occupation would not have the same property law incidents as a lease, would be determinative as a matter of planning law. Quite apart from the clear legislative intention of the Measure not to endorse the complete change of use of a church in the absence of a scheme under its other provisions, it would be imprudent, in the case of a listed church, to fail to observe the primacy principle because of the risk of losing the Ecclesiastical Exemption.

3.5 The primacy principle enshrined in s.68 of the Measure sits well with the secular notion of primary and ancillary uses and it is difficult to conceive of planning problems arising, provided the ecclesiastical law principles set out above are observed.

3.6 Another secular planning concept is that of mixed uses. Such situations are to be distinguished from those where there is a primary use to which other uses are incidental or ancillary. Mixed uses exist when it is not possible, amongst two or more activities, to discern one which has primacy to which others are ancillary. In such situations, where there was previously a single use, development will be held to have occurred. Here, it seems to the Commission, there is greater scope for a mismatch between ecclesiastical and secular law. This is because the secular arm might have a narrower view of '*ecclesiastical purposes*' or '*primarily as a place of worship*' than the ecclesiastical court which would, as a matter of practice, have regard to the role of a church as a local centre of worship and mission[9].

3.7 Once again, however, having regard to the primacy of worship principle set out in s.68 of the Measure, we do not foresee difficulties in terms of the Ecclesiastical Exemption. '*Ecclesiastical purposes*' in the LBA 1990 is, plainly, a wider phrase than the Measure's words, '*used primarily as a place of worship*'. In Whitstable, St Peter [2016] ECC Can 1, a faculty was granted for the temporary siting of a Post Office '*pod*' inside the church. Planning permission had already been granted for change of use. The Commissary General had regard to the size and positioning of the '*pod*' and the practical implications for worship, concluding that they would be

---

[9] In *Re St Luke Maidstone* [1995] 1AER 321, the Court of Arches held that s.1 Care of Churches and Ecclesiastical Jurisdiction Measure 1991 does not apply to the ecclesiastical courts but observed that the statutory provision, had it applied, would, in any event, have added nothing to the existing duty and practice of chancellors.

acceptable, providing that provision were made in the licence for accommodating occasional offices. She also had regard to the Petitioners' mission objectives. As the church was unlisted, no question of loss of the Ecclesiastical Exemption arose.

3.8 It seems to the Commission that the particular mission of the local church, for example in terms of service to the community or consciousness-raising, would be relevant in the event that the scope of *ecclesiastical purposes*' were to be questioned in any case involving a listed building. Circumstances will vary, but even in a case of a mixed use of place of worship (Use Class D1) and something else (e.g., part time shop or broadband or mobile phone installations under licence), there would continue to be use for *ecclesiastical purposes*'. This conclusion is reached because a faculty should not have been granted without primacy of the worship function having been secured; furthermore, the mission rationale for the other use should have been clearly explained both to the Local Planning Authority and the Chancellor.

4. Rating

4.1 The Local Government Finance Act 1988 Schedule 5 paragraph 11 provides as follows:

'(1) A hereditament is exempt to the extent that it consists of any of the following –

(a) a place of public religious worship which belongs to the Church of England or the Church in Wales (within the meaning of the Welsh Church Act 1914) or is for the time being certified as required by law as a place of religious worship;

(b) a church hall, chapel hall or similar building used in connection with a place falling within paragraph (a) above for the purposes of the organisation responsible for the conduct of public religious worship in that place.

(2) A hereditament is exempt to the extent that it is occupied by an organisation responsible for the conduct of public religious worship in a place falling within sub-paragraph (1)(a) above and –

(a) is used for carrying out administrative or other activities relating to the organisation of the conduct of public religious worship in such a place; or

(b)   is used as an office or for office purposes, or for purposes ancillary to its use as an office or for office purposes.

(3) In this paragraph "office purposes" include administration, clerical work and handling money; and "clerical work" includes writing, book-keeping, sorting papers or information, filing, typing, duplicating, calculating (by whatever means), drawing and the editorial preparation of matter for publications.'

4.2 Places of worship are exempted from non-domestic rates, as is any ancillary use falling within the scope of paragraph 11. The use of the words '*to the extent that*' requires apportionment where ancillary use falls outside the scope of paragraph 11. In some cases, the apportionment will be on a spatial basis and in others, on a time basis, or both, depending on the nature of the use. Particular difficulty can arise in relation to multi-functional buildings. The question of whether or not a building is exempt and the extent of the exemption is determined on a day to day basis, at the end of each day. The place of worship must 'belong to' the Church of England in order to benefit from the exemption. The words 'belong to' do not refer to legal ownership. The status of churches build before 1855 is preserved by the Places of Worship Registration Act 1855. For buildings after this date, a building 'belongs to' the Church of England if it has been consecrated or licensed for public worship. The building must be used for public religious worship.

4.3 A church hall must be used for the purposes of the Church of England. A hall that is let for a range of purposes including wider community purposes that go beyond religious life and extend to social life will not lose its exemption, but a lease of a church hall for the exclusive occupation by a third party will not be exempt. For example, occupation by a youth group under the control of the minister or the PCC will be exempt; occupation by a scout group will not be exempt unless the Church of England sponsors the scout group and its membership is drawn predominantly from the congregation. Similarly, the position in relation to occupation by children's nurseries will depend on whether or not that nursery is under the control of the minister and PCC. The wording of any lease or licence arrangement will be a significant factor in establishing whether or not the exemption applies.

4.4 Commercial occupation, including retail premises, bookshops, gift shops, function rooms that are separated from the place of worship and religious training centres, is unlikely to be exempt.[10]

---

[10] For example: *Glenwright and Durham CC v St Nicholas PCC* [1988] RA 1 where a former vestry, which had received planning permission for a change of use to a shop subject to a condition that it should operated for the benefit of the PCC and was occupied by a charitable

4.5 The use of premises by the Church of England for office accommodation, as defined, is exempt. Such occupation is not limited to occupation by the parish office of the parish concerned. The user by the Church of England may be for other purposes connected to the Church or by a group of parishes or by the diocese. Office user by another independent body will not be exempt.

4.6 For those properties falling outside the exemption afforded by the Local Government Act 1988 Schedule 5 paragraph 11, other relief may be available. Relief of 80% of the business rate liability is given by section 43(6) Local Government Finance Act 1988:

4.6.1 where the ratepayer is a charity and the property is used wholly or mainly for the charitable purposes of that charity or another charity or charities[11], or

4.6.2 where the ratepayer is registered community amateur sports club[12] and the property is used wholly or mainly for the purposes of that registered club or another registered club or clubs.

4.7 Relief will not be available where the charity occupies a small part of the property. The amount of mandatory relief given under s43(6) is 80% of the business rate liability.

---

company, was held not to be exempt; *The Chapter of the Abbey Church of St. Alban v Booth (VO) (2004) VT* [2004] RA 309: a shop and refectory run by a separate company with a separate identity with objectives quite separate from those of the Cathedral was not exempt; compare *Ebury (VO) v Church Council of the Central Methodist Church* [2009] UKCT (LC) 138: two rooms in a church buildings used as a bookshop selling Christian books, greetings cards, devotional items and including a coffee shop run by volunteers and used part of the time for church activities were exempt. In *Romily Lifecentre v Tuplin (VO)* [2011] RVR 255 a café and bookshop run by a separate charitable company limited by guarantee in premises some distance from the church was not exempt. The *Ebury* case was distinguished because in that case the kitchen was not a commercial kitchen and the turnover was very small. By comparison, the *Romily Lifecentre* operation was commercial in appearance, operated from kitchens of a commercial standard, had a very high turnover and gave no financial support to the church.

[11] The Local Government Finance Act 1988 contains no definition of 'charitable purposes'. See the definition of 'charitable purposes' contained in the Charities Act 2011. Local Government Finance Act 1988 s.64(10) provides that property used wholly or mainly for the sale of goods donated to a charity will be treated as being used for charitable purposes where the proceeds of sale of the goods, after deduction of expenses, are applied for the purposes of a charity.

[12] The club, society or other organisation must be a community amateur sports club for the purposes of Chapter 9 of Part 13 Corporation Tax Act 2010.

4.8 The Local Government Finance Act 1988 section 47(5) gives the local authority a discretion to give relief from non-domestic rates of up to 20% if:

4.8.1 the whole or part of the property is occupied for the purposes of one or more not for profit institutions or organisations and the main objects of each such institution or organisation are charitable or otherwise philanthropic, religious or concerned with education, social welfare, science, literature or the fine arts, or

4.8.2 the property is used wholly or mainly for recreation and is occupied for the purposes of a club, society or other organisation not established or conducted for profit.

5. Conclusions

5.1 The following conclusions can therefore be drawn:

(1)   that a faculty will be required in all cases where it is intended to use part of a church or other consecrated premises for secular purposes;

(2)   that, whilst the decision whether or not to grant such a faculty will be a matter for the discretion of the consistory court, the primacy of the purpose of the premises for worship should be retained;

(3)   such an approach to the wider use of church premises for mission objectives should ensure that the benefits of the Ecclesiastical Exemption from secular listed building control and exemptions under rating law are retained;

(4)   in cases raising doubt or difficulty in relation to the implications for secular planning and/or rating law, the advice of the relevant local authorities should be sought, supplemented by independent expert advice where necessary.

(October 2016)

Baptism: Consent of parent

Involvement of parents, guardians and godparents

1. The canon law has never required the consent of a parent before a child is baptized. Indeed, had that been so, emergency baptism would have proved impossible. Although the *Common Worship: Christian Initiation*: Emergency Baptism (Note 2 at p. 105) provides that it is the parent's responsibility to request emergency baptism, it also recognizes that the parents may be absent and that they may not even have named the child (see Note 3 at p. 105). The Ministration of Private Baptism in Houses in the BCP also seems to envisage the possibility of the absence of the parents. In relation to a healthy infant, however, Canon B 22 envisages some involvement of the child's parents or guardians as the minister is required to instruct them in their responsibilities.

2. However, Canon B 22 must be construed in relation to the general law applicable in England and the word 'parent'[1] must therefore now be construed as referring only to a person having parental responsibility for the child[2]. The Children Act 1989, section 3(1), defines 'parental responsibility' as

> 'all the rights, duties, powers, responsibilities and authority which by law a parent of a child has in relation to the child . . .'

And, although the Act does not further define the scope of this responsibility, subsequent case law has made it clear that it embraces both the right to determine a child's religion and to change a child's name. This being so, the decision whether or not to baptize a child is in the Commission's view also part of parental responsibility. In consequence, no person (other than one authorized by a civil court) can lawfully authorize a child's baptism unless that person has at the relevant time parental responsibility for that child[3]. Nevertheless, more than one person may have parental responsibility at any given time (CA 1989, s 2(5)), although each of them may act alone in carrying out that responsibility unless there is any enactment to the contrary

---

[1] The word 'guardian' must similarly be construed in relation to the general law applicable in England.

[2] If one or both parents of the child are, or have been, resident other than in England and Wales since the birth of the child, it may be that different considerations apply and advice in such cases should therefore be sought from the diocesan registry.

[3] Nonetheless, the exercise of parental responsibility may be subject to an order of the civil courts and in certain circumstances a local authority is entitled to exercise parental responsibility to the exclusion of any others having that responsibility. The unusual case arising in relation to section 3(5) of the Children Act 1989 is referred to later in this opinion.

(CA 1989, s 2(7)). In addition, a person who has parental responsibility may arrange for some or all of his or her responsibility to be met by one or more persons acting on his or her behalf (CA 1989, s 2(9)). In the latter circumstance a minister should not baptise the child until he or she is satisfied by reference to the original document making such an arrangement that the person applying for the baptism to take place does, indeed, have the requisite authority.

3. The Commission recognises the pastoral situation of the minister when asked to baptise a child and that any enquiries as to parenthood and who has parental responsibility requires sensitivity. Nevertheless, it is necessary for the minister to make some enquiry into these matters as to proceed without the requisite authority could in theory amount to an assault on the child. For this reason it may be best practice to provide a simple questionnaire to be filled out by those bringing the child to baptism. Such a questionnaire should include simple questions as to who are the natural parents of the child and who has parental responsibility for the child. (A table as to who in law has parental responsibility is set out in the Appendix but in the case of any complication the advice of the diocesan registry should be sought before proceeding further.)

4. Although any one person having parental responsibility may in law act alone (see above) and therefore may bring a child to baptism without the knowledge or agreement of others having contact with or responsibility for the child, the minister should not proceed without attempting first to ascertain the views of those other people. To act otherwise may cause a difficult pastoral situation and in any event it is always open to another person to apply to the civil courts for an order preventing the baptism. In the event of any disagreement the minister should seek the direction of the diocesan bishop.

5. There is also the duty under Canon B 22, paragraphs 3, to instruct the parents or guardians that 'the same responsibilities rests on them as are in the service of Holy Baptism required of the godparents'[4] and this may prove difficult if others having parental responsibility are not involved from the outset. In addition, in a case such as the natural father who may not have parental responsibility but nevertheless has involvement with the upbringing of the child, the spirit of the Canon would suggest that such persons should similarly be instructed. In all such cases, if that person should refuse to be instructed, the direction of the diocesan bishop should again be sought.

---

[4] See, too, Canon B 23, paragraph 2.

6. In English law, including the ecclesiastical law, a child is any person under the age of 18. Therefore, although Canon B 24 (Of the baptism of such as are of riper years) makes no mention of an actual age, it must be read as referring to adults, rather than to older children. The relevant rite in the Book of Common Prayer is entitled *The Ministration of Baptism to such as are of Riper Years and Able to Answer for Themselves* but the latter words should not be read as referring to children who are able to answer for themselves as the final rubric to that rite makes clear.

Who has parental responsibility?

7. Unfortunately, the question who has parental responsibility in any given circumstance in English law may often be complicated: see the Appendix. Where there is any doubt, guidance should always be sought in the first instance from the diocesan registrar. This is particularly so in cases where care proceedings are ongoing or the mother has undergone treatment for assisted reproduction and the creation of the embryo carried by the mother was not brought about by the sperm of the other party to the relationship (see CA1989, s 2(1A)(1B); Human Fertilisation and Embryology Act 2008, ss 35, 42 & 43) and also in cases of surrogacy (HFEA 1990, s 30).

8. Those having parental responsibility may in certain circumstances lose that responsibility (for example, when the child is adopted by some other person or persons or by order of a civil court) or have the power to exercise that responsibility restricted by order of a civil court. The responsibility is similarly lost if the original order which conferred the parental responsibility of the person concerned ceases to have effect, for example, if it is revoked by the court.

9. There are also some rare occasions (for example, when not all the above conditions required in law as to surrogacy have been fulfilled) where there has been no court order, no-one holds parental responsibility and a child remains in the everyday care of a person or persons who is, or are, not his biological parents and with whom he or she has no kinship relationship. In the last situation section 3(5) of the Children Act 1989 provides that he or she may (subject to the other provisions of the Act) –

> 'do what is reasonable in all the circumstances of the case for the purposes of safeguarding or promoting the child's welfare.'

In effect, such a person stands in loco parentis and within a Christian context this would seem to embrace bringing a child to baptism.

10. Usually a child will be brought to baptism by the natural or adoptive parents or the guardian or guardians. However, as has been seen,

circumstances can vary widely and it may happen that only one parent, or only one person having parental responsibility, may bring a child to baptism; the other parent or person having parental responsibility may have died; the natural parents may never have married or may now be divorced; the other parent may have a different religion or be an atheist or agnostic; the other person may object to the baptism or merely be uninterested. The minister can only discover the true state of affairs by making enquiries; in the first instance this will be from the person who requests the baptism. In any case where a claim to parental responsibility depends upon any written documentation (such as a court order, birth certificate or arrangement) the minister should not perform the baptism without first seeing written evidence in support of that contention. It is the Commission's view that in all these cases 'due notice' within the meaning of Canon B 22, paragraph 1, includes the provision of such written documentation or other proof that the person has legal authority to request the baptism. (It is always good practice to keep a copy of any such documentation.)

11. Even though section 2(7) of the Children Act 1989 permits one person having parental responsibility to act without the authority of another such person, if the child is brought by one such person alone, the minister remains under a duty (save in an emergency) to instruct those having parental responsibility in the responsibilities that rest upon them (Canon B 22, paragraph 4). The minister should therefore enquire as to the reason for the absence of the other natural parent or person having parental responsibility and, if there is another such person who cannot be located, the minister must endeavour to instruct them all[5]. In order to do so the minister may postpone the baptism (save in an emergency) (Canon B 22, paragraph 3).

12. If the other person or persons having parental responsibility cannot be found, the minister is entitled then to baptise the child. On the other hand, if they do not agree to a baptism, or refuse to be prepared or instructed, the minister should apply to the diocesan bishop for guidance and directions under Canon C 18. If the minister learns that a court order to prohibit baptism has been made or is being sought, the minister should refuse baptism until the matter has been resolved by the court; in the meantime the minister should inform the bishop of the reasons for refusal.

13. If the child is brought for baptism by persons other than those with parental responsibility, the minister's obligations in relation to those having

---

[5] It is the Commission's view that in the case of a local authority the minister's duty will be fulfilled if he or she draws its attention to the fact that ecclesiastical law places on those exercising parental responsibility the same responsibilities as are required of godparents in the service of Holy Baptism (see Canon B 22, paragraph 3).

parental responsibility still remain under Canon B 22, paragraph 3, to prepare or instruct them.

14. If the minister refuses to baptise the child, or unduly delays in so doing, a person having parental responsibility who brought the child to baptism or authorised that someone to do so may apply to the bishop under Canon B 22, paragraph 2, and after consultation with the minister the bishop may give such directions as he or she thinks fit.

Emergency baptism

15. Canon B 22, paragraph 6, provides:

> 'No minister being informed of the weakness or danger of death of any infant within his cure and therefore desired to go to baptise the same shall either refuse or delay to do so.'

There is no exception to the duty upon a minister having the cure of souls to attend upon an emergency under Canon B 22, paragraph 6, for example, to await the presence of those having parental responsibility or godparents or to give instruction; indeed, the summons may come from someone entirely unconnected with the family. However, if upon attendance the minister were to find that the child was perfectly healthy, he would not be under any obligation to administer baptism then and there, as private baptism should only occur 'in case of great danger' (see the rubric at the end of The Ministration of public Baptism to such as are of Riper Years in the BCP) or 'emergency' (see Note 1 of *Common Worship: Christian Initiation*: Emergency Baptism at page 105). Canon B 22, paragraph 6, obliges the minister to attend without refusal or delay rather than expressly to administer the Sacrament.

16. Nevertheless, if the child is in danger of death, or will remain at risk (which would seem to be the purpose of the word 'weakness' in Canon B 22 paragraph 6), there is a clearly implied duty (subject to what is said below) to administer the Sacrament (see Canon B 22, paragraph 7) unless there is an order from the civil courts forbidding such a baptism. In this regard the minister should be guided by any available medical opinion. The minister should not claim medical expertise unless actually qualified to make such a claim. If there is any doubt as to the emergency, the child should still be baptised. The decision as to whether the child should be baptised is in no way dependent upon whether it is 'within his cure'; these words only delineate upon whom the duty of attendance falls.

17. If told of the existence of an order of the court forbidding the baptism, or an application for such an order, a minister who nevertheless administered baptism would be in danger of having to answer to the civil court.

18. Does the duty to baptise in an emergency exist in relation to every child irrespective of the views or religion of one or more of those having parental responsibility? The duty to attend under Canon B 22, paragraph 6, is absolute and only when present will the minister be able to appreciate the situation. Hospital admission records or other information may reveal that those having parental responsibility are not Christian and in those circumstances the minister's duty to baptise has to be considered within the context of the significance of baptism in the universal Church. Baptism is the Sacrament instituted by Christ for those who wish to become members of his Church (see The Welcome and Peace in *Common Worship: Christian Initiation*: Holy Baptism at pages 75 and 120) and, as such, the congregation '. . . shall receive him as one of the flock of true Christian people (rubric after the questions to those who bring a child to church after emergency baptism in the Ministration of Private Baptism of Children in Houses in the BCP). This being so, and especially as baptism is not a prerequisite of ultimate salvation[6], it can no longer be argued that baptism ought to be administered against the wishes or beliefs of those having parental responsibility for the child on the ground that the salvation of the child must be of paramount concern. Therefore, although there is no exception expressly mentioned in Canon B 22, paragraph 6, it can nevertheless be implied that the minister should not baptise a child in an emergency where it is likely to be contrary to the wishes of those having parental responsibility.

19. In an emergency anyone may lawfully baptise (see, e.g., Note 1 at page 105 in *Common Worship: Christian Initiation*), although the duty under Canon B 22, paragraph 6, only falls upon a minister having a cure of souls. Subject to the general cure of the bishop, it is usually only the incumbent who has an exclusive cure of souls within a parish (*Halsbury's Laws of England*, 5th edn, 2011, vol. 34, at para 452), although the minister of a conventional district has a cure of souls, as does a vicar in a team ministry where a special cure of souls in respect of the parish has been assigned to that team vicar by a scheme under the Mission and Pastoral Measure 2011 or by a licence from the bishop. A priest-in-charge licensed to a parish during a vacancy has the cure of souls in that parish (*see also* **Clergy: priest-in-charge**). On the other hand, an assistant curate has no cure of souls except as the minister in charge of the parish by reason of a vacancy. Moreover, hospital chaplains who are licensed under the Extra-Parochial Ministry Measure 1967 are to be regarded as having a cure of souls within the meaning of Canon B 22.

(February 2017)

---

[6] See *Common Worship: Christian Initiation* Emergency Baptism (Note 2 at page 105).

Appendix

The circumstances (other than those concerning assisted reproduction and surrogacy) giving rise to parental responsibility are as follows:

(a)   *Mother*: a mother always has parental responsibility (CA 1989, s 2(1)(2)) unless the child has subsequently been adopted or a parental order[1] is made.

(b)   *Father*: a father has parental responsibility if –

    (i)   he and the mother were married[2] at the time of the child's birth (CA 1989, s 2(1); or

    (ii)   (ii) they were unmarried at the time of the birth but (subject to certain exceptions) his name has been registered on the birth certificate (CA 1989, s 4(1)(a)); or

    (iii)   they were unmarried but he and the mother have made a parental responsibility agreement[3] providing for him to have such responsibility (CA 1989, s 4(1)(b)); or

    (iv)   they were unmarried but he has obtained a court order granting him parental responsibility (CA 1989, s 4(1)(c)); or

    (v)   they were unmarried but he has been named by the court in a child arrangement order as a person with whom (α) the child is to live (CA 1989, s 12(1)) or (β) the child is to spend time or have contact with him and the court decides it is appropriate to grant him parental responsibility (CA 1989, s 12(1A).

Additionally, the father may gain parental responsibility by marrying the child's mother, being appointed as its guardian or by adoption (CA 1989, s 4(1)).

---

[1]   This latter provision only applies where there has been assisted reproduction: see HFEA 2008, s 54.

[2]   References to whether a father and mother were married to each other at the time of the child's birth must be read with section 1 of the Family Law Reform Act 1987 (which extends its meaning): see CA 1989, s 2(3).

[3]   The agreement must be in the prescribed form and recorded in the Principal Registry of the Family Division: CA 1989, s 4(2)(a).

(c)   *Other female parent* (save for cases involving fertilisation): A female who is not a parent has parental responsibility if –

    (i)   her name is registered on the birth certificate (CA 1989, s 4ZA(1)(a)); or

    (ii)   she has entered into a parental responsibility agreement[4] with the mother (CA 1989, s 4ZA(1)(b)); or

    (iii)   she has on her application obtained a court order for parental responsibility (CA 1989, s 4ZA(1)(c)); or

    (iv)   she is named in a child arrangements order as a person with whom (α) the child is to live (CA 1989, s 12(1)) or (β) the child is to spend time or have contact with her and the court decides it is appropriate to grant her parental responsibility (CA 1989, s 12(1A).

(d)   *Step parent*: A step-parent has parental responsibility where –

    (i)   a child's parent who has parental responsibility for a child is married to, or is the civil partner of, a person who is not the child's parent (the step parent), and the child's parent or parents having parental responsibility have by a parental responsibility agreement[3] with the step parent provided for the step parent to have parental responsibility (CA 1989, s 4(1)(a)); or

    (ii)   on the application of the step parent the civil court has ordered that the step parent shall have parental responsibility (CA 1989, s 4(1)(b)).

(e)   *A person with whom the child is to live*: Where the court makes a child arrangements order and a person who is not the parent or guardian of the child concerned is named in the order as a person with whom the child is to live, that person has parental responsibility while the order remains in force so far as providing for the child to live with that person (CA 1989, s 12(2)).

(f)   *Guardian*: A guardian if –

    (i)   he or she is appointed guardian by the court when no-one has parental responsibility or a parent, guardian or special

---

[4] 3

guardian who was named in a child arrangements order as a person with whom the child was to live and has died while that order was in force (CA 1989, s 5(1)); or

    (ii)   a parent having parental responsibility has appointed[5] him or her guardian in the event of that parent's death (CA 1989, s 5(3)); or

    (iii)   a guardian or special guardian of a child has appointed[3] another individual to take his or her place in the event of their death (CA 1989, s 5(4)).

(g)   *Special guardian*: A special guardian has parental responsibility if he or she is appointed as special guardian by the court (CA 1989, s 14A)).

(h)   *Local authority*: The local authority has parental responsibility

    (i)   if there is a care order or an interim care order in force[6] (CA 1989, s 33(3)(a)); or

    (ii)   while an emergency protection order is in force and the local authority assumes responsibility for the order (Emergency Protection Order (Transfer of Responsibilities) Regulations 1991, reg. 2).

(i)   *Emergency protection order*: An authorised person has parental responsibility if he or she has been granted an emergency protection order (CA 1989, s 44(4)(c)) as long as the local authority has not assumed responsibility for the order (see above).

(j)   *Adoption*: An individual or individuals obtain or obtains parental responsibility _

---

[5] The appointment must be in accordance with the provisions of section 5(5) of the CA 1989. The appointment will only take effect if on the death there is no other parent with parental responsibility or immediately before the death a child's arrangements order was in force in which the person was named as a person with whom the child was to live was the child's only or last surviving special guardian.

[6] In this case the local authority has the power in certain specified circumstances to determine the extent to which (i) a parent, guardian or special guardian of the child, or (ii) a person who by reason of section 4A has parental responsibility for the child, may meet his o or her parental responsibility (CA 1989, s 33(3(b)).

(i)   on the making of an adoption order by the court giving that person parental responsibility (Adoption and Children Act 2002, s 46(1)); or (ii) while a child is placed for adoption[7] or an adoption agency is authorised to place a child for adoption or a placement order is in force in respect of the child, parental responsibility is given (a) to the adoption agency; (b) to the prospective adopters while the child is placed with them (although the adoption agency has the power to restrict the extent of the parental responsibility) (ACA 2002, s 25); or (iii) on the application of the persons who intend to adopt a child under the law of a country or territory outside the British Isles the High Court may make an order giving them parental responsibility (ACA 2002, s 84(1)).

(See, too, **Baptism of Children: parental responsibility and same sex couples**: retitled as **Baptism and Same Sex Parents**) If a person has acquired a new gender under the Gender Recognition Act 2004 his or her status as the father or mother of a child is nevertheless unaffected: see section 9 of the Act.

(February 2017)

---

[7] Under section 19 of the Adoption and Children Act 2002.

Burial and cremation: Funerals in undertakers' private chapels

1. There are a number of statutory provisions with respect to services taken outside a church or churchyard[1]. In certain circumstances an incumbent is under an *obligation* to perform funeral services in the consecrated part of a public cemetery (see article 17(1) of the Local Authorities' Cemeteries Order 1977, SI 1977/204). Although there is no corresponding provision in respect of local authority crematoria, the Church of England (Miscellaneous Provisions) Measure 1992, section 2, confers certain rights, and imposes certain *obligations,* on ministers concerning the conduct of funeral services there (see **Burial and cremation**). In so far as the unconsecrated parts of cemeteries are concerned, section 12 of the Burial Laws Amendment Act 1880 provides that a minister of the Church of England shall not be liable to any censure for officiating at a burial service according to the rites of the Church of England 'in any unconsecrated ground or cemetery . . . or in any building thereon, in any case in which he might have lawfully used the same service, if such burial ground . . . had been consecrated'. However, this latter provision did no more than to give statutory confirmation to the law as previously set out in *Rugg v Kingsmill* (1867) LR 1 A & E 343 (on appeal (1868) LR 2 PC 59).

2. None of these statutory provisions relate to the case of an undertaker's chapel, which at least in the past was seen as essentially a place provided as a resting place for the corpse and its 'viewing' by relatives and friends, and which is neither a church nor a building on a burial ground or within the boundaries of a crematorium. Nevertheless, there is a growing demand for funeral services to be conducted in such chapels before bodies are taken to the crematorium or cemetery; this may in part be due to the limited time often allotted to individual services at busy crematoria. As these chapels are not private chapels with their own Anglican ministers (see 34 *Halsbury's Laws of England* (5th ed, 2011) at paragraph 992), the provisions of Canon B 41 do not apply to them.

3. In the light of *Rugg v Kingsmill* it is the Commission's view that it is lawful for an Anglican minister to use one of the burial rites in the BCP, *Alternative Services: Series One* or *Common Worship* at an undertaker's chapel. However, before conducting any such service the minister must obtain permission to do so from the incumbent of the parish in which the chapel is situated. The minister may in his or her discretion make and use variations to such a service as long as they are not of substantial importance

---

[1] In proprietary cemeteries with consecrated ground the company may appoint an Anglican chaplain (Cemeteries Clauses Act 1847, section 27, as amended by the Church of England (Miscellaneous Provisions) Measure 1992, Sch 3, paragraph 1).

and are reverent and seemly and are not contrary to the doctrine of the Church of England in any essential matter: see Canon B 5, paragraphs 1 & 3. Alternatively, if a service is required that is not related to a funeral rite (or a committal), the minister having the cure of souls may use a form of service considered suitable for the occasion by him or her; he or she may also permit another minister to use that service: Canon B 5, paragraph 2.

4. No statutory fees are currently (2017) payable for any service taken in an undertaker's chapel but care should be taken to ascertain the position in the future[2]. The usual fees are chargeable[3] for a subsequent burial of the body in a churchyard and for any burial of cremated remains in a churchyard or other lawful disposal of those remains[4]: Ecclesiastical Fees Measure 1978, Sch. 1A, Pt I.

(February 2017)

---

[2] As to what charges may be made in such circumstances, see *A Guide to Church of England Parochial Fees* (January 2015) at paragraph 26.

[3] No fees are chargeable for the burial of a still born infant or of a child under the age of 16: Ecclesiastical Fees Measure 1978, Sch. 1A, Pt II, note 2.

[4] It is unlawful for an Anglican minister to scatter (as opposed to strewing) cremated remains as to do so is irreverent: see Canon B 38, paragraph 4(b); see, too, the resolutions adopted by the Convocation of Canterbury on the 25th and 26th May, 1943, and by the Convocation of York on the 23rd May 1951 (*Acts of the Convocations of Canterbury and York 1921– 1970* (SPCK, 1971) at pp 98–101).

Celebrity Marriages in Anglican Cathedrals and Churches

1. The same law applies to the weddings of celebrities in Anglican cathedrals and churches as it does to the weddings of any other persons, although there may be added complications if the couple have entered into an agreement for exclusive publicity with a magazine or other form of media. Slightly different considerations will arise if the marriage is to be celebrated in a private institution such as a peculiar or a college chapel; this is because in such circumstances there may not be a right for the public at large to enter such premises.

2. However celebrated the couple may be, the preliminary requirements before a marriage may be celebrated remain the same as for any other marriage, namely, the calling of banns, a special licence, common licence or a superintendent's registrar's certificate[1]. Nonetheless those requirements (other than a special or common licence) necessitate some publicity and that in itself may cause problems that are considered below.

3. Whether or not the couple have entered into an exclusivity agreement they may not wish persons other than those they have themselves invited to attend the marriage ceremony itself. Nonetheless, a marriage is a public ceremony which at the least all parishioners[2] (including those whose names are on the electoral roll) are entitled to attend; it is also possible that those who are not parishioners are similarly entitled whether at common law (see *Cole v Police Constable 443A* [1937] 1 KB 316 *per* Goddard, J; *Cripps on Church and Clergy* (Sweet & Maxwell Ltd, 8th ed., 1937) at page 121) or by reason of the fact that anyone is entitled to raise genuine impediments to the formalisation of the marriage (see *Williamson v Dow* (unreported, 16th April, 1994); *R v Bishop of Bristol, ex parte Williamson*, 25th March 1994, CO/764/94; see, too, the Commission' opinion entitled **Cathedrals: disturbances during services and admission to episcopal enthronements and other services**[3] at pages 302–306). Such persons are entitled to attend as long as there is available seating or standing room unless a genuine question of safety or security arises. Any person with a right to seating in a particular pew cannot be denied that right.

---

[1] See, too, the requirements of Canon B 30, paragraph 3.

[2] This is so whether or not the person is an Anglican: see *In re Perry Almshouses* [1898] 1 Ch 391 at pages 399–400 *per* Stirling, J; *In re Avenon's Charity, Attorney-General v Pelly* [1913] 2 Ch 261 at page 278 *per* Warrington, J). In the case of cathedrals it is arguable that all residents of the diocese are entitled to attend: see *Re St Colomb, Londonderry* (1863) 8 LT 861.

[3] *Legal Opinions concerning the Church of England* (Church House Publishing, 8th ed., 2007).

4. It is unclear whether any service for divine worship may be ticketed[4] as the question was left open in *R v Bishop of Bristol, ex parte Williamson*. Even if it may, it is likely that there must be sufficient publicity to permit those otherwise entitled to attend to apply for a ticket (*ibid*; Hill *Ecclesiastical Law* (OUP, 3rd ed., 2007) at page 88, note 222).

5. As with any other weddings the final decisions in relation to music, furnishings and flowers rests with the minister of the parish: Canon B 35, paragraph 5; Canon B 20, paragraph 3.

6. The use of the organ is also subject to the approval of the minister of the parish, the parochial church council and (in some cases) the resident organist: *Legal Opinions* at page 108. The use of the bells and choir, too, are subject to the approval of the minister: see *Harrison v Forbes and Sisson* (1860) 6 Jur NS 1353; *Redland v Wait* (1862) 31 JP Jo 742); Canon B 20, paragraph 1. The minister must, however, be careful to respect any contract that may exist with the resident organist or choir.

7. No videos should be made without the agreement of the minister taking the service but, in addition, no video may be made while the organ is being played without the consent of the organist[5]. The organist may make his or her consent contingent upon the payment of remuneration or fees although in practice the organist often agrees in his or her written agreement specifically to include the payment of such monies either within his or her ordinary remuneration or within the calculation of the PCC's fees for such occasions. However, an exclusivity agreement is likely to require that all photographs and videos of the ceremony are the exclusive right of the magazine or media involved. However, the agreement is only binding upon the parties to that agreement and can in no way bind non-parties, such as the minister and organist.

8. It is always the right of the minister of the parish to decide what photographs or videos (if any) are permitted during any service or within the church precincts; this is so whether or not the photograph or video is intended for private consumption only. Any such decision should be communicated both to the couple themselves (especially as it may impinge on their own contractual agreement) and to any persons attending the wedding.

---

[4] A wedding invitation is not the same as a ticket to a service and cannot *per se* entitle a person to entrance to the church.
[5] The taking of any video without such consent would be an infringement of the Copyright, Designs and Patents Act 1988, s 182(1).

9. There is a common law right for anyone to remove a person who is causing a disturbance during divine service: *Glever v Hynde* (1673) 1 Mod Rep 168; *Burton v Henson* (1842) 10 M & W 105 at page 108 *per* Alderson, B). This apart, whether or not there are ushers and/or security personnel the enforcement of good order and decency in the church and churchyard lies in the hands of the churchwardens; they may be assisted by properly appointed sidesmen or women[6]: Canon E I, paragraph 4; Canon E 2, paragraph 3; see, too, Bursell *Liturgy, Order and the Law* (Clarendon Press, 1996) at pages 257–260.

(February 2017)

---

[6] They are the churchwardens' assistants referred to in Canon F 15, paragraphs 2 & 3.

Parish Music: Organists and choirmasters and church musicians (This opinion supersedes that previously published under this title.)

General

1. Canon B 20 was amended in 1988. Although the body of the Canon refers to 'any organist, choirmaster (by whatever name called) or director of music', the Canon is entitled 'Of the musicians and music of the Church' and what is said in the Canon itself should be understood as including all musicians in similar positions. References in this opinion to 'the organist' therefore include all such musicians and music directors and the term 'choirmaster' includes choir mistresses and choir directors.

2. In spite of what is said below in relation to organists and the law of employment, the Commission recognises that there are many cases (especially in small parishes) where both the organist and the parish have no intention, or desire, to enter into any legally binding contract; this is so whether the organist plays on an *ad hoc*, or on a more permanent, basis. In all such cases it is best practice to set out that determination in writing, spelling out the reasons for so deciding and stating that there is no intention to create any legal relationships; this is particularly so if the organist receives any remuneration for his or her services. All such cases depend upon the particular circumstances; for example, however, there would no requirement upon the organist to pay a substitute in the case of his or her absence. Nevertheless, it is necessary to stress that the final determination of the legal relationship in such cases will always fall on a civil court or tribunal if the matter were ever to be litigated.

3. It is also necessary to stress that what is said below in relation to safeguarding and DBS checks applies whether or not there is a contract of employment.

Minister

4. The words 'the minister' have at different times been given specific, and slightly differing, statutory meanings (see *Halsbury's Laws of England*, 5th ed., 2011, volume 34 at paragraph 382, note 1, and paragraph 451, note 2). However, Canon B 35, paragraph 5 (which is concerned with the music to be played at marriage services), speaks of 'the minister of the parish' and, as both Canon B 20 and Canon B 35 are concerned with music in church, it is the Commission's view that Canon B 20 should be read in the same way.

The word does not include a curate or assistant priest even during a vacancy in the benefice. It does include a priest-in-charge (see **Clergy: priest-in-charge**) and a team vicar assigned a special cure of souls (see the Mission and Pastoral Measure 2011, section 34(7)). However, in Canon B 1, paragraph 2, 'the minister' refers to the person actually conducting the service and, for example, will include a reader.

5. The minister must pay heed to the advice and assistance of the organist or choirmaster in the choosing of chants, hymns, anthems or other settings and in the ordering of the music of the church. However, the final responsibility and decision in these matters rests with the minister (Canon B 20, paragraph 2, and Canon B 35, paragraph 5).

6. It is the duty of the minister (that is, the minister of the parish) to ensure that only such chants, hymns, anthems, and other settings are chosen as are appropriate, both the words and the music, to the solemn act of worship and prayer in the House of God as well as to the congregation assembled for that purpose; it is also his or her duty to banish all irreverence in their practice and in their performance (Canon B 20, paragraph 3; see, too, Canon B 35, paragraph 5). In the Commission's view Canon B 1, paragraph 2 (which imposes a duty on the minister conducting the service to 'endeavour to ensure that the worship offered glorifies God and edifies the people') does not permit the person conducting the service to overrule any decision already made by the minister of the parish but is primarily concerned with the actual performance of the worship, especially by the congregation. The organist may not play the organ in opposition to the minister of the parish's direction although, if the minister were to act in an arbitrary fashion, the organist may seek the bishop's directions to the minister (*Wyndham v Cole* (1875) 1 PD 130).

7. During a vacancy or during a suspension of the minister, and if there is no organist already appointed, the churchwardens or PCC may invite an organist to play during services, although it should always be made clear that this is on an *ad hoc* basis until there is a minister who may make a formal appointment. In these circumstances the organist should co-operate in the choice of music with such minister as is to conduct the service. The latter has the final determination if in the minister's opinion the choice would not glorify God or edify the congregation.

Recruitment

8. For the safeguarding of children and vulnerable adults the process for appointing any organist must follow all Safer Recruitment procedures applicable in the diocese and parish concerned (see also paragraph 33 below).

Appointment

9. In all churches and chapels (except cathedral or collegiate churches or chapels[1]) the appointment of an organist must be by the minister (subject to the terms of any contract thereafter entered into) together with the agreement of the PCC (Canon B 20, paragraph 1)[2]. It is important that the actual contract of employment is entered into between the PCC and the organist[3]; this is so in spite of the difficulties that may be caused if the archdeacon exercises his or her discretion under Canon B 20, paragraph 2, to dispense with the PCC's agreement to termination. A draft contract of employment can be obtained from the Guild of Church Musicians, although care must be taken to ensure that the terms of any contract finally agreed are consistent with the provisions of Canons and incorporate all the terms suitable to the church (see below) and are agreed to by both parties.

10. A purported appointment other than by the minister (such as by an archdeacon, churchwarden or the PCC) is *ultra vires*. Nevertheless, a legally enforceable unwritten contract may thereafter arise by conduct if the minister and PCC thereafter go along with such a purported appointment.

11. If during a vacancy in the benefice or the suspension of the minister the PCC or other person or persons purport to appoint an organist or arranges for the services of an organist to be provided, the arrangement should specifically state that it will terminate upon the filling of the vacancy or suspension. (See above.)

12. Subject to what has been said in paragraph 2 above, any agreement between the PCC and the organist will in nearly all circumstances constitute a contract of employment[4]. It is therefore essential in every instance that the agreement is reduced to writing and signed by both parties. Oral

---

[1] These are expressly excluded by the wording of Canon B 20, paragraph 1, as they are likely to have their own statutes governing such matters.

[2] This is so whether or not the organist is to be employed under a contract of employment. The resolution should be formally minuted. The minister, if chairing the meeting, has a casting vote: *Church Representation Rules 2017* (Church House Publishing, 2017), appendix II, paragraph 11.

[3] This is because of the recent developments in employment law.

[4] In the case of *Ready-Mixed Concrete (South East) Ltd v Minister of Pensions and National Insurance* [1968] 1 All ER 433 the court provided that 'A contract of employment exists if these three conditions are fulfilled: (i) the servant agrees that, in consideration of a wage or other remuneration, he will provide his own work and skill in the performance of some service for his master; (ii) he agrees, expressly or impliedly, that in the performance of that service he will be subject to the other's control in a sufficient degree to make that other master; (iii) the other provisions of the contract are consistent with it being a contract of service.'

agreements or agreements by conduct should in every case be avoided. It is good practice expressly to include in that agreement reference to the provisions of Canons B 20 & B 35, although it is the Commission's view that the provisions of those Canons are in any event included by operation of law. It is a well established principle that 'the labels parties attach to the arrangement are not determinative of employment status' (see *Sholl v PCC of St Michael's with St James, Croydon* [2011] ET 2330072/2010); it follows that there may be a contract of employment even though the parties may have expressly said that they do not intend that there should be one or the word 'employment' is never used.

Content of the agreement

13. The agreement should also always include amongst other matters:

(a)   the names of the parties entering into the contract;

(b)   a recital of the PCC's agreement to the appointment of the organist by the minister;

(c)   the date on which it begins;

(d)   the amount of remuneration (or other recompense) on appointment[5] (if any) and when it is payable;

(e)   a clause that the termination of the agreement is exercisable by the minister with the agreement of the rest of the PCC except that, if the archdeacon[6] of the archdeaconry in which the parish is situated considers that the circumstances are such that the requirement of the agreement of the PCC should be dispensed with, the archdeacon may direct accordingly (see Canon B 20, paragraph 1);

(f)   the length of notice required to be given by either the minister or the organist to terminate the appointment under the terms of the agreement in the absence of conduct amounting to gross misconduct or other repudiatory breach of contract (this should be the same period for both sides of the agreement);

(g)   a term that, although the minister of the parish must pay attention to the views of the organist in relation to the choice of music on

---

[5] This should include the payment of fees (if any) for occasional services such as weddings and funerals (see below).

[6] If the minister is also the archdeacon, the function of the archdeacon must be exercised by the diocesan bishop.

any given occasion, (i) the final decision on all such matters rests with that minister alone (see Canon B 20, paragraph 3, and Canon B 35, paragraph 5); and (ii) the minister conducting the service has the final decision whether the worship (including the playing and singing of any music) offers glory to God and edifies the people (see Canon B 1, paragraph 2);

(h)   a term setting out the duties of the organist or choir director, including perfoming at any occasional services;

(i)   an appropriate, and carefully worded, condition making it clear what conduct is to be regarded as gross misconduct and what behaviour will amount to a repudiatory breach of the agreement, for example, in relation to DBS certification or its equivalent and safeguarding (see below);

(j)   a pre-condition insisting both on the organist providing a satisfactory DBS certification (or any similar statutory requirement) prior to his or her taking up the post of organist and thereafter taking part in ongoing safeguarding training (see below). A failure to undergo such training and/or to provide evidence of having done is to be regarded as serious misconduct; and

(k)   a term recognising that the PCC is bound to pay due regard to the House of Bishops' guidance on the safeguarding of children and vulnerable adults (see section 5 of the Safeguarding and Clergy Discipline Measure 2016).

14. The contract will in almost all circumstances constitute a contract of employment[7] (see above) and in these circumstances there are a number of obligations imposed by statute upon the employer, that is, the PCC: see the Appendix (below). However, it must be borne in mind that these obligations may change from time to time and therefore care must be taken to ensure that all current obligations are fulfilled. (A further complication is provided by the possibility that an employment tribunal may rule that an agreement is one of employment in spite of the express wording of the agreement.)

15. In all cases the agreement must be subject to a pre-condition of obtaining of a satisfactory DBS disclosure (or any similar statutory requirement) where such a disclosure is required and it is good practice for the agreement specifically to refer to the safeguarding guidance given by

---

[7] Assistance can be found in a number of diocesan websites such as https://www.london. anglican.org/kb/employment-status (see, especially, the FAQs section).

the House of Bishops. The agreement should also cover other points referred to below and it is therefore advisable to consult the diocesan registry about the content of the draft agreement before finalising it.

Termination

16. Subject to the general provisions of employment law, the contract may be terminated either by the organist or (with the agreement of the PCC) by the minister except that, if the archdeacon considers that the circumstances are such that the requirement as to the agreement of the PCC should be dispensed with, the archdeacon[8] may direct accordingly (Canon B 20, paragraph 1). The PCC's agreement was introduced as a requirement in 1988 to prohibit 'shot-gun' dismissals or summary dismissal by the minister acting solely on his or her own initiative.

17. If the organist has been employed for two or more years the minister must be satisfied before terminating the employment that any dismissal is a 'fair dismissal' for the purposes of the applicable employment law. Before dismissing the organist the minister should therefore obtain legal advice as necessary.

18. Where the minister is of the opinion that there cannot be a proper discussion or 'fair' hearing of the matter in the PCC then the minister may ask the archdeacon to consider dispensing with the PCC's agreement. If the PCC's agreement is dispensed with, the decision is solely that of the minister. The circumstances which the General Synod had in mind included where there is a dispute concerning the choir and many members of the choir are also members of the PCC, or where an improper relationship has developed and for the sake of avoiding scandal it is desirable that one person only, i.e. the archdeacon, and not a group of persons, i.e. the PCC, should be consulted. However, it must be remembered that an employment tribunal will look at each case of dismissal on its own facts and an organist's immoral or scandalous conduct may not be sufficient grounds for dismissal (see *Obst v Germany* [2010] ECtHR (no. 425/03); *Schüth v Germany* [2010] ECtHR (no. 1620/03); and *Siebenhaar v Germany* [2011] ECtHR (no. 18136/02)). For this reason it is essential to include in the agreement an appropriate, and carefully worded, condition making it clear what conduct is to be regarded as gross misconduct and what behaviour will amount to a repudiatory breach of the agreement, for example, in relation to DBS certification or its equivalent and safeguarding (see below)[9].

---

[8] If the minister is also the archdeacon, the function of the archdeacon must be exercised by the diocesan bishop.

[9] See, too, *Neary v Dean of Westminster* (1985) 5 Ecc L J 303

Nevertheless, no condition may be contrary to the general laws against discrimination.

Duties of the organist (These should be included in the written agreement.)

19. It is the duty of the organist:

(a) to devote his or her best efforts towards securing a devout and appropriate rendering of the musical portions of the church services so far as the means available permit;

(b) to recognise the authority of the minister in all matters relating to the conduct of the service, including what parts are to be said and sung respectively and the amount of musical elaboration suited to the needs of the congregation;

(c) to play the organ (or take such part in the service as his or her position requires) at all chief services on Sundays, the Great Festivals and major Holy Days as defined in the terms of the agreement;

(d) to play the organ (or take such part in the service as his or her position requires) at such services on the Lesser Festivals and weekdays (including occasional services) as the organist's agreement with the PCC requires; and

(e) to assist the choirmaster and/or choir director (if any) at choir practice, if the offices are distinct.

Duties of the organist, if also the choirmaster or choir director (These should be included in the written agreement.)

20. If the organist is also the choirmaster or choir director, the duties include:

(a) the training of the choir;

(b) the conduct of suitable practices as specified in the written agreement; and

(c) generally, the advancement of the interests of the church in musical matters.

21. It should be noted that none may be admitted to, or dismissed from, the choir save with the approval of the minister of the parish.

Holidays and maternity/paternity leave

22. The agreement should make provision for holidays (at least as provided by statute) during which the organist should be required to find a suitable deputy (to be paid, if payment is required, by the PCC). If the organist is absent on any other occasions in the year, apart from illness and maternity/paternity leave, the organist must find (and make appropriate payment to) a deputy approved by the minister. If the organist is absent through illness or maternity/paternity leave, the organist should (unless prevented by illness) assist in finding a deputy acceptable to the minister. The remuneration of such a deputy is a matter for decision between the deputy and the PCC.

Other absences

23. If the organist is absent for any reason other than those referred to in paragraph 22, he or she must assist in finding a suitable deputy approved by the minister (or, during a vacancy, by the churchwardens). Where the organist is employed and the deputy requires remuneration, the deputy should be paid by the PCC which should in turn be reimbursed by the organist.

Use of the organ

24. The use of the organ should not be granted to anybody save the organist (or a deputy in the case of holiday, illness and maternity/paternity leave), except by joint permission of the minister and the organist.

25. The use of the organ should be granted to the organist for the purposes of:

(a)   the organist's own private practice;

(b)   the occasional practice of the organist's friends; and

(c)   the instruction of the organist's pupil or pupils.

However, care must be taken by the organist and the PCC to ensure that proper safeguarding requirements are in place at all times.

Use of the organ at weddings, funerals and other occasional services

26. As an organist's entitlement to remuneration or fees for occasional services (such as weddings and funerals) has on occasion proved to be a contentious issue, it is best practice that any contract entered into specifically deals with entitlement to play at such services and with entitlement to

remuneration (if any) for such services. What is said in this section is subject to whatever is specified in the contract.

27. Care should be taken in any advertisement for a vacant position to state that entitlement to remuneration or fees for occasional offices is a matter for negotiation between the organist and the PCC.

28. The use of the organ at weddings, funerals and other services of a similar character is subject to the approval of the minister. If so stated in the agreement, the organist has the right to play if organ music is required[10]; in these circumstances he or she is entitled to be paid such remuneration or fees as may have been set by the PCC[11] for such occasions. If the organist does not wish to perform these duties on any particular occasion, then another suitable organist (chosen by the organist with the approval of the minister) may play; in these circumstances any remuneration should be agreed between the organist and the substitute organist.

29. Where there is any such agreement as is referred to in paragraph 28, if for any reason those for whom the service is held desire that the organ be played by a relative or friend rather than by the organist of the church, it is subject to the agreement of both the latter and the minister; in these circumstances the organist of the church is still due the normal fee. Similarly, if there is any such agreement, the organist is still entitled to the normal remuneration or fee whenever any music is played or performed at any such service. This includes the playing of any CD or other recorded music.

30. The organist is entitled to composer's fees if his or her musical works are publically performed at an occasional service. However, the Performing Rights Society has the right to collect these fees on behalf of those composers who are members of that Society and it has decided not to exercise that right in respect of divine worship (including weddings and funerals) in the United Kingdom[12]. The playing of recorded music during divine worship falls within the purview of the Mechanical Copyright Protection Society and the MCPS in practice makes a similar concession.

31. No videos or recordings should be made without the agreement of the minister taking the service but, in addition, no video or recording may be

---

[10] There is no such entitlement if a CD is to be used or a string quartet (or similar) is to be provided apart from the organist

[11] The Parochial Fees Order does not include fees for any music provided.

[12] If any question arises in relation to this concession reference should in the first instance be made to the PRS

made while the organ is being played without the consent of the organist[13]. The organist may make his or her consent contingent upon the payment of remuneration or fees although in practice the organist often agrees in his or her written agreement specifically to include the payment of such monies either within his or her ordinary remuneration or within the calculation of the PCC's fees for such occasions.

Children

32. For the purposes of the provisions of the Children and Young Persons Acts 1933 and 1963 and any subsidiary legislation or regulation made under them relating to the employment of children, a chorister taking part in a religious service, or in a choir practice for a religious service, is not deemed to be employed whether or not the chorister receives any reward: see the Children and Young Persons Act 1933, s 30(1).

Safeguarding

33. It is of fundamental importance that, before being appointed, all organists and choir directors (whether they are employed or not) are required to apply for a DBS check (or any similar statutory requirement) at the appropriate level and to provide the requisite certificate; thereafter they must undergo ongoing training approved by the diocese in accordance with any guidance from the House of Bishops on safeguarding; in addition the organist must apply for updated DBS checks at the intervals required by the safeguarding policy as well as providing certificates to show that they have done so. The written contract should provide for any such subsequent training to be paid for by the PCC. Failure to comply with these requirements must be treated as misconduct rendering the organist liable to dismissal. Each diocese has established a procedure for carrying out these checks, and for conducting risk assessments where necessary. The PCC must pay due regard to any such House of Bishops' guidance and comply with its own parish safeguarding policy as well as seek guidance from the diocesan safeguarding officer as needed. Failure to carry out such checks, and to put in place reasonable steps to manage any risk, could expose the PCC to legal liability if a child or an adult at risk is harmed.

---

[13] The taking of any video without such consent would be an infringement of the Copyright, Designs and Patents Act 1988, s 182(1)

Appendix

Obligations imposed by statute on the PCC as employer

(It must be remembered that the organist may be an employee whatever terminology may be used in the wording of the agreement).

(a) Where an employee begins employment, the employer not later than two months after the commencement of the employment must give to the employee a written statement of specific particulars of employment; subject to certain exceptions some of these particulars may be given in instalments: see the Employment Rights Act 1996, sections 1, 2 & 3. These particulars include any terms or conditions relating to holidays and holiday pay; incapacity for work due to sickness or injury (including any provision for sick pay); and pensions and pension schemes: see the 1996 Act, s 1(4)(d).

(b) Where any changes to the terms of employment are agreed, the employer must provide details of these changes to the employee within one month: Employment Rights Act 1996, s 4.

(c) Every payment to an employee must be accompanied by an itemised pay slip (or statement) giving specific particulars: Employment Rights Act 1996, s 8.

(d) If an organist has a contract or other arrangement for work or services personally for reward and is between the ages of 16 and 24, he or she is entitled to the national minimum wage; if the organist is over the age of 25, the entitlement is to the national living wage: National Minimum Wages Act 1998, s 1. This does not apply if the employer is a charity (such as the PCC) and the organist receives (i) no monetary payment of any description or only receives expenses actually incurred in the performance of his or her duties or reasonably estimated as such; and (ii) no benefit[14] (other than in relation to subsistence or accommodation) in kind of any description: see the 1998 Act, s 44.

(e) If the organist is employed, the employer is under a duty to deduct income tax and national insurance at source under PAYE and to inform HMRC using the online service: see https://www.gov.uk/paye-for-employers.

---

[14] A benefit would include the right to practice on the church's organ or to use it for the purposes of teaching.

(f)   If the organist is female she is entitled to maternity leave; a male organist may in certain circumstances be entitled to paternity leave: see the Employment Rights Act 1996, ss 71 & 76.

(g)   The auto-enrolment pensions scheme may in certain circumstances apply to employed organists: see www.thepensionsregulator.gov. org

(February 2017)

Delegation of Episcopal Functions

Opinion

1. The purpose of this Opinion is to give guidance in relation to the circumstances in which instruments in writing under section 13 of the Dioceses, Pastoral and Mission Measure 2007 are required for the delegation of episcopal functions.

2. The role of the diocesan bishop as the chief pastor having ordinary jurisdiction within the diocese is enshrined in Canon C18.1 and 2. A diocese may also be served by one or more suffragans holding titular sees within it, and being office holders appointed under the Suffragan Bishops Act 1534. A suffragan's 'jurisdiction or episcopal power or authority' is by Canon C20.2 derived from the diocesan bishop. In addition, episcopal ministry within a diocese may be provided by assistant bishops about whom the Canons are silent. Such bishops are often retired, but may hold some appointment (stipendiary or otherwise) in that or a neighbouring diocese or may be stipendiaries exercising special episcopal ministry. It is, indeed lawful for a diocesan bishop to serve as the assistant bishop of another diocese. An assistant bishop's legal powers are invariably conferred by the diocesan bishop.

3. Section 13(1) of the Dioceses, Pastoral and Mission Measure 2007 enables the diocesan bishop by an instrument under his or her hand to delegate such episcopal functions as may be specified in it to a suffragan bishop or, by the extension contained in section 13(16), to an assistant bishop. Normally, by subsection (8) the approval of the diocesan synod is required, but in cases of urgency the approval of the bishop's council and standing committee of the diocesan synod is sufficient. Plainly the making of an instrument of delegation under section 13 is intended to be a formal legal act. The power of delegation in section 13 is interconnected with the provisions in section 14 for the discharge of the diocesan bishop's functions during a vacancy in see. If there has been a delegation within section 13 before the vacancy, it remains operative during the vacancy and for six months thereafter. Delegation under section 14 is, however, required where there has been no section 13 delegation, or where the previous delegation is in limited terms insufficient to cover all the functions arising during the vacancy.

4. Section 13 does not itself specify the class of delegable functions in respect of which an instrument is required. Comprehended within the Section must be those functions for which formal delegation is necessary as a matter of law. Although instruments made under section 13 sometimes confer authority in very broad and general terms, the better practice is to

specify in some detail the functions which are the subject of delegation, so that there can be no doubt about the extent of the powers of the suffragan or assistant. In strict law, however, delegation under section 13 is obligatory only in the circumstances explained in paragraph 5 below.

5. *Act of Parliament or Measure*

Functions vested in a diocesan bishop by statute (i.e. an Act of Parliament or Measure, or subordinate legislation made thereunder) normally require a delegation to a suffragan or assistant bishop under section 13. Important examples of such functions are to be found in the Patronage (Benefices) Measure 1986, the Clergy Discipline Measure 2003 and the Mission and Pastoral Measure 2011 as well as elsewhere. Unless the statute or measure itself deals specifically with the issue of delegation, all functions derived from primary legislation are, with one current exception contained in section 13(1) capable of delegation by instrument under section 13. The exception relates to section 9(2) of the Clergy (Ordination and Miscellaneous Provisions) Measure 1964 and the related Canon C4.5, whereby an application to the archbishop for a faculty to enable a divorced and remarried candidate to be ordained may be made only by a diocesan bishop. (The further exception, concerning functions under section 2 of the Priests (Ordination of Women) Measure 1993, was repealed by the Schedule to the Bishops and Priests (Consecration and Ordination of Women) Measure 2014).

6. *Canon*

A diocesan bishop's functions specified in the Canons Ecclesiastical are generally capable of being delegated to a suffragan or assistant bishop pursuant to section 13. This may be achieved either by reference in the instrument of delegation to particular canons or by means of comprehensive words of delegation. Canon C 20 provides for suffragan bishops to exercise such episcopal functions 'as shall be licensed or limited to [them] to use, have, or execute by the bishop of the [diocese]'. Such authority may take the form of an instrument made under section 13. But if no statutory functions are being delegated, a diocesan bishop's functions may be delegated to a suffragan or assistant bishop by way of a commission as envisaged by paragraph 3 of Canon C 18, under which 'formal' commissioning ought to be effected or confirmed in writing. (It should be noted that the power to grant a commission under Canon C 18.3 is unaffected by the abolition in section 15(1) of the Dioceses Measure 1978 (itself now repealed) of the statutory commissioning of suffragan bishops pursuant to the Suffragan Bishops Act 1534.)

7. There are Canons which themselves make provision for a deputy or commissary to act on behalf of the diocesan bishop. Canon B27.1 requires

the rite of confirmation to be administered by the bishop of the diocese or by another bishop 'lawfully deputed in his stead'. Deputing another bishop for this purpose could be given effect by an instrument under section 13; alternatively a purely informal delegation to the other bishop is sufficient in law. Although no specific provision for a deputy is made in Canon C 3, the same considerations apply in the case of the ordination of priests and deacons. By contrast, a diocesan bishop's delegation of the giving of institution to a benefice under Canon C10.7 (although capable of delegation to a bishop under section 13) is wider, because delegation is to 'some commissary in holy orders' who need not be a bishop.

8. *Other Circumstances*

There are numerous occasions upon which a suffragan or assistant bishop may act on behalf of the diocesan bishop, and which do not involve the discharge of specific functions under statute, measure or canon. These might include attendance on behalf of the diocesan bishop at acts of public worship; visits to schools, hospitals or other institutions; the giving of pastoral guidance; the conduct of interviews; and conciliation in the event of disputes. Subject to compliance with relevant safeguarding requirements, such activities may be undertaken on a purely informal basis at the diocesan bishop's request. No transfer of legal power is involved. Accordingly, it is unnecessary for an instrument under section 13 or a commission to cover public or pastoral work of this nature.

(February 2018)

Friends' Charities: Conflicts of Interest

1. A number of unincorporated charitable associations have been established as 'friends' of a particular church whose aims or objectives typically include the preservation, repair, maintenance, restoration and improvement of the fabric, furniture, ornaments and contents of that church and its churchyard for the benefit of the public. The underlying basis of such friends' charities has been to provide a vehicle for building up a supporter base for church buildings amongst those who, while not necessarily interested in their religious purposes, nevertheless value them as heritage and community assets. Such support may involve both financial support and the volunteering of time for fundraising, events organisation and the administration of the friends' charity. These bodies exist independently of the relevant Parochial Church Council (PCC) which is the body that (subject to the faculty jurisdiction) has the obligation to maintain the church and its churchyard. (Legal ownership of the church and its churchyard is, of course, vested in the incumbent whilst the churchwardens are the legal owners of the church's ornaments and furnishings.) The constitution of such friends' charities often provides for the incumbent or priest-in-charge and the churchwardens to be trustees of the charity by virtue of their office, recognising that the only way that such organisations can further their charitable objectives is through the PCC applying the charity's funds to maintain and implement repairs and improvements to the church and churchyard (subject to the grant of any necessary faculty).

2. In May 2014 the Charity Commission published 'Conflicts of interest: a guide for charity trustees' (CC29). This recognises that a trustee's personal or professional connections can bring benefits to the work of a charity, and often form part of the reason why an individual has been asked to join the trustee body, but that they can give rise to conflicts of interest to which the trustees must respond effectively. A particular type of conflict of interest with relevance in the present context is a 'conflict of loyalty', in which a trustee's loyalty or duty to another person or organisation could prevent the trustee from making a decision solely in the best interests of the charity. As a result of this guidance, concerns have been expressed as to whether it is appropriate for the incumbent and churchwardens to continue to act as trustees of a friends' charity or whether their role should be relegated to one of being invited to attend and speak at meetings but withdrawing prior to any decision or vote being taken. A further concern is whether a trustee of a friends' charity should also properly serve on the relevant PCC.

3. Those who entertain such concerns point to the fact that the Charity Commission are clearly very concerned about conflicts of interest and expect charity trustees to identify and address effectively any such conflicts that affect them or their charity. They emphasise that a conflict of interest is

any situation in which a trustee's personal interests or loyalties *could*, or *could be seen to*, prevent the trustee from making a decision *only* in the best interests of the relevant charity. It is argued that the incumbent and churchwardens are members of a body which seeks funds from the friends' charity and that, when viewed objectively, it is difficult to see that a conflict of loyalty will ever cease. There is said to be the potential for a PCC to be held to ransom by a friends' charity as to the provision of funds for works in relation to which it might be seeking to attach conditions, such as a grant for urgent roof repairs being made subject to the PCC dropping a separate reordering scheme or (in an alternative scenario) the PCC being invited to implement a reordering scheme that the friends' charity might want but the PCC does not.

4. The response to such concerns has been to point to the identity between the aims or objectives of the relevant PCC and the friends' charity and the consequent difficulty in envisaging the possibility of a conflict of interest or loyalty between members of the two bodies. It is pointed out that it is not the role of a friends' charity to debate whether or not a particular project should be pursued; that is said to be the role of the PCC, with the advice of the Diocesan Advisory Committee, and, ultimately, subject to the jurisdiction of the diocesan chancellor. The role of a friends' charity is to consider whether any request for funding falls within the scope of the charity's objects and is one which should be supported and, if so, to what extent and on what basis. It is said to be important that those responsible for initiating and delivering a project should be present during any relevant discussions of a friends' charity to advise on the reasons for, and details of, any proposed works and to answer any questions, and correct any misunderstandings, that may arise. An extremely close working relationship between a friends' charity and the relevant PCC is vital to the effectiveness of the former body because a friends' charity is powerless to achieve its objects unless the PCC is prepared to implement particular projects.

5. We recognise that it is a general principle applicable to all trustees, and others in a fiduciary position, that persons must not put themselves in a position where their duty to the relevant body may conflict with some personal interest (a 'conflict of interest') or some duty owed to another body (a 'conflict of loyalty'). As Lord Cranworth LC observed in *Aberdeen Railway v Blaikie*[1]:

> '. . . it is a rule of universal application, that no one, having [fiduciary] duties to discharge, shall be allowed to enter into engagements in which he has, or can have, a personal interest

---

[1] (1854) 1 Macq 461 at 471.

conflicting, or which may possibly conflict, with the interests of those whom he is bound to protect.'

In *Boardman v Phipps*[2] Lord Upjohn considered the meaning of the phrase 'possibly may conflict' in Lord Cranworth's 'celebrated speech'. Lord Upjohn said that:

'In my view it means that the reasonable man looking at the relevant facts and circumstances of the particular case would think that there was a real sensible possibility of conflict; not that you could imagine some situation arising which might, in some conceivable possibility in events not contemplated as real sensible possibilities by any reasonable person, result in a conflict.'

6. In the case of a charitable body, it is important that its trustees act only in the interests of the charity and take their decisions solely in the interests of furthering its charitable purposes. Thus, when an incumbent of a church or members of a PCC act as trustees of a related friends' charity, they have to make sure that they act solely in the interests of that charity and not of the PCC. It is important, however, to view that fiduciary duty in the light of the similarity, if not the identity, of the charitable objectives of both bodies. CC29 recognises (at page 10 and in Example 4) that although there may be a decision at one charity that also affects another body, the similarity of charitable purpose between the two bodies may mean that any conflicts of loyalty which do occur pose no risk, or only a low risk, to decision-making in the best interests of the former charity, and that the affected trustee(s), having declared their other interest, can then participate in its decision-making. We consider that this is the position in the case of a friends' charity and the relevant incumbent and PCC members. We do not consider this situation to be analogous to that considered by the Charity Commission in Examples 2 and 5 of CC29 where an individual is a trustee for two charities planning to bid for the same service provision contract. There the two charities are in clear competition with each other so that there is a clear conflict of loyalty. Because the trustee's decision at either charity could be influenced by the trustee's knowledge of, and duty to, the other charity this means that he or she cannot fulfil their duty to either charity to make decisions only in its best interests. In the case of an incumbent or PCC member participating in a decision of a friends' charity, the duty to each body should coincide. In our view, it is sufficient, in order to address any conceivable conflict of loyalty, for a PCC member to declare that

---

[2] [1967] 2 AC 46 at 124 B-C. Lord Upjohn's was a dissenting speech, but his dissent is not material for present purposes. His observations are cited at page 2 of the Charity Commission's published summary of its view of the law underpinning its publication CC29.

membership to the friends' charity and to disclose the nature of any decision that the PCC may already have arrived at relevant to the decision which is being considered by the friends' charity. We are not aware that PCC representation on the board of a friends' charity has given rise to any difficulties in the past. Rather, it reflects the realities of the PCC's role, recognising the inherently close relationship between a friends' charity and the relevant PCC, and engendering confidence in subscribers to friends' charities that their donations are likely to be applied in a timely and effective manner for the benefit of the church and its fabric. Indeed, some subscribers might be deterred from membership of, or contributing to, a friends' charity if it did not appear to have the support of the church, as evidenced by the incumbent and churchwardens being trustees of the friends' charity.

7. For the future, it may be sensible for the governing constitutional documents of a friends' charity to include some provision expressly recognising the inherently close relationship between the charity and the relevant PCC and expressly recognising the need to make the declaration and any disclosure referred to in paragraph 6 above. Alternatively, before a PCC considers supporting the establishment of a friends' charity, it may wish to consider the simpler route of using a restricted fabric repair fund within the PCC's control associated with the establishment of a committee of its own (which could include persons who are not members of the PCC) to promote the church building and its fabric as a heritage and community asset.

(February 2018)

Part 1
Benefice and Patronage

Benefice: plurality

1. By plurality is meant the holding of more than one benefice by one person at the same time. Under section 85 of the Pastoral Measure 1983, no person may hold benefices in plurality without authority under the Measure, and institution to one benefice without such authority while already in possession of another benefice involves loss of the original living. 'Benefice' for this purpose includes the office of team vicar, and there are also special provisions regarding those holding cathedral preferment.

2. Authority for the holding of two or more benefices in plurality may be given by a pastoral scheme pursuant to section 18(1) of the 1983 Measure or by a pastoral order by virtue of section 37(1)(c). The former procedure for authorizing a plurality by licence or dispensation from the Archbishop of Canterbury was abolished by the Pastoral Measure 1968.

3. A plurality does not automatically terminate on a vacancy in the benefices, but may be brought to an end on a vacancy or impending vacancy by notice from the bishop or any of the PCCs concerned (1983 Measure, s18(2)). The pastoral scheme or order may also provide for the exercise of rights of patronage during a plurality or on the renewal of a plurality.

4. Except with the leave of the bishop, a pluralist incumbent may not resign any of the benefices without resigning the other or others. If the incumbent resigns one or more of the benefices with the bishop's leave and there are at least two other benefices remaining, the holding in plurality of those other benefices will not be affected, but the Church Commissioners have power to make any necessary consequential amendments to the pastoral scheme providing for the plurality (1983 Measure, s18(4)).

(Revised 2003)

Benefice: vacancy

1. When an incumbent ceases as such to serve the duties of the cure there is said to be an 'avoidance' of the benefice. This may occur by death, attainment of the appropriate age under the Ecclesiastical Offices (Age Limit) Measure 1975, earlier retirement or resignation, exchange, cession or removal from office.

2. A benefice may be resigned either personally before the bishop or in writing. If in writing the resignation must be in the form prescribed by section 11 of the Church of England (Miscellaneous Provisions) Measure 1992, signed by the incumbent and tendered to the diocesan bishop. Resignation may be made to take effect at a future date, but must, except on an exchange, be unconditional, and if in writing will be irrevocable. It only becomes valid when accepted by the bishop, either personally or in writing.

3. Cession takes place when an incumbent is created a diocesan bishop or is appointed to another benefice or preferment which cannot lawfully be held with the benefice or preferment held at the time of the new appointment.

4. Removal from office takes effect

    (a)   when there has been simony in connection with the presentation, institution, collation or admission to the benefice, whether the incumbent was or was not a party thereto, the benefice being void under section 4 of the Simony Act 1588;

    (b)   where the incumbent otherwise lacks a legal qualification for holding it;

    (c)   as a penalty imposed under the Clergy Discipline Measure 2003 (or in cases involving doctrine, ritual or ceremonial, the Ecclesiastical Jurisdiction Measure 1963); or

    (d)   upon the benefice being declared void by the bishop under the Incumbents (Vacation of Benefices) Measure 1977 in a case of pastoral breakdown or disability.

5. An incumbent ceases to have any rights to the emoluments of the benefice on the date when the incumbency ceases. If the avoidance is brought about by death, and the incumbent was then residing in a parsonage house annexed to the benefice, the incumbent's widow or surviving civil partner may continue to occupy and enjoy the parsonage

house and garden for two calendar months thereafter. If the vacancy arises under the 1977 Measure the incumbent must leave the house not later than three months after the date of the vacancy (s12(2)).

(*See also* **Clergy: priest-in-charge**)

(Revised 2003)

Benefice: vacancy: ownership of ecclesiastical property

1. This Opinion deals with cases when an incumbent holds the freehold of land, and is concerned with the legal position when the benefice is vacant.

The incumbent's freehold

2. It is first necessary to consider what is meant by an incumbent's freehold. For the present purpose there is no need to distinguish between property of the benefice (the parsonage and, formerly, glebe) and property vested in the incumbent in right of office (church and churchyard), although there are profound differences in other respects.

3. In modern times 'the freehold', in other contexts, is synonymous with a legal estate in fee simple, but as will be seen an incumbent has something less than that. Historically the expression 'freehold' was applied both to the way in which an interest in land was held (tenure) and to the extent of that interest (estate). Freehold *tenure* was distinguished from copyhold tenure, but the distinction ceased to be of major importance when copyhold was converted to freehold by the 1925 property legislation: all land is now held from the Crown. A freehold *estate* is one which is of uncertain duration, as opposed to a leasehold. It may pass by inheritance (a fee simple or a fee tail) or it may end with a life, either that of the holder or of another person. Since 1925 the only *legal* freehold estate is the fee simple absolute in possession, but before that date a legal life estate could be followed by a legal estate in fee simple in remainder. It is against that background that the nature of an incumbent's freehold must be examined.

4. In the case of *Re St Paul's, Covent Garden* [1974] Fam 1 at 4E, Chancellor Newsom, after quoting a statement by Chancellor Tristram in 1896 to the effect that 'the freehold of a churchyard is in the rector, the fee being in abeyance', went on to say:

> 'At the date of that decision there could of course be a legal life estate, which was a freehold estate. In my judgement, it was that to which Tristram Ch was referring as being the freehold vested in the incumbent. There is nothing so far as I can find in the transitional provisions of the Law of Property Act 1925 or in the Settled Land Act 1925 which has given the incumbent the legal fee simple and, in my judgement, the fee simple is, as it always was, in abeyance.'

5. The expression 'in abeyance' derives from a French word and means 'in expectation'. At the time when legal patterns for holding land were evolving it was recognized that an incumbent needed to be supplied with certain property to assist him in providing an effective cure of souls, but to ensure that any such land would continue to be available to his successors for that purpose he was not given the fee simple but a qualified fee; thus any attempt by the current incumbent to alienate the land would take effect at the most for the duration of his life and his successor would take the land free of the temporary interest created. The precise legal nature of 'the incumbent's freehold' is thus rather elusive: it is of freehold *tenure*, and a freehold *estate* but not a legal estate, and such powers as an incumbent has of disposing of the land are entirely dependent on statute.

Corporation sole: vacancy in holder of office

6. An incumbent is a corporation sole. The position after one holder of the office leaves and before a successor is appointed was described in *Cripps on Church and Clergy*, 8th edn, 1937, p. 429, as follows:

'Upon the death of the parson of a church, or other ecclesiastical person seised jure ecclesiae, the freehold of his glebe, or other ecclesiastical lands, is in abeyance, that is, in expectation, remembrance or contemplation of law, until a successor is appointed, and the fee simple in such lands may be said to be always in abeyance. This is one of the few instances in which a freehold estate can be in abeyance, for it is a principle of the highest antiquity in our law that there should always be a known and particular owner of every freehold estate, for the reasons derived partly from general convenience and partly from feudal times.'

7. During a vacancy, then, the fee simple is in abeyance as always, but the freehold is in abeyance as well. As has been noted, an incumbent has certain statutory powers of dealing with the land while in office, for example under the Parsonages Measure 1938, and frequently supplementary provision has been made to enable the powers to be exercised by the diocesan bishop during a vacancy. But, apart from that, the position at common law is that the incumbent's interest in the land, however vestigial, continues to be vested in the corporation sole (it does not pass, as has sometimes been suggested, to the diocesan bishop) but during a vacancy there is no means of animating the corporation. The only interest that can be created, so far as the land is within the jurisdiction of a consistory court, is a licence granted by or under the authority of the chancellor, in the course of faculty proceedings brought by the PCC or other party recognized by the chancellor as having the necessary locus. Otherwise land vested in 'the incumbent' during a

vacancy can only be dealt with by or under statute, a notable example being the Pastoral Measure 1983.

Secular legislation

8. Provision has frequently been made in secular legislation with a view to overcoming this difficulty in the public interest. Section 52(1) of the Town and Country Planning Act 1944 reads:

> 'Where the fee simple in any ecclesiastical property is in abeyance it shall be treated for the purposes of a compulsory purchase of the property authorised under this Part of this Act as being vested in the Ecclesiastical Commissioners, and any notice to treat shall be served, or be deemed to have been served, accordingly.'

Subsection (2) required a copy of any notice served on the 'owner' of ecclesiastical property to be served also on the Ecclesiastical Commissioners, and in effect subsection (3) defined 'ecclesiastical property' as land vested in an incumbent whether in right of his office or his benefice.

9. The section was inserted in the Bill at the committee stage in the House of Lords, and the Bishop of London in introducing it explained the purpose behind it. Subsection (2) was designed to overcome the difficulty that an incumbent did not fit the definition of 'owner', eventually contained in section 65(1) of the Act, as 'a person entitled to dispose of the fee simple of land': the incumbent could only dispose of ecclesiastical property under certain statutory provisions of which the Ecclesiastical Commissioners were the guardians. As for subsection (3), the Bishop said:

> 'At present, owing to war conditions, some benefices are being kept vacant for a considerable time. In that case there would be nobody to protect the interests of a benefice or give a discharge as temporary owner of ecclesiastical property. Subsection (1) of the new clause, therefore, secures that where there is no incumbent the property shall be regarded for the purposes of this Bill as being vested in the Ecclesiastical Commissioners.'

10. Thus the provision had its origin in the exceptional circumstances created by wartime conditions; a fact exemplified by another provision, section 28, which authorized consecrated land to be put to secular use, subject to certain conditions, and so opened the way to the redevelopment of land which would not have been contemplated before the war.

11. The precedent thus set has been followed (with two exceptions) in many subsequent Acts and Measures, but as appears from what has been said above it was inappropriate for it to refer to the fee simple being in abeyance during a vacancy: it is in abeyance then, of course, but it is also in abeyance when the benefice is full. The reference should have been to the freehold being in abeyance. If the provisions were interpreted strictly the Church Commissioners and not the incumbent would have power to convey ecclesiastical property on a compulsory purchase; in practice they were understood in the way the Bishop of London intended them to be in 1944.

12. The two exceptions mentioned above occur in section 19(1)(g) of the Commons Registration Act 1965 and section 67(1)(a) of the Water Resources Act 1991, where the references are simply in terms of land belonging to a vacant benefice.

13. Many pieces of legislation are amended by the draft Church of England (Miscellaneous Provisions) Measure (awaiting parliamentary approval in 2006) to refer to land vested in the incumbent of a benefice which is vacant rather than the language of abeyance derived from the 1944 Act.

(October 1995, revised 2006)

Patronage: Patronage (Benefices) Measure 1986 section 11

1. This Opinion deals with the position under section 11 of the Patronage (Benefices) Measure 1986 where there is an overlap between membership of the PCC and of a corporation or a board of trustees or other unincorporated body exercising the functions of a patron.

2. In dealing with meetings of the PCC called under section 11(1) of the Patronage (Benefices) Measure 1986, section 11(2) provides that:

> '. . . no member of (the) council who is . . . the registered patron, or . . . the representative of the registered patron, shall attend the meeting.'

Section 11(3) further provides that such a person shall not be qualified for appointment by the PCC as one of its representatives in connection with the selection of an incumbent.

Section 39 (the interpretation section) of the Measure provides that:

> '. . . "patron" in relation to any benefice means the person or persons entitled . . . to present to that benefice upon a vacancy, including . . . in any case where the right to present is vested in different persons jointly, every person whose concurrence would be required for the exercise of the joint right . . .'.

3. If the right of patronage is vested in a corporate body, then the corporation itself, as distinct from its individual members, will be registered as patron. Since the corporate body is a legal entity separate from its members (*Salomon v Salomon & Co* [1897] AC 22) any member of the PCC who is also a member of the corporate body will not be caught by section 11(2) and prevented from attending the section 11 meeting, nor from being appointed as the PCC representative. The position is unaffected by the prohibition in section 11(2) upon the involvement of the representative of the registered patron, because this expression refers specifically to a representative appointed under section 8(1)(b) of the Measure, and not to any other person.

4. If the right of patronage is vested in an unincorporated body, then the primary question is whether individual members of that body can be described as 'the registered patron'. In this connection, section 1(1) of the Measure provides that:

> 'the registrar of each diocese shall compile and maintain a register indicating in relation to every benefice in the diocese the person

who is the patron of the benefice and containing such other information as may be prescribed'.

Section 39 indicates that where there is more than one person entitled to present, as in the case of a body of trustees, the names of the individual members of the trustee body should be registered in the patronage register as patrons.

5. A difficulty arises over section 8(2) of the Measure which provides that:

'(2) Where the registered patron of a benefice is a body of persons corporate or unincorporate then, on receiving notice of a vacancy in the benefice ... that body shall appoint an individual ... to act as its representative to discharge in its place the functions of a registered patron.'

The implication of this is that it will be the name of the unincorporated body, for example, 'The Peache Trustees', or 'The Executors of XYZ deed' that is to be entered on the register, and not the names of the individual members of the body. On balance, however, it seems right that section 1(1), as interpreted by section 39, should be followed, and the names of the individual members of the unincorporated body entered on the register as patron, in which event they will not be able to attend the section 11 meeting, or be appointed as representatives of the PCC.

6. The combined effect of section 11(2) and section 39 is thus to exclude a trustee or member of an unincorporated body from the PCC meeting and to disqualify such person from acting as a PCC representative. This is the result of the extended definition of the term 'patron' in section 39 to include the case where the right of patronage is 'vested in different persons jointly'. Each of these persons has to be treated as the patron for the purposes of section 11(2) and (3), so each is subject to the same legal constraints.

7. This is, more or less, in accordance with the Code of Practice issued with the Measure which states:

'... the presenting patron. (This includes anyone who is a joint patron as well as a PCC member. For example where the rights (*sic*) of presentation is held by trustees whose names are entered on the register of patronage, and who include persons representing the PCC or the churchwardens, anyone who is a trustee will be excluded from a meeting under section 11. The same does not apply in the case of a special patronage board established under the

Pastoral Measure 1983 . . . because the board is a corporate body and, as a matter of law, is a separate person from its members.'

It is assumed that 'persons representing the PCC' in the third line of this extract should read 'members of the PCC', but the basic advice given by the Code would appear to be correct.

8. The operation of section 11(2) will inevitably prevent some PCC members from assuming a dual role, and in certain circumstances may give rise to inconvenience. The most straightforward remedy is for the person involved in the exercise of the patron's right to absent himself from the PCC meeting and for someone other than that person to be appointed as the representative of the PCC. The alternative involves the person's resignation from the board of trustees or other unincorporated body. Any adverse consequences (such as an insufficiency in the number of trustees) depend upon the terms of the trust instrument and are not, therefore, a matter of general law.

(September 1999, revised 2003)

Patronage: vacancy in see: bishop's joint patronage

1. It is a well-settled rule of law that where an advowson vests in a diocesan bishop by virtue of his office, and a vacancy in the benefice occurs when the see in question is also vacant, the Crown has the right to present to the benefice (see e.g. Burn, *Ecclesiastical Law*, 9th edn, 1842, vol. 1, pp. 139–41; *Mirehouse v Rennell* (1833) 1 Cl & Fin 527, HL). The basis of this principle lies either in the Crown's position as patron paramount of all benefices, with the right to fill those which are not regularly filled by others (see Burn, vol. 1, p. 140) or in the Crown's right to guardianship of the temporalities of a see during a vacancy, or both. The principle is preserved by section 31 of the Patronage (Benefices) Measure 1986, which abolishes any rule of law under which a right of patronage lapses to a bishop or Archbishop or to Her Majesty, but goes on to provide that this shall not affect, inter alia 'any right of presentation which on a vacancy in a benefice is exercisable by Her Majesty . . . by reason of a vacancy in the see of a diocesan bishop who is a registered patron of the benefice concerned' (s31(2)(b)).

2. Where the bishop and other persons or bodies are entitled to exercise a right of presentation by turns, and the vacancy in the see coincides with a vacancy in the benefice which it would otherwise be the bishop's turn to fill, the Crown clearly takes that turn. On the other hand, there appears to be no direct authority on the position where the bishop and other persons or bodies are joint patrons, all of whom would normally need to concur in each presentation. However, it is considered that the Crown has the sole right to present (which it is understood is also the view of the Crown's advisers), on the basis that the right to present to a benefice which has fallen because the benefice has become vacant is personal property (see Burn, p. 139), and where the Crown and a subject would otherwise have joint ownership of personal property the whole goes to the Crown.

3. That principle is stated by Blackstone *Commentaries*, 4th edn, 1876, vol. II, pp. 366–7 as follows:

> '. . . the crown cannot have a *joint* property with any person in one entire chattel, or such a one as is not capable of division or separation; but where the titles of the crown and a subject concur, the sovereign shall have the whole: in like manner as the crown cannot, either by grant or contract, become a joint-tenant of a chattel real with another person, but by such grant or contract shall become entitled to the whole in severalty. Thus, if a horse be given to the sovereign and a private person, the sovereign shall have the sole property: if a bond be made to the sovereign and a subject, the sovereign shall have the whole penalty, the debt or duty being

one single chattel; and so, if two persons have the property of a horse between them, or have a joint debt owing them on bond, and one of them assigns his part to the sovereign, the sovereign shall have the entire horse, or entire debt. For, as it is not consistent with the dignity of the crown to be partner with a subject, so neither does the sovereign ever lose his right in any instance; but where they interfere, his is always preferred to that of another person; from which two principles it is a necessary consequence, that the innocent, though unfortunate partner, must lose his share in both the debt and the horse, or in any other chattel in the same circumstances.'

4. It is also clear that the Measure assumed the Crown would never have the right to present jointly with any other person or body. Indeed, section 31(2)(b) (see para 1) seems to have accepted the position set out above, as it refers to a right of presentation exercisable by Her Majesty by reason of a vacancy in the see of a diocesan bishop who is '*a* registered patron' (not '*the* registered patron') of the benefice concerned.

5. On that basis, the other question which arises is how far the normal provisions of the 1986 Measure apply to the presentation by the Crown in the type of case under consideration. The general principle of construction is that legislation does not apply to the Crown except so far as there is an express provision to that effect or a necessary implication that the Crown is intended to be bound. Subject to anything to the contrary in the 1986 Measure, the provisions which, for example, give the diocesan bishop and the parish representatives a right of veto over the patron's choice of incumbent will not operate.

6. However, the 1986 Measure contains a provision – section 35 – which deals expressly with benefices in the patronage of the Crown or the Duke of Cornwall. It applies to:

'. . . any benefice the patronage or any share in the patronage of which is vested in or exercisable by Her Majesty . . . or . . . the possessor for the time being of the Duchy of Cornwall (in this Measure referred to as a "Crown benefice") (s35(1)).'

7. Under section 35 most of the provisions of the 1986 Measure are excluded but a few, including section 7, are specifically stated to apply (s35(7)). In addition, section 35(7)(c), which comes into operation where the patronage is vested wholly in Her Majesty or the Duke of Cornwall 'or in the case of a shared benefice, if the right of presentation upon the vacancy in question is exercisable by Her Majesty or the Duke of Cornwall', gives the PCC the right to send Her Majesty or the Duke of

Cornwall a statement describing the conditions, needs and traditions of the parish.

8. Section 35 was apparently *not* drafted with this kind of case in mind. Taken literally, the definition of a 'Crown benefice' in section 35(1) seems to be applicable, as the right of presentation is *for the time being* exercisable by the Crown. However, section 35(2) and (3), dealing with registration of Crown benefices, provide only for cases where Her Majesty (or the Duke of Cornwall) is the sole patron, and with 'shared benefices', where 'a share only' of the patronage is vested in Her Majesty, and those provisions do not seem appropriate to cover the type of case in question here. Section 35(7), on filling vacancies to Crown benefices, is drafted on the same basis, and reinforces the view that 'a share' in this context was intended to mean 'a turn'. Nevertheless, it is considered that, to make the Measure (and s35 in particular) workable in these circumstances, the benefice should be treated (albeit only temporarily) as a 'Crown benefice' for the purposes of section 35 and as a 'shared benefice' for the purposes of section 35(7), so that the PCC's special position under section 35(7) applies.

(January 1991)

Patronage: vacancy in see: team ministries

1. When a team ministry is established by a pastoral scheme there are several ways in which the question of presentation can be dealt with, namely:

(a)   if the bishop is the sole patron, the pastoral scheme *may* provide for presentation of the rector to be either:

   (i)   by a patronage board constituted by the scheme; or

   (ii) by the diocesan board of patronage;

(b)   if the bishop is the sole patron and the scheme does not provide for (i) or (ii) in (a) above, then the bishop acts alone in choosing the rector.

(c)   if the bishop is *not* the sole patron of the benefice concerned then (subject to any rights of the Crown or the Duke of Cornwall) the pastoral scheme *must* provide for presentation of the rector to be either:

   (i)   by a patronage board constituted by the scheme; or

   (ii) by the diocesan board of patronage.

(*See* para 1 of Sch 3 to the Pastoral Measure 1983.)

2. Both the patronage board and the diocesan board of patronage are bodies corporate (see para 1(8) of Sch 3 to the Pastoral Measure 1983 and s26 of the Patronage (Benefices) Measure 1986). The bishop is required to be a member of any patronage board constituted by a pastoral scheme and its chairman. Under the Patronage (Benefices) Measure 1986 he is not eligible to be chairman of the diocesan board of patronage (Sch 3 para 3). Prima facie the bishop's membership of a patronage board is no different from his membership of the diocesan board of patronage. The right of presentation is exercisable by the board as a corporate body with members entitled to vote. (Under para 1(7A) of Sch 3 to the Pastoral Measure 1983, amended by the Team and Group Ministries Measure 1995, the team vicars and certain other members of the team are also entitled to one vote between them.) Certainly the right to present does not pass to the Crown during a vacancy in the see because it is not exercisable by the bishop as holder of his office, having been transferred to the patronage board by the pastoral scheme.

3. Where presentation is exercisable by a diocesan board of patronage a vacancy in the see will not affect the powers of the board because it is expressly provided that 'the Board may act notwithstanding any vacancy in its membership' (para 5(2) of Sch 3 to the Patronage (Benefices) Measure 1986). But where presentation is to be by a patronage board constituted by a pastoral scheme, because the bishop is required to be chairman provision has to be made for someone to take his place as chairman during a vacancy in the see. This may be done by the bishop on his resignation making an instrument delegating his episcopal functions (which will include his functions as a member of the patronage board) to another bishop; if he is not able to or does not do so, and the see is vacant, the Archbishop of the Province must delegate such functions to another bishop (s8(1) and (3) of the Church of England (Miscellaneous Provisions) Measure 1983). Thus during a vacancy in the see the patronage board will still be able to make a presentation.

4. Where there is a vacancy in the membership of a diocesan patronage board it can still function because of the express provision in paragraph 5(2) of Schedule 3 to the 1986 Measure, already referred to. There is no similar provision in paragraph 1 of Schedule 3 to the Pastoral Measure 1983 in relation to a patronage board constituted by a scheme. However, Schedule 3 to the 1983 Measure has effect without prejudice to the powers conferred by section 38(1) (see s40) and, in consequence, the Church Commissioners have the power to include in a pastoral scheme such supplementary provisions as appear to them 'to be necessary or expedient for giving effect to the purposes of the scheme'. This power should be exercised to provide in the scheme for a quorum of the patronage board and for it to act notwithstanding any vacancy in its membership (excluding the chairman). These are matters of substance warranting inclusion in the scheme. The patronage board's power to regulate its procedure conferred by paragraph 1(8) of Schedule 3 to the 1983 Measure is available to deal with other matters such as appointment of a vice-chairman, sealing of documents and arrangement for meetings.

(October 1986, revised 2003)

Part 2
Clergy

Clergy: assistant curates

Stipendiary curate

1. Whether or not there shall be an assistant curate is a question for the incumbent, subject to the bishop's licence. Matters of stipend are dealt with by the diocesan office.

2. The position of a stipendiary curate is the same whether the curate comes to a parish on ordination or from another parish. The curate must be licensed by the bishop after the relevant letters of orders (both deacon's and priest's if the curate is a priest) have been sent to the bishop together with testimony from the bishop of the curate's former diocese (Canon C 12 para 2), and after the curate has made the declaration and oaths required by Canon. The bishop's licence may be for a term of years (Canon C 12 para 1).

3. The effect of the licence is that the incumbent cannot terminate the stipendiary curate's engagement without the latter's consent, except by leave of the bishop and on giving six month's notice.

4. The Employment Rights Act 1996 and most other secular employment legislation does not apply to the office of an assistant curate (see *Diocese of Southwark v Coker* [1998] ICR 140, CA). Where an assistant curate has been granted a licence for a term of years, if the licence is revoked by the bishop before the full term has expired, the assistant curate is not able to claim compensation for loss of office. A licence is not a contract but merely an authority to perform the duties of an assistant curate and therefore if the licence is revoked summarily there can be no claim for compensation. Under Canon C 12 para 5 the assistant curate is, however, entitled to have the opportunity to show reason why the licence should not be revoked, whilst in the event of its summary revocation he or she is to be informed that there is a right of appeal to the Archbishop, exercisable within twenty-eight days of the date of receipt of the notice of revocation.

Non-stipendiary curate

5. The rights and obligations of a non-stipendiary curate are substantially the same as those of a stipendiary curate. In particular the licence is subject to revocation in a similar manner.

Perpetual curate

6. Under section 87 of the Pastoral Measure 1968 all perpetual curates became vicars.

Accommodation and recovery of vacant possession

7. Where the right of presentation to a benefice has been suspended pursuant to section 67 of the Pastoral Measure 1983, the sequestrators appointed under section 68 have power (subject to the consent of the Diocesan Board of Finance (DBF) and under the authority of the diocesan bishop) to grant a lease of the parsonage house. The power to let parsonage land, including the parsonage house, in such circumstances is now contained in section 38(2) of the Endowments and Glebe Measure 1976 as amended by Schedule 5 to the Church of England (Miscellaneous Provisions) Measure 2000. Following the amendment of section 38(2) a lease granted under these provisions to a priest-in-charge or assistant curate is governed exclusively by the secular law relating to landlord and tenant. In particular, if an assured tenancy is created under Part 1, Chapter 1 of the Housing Act 1988 in respect of a residence to be made available for a minister of religion, possession for that purpose may be recovered as of right providing notice at the commencement of the tenancy was given under Ground 5 of Schedule 2.

8. In the absence of a lease or tenancy agreement, the Legal Advisory Commission regards it as highly desirable for a curate to receive a licence to occupy accommodation and recommends at least the essential provisions (which may be supplemented as appropriate) contained in the model licence drafted by the Ecclesiastical Law Association and the Commission's predecessor, the Legal Board, which are set out below.

9. For the purpose of the following paragraphs it is assumed that neither a lease nor a tenancy agreement has been created and the curate is occupying the property by virtue of a licence under which no payment is made. In those circumstances the occupier would not be entitled to remain in possession after the licence came to an end. It is possible that a licence granted on other terms could be claimed by the occupier to take effect as a tenancy, because the courts look at the substance and not the form in such cases, and unless there is a low rent (for tenancies created after 1 April 1990 this means rent not for the time being exceeding a prescribed amount – at the date of this Opinion, £1,000 a year in Greater London and £250 elsewhere) that tenancy may be protected under the Housing Act 1988 and obtaining possession of the accommodation could not be taken for granted. Where it is intended to charge a rent higher than the Housing Act limit it may be possible to grant an assured shorthold tenancy, which would entitle the grantor to possession at the end of a fixed term of at least six months.

10. A licence does not create any estate or interest in the property to which it relates; it only makes an act lawful which would otherwise be

unlawful. The model licence makes it clear that the licence shall be personal to the curate and it specifically prohibits the licensee from taking in any lodger. If a curate permits someone to share his or her accommodation, that person would have no better title against the licensor than the curate but there may be rights which that person may have against the curate. It is equally important that no rent or other payment should be taken by the PCC from any lodger who may be sharing the curate's accommodation.

11. Under the Family Law Act 1996 section 30, as amended, a spouse or civil partner has a right not to be evicted or excluded from a dwellinghouse which the other spouse or civil partner is entitled to occupy by virtue of a beneficial estate or interest or contract or by virtue of any enactment. A spouse or civil partner not in occupation may obtain a court order to enable him or her to enter the matrimonial (or civil partnership) home. In most cases, the spouse's or civil partner's right is no greater than the licensee's, so that the spouse or civil partner of a curate holding under a licence (whether in fact it is a licence or an unprotected tenancy) would lose his or her rights on the expiration of a notice of appropriate length given to the curate by the licensor.

12. The PCC will usually be the licensor (Parochial Church Councils (Powers) Measure 1956). If the parish has adopted an independent line and appointed private trustees to circumvent the authority of the DBF the position will still be the same.

Model licence to assistant curate to occupy premises belonging to a PCC

THIS AGREEMENT is made the .... day of ....
BETWEEN the Parochial Church Council of the Parish of
.... in the County of .... and the Diocese
of .... (hereinafter called 'the Council') of the one part
and the Reverend .... of (address etc) in the County
of .... Clerk in Holy Orders (hereinafter called 'the
Licensee') of the other part

WHEREAS the Premises known as .... (hereinafter
called 'the Premises') are held for and on behalf of the Council as
(inter alia) a residence for an assistant curate in the said parish of
....

NOW IT IS HEREBY AGREED as follows:

1   The Council in right of its interest in the Premises hereby permits
the Licensee to occupy the same during such time as s/he holds office as an
assistant curate in the parish of .... or until such time as this
licence is determined as hereinafter provided

2   The licence shall be personal to the Licensee and s/he shall not take in
any lodger

3   The Licensee shall not allow or permit any nuisance or annoyance to
be created on the Premises and will keep the Premises in good and clean
condition (fair wear and tear excepted) and the garden belonging thereto
clean and tidy

4   The Council may by giving to the Licensee [three] months' notice in
writing signed by the secretary of the Council determine this licence and
the Licensee shall on the expiration of such notice vacate the Premises

5   Nothing herein contained shall create the relationship of landlord and
tenant between the parties hereto or derogate from the rights of the
Council to enter upon the Premises from time to time and repair the same

[Add such other conditions as may be desired]

AS WITNESS whereof the chairman presiding and two other members
of the Council present at a meeting of the Council held on the ....
day of .... at which a resolution was passed authorizing the
execution of this licence have on behalf of the Council hereunto set their

respective hands and the Licensee has hereunto set his/her hand the day and year first above written

(Signatures of chairman presiding and two members present at the meeting of the Council and the Licensee).

Notes:

(i)   This form of licence is drawn on the assumption that the PCC will pay the rates and other outgoings, will insure and will be responsible for all repairs and maintenance. It is probably inadvisable to insert a clause as to this liability in the form of licence, as usually the Council would not desire to give any detailed undertaking as to repairs or otherwise. The assistant curate would, under this form, be prohibited from committing waste and must keep the property clean and the garden in reasonable order. No provision for payment of rent and no right to enter and view are included in the licence as the payment of rent (as such) would, and a specific right to enter and view might, make the assistant curate a lessee.

(ii) As to the sufficiency of signature in this form on behalf of the PCC, see the Parochial Church Councils (Powers) Measure 1956, section 3.

(*See also* **Clergy: priest-in-charge**)

(Revised 2003)

Clergy: breakdown of clergy marriages: potential liability for advice given by diocesan Visitors

1. In 1985 the House of Bishops published a report 'The Breakdown of Clergy Marriages: Pastoral Care and Practical Provisions' (GS Misc 222), dealing with the matters to which its title refers. The Report contained a Code of Procedure, which is now set out as part of a much longer document with restricted circulation.

2. This Opinion is concerned with whether such Visitors are liable to be sued by spouses whose marriages to members of the clergy have broken down for giving wrong, insufficient or no advice, and if so whether insurance cover should be sought to cover the potential liability.

3. A Visitor acting in accordance with paragraph 9 of the Code may be thought likely to give counsel and advice on possible courses of action open to the wife. If such advice is given negligently, and the wife relies upon it to her detriment, she will have a cause of action under the principles formulated in *Hedley Byrne & Co Ltd v Heller & Partners* [1964] AC 465. The four marks identified in that case as giving rise to possible liability would be present – mutuality, special relationship, reliance and undertaking of responsibility. There would be mutuality and a special relationship because the Visitor would present himself or herself as a person specially appointed by the bishop to help and counsel the wife and, it must be assumed if any advice is offered, that the wife had sought or, at the least, accepted such help and counsel. There would be undertaking of responsibility because the Visitor had accepted the appointment and offered help. Unless there were reliance there would be no connection between the advice and any loss the wife might have suffered and therefore no cause of action.

4. The above statement of principle requires the following qualifications and definitions:

(a)   Advice must be distinguished from pastoral care and help. One may shade into the other but there can be no valid claim unless the Visitor advises the wife to take a course of action, which causes her a loss which she would not otherwise have suffered, or fails to advise her on a course which she should take to avoid loss;

(b)   Advice can only be stigmatized as negligent if it falls below the standard of competence and knowledge and care to be expected of a person accepting the appointment of a Visitor. If a Visitor has some professional qualifications, e.g. as a solicitor or social worker, then, in that particular case, the standard would be that of an ordinary competent member of that profession. But if the Visitor has no particular qualifications the standard must simply be that to be expected of a sensible, practical person undertaking the responsibilities set out in paragraphs 6, 9 and 10 of the Code;

(c)   The wife will have no cause of action unless she can show that wrong, misleading or insufficient advice was given, or that advice which should have been given, in her particular situation, was not given and that, in reliance upon the advice given, or, because of the absence of advice which should have been given, she has suffered loss. That loss must be capable of being quantified in money.

5. Although the legal possibility of a claim must be acknowledged the likelihood of establishing liability must be small. Although difficult to define in general terms a real distinction exists between sympathetic and practical counselling and advice, or failure to advise, on specific courses of action. Wrong advice or a failure to give advice on a sensible course of action is a theoretical possibility but it is not easy to imagine examples of how these might occur in the context of Visitor and distressed wife.

6. In the preceding paragraphs it has been assumed, from the terms of the Code, that the person to be counselled is a wife deserted in a parsonage. Now that a benefice may be filled by a woman the opinions expressed above apply equally to a husband left to live on his own in a parsonage house by his ordained wife.

7. It follows from what is said above that answers to both the questions in paragraph 2 above are in the affirmative. While it is not for the Legal Advisory Commission to estimate the risk from an underwriting point of view, the Commission would suggest that the potential damages in any given case are unlikely to be large and the chances of success in an action, having regard to the difficulties a plaintiff would face in proving the elements of firm advice, or the absence of advice which should have been given, reliance and loss, are small. These factors should indicate that any premium should be negotiated nationally or provincially and on a competitive basis.

8. The admittedly small risk of legal action against a Visitor can be reduced even further by it being made abundantly clear to the Visitor that he or she must observe the Code of Procedure, and not go beyond offering pastoral care and practical assistance. In addition the Visitor could leave with the deserted spouse a leaflet indicating how the Visitor can be

contacted again, and making it clear that a Visitor is only able to offer pastoral care and practical assistance, and not expert advice. Even these steps cannot guarantee that an action will not be pursued by a determined litigant, and for that reason also DBFs need to consider taking out suitable insurance or guaranteeing to underwrite the legal costs of a Visitor involved in an action for negligence while acting in that capacity.

(October 1995, revised 2003 and 2006)

Clergy: confidentiality

1. The Legal Advisory Commission was asked by the House of Bishops for advice on the circumstances in which a minister is:

(a)   entitled, and

(b)   under a legal duty

to refuse to disclose to a third party an admission or confession made to the minister that the person who made it has been guilty of a criminal offence, or other misconduct, or any other information given to the minister by that person in the course of admitting misconduct.

2. In addition to a general pastoral responsibility to respect all information gained through personal ministry to individuals, the position of a minister who receives confidential information in the course of his or her ministry is affected by a number of different legal principles:

(a)   the equitable doctrine of confidence or confidentiality which may place the minister under a duty not to make a disclosure;

(b)   the Human Rights Act 1998, giving effect to the European Convention on Human Rights, has introduced an enhanced concept of privacy, the violation of which (in certain circumstances) is unlawful;

(c)   Canon law, which seeks to impose an almost absolute obligation of secrecy where sins are confessed to a minister with a view to the person making the confession receiving the benefit of absolution, spiritual counsel and advice, for the quieting of his or her conscience;

(d)   exceptionally, express statutory provisions which may make it an offence not to disclose information however received.

These issues are considered in turn.

The equitable doctrine of confidence

3. A person seeking pastoral guidance and counsel from the clergy has the right to expect that the minister concerned will not pass on to a third party confidential information so obtained, without consent. There are, of course, cases in which the person concerned is advised, and is willing that the information should be given to others. If the minister seeks to do this

without such consent, he or she can be restrained by injunction, and may also face a claim for damages.

4. To enjoy this right it must be clear from the circumstances in which the information was received that an obligation of confidence was expected. In the case of the clergy this must have a wide application, and include most information that they receive in the course of their pastoral work. Further, the information must be of limited availability – protection will not be given to information that is generally known – and it must be of a specific character, that is, it must be possible to say with certainty what information is being restricted from disclosure. A claim to restrict, for example, 'anything about X as a young man' is likely to be unsuccessful as being too uncertain. The information need not be detrimental – for example a person may not wish to be publicly identified as the maker of a large donation to the church repair fund, although that would generally be regarded as a highly creditable action.

5. The general duty not to disclose does not extend to information concerning the commission of a crime or other misconduct, for example sexual misconduct, either in the past, or in the future, provided that it is in the public interest that disclosure should happen. If someone tells a minister that he or she has committed a crime or is about to do so, the court will not intervene to restrain disclosure if, as is likely, disclosure would be in the public interest. Outside the area of crime the test of whether disclosure is in the public interest is more difficult to apply and is dealt with below with particular reference to human rights issues.

6. The general equitable duty not to disclose confidential information does not extend to disclosure if a minister is summoned to give evidence in court. Confidential communications passing between a client and his legal adviser, and made for the purpose of obtaining or giving legal advice, are privileged from disclosure, that is, the legal adviser cannot be compelled to give evidence against his client on matters confided to him. The reason is that it is necessary for the proper administration of justice that a client should be able to speak freely to his or her legal adviser without the fear that the legal adviser might later be compelled to reveal what the client had said. This privilege does not extend to other professions, who are subject to the general rule that a witness must tell what it is that he or she knows. Where the minister is under a canonical duty of silence (see para 18 below) it can be argued that the information may also be privileged. In the case of information received in other circumstances however, dishonourable and unpleasant though it may seem, a minister who is summoned to give evidence in court is obliged to disclose the information that he or she has, or face the consequences, possibly imprisonment for contempt of court, unless the judge is prepared to exercise such discretion

as is available and say that the question need not be answered. In criminal proceedings, the guiding principle is the fairness of the proceedings and therefore the interests of the defendant will be given greater weight than doctrinal sensibilities of the attesting witness. The possible relevance of the Human Rights Act 1998 to this matter is considered below (see para 14 et seq below).

The European Convention on Human Rights and the Human Rights Act 1998

7. There are three Articles in the European Convention on Human Rights ('the Convention') which are relevant. Article 8 of the Convention, entitled 'Right to respect for private and family life', is as follows:

'1   Everyone has the right to respect for his private and family life, his home and his correspondence.

2   There shall be no interference by a public authority with the exercise of this right except such as is in accordance with the law and is necessary in a democratic society in the interests of national security, public safety or the economic well being of the country, for the prevention of disorder or crime, for the protection of health or morals, or for the protection of the rights and freedom of others.'

The former Commission held that 'private life' went beyond 'privacy' and included the establishment of relationships with other human beings especially in the emotional field: *App 6825/74 X v Iceland*. Most of the case law on Article 8.1 is on prisoners' correspondence.

Article 9, entitled 'Freedom of Thought, Conscience and Religion' is as follows:

'1   Everyone has the right to freedom of thought, conscience and religion; this right includes freedom to change his religion or belief and freedom, either alone or in community with others and in public or private, to manifest his religion or belief, in worship, teaching, practice and observance.

2   Freedom to manifest one's religion or beliefs shall be subject only to such limitations as are prescribed by law and are necessary in a democratic society in the interests of public safety, for the protection of public order, health or morals, or for the protection of the rights and freedoms of others.'

Article 10, entitled 'Freedom of Expression' is as follows:

'1   Everyone has the right to freedom of expression. The right shall include freedom to hold opinions and to receive and impart information and ideas without interference by public authority and regardless of frontiers. This article shall not prevent States from requiring the licensing of broadcasting, television or cinema enterprises.

2   The exercise of these freedoms, since it carries with it duties and responsibilities, may be subject to such formalities, conditions, restrictions or penalties as are prescribed by law and are necessary in a democratic society, in the interests of national security, territorial integrity or public safety, for the prevention of disorder or crime, for the protection of health or morals, for the protection of the reputation or rights of others, for preventing the disclosure of information received in confidence, or for maintaining the authority and impartiality of the judiciary.'

8. Section 6(1) of the Human Rights Act 1998, which came into force on 1 October 2000 provides that:

'It is unlawful for a public authority to act in any way which is incompatible with a Convention right.'

and sub-section 3(3)(b) provides that the term 'public authority' includes:

'any person certain of whose functions are functions of a public nature . . .'.

9. There is a tension between the privacy rights of Article 8 and the freedom of imparting information in Article 10(1), but Article 10(2) makes it clear that the freedom of expression is made subject to other rights including those derived from the law as to confidence. It should be remembered that the right to privacy and that of free expression are qualified and not absolute rights; and that any court in defining the legitimate limits of such right must make a value judgement. The courts have to strike a balance between the conflicting interests, so that the Convention rights are absorbed into the action for breach of confidence, which acquires a new strength and breadth: *Douglas v Hello! Ltd (No 3)* [2005] EWCA Civ 595, [2006] QB 125.

Article 8 of the Convention

10. The extent to which component institutions and personnel of the Church of England are public bodies remains somewhat unclear despite a decision of the House of Lords on the matter. In the solemnization of matrimony, a minister will be regarded as a 'public body' but in other acts of spiritual ministry such categorization is less likely. Only when exercising 'functions of a public nature' will a person's actions be unlawful if they are incompatible with a Convention right. Administration of the Sacrament of Penance is likely to be considered a private act, as also conversations in the course of counselling. The mere fact that the Church of England has the status of an established church does not render it (or its parts) a public authority. It is therefore unlikely that Article 8 will be engaged in most instances when confidentiality is an issue. The most relevant rights among those guaranteed by Article 8, are respect for private and family life. Divulging confidential information about a person might result in a considerable interference with his private and family life, and will be unlawful unless it is covered by one of the limitations in paragraph 2 of Article 8. Any minister considering divulging such information will, therefore, have to weigh carefully the right of the person who is the subject of the information to respect for his private and family life, against the exceptions in paragraph 2 of Article 8, the most relevant of which will probably be '. . . the protection of health or morals, or for the protection of the rights and freedoms of others'.

11. Of particular concern at present are cases where information concerning child abuse comes into the possession of the clergy, and a decision has to be taken as to whether or not that should be disclosed. A minister may be asked to supply a reference, or may be aware that the subject of the information is about to be appointed to, or is actually in, a post which gives access to children. Possible situations that might arise are set out below. Of course there are many gradations between them.

(a) A minister is told by X, or is made aware in some other way (given that Article 8 applies whether the information comes from the person concerned, or from a third party), that X has been convicted at some time in the past of an offence involving child abuse;

(b) A minister is told by X, or is made aware in some other way, that X had been charged with offences involving child abuse, but was found not guilty, and was discharged;

(c) A minister is told by X, or is made aware in some other way, that there are reasons to suspect that X might have been involved in child abuse, but that X has never been prosecuted;

(d)   A minister is told by X that he (X) is concerned that he might have paedophile tendencies, and be tempted to commit child abuse.

12. What is the minister to do? So far as the Convention is concerned, each and every case has to be considered on its own facts. It has been held (*R v Local Authority and Police Authority in the Midlands ex parte LM* [2000] 1 FLR 612) that a 'blanket approach' is not permissible. The minister cannot say that matters involving child abuse are so serious that whenever there is any possibility of someone being involved with it this should be disclosed. Nor can he or she claim that disclosure is necessary to avoid being sued for negligence, as might happen if information is withheld and problems arise later.

13. Bearing in mind the provisions of Article 8(2), disclosure should only be made if there is a 'pressing need', taking into account such matters as (i) the minister's own view as to the truth of what is alleged, (ii) the interest of the third party in obtaining the information (much greater if, for example, X is seeking employment in a children's hostel, than if X is seeking to work in an old peoples' home), and (iii) the degree of risk likely to arise if the disclosure is not made, which will involve consideration of such matters as the length of time that has passed since the behaviour the minister is aware of took place, the age of the children to which X will have access, and which of the above categories applies. The decision is rarely likely to be easy, and the consequences of making a wrong decision could be serious. Clergy are strongly advised to consult the diocesan registrar who, in the light of this Opinion, will be able to advise whether further legal advice is needed on the fact of a particular case.

Article 9 of the Convention

14. It is arguable that the freedom of thought, conscience, and religion covered by Article 9, as reinforced by section 13(1) of the Human Rights Act might provide some protection to a minister against a claim that disclosure should be made, on the basis that the reception and retention of confidences is part of the practice and observance of religion. Section 13(1) provides as follows:

'13. Freedom of thought, conscience and religion

(1)   If a court's determination of any question arising under this Act might affect the exercise by a religious

organisation (itself or its members collectively) of the Convention right to freedom of thought, conscience or religion, it must have particular regard to the importance of that right.'

It does not seem, however, that section 13 adds anything to the underlying Article. The same Article might also be relevant to the question of whether a minister can or should be compelled to give evidence of the contents of confidences received.

15. Some assistance may be found in the experience under the Canadian Charter of Rights and Freedoms, a document serving purposes broadly similar to that of the Human Rights Act 1998. The Canadian Charter guarantees, among the 'fundamental freedoms' in section 2 'freedom of conscience and religion'. In the Charter there is no right to privacy as such and the fundamental rights are 'subject only to such reasonable limits prescribed by law as can be demonstrably justified in a free and democratic society' (s1).

16. The Canadian courts follow the common law view, reflected in paragraph 2.4 of this Opinion, that there is no general privilege attaching to communications to clergymen. See *Re Church of Scientology and The Queen (No. 6)* (1987) 31 CCC (3rd) 449, 537 Ont. CA, citing Jessel M. R. in *Wheeler v Le Marchant* (1881) 17 ChD 675; *R v Medina* (1988) 6 WCB 2nd 358, Ont, where some cases to the contrary are cited: *Cook v Carroll* [1945] IR 515 (Irish case on advice by parish priest on pregnancy out of wedlock); *R v Griffin* (1853) 6 Cox CC 219 (per Alderson B; statement made to workhouse chaplain). That common law position was, however, reviewed in the light of the Charter by the Ontario Court of Appeal in *Re Church of Scientology and The Queen (No. 6)* (1987) 31 CCC (3rd) 449. The Court held that the position at common law was modified by protection which the Charter affords to religious activity and observed (at 540):

'This protection will no doubt strengthen the argument in favour of the recognition of a priest-and-penitent privilege. The restrictive common law interpretation of the privilege may have to be reassessed to bring it in conformity with the constitutional freedom. In our view, however, while s.2 of the Charter enhances the claim that communications made in confidence to a priest or ordained minister should be afforded a privilege, its applicability must be determined on a case-by-case basis. The freedom is not absolute.'

17. In *R v Medina* (1988) 6 WCB 2nd 358, the Ontario High Court held

that the case-by-case analysis involved the use of four principles elaborated in Wigmore's treatise on the law of evidence: (1) The communication must originate in a confidence that they will not be disclosed; (2) This element of confidentiality must be essential to the full and satisfactory maintenance of the relation between the parties; (3) The relation must be one which in the opinion of the community ought to be sedulously fostered; and (4) The injury that would inure to the relation by the disclosure of the communications must be greater than the benefit thereby gained for the correct disposal of litigation.

18. In examining more closely what area was protected as amounting to religious practice, the Court said that it might be helpful to ask the following questions: (1) Does the communication involve some aspect of religious belief, worship or practice? (2) Is the religious aspect the dominant feature or purpose of the communication? (3) Even if the religious aspect is not the dominant purpose, how significant is it? Would the communication have been called into being without the religious aspect? Even if not the *causa causans*, is the religious aspect the *causa sine qua non* of the communication? (4) Is the religious aspect of the communication sincere or is it colourable? Does it amount to a good faith manifestation of religious belief, worship or practice? If sincere and asserted in good faith, the truth or falsity of the religious belief was irrelevant.

19. The Supreme Court of Canada considered the issue in *Gruenke v The Queen* (1991) 67 CCC 3rd 289. The majority (Lamer C. J. C., La Forest, Sopinka, Cory, McLachlin, Stevenson and Iacobucci JJ.) held that notwithstanding the value of freedom of religion embodied in section 2(a) of the Canadian Charter of Rights and Freedoms, the court would not recognize the prima facie protection of religious communications. Religious communications, notwithstanding their social importance, were not inextricably linked with the justice system in the way that solicitor–client communications are. The proper approach was to consider whether the communication should be excluded in the particular case applying the Wigmore criteria. Those criteria would, however, be 'informed' by the guarantee given in the Charter to freedom of religion. L'Heureux-Dube and Gonthier JJ. Agreed on the facts of the instant case but took the view that the court ought to recognize a privilege for religious communications. The inclusion of the guarantee of freedom of religion in section 2(a) of the Charter indicated that a legal privilege for confidential religious communications was commensurate with Canadian values. Recognition of this privilege could also be supported by the interests in privacy. This privacy interest did not simply address the interest all people have in the privacy of their conversations, but the interest that an individual has in privacy when seeking out a religious leader for spiritual guidance and

assistance. In their view, an ad hoc or case-by-case approach to privilege was not sufficient: if society truly wished to encourage the creation and development of spiritual relationships, individuals must have a certain amount of confidence that their religious confessions, given in confidence and for spiritual relief, will not be disclosed.

20. It will be seen that there are a number of strands in this approach, and it is very difficult to predict which will be adopted in case law under the Human Rights Act 1998.

Canon law

21. The relevant provision is contained in Canon 113 of the code of Canons that was confirmed by Letters Patent of James I in 1604, but are usually referred to as the Canons of 1603. Canon 113 is entitled 'Minister may Present'. Its principal purpose was to provide that because 'churchwardens, sidesmen, questmen and such other persons of the laity' often failed, through negligence or fear of their superiors, in their duty to suppress sin and wickedness in their parishes by presenting those considered guilty to the Ordinary (this was at a time when, for example, sexual offences such as fornication or adultery were punishable by the ecclesiastical courts), then the minister, in order to encourage the churchwardens etc., may join with them in making presentments, or indeed, make the presentments himself. The Canon ended with the following proviso:

> 'Provided always that if any man confess his secret and hidden sins to the minister, for the unburdening of his conscience, and to receive spiritual consolation and ease of mind from him; we do not in any way bind the said minister by this our constitution, but do straightly charge and admonish him that he do not at any time reveal and make known to any person whatsoever any crime or offence so committed to his trust and secrecy, (except they be such crimes as by the laws of this realm his own life may be called into question for concealing the same) under pain of irregularity.'

22. Canon 113 was a new Canon, but, apart from the words in brackets, this proviso to the new Canon was not itself new; it was rather a restatement of the existing canon law dating back to Canon 21 of the Fourth Lateran Council of 1215, and would appear to have been inserted to remind the clergy that although they ought now themselves present wrongdoers to the Ordinary, this did not extend to those whose wrongs were known to them through the confessional. The meaning of the words in brackets is not clear, indeed it has been argued by Badeley, in *The*

Privilege at Religious Confessionals English Courts of Justice, 1865, at pp. 31–2, that they have no meaning at all. It is thought possible, however, that they refer to a confession of high treason. According to J. P. Winckworth in *The Seal of the Confessional and the Law of Evidence*, at p. 4, 'under pain of irregularity' meant that the punishment for breaking the seal of the confessional was deprivation, accompanied by incapacity for taking any benefice whatever, whilst under its operation.

23. It is, perhaps, surprising that the proviso to Canon 113 of the 1603 code is still in effect and states the present law on the subject. The draft revised canons annexed to the 1947 Report of the Archbishops' Commission on Canon Law included the following:

> 'If any man confesses any secret or hidden sin to a Priest for the unburdening of his conscience and to receive spiritual consolation and ease of mind and absolution from him, such Priest shall not either by word, writing, or sign directly or indirectly, openly or covertly, or in any other way whatsoever, at any time reveal and make known to any person whatsoever, any sin, crime, or offence so committed to his trust and secrecy; neither shall any Priest make use of knowledge gained in the exercise of such ministry to the offence or detriment of the person from whom he has received it, even if there be no danger of betraying the identity of such person; neither shall any Priest who is in a position of authority in any place, make use of any such knowledge in the exercise of his authority.'

24. This draft canon was not included in the new code of canons promulged in 1964 and 1969. It appears that advice was received that a new canon in this form was unlikely to receive the Royal Licence, and, rather than risk a refusal, it was decided to retain the proviso to the old Canon 113, whilst repealing the rest of the code of 1603. Resolutions were, nevertheless passed in the Convocations of Canterbury and York on 29 April 1959, as follows:

> 'That this House (*York*, That this Synod) reaffirms as an essential principle of Church doctrine that if any person confess his secret and hidden sin to a priest for the unburdening of his conscience, and to receive spiritual consolation and absolution from him, such priest is strictly charged that he do not at any time reveal or make known to any person whatsoever any sin so committed to his trust and secrecy.'

25. In the case of Canterbury the resolution was declared to be an Act of Convocation. Acts of Convocation have moral force, but are not law.

26. The reason why advice was given that the draft new canon might not receive the Royal Licence is that it was questioned whether it was in accordance with the law. The implication of the canon being passed in these absolute terms was that the clergy have the privilege of not being obliged to disclose information received in the confessional, if called to give evidence in court. It was thought that whilst that privilege might have existed in the past, the modern law of evidence had evolved without reference to it, and that it was, at the least, doubtful whether the privilege existed under the civil (as opposed to ecclesiastical) law. Rather than put the point to the test, it was decided to retain the status quo, and the proviso to Canon 113 was not repealed.

27. The question of whether a priest can claim privilege, and not answer questions put to him or her in the witness box, concerning information received in the confessional is, therefore, an open question. Writers such as Philimore (*The Ecclesiastical Law of the Church of England* 2nd edn at p. 584 et seq), Winckworth (*The Seal of the Confessional and the Law of Evidence*) and Bursell (*The Seal of the Confessional* 3 ECC LJ 84) have argued persuasively that canon law has never changed since pre-Reformation times, and that, as this is part of the law of the land, the privilege exists at law. Most, if not all, modern writers on the law of evidence do not accept this. It may be that the case is not one of privilege as such, but one in which the priest may ask the court to excuse him, with some prospect of obtaining that concession. The existence of the canonical provision, together with Article 9 of the Convention and the Canadian case law already noted, provide a basis for an argument to that effect, but there is no clear modern authority.

Statute

28. One such provision is section 38B of the Terrorism Act 2000 (as inserted by the Anti-Terrorism, Crime and Security Act 2001) which provides in part:

'(1) This section applies where a person has information which he knows or believes might be of material assistance –

(a) in preventing the commission by another person of an act of terrorism, or

(b) in securing the apprehension, prosecution or conviction of another person, in the United Kingdom, for an offence involving the commission, preparation or instigation of an act of terrorism.

(2) The person commits an offence if he does not disclose the information as soon as reasonably practicable in accordance with subsection (3)

(3) Disclosure is in accordance with this subsection if it is made –

(a) in England and Wales, to a constable,

(b) in Scotland, to a constable, or

(c) in Northern Ireland, to a constable or a member of Her Majesty's forces.

(4) It is a defence for a person charged with an offence under subsection (2) to prove that he had a reasonable excuse for not making the disclosure . . .'

29. The section provides a defence of 'reasonable excuse', and it is possible (although in the circumstances of terrorism unlikely) that some judges might be persuaded that the failure to divulge confessional secrets would fall within that defence. Subject to that, there is no doubt but that the section considerably, if not entirely, restricts any right or duty to remain silent.

30. Similar provisions apply in relation to terrorist funds, fundraising and money laundering. Section 19(1) of the 2000 Act makes it an offence not to disclose information to specified persons in relation thereto:

'This section applies where a person –

(a) believes or suspects that another person has committed an offence in relation to [providing financial assistance for terrorism];

(b) bases his belief or suspicion in information which comes to his attention in the course of a trade, profession, business or employment.'

Subsection (3) again provides the defence of reasonable excuse; subsection (5) excludes privileged communications to legal advisers.

31. Whatever the precise status of a priest in relation to employment, the priest will be caught by the breadth of wording in subsection (1)(b). In this case, it is even more unlikely that the defence of reasonable excuse would be interpreted to cover confessional secrets, not only because of the

specific provisions of subsection (5) but also because of the provisions of section 20(4).

Section 20 provides:

'(1) A person may disclose to a constable –

    (a) a suspicion or belief that any money or other property is terrorist property or derived from terrorist property;

    (b) any matter on which the suspicion or belief is based.'

'(4) Subsection (1) . . . shall have effect notwithstanding any restriction on the disclosure of information imposed by statues or otherwise.'

The words 'restriction . . . imposed by statute or otherwise' are clearly apt to embrace the legal duty of confessional confidentiality.

Clergy discipline issues

32. It is, prima facie, an offence against the laws ecclesiastical (see s8(1) of the Clergy Discipline Measure 2003) for a priest to reveal information received by him or her in circumstances described in Canon 113. If, however, a priest were to be summoned to give evidence in court, and the court were to hold, after due argument, that despite Canon 113 that priest was not entitled to refuse to answer questions, it is considered that an ecclesiastical offence would not be committed if such information were to be revealed. The law of the land must be one and the same in all courts, and the ecclesiastical courts cannot take a different view from the civil courts.

33. There will almost certainly be those who consider that whatever the law of the land may be they must nevertheless keep confidence. For this reason, it is important that if a priest with knowledge received in the circumstances described in Canon 113 is summoned to give evidence in court, he or she should seek legal advice, if possible, and should certainly claim privilege, even though this might not be upheld.

34. In other cases, that is, in cases where the information is received in circumstances other than those described in the Canon, it is considered that if a minister discloses information in breach of the equitable doctrine of confidence, or in a way that would be unlawful under the provisions of the Human Rights Act 1998, this will almost certainly amount to 'conduct unbecoming or inappropriate to the office and work of a clerk in Holy

Orders' and fall to be dealt with under the Clergy Discipline Measure 2003.

Conclusion

35. Given the present uncertain state of the law as regards the effect of both Canon 113 of the 1603 Canons and the Human Rights Act 1998, it is not possible to answer the questions raised by the House of Bishops in a series of short and simple propositions. It is hoped, however, that this Opinion, which is intended to provide such advice as can be given on the basis of the law as it now stands, will be helpful.

(May 2000, revised September 2003)

Clergy: deacons: ordination, licence and title

1. Paragraph 1 of Canon C 5 provides that a person may not be admitted into Holy Orders – that is, ordained deacon – without having first exhibited a certificate to the bishop of the diocese in which ordination is sought that 'he is provided of some ecclesiastical office within such diocese, which the bishop shall judge sufficient, wherein he may attend the cure of souls and execute his ministry'. There are certain exceptions to this requirement listed in the next paragraph, permitting a bishop to ordain as deacon a person holding office in a university or a fellow of a college or hall in a university, a schoolmaster, a school, college or university chaplain, a member of staff of a theological college or a person living under vows in the house of a religious order or community.

2. In the Commission's view, a bishop needs to be satisfied (subject to the exceptions in paragraph 2 of the Canon) that he is ordaining a person as deacon to some recognized ecclesiastical office of the kind wherein he (and now she) may attend to the cure of souls and execute his or her ministry. This is what is meant by Title to Orders. It follows that serving a title requires that the work of the office be both parochial and diaconal (i.e. a ministry where he or she may carry out the normal duties of a deacon as defined in the Ordinal). Thus, the Commission considers that, subject to the exceptions in paragraph 2, a deacon should, on ordination, be licensed to the office of assistant curate. A sector or specialist ministry does not of itself involve a 'cure of souls' (however pastoral it may in fact be), and no person should be ordained as deacon to such a ministry alone unless it falls within the terms of paragraph 2 of the Canon.

3. It is the view of the Legal Advisory Commission that the wording used in the licence which is signed and sealed by the bishop is important, and should stipulate that the deacon is being licensed to the office of assistant curate. Certain duties and responsibilities are placed on assistant curates by the Canons and in particular the incumbent has certain rights and authority in relation to his curates.

4. There is no legal objection to styles or descriptions such as 'parish deacon' or 'minister in charge' being used for the deacon in practice, provided the deacon is formally licensed as an assistant curate (although it is suggested, with respect, that when a person is first ordained there is much to be said for the style 'curate' being used, since this reflects the office of 'assistant curate' to which he or she is licensed). However, there is no established ecclesiastical office of 'parish deacon', and it is doubted that a new ecclesiastical office can be created in law by a decision of the House of Bishops alone. The offices of deacon and priest are not ecclesiastical offices as such, but offices or orders of ministry. The office of

bishop is both an order of ministry and an established ecclesiastical office (see Canon C 1 and the Schedule to the Ecclesiastical Offices (Age Limit) Measure 1975).

5. The Commission recognizes that the principle laid down by paragraph 1 of Canon C 5 has sometimes created problems. In particular, the ordination in 1987 of mature and experienced deaconesses to the diaconate, some of whom were already in specialist ministries, was exceptional and understandably some were not ordained to a title, even though this was irregular. However, the problems over deciding to what office a person about to be ordained deacon should be licensed did not begin when it became possible in law to make women deacons, but with the development of the non-stipendiary ministry. Many men in very senior positions in secular life have, on being made a deacon, received the usual licence from the bishop to exercise the ministry of assistant curate. No doubt they will be referred to and addressed in a variety of styles, but their licence will remain that of an assistant curate.

6. Once a deacon has served his or her title, it is for the bishop to decide upon the description or style by which he or she is to be known, particularly in the case of those who are not subsequently ordained to the priesthood. A deacon in that position may take up a sector ministry post, or the bishop may, under Canon C 12 para 1(a) grant a general licence under seal.

7. The office of team vicar carries the status and authority of an incumbent under section 20 of the Pastoral Measure and involves sharing in the cure of souls. Thus a deacon cannot be a team vicar (see s10 of the Act of Uniformity 1662), but section 20(1)(b) of the Pastoral Measure 1983 does permit a deacon, licensed as stipendiary curate to a team ministry, to be a member of the team. The new paragraph (3A) added to section 20 by the Team and Group Ministries Measure 1995 also makes it possible for the bishop to include in the licence of a deacon as a member of the team a provision authorizing the deacon to perform, for the purposes of the team ministry and so far as consistent with his or her office, all such offices and services as may be performed by an incumbent. In that case the deacon will also enjoy tenure of office equivalent to that of the team vicars in the team ministry concerned. However, it is suggested that the use of paragraph (3A) would only be appropriate in the case of an experienced member of the clergy who, if a priest, would have been regarded as qualified for appointment as a team vicar.

(Revised 2003)

Clergy: Ecclesiastical Offices (Age Limit) Measure 1975

Section 1(3) of the Ecclesiastical Offices (Age Limit) Measure 1975 states that the holder of an office specified in the Measure 'shall vacant that office on the day on which he attains the age of seventy years'. These words correspond to those used in section 2(1) of the Judicial Pensions Act 1959. In that case the relevant judge's office is automatically vacated at the age specified in section 2 without a deed of resignation being required. In the Legal Advisory Commission's Opinion, a formal resignation is not required in the case of an office within the provisions of the 1975 Measure, and such an office is vacated by operation of law once the holder reaches the age of 70.

(Revised 2003)

Clergy: Incumbents and Churchwardens (Trusts) Measure 1964

1. The Commission was asked:

(a)   Whether a priest-in-charge is an 'incumbent' for the purposes of the Incumbents and Churchwardens (Trusts) Measure 1964 and,

(b)   whether the incumbent's rights and duties in respect of property to which the 1964 Measure applies would vest in a priest-in-charge by virtue of section 74 of the Pastoral Measure 1983.

2. The 1964 Measure applies (with certain exceptions) to land, and personal property (if held on permanent trusts) which is acquired or held on charitable trusts, established for ecclesiastical purposes of the Church of England, and whereof no present or past trustee is, or has been, any person other than an incumbent or churchwardens, or, an ecclesiastical corporation sole acting as a joint trustee with an incumbent or churchwardens. The Measure provides for such property to vest in the Diocesan Authority. Before the vesting takes place, the Diocesan Authority is to serve a notice upon the persons believed by the authority to have or be entitled to the general control and management of the property, the incumbent, and the Charity Commission. On the vesting taking place, the Diocesan Authority is to establish a Scheme for the management of the charity, limited to securing the establishment and continuation of managing trustees who shall be the incumbent or churchwardens, and, where appropriate, an ecclesiastical corporation sole to act as joint managing trustee with them or any of them.

3. Section 1 of the Measure provides that 'incumbent' includes any minister with a separate cure of souls but shall not include a curate in charge of a conventional district. The Commission is of the view that a priest-in-charge has the cure of souls with the responsibilities that this entails and the rights flowing from those responsibilities or needed in order to discharge them effectively. (*See* **Clergy: priest-in-charge**.) If the Commission is correct in that view, a priest-in-charge is an 'incumbent' for the purposes of the 1964 Measure.

4. The effect of this statement would appear to be somewhat limited, because there are unlikely to be many trusts where the trustees are named as the priest-in-charge and the churchwardens of a parish. If there are any such trusts, however, they will come within the purview of the Measure. Further, if a Diocesan Authority is proposing to make a Scheme for the

vesting of property under the Measure, and there is a priest-in-charge and no incumbent at that time, then he, or she, will be entitled to receive the notice that the authority is required to serve upon the incumbent.

5. Question (b) relates to cases where property has been vested in the Diocesan Authority under the 1964 Measure, and the authority has made a Scheme appointing the incumbent and churchwardens of the parish as the managing trustees of that property. In these cases does a priest-in-charge have the same powers as an incumbent would have in relation to the property?

6. Section 74(1) of the Pastoral Measure 1983 provides the answer. This states that:

> 'where any property of a charity established for ecclesiastical purposes of the Church of England is vested in, or under, the management or control of the incumbent of a benefice (with or without other persons) . . . and the benefice becomes vacant or the bishop declares a suspension period in respect of the benefice, then during the period of the vacancy, or during the suspension period, as the case may be, the trusts of the charity . . . shall have effect with the substitution for the incumbent of that benefice of the priest-in-charge of that benefice.'

7. We have seen that the 1964 Measure applies to property held on charitable trusts established for ecclesiastical purposes of the Church of England. Section 74 of the 1983 Measure must, therefore, apply, and any reference in a Scheme made by the Diocesan Authority under the 1964 Measure to the appointment of an incumbent and/or churchwardens as managing trustees must include a priest-in-charge in cases where there is no incumbent, and a priest-in-charge has been appointed.

(October 1997)

Clergy: institution and induction

1. By the process of institution the bishop places a priest in possession of the spiritualities of the benefice, i.e. places in his or her hands the cure of souls in the parish. Before this takes place, three weeks' notice of the intention to institute must be sent to the secretary of the PCC, and the secretary must cause the notice or a copy to be fixed on or near the principal door of every church in the parish, where it must remain for two weeks. The priest must make a Declaration of Assent to the doctrine of the Church of England, and must take the oaths of allegiance to the Queen and of canonical obedience to the bishop. It is an offence against the laws ecclesiastical for a bishop to institute a woman as incumbent of a benefice in contravention of a resolution passed by the PCC under the Priests (Ordination of Women) Measure 1993, section 3.

2. Induction is performed by the archdeacon (after institution) acting on the directions of the bishop, or by the rural dean or some other clergyman acting on the authority of the archdeacon. By it the incumbent is placed in possession of the temporalities of the benefice. In case of dire necessity an incumbent may be inducted by proxy.

3. The legal elements of these services of institution and induction must comprise:

(a)   the report of the presentation by the patron (or by the Archbishop where the right to present has passed to him), or collation where the bishop is patron;

(b)   the institution by reading or proclaiming the delivery of the cure of souls to the incumbent; and

(c)   the induction by a token livery of seisin by both words and action, e.g. ringing the bell, putting a hand on the door knob, or receiving a clod of earth.

4. A new incumbent is no longer required to read the Thirty-Nine Articles and make the declaration before the congregation at the beginning of his or her ministry.

(Revised 2003)

Clergy: meaning of 'minister of religion' for the purposes of the Housing Act 1988

1. Section 7 of the Housing Act 1988 (as amended by the Housing Act 1996), read with Ground 5 in the Second Schedule, obliges the court in appropriate circumstances to make an order for possession of a dwellinghouse let on an assured tenancy if it is required for occupation by a minister of religion as a residence from which to perform the duties of his or her office.

2. Ground 5 requires that:

> 'The dwellinghouse is held for the purpose of being available for occupation by a minister of religion as a residence from which to perform the duties of his office and –
>
> (a)   not later than the beginning of the tenancy the landlord gave notice in writing to the tenant that possession might be recovered on this ground; and
>
> (b)   the court is satisfied that the dwellinghouse is required for occupation by a minister of religion as such a residence.'

3. This Ground, in relation to assured tenancies, serves the same purpose as Case 15 of Schedule 15 to the Rent Act 1977 in relation to regulated tenancies. That Case in turn derives from section 15(1) of the Rent Act 1965, which was new in 1965, and began as follows:

> '15(1) Where a dwellinghouse is held for the purpose of being available for occupation by a minister of religion as a residence from which to perform the duties of his office and the dwellinghouse has been let on a regulated tenancy . . .'

4. The 1965, 1977, 1988 and 1996 Acts do not contain any definition of 'minister of religion'.

Use of term 'minister' in legislation relating to the Church of England

5. The use of the word 'minister' in statutes having a religious context goes back at least to the Act of Uniformity of 1548. The office of lay reader existed in England before the Reformation but was allowed to lapse after it. Therefore until it was revived, and other lay offices added to it, there can have been no doubt that the word referred only to a minister who had been ordained. With the development of the lay ministry in the

Church of England in the twentieth century it is no longer possible to make such a simple assumption.

6. In the cases where the word 'minister' is defined for the purposes of a particular statute it is nevertheless almost invariably confined, so far as the Church of England is concerned, to the ordained ministry. Examples are section 2 of the Clerical Disabilities Act 1870 ('priest or deacon') and the CRR rule 54(1) (where it means, briefly, an incumbent, a curate, a priest-in-charge or a team vicar, a definition which has been adopted for the purposes of the Parochial Church Councils (Powers) Measure 1956 (see s1) and the Churchwardens Measure 2001 (see s13(1)). It could be argued that such a definition in itself indicates that, to the mind of the draftsman at least, the word would have a wider meaning if left undefined.

7. In other cases, although the statute contains no definition the meaning is clear from the context; for example sections 10 (now repealed) and 11 of the Clergy (Ordination and Miscellaneous Provisions) Measure 1964 and section 7(1) of the Church of England (Legal Aid and Miscellaneous Provisions) Measure 1988 (revocation of licences granted to 'ministers, deaconesses, lay workers and readers').

8. The definition of 'minister of a parish' in section 3 of the Extra-Parochial Ministry Measure 1967 is 'inclusive', but again the context indicates an ordained minister.

9. The Parochial Registers and Records Measure 1978 is particularly carefully worded, and contains three different definitions of the word: section 2(5) (where in relation to a parish, as regards baptism, it has much the same meaning as in the CRR), section 3(5) (where as regards burial it means any person authorized to bury the dead according to the rites of the Church of England) and section 9(8) (where among the persons to receive the result of an inspection of register books and records are 'an incumbent or priest in charge').

10. Section 3(5) of the Parochial Registers and Records Measure 1978 clearly reflects section 1 of the Deaconesses and Lay Ministry Measure 1972 and the Canons made under it (Canon D 1 para 4, Canon E 4 para 2A and Canon E 7 para 5). Indeed the 1972 Measure not only uses the word 'minister' in such a way as to make it clear that it does not include deaconesses or other lay persons, but in section 1(4) it provides as follows:

> 'References to any enactment or Measure relating to burial or cremation to a clerk or minister in Holy Orders, or to qualified persons authorised by an incumbent or minister, or to a minister of religion, shall be construed as including references to a person

authorised in pursuance of subsection (1) of this section to perform the duties specified in paragraph (c) thereof, but not so as to enable any such person to perform those duties otherwise than in accordance with the conditions prescribed by Canon.'

Use of term 'minister' in other legislation

11. In legislation not directly relating to the Church of England it is usual for the word 'minister' to appear in the second part of a more comprehensive expression; for example:

(a)   Section 36 of the Offences Against the Person Act 1861 makes it an offence to obstruct 'any clergyman or other minister' in the performance of the duties referred to in the section. Among those duties is the lawful burial of the dead in any churchyard or other burial place, so that in this respect at least a deaconess or other lay person authorized under the Deaconesses and Lay Ministry Measure 1972 should qualify as a minister.

(b)   Section 332 of the Income and Corporation Taxes Act 1988 conferred certain tax exemptions on 'persons holding any full time office as clergyman or minister of any religious denomination' (see now the more limited exemptions in s351 of the Income Tax (Earnings and Pensions) Act 2003, which uses the phrase 'minister of a religious denomination'). The Inland Revenue refused to accept that this exemption is available to deaconesses and licensed lay workers, partly in reliance on the authorities referred to in paragraphs 12 and 13 and partly because the existing provision can be traced back at least to the Income Tax Act of 1853, at which date the expression would not have been regarded as capable of extending to laymen.

12. The first of the authorities referred to in paragraph 11(b) is *Simmonds v Elliott* [1917] 2 KB 894, DC, where a lay reader unsuccessfully claimed exemption from military service as 'a regular minister of a religious denomination' within the meaning of the Military Service Act 1916. The full exemption applied to 'men in Holy Orders or regular ministers of any religious denomination', and the court held that the exemption for a regular minister of a religious denomination was only available in the case of denominations which did not have Holy Orders.

13. The other authority is *Walsh v Lord Advocate* 1956 SC (HL) 126, [1956] 3 All ER 129, where a Jehovah's Witness claimed exemption from service in the armed forces under the National Service Act 1948, which included among the persons not liable to be called up for service 'a man in

Holy Orders or a regular minister of any religious denomination'. The House of Lords held that since any baptized member of the Jehovah's Witnesses was considered by them as a minister the appellant did not fall within the exemption. Lord Mackintosh said:

> 'In my view Parliament had in view religious denominations where there was a clear and definite distinction drawn and preserved between the clergy and the laity and where a person could qualify as a "regular minister" within the meaning of the Schedule only if he belonged to the clergy class as distinct from the laity.'

Conclusion

14. A general proposition which can be drawn from all this is that where a combined expression is used, part of which can only apply to a Church which ordains its ministers, the remainder of the expression does not apply to that Church. Ground 5 of Schedule 2 to the Housing Act 1988, however, only contains the expression 'minister of religion'. This expression derives from the Rent Act 1965, and by the time that Act was passed it was accepted that the Rent Acts did not apply to a parsonage house. To that extent therefore it was not necessary for the expression to extend to the incumbent of a benefice in the Church of England. That may explain why a simplified expression was adopted, although the purpose cannot have been to rule out other clerks in Holy Orders – deacons, for example, and ordained ministers of the Roman Catholic Church.

15. It is very common for housing accommodation to be provided for occupation by a deaconess or licensed lay worker. Normally the house is owned or acquired by the DBF, and occupied by successive holders of the particular office. There would be no incongruity, therefore, in the application of Ground 5 to such persons. Nor is it considered inappropriate to regard them as ministers, albeit lay. The Deaconesses and Lay Ministry Measure 1972 gave statutory authority to the expression 'Lay Ministry' in its title, and it cannot be a misuse of language to regard a person exercising a ministry as a minister.

16. It is considered significant that in the 1988 Act a single expression is used – 'minister of religion' – and not the combined expression which statutes normally adopt. It is not opposed, as the word 'minister' usually is, to 'a man in Holy Orders', and so is not open to the argument which prevailed in *Simmonds v Elliott*. The broad principle of *Walsh v Lord Advocate* would no doubt apply, although the distinction would not be between clerical and lay but between minister and non-minister. Moreover the expression first appeared, in the context of landlord and tenant, in

1965, when the lay ministry was beginning to flourish, and there could not be the presumption, as there could in the case of much earlier legislation, that it could only relate to a minister who had been ordained.

17. It is therefore considered that the expression 'minister of religion' appearing in Ground 5 of Schedule 2 to the Housing Act 1988 is not limited to Holy Orders, and is capable of applying to a deaconess, licensed lay worker or other person who is licensed by the bishop to exercise a lay ministry within the Church of England.

18. It should be noted, however, that the abolition of the preliminary notice provisions and six-month minimum letting period for assured shorthold tenancies by the Housing Act 1996 means that assured shorthold tenancies will now in many cases be the preferred letting method in relation to vacant clergy housing (including the letting of official houses of residence, following the abolition of lettings by sequestrators under the Pluralities Act 1838, by the Church of England (Miscellaneous Provisions) Measure 2000). There remains an inflexibility in assured shorthold tenancies, however, in that possession cannot be recovered by court order less than six months from the commencement date of the letting; Ground 5 may therefore continue to be used in a number of cases, notwithstanding the uncertainties identified in this Opinion.

(October 1990, revised 1993)

Clergy: non-stipendiary ministers: appointment as incumbents

1. The Legal Advisory Commission has been invited to consider the legality of appointing as incumbents non-stipendiary ministers (NSM) who would not, after appointment, be entitled to a stipend or the profits of the benefice to which they were admitted. Regulation 1.2 of the House of Bishops' Regulations for Non-Stipendiary Ministry (which strictly have no legal effect) states that 'Non-Stipendiary Ministers are those whose main financial income comes from sources other than their work or ministry, and who receive no direct salary or stipend for their ministerial work'; the accompanying notes state that non-stipendiary ministry does not generally include, among others, those who are receiving a stipend from the Church Commissioners or who are paid by diocesan boards of finance.

2. An arrangement of the kind set out at the beginning of the previous paragraph cannot lawfully be made simply by the proposed incumbent agreeing in advance (by deed or otherwise) to disclaim the financial entitlements which would otherwise attach to the incumbency. Such an agreement is simoniacal (*R v Bishop of Oxford* (1806) 7 East 600) and will result in the benefice being avoided under section 4 of the Simony Act 1588, with the presentation upon such avoidance being exercised by the Diocesan Board of Patronage pursuant to section 28 of the Patronage (Benefices) Measure 1986. Even an agreement which is not morally corrupt, and reflects genuine pastoral requirements, will still be struck down under the mandatory terms of the Elizabethan Act.

3. Apart from avoidance on the grounds of simony, the effect of an incumbent's disclaimer of his income in relation to his liability to pay income tax is at best uncertain. The general principle, as stated by Finlay J in *Reade v Brearley* (1933) 17 TC 687 at 693, is that:

> 'If a person holds an office and the office is an office of profit, it is perfectly clear that no application of the income, which he may think proper to make as between himself and other persons, can for a moment affect his liability as being the holder of an office of profit . . . I think it is clear that at least in a large number of cases the voluntary foregoing of a salary due to a person ought to be regarded by the Court, and would be regarded, simply as being an application of the income and that in such circumstances, the office would not the less be an office of profit and the assessment would therefore not the less be made.'

The application of this principle is not inexorable. On the special facts of *Reade v Brearley* Finlay J found there to have been disclaimer, effective for tax purposes, of part of a salary. In *Whiteman on Income Tax*, 3rd edn, paras 14–16, it is suggested that a person who voluntarily renounces the emoluments of his employment is clearly not liable to tax on them. No authority, however, is cited in support of this proposition (but see *Dewar v Inland Revenue Commissioners* [1935] 2 KB 351, CA). The efficacy of an incumbent's agreement to renounce all or part of the profits of his benefice would at the very least be viewed with scepticism both by the Inland Revenue (now HM Revenue & Customs) and the court, and it is impossible to advise with confidence that an incumbent would escape liability to pay tax upon the notional income of the benefice. However, the position would be different, and tax would not be payable, if the income itself was not payable under some statutory provision.

4. Although section 33 of the Pastoral Measure 1983 provides a mechanism whereby certain income can be withheld from an incumbent, this power can only be used where there is continuing income from specified sources which income is 'sufficient to support' the incumbent. (Presumably, though the matter is not free from doubt, account may be taken, in assessing the sufficiency of the income, of other sources of income or capital which the incumbent is happy to rely upon.)

5. In the past, the particular problem over the appointment of NSMs as incumbents of some benefices arose from the entitlement of an incumbent under section 1 of the Endowments and Glebe Measure 1976 to a 'guaranteed annuity' of £1,000 or such lesser sum as represented the net annual endowment income (if any) immediately before 1 April 1978. However, these payments were abolished for all new appointments by the Stipends (Cessation of Special Payments) Measure 2005, and the legal obstacle preventing the appointment of an NSM to a benefices for which the 'guaranteed annuity' had been payable was therefore removed.

6. What was formerly described as 'augmentation' of stipend is made under section 5 of the Diocesan Stipends Funds Measure 1953 (as substituted by the 1976 Measure). Moneys in the income account of the Diocesan Stipends Fund are to be applied (inter alia) 'in providing or augmenting the stipends or other emoluments of incumbents' in accordance with directions given by the bishop or a person authorized by him with the concurrence of the DBF. It would be possible for the bishop to direct that no augmentation be made to the income of a 'non-stipendiary' incumbent.

7. There remain, despite the 2005 Measure, some subsidiary issues concerning the appointment of NSMs as incumbents. It might be that the

matter as a whole could best be clarified in the legislation following the Review of Clergy Terms of Service conducted in 2003 and 2004.

8. One of these issues is that the House of Bishops' Regulations referred to in paragraph 1 above envisage appointment under licence for a term of years, and are thus not apt for an incumbency.

9. In some cases, the incumbent of a benefice receives payments from local charitable trusts. If an NSM priest was to be appointed to such a benefice, the first question would be whether, depending on the circumstances, including the terms of the trusts, it was appropriate for him or her to receive the payments and, if not, whether the difficulty could be resolved in a way that was consistent with the trust instrument as it stood. Failing that, it would be necessary to consider the possibility of having the terms of the trusts altered, if necessary, by the Charity Commissioners.

10. The third subsidiary issue to which attention has been drawn concerns the incumbent's entitlement to occupy the parsonage house. The legislation dealing with the use of the parsonage house appears in the Pluralities Act 1838, which treats the requirement of occupation of the house of residence as a duty rather than a benefit. Section 33 of the Pluralities Act permits the bishop to grant a licence for the incumbent to reside in 'some fit and convenient house' if there is 'no house or no fit house of residence', while section 43 enables a similar licence to be granted permitting an incumbent who owns a 'mansion or messuage' within the parish to live in it. Reliance on these provisions within the Pluralities Act 1838 concerning licences for non-residence, ought to meet the case of a non-stipendiary minister who elects to live in his or her own accommodation. Housing arrangements are unlikely to be tainted by simony provided they are made for the convenience of the incumbent. The law concerning parsonage houses is not in itself an insuperable obstacle to the creation of a non-stipendiary incumbency; but legislation of the kind envisaged in paragraph 6 would doubtless substitute some straightforward arrangement with regard to housing for the technicality of the Pluralities Act 1838.

(July 2001, revised 2006)

Clergy: non-stipendiary ministers: licences

1. A non-stipendiary minister (NSM) should be licensed by name (and not office) 'as an assistant curate/priest/minister in the parish of . . .'. It would be contrary to Canon C 5 for an NSM to be licensed to the rural dean to serve his title on ordination. However, the Legal Advisory Commission's opinion is that if an NSM were to be licensed 'as an assistant curate in the parish of . . . for duties/ministry in the rural deanery of . . .' that would not be contrary to Canon C 5.

2. It is becoming increasingly common for clergy to be appointed, without stipend, as ministers in team ministries or in charge of benefices in suspension. In such cases, the Legal Advisory Commission's view is that the licence may read 'as team minister/minister in charge [as the case may be] of . . . . *without stipend* . . .' (editor's emphasis).

(*See also* **Clergy: non-stipendiary ministers: appointment as incumbents**)

(Revised August 2004)

Clergy: oath

Affirmation by clergy

1. Any person who objects to being sworn shall be permitted to make a solemn affirmation instead of taking an oath (Oaths Act 1978 s5). There is now an absolute right to affirm for any person in all places and for all purposes where an oath is or shall be required by law. As the canon law cannot be repugnant to the statute law, a member of the clergy may lawfully affirm rather than take the oaths required by the Canons.

Foreign nationals

2. Subject to section 2 of the Overseas and Other Clergy (Ministry and Ordination) Measure 1967 an ordinand or clergyman who is not a British national must take the Oath of Allegiance under Canon C 13 if he or she is to serve in the Provinces of Canterbury or York. If this causes difficulties in relation to the country of nationality, that is a matter for the ordinand or clergyman to sort out with the relevant embassy.

3. Any national of a foreign state living in the United Kingdom owes a duty of local allegiance to the Sovereign on the grounds that, by residing here, he is living under the protection of the British Crown: *Johnstone v Pedlar* [1921] 2 AC 262; *Falema'i v Att-Gen for New Zealand* [1983] 2 AC 20.

(1989)

Clergy: ordination: remarriage after divorce

1. Canon C 4 paras 3 and 3A provide as follows:

'3. Subject to paragraph 3A of this Canon no person shall be admitted into holy orders who has remarried and, the other party to that marriage being alive, has a former spouse still living; or who is married to a person who has previously been married and whose former spouse is still living.

3A. The archbishop of the province, on an application made to him by the bishop of a diocese on behalf of a person who by reason of paragraph 3 of this Canon could not otherwise be admitted to holy orders, may grant a faculty for the removal of the impediment imposed by that paragraph to the admission of that person into holy orders, and any request made to a bishop for an application to be made on his behalf under this paragraph shall be made and considered, and any application made by the bishop to the Archbishop shall be made and determined, in accordance with directions given from time to time by the Archbishops of Canterbury and York acting jointly.'

2. Canon C 4 was modified in 1991 (following the passing of the Clergy (Ordination) Measure 1990, which amended the Clergy (Ordination and Miscellaneous Provisions) Measure 1964 by substituting a new s9) to make it possible for a person who is divorced and remarried with a former spouse still living, or who is married to a divorced person with a former spouse still living, to be ordained where the Archbishop of the Province has granted his faculty for the removal of the impediment imposed by paragraph 3 of the Canon (see Canon C 4 para 3A). The Archbishops have issued revised Directions dated 9 May 2002 with regard to applications for faculties; a copy can be obtained from the Secretary to the House of Bishops.

3. In the Legal Advisory Commission's opinion a faculty is not required in the case of a person who has been married twice but both of whose marriages have ended in divorce, but that does not of course mean that the candidate's marital history should not be taken into account in assessing his or her suitability for ordination.

(April 1991, revised 2003)

Clergy: priest-in-charge

Description of priest-in-charge

1. The authority for a bishop to appoint a priest to be in charge of a vacant benefice is contained in Canon C 12 ('Of the Licensing of Ministers under Seal').

2. The expressions 'priest-in-charge' and 'curate-in-charge' are sometimes used to describe a minister so appointed. The former is more commonly used at present although there are many Acts, Measures and instruments which refer to 'curates-in-charge'. The word 'curate', however, can give a wrong impression, and in the opinion of the Legal Advisory Commission it would be desirable for the expression 'priest-in-charge' to be adopted, so far as practicable, for official use and in legal documents.

Status, rights and duties

3. A priest-in-charge is not an incumbent. Although appointed to a benefice a priest-in-charge is unbeneficed, with no 'parson's freehold' or property rights in parsonage house, church or churchyard. Frequently a priest-in-charge is authorized to live in the parsonage house, and if presentation to the living is suspended, the bishop may so require (see Pastoral Measure 1983, s68(4)). But in the absence of any such authority or requirement a priest-in-charge is neither entitled nor bound to live in the parsonage house.

4. A licensed priest-in-charge is within the definition of a 'minister' in the CRR, which is also referentially applicable to the Parochial Church Councils (Powers) Measure 1956 and the Churchwardens Measure 2001. As a result a priest-in-charge:

(a) is a member of the PCC and acts as its chairman;

(b) is entitled to attend and is the ex officio chairman of parochial church meetings, and meetings of parishioners for the appointment of churchwardens;

(c) has the same rights as an incumbent as regards the choice of churchwardens;

(d) has the same rights as an incumbent as regards the employment of a parish clerk or sexton or of a person to perform equivalent duties, and as regards the allocation of church collections (see s7 of the 1956 Measure);

(e)   is a member of the House of Clergy of the deanery synod (by virtue of being licensed to a parish in the deanery);

(f)   has a vote at elections to the Lower House of Convocation and to the House of Clergy of the diocesan synod, and is eligible for election.

5. As regards duties, the very fact that a priest-in-charge is appointed and licensed to a benefice seems to import a responsibility in pastoral matters, and for the maintenance of the services of the Church, comparable with that of an incumbent. Moreover many duties are specified in the rubrics of the BCP and in the Canons in terms which are apt to cover the case of a priest-in-charge. Such expressions as 'the minister', 'the curate' and 'the priest' which are frequently used in these contexts are, in the opinion of the Legal Advisory Commission, sufficient for the purpose.

6. An issue which has implications for the whole range of a priest-in-charge's powers and duties is whether a person licensed to the office of priest-in-charge has the 'cure of souls' within the benefice, as does an incumbent. There is no clear definition of the term 'cure of souls', either in legislation or in textbooks on ecclesiastical law (although there is an explanation in *Halsbury's Laws of England*, 4th edn, 1975, vol. 14, para 690). Moreover, the word 'cure' in the sense of 'care' is not in common use in modern times. However, the term 'cure of souls' is used in the Canons, and Canon C 24 lays certain obligations on a priest 'having a cure of souls'. When a bishop institutes an incumbent, and directs him to 'take this cure, which is both yours and mine', he is laying certain responsibilities towards the parishioners on the priest. It is clear that the purpose of licensing a priest-in-charge to a vacant benefice is to provide someone to discharge those responsibilities in the absence of an incumbent. Thus, in the Legal Advisory Commission's view, a priest-in-charge has the 'cure of souls', with the responsibilities this entails and the rights flowing from those responsibilities or needed in order to discharge them effectively, and the wording of licences to priests-in-charge make it clear that the cure of souls is being conferred (*see also* **Baptism: consent of parent**).

7. As regards rights, at the very least a priest-in-charge must by necessary implication be entitled to whatever rights and authorities are essential for the efficient performance of the duties of the office. But even if this is the true criterion (and the Legal Advisory Commission would be inclined to put the extent of his rights more widely), it would be a rather vague one, and difficult to apply to particular cases that might arise in practice. The following questions would arise:

(a)   Has a priest-in-charge the same general control of the church and churchyard as is enjoyed by an incumbent?

(b)   Has a priest-in-charge the legal custody of the keys of the church?

(c)   Has a priest-in-charge the same rights as an incumbent to decide, in conformity with the law, on the nature, form, frequency and times of church services?

(d)   Has a priest-in-charge the same right as an incumbent to decide the place in the churchyard in which a body is to be buried?

(e)   Has a priest-in-charge the same right as an incumbent to invite or permit other clergy to minister within the parish?

(f)   Should a priest-in-charge be a party to a sharing agreement under the Sharing of Church Buildings Act 1969?

8. The following points can be made about these questions:

(a)   The freehold of the church and churchyard is vested in an incumbent but not in a priest-in-charge. In the event of proceedings being necessary against a trespasser or any other person responsible for a civil wrong or criminal offence in the church or churchyard the proper plaintiff or prosecutor would be the incumbent. The priest-in-charge would not be able to initiate such proceedings, not having a proprietary interest in the church or churchyard, and a priest-in-charge cannot act in other respects as if he or she is a freeholder. Under the Open Spaces Act 1906 there is a scheme whereby an incumbent may convey the freehold (and fee simple) of a disused burial ground (churchyard) to a local authority so that the authority will thereafter be responsible for its maintenance. A priest-in-charge cannot invoke this scheme. Generally the priest-in-charge cannot be regarded as having any of the same rights and powers as the incumbent where the latter's position arises from the freehold.

(b)   An incumbent has property in the keys of the church. Subject to the right of churchwardens to have access, the incumbent controls entry into the church. Again this arises from the freehold. A priest-in-charge may have possession of the keys in order to carry out the duties of the office, but that possession does not symbolize any greater right to control the use of the

church than that of churchwardens, the PCC or the bishop (in their own spheres), and a priest-in-charge cannot exclude the bishop. However, the rights of even an incumbent in relation to the bishop are also subject to the bishop's rights, powers, duties and jurisdiction, as set out in Canon C 18 paragraphs 2 and 4. The incumbent's rights as against the archdeacon are likewise subject to the rights, powers, duties and jurisdiction of the archdeacon, as set out in Canon C 22.

The incumbent must hold services in the church and admit the congregation to them, but he can close the church at other times. The priest-in-charge does not have these wide powers. In practice an incumbent is most unlikely to use the powers in the way described and in practice a priest-in-charge may have a great measure of authority over the opening and closing of the church (and over the use of the churchyard) but the legal distinction remains.

(c)   Because of the provisions of section 1(3) and 5(2) of the Church of England (Worship and Doctrine) Measure 1974, and the provisions of Canons B 3, B 5 and B 20, which refer to the 'minister' or the 'minister having the cure of souls', a priest-in-charge is in the same position as an incumbent in relation to decisions as to the nature, form, frequency and timing of services in the parish, including control of the music and singing.

(d)   The designation by an incumbent of a burial plot is a consequence of freehold status. The priest-in-charge does not have the same degree of independence, but most co-operate with the churchwardens, the PCC and bishop in reaching any decision as to the place in the churchyard where a body is to be buried.

(e)   Under Canon C 8 a priest-in-charge has the same rights as the incumbent to invite or admit other clergy to minister within the parish or to exclude them.

(f)   A priest-in-charge should not be a party to a sharing agreement under the Sharing of Church Buildings Act 1969, as section 1 of that Act specifically refers to the 'incumbent', but a priest-in-charge should have an opportunity to be involved in the agreement as a member of the PCC and can be taken to have the same duties as an incumbent in relation to the operation of a sharing agreement.

9. Other similar questions could doubtless be devised. If any such questions were ever to come to a court for decision (which is perhaps unlikely) the tendency would be to approximate the rights of a priest-in-charge as nearly as possible to those of an incumbent wherever this was considered necessary for the effective performance of the duties of the office. During an interregnum conflict might arise between the functions of a minister-in-charge and those of the sequestrators.

Priest-in-charge responsible for more than one benefice

10. Paragraph 4 of Canon C 12, which provided that 'No stipendiary curate shall be licensed to serve in more than one church or chapel, except they be churches of one united benefice or held in plurality, or the chapel be dependent on the parish church', has been repealed by Amending Canon No. 19.

11. It is not uncommon for presentation to a benefice to be suspended, and for the incumbent of a neighbouring benefice to be appointed as priest-in-charge, in effect to enable an experiment to see whether a pastoral scheme for uniting two benefices or holding them in a formal plurality would work.

The service of licensing

12. Questions have been raised as to the form of service to be used at the licensing of a priest-in-charge. Congregations are familiar with the various acts which take place at the induction following the institution of an incumbent, and some feel that something is lacking when there has been a licensing without any further ceremony.

13. It must be emphasized that induction is a legal requirement when a new incumbent is admitted to a benefice but is not appropriate to the ceremony of licensing a priest-in-charge. Notwithstanding this, there is no legal objection to a short ceremony being performed following the licensing. Placing the priest-in-charge in the priest's stall in the church and tolling the bell to signify the start of a new ministry are symbolic acts which may appropriately be included. However, care should be taken that no words or actions are employed, such as placing the priest-in-charge's hand on the church door or handing over the keys, which would suggest that the priest-in-charge is being put into corporeal possession of the 'freehold'.

Faculty proceedings and churchyard monuments

14. A priest-in-charge is included within the definition of 'minister' in section 31(1) of the Care of Churches and Ecclesiastical Jurisdiction Measure 1991 and consequently has the right under section 16(1)(b) of the same Measure to institute faculty proceedings, together with the churchwardens.

15. As regards monuments in churchyards:

(a) The position is that, in law, the erection of any such monument requires a faculty. But by long standing custom an incumbent of a parish is assumed to have delegated authority from the diocesan chancellor to sanction the erection, without a faculty, of a monument over a grave. (In most dioceses the chancellor has issued rules as to the sort of monuments which may be sanctioned, and the incumbent must of course, in exercising the delegated authority, comply with these rules.)

(b) Whether a priest-in-charge has such authority depends on how far the diocesan chancellor has expressly delegated it to priests-in-charge in the diocese. However, a parishioner who was unaware of a churchyard regulation or a practice direction of the diocesan chancellor on the extent of the delegated authority of a priest-in-charge might reasonably assume that a priest-in-charge did have the necessary delegated authority to sanction the erection of a gravestone or other monument. It follows that in the Legal Advisory Commission's view this is a matter for action by the chancellors in their several dioceses. For instance any chancellor could publish a practice direction or churchyard regulations to the effect that every priest-in-charge, as regards any parish in his or her care, should henceforth have the same authority in faculty matters as if he were the incumbent. It is understood that in some dioceses this has already been done. Alternatively a chancellor who did not do this could take steps to ensure that parishioners knew that during a vacancy they must apply to the rural dean, if that was the relevant office-holder specified in the regulations.

16. There are certain actions which a priest-in-charge, as opposed to an incumbent, cannot take even pursuant to a faculty, for example, granting a licence for a right of way over the churchyard or for the use of the crypt of the church by a third party, as a priest-in-charge has no legal or equitable interest in the church and churchyard (see *Re St Mary, Aldermary* [1985] Fam 101).

Parochial charities

17. Section 74 of the Pastoral Measure 1983 provides that where any property of a charity established for ecclesiastical purposes is vested in the incumbent of a benefice (with or without other persons) and where, during a suspension period, a priest-in-charge has been appointed, the trusts of the charity shall have effect with the substitution for the incumbent of that benefice of the priest-in-charge of that benefice. However, section 74 does not apply to non-ecclesiastical charities, nor to charities whose property is vested in a corporate trustee other than the incumbent.

(*See also* **Clergy: assistant curates**)

(October 1996, revised 2003)

Clergy: residence by incumbent

1. It is the duty of an incumbent to reside within his or her parish, and if there is a house of residence to inhabit it unless the bishop has licensed the incumbent to reside elsewhere. An incumbent who is absent without such licence for more than three months in any year is liable to certain penalties, and residence may be enforced by sequestration of the benefice. If the benefice remains sequestered for a whole year or is twice sequestered in any year, it becomes void without further formality unless otherwise directed by the bishop. An appeal lies to the Archbishop against the refusal of a licence or the revocation of an existing licence. An incumbent who is also a member of a cathedral or collegiate body may reckon residence at the latter as equivalent to residence in the parish provided that he or she is not absent from his parish for more than five months altogether in any calendar year. (See the Pluralities Act 1838, ss32–58.)

2. When a house of residence is erected, purchased or improved under the Parsonages Measures 1938 and 1947, or where a house or residence is divided into parts, the bishop may certify the house or part (as the case may be) to be the residence house of the benefice.

3. Subject to the provisions of the Incumbents (Vacation of Benefices) Measures 1977 and 1993, the bishop may give to an incumbent, reported to him as unable to discharge his or her duties, leave of absence for a period not exceeding two years (1977 Measure, s11(2)(c)).

(Revised 1984)

Clergy: revocation of licences

General principles

1. The scope for revocation of licences was curtailed by section 8(2) of the Clergy Discipline Measure 2003. Where a minister is licensed by the bishop to serve in a diocese, the licence may not be terminated by reason of that person's misconduct otherwise than by way of disciplinary proceedings under the Measure; but this does not apply to deaconesses, readers and lay workers, nor (as the Measure does not apply) where the grounds of the revocation are misconduct involving matters of doctrine, ritual or ceremonial. What follows is subject to that provision.

2. When a bishop has granted a licence to a minister in Holy Orders to serve within his diocese under Canon C 12 para 1, it may be summarily revoked by the bishop under para 5 of the same Canon for any cause which appears to him to be good and reasonable. The bishop must explain the reasons for the revocation as well as giving the minister sufficient opportunity of showing reason to the contrary before the licence is revoked; the bishop should normally offer the minister a meeting at which the bishop can explain his reasons and the minister can respond. The revocation must be by notice in writing, which must inform the minister of his or her right to appeal to the Archbishop of the Province within 28 days from the date of receipt of the notice. Substantially the same provisions apply to deaconesses under Canon D 3, to readers under Canon E 6 and to licensed lay workers under Canon E 8.

3. Under paragraph 6 of Canon C 12, when a bishop has granted a licence to a minister to serve within his diocese for a term of years, the licence does not terminate automatically when the term expires. The bishop may give notice in writing to the minister before the end of the term, requesting him or her to vacate the office concerned when the term expires, and the licence will then come to an end on the expiration of the term. If the bishop does not give such a notice, the minister may continue in office after the end of the term, but may subsequently be given three months' notice in writing by the bishop requesting him or her to vacate the office concerned.

4. Where a minister's licence is granted for an indefinite period, as opposed to a fixed term of years, the bishop may withdraw it on reasonable notice unless the licence itself provides to the contrary. What period of notice is reasonable will depend on all the circumstances of the particular case. No appeal lies against the revocation of a licence on reasonable notice. However, a licence granted for a fixed period may not be revoked on this basis unless the licence provides for that possibility.

5. A minister in Holy Orders may also cease to hold a preferment to which he or she is licensed, as a result of proceedings under the Clergy Discipline Measure 2003 leading to a penalty of removal from office (or, in the case of matters of doctrine ritual or ceremonial, the Ecclesiastical Jurisdiction Measure 1963) or, in the case of a member of the clergy licensed by a bishop to serve in his diocese, revocation of the licence. (This may be coupled with prohibition from exercising the functions of his Orders, either permanently or for a limited period.)

6. Subject to paragraph 11 below, no form of compensation is payable in any of these situations.

Team ministries

7. Special provisions apply in the case of team ministries. Paragraph 6 of Canon C 12, explained in paragraph 3 above, does not apply to members of team ministries. The licences of members of team ministries (other than the team rector who does not serve under a licence) cannot be revoked summarily. Given that, under section 20(3B) of the Pastoral Measure 1983 as amended by the Team and Group Ministries Measure 1995, a member of a team must serve for a term of years, the possibility of revocation on reasonable notice will also not normally arise.

8. Under section 20 of the Pastoral Measure 1983, a vicar in a team ministry is appointed to that office by licence of the bishop and holds it for a term of years (fixed in accordance with the provisions of the Measure) but has the same security of tenure during the term as an incumbent of a benefice. Thus the team vicar cannot be removed from office except as a result of proceedings under the Clergy Discipline Measure 2003 (or the Ecclesiastical Jurisdiction Measure 1963) or under the provisions on pastoral breakdown or on incapacity as a result of age of infirmity in the Incumbents (Vacation of Benefices) Measures 1977 and 1993. (A team rector who holds office for a term of years has the same security of tenure during the term; however, the team rector, as incumbent, is not appointed by licence from the bishop, but is presented and collated to the benefice.)

9. Section 20(3A) of the 1983 Measure, inserted by the Team and Group Ministries Measure 1995, provides that a person ordained to the office of deacon who is authorized by the bishop's licence to serve as a member of a team (other than a team rector or team vicar) and to perform, so far as consistent with the office of deacon, all such offices and services as may be performed by an incumbent for the purposes of the team ministry, shall serve for a term of years (fixed in accordance with the provisions of the Measure) but, during that term, also has the same security of tenure as an

incumbent. The deacon may be removed from office as a result of proceedings under the Clergy Discipline Measure 2003 (or the Ecclesiastical Jurisdiction Measure 1963). However, under section 7(1A) of the Church of England (Legal Aid and Miscellaneous Provisions) Measure 1988, also inserted by the 1995 Measure, the licence of a deacon to whom section 20(3A) applies may not be revoked unless the bishop is satisfied either that there has been a serious breakdown of the pastoral relationship (construed in accordance with the Vacation of Benefices legislation) between the deacon and the parishioners concerned, or that the deacon is unable to discharge his or her pastoral duties adequately by reason of age of infirmity.

Contracts of employment

10. In certain circumstances a minister who holds the bishop's licence may also have a contract of employment either with a church body (normally the DBF) or with a secular employer. In particular, an ordained or lay person engaged as a sector minister will normally be an employee. Where there is such a contract of employment the termination of the contract may give rise to a claim for breach of contract or unfair dismissal in the secular courts if the dismissal was wrongful or unfair or, in appropriate circumstances, to a claim for redundancy pay. It is considered that where the continuance of the employment is to be dependent on the continuance of the licence it is important to spell that out at the outset in the particulars of employment, so as to help avoid a successful claim for unfair dismissal if the employment is terminated following the termination of the licence. Likewise, if the continuance of the employment is to be an essential condition of the continuance of the licence, it is considered desirable for the licence itself to include a provision to that effect.

(2006)

Clergy: women bishops of churches in communion with the Church of England: effect of acts

1. The Commission was asked by the House of Bishops' Working Party on Women in the Episcopate to give an Opinion on the legal aspects of the issues regarding the recognition of women bishops and ordinations and confirmations carried out by them. These issues were addressed in the Presidential Statement made by Archbishop Runcie in November 1988. The relevant part of that Statement is reproduced as an Annex to this Opinion. The Statement was made after the General Synod had failed to give approval to the draft Women Ordained Abroad Measure which would have permitted women ordained priests elsewhere than in England to be given permission to officiate in the Province of Canterbury or York. At the time that draft Measure was considered, and at that time of the Archbishop's Statement, women could not be ordained priest in England as has been possible since 1994.

2. Archbishop Runcie's Statement is principally concerned with the question whether the non-recognition of the ministry of a woman bishop was compatible with the relationship of communion existing between the Church of England and the Church in which she served. He touched on the legal issues in the following passage:

'In this case [of ordination by a woman bishop] it is clear enough that women priests so ordained would be unable to minister as priests within the Church of England. But it has been put to me that the same might not be the case for men ordained by a woman bishop. It might be argued that, on a strict interpretation of the [Overseas and Other Clergy (Ministry and Ordination) Measure 1967], they could be licensed simply because the Archbishops of Canterbury and York can give this permission to male clergy episcopally ordained overseas or in a Church in communion with the Church of England. I do not, however, think that I can accept and act upon such a theologically paradoxical understanding of the Measure because, as I have already indicated, the real grounds for archiepiscopal permission do not seem to be simply ordination within a Church in communion, since precisely the same permission may be given to clergy ordained in Churches not in communion. The implied ground is surely the recognition of orders. The other interpretation would involve the theological absurdity of being able to recognise and accept the ministry of male priests or deacons but not the ministry of the woman bishop who ordained them.'

Legal principles

3. A legal analysis of the issues addressed in this Opinion must begin with a recognition that the facts have connections with more than one system of ecclesiastical law, those of England and of the other relevant Church or Province. That means that the cases fall within that branch of law known as the Conflict of Laws. This deploys techniques devised especially to deal with cases which have foreign fact-elements. The techniques are used to determine which system of law most appropriately governs a particular issue. This entails a recognition that any rule of law (statutory or not, ecclesiastical or secular) has a spatial limitation. So, the English definition of a crime applies only to acts taking place in England, in the absence of an explicit provision to the contrary. A well-known example in another context is the rule in what is now section 2 of the Marriage Act 1949, which provides 'A marriage solemnized between persons either of whom is under the age of sixteen shall be void'. This is not read literally: if the parties have their domicile (roughly, permanent home) outside England and the marriage is celebrated abroad lawfully according to the law of that country, the marriage will be regarded as valid in England despite the express words of section 2. The courts have to examine the functional context of a rule: in effect 'persons' in this section of the 1949 Act is given a more restrictive meaning than it would bear in other contexts, even in the same Act.

4. In the case of the issues examined in this Opinion, it seems appropriate using these techniques to advance two propositions: the first is that the validity of any ecclesiastical act is governed by the law of the ecclesiastical jurisdiction in which it was done; the second, that the exercise of ecclesiastical functions is governed by the law of the ecclesiastical jurisdiction in which they are to be exercised. The rules of English law must be interpreted in the light of these principles.

The 1967 Measure

5. Many of the legal issues that have been raised concern the Overseas and Other Clergy (Ministry and Ordination) Measure 1967. It must be interpreted in the light of the principles set out above. The Measure deals with

    (a)   the performance of episcopal functions in England by 'overseas bishops';

    (b)   the performance in England of episcopal functions by other bishops 'consecrated in a Church not in communion with the Church of England whose Orders are recognised and accepted by the Church of England';

(c)   the grant of permission to 'overseas clergymen' to officiate as deacon or priest in England;

(d)   the grant of similar permission to any person episcopally ordained priest or deacon in a Church not in communion with the Church of England whose Orders are recognized and accepted by the Church of England; and

(e)   ordinations in England at the request of an 'overseas bishop'.

It does not apply to clergy from other Anglican Provinces in the British Isles. The effect of a grant of permission is that the priest or deacon concerned can exercise his or her orders as if ordained in the Church of England, and in so doing is subject to the rules and obligations applying to all other clergy so ordained.

6. 'Overseas bishop' is defined (s6(1)) to mean

'a bishop of the Church of England or a Church in Communion with the Church of England having a diocese or office elsewhere than in the province of Canterbury, the province of York, Ireland, Wales or Scotland.'

7. 'Overseas clergyman' is defined in the same sub-section to mean

'a clergyman who has been ordained priest or deacon by an overseas bishop or under section 5 of this Measure [which enables an English bishop to ordain at the request of an overseas bishop].'

8. The 'strict interpretation' to which Archbishop Runcie referred is presumably the simple argument that a male priest is a 'clergyman' and a woman bishop in another Anglican Province falls within the definition of 'overseas bishop'. On the plain meaning of the words, that is clearly correct; but there are other considerations, and an earlier legal Opinion (though not of the Commission itself) addressed analogous issues.

9. The Opinion was given in 1976 by the then Dean of the Arches (Sir Harold Kent), the then Provincial Registrar of Canterbury and the then Solicitor to the General Synod. This addressed the question of women ordained priest in overseas provinces. The authors noted that the Interpretation Act 1889 (now the Interpretation Act 1978) provided that words importing the masculine gender include the feminine gender unless the contrary intention exists. On the ground that no woman could be a priest in England, the authors rejected the suggestion that the masculine term 'clergyman' in the Overseas and Other Clergy (Ministry and

Ordination) Measure 1967 could be read as including the feminine: a contrary intention did exist.

10. Since that Opinion was issued, it has become possible for women to be ordained to the priesthood in England, but the masculine language of the 1967 Measure has not been amended. 'Clergyman' in the 1967 Measure is now assumed to refer to both men and women: the original 'contrary intention' has dissolved. This illustrates a principle of statutory interpretation under which an Act or a Measure can be regarded as 'always speaking': if it is designed to deal with practical issues, its interpretation is 'ongoing' and must reflect current circumstances and is not fixed by reference to the circumstances existing when it was first enacted.

11. In the cases with which this present Opinion deals, the principal issue concerns the definition of 'overseas bishop', not that of 'clergyman'. Given that there are no women bishops in the Church of England, it is possible to construct an argument as to the meaning to be given to the term 'overseas bishop' which parallels that advanced in the 1976 Opinion.

12. In considering this, it is important to examine more closely the various provisions in the 1967 Measure which concern 'overseas bishops':

Ordinations in England at the request of an overseas woman bishop

13. Section 5 deals with the case in which an overseas bishop requests a bishop in the Province of Canterbury or York to ordain a named person as priest or deacon with a view to that person exercising his or her ministry in the overseas diocese. The ordination is necessarily by a male bishop, and the candidate may be male or female. The overseas bishop is acting in his or her official capacity but is not the minister of ordination. The request is an ecclesiastical act done under the law of the woman bishop's own jurisdiction, and she is to exercise no function in England. There seems therefore to be no reason to give the term 'overseas bishop' in section 5 anything other than its natural meaning, which would include a woman. It follows that a bishop of a diocese in England *may* under section 5 accede to a request from a woman bishop. He is not obliged to do so.

Performance of episcopal functions in England by an overseas woman bishop

14. Section 4 enables an 'overseas bishop', subject to certain approvals and consents, to perform episcopal functions in England. This is the case most clearly analogous to the matters considered in the 1976 Opinion, and the argument accepted in that Opinion would indicate that a woman

bishop could not be given permission so to act. The exercise of episcopal functions in England must be governed wholly by English law.

15. It is this question, of the performance of episcopal functions in England, which is the subject of the first question formulated on behalf of the House of Bishops' Working Party:

> If it is desired that a woman bishop from another Anglican Province (other than Scotland, Wales and Ireland) should perform episcopal functions in the Church of England under section 4 of the Overseas and Other Clergy (Ministry and Ordination) Measure 1967, what constraints, if any, are placed upon such performance by section 6(2) of the Measure where the Archbishops of Canterbury and York would appear to have power to determine conclusively whether a Church is in communion with the Church of England or whether the Orders of any Church are recognized and accepted by the Church of England?

16. Section 6(2) provides as follows:

> 'If any question arises whether, for the purposes of this Measure, a Church is in Communion with the Church of England or whether the Orders of any Church are recognised and accepted by the Church of England, it shall be determined by the Archbishops of Canterbury and York, whose decision shall be conclusive.'

17. Despite its heading, which refers to 'overseas bishops', section 4 deals with two different cases,

(a)   the performance of episcopal functions in England by 'overseas bishops', who are bishops in a Church in Communion with the Church of England; and

(b)   the performance in England of episcopal functions by other bishops 'consecrated in a Church not in communion with the Church of England whose Orders are recognised and accepted by the Church of England'.

18. Section 6(2) also deals with both cases, enabling the Archbishops to determine conclusively the issues of Communion with the Church of England (relevant to case *a*) and of the Orders of a Church being recognized and accepted (relevant to case *b*). It is only case *a* that is relevant to the question posed by the House of Bishops' Working Party. The answer to that question must be that section 6(2) places no *additional* constraint on the performance by a woman overseas bishop of episcopal

functions in England. It follows from the argument advanced in paragraph 14 above, that the Archbishops could not grant permission, but that arises independently of section 6(2).

19. Were the Archbishops to declare that a particular member Church or extra-provincial diocese of the Anglican Communion was not in communion with the Church of England – and the issue must be answered in those terms, not by reference to any individual – then the woman bishop concerned would cease to be an 'overseas bishop' within the Measure. She might claim, in those circumstances to be a bishop 'consecrated in a Church *not* in communion with the Church of England whose Orders are recognised and accepted by the Church of England' and so fall within case *b* above. Again the Archbishops could rule whether the Orders of the Church in which she was consecrated – and again it is a question of the Orders of a Church not an individual – were or were not 'recognised and accepted' (the Commission would take that phrase as a whole, and not distinguish between 'recognition' and 'acceptance'). But for the reason already given, permission under section 4 could not be given.

Deacons and priests ordained by overseas bishops

20. The questions from the House of Bishops' Working Party include a number relevant to this case. The first is as follows:

> What bearing if any does section 6(2) have on the application of the Measure to priests ordained by a woman bishop from another Province (other than Scotland, Wales and Ireland)?

21. Section 1 of the 1967 Measure regulates the position of deacons and priests ordained by 'overseas bishops'. As has already been stated, whether a woman bishop is an 'overseas bishop' for the purposes of the Measure depends on whether her Church is in Communion with the Church of England, and section 6(2) enables the two Archbishops to rule on that question. If it is assumed that the Province concerned is in Communion with the Church of England, section 6(2) has no further significance. The more important issue concerns the principles developed in this Opinion as to the proper field of application of the canon law of different Provinces. In this context, the relevant function of the overseas bishop in that context is the act of ordination, carried out in her own jurisdiction under the Canons of the relevant Province. She exercises no functions in England. The validity of the ordination is therefore a matter for the law of the overseas Province.

22. It follows that permission may as a matter of law properly be given in such cases under section 1 of the Measure. The giving of permission is a

matter of discretion, though the manner in which that discretion has been exercised hitherto is principally concerned with the suitability of the priest or deacon. Any exercise of discretion must give proper weight to the sensitivities of the relevant issues, but were the discretion under section 1 to be exercised in a way which questioned the validity of the ordination, it is arguable that would be open to challenge as seeking to apply English law to an issue properly governed by the law of another Province.

23. It might be argued that English ecclesiastical law is relevant to the recognition of an overseas bishop's orders; this is close to Archbishop Runcie's theological approach. However, as he observed:

> 'In [the 1967] Measure there is an implicit assumption, correct at the time of its being passed, that the orders of clergy of overseas Anglican provinces were indeed recognised by the Church of England. This is made clear by the explicitly stated ground for the granting of archiepiscopal permission to minister for clergy ordained in Churches not in communion with the Church of England: namely, that their orders are recognised and accepted by the Church of England.'

24. He is contrasting the language used in the definition of 'overseas bishop' with that in section 3 of the Act. It is only in section 3, dealing with those episcopally ordained in churches *not* in communion with the Church of England, that a requirement of recognition of orders is included. See also paragraph 1 of Canon C 1 which does not draw the same distinction and paragraph 5 of Canon C 8 which (in the directly relevant context) does. So far as the Measure is concerned, the natural meaning of the words in the definition of 'overseas bishop' is that the term includes any bishop of another Anglican Province or of another Church in communion with the Church of England. In other words it assumes that in these cases the validity of orders is a matter for the canon law of the Province or Church in which they were conferred.

25. The second question from the House of Bishops' Working Party relevant to this issue is:

> Was the Statement to the General Synod in 1988 by Archbishop Runcie a statement of policy at that time, before the ordination of women had been decided in the Church of England, rather than a determination of recognition of orders under section 6(2) of the Overseas Clergy Measure?

26. In the Commission's view, neither description of the Statement is correct. It is clear from its opening words that Archbishop Runcie was

addressing issues of ecclesiastical law and not of policy. In part, Archbishop Runcie was relying on a legal Opinion which cannot be relied upon in the changed circumstances of today. As has already been explained, in the context of the acts of 'overseas bishops' the question of Orders being 'recognised and accepted' does not arise. The Statement was less than clear on the relationship between the two issues of Communion and the validity of the acts of a woman bishop as the minister of ordination. The South India example used in the Statement does not assist, for the priests concerned were not ordained by a bishop, and on that ground did not satisfy the requirements of section 1 of the Measure. The principles developed in this Opinion were not considered, and it is the view of the Commission that the Statement cannot now be relied upon.

27. The third question from the House of Bishops' Working Party relevant to this issue is:

> What bearing, if any, does section 1 of the Priests (Ordination of Women) Measure 1993 have on any exercise of recognition by the Archbishops under section 6(2) of the Overseas Clergy Measure?

28. The Commission has already explained that since promulgation of Canon C 4B under the 1993 Measure, permission has been granted to women ordained in overseas Provinces despite the 1976 Opinion. Where permission is given under the 1967 Measure, Resolution A or B under the Priests (Ordination of Women) Measure 1993 may limit the scope of the ministry a woman priest may exercise. It is difficult to answer the question as posed: the 1993 measure is part of the background to the whole set of issues but has had no direct bearing apart from the points just noted.

29. On the general issue of priests ordained abroad, the approach adopted in this Opinion makes it easier to deal with some fact-situations which otherwise present further difficulties:

(a) A man is ordained deacon by a woman bishop and priest by a male bishop;

(b) A man is ordained deacon by a male bishop and priest by a male bishop; one or both ordinations is by a bishop who is either a suffragan or assistant bishop commissioned by a woman bishop or a bishop acting under letters dimissory from a woman bishop; cf. section 4(2) of the 1967 Measure, deeming a person ordained by an overseas bishop *in England* on the request and by the commission in writing of an English bishop to have been ordained by the bishop making the request.

(c)   A man is ordained at an ordination presided over by a woman bishop but another, male, bishop joins in the laying on of hands and the accompanying words. It is not clear whether letters of orders would necessarily make this participation clear, or indeed the gender of the bishops.

In all these cases, the validity of the ordination will fall to be assessed by reference solely to the law of the ecclesiastical jurisdiction in which it takes place.

30. To summarize, the position in law appears to differ from that set out in 1988 by Archbishop Runcie. The validity of ordinations carried out under the canon law of a Province of the Anglican Communion or of another Church in communion with the Church of England is treated by the 1967 Measure as a matter for that law, and the assumption is that those ordinations are valid. A bishop acting under that law is an 'overseas bishop' under the Measure, whether male or female. However, there are reasons – in legal terms, of public policy – under which this approach cannot be followed in the case of section 4 of the Measure, so that a woman bishop cannot be permitted to exercise episcopal functions in England.

Women bishops in Scotland, Ireland or Wales

31. The House of Bishops' Working Party asks a number of questions concerning the possibility of women bishops in the other Anglican Provinces in the British Isles. There is no reason why the legal principles set out in paragraph 4 of this Opinion should not apply equally as between the different Anglican Provinces in the British Isles. The first question posed by the Working Party in this context is:

What legal constraints, if any, are there upon any eventual women bishops in the Episcopal Church of Scotland functioning episcopally in the Church of England, or from the Church in Wales should it change its legislation to allow for the provision of women bishops?

32. A woman bishop, were there to be any, of the Episcopal Church of Scotland, the Church of Ireland or the Church in Wales would not be an 'overseas bishop' for the purposes of the 1967 Measure, which therefore would have no application. There is therefore no question of the consent of the relevant Archbishop being required were such a bishop to be asked to 'function episcopally' in England. The phrase appears to mean ordain or confirm, and it is clear from the Canons that these acts are within the control of the bishop of the diocese. It would be misconduct for a woman

bishop to act without the diocesan bishop's authority, and the application of the principle expounded in this Opinion suggests that the diocesan bishop could not lawfully invite a woman bishop to act.

33. The second question on this issue is:

> Does the Episcopal Church (Scotland) Act 1864 give an English Diocesan absolute discretion to institute to a benefice, or licence, a priest ordained by a Scottish woman bishop, or to refuse to do so?

34. Section 5 of the 1864 Act seems, consistently with the approach taken above, to assume the validity of ordinations carried out in Scotland and Ireland under the ecclesiastical law of the churches there. Section 5 does appear to give the bishop wider powers of *refusal* than are available to him under Canon C 10 paragraph 3 in the case of priests ordained in England. Despite the emphatic language of the statutory provision, the courts might entertain an application for judicial review were the bishop to act in an obviously unreasonable way. The bishop's power to institute or licence is in other respects governed by the normal rules; section 5 does not add to those powers.

35. The third question on this issue is:

> Does the Episcopal Church (Scotland) Act 1964 give an English Incumbent (or equivalent) absolute discretion to invite a priest ordained by a Scottish woman bishop to officiate without consent of the bishop? Could this apply to a bishop ordained in Scotland in terms of Episcopal functions such as Confirmation or Ordination?

36. Section 1(1) of the Episcopal Church (Scotland) Act 1964 has the effect of enabling a priest ordained in Scotland to be invited to officiate in England under Canon C 8 para 2 on the same terms as one ordained in England. So the short answer to the first part of the question is 'yes'. An incumbent cannot authorize services of confirmation or ordination, so this provision cannot have the effect envisaged in the second part of the question. An Opinion prepared by a former Dean of the Arches (the Revd Kenneth Elphinstone) and others addressed this legislation in the context of women priests. It is mainly of historical interest, but the view expressed by Sir Harold Kent and quoted at paragraph 7 of that Opinion shows a functional analysis being used to give an interpretation of the clear words of the 1964 Act to restrict their meaning, so giving effect to the public policy considerations prevailing at that time concerning the exercise of ministry by women.

The Lambeth Conference

37. Finally, the House of Bishops' Working Party asks:

> Do invitations to the Lambeth Conference by the Archbishop of Canterbury (with or without conditions) have any formal bearing on legal recognition of Episcopal or other ministry?

The Lambeth Conference is not mentioned in any relevant legislation or in the Canons. Given that the question whether a Church's Orders are recognized and accepted by the Church of England for the purposes of the Overseas Clergy Measure is a matter for the two Archbishops acting jointly, the acts of one Archbishop cannot have any binding effect in that context. However, invitation to the Conference by the Archbishop of Canterbury is of very great symbolic significance to those concerned; and the approach taken by Archbishop Carey in relation to women bishops in 1998 (when women bishops were invited to the Conference, but were asked not to undertake any Episcopal functions during their stay in the Province of Canterbury) illustrates the policy underlying the legal analysis set out in this Opinion.

(May 2004)

Annex

Extract from the *Report of Proceedings, Monday 7 November 1988.*

PRESIDENTIAL STATEMENT

by the Archbishop of Canterbury (Dr R A K Runcie).

I now turn for the moment to my second question: Do we recognise a woman bishop? This brings me to speak of ecclesiastical law. But before that, a necessary disclaimer. To state what the official position of the Church of England currently appears to be – that is, to speak of the formal position in ecclesiastical law – is not to make a final judgement on the theology of women priests or bishops. Still less is it to deny the spiritual fruitfulness of the ministry of a woman bishop or priest. In a divided Church we have long since learned to acknowledge the gifts of grace given through ministries that Anglicans cannot yet regard as juridically interchangeable with their own. This must be borne in mind in all that now follows.

The Synod will need no reminding that it is necessary to change the ecclesiastical law if the orders of women priests are to be accepted. By declining to pass the Women Ordained Abroad Measure the General Synod maintained the bar on women priests ministering in the Church of England under the terms of the Overseas Clergy Measure. In that Measure there is an implicit assumption, correct at the time of its being passed, that the orders of clergy of overseas Anglican provinces were indeed recognised by the Church of England. This is made clear by the explicitly stated ground for the granting of archiepiscopal permission to minister for clergy ordained in Churches not in communion with the Church of England: namely, that their orders are recognised and accepted by the Church of England. I believe that this principle is important in interpreting the present official position.

The 1967 Measure also makes provision for the two archbishops, with the concurrence of the bishop of the diocese, to give their consent and licence for bishops consecrated in other provinces, or Churches in communion, to perform episcopal functions within the Church of England. But as with priests, so with bishops: the implication of the legislation is that their orders are accepted by the Church of England. This is again made explicit for bishops consecrated by Churches not in communion, where the ground for the archiepiscopal licence is the recognition and acceptance of their episcopal orders by the Church of England. I have laboured this point because of complications which may follow when we come to the question of those ordained by a woman bishop.

In this case it is clear enough that women priests so ordained would be unable to minister as priests within the Church of England. But it has been put to me that the same might not be the case for men ordained by a woman bishop. It might be argued that, on a strict interpretation of the 1967 Measure, they could be licensed simply because the Archbishops of Canterbury and York can give this permission to male clergy episcopally ordained overseas or in a Church in communion with the Church of England. I do not, however, think that I can accept and act upon such a theologically paradoxical understanding of the Measure because, as I have already indicated, the real grounds for archiepiscopal permission do not seem to be simply ordination within a Church in communion, since precisely the same permission may be given to clergy ordained in Churches not in communion. The implied ground is surely the recognition of orders. The other interpretation would involve the theological absurdity of being able to recognise and accept the ministry of male priests or deacons but not the ministry of the woman bishop who ordained them.

But is the non-recognition of the ministry of a woman bishop, as the law now stands, incompatible with our communion with the Episcopal Church? It certainly places restrictions on our communion but surely does not render us out of communion.

I have already given reasons for my mistrust of an over-simplistic understanding of being either in or out of communion. Ecumenical experience furnishes an interesting analogy with the present situation, we are in communion with the Church of South India, yet this makes no difference in ecclesiastical law to the question of the few remaining non-episcopally ordained presbyters; they could not minister in the Church of England under the Overseas Clergy Measure, but we do not go on to say that we are not in communion. On this analogy, our communion with the Church in the United States remains – although there are restrictions on communion brought about by our different practices regarding the ordination of women.

I ought finally to say something about those confirmed by a woman bishop. Here at least I can be simple and brief. Though confirmation is important, canon law clearly states that admission to communion is to be given to those who are episcopally confirmed, or ready and desirous to be confirmed. It surely cannot be in doubt that those who have been confirmed by a woman bishop are in such a state. We can affirm this about those confirmed by a woman bishop without implying the recognition of the episcopal ministry of the woman bishop.

As I see the position, it seems clear enough that the Church of England does not canonically accept the ministry of either women priests or bishops of other Churches, unless and until the ecclesiastical law is changed specifically to allow this or to allow the Church of England itself to ordain women to the orders of priest or bishop. Nor are we able to accept clergy ordained by a woman bishop as long as her episcopate is not officially accepted. Nevertheless, this by no means destroys all communion. There are many shared holy things which maintain our communion, and we must also recognise that there is still an official recognition and acceptance of the major part of the orders of the American Church. If we do not share the richness of communion that we once did, we still share much more than we presently do with our Catholic, Orthodox and Protestant ecumenical partners, where no ministry is yet officially interchangeable.

Whatever the differences, I hope that neither we nor the other provinces that ordain women to the episcopate will forget all those things which continue to unite us as well as the profound experience of communion in the One Lord that we experienced at the Lambeth Conference. With the assistance of the Eames Commission I hope that we shall now begin to work out the painful but honest relationship between our provinces, not only in faithfulness to where our Churches actually are in the matter of the ordination of women but also in faithfulness to each other's experience of the living tradition of the One Church of Jesus Christ.

Part 3
Parish

Parish: annual parochial church meeting

Failure of minister to convene

1. If the minister or other person appointed by rule 7 of the CRR fails to convene the annual parochial church meeting (APCM), such failure should be reported to the bishop by the rural dean under rule 53(5), and the bishop may appoint someone else to carry out the duty under rule 53(1)(b). Under the general powers conferred on him by rule 53 the bishop may also in cases of difficulty give directions as to elections.

Business of APCM

2. The business of the APCM is governed by rule 9 of the CRR.

(a) Electoral roll: The meeting cannot amend the revised roll but it can discuss it under rule 9(1)(a) and can make recommendations to the PCC under rule 9(7).

(b) Discussion of accounts: The meeting is entitled to discuss the accounts, to comment on them and to make such recommendations as it thinks fit to the PCC. It can give or withhold approval (r9(3)). The meeting cannot alter the past but has every right to make proposals for the future.

(c) Election to deanery synod by reference to office: A person cannot be elected by reference to his or her office. Accordingly if an APCM elects e.g. churchwardens ex officio to be members of the deanery synod for three years, the persons who were actually churchwardens at the time of the election should be considered elected and remain members of that synod, even though they have ceased to be churchwardens.

(d) Failure to elect to deanery synod: The failure of the meeting to elect representatives to the deanery synod does not invalidate the election of representatives to the PCC.

(e) Confirmation of minutes: In order to have any evidential value minutes of a previous meeting should either be circulated prior to the next meeting or be read at such meeting and their confirmation recorded. Unless confirmed they are merely a record of the secretary's views as to what passed at the meeting to which such minutes relate.

Notice of raising of major matters of principle

3. The question sometimes arises whether a decision by an APCM to require, say, two weeks' notice of the raising of major matters of principle should be considered as a legitimate rule of procedure under rule 9(7) of the CRR or as adversely affecting the rights given by rule 9(6). In the Legal Advisory Commission's Opinion a reasonable interpretation of rules 9(6) and 9(7) would be as follows:

(a)   an APCM cannot bind a future parochial church meeting by any rule of procedure made under rule 9(7);

(b)   an APCM cannot refuse to allow a matter to be raised under rule 9(6) on the ground that no notice (or insufficient notice) has been given;

(c)   if, however, after preliminary consideration of the matter, the meeting decides that it cannot satisfactorily be disposed of there and then, it may be justified in taking one of the following courses:

(i)   adjourning with a view to further discussion after a suitable interval;

(ii)   closing the discussion and suggesting that recourse be had to the provisions of rules 22 or 23 concerning special and extraordinary meetings; or

(iii)   in appropriate cases, closing the discussion and advising that the matter be placed on the agenda for the next APCM, possibly with a recommendation that it be considered in the meantime by the PCC.

(Revised 2003)

Parish: annual parochial church meeting – elections

Non-communicant candidate

1. The chairman of the APCM has the right to ask any candidate for election to the PCC whether he or she is an actual communicant. If the answer is 'yes', no further question can properly be put by the chairman. If the answer 'yes' is challenged by anyone else the onus of proof is on the objector.

2. A candidate who answers 'no' or refuses to answer cannot be elected. In the case of dispute, any appeal will be dealt with in accordance with rule 44 of the CRR.

3. A non-communicant who has been elected to a PCC should be asked whether he or she is a communicant, but cannot be compelled to reply. Anyone replying in the negative should be informed that any vote which he or she gives will be disallowed. The incumbent should endeavour to persuade a person in this position to retire from the PCC.

Nominations at elections by APCM

4. Rule 11(2) of the CRR cannot be altered by resolution of the APCM or the PCC so as to make nominations which would otherwise fall within the sub-rule invalid. For example:

(a) an incumbent is not justified in declining to accept nominations for election to the PCC, made at the APCM, on the ground that notice had been given that all nominations must be made in writing prior to the meeting; and

(b) the following resolution framed by a PCC is invalid: 'That all candidates at elections of lay representatives by the Annual Meeting shall be nominated and seconded in writing on the special forms provided by the purpose, and that no nominations shall be accepted which are not delivered to the secretary of the PCC at least three clear days before the date of the Annual Meeting.'

Mode of publication of the results of elections to PCC

5. The requirements of rule 11(9) of the CRR are satisfied by the announcement of the names of the candidates elected and affixing notices giving that information. If the presiding officer is asked by the person interested for the number of votes secured by any candidates, the

presiding officer should give the information, and there is no reason why such information should not be published.

Failure to elect deanery synod representative

6. The failure of an APCM to elect representatives to the deanery synod under rule 9(4) of the CRR does not invalidate the constitution of the PCC. The omission can be dealt with under rule 53(1)(b) and in the meantime the proceedings of the PCC cannot be invalidated on account of any vacancy in its membership (r53(3)).

(Revised 1997)

Parish: attendance at church meetings: public and press

1. Unless the matter is regulated by law or by a body's terms of reference, each body is free to decide for itself whether its proceedings are to be public or private.

2. The proceedings of the General Synod are usually open to the public, but the Business Committee of the General Synod chooses to conduct its proceedings in private. The Archbishops' Council also chooses to hold its meetings in private.

3. A PCC may decide for itself which to do. A PCC has to perform some functions which are at a lower level akin to proceedings of General Synod and other functions which are akin to the confidential deliberations of the Archbishops' Council.

4. If a PCC decides to open its meetings to non-members it must decide whether to restrict attendance to persons whose names are entered on the electoral roll or to admit the public generally. In either event it should be made clear to non-members that they have no right to speak (without permission) or to vote.

5. A PCC cannot bind its successors. Its decision can be changed by a later PCC or by the same PCC at a later meeting.

6. The Public Bodies (Admission to Meetings) Act 1960 applies only to the authorities specified in the Schedule to that Act, which do not include PCCs. Consequently the press has no right to attend PCC meetings unless expressly authorized by the PCC itself.

7. The position on all the above matters is the same for deanery and diocesan synods.

8. The parochial meeting for the purpose of choosing churchwardens must consist of:

(a)   persons whose names are entered on the church electoral roll of the parish, and

(b)   persons resident in the parish whose names are entered on a register of local government electors by reason of such residence (Churchwardens Measure 2001 s5(1)).

No reference is made in the measure to members of the public other than those referred to in (a) and (b), so they may only attend with permission of the meeting.

If a representative of the press comes within categories (a) or (b) he or she is entitled to attend the meeting, but is not entitled to report the proceedings except with the permission of the meeting.

Annual Parochial Church Meeting (APCM)

9. Under rule 6(2) of the CRR 'All lay persons whose names are entered on the [church electoral] roll of the parish shall be entitled to attend the annual meeting and to take part in its proceedings, and no other lay person shall be so entitled.'

(Revised 2003)

Parish: archdeacon's visitation: replies to articles of enquiry

1. It has long been customary for an archdeacon to carry out annual visitations of the parishes in his or her archdeaconry. To this end, the archdeacon is authorized to deliver to the incumbent or priest-in-charge and to the churchwardens articles of enquiry relating to the administration of the parish, the state of the church buildings, the arrangements made for services, and the life and health of the parish generally. These articles must be answered by the incumbent and churchwardens in their presentments which they are to frame 'advisedly and truly according to their consciences' (Canon G 6 para 2). Moreover the churchwardens, as the bishop's officers, are also under a duty to report on any matters which are amiss or irregular in the parish or about which they feel the archdeacon should be made aware. This remains a continuous duty throughout their tenure of office and is not limited to the archdeacon's visitation. The incumbent may join with the churchwardens in making such complaints or may make such complaints personally.

2. Although these presentments will normally be concerned with the factual state of the parish, they may also include sensitive material e.g. complaints by the incumbent or churchwardens about each other's conduct or complaints about individual parishioners.

3. The information included in these presentments is not intended to be restricted to the archdeacon, as the whole object of the exercise is to enable the archdeacon to become aware of the situation in the parish and to act accordingly. The archdeacon may feel obliged to communicate such information to others – to the bishop, the chancellor, the diocesan pastoral committee, the DBF and so on, and may also feel obliged to take other action in the light of the information, e.g. by calling a meeting of the PCC or by presenting a petition for a faculty for the removal of something unlawfully put into a church.

4. While a person can seek an injunction to restrain a breach of confidential relationships by the disclosure of material supplied in confidence, there cannot in the Legal Advisory Commission's view be any question of confidentiality regarding these communications from the minister and churchwardens to the archdeacon such as to give rise to such a remedy in the event of the archdeacon making use of the information received as both the minister and the churchwardens are under a duty to make such presentments. Indeed it would be quite wrong for the archdeacon to agree not to disclose the information provided in this way. Moreover, it would not, in the Legal Advisory Commission's Opinion, make any difference if the presentments were marked 'confidential'.

5. The archdeacon is under a duty only to make proper use of such information and if the archdeacon improperly or maliciously discloses the information to a newspaper or to someone wholly unconnected with the subject matter, then it may be that the archdeacon could be made the subject of disciplinary proceedings.

6. If an aggrieved party sought to sue the incumbent, churchwardens or the archdeacon for libel in respect of these presentments or their subsequent disclosure, then the incumbent and churchwardens would have a defence on the ground that they had a common interest in communicating the material to the archdeacon, unless of course there was express malice on their part. So far as the archdeacon was concerned, there would likewise be a defence on the basis of the common interest between the archdeacon and the person to whom the information was communicated, though, once again, express malice could defeat the defence if available. If the incumbent or churchwardens disclosed their presentments to others or if the archdeacon disclosed such material to persons who were not in the class of those referred to above, the position might be very different.

7. The incumbent and churchwardens are under a duty to include in their presentments information received by them from third parties provided that such information could properly be included even though the information was disclosed to them by the third party 'in confidence'.

8. It follows from this analysis that the archdeacon, having ordinary jurisdiction throughout the archdeaconry as well as duties allocated from time to time by the bishop and others, should probably be regarded as a 'data controller' for the purposes of the Data Protection Act 1998. Whether strictly required to do so or not, the archdeacon should register with the Information Commissioner in the usual way. While the matter is not wholly free from doubt (and in some dioceses it is the practice to treat the archdeacon as a 'data processor' for the purposes of the Act, with the handling of data strictly controlled by the diocesan or area bishop with whom the archdeacon works) the advantage of registering is that the archdeacon can specify his or her purposes as widely as necessary and then do everything so specified.

9. Be that as it may, what is beyond doubt is that the archdeacon must comply with the requirements of the 1998 Act in respect of any material kept by him or her as mentioned in this Opinion. Thus any personal data included in the presentments must be held, kept and used by him or her in accordance with the eight Data Protection Principles. The archdeacon should ensure, as a matter of good practice as well as law, that the minister and churchwardens are made aware of how any personal data included in

their replies to the articles of enquiry will be used. While the consent of the data subject is not generally required where personal data is processed in pursuance of a legal obligation, the position is not always straightforward in the case of material which falls within the term 'sensitive personal data' in the 1998 Act. This includes information relating to an individual's religious beliefs, racial or ethnic origin, political opinions, physical or mental health or sexual life, or the commission or alleged commission by him or her of an offence. Advice should be sought on all these matters from the diocesan registrar.

10. This Opinion refers expressly to an archdeacon's visitation, but the same principles apply generally to a visitation by the bishop to either a parish or the cathedral church.

(October 1986, revised December 2003)

Parish: bishop's visitation

In the Legal Advisory Commission's Opinion, a diocesan bishop may go into any parish in his diocese and exercise his episcopal ministry there. This principle, which is of general application, is subject to any arrangements as regards oversight made under the Episcopal Ministry Act of Synod 1993.

(April 1994)

Parish: collections

Alms at Holy Communion

1. Money given at services of Holy Communion, whether according to the BCP or Common Worship, forms part of the general funds of the PCC and must be disposed of in accordance with section 7(iv) of the Parochial Church Councils (Powers) Measure 1956. The rubric placed at the end of the service in the BCP is no longer binding as a result of the change in the law effected by the Church of England (Legal Aid and Miscellaneous Provisions) Measure 1988, section 13 and Canon B 17A.

Collections at institutions, inductions and confirmations

2. The bishop has the right to say whether or not there shall be a collection at any service he conducts but, if there is a collection, strictly its destination rests with the incumbent and PCC in accordance with section 7(iv) of the Parochial Church Councils (Powers) Measure 1956.

Collections at other services

3. The purposes to which collections at other services are to be allocated are to be determined by the PCC jointly with the incumbent, and in case of disagreement the bishop may give directions (see s7(iv) of the Parochial Church Councils (Powers) Measure 1956). The PCC must keep accounts of all moneys so collected. The treasurer or treasurers of the PCC are the responsible officers for this purpose.

4. The churchwardens are the proper officers to make and receive the collection, either alone or with the aid of the sidesmen or other persons selected by them, and, where they are not themselves the treasurers, they hold the money as agents for the incumbent and the PCC until handed over to the PCC treasurer or other authorized person.

Money placed in alms boxes

5. Canon F 10 provides that alms placed in the alms box (which should be provided in every parochial church and chapel) are to be applied to such uses as the incumbent and PCC think fit, and if they disagree the Ordinary (usually the bishop) is to determine how the alms are to be disposed of.

(Revised 2003)

Parish: Easter offering and Easter collection

1. The payment known as the Easter offering was one which certain incumbents claimed the right to demand at common law, amounting to a penny (unless a larger sum was traditionally paid) per household within the parish. It is believed to be no longer demanded and to have fallen into desuetude.

2. The voluntary collection made on Easter Day was originally intended to supplement the stipend which an incumbent received from other sources. It may still be given to him, if the PCC so decides: the congregation should normally be informed before the collection is made. If it is given to the incumbent it will be taken into account in calculating his income for the purposes of determining his augmentation grant. The collection will thus not benefit him directly, but will increase the funds generally available for the payment of stipends in the diocese.

3. Both the Easter offering (where paid) and the Easter collection are held to be profits of office and are taxable, even though the collection is voluntary and made as a gift.

(April 1986)

Parish: electoral roll

1. The Church Representation Rules (CRR) require that a Church Electoral Roll is prepared for every parish. It is a roll of names of laity only, and a clerk in Holy Orders (including a retired clerk) may not be entered on the roll. The qualifications for a lay person's name being included on the roll are set out in Rule 1. A lay person may have his or her name entered on the roll of more than one parish if he/she is entitled by the terms of qualification in the Rules.

Residence

2. What amounts to residence is in each case a question of fact and degree, from which it follows that there must be many borderline cases.

3. A person may have more than one residence if he or she has more than one residence which is of some permanence and can be described as a regular abode or home. For example a person may have a residence with his or her parents and also a residence at the term time address where he or she is a student and resides during the university or college term. Similarly a person who has a second home e.g. living in London at the same address during the week may be treated as having a residence at the home out of London and at the regular abode in London. In this context a hotel or bed and breakfast accommodation would not be usually regarded as a London home but a room with facilities where possessions are left from week to week would be.

4. When a person is thus qualified to be a resident elector, members of that person's household ordinarily living with the elector are similarly qualified.

Qualification by residence

5. It is to be noted that the requirement of habitual attendance at public worship in the parish does not apply to electors on the Civil Register of Electors who are qualified by residence; consequently the name of a parochial elector so qualified cannot be removed from the roll upon the ground of failure to attend public worship in the parish. But in such a case it would be reasonable to suggest to the elector withdrawal from the roll.

Addition or removal of names

6. Names can be added to or removed from a roll by or under the direction of the PCC at any time except during the closed period indicated in rule 2(3). The addition or removal takes immediate effect.

Data Protection Act 1998 and copyright

7. The CRR provide for the roll to be exhibited annually for at least fourteen days (when either a new roll is drawn up or an existing roll is revised) and for it to be made available for inspection by bona fide enquirers (rr1 and 2). There is no requirement to be registered under the Data Protection Act 1998 where the sole purpose of processing is the maintenance of a public register. Data Protection Act 1988 section 17(4). Most PCCs will be exempt from registration anyway (under the Data Protection (Notification and Notification Fee) Regulations 2000, Sch, para 5).

8. Similarly, under the Data Protection Act 1998 section 34 the information in the roll is exempt from the subject information provisions, the fourth data protection principle (accuracy), sections 14(1)–(3) (rectification, blocking, erasure and destruction); and the non-disclosure provisions. Because the roll is in practice a public document, any member of the general public may ask the incumbent, the secretary to the PCC or the electoral roll officer to see a copy of it.

9. However, if any further information is kept beyond what is required for the roll, e.g. telephone numbers, then the Data Protection Act 1998 section 34 does not apply to that information. In practice therefore PCCs should confine the electoral roll to the information strictly required by the CRR, i.e. names and addresses: see rule 1(1) and 1(11); any further information about electors should be kept elsewhere.

10. Copyright exists in an electoral roll as it is a table or compilation within the terms of the Copyright, Designs and Patents Act 1988 (s3(1)). It is a matter for the PCC to decide whether a copy of the roll should be supplied to a third party for purposes other than those of the CRR. The electoral roll officer acts under the direction of the PCC and the PCC is entitled to charge a fee for the supply of a copy.

(January 1986, revised 2003)

Parish: legacies affected by pastoral reorganization or redundancy of a church

1. Legacies may be affected where, before the testator dies, one of the following situations arises:

(a)   The church, for the repair and maintenance of which the legacy was to be applied, is declared redundant;

(b)   The legacy is expressed to be for repair and maintenance of 'the parish church of the parish of X' and, at the time of the testator's death, the parish has no parish church;

(c)   The legacy names a particular PCC, or is otherwise expressed to be for the benefit of a particular parish, and that parish has been merged with another parish, or divided between two or more other parishes.

2. It is equally possible that the situations described above could arise after the testator's death.

Summary

3. If pastoral reorganization or the redundancy of the church occurs after the testator's death, it is likely that the provisions of the Pastoral Measure 1983 will ensure that the underlying object of the gift is preserved.

4. If, however, pastoral reorganization or the redundancy of the church takes effect before the date of the testator's death, the provisions of the Pastoral Measure will not apply and, in the absence of some suitable clause in the will, the executors will need to apply to the Charity Commissioners for a cy-pres scheme, assuming that a general charitable intention can be demonstrated.

Pastoral Measure 1983

5. The Pastoral Measure 1983 contains provisions which can usefully be applied here, but only where the testator has died *before* the pastoral reorganization or redundancy has occurred.

6. Section 40 of the 1983 Measure provides that Schedule 3 to that Measure shall have effect with regard to schemes which create new parishes, or which dissolve or alter the areas of existing parishes.

7. Paragraph 11(5) of Schedule 3 provides that in the case of a union of

parishes or where the area of a parish is altered, and property is held by reference to one of the constituent parishes or to the parish affected by the alteration, the trusts of the charity shall (subject to any scheme of the Charity Commissioners) have effect with the substitution of the parish created by the union, or the parish as altered.

8. Paragraph 11(6) of Schedule 3 allows the Charity Commissioners to make cy-pres schemes (see below) in cases affected by pastoral reorganization on the application of the DBF.

9. Paragraph 11(8) of Schedule 3 provides that so far as not dealt with by the foregoing provisions of paragraph 11, property vested in or held on behalf of a PCC which ceases to exist is to vest in or be held on behalf of the PCC of the parish in which the parish church of the dissolved parish is situated 'for the like purposes, as nearly as may be, as those for which it was previously applicable in the hands of the first mentioned council'. Paragraph 11(8) also provides that any question arising as to the application of any such property or the income from it shall be determined by the diocesan bishop.

10. Where a church that has been declared redundant:

(a)   is vested in the DBF during the, so called, 'waiting period' or on terms specified in a redundancy scheme; or

(b)   becomes vested in the Church Conservation Trust (formerly the Redundant Churches Fund); or

(c)   is vested in the Church Commissioners or the DBF for a use (which usually leads to a disposal);

section 63(1) of the 1983 Measure provides that funds which were available for the repair and maintenance of the building continue to be available for that purpose but, in the last mentioned case, only if the scheme so provides. However, where the church is being disposed of, a cy-pres scheme (see below) may be more appropriate. Section 63(2) provides that where the churchyard, or part of the churchyard, is also vested in the DBF or the Churches Conservation Trust, any property of a charity applicable for the maintenance of the churchyard shall continue to be so available, but in the case of part only of the churchyard being so vested then only if and to the extent that the scheme so provides. By virtue of section 63(3) the provisions of sections 63(1) and 63(2) do not affect the powers of the Charity Commissioners to make cy-pres schemes, and section 63(3) provides that those powers may also be exercised in these cases on the application of the DBF.

Cy-pres schemes

11. In cases where the testator dies *after* the pastoral reorganization or redundancy has occurred, it appears that, in the absence of some express provision in the will, application will need to be made to the Charity Commissioners for a cy-pres scheme, under section 13 of the Charities Act 1993.

12. Section 13 provides that application for a cy-pres scheme may be made where, inter alia:

(a)   the original purposes of the gift cannot be carried out, in whole or in part, or not according to the directions given;

(b)   the property available can be more effectively used in conjunction with other property;

(c)   the original purposes of the gift were laid down by reference to an area which was then a unit for other purposes, but which has ceased to be such a unit; or

(d)   the original purposes have ceased to be suitable and effective, regard being had to the spirit of the gift.

13. However, it is important to bear in mind that for a gift to be saved through the application of the cy-pres doctrine, a general charitable intention must have been shown on the face of the will. It is a matter of construction to be determined in each case whether the dominant intention of the testator was the specific purposes which has failed or a wider charitable purpose (see *Re Spence's Will Trusts, Ogden v Shackleton and Others* [1979] Ch 483). If the gift fails, it will fall into residue or, if it was a residuary gift, the property will pass as on an intestacy.

Provisions in the will

14. It is always open to a testator to make express provision in the will for what is to happen in a situation where the object of the gift is frustrated through supervening events.

15. There is a published precedent for a gift over in the case of failure, to a named alternative charity (*Encyclopaedia of Forms and Precedents*, 5th edn, 1998 Re-issue, vol. 42(1), precedent 451).

16. It is also possible for the testator to confer on his executors and trustees special powers to declare the trusts for the use and application of

that part of his estate which he or she wishes to leave to charity. Again there is a published precedent, though it is not particularly helpful in this context (see *Encyclopaedia of Forms and Precedents*, vol. 42(1), precedent 503).

17. Equally it appears possible for a testator to provide in his will for his executors to select another charity or charities, in keeping with the general charitable intention of the original gift. However, this could give rise to difficulties in:

(a)   defining the circumstances in which the original gift would be deemed to have failed; and

(b)   defining the scope of the executors' choice.

There is now a published precedent (*Encyclopaedia of Forms and Precedents*, vol. 42(1), precedent 452), directing the testator's trustees to substitute another charitable institution if a charity or charitable organization named in the will has never existed or has ceased to exist before the testator's death, and in certain other circumstances. The precedent includes the possibility for the testator of expressing a wish, but without imposing any binding obligation, that the gift should go to an institution whose purposes are 'as close as possible' to those of the charity named in the will. However, this is not altogether appropriate where, for example, the gift was intended for the upkeep of a particular church which has been declared redundant.

18. Given the wide variety of circumstances in which the need to include some 'alternative' provision in the will may arise, it is impractical to provide a perfect precedent. However, depending on the circumstances and the wording of the will, something on the following lines *may* be appropriate:

> 'If at the date of my death [the said church of . . . . has been declared redundant] [the said ecclesiastical parish of . . . . has been merged with another parish or divided between two or more other parishes] the gift contained in clause of this my will shall have effect with the substitution for [the said church/the repair and maintenance of the said church] [the said parish] of such other ecclesiastical charitable purposes as my executors/trustees shall in their absolute discretion select.'

(*Encyclopaedia of Forms and Precedents*, 5th edn, 2000 Re-issue, vol. 13(2)) contains a precedent (precedent 107) along these lines for use with a gift to a PCC.)

19. Alternatively, instead of a gift for the repair and maintenance of a particular church, the testator may wish to consider a legacy to the PCC for its general purposes, coupled with a wish that the money should be used for the upkeep of a named church, though expressly without creating any binding trust or obligation in that respect. (In *Re Broadbent* [2001] EWCA Civ 714 where a gift by will was on similar lines, the Court of Appeal held that it took effect in favour of the trustees of a mission church even though the church building had been sold before the testator's death.)

20. In each case it will be for the solicitors preparing the will to be satisfied that they have correctly interpreted their client's instructions, and have advised the testator as to the most appropriate wording to give effect to his or her wishes if the original purpose fails in some way.

21. Information as to the status of and proper description for a particular church, and as to whether redundancy or pastoral reorganization are being contemplated, will usually be available from the diocesan registrar or the diocesan secretary.

(November 1994, revised 2003)

Parish: organist and choirmaster and church musicians

General

1. Canon B 20 was amended in 1988. References here to the organist include the choirmaster and other church musicians.

2. The incumbent must pay due heed to the advice and assistance of the organist or choirmaster in the choosing of chants, hymns, anthems or other settings and in the ordering of the music of the church. However, the final responsibility and decision in these matters rests with the incumbent (Canon B 20 para 2).

Appointment

3. Appointment is by the incumbent, with the agreement of the PCC (Canon B 20 para 1).

4. It is essential in every instance that the appointment should be subject to an agreement in writing signed by the contracting parties. A precedent form of agreement is published by the Royal School of Church Music. Oral arrangements must be avoided. The agreement should always include:

(a)   the names of the parties making and accepting the appointment;

(b)   the date on which it begins;

(c)   the amount of the salary (if any) and when it is payable; and

(d)   the length of notice required to be given by either the incumbent or the organist to terminate the appointment by mutual agreement.

The agreement may also cover other points referred to below.

Termination

5. Termination is by the incumbent with the agreement of the PCC, except that if the archdeacon considers that the circumstances are such that the requirement as to the agreement of the PCC should be dispensed with the archdeacon may direct accordingly (Canon B 20 para 1). The PCC's agreement was introduced as a requirement in 1988 to prohibit 'shot-gun' dismissals or summary dismissal by the incumbent acting solely on his or her own initiative.

6. Where the incumbent is of the opinion that there cannot be a proper discussion or 'fair' hearing of the matter in the PCC then the incumbent may ask the archdeacon to consider dispensing with the PCC's agreement. The circumstances which the General Synod had in mind included where there is a dispute concerning the choir and many members of the choir are also members of the PCC, or where an improper relationship has developed and for the sake of avoiding scandal it is desirable that one person only, i.e. the archdeacon, and not a group of persons, i.e. the PCC, should be consulted.

Duties of the organist

7. It is the duty of the organist:

(a)   to devote his or her best efforts towards securing a devout and appropriate rendering of the musical portions of the church services so far as the means available permit;

(b)   to recognize the authority of the incumbent in all matters relating to the conduct of the service, including what parts are to be said and sung respectively and the amount of musical elaboration suited to the needs of the congregation;

(c)   to play the organ at all the chief services on Sunday and the Great Festivals as defined in the terms of the appointment;

(d)   to play the organ at such services on the Lesser Festivals and weekdays as the organist's agreement with the incumbent requires; and

(e)   to assist the choirmaster at choir practice, if the offices be distinct.

Duties of the organist, if also choirmaster

8. If the organist be also choirmaster the duties include:

(a)   the training of the choir;

(b)   the conduct of suitable practices at least once a week; and

(c)   generally, the advancement of the interests of the choir as a whole.

9. It should be noted that none may be admitted to or dismissed from the choir save with the approval of the incumbent.

Parish

Holidays

10. The agreement should make provision for holidays during which the organist should be required to find a deputy, to be paid, if payment be required, by the PCC. If the organist is absent on other occasions in the year, apart from illness, the organist must find and make personally an appropriate payment to a deputy approved by the incumbent. If the organist is absent through illness the organist should find a deputy approved by the incumbent, and the deputy's remuneration, if any, must be approved by the organist.

Use of the organ

11. The use of the organ should not be granted to anybody save the organist, or a deputy in case of holiday or illness, except by joint permission of the incumbent, the PCC and the organist.

12. The use of the organ should be granted to the organist for the purposes of:

(a)   the organist's own private practice;

(b)   the practice of the organist's friends; and

(c)   the instruction of the organist's pupils.

13. For these purposes, if the mechanism of the organ is by hand, the remuneration of the blower must be defrayed by the organist. If the blowing apparatus is electric or hydraulic the organist may be required by agreement to refund to the PCC, which is responsible for this cost, a fixed proportion thereof.

Use of the organ at weddings, funerals and other services

14. The use of the organ at weddings, funerals and other services of a similar character is subject to the approval of the incumbent. If approval is given, the organist has the right to play and to be paid the customary fee by those who desire its use. If the organist does not wish to perform these duties on any such occasion then another organist, chosen with the approval of the incumbent and the organist, may play; and the fees receivable on such occasions should be fixed and paid by agreement between the parties. If for private reasons those for whom the service is held desire that the organ shall be played by a relative or friend, the normal fee will be due to the organist of the church.

Children

15. For the purposes of the provisions of the Children and Young Persons Acts 1933 and 1963 and any byelaws made under them relating to the employment of children, a chorister taking part in a religious service, or in a choir practice for a religious service, shall not, whether the chorister receives any reward or not, be deemed to be employed (Children and Young Persons Act 1933, s30(1)).

16. It is of fundamental importance that, before being appointed, all organists and choirmasters whose duties give them the opportunity for contact with children or vulnerable adults should be asked to apply for a Criminal Records Bureau disclosure at the appropriate level. Each diocese has established a procedure for carrying out these checks, and for conducting risk assessments where necessary. The PCC should comply with its own parish child protection policy and seek guidance from the Diocesan Child Protection Adviser as needed. Failure to carry out such checks, and to put in place reasonable steps to manage any risk, could expose the PCC to legal liability if a child or vulnerable adult is harmed.

(Revised 2003)

Parish: parish clerk and sexton

1. By the Parochial Church Councils (Powers) Measure 1956, section 7(iii), the power to appoint and dismiss the parish clerk and sexton and to determine their salaries and the conditions of their tenure of office or employment is vested jointly in the incumbent and the PCC. These offices are the subject of a contract of service between the parish clerk or sexton on the one hand and the PCC and the incumbent on the other, and the ordinary law as to contracts of service applies.

2. The office of parish clerk may be held by a layman or by a person in Holy Orders. The office of sexton or clerk may be held by a woman.

3. Occasionally the situation arises where a parish officer seeks election to the PCC. Although there is nothing in law to prevent the election, the disadvantages of having a paid servant sitting on the body which is the employer must be obvious.

(*See also* **Parochial Church Council; Parochial Church Council: legal position of members**)

(Revised 1997)

Parish: provision of flowers under charitable trust

1. A gift made to a DBF for the purpose of providing flowers for a chancel and altar is a good charitable trust.

2. In the case of *Elphinstone v Purchas* (1870) LR 3 A & E 66 at 106, it was held by Sir R Phillimore, in the Arches Court, that there was nothing unlawful in a 'profuse decoration' of the altar with flowers. He described them as an 'innocent and not unseemly' adornment of the church and as analogous to the 'holly at Christmas and willow-blossom on Palm Sunday with which our churches have very generally been adorned'.

3. There appears to be no difference in principle between a weekly renewal of flowers and an annual renewal of whitewash; both are matters of reasonable and proper expenditure upon the upkeep and maintenance of the church as a place of worship. All decorations are perishable, more or less, and a permanent endowment for the provision periodically of that particular lawful decoration which needs the most frequent renewal appeals to be not less 'charitable' than one for the provision of other adjuncts to worship, upon which expenditure would fall to be made at longer intervals. In the case of *Turner v Ogden* (1787) 1 Co Eq Cas 316, a bequest for keeping 'the chimes' in repair was held to be charitable: that was a purpose analogous to the provision of flowers, because neither chimes nor flowers are necessary, though both are legal and each requires the periodical expenditure of money.

(1994)

Parish: verger

1. The name 'verger' is derived from one who carries the verge, or mace, before a dignitary. Today his or her mace-bearing duties are few and the verger's main duties are to care for the interior fabric of the church.

2. Occasionally the situation arises where the verger or other parish officers seek election to the PCC. Although there is nothing in law to prevent their election the disadvantages of having a paid servant sitting on the body which is the employer must be obvious.

(*See also* **Parochial Church Council: legal position of members**)

(1997)

Parish: visitation: inspection of parochial documents

A visitation of a parish by a rural dean is made only as agent for and on behalf of the archdeacon or the bishop (see Canon C 22). Such visitation is made primarily to the clergy and churchwardens and sidesmen of the parish and not to the PCC, and although the visitor has a right to inspect documents in the rightful custody of the clergy and churchwardens there is no authority for extending that right to documents in the custody of the PCC or of any other body. However, production of the minutes of the PCC can be insisted on if the rural dean has been so authorized by the bishop or archdeacon (CRR App II, para 12(d)).

(1997)

Part 4
Conventional Districts

Conventional districts

1. Where a large new population grows up, for example as a result of a housing scheme, the question may arise of making special provision for its spiritual oversight without forming, or (more often) as a preliminary to the formation of, a new parish. One method of doing this is to constitute the area a 'conventional district', by means of an agreement between the bishop and the incumbent or incumbents of the parish or parishes concerned. By such an agreement the area is taken out of the incumbent's charge and placed under that of a separate 'curate in charge', who is licensed by the bishop, has the cure of souls of the district, and is given by his or her licence a degree of independence in ministering to its population and building up the work towards its legal separation.

2. Since the status of the district rests upon agreement only, the legal position of the parishioners remains unaffected, and they remain parishioners of the parish of which the area where they reside forms part. Their rights and obligations as to marriage, burial and attendance at their parish church and so forth remain unaltered. So far as marriages are concerned, the bishop may license the place of worship of the conventional district under section 20 of the Marriage Act 1949, but this does not take away the parishioners' right to be married in the parish church.

3. The area as a whole is, however, able to organize itself as a distinct parochial unit. In particular, for the purposes of the CRR, 'parish' is defined as meaning:

> '(a)   an ecclesiastical parish; and

> (b)   a district which is constituted a "conventional district" for the cure of souls' (CRR r44(1)).'

4. Thus a conventional district should have its own church electoral roll and PCC. Those who reside in the district or who have habitually attended public worship there for the period stipulated by the CRR are entitled to have their names entered on the church electoral roll of the district.

5. In addition, the Legal Advisory Commission is of the opinion that a resident in the district is entitled to be enrolled on the church electoral roll of the ecclesiastical parish of which the district forms part, even if he or she worships only within the district. This is because the CRR do not show any clear intention to deprive those resident in the district, whether they approved of its formation or not, of their rights as residents of the ecclesiastical parish.

6. While an agreement for the formation of a conventional district may strictly bind only the individual parties to it and requires to be renewed on any change of incumbent, such renewal is, in the absence of any steps to renounce it, ordinarily assumed. In some cases a greater degree of stability is sought by joining the patron or patrons in the agreement.

7. Section 2A of the Pastoral Measure 1983 (inserted by the Synodical Government (Amendment) Measure 2003, s2(1), (2)) places a duty on the pastoral committee of a diocese from time to time as may be directed by the bishop, and in any event at least once every five years, to review the arrangements for pastoral supervision in each conventional district in the diocese and, in cases where they consider it desirable, to make recommendations to the bishop for action under the Measure.

(*See also* **Baptism; Conventional districts: building project by parochial church council**)

(Revised 1988 and 2006)

Conventional districts: building project by parochial church council

1. This Opinion is concerned with issues which arise when the PCC of a conventional district wishes to carry out a building project within its district. In particular, what is the position, especially in relation to the PCC of the parish out of which the conventional district was created, should the conventional district cease to exist?

2. Conventional districts are created by agreement between the bishop and the incumbent or incumbents of the parish or parishes concerned; the status of the district rests upon the agreement only. As the agreement binds only the parties, a new incumbent received the cure of souls of the whole parish, and takes free of the agreement, which must be renewed if the conventional district is to continue. Although such renewal is, in the absence of any steps to renounce it, ordinarily assumed, difficulties could arise were the new incumbent to express uncertainty and delay renewal; it is unclear how long the period of hesitation may be, i.e. for how long the assumption of continuance can be maintained. It is arguable whether, where two or more parishes are involved, the arrival of a new incumbent in one party, Parish A, affects the position as between the bishop and the other incumbent, of Parish B. If the new incumbent of Parish A were to renounce the agreement, it is doubtful whether that part of the conventional district carved out of Parish B would retain its status. If so (or if, to avoid any doubt, a fresh agreement to that effect were entered into between the bishop and the incumbent of Parish B) it is an unresolved question whether it would be the same district with altered boundaries, or a new district.

3. A conventional district is a 'parish' for the purposes of the CRR (see rule 54(1)), and so should have a PCC. That council will have the status and powers conferred by the Parochial Church Councils (Powers) Measure 1956; the term 'parish' in that Measure has the same meaning as in the CRR (1956 Measure, s1).

4. The PCC of a conventional district can hold property in the same way as any other PCC (1956 Measure, s5). Were the district to disappear, a range of issues would arise, including issues as to church and parochial trusts and other property. Where a *parish* disappears, there are relevant provisions on all these matters in Schedule 3 to the Pastoral Measure 1983. However, a conventional district is expressly excluded from the meaning of 'parish' for the purposes of that Measure (see s86(1)), and none of the provisions of Schedule 3 can have any application.

5. Were a conventional district to come to an end (let it be assumed on a positive act of renunciation, to use the term in paragraph 6 of the Opinion on **Conventional districts**, though denunciation might be better, by the new incumbent), there would no longer be a 'parish' for the purposes of the CRR. The provisions in the CRR as to a church electoral roll, the election of representatives, and the working of the PCC will all cease to be operative.

6. It is, however, unclear whether the PCC of the conventional district actually ceases to exist in law. Section 3 of the Parochial Church Councils (Powers) Measure 1956 renders every PCC, including the PCC of a conventional district, a body corporate with perpetual succession. A corporation is a hardy creature; it can survive the disappearance of its membership, and the question has to be asked how and by what means its existence is terminated. A company may be wound up; a chartered corporation may surrender its charter; a statutory corporation may be dissolved by a subsequent statute; but there is no clear provision governing the position in respect of a corporation created under section 3 of the 1956 Measure. (It may be added that all this can become relevant not only on the total disappearance of a conventional district, but also on its renewal within altered boundaries.)

7. When a parish is dissolved by a pastoral scheme under section 17(1)(b) of the Pastoral Measure 1983, paragraph 11(8) of Schedule 3 to the Measure assumes that its council also ceases to exist: 'Where, by reason of the dissolution of a parish by a pastoral scheme, the parochial church council of that parish ceases to exist . . .', and makes provision for the vesting of its property. It has been noted that the provisions of the Schedule are of no direct application, but the assumption as to the council ceasing to exist is significant. However, the analogy is imperfect: the parish is formally dissolved by a scheme made under statutory powers, and the dissolution of the organs of the parish is a natural consequence. In the conventional district case, the new holder of a benefice refuses to waive any of his or her rights; there is no clear authority for the proposition that that refusal will *ipso facto* operate to dissolve a corporate body.

8. It may well be, therefore, that the PCC of the defunct district enjoys some shadowy existence. In so far as the Parochial Church Councils (Powers) Measure 1956 defines 'parish' by reference to the CRR, any powers of the council under the Measure would seem to fall away on the disappearance of the district. It might be argued that this includes the holding of property, a power governed by section 5 of the Measure, but the power to hold property seems a necessary part of what it means to be a corporate body. It seems clear that if the corporation continues to exist, it cannot act; it cannot meet and it cannot deal with any property, and it

certainly cannot vest it in any other body. There is no power to end the resulting stalemate by use of the powers in Schedule 3 to the Pastoral Measure.

9. If the PCC of a conventional district wishes to build on land acquired by the parish PCC (this term indicating the council of the parish out of which the district was carved, in contrast to 'the district PCC'), that land will be vested in the Diocesan Authority under section 6(2) of the 1956 Measure, and the parish PCC (and no other body) will be under a duty to keep the Diocesan Authority indemnified under section 6(4) (where 'the council' must refer to the council which 'holds or acquires an interest in land' in section 6(2)). For the same reason, the powers of management reserved to the council under section 6(3) must be those of the parish PCC, however awkward this may be in pastoral terms. In terms of property rights, the existence or otherwise of the district PCC seems, in such a case, to be immaterial. Nothing in the relevant provisions of the 1956 Measure turns on the location of the land, as being within or outside the district boundaries.

10. In other cases, there is no reason in law why a district PCC should not enter into contracts, including major contracts such as those entailed in building contracts. While the parish PCC cannot escape its duty to indemnify the Diocesan Authority in cases falling within section 6(4) of the 1956 Measure, it does not become liable in any other context for the debts of the district PCC. However, a third party would be ill-advised to enter into such a contract with a district PCC without ensuring that payments under the contract would be guaranteed by some body with a more secure future than the district PCC.

11. Once the conventional district becomes a separate parish, the relevant provisions in the Pastoral Measure 1983 apply as to any other parish.

(January 1996)

Part 5

Churchwardens

Churchwardens

Qualification and election

1. The number and qualifications of and the time and manner of choosing churchwardens are regulated by the Churchwardens Measure 2001, which replaces the Churchwardens (Appointment and Resignation) Measure 1964. The 2001 Measure also provides for their admission to office as well as resignation and vacation of office. Subject to local custom and statutory provision to the contrary, there are to be two churchwardens of every parish, to be chosen from persons who are on the church electoral roll of the parish (ss1(1)–(3), 11). (Where a parish has more than one designated parish church two churchwardens are to be appointed for each church but will take office as churchwardens of the whole parish unless they agree to perform separate duties in the respective churches.) They must be 21 or over and communicant members of the Church of England (s1(3)). The bishop has power, in exceptional circumstances, to dispense with the statutory qualifications. No one who has not consented to serve can be chosen to be a churchwarden (s1(5)).

2. Churchwardens should be chosen annually not later than 30 April in each year (s4(1); CRR r13(1)). They must be chosen at a joint meeting of the persons whose names are on the church electoral roll and the persons resident in the parish whose names are on the register of local government electors. The 2001 Measure gives the minister a limited right of objection to one candidate if he or she considers that the election of the person nominated might give rise to 'serious difficulties' between that candidate and the minister. When such an objection is made the minister has to appoint one churchwarden from among the persons nominated, and the other is elected by the meeting (s4(5)).

3. The fact that for many years it had been the practice in a parish for an incumbent to nominate one warden does not necessarily indicate or prove an 'existing custom' preserved by section 11(2) of the 2001 Measure. It normally indicates an assumed disagreement between the two appointing parties, which brought into play the old procedure laid down in sections 2 and 3 of the 1964 Measure. In other words it will be assumed that the joint consent mentioned in section 2(2) had not been signified and that the alternative procedure in section 2(3) will have been followed, the incumbent appointing one churchwarden and the meeting of parishioners the other.

Admission and resignation

4. The choosing of a churchwarden does not in itself complete the appointment procedure. Before entering upon their duties the churchwardens must each year be admitted or re-admitted to office (s6). This takes place at the archdeacon's visitation. Strictly speaking, sidesmen ought also to be admitted with the churchwardens, but this rarely happens in practice. On the rare occasions when there is an episcopal visitation the admission takes place before the bishop or chancellor or his deputy.

5. Churchwardens vacate their office on the admission to office of their successors, or their own readmission for the following year. However, a churchwarden who has been chosen and admitted under the 2001 Measure for a given term of office will not in any event hold office beyond 31 July in the year when that term ends; if at that point no successor has yet been chosen and admitted, a casual vacancy is deemed to arise (s6(2)–(3)). Before finally quitting office the churchwardens must hand over to their successors all the funds and other property and documents belonging to the church which are in their possession, and they may be sued if they do not do so. It is not possible to suspend a churchwarden.

6. A churchwarden who wishes to resign the office may serve written notice of that intention on the bishop by post. Normally office will be vacated two months thereafter, or earlier if the bishop so determines. Further, the churchwarden's office is vacated if his or her name is not on the electoral roll (s8) or he or she becomes disqualified on one of the grounds contained in section 2. If a churchwarden dies in office that person's colleague may act alone. Where, however, a vacancy occurs another person may be chosen to fill the vacancy, and will be chosen in the same way as the person being replaced.

Duties as officers of the Ordinary

7. Each year churchwardens present at the visitation the answers to such questions as are put to them; and they are at liberty to include in their response any further matters affecting the parish which may be relevant, always remembering that the object of a presentment is to inform the Ordinary whether all is well with the parish or, if not, what is amiss. Such presentments include any gross neglect of duty or impropriety of life on the part of the incumbent and, if made in good faith, are privileged communications.

8. Presentments do not mark the limit of the churchwardens' responsibilities. At any time the Ordinary can make enquiry of them as to parochial matters and at any time they can inform the Ordinary of any

such irregularities or derelictions of duty as need his intervention. It is for them to see that where a faculty is necessary a faculty is sought: they are quite the last persons who should permit any evasion of the bishop's authority, and they should keep the PCC mindful of the fact that the bishop has the original cure and guardianship of every parish in his diocese.

Duties relating to the parish

9. Of their original powers, duties and responsibilities regarding the parish church the following remain, and while the incumbent has a right to the keys of the church, it should be remembered that the churchwardens have a right of free access thereto for the performance of their duties:

(a) The property in church goods is still vested in the churchwardens as a quasi-corporation, and the churchwardens are the persons to take proceedings for their recovery if stolen or improperly removed. For this purpose they must have been duly admitted. No one has power to dispose of church goods without a faculty (*see* **Church building: improper removal of the contents**). They should ensure that the PCC provides a safe for the custody of valuable articles and documents. The churchwardens are under a duty to compile and maintain an inventory of church goods and a terrier of church lands and to make an annual fabric report to the APCM.

(b) They maintain good order at divine service by ejecting without unnecessary violence any person creating a disturbance (Canon F 15 para 2). They have statutory power to apprehend any person guilty of riotous, violent or indecent behaviour in the church or churchyard, and to take that person before a magistrate, who can punish by fine or imprisonment (Ecclesiastical Courts Jurisdiction Act 1860 s3; see also Canon F 15 para 3).

(c) They seat the congregation, without interfering with any seats held under a faculty, or by prescription (evidenced by long continued possession and repair) which implies a faculty (Canon F 7 para 2). See **Church building: seating of congregation**.

(d) They are responsible for the collection of the alms in church. Their duties in relation to collections (except those made for special purposes) extend to receiving the money and ensuring that it is paid over to the Treasurer or other recipient authorized by the PCC.

Duties as members of the PCC

10. A person chosen, appointed or elected as a churchwarden is (if a communicant member of the Church of England) a member of the PCC from the date he or she is chosen etc., not from the date of admission (CRR r14(2)). If communicants, churchwardens are also members of the standing committee of the PCC (CRR, App II, para 14). They are also joint treasurers where no other treasurer is appointed by the PCC (App II, para 1(e)).

11. It must be remembered that many questions with which the PCC is concerned are and have to be dealt with by the churchwardens in their presentments (*see also* **Parish: archdeacon's visitation: replies to articles of enquiry**), and that the admonitions of the Ordinary can only reach the PCC through the churchwardens. Consequently they are greatly concerned to see that at least on questions of this nature the PCC recognizes and acts up to its responsibilities.

(Revised September 2003)

Part 6

Parochial Church Councils

Parochial Church Council

Membership

1. A resolution of an APCM to make the elected members of the PCC consist of, say, six persons of each sex as a permanent arrangement is ultra vires the CRR.

2. Vacancies occurring in the number of representatives of the laity during the year must be filled in accordance with CRR rule 48(1). However, the PCC would be duly constituted even if such vacancies were not filled (CRR, App II, para 17).

Co-options

3. A clerk in Holy Orders, or an actual lay communicant (as defined by CRR r54(1)) of sixteen years or upwards, even if not on the roll of the parish, can be co-opted as a member of the PCC by the PCC itself (CRR r14(1)(h)) even though a clerk in Holy Orders or a lay person whose name is not on the roll of the parish cannot be elected to the PCC as a representative of the laity (CRR rl0(1)). The disqualification from membership under rule 14(3)(c) (which applies to those who are disqualified from being charity trustees under the Charities Act 1993 and those who are disqualified by the bishop from serving on the PCC under the Incumbents (Vacation of Benefices) Measure 1977 (as amended): CRR r46A) applies to co-opted members in the same way as to all other members of the PCC.

4. The number of co-opted members may not exceed one-fifth of the representatives of the laity who are elected by the APCM to the PCC, or two persons, whichever is the greater (CRR r14(1)(h)). It should be noted that representatives of the laity elected to the deanery synod are not included for the purpose of this calculation.

Term of office of PCC members

5. Unless the annual meeting decides that all representatives of the laity elected to the PCC should face re-election each year, one third of those representatives must retire from office in every year. The representatives to retire at each subsequent annual meeting shall be those who have been longest in office since last elected. As between representatives elected on the same day, those to retire shall be selected by lot unless they agree otherwise among themselves (CRR, r16).

PCC office holders

6. Officers of the PCC are governed by CRR Appendix II, paragraph 1:

(a)   Although there is nothing in the CRR or the 1956 Measure to prevent one person from combining the offices of secretary and treasurer of the PCC, the arrangement is not desirable.

(b)   A PCC can appoint its officers for such term as it thinks fit. In the absence of any provision to the contrary the appointment terminates at the first meeting of the PCC held after the APCM following the officer's appointment.

(c)   Although persons who are not members of the PCC may be remunerated for acting as secretary or treasurer, members may not (CRR, App II, para 1(d) and (e)).

PCC agenda

7. Agenda of the meetings of the PCC are governed by CRR Appendix II, paragraph 4. Best practice dictates:

(a)   Notices of motion should contain the words of the motion proposed to be moved, but notices fairly indicating the purport of the words may be accepted.

(b)   Matter which is defamatory, scandalous or entirely outside the functions of the PCC ought not to be put on the agenda paper.

Chairman of PCC

8. The chairmanship of the PCC is dealt with in CRR Appendix II, paragraphs 1(a) and (h), 5 and 11. Under rule 11, in the case of an equal division of votes at a meeting of the PCC the chairman has a second or casting vote. But the chairman's right to give a second or casting vote at meetings of a committee of the PCC depends upon any rules of procedure which the PCC itself may make. It is doubtful whether in the absence of any such rules the chairman of a committee can claim any similar right to that of the chairman of the PCC. It would be out of order for a chairman who has a casting vote to refrain from voting until the votes have been counted and then to give his original vote and his casting vote together.

PCC minutes

9. PCC minutes are subject to CRR Appendix II, paragraph 12. In addition, a resolution which is not ultra vires cannot be deleted subsequently from the minutes though subsequent resolutions can express disagreement with or rescind former resolutions. Resolutions if ultra vires can be expunged from the minutes.

Loans to a PCC

10. The power of a PCC to borrow money is inferentially recognized and therefore implicitly conferred by the Parochial Church Councils (Powers) Measure 1956. The inference may be deduced from the fact that the powers formerly conferred on or customarily exercised by the vestry or churchwardens have now passed to the PCC.

11. Money can be borrowed from anyone willing to lend it and upon any terms that may be agreed, including, it is considered, the giving of security, despite the decision to the contrary in *Re St Peter, Roydon* [1969] 1 WLR 1849. Since a PCC is a statutory corporation rather than a trust in the strict sense, it does not enjoy the powers of management of land – which would normally be seen as conferring a power to borrow by way of security – conferred by the Trusts of Land and Appointment of Trustees Act 1996. A loan can be accepted from, amongst other sources, the Diocesan Authority if willing to lend on such terms consistent with the duty of prudence as may be agreed (*see* **Parochial Church Council: legal position of members**). An interest-bearing loan from a member of the PCC would, however, infringe the rule against benefits to them described in the Opinion on **Parochial Church Council: legal position of members**. A security given for a loan in the form of a mortgage or charge on property held by a Diocesan Authority under section 6 of the Parochial Church Councils (Powers) Measure 1956 would require the consent of the Diocesan Authority but not of the Charity Commissioners provided that section 38 of the Charities Act 1993 is complied with and the advice there referred to is obtained and considered. Apart from such a security a PCC can give any security it pleases by way of bond or covenant to repay a loan either in one lump sum or by instalments or otherwise and such bond or covenant would be binding on the PCC, even though its members might change, to the extent of moneys in its hands as a corporation available for the purpose for which the money was borrowed.

12. If a PCC has property which it can mortgage to secure its overdraft with a bank, a legal mortgage of such property can be given with the necessary authorization. In the absence of such property it is unlikely that any document executed by the PCC alone would be acceptable to a bank.

Members of the PCC are under an obligation to see that the PCC's debts are duly paid. PCC members should not commit the PCC to any liabilities that they do not believe the council will be able to honour. If a particular item of expenditure is essential, and can only be funded by an overdraft, the better course would be to spread the burden of personal guarantees as widely as possible amongst the worshipping community.

Contract between PCC and member

13. As regards contracts between a PCC and any of its members, see the Opinion on **Parochial Church Council: legal position of members.**

Power to make donations to non-parochial objects

14. Whilst it should be remembered that the PCC is effectively a trustee of its assets and has a duty to exercise its powers responsibly, in view of its widely expressed functions under the 1956 Measure (as amended) a PCC has power as a matter of law to subscribe a reasonable part of its general funds to any charity the objects of which are such as to further any part of 'the whole mission of the Church'. The 'mission of the Church' for this purpose comprises not only religious objects in the narrow sense, but also the Christian duty of relieving the poor, the sick and others in need. Provided this requirement is met, the charity need not be one which operates within the parish or under which the parish or individual parishioners may benefit. Indeed, funds may be given to a non-charity, provided that they are to be used by it to further the 'mission of the Church' in some way. An example of this would be where funds are given to a deanery synod to support the work of a youth worker employed by it. However, a PCC would be well advised to seek advice, whether from the diocesan registrar or the Charity Commission, before giving funds to a non-charity.

15. It is of course important that a PCC takes all reasonable steps to ensure that funds it donates to third parties are in fact applied for the intended charitable purposes. Particular care may be needed where the funds are to be applied for the support of a Christian worker who is not employed by a charity. Failure to restrict expenditure to charitable purposes could lead to the loss of tax relief on the sums misapplied and expose the members of a PCC to claims for breach of trust. Difficulties of this kind are unlikely to arise where a donation is made to a registered charity. But care is required where funds are paid to a body which is not a charity, including bodies situated outside the United Kingdom. In such cases the advice of the Legal Advisory Commission is that, as a minimum, the donation should be accompanied by a covering letter stating that the donation should only be used for the charitable purpose for which the

PCC wishes it to be applied and requesting the donee's acceptance of that restriction.

Standing committee and other committees of PCC

Chairmanship of standing committee

16. The standing committee of the PCC is governed by paragraph 14 of Appendix II to the CRR. The incumbent (although the chairman of the PCC (see CRR App II, para 1(a)) and thus an ex officio member of the standing committee of the PCC) is not the ex officio chairman of the standing committee, but would normally act as such. The vice-chairman of the PCC (see CRR App II, para 1(b)) is not an ex officio member of the standing committee.

Powers and duties of standing committee and other committees

17. The standing committee, between the meetings of the PCC, has power to 'transact the business' of the PCC, subject to any directions which the PCC may have given it (CRR, App II, para 14(b)). Apart from any limitation which may have been set by such directions, every power which the PCC itself possesses could, in appropriate circumstances, be exercised by the standing committee in the course of the interim transaction of the PCC's business. A committee is, however, bound by the directions of and accountable to the higher authority for which it acts. The real purpose of the standing committee of a PCC is to carry on the routine work of the PCC between the meetings, and while it has powers which may be conveniently extensive for the purpose of enabling it to deal with matters of real urgency, the committee may not act outside the directions given to it by the PCC or outside the competence of the PCC whose business it has power to transact.

18. In addition to the standing committee, the PCC may appoint other committees for the purpose of the various branches of church work in the parish (CRR, App II, para 15). Any committee is similarly accountable to the PCC, and may perform such functions as may be given to it by the PCC.

Membership of committees

19. Under CRR Appendix II, paragraph 14 members of the standing committee must be members of the PCC. So far as other committees are concerned persons who are not members of the council may be included (CRR, App II, para 15), and it is within the competence of a PCC to include as members of such committees persons who are not qualified to be on the electoral roll.

20. The incumbent is ex officio a member of all committees (CRR, App II, para 15). The secretary of a PCC is not a member ex officio of any committee appointed by the PCC. However, it may be convenient that the secretary should attend some committees, in which case the PCC may consider it appropriate to include the secretary as a member. Churchwardens are ex officio members of the standing committee (see above), but not of any other committee unless expressly included by the PCC.

(Revised May 2003)

Parochial Church Council: employment of solicitors

1. It is common practice for the PCC to instruct the same solicitors as the Diocesan Authority on a purchase, sale or mortgage of land, but the PCC is entirely free to instruct other solicitors if it thinks fit. The Diocesan Authority is not entitled to withhold consent to a transaction merely on the ground that the PCC wishes to instruct different solicitors.

2. In the case of a purchase by the PCC:

(a)   It is for the solicitors to the PCC to investigate the title to the land being purchased and to prepare the conveyance.

(b)   The solicitors to the PCC are entitled to a fee calculated in accordance with the Solicitors' (Non-Contentious Business) Remuneration Order 1994, SI 1994/2616.

(c)   It is for the solicitors to the Diocesan Authority to peruse the conveyance and to approve the same on behalf of the Authority. There may be ancillary work arising out of that approval.

(d)   The solicitors to the Diocesan Authority are entitled to a fee in accordance with the Solicitors' (Non-Contentious Business) Remuneration Order 1994 in respect of the work undertaken. They will be likely to send their fee account to the PCC for convenience of collection. Both sets of legal costs are payable by the PCC.

(e)   It is common practice in certain dioceses for the solicitors to the PCC to investigate title, and to ask the solicitors to the Diocesan Authority to prepare the draft conveyance. Where this practice is followed the additional work and responsibility will be reflected in the fees charged by the solicitors to the Diocesan Authority.

3. In the case of a sale of land belonging to the PCC the cost should be dealt with on a similar footing, having regard to the respective duties of the solicitors to the Diocesan Authority and to the PCC in such a case.

4. In the case of a mortgage of land belonging to the PCC where the money is advanced otherwise than by the Diocesan Authority, the costs should be dealt with as above. Where however money is advanced or given by way of grant by the Diocesan Authority, the Authority is entitled to require that its solicitors shall be satisfied as to the title as well as with the

form of conveyance if the loan is made on the occasion of a purchase, and generally in such a case a loan is governed by ordinary mortgage rules, and a gift or grant will be made on such terms and subject to such conditions as the Authority may impose.

5. The principles set out above also apply to transactions under the Incumbents and Churchwardens (Trusts) Measure 1964 when different firms of solicitors are instructed to act.

(1997)

Parochial Church Council: legal position of members

Legal status of a PCC

1. A PCC is a body corporate (Parochial Church Councils (Powers) Measure 1956 s3).

2. The Charity Commission accepts that PCCs are charities. However, as the law now stands they are excepted from registration and so not required to register under the Charities Act 1993.

3. The affairs of a PCC must be conducted, and the assets of a PCC must be held and applied, solely to promote the charitable purposes which the PCC is established to promote, and not for other purposes (even if charitable) nor, a fortiori, for the private purposes of individuals, such as members of the PCC.

Fiduciary position of members of PCC

4. The members of a PCC are appointed to promote its charitable and other purposes whether statutory or otherwise. In promoting those purposes, the members of a PCC control the conduct of its affairs and the use and application of its assets.

5. The position of a member of a PCC is analogous to that of a trustee of trust property who holds the trust assets for the benefit of the beneficiaries or for the advancement of charitable purposes (see *Harries v Church Commissioners* [1992] 1 WLR 1241).

6. The duties of a trustee apply to all persons who occupy a fiduciary position analogous to that of a trustee. The duties have been held to apply, for example, to directors of a company in relation to the company's assets.

7. Those duties are stringent and include the following:

    (a)   the duty not to receive a financial benefit, whether directly or indirectly, from the trust;

    (b)   the duty not to take advantage of knowledge, information or opportunities acquired while a trustee;

    (c)   the duty not to put himself in a position where his duty to the trust and his personal interest conflict: for example, the acquisition of an interest in the property of the trust, whether by way of sale or lease, is liable to be set aside at the instance of a beneficiary (or of the Attorney General in the case of a charity).

8. Those duties are based on the trustee's status, not on the nature of the trustee's conduct or the effect of that conduct on the trust and its assets. Thus, the liability of a trustee to account to the trust for profits made in breach of duty is not dependent in any way on proof of lack of good faith in the conduct of the trust's affairs or on the proof of any loss suffered by the trust.

Breach of duty

9. Prima facie, a breach of duty will occur if a member of a PCC enters into any contract with a PCC under which he or she derives a financial benefit: for example, a lease or an agreement to take a lease of PCC property or an agreement between the PCC and the member under which the member is paid for the supply of goods or services to the PCC.

10. If a breach of duty occurs, a PCC member who receives any benefit must account to the PCC for that benefit unless the retention of the benefit is agreed by the Charity Commission or the court. The charity's right to enforce this is an asset of the charity and it is the responsibility of all the trustees to ensure that it happens.

11. Fortunately, there is a mechanism by which difficulties in this respect can be addressed in advance by seeking authority for the intended benefit from the Charity Commission. Although its starting point, following the lead of the court, is that the office of trustee is unpaid, it is able and willing to authorize trustee benefits if a charity can show that the benefit in question is necessary and reasonable for the proper administration of the charity. In considering whether or not to authorize a benefit, the Commission will take into account a number of factors such as the procedures the PCC will put in place to manage the conflict of interest and the number of trustees to benefit. In the case of payment for services rendered, other factors will include whether the contract contains features to protect the PCC's interests, whether the PCC can demonstrate that the contract is in its interests in terms of value for money and whether the PCC has any arrangements for testing or challenging bills which might be disputed. The PCC will need to demonstrate in its application to the Commission that they have considered these factors.

12. PCCs with an annual income of less than £10,000 can take advantage of a special concession introduced by the Charity Commission. This allows payments to trustees (except remuneration for carrying out trustee functions and duties) to be made without the Commission's express

authority, provided that (a) the total payments to trustees in any financial year do not exceed £1,000; (b) at all times a majority of the trustees is unpaid; and (c) that the trustees reasonably believe the payments to be in the best interests of the charity. There is also a fast-track procedure for authorizing payments above this de minimis limit. More detailed information is available on the Charity Commission website.

(Revised 2004)

Parochial Church Council: parochial investments and property

Investments generally

1. A PCC being a trustee can invest its money only in investments authorized by law for the investment of trust funds, such as funds held by the Central Board of Finance under the Church Funds Investment Measure 1958 as amended by the Church of England (Miscellaneous Provisions) Measure 1995.

2. In a case in which the PCC is the administrative trustee of a trust, the securities are held by the Diocesan Authority, and their relationship is governed by section 6 of the Parochial Church Councils (Powers) Measure 1956. Decisions as to investment rest with the PCC as one of its powers of management, but the consent of the Diocesan Authority to the investment of the PCC's choice is required because a change of investment is an exchange within the meaning of section 6(3) of the 1956 Measure. Where, on the other hand, the Diocesan Authority has been expressly appointed custodian trustee, with the result that the relationship is governed by section 4(2) of the Public Trustee Act 1906 (e.g. by scheme of the Charity Commissioners), the decision lies wholly with the PCC and the Diocesan Authority must concur in carrying it out unless it involves a breach of trust.

3. As regards investment in the Charities Official Investment Fund, section 24(7) of the Charities Act 1993 is of absolutely general application and overrides the provisions of the 1956 Measure as regards funds which the PCC wishes to be transferred to this Fund.

Diocesan Authority consent

4. The Diocesan Authority may give or withhold its consent in its discretion and, if it is withheld, the PCC cannot acquire property of the nature mentioned in section 6(1) of the 1956 Measure (i.e. property of any nature to be held on permanent trusts) in any other way. Where money will have to be raised to finance the purchase or the property intended to be acquired is already mortgaged, it would be reasonable for the Diocesan Authority to consider the extent of the liability and the value of the statutory indemnity afforded to it in the particular case under section 6(4) of the Measure.

5. Whether the consent of the Diocesan Authority is required or not, it is desirable that stocks and shares held on behalf of a PCC should be in the

name of the Authority and that any papers and certificates should be deposited in the diocesan office for safe keeping.

6. Where a PCC has been in exclusive possession of land adverse to the true owner for the statutory period of twelve years or upwards under the Limitation Act 1980, section 15(1), but the consent of the Diocesan Authority to the original acquisition has not been sought, the PCC should acquaint the Authority with the circumstances and ask consent for the acquisition. This having been obtained, the PCC should forthwith convey and assign to the Authority all its estate and interest in the land so as to comply with section 6(2) of the 1956 Measure.

Relationship between Diocesan Authority and PCC

7. The relationship between the Diocesan Authority and the PCC with regard to trust property vested in the Authority under the Parochial Church Councils (Powers) Measure 1956 is not identical with that between custodian and managing trustees laid down in section 4 of the Public Trustee Act 1906, because under the Measure the consent of the Authority is necessary before any change of investment can be made. On the other hand, although consent to the making of an investment or change of investment has to be obtained, it is the duty of the PCC, not the Authority, to select and control the investments of the trust property.

8. In the following cases trust property need not be vested in the Diocesan Authority:

(a)   where land is held by private trustees for church purposes, as for instance for the upkeep of the fabric, but no reference is made in the trust document to the PCC;

(b)   if capital monies are held under a trust deed by local trustees, the income to be applied either for church purposes in the parish direct or to the PCC for application by it for such purposes.

9. Where a trust exists to provide income for a specific purpose within a parish and the Diocesan Authority acts as sole trustee, the Diocesan Authority is obliged to make enquiries of the PCC. The PCC should provide an account or certificate relating to the trust to the Diocesan Authority by way of a receipt. It is generally advisable for trust income to be shown clearly in the PCC's accounts.

10. Where land is held on behalf of a PCC, in most cases the Diocesan Authority will not be entitled to enter on the land and repair buildings

thereon. It is doubtful therefore whether the Authority is liable in respect of an accident causing injury to a person using such property, whether the accident occurs due to failure to effect necessary repairs or through the negligence of the PCC. In any case, section 6(4) of the 1956 Measure provides a statutory indemnity for the Authority in cases where it holds the land under that Measure. However, it is important that the Diocesan Authority should ensure that the PCC does take out adequate insurance cover against third party and other risks, protecting the interests of both parties (*see also* **Church building: insurance**).

11. When selling property belonging to a PCC, the solicitor acting for the Diocesan Authority or the PCC should retain any original deed which contains the trust upon which the property is held even if the deed comprises only the particular property and would otherwise have been handed over to the purchaser (see the Law of Property Act 1925, s45(9)).

Letting or mortgaging of property

12. Because the provision of a dancing hall is not an ecclesiastical purpose, any cause providing for the letting of a hall for entertainments should be included in the powers of the trustees and not in the objects of the trust. The objects of a trust do not detract from the ordinary power of trustees to let for any reasonable purpose.

13. Where property is held on behalf of a PCC, for charitable purposes, whether subject to an express power to sell or mortgage or not, the assent of the Diocesan Authority will usually now be sufficient; the consent of the Charity Commissioners will not normally be required (see section 38 of the Charities Act 1993).

14. If, as is usually the case, a Diocesan Authority is a limited company, particulars of a mortgage created under section 6 of the Parochial Church Councils (Powers) Measure 1956 by such a Diocesan Authority over land conveyed to a Diocesan Authority on trust for a PCC need not, it is thought, be registered under sections 395, 396 and 401 of the Companies Act 1985, as amended by the Companies Act 1989. The charges which must be registered under section 399 are those falling within section 395 and 196. The charges referred to in those sections are only such as affect a company's own property which, if uncharged, would be available to pay the creditors of the company on a winding up. The object of sections 395, 396 and 401 is to enable unsecured creditors to know how far they can look to property ostensibly belonging to the company for payment of their debts. If a Diocesan Authority, which is a limited company, were to go into liquidation its unsecured creditors would have no claim against the property held by it in trust for a PCC. Further, a Diocesan Authority

cannot charge such property for its own purposes. The wording of section 395 appears to indicate that it is not necessary to register mortgages created by or on behalf of companies upon property held by them in trust for some other person or body.

Leases by Diocesan Authority

15. The main principles of, and the clauses to be included in, a lease by a Diocesan Authority on behalf of a PCC should be the following:

(a)   the parties should, as a rule, be the Diocesan Authority, the PCC and the lessee;

(b)   the Authority (as owning the legal interest) should demise the property; and the PCC with the consent of the Authority should demise and confirm it to the lessee;

(c)   the lessee's covenants should be entered into with the Authority and also separately with the PCC;

(d)   the power of re-entry should be in favour of the Authority and the PCC according to their respective rights and interests;

(e)   each of them, so far as relates to its own acts and deeds, should covenant for quiet enjoyment; and

(f)   any other 'lessor's covenants' should be entered into by the PCC 'with the consent of the Authority'.

Leases by PCC

16. Under section 6 of the Parochial Church Councils (Powers) Measure 1956 a 'short lease' as defined in section 6(6) can be acquired by the council without the consent of the Diocesan Authority and such lease need not be vested in the Authority. Under section 6(3) the Authority's consent to a letting of any property vested in it is required. The result is that if a PCC acquires a 'short lease' and grants a shorter one out of it, no consent is required, whereas, on the other hand, if it acquired the freehold or a leasehold interest which is not a 'short lease', consent for a letting of that property, being vested in the Authority, is required.

Incumbents and Churchwardens (Trusts) Measure 1964: repairs

17. The Legal Advisory Commission is of the Opinion that generally managing trustees of property could not assert that a Diocesan Authority

is legally responsible for repairs to trust property vested in the Authority under section 3 of the Incumbents and Churchwardens (Trusts) Measure 1964 if the managing trustees have no money. Section 3(5) of the 1964 Measure is concerned only with making it clear that the vesting under the section does not override any incumbrances; the subsection is not concerned with the question of who is responsible. Unless the Diocesan Authority has been at fault or has concurred in some act of the managing trustees, the Authority is not responsible for any act or default on the part of the managing trustees. Failure to make due payments could be regarded as a default on the part of the managing trustees; but so long as the action was *in personam* the Diocesan Authority could disclaim liability. However, if there was some incumbrance that gave rise to an action *in rem*, the Diocesan Authority would have to meet the claim and look to the managing trustees for repayment. The Legal Advisory Commission considers that it would make no difference if the Diocesan Authority put a disclaimer clause in the vesting deed; it would be overridden by section 3.

(Revised 2003)

Parochial Church Council: status of joint parochial church councils

Legislation before 1981

1. Provision for the establishment of PCCs was made in the Schedule to the Church of England Assembly (Powers) Act 1919. They were made corporate bodies by section 3 of the Parochial Church Councils (Powers) Measure 1921. The 1921 Measure was subsequently replaced by the Parochial Church Councils (Powers) Measure 1956, section 3 of which was in all material respects in the same form as section 3 of the 1921 Measure.

2. The first mention of joint PCCs was contained in the Pastoral Measure 1968. Paragraph 13 of Schedule 3 to that Measure reads as follows:

> '13. Where there are two or more parishes within the area of a single benefice or two or more benefices are held in plurality, a pastoral scheme or order may provide for constituting a joint PCC for all or some of the parishes of the benefice or benefices and for empowering that council to exercise such of the powers of the PCCs of the several parishes concerned as may be determined by or in accordance with the scheme or order, and the scheme or order may apply in relation to the joint PCC, with such modifications as may be specified, the provisions of any Measure relating to PCCs, and may make provision for vesting in the joint PCC any property, rights and liabilities of the PCCs of the several parishes concerned.'

Legislation from 1981 onwards

3. Until 1981 joint PCCs were only briefly referred to in the CRR, rather as a footnote to the Pastoral Measure 1968. What is now rule 19 was inserted by paragraph 8 of the Church Representation Rules (Amendment) Resolution 1981 (SI 1981/959). (In its present form the rule is as amended by a further resolution, the Church Representation Rules (Amendment) (No. 1) Resolution 1984, SI 1984/1039, para 10, and by the Patronage (Benefices) Measure 1986, Sch 4, para 13(b)). That rule now enables a joint PCC to be formed independently of the making of a pastoral scheme.

4. Paragraph 13 of Schedule 3 to the Pastoral Measure 1968 was repealed and re-enacted in a substantially revised form as paragraph 13 of Schedule 3 to the Pastoral Measure 1983. Paragraph 13(1) (as amended by

the Patronage (Benefices) Measure 1986, Sch 4, para 25(d) now reads as follows:

'13(1) Where a pastoral scheme provides for two or more parishes to be comprised in the area of a single benefice or a pastoral scheme or order provides for two or more benefices to be held in plurality, the scheme or order may make provision or authorise the bishop by instrument under his hand with the concurrence of the incumbent of the benefice or benefices to make provision, –

(a)   for establishing a joint PCC for all or some of the parishes of the benefice or benefices;

(b)   for the chairmanship, meetings and procedure of that council; and

(c)   subject to paragraph 20 of Schedule 2 to the Patronage (Benefices) Measure 1986, for the functions of the PCC of any such parish which must or may be delegated to the joint PCC,

being provisions to the same effect as those which may be made by a scheme under the Church Representation Rules in the like case.'

5. Paragraph 13(2) goes on to provide that any such provisions and pastoral scheme or order or a bishop's instrument are to cease to have effect at the end of the period specified in the scheme, order or instrument; the period may not exceed five years from the date when the scheme or order came into operation and may not be extended or renewed. In addition, under paragraph 13(3), any provisions included in a pastoral scheme or order by virtue of paragraph 13 of the 1968 Measure are to cease to have effect at the end of five years from the establishment of the joint PCC or, if later, three years from the date of coming into operation of the 1983 Measure (i.e. 1 November 1986).

6. Two significant differences from the 1968 Measure are:

(a)   that joint PCCs created by a pastoral scheme can now only have a limited life because of paragraph 13(2); and

(b)   that the pastoral scheme may now only provide for the delegation of functions in accordance with the CRR, the power 'to apply the provisions of any Measure relating to PCCs', and to 'make provision for vesting in the joint PCC any property, rights and liberties of the PCCs of the several parishes concerned' not being re-enacted.

7. It seems clear that as a matter of policy the General Synod decided that a joint council should not be established on a permanent basis in every case of a multi-parish benefice. A joint council could be provided, if thought necessary, to enable parishes to adjust to a new situation, but if it were to be retained indefinitely that should be by the positive decision of those most closely involved, under the CRR.

Conclusion

8. Under the Pastoral Measure 1968 a scheme establishing a joint council could have applied section 3 of the Parochial Church Councils (Powers) Measure 1956 in relation to the council, and then made provision for vesting property in it. Where such provision was made in the scheme, it is considered that the joint PCC constituted by that scheme was not incorporated. But whether the council was incorporated or not, if its constitution rested only on the scheme then paragraph 13(3) of Schedule 3 to the Pastoral Measure 1983 would have dissolved it on 1 November 1986 (or, if later, five years after the establishment of the council), and a scheme under rule 19 of the CRR would be needed to revive it.

9. It is not considered that a joint PCC can be incorporated under any Measure passed by the General Synod since the Pastoral Measure 1983 came into operation. Paragraph 13 of Schedule 3 does not provide for incorporation, nor does it authorize section 3 of the 1956 Measure to be applied; and there is nothing contained in the CRR to enable a council formed under rule 17 to be made a corporate body. Nor, since the authority of the joint councils permitted by the Measures depends on the provisions of the schemes establishing them, is there any scope for conferring functions on a body described as a joint PCC but established as a company registered under the Companies Acts, and certainly not for vesting property in any such body.

(January 1990, revised 1997)

Part 7
Church Building

Church building: bells

Ringing of church bells: potential liability under the Environmental Protection Act 1990 and for nuisance at common law

Church bells

1. There are at present over 5,200 churches in England with rings of five or more bells and there are over 3,000 bells cast in medieval times that are still rung. Church bells have been ringing in England since the seventh century but change ringing was not introduced until the middle of the seventeenth century. Change ringing is an art (or exercise) unknown outside the Anglican Communion, where it is principally confined to England and Wales. Bells are rung to summon the faithful to worship, to celebrate weddings and festivals and to mark national thanksgivings. Muffled bells are sometimes rung at funerals and at times of local or national disasters. During times of national emergency it has always been understood that church bells would be rung as a warning of invasion.

2. Canon F 8 'Of Church Bells' states that:

> '1. In every church and chapel there shall be provided at least one bell to ring the people to divine service.
>
> 2. No bell in any church or chapel shall be rung contrary to the direction of the minister.'

Nuisance at common law

3. A nuisance at common law consists of an unlawful interference with a person's use and enjoyment of his property. Making unreasonable noise is actionable as a nuisance and there are a number of earlier authorities which accept that the ringing of noisy church bells may constitute a nuisance (see *Soltau v De Held* (1851) 2 Sim NS 133, and *Martin v Nutkin* (1724) 2 P Wms 266). In the Australian case of *Haddon v Lynch* [1911] VLR 5 complaint was made of an unmelodious church bell rung in the valley of an iron roof which served as a sounding board. The judge made an order that the bell should not be rung before 9.00 a.m. In *Hardman v Holbertson* [1866] WN 379, however, an injunction restraining the ringing of church bells was refused on the ground that the noise was not sufficient materially to interfere with comfort.

4. Those who complain about the ringing of church bells are invariably those who live close to a church. Often newcomers to the locality buy houses close to churches and then complain. This fact does not prevent

such a person from proving an actionable nuisance and recovering damages or an injunction. Coming to the nuisance is not a defence. Nevertheless it is a general principle that in the case of a nuisance interfering with comfort and amenity, the local character of the neighbourhood is relevant in determining liability. A person who chooses to live near a church cannot reasonably expect the same freedom from noise as he or she would expect in some other place. Whether an actionable nuisance exists is not an abstract consideration; it has to be determined by reference to all the circumstances.

5. The duration of the interference is an element in assessing its actionability. Few, if any, complaints appear to have been made in respect of short periods of bell ringing prior to mid-morning or early evening service. Complaints have been made in connection with periods of week day practising where bells may be rung for an hour or so. It is not unreasonable that bell ringers should need to practise; but practising in the late evening is more likely to create a nuisance than the early evening. The test is whether the bells materially interfere with the ordinary comfort and amenity of those living in houses near the church. Each case must be determined according to its own merits. The courts are unlikely to restrain bell ringing practice except in extreme cases. But if, for example, for an hour or so normal communication is substantially interfered with or listening to a broadcast is made extremely difficult, then bell practising could be restrained as an actionable nuisance. The visit of a team of change ringers intent on ringing a full peal of 5,000 changes of Grandsire, Treble and Bob, Surprise and so on in a residential area is more than likely to constitute an actionable nuisance.

Statutory nuisance under the Environmental Protection Act 1990

6. Section 79 of the 1990 Act defines a statutory nuisance as constituting inter alia 'noise emitted from premises so as to be prejudicial to health or a nuisance' (s79(1)(g)). Noise, which includes vibration, may fall into this category either because it is prejudicial to health or because it is a nuisance at common law, in the sense of interfering unduly with the comfort and convenience of neighbouring occupiers. The Act does not depart from the common law definitions and standards but it provides additional remedies through the magistrates' court. Where a local authority is satisfied that a statutory nuisance exists or is likely to occur or recur, it is the duty of the local authority to serve a notice requiring the abatement of the nuisance or the prohibition of its recurrence (s80(1)). Such an abatement notice may require works to be done or steps to be taken to abate the nuisance. A person who receives such an abatement notice may appeal against it to the magistrates' court (s80(3)). If there is no appeal, and if the abatement notice is not complied with, then an offence is committed. Such an offence

may be prosecuted in a magistrates' court when evidence given by an environmental health officer who measured the noise in decibels may be sufficient. Independent of the local authority, a person aggrieved by a statutory nuisance may make a complaint to the magistrates' court direct (s82(1)). If the magistrates are satisfied that the alleged nuisance exists they must make an order directing the nuisance to be abated and they may order the exclusion of the necessary works for that purpose (s82(2)). Although those who drafted the 1990 Act and the provisions of Part III of the Control of Pollution Act 1974 may not have contemplated noise occasioned by the ringing of church bells, there can be little doubt that a statutory nuisance can arise and be controlled in this way.

7. Cases on statutory nuisance involving church bells do not appear to have reached the Law Reports and this is no doubt due to the common sense of the ringers and local authorities concerned. However, one such case relating to St Peter Harrogate was settled by compromise, and reported in the 28 January 1977 issue of *The Ringing World*. There, ringing before services was restricted to 45 minutes and a further 60 minutes per week for general ringing. Bell practice time was restricted to 90 minutes between 6.00 p.m. and 9.00 p.m. on one week day evening. There were other generous special provisions for peal attempts.

Summary

8. Every case remains a question of fact and degree, and evidence of noise levels is very relevant. If the level of comfort is reduced to the extent stated above, the ringing of church bells for the normal period of practice of about one and a half hours may constitute an actionable nuisance at common law giving rise to claims for damages and/or an injunction. It could also be prosecuted in the magistrates' court as a statutory nuisance. It may therefore be wise for a parish to consider the question of abatement by ensuring that practices take place as early in the evening as possible. Consideration should also be given to the fitting of sound-proof shutters to the inside of the belfry louvres which can be closed during practice periods. The ringing of bells for relatively short periods before public worship or a wedding or festivities is probably not actionable at the suit of those who have lived near churches for many years or of those who have bought or tenanted houses close to a church where bells are habitually rung.

Note: *Information and advice on the conservation of church bells and bell-frames can be obtained from the Council for the Care of Churches and the Central Council for Church Bell Ringers.*

Control of church bells and bell-ringers

9. The control of the church bells and bell-ringers does not belong to the PCC but jointly to the incumbent and churchwardens. Accordingly anyone who wishes to ring the bells must comply with their requirements which could, if they thought fit, include the levying of a charge.

Who is liable

10. Clearly the persons who can give directions regarding bell ringing may be liable, usually the incumbent or churchwardens and, during an interregnum, possibly the PCC for authorizing it. However, the ringing of bells in a parish church which might constitute a nuisance is not actionable against the bishop of the diocese in which the church is situated (*Calvert v Gardiner and Others* (*The Times* 22 July 2002))

(June 1992, revised 2003)

Church building: chancels

Liability of lay rector

1. Many parish churches have lay rectors as a result of impropriation (the transfer of an ecclesiastical benefice to a lay person: see *Representative Body of the Church of Wales v Tithe Redemption Commissioners* [1944] AC 228). The number of cases in which a lay rector continues to be personally liable for the repair of a chancel has been diminished by the effect of section 52 of the Ecclesiastical Dilapidations Measure 1923 (which provides for the compounding of liability by payment of a lump sum) and much more so by the Tithe Act 1936 which came into force on 2 October 1936. Where, in lieu of tithe rentcharge extinguished by the Act, redemption stock was issued to a lay rector who was previously liable to repair a chancel, a portion of the stock was issued to the Diocesan Authority. Out of this portion of the stock the former liability of the lay rector in respect of the chancel is to be discharged.

2. There are at least five cases left in each of which the liability of a lay rector to repair a chancel continues as before the Tithe Act 1936, namely:

(a)   where land was allotted to the lay rector under an Inclosure Act in lieu of tithe or unenclosed glebe. This case is not touched by the Tithe Act 1936, which only applies to tithe rentcharge created under the 1836 Act;

(b)   if he is the owner of land or corn rents given in lieu of tithe by the Tithe Act 1836. This is similarly not touched by the Tithe Act 1936;

(c)   if he is the owner of land in respect of which merger of the tithe payable thereout has taken place in accordance with the Tithe Act 1839 (see s1 of the Tithe Act 1839; s31(1)(c) and (4) of the Tithe Act 1936);

(d)   if he is the owner of land where the land and the tithe rentcharge issuing thereout were in the hands of the same owner between the dates specified in section 21 of the Tithe Act 1936 but no merger had taken place in accordance with the Tithe Act 1839 (see ss1, 21 and 31(3) of the Tithe Act 1936);

(e)   if the lay rectory is vested in any of the bodies mentioned in the proviso to section 31(2) of the Tithe Act 1936.

(for more detail, see *Nugee* 'The Consequences of *Aston Cantlow*' (2004) 7 Ecc LJ 452).

3. The liability does not constitute a charge on the rectorial land but is a personal liability imposed on whoever is from time to time the owner of rectorial property. Where there are several owners of such property, each is severally liable for the whole amount though a person liable can seek contribution from co-owners (*Wickhambrook Parochial Church Council v Croxford* [1935] 2 KB 417; *Chivers & Sons Ltd v Air Ministry* [1955] Ch 585; but see also the doubt expressed by Lord Scott of Foscote in *Parochial Church Council of Aston Cantlow v Wallbank* [2004] 1 AC 546 para 108).

Importance of registering the right

4. Under the Land Registration Act 2002, liability to repair the chancel is treated as being an overriding interest for a transitional period of ten years following 13 October 2003 (see The Land Registration Act 2002 (Transitional Provisions) No. 2 Order 2003). At the end of that period the liability to repair will lapse on a transfer of ownership of the rectorial land unless, if the title to the land is unregistered, a caution against first registration of the land has been lodged, or, in the case of registered land, a notice has been entered against the register of the title to the land. Therefore it is important that the Parochial Church Council applies for the registration of a caution or notice in respect of each part of the rectorial land. As no registration fee is payable for applications to protect similar ancient property rights, such as payments in lieu of tithe, Crown rents and manorial rights (see s117), the Land Registry intends to waive the fee for applications to protect chancel repair liability for the 10 year period: statement by the Parliamentary Under-Secretary of State for Constitutional Affairs, Hansard, House of Commons, 14 October 2003.

5. A lay rector is bound not only to repair but also to restore and rebuild if necessary (*Wise v Metcalfe* (1829) 10 B&C 299), and put the chancel into substantial repair, without ornament (*Bell v Addison* (1860) 2 F&F 261). Thus while the rector must bear the cost of repairing windows glazed with plain glass or a plain chancel screen, as part of his ordinary liability in respect of the chancel, where windows of stained glass or an ornamental chancel screen have at any time been substituted for the original plain glazing or chancel screen for any reason, he need not accept responsibility for the increased cost of repair or replacements due to the existence of the ornamental windows or chancel screen. This applies equally to the cases where the lay rector's liability has been replaced by a sum of stock issued to the Diocesan Authority for the purpose of

providing for the repair of the chancel in accordance with section 31(2) of the Tithe Act 1936.

6. Incumbents and PCCs are strongly advised to include among the risks against which they insure the risks of damage to or destruction of all ornamental fittings and stained glass in the chancel, since it would be for the PCC and not for the lay rector to replace such ornaments in the event of damage or destruction (*see also* **Church building: insurance**).

7. Neither a parochial chapel nor a chapel of ease can be a rectory, though a chapel may prescribe for the tithe against the mother church, but only apparently where a separate clerk to say divine service has been found by the chapelry and by way of composition (see *Saer v Bland* (1548) 4 Leon 24). It would appear, therefore, that the lay rector would be responsible for the repair of the chancel of the parish church, but not for the repair of the chancel of the chapel.

Ecclesiastical Dilapidations Measure 1923

8. In cases where the liability of an incumbent to repair the chancel has become extinguished by section 52(1) of the Ecclesiastical Dilapidations Measure 1923, the chancel becomes repairable in the same manner as the remainder of the church and any funds applicable generally to church repairs may be applied to repair the chancel. A repair fund held on trusts limiting its application to the body of the church excluding the chancel is not applicable under the 1923 Measure to the repair of the chancel. Such application could be a breach of trust unless the scope of the trust were extended by order of the Charity Commissioners or otherwise.

9. The income of a fund representing the money for which a lay rector has compounded his liability for the repair of a chancel can under section 52(2) be used for the repair of stonework in the nave of a church.

Proceedings for neglect to repair

10. The Chancel Repairs Act 1932 provides a procedure by which the PCC can recover the cost of chancel repairs from a defaulting lay rector. In following the statutory procedure a PCC is not acting as a public authority so as to engage the provisions of the Human Rights Act 1998. Even if it were, the procedure does not amount to a violation of such rights as the lay rector may enjoy under the European Convention on Human Rights (see *Parochial Church Council of Aston Cantlow v Wallbank*, above)

11. As regards parties, when there are more impropriators than one it is not necessary to make every impropriator a party (see *Wickhambrook Parochial Church Council v Croxford*, above).

12. The following are some cases in which proceedings have been taken against a lay rector for neglect to repair a chancel: *Morley v Leacroft* [1896] P 92; *Neville v Kirby* [1898] P 160, Arches Ct; *Hauxton Parochial Church Council v Stevens* [1929] P 240; *Wickhambrook Parochial Church Council v Croxford*, above; *Chivers & Sons Ltd v Air Ministry*, above; *Parochial Church Council of Aston Cantlow v Wallbank*, above.

13. The PCC is a trustee for the parishioners as a whole and its members have the fiduciary duties of charity trustees, so that it will only be in exceptional circumstances that they can properly decide not to make enquiries to ascertain what land may be burdened and the identity of its owner, and to take proceedings under section 2 of the Act to enforce the lay rector's repairing liability where it is known to exist. Their failure to do so without good cause may render members personally liable for the cost of the repairs.

Rights of lay rector

14. The most valuable of the lay rector's former rights, the right to receive tithes, has been either commuted for land under the Inclosure Acts or commuted or extinguished under legislation culminating in section 56 of the Finance Act 1977.

15. Legislation has not however divested a lay rector of his freehold in the chancel upon which his rights are founded. He will therefore be entitled to enjoy the same rights as before the Tithe Act 1936 in so far as his claims to be the lay rector can be substantiated. An application for a faculty however, which would, before the passing of the Tithe Act 1936, have increased the rector's obligation to repair and thus required his consent, will in cases where the rector's obligation has been removed by the Act no longer require his consent.

Lay rector's right to seats

16. The land upon which a chancel stands is the rector's freehold and his right to the 'chief seat', which may be a pew and not merely one sitting, rests upon the theory that he has reserved to himself the exclusive property in a portion of his own land. Consequently the churchwardens, whose duty it is to seat the congregation, are not entitled to authorize anyone to use the lay rector's seat or seats even though unoccupied after a service has begun. It also follows that a lay rector's rights do not depend

on his being a parishioner and that he can, in the absence of any special user altering the usual nature of the reservation, authorize anyone he pleases to occupy his seat or seats. The only case in which a lay rector's rights might be lost would occur if he removed his seating accommodation, including the enclosure of his pew, since the nature of the reservation is probably the retention of a seat and not of a site for a seat.

Rights to seats of several owners of land allotted in lieu of tithe

17. There is little authority on the question of the rights to seats of several owners of land allotted in lieu of tithes. In *Lanchbury v Bode* [1898] 2 Ch 120, Kekewich J seems to have thought that owners of land allotted in lieu of tithes could not claim any rectorial rights. This was however merely *obiter* and does not carry much weight; and in *Stileman-Gibbard v Wilkinson* [1897] 1 QB 749, Charles J said (at p. 762) that the parson was entitled to the chief seat whether impropriator or instituted rector (see also *Spry v Flood* [1840] 2 Curt 353). A somewhat analogous case is *Harris v Drewe* (1831) 2 B & Ad 164, in which it was decided that when a pew had been appropriated by faculty to a house which had come into two occupancies the pew should be apportioned, and if the persons entitled became too numerous and should disagree, they must settle their differences between themselves. The right of sitting in the allotted space was compared to a right of common pasture. The pew in that case was in the nave, but the same principle would apply to a seat in the chancel.

18. In the event of persons coming under this heading failing to agree so that confusion resulted, there would probably have to be an application to the consistory court to settle the matter (see Prideaux's *Churchwardens Guide*, 16th edn, 1895, p. 29, cited with approval by Charles J in *Stileman-Gibbard v Wilkinson*, above, at p. 763).

(2004)

Church building: clocks

District councils and parish councils have certain powers to provide and light public clocks (*see* Public Health Act 1875, s165, and Parish Councils Act 1957, s2). Local authorities have power to bear the reasonable cost of repairing, maintaining, winding up and lighting any public clock in their area, whether or not the clock belongs to the local authority (*see* Public Health Acts Amendment Act 1890, s46).

(1994)

Church building: consecrated chapels and the faculty jurisdiction of the consistory court

1. The Council for the Care of Churches ('the Council') asked for an Opinion about the extent of its duty, pursuant to section 1 of the Care of Places of Worship Measure 1999 ('CPWM'), to compile and maintain a list of buildings, at present outside the faculty jurisdiction, which will result in them becoming subject to the jurisdiction of the consistory court (ss1(1)(2), 3(2). An issue had arisen as to whether certain buildings used for worship were already subject to the faculty jurisdiction. If they were there was no requirement for them to be included in the list and, indeed, the Council had no power to do so (s1(5)).

2. The buildings about which the Council sought advice were those listed in section 1(2) of the CPWM, namely:

'(a)   a building which is subject to any peculiar jurisdiction and which is used for worship according to the rites and ceremonies of the Church of England;

(b)   a building which is a chapel forming part of an episcopal house of residence;

(c)   a building which is a chapel or other place of worship owned or leased by or held by deed in trust for a religious community;

(d)   a building (not being one falling within any of the foregoing paragraphs) which is part of a university, college, school, hospital, Inn of Court, almshouse or other public or charitable institution and of which the primary use is for worship according to the rites and ceremonies of the Church of England or for joint worship by members of the Church of England and other Churches.'

No reference is contained in the CPWM to the consecration of such building or its effect.

3. If such buildings are *unconsecrated*, they are not subject to the faculty jurisdiction unless they are parish churches, or are buildings which have been licensed for public worship by order of the bishop (Care of Churches and Ecclesiastical Jurisdiction Measure 1991 (s11(1)(2))). With those exceptions such buildings are therefore eligible for inclusion in the list which will bring them within the jurisdiction of the consistory court. If they are *consecrated* the matter is not so simple.

4. A building becomes consecrated when the bishop of the diocese signs a sentence 'by which he separates and sets apart the building from all profane and common uses whatsoever, dedicates the same to the service of Almighty God for the performance therein of divine offices and consecrates the same for the celebration of such offices' (*Re St John, Chelsea* [1962] 1 WLR 706, 708 per Newsom, Ch). He went on to say that, in consequence of the sentence of consecration, 'the building, and with it the land on which it stands, becomes consecrated land, held to sacred uses and subject to the jurisdiction of this court'.

5. In these circumstances it might be thought that all buildings referred to in section 1(2) (see para 2 above) would be subject to the faculty jurisdiction if consecrated by the bishop. However, such buildings, all of which are referred to popularly as 'peculiars', have long been the subject of claims, by those responsible for them, that the faculty jurisdiction does not apply to them. Indeed such claims were often accepted by the bishop and chancellor in relation to alterations proposed to be made to those buildings, on the ground that the bishop was not the Ordinary, the Ordinary being the governing body of the institution in question. (*Halsbury's Laws of England*, 4th edn, 1975, vol. 14, para 1309; *Moore's Introduction to Canon Law*, 3rd edn, pp. 45–6; *Hill on Ecclesiastical Law*, 2nd edn, pp. 84–5.)

6. At one time there were 300 or more places of worship in respect of which such claims were made and often accepted or, at least, not challenged. However, by the Ecclesiastical Commissioners Acts 1836 and 1850 many peculiar jurisdictions were abolished. Moreover, as already indicated, any building which is subject to a peculiar jurisdiction and which is also a parish church, is now deemed to be subject to the faculty jurisdiction.

7. Neither has it always been the case that a governing body has claimed that the faculty jurisdiction did not apply. In *Re Tonbridge School Chapel (No 1)* [1993] 1 WLR 1138, the school governors, who petitioned for a faculty to rebuild the chapel which had been almost burnt to the ground in a fire, and the party opponents, jointly submitted to the jurisdiction of the consistory court which duly accepted jurisdiction. There had indeed been at least four previous petitions for faculties in respect of proposed alterations to the chapel since its foundation towards the end of the nineteenth century and no one had ever questioned the application of the faculty jurisdiction to the school's chapel. In the course of his judgement, Goodman, Ch commented as follows:

'Generally speaking, the faculty jurisdiction is applied to parish churches and other consecrated buildings within a parish. Certain buildings are clearly outside faculty jurisdiction, for example cathedrals ... The position with regard to consecrated school chapels, and the consecrated chapels of certain other institutions "is not sufficiently clear to justify any general statement of the law:" see *Halsbury's Laws of England*, 4th edn, 1975, vol. 14, p. 725, para 1309. It may depend to some extent on whether the bishop is ordinary in respect of the chapel in question and whether the building was consecrated for public worship. However, in the present case the chapel was consecrated by the Archbishop of Canterbury "to the service of Almighty God and Divine Worship according to the rites and ceremonies of the Church of England", and I note that in a faculty of 1907 the Bishop of Rochester described himself as acting "by virtue of our authority ordinary and Episcopal".'

8. The submission to the jurisdiction of the consistory court in relation to Tonbridge School Chapel has, it is understood, been echoed in relation to other such chapels, where the bishop of the diocese in which the chapel was situated was Ordinary. Lincoln's Inn Chapel has been dealt with under the faculty jurisdiction upon proof of consecration.

9. Therefore the questions which the Council should ask in the case of an application to be included in the list are:

(1)   Was the building consecrated? If not, then it is almost certainly outside the faculty jurisdiction and eligible for inclusion in the list.

(2)   If it was consecrated, who has authority as Ordinary in exercising jurisdiction over the building? If it is the governing body of the institution and not the bishop, the building is outside the faculty jurisdiction and can be included in the list. If the bishop is Ordinary, the building is already subject to the faculty jurisdiction and is ineligible for inclusion in the list. It will be necessary to examine the available evidence, including the Sentence of Consecration (if still in existence) and other documents relating to the building's foundation. The fact that the building was consecrated by the bishop is only the beginning of the enquiry and not the end. Evidence that the bishop is visitor is likely to be highly relevant, as is evidence about faculties being granted or refused in the past in respect of the building. If the terms of the consecration are known and they specify that the building is consecrated for public worship that would be a strong indicator that the bishop acted as Ordinary, and the building could reasonably be assumed to be

within the faculty jurisdiction already. However, the Council can only be expected to make reasonable enquiries and if, having done so, the position remains doubtful, then the Council will be justified in including the building in the list.

10. One of the problems, until the passing of the CPWM, was that, in the case of many institutions where the bishop was Ordinary, the governing bodies of the institutions in question did not submit to the jurisdiction of the consistory court, neither were they encouraged to do so, probably because it was not then appreciated that such buildings could be brought within its jurisdiction. It is therefore important, where an application is made in the case of a consecrated building for it to be included in the list maintained by the Council and if it is refused, that the Council notifies the governing body of the building in question that it is already subject to faculty jurisdiction and reports that fact to the registrar of the diocese.

11. The provision in the CPWM, whereby places of worship outside the faculty jurisdiction can be included in the Council's list and therefore become subject to the faculty jurisdiction of the consistory court, is particularly important. This is because, in the past, when it was successfully claimed that a peculiar was outside the faculty jurisdiction, then, if it was a listed building, it was also exempt from the need to obtain listed building consent to changes to the building (Planning (Listed Buildings and Conservation Areas) Act 1990 s60). The result was the listed building could end up being subject to neither ecclesiastical nor secular control, to the detriment of the building itself. This should not be allowed to happen again.

(May 2002)

Church building: customary rights of church way

Introduction

1. The Commission considered customary rights of church way, under which parishioners are entitled to cross land which does not belong to them to reach the parish church even though it is not possible to establish the existence of a public right of way. The Commission's specific advice was sought on three matters:

(i)   Whether the customary right can be exercised with vehicles and whether it can include a right to park vehicles;

(ii)   Whether the right extends only to parishioners seeking to attend the church for regular Sunday or weekday services, or whether it also applies to occasional services and the use of the church for personal prayer and

(iii)   How far customary rights of church way survive after the church has been made redundant.

Guidance from textbooks

2. Limited assistance is available in the principal textbooks in relation to the questions under consideration. The authors draw a distinction between public highways and the special features of a church way as a way to the church for persons from a defined locality. Thus:

(i)   Rogers, *Ecclesiastical Law* (London, 1849) at pp. 263–4 says 'The right to a church way may be claimed and maintained in the spiritual court; for a way leading to the church terminating at the churchyard is not a highway, because it does not belong to all the subjects of the realm, but to the inhabitants of a particular house, hamlet, village or parish, each of which may maintain an action at law for a nuisance therein; but if it were a public way the private would be merged in the public injury and then the remedy would be by indictment . . .'. Claims that the way is a highway or belongs to all the parishioners by prescription are triable in the temporal (and not spiritual) courts. Rogers also states 'Individuals or the public may by prescription have a right of way, and parishioners have a right of way in order to attend divine worship, vestries, and for going to the church on other fit occasions.'

(ii)   Phillimore, 2nd edn, 1895, uses similar terms at p. 1444 describing a church way as a 'private way' because it belongs to a particular class of inhabitants.

(iii)   Cripps, *Law relating to the Church and Clergy*, 7th edn, 1921, at pp. 421–2 says that a church way is a customary right of use (or quasi-easement) of land for the parishioners at large to have a way to the church. It is a 'private and limited right' in contrast to a public right of way. The right may include a portion of the way which is consecrated ground as well as the rights 'in alieno solo'.

(iv)   *Halsbury's Laws of England*, 4th edn, 1989 re-issue, vol. 12(1), at para 637 refers to a customary church way as 'a right of way in favour of the parishioners to go to and from the parish church over the land of a private individual owner and is enjoyed by the parishioners as a means of access to the parish church'.

3.   None of the textbooks consulted expressly states that the church way is limited to access on foot only, although there are references to 'footway' (Rogers at p. 264) and 'ancient footpath' (*Walter v Montague* (1836) 1 Curt p 261 cited in Phillimore at p. 1414). From a practical point of view it is reasonable to assume that the private landowner did not object to parishioners crossing his land on foot to reach the church but that those on horseback or travelling with a horse and carriage would have been expected to use a route which was a public highway. However, because custom is local law (*Halsbury's Laws of England*, vol. 12 (1), paras 602–4) the nature of use of a particular way would depend upon the evidence of user in that locality. Thus there could have been limited use by those on horseback, horse-drawn hearses, wheeled biers and such like using a church way in a particular parish. When the ground was dry perambulators or early forms of wheelchair for the disabled could have been used.

Authorities

4. The case of *Brocklebank v Thompson* [1903] 2 Ch 344 is not inconsistent with this approach. In that case the parish church was situated in the midst of fields and the action was for an injunction to restrain the defendant from trespassing upon a footpath crossing the plaintiff's park and terminating at the church (p. 345). The evidence as to user of the disputed way was that the parishioners used it on foot only (p. 346), although corpses were carried along the way for burial in the churchyard (p. 353). It is hardly surprising that the judge approached

the matter as one relating simply to a church way on foot. The plaintiff sought to argue that the custom was limited to tenants of the manor but this argument failed as the Judge held that the customary church way was available to parishioners at large.

5. In *Farquhar v Newbury Rural District Council* [1909] 1 Ch 12 the facts disclosed that from time immemorial there had been several church ways across the estate 'for the most part merely undefined tracks'. The church was rebuilt in 1841 and in 1942 the church ways were diverted and replaced by a road suitable for vehicular traffic. The Court of Appeal held that the church way had been subsumed in the public highway and the owners could not argue that they had only intended to create a new church path when they had in reality created a highway. It was pointed out that a church way arises from time immemorial and 'cannot now be created anew' (at p. 19).

6. It is worth noting that Joyce J in *Brocklebank v Thompson* did not regard 'occasional use by other persons, or for purposes not strictly within the limited legal right' as detracting from the legal right of church way established to exist (p. 351).

Purposes for which church way may be used

7. Both Rogers and Phillimore cite *Walter v Montague* for the proposition that the parishioners' right of way is 'for attendance on divine worship, vestries, and other fit occasions'. The reference to 'vestries' shows that the user was assumed to be of considerable frequency and not limited to the twentieth-century notion of church attendance on Sunday. Prior to the formation of local authorities the vestry was an 'assembly of the whole parish met together in some convenient place for the dispatch of the affairs and business of the parish'. Thus in so far as there is now some revival of community use of churches and church hall extensions there is no obvious reason why a church way, being a way to the church, should not be used by parishioners going to the church for a particular group meeting.

8. Going to the church 'on other fit occasions' is also a wide expression, which in a modern context could be interpreted as covering attendance by a parishioner at an occasional service, for personal prayer or attending a flower festival and such like. The same applies to parishioners tidying the churchyard or tending graves in the churchyard. Furthermore, use of the church way by non-parishioners (certainly on foot) would in practice be overlooked at a court as being de minimis and not in any event, detracting from an established right of way (as was made clear by Joyce J in *Brocklebank v Thompson*, para 6 above).

9. The same point can be made in respect of weddings and funerals. Although the rights of burial and to marry at common law are vested in the parishioners, and the extension of the rights to those on the electoral roll could not create a new customary church way, the use of the church way by some non-parishioners to attend a lawful burial and a wedding could be regarded as de minimis. Any visit to a parsonage house in connection with a funeral or a wedding would simply be incidental to the use of the church way to the church and not a separate church way.

10. But use of the way for purposes outside or beyond those described in *Walter v Montague* by non-parishioners, for example by those who wish to visit the building for purposes such as to admire the architecture or the stained glass, to play the organ or to ring the bells (other than as part of or in preparation for church services), cannot be regarded as de minimis and so cannot be claimed as a right of church way.

Non-parishioners

11. There is no guidance in the cases or legal textbooks on the point whether a person whose name is on the electoral roll but is not a parishioner has the right in law to use a church way 'for attendance on divine worship, vestries and other fit occasions'. This is not surprising as the principles relating to a church way were established in law at a time when the emphasis was upon the residence within the parish of those who used it to reach their parish church.

12. A church way has its validity and authority in custom from time immemorial and a particular custom may develop and change over the years. The Commission's view is that a church way may afford a right of way to those on the electoral roll who are not parishioners to exercise their statutory rights in relation to the parish church on whose roll their name appears. Persons whose names are on the electoral roll have a right to be married in the parish church and to be buried in the churchyard (Church of England (Miscellaneous Provisions) Measure 1976, s6). They may be elected members of the PCC and if elected, are required to attend PCC meetings, and may be chosen as churchwardens. To maintain an entry on the electoral roll a person is required to attend public worship regularly 'to have habitually attended public worship in the parish during a period of six months prior to enrolment . . .' (CRR, r1(2)).

Church ways and ways of necessity

13. Although a church way may have originated as a necessary means of access to an ancient church the right vested in parishioners at large is

separate and distinct from any easement which may belong to the church as a dominant tenement.

14. The statement by Sir John Pennycuick in *St Edmundsbury and Ipswich DBF v Clark (No 2)* [1975] 1 WLR 468 that 'the church authorities may have a vehicular right of way of necessity to the church for the purpose of taking up building materials and the like' (p. 481) was *obiter dictum* and made in the context of a right of way reserved in a conveyance. The existence of a private easement of necessity over another person's land would depend upon the existence of a grant and have to be determined in accordance with the established principles of law (see *Halsbury's Laws of England*, 4th edn, 1975, vol. 14, para 152). Similarly any other easement of way for employees of the PCC (e.g. a verger) or independent contractors could exist if established by user for the purposes of prescription or presumption of a lost modern grant.

Parking vehicles

15. There seems to be no scope for arguing that a right of parking modern vehicles is incidental to a customary right of way – consistent with what is said above (para 3) perambulators and wheelchairs could possibly have been 'parked' or even a horse tethered but this would almost certainly have been on church property (i.e. the churchyard) and not on the adjoining owner's land. Any right to park on adjoining land (church way or not) would, therefore, have to be acquired by long user sufficient to satisfy the requirements of prescription or lost modern grant (20 years user).

Effect of redundancy

16. Pastoral Measure 1983, section 60(2) has amended the customary law on rights of church way: it makes provision for the use of rights of way over land adjoining or adjacent to a church which has been declared redundant in whole or in part. The test is whether rights of way 'were, before the declaration (of redundancy) took effect, enjoyed by persons attending the church'. This is a question of fact as in the case of any church way.

17. On the assumption that enjoyment of a right of way over land adjoining or adjacent to the church when in use can be proved, the effect of section 60(2) is to enable that right of way (or ways) to continue to be enjoyed after redundancy in certain circumstances. It is a prerequisite that the church or the relevant part of it vests in the Churches Conservation Trust or in the DBF. Vesting in any other owner (particularly a private owner) is therefore excluded from the section.

18. The rights of way are continued in existence following redundancy by virtue of the express terms of section 60(2) and are exercisable in a different way from the rights originally acquired as a church way 'by persons attending the church'. This is because the section enables the rights to be enjoyed

(i)   by the Trust or the Board (depending upon the body in which the church or the relevant part is vested) for the performance of its functions

(ii)   by members of the public for the purpose of visiting the church.

19. The effect of the section is, therefore, to convert pre-existing rights of church way into rights of a different nature exercisable for different purposes and by different bodies and persons. Parishioners and those on the electoral roll are members of the public and so their right to visit the redundant church will be based on the Measure and no longer upon any customary right.

20. Where the scheme makes the church (or part of it e.g. an aisle or chapel) but not the churchyard or curtilage (or the whole or it) (or vice versa) redundant it is submitted that the right of church way remains unaffected and undiminished in so far as that part of the building or land which has not been made redundant is concerned. So where the churchyard is not declared redundant it seems likely that the right of church way over adjoining land may continue to be lawfully used e.g. to go to the churchyard to visit a grave or bring in materials for repair of paths, gravestones etc.

General conclusions

21. It would seem that a right of church way has the following characteristics:

(i)   it is a customary right of way arising from user from time immemorial and cannot now be created anew: it is not an easement as there is no dominant tenement

(ii)   it is a private right of way for the parishioners leading to the church terminating at the churchyard

(iii)   the church way may be used to attend public worship, other services and private prayer but also on other occasions to attend other lawful uses of the building or churchyard both being used for ecclesiastical or spiritual purposes

(iv)   it is a right of way on foot: whether the user is more extension, e.g. horses or vehicles, depends upon the customary law established in a particular case in a particular parish

(v)   it is not a public right of way or highway: the general public, i.e. persons who are not parishioners or on the electoral roll do not have the right to use the church way (where one exists for the parishioners): but any member of the public using the church way in order to attend the church for public worship, private prayer, funerals, tending the graves in the churchyard, or other lawful uses of the church whilst being used as an ecclesiastical building or burial ground, could be regarded as de minimis

(vi)   it does not include a right to park carts, carriages or vehicles on the land over which the right of church way runs

(vii)   where a redundancy scheme has been made in respect of a church or part of a church, the right of church way will have been modified by section 60(2) of the Pastoral Measure 1983 and replaced by a new right for members of the public to use the right of way to visit the redundant church.

Response to the enquiry made of the Commission

22. In response to the three matters identified in paragraph 1 the Commission's opinion is:

(i)   A church way is a customary right from time immemorial and is primarily to enable parishioners to have access to their church on foot. The custom will depend upon the actual user in a particular parish so that a wheeled bier, perambulators etc may use the particular church way (para 3). It is highly unlikely that it could be proved that vehicles used a church way unless it was also a public highway. Parking would not be incidental to the use of a church way and would have to be proved to exist as a private easement, if at all (para 15).

(ii)   The purposes for which parishioners could use the church way were wide at common law including 'vestries and other fit occasions'. There is no reason why modern usage should be construed more strictly. When services are held which parishioners are invited to attend the landowners could not properly contend that parishioners were not using the church way for access to the church building either for 'divine worship' on 'a fit occasion'. Private prayer would come within the latter category (paras 7 to 9).

(iii)   Continuance of the church way would depend upon the terms of the redundancy (para 16).

(May 2000, revised 2003)

Church building: ecclesiastical exemption: churches in use and churchyards

The ecclesiastical exemption generally

1. Many churches in use are included in a list of buildings of special architectural or historic interest, now maintained under the provisions of the Planning (Listed Buildings and Conservation Areas) Act 1990. The listing of the church covers not only the building but also objects and structures fixed to the building, and free-standing objects or structures within the curtilage of the building which have formed part of the land since before 1 July 1948 (s1(5) of the 1990 Act).

2. All secular listed buildings are subject to the controls laid down in the Act and listed building consent must be obtained from the local planning authority or the Secretary of State in respect of works for the demolition of a listed building, or its alteration or extension in any manner which would affect its character as a building of special architectural or historic interest. Listed churches have, however, long enjoyed an exemption known as the 'ecclesiastical exemption' from such statutory controls. This is in recognition of the fact that the Church of England operates its own regulatory system of control over alterations to its churches through the faculty jurisdiction.

3. The Secretary of State has exercised the new power conferred by section 60(5) of the 1990 Act to restrict the extent of the ecclesiastical exemption, primarily in relation to other denominations.

4. The extent of the ecclesiastical exemption in relation to Church of England churches and churchyards is controlled by the Ecclesiastical Exemption (Listed Buildings and Conservation Areas) Order 1994, SI 1994/1771, which came into force on 1 October 1994. This has made relatively few changes to the previous position, such changes being limited to objects or structures fixed to the exterior of a church building or within its curtilage, which will need listed building consent if they have been listed separately and apart from the building in their own right.

5. Consequently the ecclesiastical exemption continues to apply and no listed building consent is required in respect of:

   (a)   alterations or extensions to a church building, which is defined as a building whose primary use is as a place of worship;

   (b)   works to any object or structure within a church building (as so defined);

(c)   works to any object or structure fixed to the exterior of a church building (as so defined) unless the object or structure has been listed in its own right;

(d)   works to any object or structure within the curtilage of a church building (as so defined) and forming part of the land unless such object or structure has been listed in its own right.

Even if the object or structure in (c) or (d) has been separately listed, it is not every item or work which requires listed building consent. Demolition of the object or structure clearly needs such consent – other works require listed building consent only if they would affect the character of the object or structure as an item of special architectural or historic interest.

6. The need for listed building consent in respect of objects or structures if, and only if, they have been separately listed is additional to the requirement for a faculty which applies to all works (other than those which are specified by the chancellor as de minimis). A churchyard which has been closed by Order in Council remains within the faculty jurisdiction and the same principles apply to it.

'Object or structure'

7. Although not defined in the Order, the words 'object or structure' clearly have a wide meaning. 'Structure' is defined in the *Shorter Oxford Dictionary* as 'a fabric or framework of material parts put together' and 'object' as 'a material thing'.

8. Thus chapels, church halls, potting sheds, shelters and so on can properly be regarded as structures, whether free-standing or affixed to a church building. Similarly mausoleums, vaults, tombs, statues, headstones and other monuments would be objects even if some could not properly be said to be structures. Indeed virtually everything would be covered by the words 'object or structure'. Moreover by virtue of the Order it is unnecessary to prove that such objects or structures are themselves specifically used for ecclesiastical purposes.

Curtilage: churchyard

9. The Order refers to 'curtilage' rather than to 'churchyard' and it is therefore necessary to consider whether the word curtilage would cover the whole of a churchyard, some of which are very large. There is no definition of 'curtilage' in the legislation. In the *Shorter Oxford Dictionary* it is defined as 'a small court, or piece of ground attached to a dwellinghouse and forming an enclosure with it'. In *Termes de la Ley*,

1671 edn, it is defined as a 'garden, yard, field or piece of void ground lying near and belonging to the messuage'.[1]

10. Thus 'curtilage' would seem to cover any land near to and belonging to[2] the church building but probably not land physically separated from it, for example, by a road. All consecrated and most unconsecrated churchyards, at least if they are in the same enclosure as the church, would be regarded as being within its curtilage.[3]

11. In practical terms the question for the future will be – is the object or structure listed in its own right? If it is, then the boundary of the curtilage will not matter, because whether the object or structure is inside or outside the curtilage, listed building consent will be required for certain works to it. If, on the other hand, the object or structure is not separately listed but is within the curtilage of a listed church building (and thus treated as part of the building) the ecclesiastical exemption will apply, and no listed building consent will be required.

12. Different principles apply in the case of cathedrals, redundant churches and detached burial grounds.

(May 1995, revised 2003)

---

[1] In *Philbrow v St Leonard's, Shoreditch, Vestry* [1895] 1 QB 33 at p. 37 Matthew J described curtilage as a 'courtyard, backside or piece of ground lying near or belonging to the premises'.

[2] 'belonging to' means 'belong, or go, together in a physical sense' see *Re St John's Church, Bishop's Hatfield* [1967] P 113.

[3] In *Re St George's, Oakdale* [1976] Fam 210 at p. 220 Chancellor Ellison said of the word curtilage in a case under section 7(1) of the Faculty Jurisdiction Measure 1964 that 'its territorial extent will depend on the facts of the individual case and the circumstances of the particular site'. In *Re St Mary Magdalene's, Paddington* [1980] Fam 99, Chancellor Newsom observed that, where the churchyard is unconsecrated, the churchyard may be greater than the land forming the curtilage of the church for the purposes of the faculty jurisdiction. See also *Re Christ Church, Chislehurst* [1973] 1 WLR 1317. More recently in relation to the planning legislation it has been said that what constituted the curtilage is 'quintessentially a matter of fact': *James v Secretary of State* [1991] 1 PLR 58. In *Skerrits of Nottingham v Secretary of State for the Environment, Transport and Regions* [2001] 1 QB 59, the Court of Appeal went further and held that 'the curtilage of a building need not always be small, nor was the nature of smallness inherent in the expression; that the word "curtilage" could not usefully be described as a term of art and the question of what fell within the curtilage of a building was one of fact and degree'.

Church building: flags

Without making it compulsory, the Earl Marshal laid down in 1938 that the flag proper to be flown on any church in the Provinces of Canterbury and York is a St George's Cross with the arms of the see (which should not be surmounted by a mitre except where used by the bishop personally) in the first quarter. Detailed guidance was given in the *8th Report of the Council for the Care of Churches*, published in 1940.

(1994)

Church building: improper removal of the contents

Ownership of contents

1. The contents of a parish church belong to the parishioners. 'Contents' may be defined as the ornaments, utensils and goods of a church, viz. those things in and appertaining to the church and its curtilage which are not affixed to the fabric or the soil and which are therefore not part of the realty. The legal possession, sometimes referred to in the authorities as the 'title to' or 'property in' the contents, is in the churchwardens. The churchwardens are in law deemed to be a quasi-corporation for this purpose, viz. they are in possession of the goods jointly, in virtue of their office, and not severally as individuals. Whatever expression is used, whether it be 'property in', 'the vesting of the property in', 'possession of' or 'legal title to' the contents, the right so described is not an absolute right of ownership, but is held and to be exercised for and on behalf of the parishioners, in other words the contents are vested in the churchwardens for the use and benefit of the parishioners.

Authorities

Sir Alfred Kempe, Chancellor London, in *St Mary Northolt (Vicar and Churchwardens) v Parishioners* [1920] P 97, citing Prideaux's *Churchwardens Guide*, 16th edn, 1895, p. 333; and *Jackson v Adams* (1835) 2 Bing NC 403; Canon E 1 para 5; also authorities cited in Phillimore, *Ecclesiastical Law*, 2nd edn, 1895 vol. 2, p. 1484.

2. The reference to a church and its curtilage in paragraph 1 is to a consecrated church and its churchyard and to the curtilage of a consecrated church, whether the curtilage itself is consecrated or not (see s7 of the Faculty Jurisdiction Measure 1964). The principles mentioned in paragraph 1 will also apply to the contents of buildings licensed for public worship which are subject to the faculty jurisdiction (see s6 of that Measure and s11(2) of the Care of Churches and Ecclesiastical Jurisdiction Measure 1991).

3. No opinion is expressed upon the ownership of or right to remove the contents of buildings which are licensed for public worship but not subject to the faculty jurisdiction.

Disposal of contents

4. The churchwardens may lawfully dispose of any of the contents of a church with the consent of the parish and a faculty granted by the chancellor of the diocese. Such disposal may be by sale, whether at a full

value or less, bailment, whether gratuitous or for valuable consideration, or gift.

5. Before the Church of England Assembly (Powers) Act 1919 the consent of the parish was signified by an affirmative vote at a meeting of the vestry of the parish. The powers of the vestry in such a matter have devolved upon the PCC (see s4(1)(i) of the Parochial Church Councils (Powers) Measure 1956). Therefore the consent of the parish should be given by a resolution of the PCC passed by a majority of those present at the meeting, due notice of the resolution having been given in accordance with the CRR.

6. The licence of the Ordinary will, in the case of a parish church, be signified by the issue of a faculty bearing the seal of the consistory court and authorizing the disposition. The consistory court appears to have no jurisdiction to authorize, by faculty, the permanent alienation (as opposed to the temporary disposition as by loan) of any of the contents of a parish church in the absence of the consent of the parish. The faculty will, therefore, in the absence of evidence to the contrary, be sufficient proof that the consent of the parish to the disposition has been obtained.

7. The conditions precedent which must be satisfied before there can be a valid disposition of any of the contents of a church are therefore:

(a)   an affirmative resolution of the PCC, convened in accordance with the CRR;

(b)   a faculty authorizing the disposition; and

(c)   the joint assent of both churchwardens. (If there is only one churchwarden, through death or other cause, it may be that the assent of that one is sufficient, though it is preferable that the vacant office should be filled and a joint assent given.)

Trustees distinguished

8. A distinction should be noticed between churchwardens and trustees. Trustees in whom personal property is vested are the owners of the legal title to the property. A disposal, otherwise than in the course of the trust, by trustees of personal property to a stranger to the trust, who has no notice of the trust and who gives valuable consideration, passes the legal title of that property to that person. Churchwardens who dispose of the contents of a church improperly do not give a good title to those contents to the person receiving them, whether or not that person has notice whence they came or gives valuable consideration for them. The reason is

that the churchwardens have no power to dispose of any of the contents of the church until express authority for such disposal has been given by parish and Ordinary (*Re St Mary's Barton-upon-Humber* [1987] Fam 41).

Effect of valid disposal

9. Once a valid disposal, by way of sale or gift, of the contents of a church has been made, the goods in question become ordinary things in commerce and are wholly divested of any sacred character. This general proposition may be qualified by the nature of any particular transaction – as where ornaments are disposed of to another church.

Fixtures

10. Some of the contents of a church may be so affixed to the fabric of the church or the ground upon which it stands as to be in law fixtures and so part of the realty. Examples are: organs, pews, fonts and panelling. In the case of these contents which, as fixtures, are part of the church there is a statutory bar on their disposal. Section 56(2) of the Pastoral Measure 1983 provides that unless a faculty be granted it shall not be lawful to 'sell, lease or otherwise dispose of any ... part of a church ... except in pursuance of powers under' section 30 or Part III of the Measure, viz. except under a pastoral or a redundancy scheme.

Invalid disposal of contents

11. If a disposal of the contents of a church is made, in respect of which any of the above-mentioned conditions precedent to the disposal are not satisfied, the property in the goods does not pass but remains in the churchwardens. This is true however many subsequent disposals of the goods there may be and whatever the terms of such subsequent disposals. This general proposition is subject to the special cases mentioned in paragraphs 23–4 below.

12. Churchwardens do not have the general property in the contents of a church but only a special property. Therefore churchwardens who purport to sell any of the contents, when the above-mentioned conditions precedent are not satisfied, are not making a sale within the meaning of the expression in the Sale of Goods Act 1979. Sales to which the Act applies are sales of the general property in goods (see s2(1) of the 1979 Act and the definition of 'property' in s61(1)), whereas the churchwardens have only a special property. They have only a special property because the general property is divided between the parishioners, the PCC and the churchwardens, although the right to possession is in the churchwardens. (For an instance of the general property being divided between owners

but the right to possession being in one alone, see *Nyberg v Handelaar* [1892] 2 QB 202.)

13. The former powers, duties and liabilities of churchwardens of a parish with respect to the care, maintenance, preservation and insurance of the goods and ornaments of the parish church are now vested in the PCC of the parish under the Parochial Church Councils (Powers) Measure 1956, section 4(1)(ii)(b). That section states that this provision does not 'affect the property of the churchwardens in the goods and ornaments of the church', but care, maintenance, preservation and insurance are all aspects of both general and special property. The section is therefore consistent with the proposition that the property of the churchwardens in the contents of a parish church is a special property, viz. the right to possession of them.

14. If upon a purported sale by churchwardens, the goods in question are received by a person in good faith and without notice of any claim or right of the parishioners, such a person cannot invoke the provisions of the Factors Act 1889 or the Sale of Goods Act 1979 to validate his title. It has been held in the House of Lords in the case of *National Employers' Mutual General Insurance Association Ltd v Jones* [1990] 1 AC 24 that no subsequent dealings after a purported sale by a thief can ever supply the initial want of title. The reasoning in that case applies equally to a purported sale by a person with a special property only.

Dishonest disposal

15. At common law churchwardens could not commit larceny of the contents of a church as they were in lawful possession of them (see *Jackson v Adams* (1835) 2 Bing NC 403). However, the common law offence of larceny has been abolished (s32(1)(a) of the Theft Act 1968). By the 1968 Act theft is the dishonest appropriation of property belonging to another with the intention of permanently depriving the other of it (s1(1)). By section 5(3) of the Act 'Where a person received property from or on account of another, and is under an obligation to the other to retain and deal with that property or its proceeds in a particular way, the property or proceeds shall be regarded (as against him) as belonging to the other.' Churchwardens receive the contents of the parish church for or on account of the parishioners at large and are under obligation to retain and deal with them in a particular way. If therefore one or other disposes, or both dispose, of the contents (viz. appropriate them) dishonestly it is arguable this amounts to stealing the contents. If, therefore, a dishonest disposal can be proved the goods taken may be treated as having been stolen, which should simplify a claim for their recovery.

Abolition of market overt

16. For centuries, if goods, for example altar candlesticks, were stolen from a church and sold in market overt, the buyer could, subject to satisfying the conditions of section 22(1) of the Sale of Goods Act 1979, claim a good title, to the great disadvantage of the unfortunate parish.

17. However, as from 3 January 1995, by virtue of the Sale of Goods (Amendment) Act 1994, the law relating to market overt was abolished, and proceedings can be taken to recover from an innocent third party contents of a church which are improperly disposed of in circumstances formerly covered by the market overt rules.

Recovery of contents improperly removed

18. If the contents of a church are improperly removed, the proper plaintiffs in proceedings at common law to recover them are the churchwardens (see Prideaux's *Churchwardens Guide*, 10th edn, 1865). While the churchwardens are undoubtedly competent and unassailable plaintiffs, the PCC is arguably a competent plaintiff. In order to maintain an action for conversion and a right of property in the goods at the time of conversion or detention, the plaintiff's property need not be absolute (see *Halsbury's Laws of England*, 4th edn, 1975, vol. 45, at para 1433) and as statutory successor to the churchwardens' powers and duties with respect to the care, maintenance and preservation of the goods and ornaments of the church, a PCC could presumably sue (see para 13 above). If the churchwardens are unable or unwilling to act the PCC would appear to have a statutory duty to sue and would, therefore, be a competent plaintiff but should, in such a case, join the churchwardens as parties, viz. as defendants.

19. If the defence of estoppel may be raised against churchwarden-plaintiffs it may be wise for any action to be commenced in the name of the PCC. Similarly if the disposal was made pursuant to a resolution of the PCC it may be wise for any action to be begun in the names of the churchwardens who were not members of the council when the resolution was passed.

20. In the specific case put to the Legal Advisory Commission it was suggested that the defence of estoppel might be raised against the incumbent (though the incumbent would not be a competent plaintiff), churchwardens and PCC since all were party to a sale of a pair of valuable gates to the suggested defendant. No doubt this would be an embarrassing situation but a person cannot raise an estoppel so as to cause a state of things which that person is legally disabled from creating.

To quote *Halsbury's Laws of England*, 4th edn, 1975, vol. 16, para 1596, 'thus a corporate or statutory body cannot be estopped from denying that it has entered into a contract which it was ultra vires for it to make. No corporate body can be bound by estoppel to do something beyond its powers or to refrain from doing what is its duty to do, and the same principle applies to individuals.' As the churchwardens and PCC had purported to make a sale which was not authorized by faculty they had no lawful power or authority to make such a sale. It follows that they could not be estopped from denying that they had a good title to sell the gates in question.

21. It has been suggested that there may be circumstances in which both PCC and churchwardens may be unwilling to commence proceedings, even though a duty to do so to recover contents of the church improperly disposed of may be shown. Should this occur, then the archdeacon might be able to apply to the High Court for a judicial review, making the churchwardens and PCC respondents, and by this means obtain an order of mandamus compelling them to sue. The remedy of mandamus is available as the power and duty of the churchwardens and PCC to protect and maintain the contents of the parish church is a public duty.

Allowance for improvement of contents invalidly disposed of

22. If any of the contents of a church have been improperly removed and have passed into the hands of persons who have acquired them in good faith and have also improved them, as by repair or restoration, statutory allowances may fall to be made under the Torts (Interference with Goods) Act 1977. The allowance is the extent to which the value of the goods is attributable to the improvement and is to be made in reduction of damages awarded for wrongful interference with the goods. If, as will normally be the case, the relief sought is an order for the delivery up of the chattel in question, the court may make it a condition for the grant of that relief that the statutory allowance is made (see s3(7) of the 1977 Act).

Expiry of right to recover

23. If any of the contents of a church are improperly removed, otherwise than by theft, the churchwardens', and the PCC's, cause of action in respect of the conversion is lost after the expiry of six years from the date of the conversion, under section 2 of the Limitation Act 1980. Furthermore if, during those six years, the churchwardens have not recovered possession of the goods, their title, and so that of the parishioners, to the goods is extinguished (s3(2)). This bar operates even though there may have been successive conversions following the original conversion while the goods have been out of the churchwardens'

possession. No action in respect of any succeeding conversion, whether for damages or for recovery of the goods, may be brought by the churchwardens more than six years after the date of the original conversion (s3(1)).

24. Where goods are stolen from a church there is no time bar in recovering damages or the goods themselves from the thief or from a person receiving the goods from or claiming through a thief unless the person from whom their recovery is sought is a buyer in good faith. A buyer in good faith will acquire title to goods six years from his or her purchase; if there be more than one such buyer the six years will begin to run from the first purchase by such a person. The parishioners, should the stolen goods come into the hands of such a buyer, may thus be deprived of their title to the goods themselves, but will still be able to claim damages, without limit of time, against the thief or any dishonest handler of the goods (Limitation Act 1980, s4).

(January 1989, revised 2003)

Church building: Inspection of Churches Measure 1955: approved architects and surveyors

1. The Commission was asked to advise whether there was any realistic possibility of an architect or surveyor mounting a legal challenge or claim, following the withdrawal of his or her approval by a Diocesan Advisory Committee exercising its powers under section 1 of the Inspection of Churches Measure 1955, as amended. If so, the Commission was asked what precautions could be taken to reduce or prevent the risk of a successful challenge or claim.

2. Under section 1 of the Inspection of Churches Measure 1955 ('the 1955 Measure'), as amended by the Care of Churches and Ecclesiastical Jurisdiction Measure 1991 ('the 1991 Measure'), each diocese of the Church of England has established a scheme to provide for the inspection of every church in the diocese at lease once in every five years ('the quinquennial inspection'). The inspection must be carried out, and the report made, by a qualified professional person approved by the Diocesan Advisory Committee (DAC) for any particular diocese. Under the original 1955 Measure the qualified professional person had to be an architect, but, by virtue of the 1991 Measure, it is permissible now to approve either an architect, or a chartered building surveyor who is a member of the Royal Institution of Chartered Surveyors.

3. Although inspecting architects and surveyors have to be approved by the DAC, they are chosen and appointed by the individual parishes. A contractual relationship thus comes into existence between the parish and the architect/surveyor, with the parish being legally responsible for the payment of the fee due. The 1955 Measure, as amended, lays down specific requirements with regard to the extent of the inspection necessary on each occasion.

4. Each DAC has its own system and criteria for approving architects and surveyors to undertake quinquennial inspections. Some dioceses have a two-tiered system, with the upper tier reserved for those persons approved for all churches within the diocese, and the lower tier reserved for those of more limited experience or competence, whose appointment is approved for churches of less architectural or historic significance.

5. Each DAC clearly has a right, and perhaps a duty, to review from time to time its list of approved architects and surveyors. If, on the basis of perceived skill and experience, it chooses to approve, or to promote to a higher tier or category, an architect or surveyor, it may, of course, do so. In the converse situation, how should a DAC respond if it considers that an approved architect or surveyor (i) has produced a sub-standard

quinquennial report or reports, (ii) is guilty of persistent delay in producing reports, or (iii) for some other reason, may no longer be a fit and proper person to remain on the approved list or lists? Examples of the latter could be, for instance, conviction of a serious criminal offence, bankruptcy, or long-term illness, whether physical or mental (including, perhaps, alcoholism), sub-standard work in areas other than the production of quinquennial inspections and advising a PCC to act in clear breach of the faculty jurisdiction.

6. It is of prime importance to recognize and accept that a decision by a DAC to withdraw approval from (or, as the case may be, to relegate to a lower category or tier) an individual architect or surveyor will, or is likely to, have an effect on that person's professional livelihood. The decision could have far-reaching consequences for the individual concerned. In the circumstances we are in no doubt that, in exercising its statutory function, the DAC is under a duty to act fairly and in accordance with natural justice. If it fails so to act, then an aggrieved individual would be entitled to apply to the Divisional Court of the High Court of Justice for judicial review of the decision of the DAC. This, in turn, could lead to the Court's quashing of the DAC's decision, together with a requirement that the matter be reconsidered by the DAC fairly and in accordance with natural justice.

7. What, in practice, does it mean to say that a DAC should act fairly and in accordance with the principles of natural justice? In the first place, its decision should be based only upon the evidence before it, and not upon unsubstantiated comment, gossip or rumour. Secondly, it is under a duty to investigate that evidence carefully and objectively. Thirdly, it should bear in mind that all professional people can make the occasional mistake or be criticized for a particular decision, but an occasional mistake or questionable decision, in itself, is insufficient to suggest or confirm general incompetence. To decide that someone is incapable of dealing satisfactorily with any ecclesiastical work within the diocese, and thus depriving that individual of what may be a substantial part of his or her professional livelihood, is a conclusion that should normally only be reached after receiving considerable persuasive evidence to that effect. Fourthly, and this is of paramount importance, such a decision should only be reached, if at all, after giving the individual concerned a proper opportunity to respond to the specific evidence of persistent sub-standard work. Fifthly, if requested so to do, a DAC should be prepared to give succinct written reasons for its decision. Since such a letter would be subject to qualified privilege, then, provided the DAC has reached its decision fairly and objectively on the evidence before it, it need have no fear of a libel action resulting.

8. A similar approach should be taken if the issue is whether or not to relegate an approved architect or surveyor from a higher to a lower grade of work within the diocese. In our view it would be wrong to reach such a decision arbitrarily and without careful consideration of all the relevant evidence, including his or her response, if any, to the specific allegations of sub-standard work upon which reliance is being placed.

9. It is important, however, that each DAC makes it clear to all approved architects and surveyors precisely (a) what areas it expects a quinquennial inspection to cover, and (b) what standard it expects an inspection report to reach. Otherwise, to speak of a report or reports being sub-standard begs the question. In some dioceses, arrangements are in place for the DAC to review all quinquennial inspection reports and to advise with regard to their adequacy. Such a system enables the standard of reports from an individual architect or surveyor to be monitored. If, at any stage, the DAC perceives the standard to be falling, then the individual concerned can be duly notified and, if the situation is sufficiently serious, warned of the possible consequences of continuing to submit sub-standard reports.

10. The other possibilities posed at the end of paragraph 5 above are, in practice, likely to be rare. In the event of such a situation arising, however, we would advise a DAC to act with caution before deciding to remove an individual from its approved list. It would be sensible first to find out the response (if any) to the situation adopted by the disciplinary body of the professional association to which the individual belongs. In any event, each situation is likely to be unique on its own facts, and in particular consideration should be given to the danger of involving the parish in a breach of contract with its architect or surveyor. If in doubt, the DAC should always seek appropriate legal advice.

(January 1997)

Church building: insurance

1. The insurance of the fabric of the parish church and all other ecclesiastical or parochial buildings in the parish, of the ornaments and furnishings of the churches within the parish and in respect of public liability is a matter which the incumbent, churchwardens and PCC must consider with care.

2. The PCC has the like powers, duties and liabilities as, on 21 July 1921, the churchwardens had with respect to the care, maintenance, preservation *and insurance* of the fabric of the church and the goods and ornaments thereof (s4(1)(ii)(b) of the Parochial Church Councils (Powers) Measure 1956). This statutory provision requires an assessment of what the scope and nature of the powers, duties and liabilities of churchwardens were in 1921 and then a decision how, if the Measure of 1956 had not been passed, churchwardens would exercise their powers and duties and the extent of any liability upon them in the changed circumstances of the present. The answer gives the measure of the powers, duties and liabilities of a PCC at the present time.

3. Churchwardens had, in 1921, duties in respect of the parish church which corresponded with the duties of a trustee. Although the legal title to the parish church was (and still is) in the incumbent the churchwardens were, to use the old phrase, 'guardians and keepers' of it. They, on behalf of the parishioners, had the duty of keeping the church in good and sufficient repair. (Distinctions between the duties in respect of nave and chancel may be overlooked for this purpose.)

4. In the absence of special legislation to the contrary, the goods and ornaments of a parish church belong to the parishioners, but the legal possession, sometimes referred to in the authorities as the 'title to' or 'property in' them, is in the churchwardens. In 1921 it would have been proper for the churchwardens to have insured the goods and ornaments in their joint names, as churchwardens. Again, since the churchwardens have no absolute right of ownership in the goods and ornaments of the church, but hold, and must exercise, the right for and on behalf of the parishioners, the churchwardens' duty to insure would, in 1921, have corresponded with the duty trustees of those goods, for the use and benefit of others, would have had.

5. A trustee is bound to take as much care of the trust property as an ordinary prudent man. The standard of care expected of an ordinary prudent man will vary from generation to generation. In the opinion of the Legal Advisory Commission that standard, at the present time, requires a trustee to insure buildings on the trust estate and goods and

chattels which he holds for the benefit of others. It follows that, in the opinion of the Legal Advisory Commission, churchwardens would, if the Measure of 1956 had not been passed, and PCCs, as it has been passed, have a duty to insure the church and other buildings of the parish and the goods and ornaments of the church against all usual risks. There is also a duty to insure against what is known as third party liability in its various forms.

6. The duty to insure is, nevertheless, not unqualified. In deciding how much to spend on insurance a PCC must take account of other proper claims on its income. A trustee is not obliged to pay insurance premiums out of his or her own pocket – the trustee's ability to pay the premiums required may be limited by the trust income. A PCC is a body corporate and therefore its members are not personally liable to discharge its obligations. While a PCC has a duty to insure, it is not an absolute duty and may be limited by the funds available to the PCC and the extent of other, proper claims on those funds. Where the insurance of a valuable article places an impossible burden upon the PCC, consideration should be given to invoking the archdeacon's powers under section 21 of the Care of Churches and Ecclesiastical Jurisdiction Measure 1991 whereby such an article may be deposited at the archdeacon's discretion in a place of safety.

7. In accordance with these principles, the Legal Advisory Commission gives the advice in the following paragraphs of this Opinion to incumbents and priests-in-charge, churchwardens and PCCs.

8. In all but the most straightforward cases PCCs should seek the advice of an insurance company experienced in the insurance of ecclesiastical buildings. The DBF would, if any difficulty exists in identifying such a company, be able to supply the names of companies known to be reputable and reliable. However, in many dioceses, the DBF has arranged a group insurance scheme or special policy to which any PCC in the diocese may subscribe. It will almost certainly be in the PCC's interest to subscribe to such a block policy.

9. Bodies such as English Heritage providing grant aid for the repair or maintenance of church buildings often impose an obligation to insure to a specified extent as a condition of making the grant. The financial implications of such a requirement must be considered with care before the grant is accepted. Thereafter insurance cover at the required level must be maintained in accordance with the contract under which the grant is payable.

10. With regard to churches and other parochial buildings, the ideal must

be to insure the building against the costs of restoring it, in the event of its destruction, to its existing condition together with such ancillary expenses as professional fees and the expense of hiring a substitute building for use during the reconstruction of the building insured. In the case of many ancient or large buildings this may be an unattainable ideal; the premium may simply be an impossible burden on the PCC's funds. Nevertheless the insurance principle of average must be borne in mind. This is the rule that if a property is insured for only a proportion of its value and damage occurs to a part of the property insurers will be liable to pay only the same proportion in respect of the loss that the sum insured bears to the full restoration cost. A possible solution is to agree with the insurers, at the commencement or annual renewal of the policy, upon a reinstatement value with the proviso that should the reinstatement value prove to be inadequate the insurers will not apply average.

11. There is a similar problem as to the amount of cover which should be provided for church treasures, such as plate and pictures, some of which can be sold in the open market at high prices, if a sale is authorized by faculty. If a valuation is made and a high value is disclosed, once again the amount of the premium could be a real burden to a parish. The advice the Legal Advisory Commission gives in such cases is that there is no legal requirement for insurance to cover the full market value and that a practical compromise may be the insurance of any such objects for a sum which would cover the cost of repair and (if beyond repair) of a good modern replacement. (See *Re St Helen's Brant Broughton* [1974] Fam 16, where the chancellor held and the Court of Arches accepted that, in the circumstances of that case, it would be sufficient for the parish to insure a valuable fifteenth-century painting for an amount which was less than its full commercial value but which in the event of a total loss would allow for a suitable replacement.) This would require a much smaller premium and PCCs could feel that in the circumstances they had carried out all their responsibilities in this respect. If a PCC takes this course, it must make a full disclosure to the insurers of the knowledge or belief of its officers about the age and value of the object to be insured, state the precise cover required in the event of total loss and make sure that in any policy issued there will be no penalty for under-insurance.

12. The solution of insuring for the cost of a good modern replacement may also meet the difficulty in which an impossibly high premium for an ancient or elaborate building places a PCC. A policy has been introduced by the Ecclesiastical Insurance Group for insuring churches as well as valuable church treasures for the cost of a good modern replacement. If the PCC can show that this option is the best use of its resources its members need not fear that they would be open to criticism for not insuring for a complete reinstatement of the church as it stands or for the

full market value of the treasure in question. In a particular case it may be decided that the remodelling of a church (internally and/or externally) would for pastoral reasons be preferable to its reinstatement. In that event the exercise may in addition to or instead of a faculty require the use of powers under the Pastoral Measure 1983.

13. Different considerations may apply to assets which are not the corporate responsibility of the PCC under the Parochial Church Councils (Powers) Measure 1956 but are held on charitable trusts of which the PCC is trustee. A church hall might be an example of this class of asset. In such cases the Charity Commissioners recommend insurance for full reinstatement value inclusive of demolition of surviving structures, site clearance, professional fees and compliance with legal requirements such as planning. The Commissioners envisage that the new building should replicate the lost original. Failure to insure adequately in circumstances in which a reasonable person would have maintained proper insurance of the trust property may well be viewed as a breach of the trustee's paramount duty to act in the interests of the charity.

14. PCCs should treat insurance against third party liability, or public liability as it is sometimes called, in its various forms as of the highest priority. The occupiers of buildings and land to which the public, or certain members of the public, are admitted owe those persons the 'common duty of care' and are liable in damages for any breach of that duty (Occupiers' Liability Act 1957). Employers have an absolute obligation to insure their liability in respect of employees suffering injury or disease arising out of and in the course of their employment (Employers' Liability (Compulsory Insurance) Act 1969, s1). PCCs should insure against liability to claims by persons using the church, churchyard or any parochial building or land and if they are employers against liability to compensate their employees, whether full- or part-time, for injury or disease suffered through their employment. The limit of indemnity should not be less than £5 million. As difficult questions may arise as to who is the occupier or employer or, in the case of a moveable object, the owner in point of strict law, any policy should insure the whole 'church interest', however expressed, viz. the respective interests of the bishop, incumbent, priest-in-charge (should there be a suspension of presentation or a vacancy), PCC and churchwardens. The policy should cover the parish church, churchyards, whether surrounding the church or detached, and all parish buildings and lands. *See also* **Churchyards** and **Churchyards: liability for personal injury accidents**.

15. With regard to the parsonage house, under section 12 of the Repair of Benefice Buildings Measure 1972 it is the duty of the Diocesan Parsonages Board to insure all parsonage houses in its diocese against all

such risks as are included in the usual form of house owner's policy relating to buildings, and such insurance must be effected with the Ecclesiastical Insurance Group or some other insurance office selected by the Board. Since the policy might not cover the incumbent, as occupier, against third party liability, enquiry should always be made of the Diocesan Parsonages Board as to the precise terms of the policy and the cover it affords. An incumbent would be well advised to insure his or her personal possessions under a 'contents' policy, and such a policy will, in the ordinary way, cover the assured against occupier's liability. However, as always, the policy should be read with care to make sure what is covered by it and the limits of such cover.

16. From whatever fund the premium for any policy is paid the payer should heed the advice given in paragraph 14. Rights of ownership, possession and occupation and liability to replace and repair can frequently be difficult to state with certainty, save that they are in one or other ecclesiastical corporation or person concerned with the parish. All policies should be drawn so that the respective interests of the bishop, DBF, incumbent, priest-in-charge, PCC and churchwardens are protected, if necessary by providing that in the event of a dispute the insurer may obtain a full release by paying any sums due under the policy to the DBF.

(May 1977, revised May 2003)

Church building: notice boards

1. Notices and notice boards in the churchyard (and possibly in the church porch) are regulated by the Town and Country Planning (Control of Advertisements) Regulations 1992, SI 1992/666, as amended. 'Advertisement' for the purpose of these regulations has a very broad meaning and (subject to some specific exceptions) includes any sign, board and notice 'in the nature of, and employed wholly or party for the purposes of advertisement, announcement of direction' (Town and Country Planning Act 1990, s336(1)). Generally, new notices and notice boards of this kind require advertisement consent from the local planning authority (in addition to any planning permission which may be necessary), although the authority is restricted to considering matters of amenity and public safety as opposed to the subject matter displayed.

2. However, there are a number of cases where an application for advertisement consent is not required, including the following:

(a)   some official notices by local authorities and other public bodies;

(b)   certain temporary notices, including those announcing 'any local event of a religious, educational, cultural, political, social or recreational character', provided the notice is not more than 0.6 square metres in area, is not erected more than twenty-eight days before the event, and is removed within fourteen days afterwards;

(c)   one permanent notice or notice board of up to 1.2 square metres (or, if the church has entrances onto more than one road frontage, a measurement of one board at each of two such entrances); and

(d)   small notices up to 0.3 square metres 'displayed for the purpose of identification, direction or warning' with respect to the church or churchyard.

3. All the notices and notice boards within the categories listed in the previous paragraph are subject to standard conditions requiring them to be kept clean and tidy. In addition, so far as churches and churchyards are concerned, those in categories (b), (c) and (d) in the previous paragraph are subject to a prohibition on illuminated signs and to restrictions on the size of the symbols or characters displayed and the height above ground. It would therefore be prudent to consult the local planning

authority in all cases before incurring expense in providing a new notice board.

4. A faculty will also be required for a notice board in a churchyard or church curtilage.

(Revised 2003)

Church building: party walls to churches and churchyards

1. In many parishes, there are buildings against the churchyard boundaries and walls. Many churches in towns have secular buildings abutting against part of them. There will, therefore, from time to time be instances where secular landowners with property adjoining a church or churchyard will wish to erect, alter or repair a building or wall on or alongside the boundary. Occasionally there may be proposals from the church which will affect adjoining property.

2. The Party Wall etc. Act 1996, modelled on earlier legislation applying only in London, the London Building Acts (now repealed), deals with the rights of landowners as against adjoining owners in such cases, and lays down procedures to be followed when works are proposed which will or may affect adjoining structures or land. This Opinion is concerned with the effect of the Act and its relationship to the faculty jurisdiction.

3. The Act covers the following categories of proposals by an adjoining landowner:

A   the erection of a new party wall or party fence wall on the line of the junction between adjoining properties (s1 of the Act), a party wall being one which forms part of a building, or separates two buildings, a party fence wall not forming part of a building (for example, it is a boundary wall to a churchyard);

B   a range of works of rebuilding, repair, cutting through, strengthening, demolishing or altering a party wall or a party fence wall on the line of the junction (ss2 and 3); and

C   the excavation of land at a specified distance from a building or structure of an adjoining owner (s6).

4. In all these cases, the 'building owner', the person initiating the proposals, is required to serve a notice outlining the proposals on the 'owner' of the property which will be affected by them. 'Owner' is defined in the Act to include a person in possession of the land. If the benefice is filled the incumbent, who has the legal title and is also the person in possession of the land, will be the 'owner'. If presentation is suspended a priest-in-charge will be the 'owner', being the person in possession. Where the benefice is vacant for any other reason the building owner may invoke section 15 of the Act and simply fix the notice to a conspicuous part of the church or churchyard and address it to the 'owner' of the named church or churchyard. Should that happen the PCC would be well advised to accept the notice as served upon it as a council. The council is, by virtue of

section 4(i),(ii) of the Parochial Church Councils (Powers) Measure 1956, liable to care for, maintain and preserve the fabric of the church and to care for and maintain the churchyard and therefore the secular courts would be likely to hold that the PCC was to be regarded as the 'owner' for the purposes of the Act.

5. Again in all types of case, the building owner can carry out the proposed work with the consent in writing of the 'owner'. Where the proposed work is likely to affect the church or churchyard, on no account should consent be given by an incumbent, a priest-in-charge or the PCC without obtaining appropriate professional advice from an architect or surveyor and authorization by faculty for the giving of consent.

Category A works: new party wall or party fence wall

6. One month's notice has to be given by the building owner to the adjoining owner describing the intended wall (s1(2)). If no consent is given in response to the notice the building owner is empowered by the Act to build a wall on his or her own land and to construct such projecting footings and foundations as are necessary for construction of the wall below the level of the church curtilage or churchyard. Any such disturbance of the ground in the churchyard requires a faculty. It is, therefore, essential that the incumbent, or whoever is accepting responsibility as the 'owner' of the church or churchyard informs the diocesan registrar immediately on receipt of a notice under section 1, and also informs the building owner that a faculty must be obtained before any work is commenced which will affect land subject to the faculty jurisdiction. The building owner is obliged to compensate the adjoining owner for any damage to the property of the adjoining owner resulting from the works (s1(7)). Such a faculty should make provision for the determination of any dispute as to damage to consecrated land in accordance with the compulsory arbitration procedure in section 10 of the Act.

Category B: works of re-building, repair, strengthening, demolishing, or altering a party wall

7. A notice, called 'a party structure notice', giving at least two months' warning of the works has to be given to the adjoining owner. The incumbent, or whoever is accepting responsibility as owner, then has three options

    (a)   to consent in writing within 14 days to the works (which the incumbent should only do after obtaining advice and under the authority of a faculty); or

(b)   to serve a counter notice on the building owner within one month of receipt of the party structure notice (again after obtaining advice and a faculty), the counter-notice requiring alternative works or imposing conditions; or

(c)   to take no action, in which case the incumbent is deemed to dissent.

If a counter-notice under (b) is not accepted, or if there is dissent as under (c), a dispute is deemed to have arisen. Such a dispute must be determined by an arbitration procedure set out in section 10 of the Act.

Category C: excavations

8. For any excavation within 3 metres of a church or structure in a churchyard, or 6 metres if the excavation is to be 6 metres deep, the building owner must give at least one month's notice to the adjoining owner describing the proposals by reference to accompanying plans. Perusal of the notice and accompanying plans should show whether a faculty should have been obtained and enquiry should be made of the adjoining owner whether one has been granted. The incumbent or whoever is accepting responsibility as owner has the same options as under (a) or (c) of Category B.

Resolution of disputes

9. Under the dispute-resolution procedure established by section 10 of the Act, the parties have the option of appointing one surveyor to act for both of them. To safeguard the church interest, it will normally be essential that the incumbent or other person accepting responsibility as owner appoint a surveyor to act for the church so that each party then has its own surveyor and the two jointly appoint a third. The sole surveyor or the three surveyors make an award which may determine (a) the right to execute any work, (b) the time and manner of executing the work, and (c) incidental matters including costs and compensation (ss1(8), 10(12)). It will therefore be essential for the church's surveyor to emphasize the need for a faculty so that this requirement can be built into the conditions of the award.

The faculty jurisdiction

10. Where a church or churchyard is affected, the works covered by the Act include many for which a faculty is required. Examples are the excavation of 'footings' and 'foundations' on neighbouring land, which might lead to the disturbance of human remains in an old burial ground,

and works involving cutting into a wall to insert a flashing or to demolish a party wall and rebuild it to a lesser height.

11. The Commission is of the opinion that the Act does not affect the need for a faculty in any such case. No mention is made in the 1996 Act of either the faculty jurisdiction or planning (including listed building) controls, whether in relation to the land of the party wishing to utilize the provisions of the Act or in relation to a neighbour's land. In the ordinary course of events no owner of land has the right to do works upon it that breach planning controls; the same applies to an incumbent in relation to the faculty jurisdiction. The Act makes no change in this position.

12. Any argument that the 1996 Act, dealing generally with party walls, excluded the special rules as to the faculty jurisdiction in relation to certain ecclesiastical property (and the same must apply to planning controls as to listed buildings) is contrary to the principle of statutory interpretation enshrined in the maxim *generalia specialibus non derogant*. Moreover, 'It is a principle of legal policy that, law should be altered deliberately rather than casually, and that Parliament should not change either common law or statute law by a sidewind, but only by measured and considered provisions' (Bennion, *Statutory Interpretation* (Butterworths, 1984) at p. 317). The intention of the sponsors of the Act was clear: the Bill was 'not designed to affect common law rights of support or conflict with other statutory requirements' (Earl of Lytton, in the House of Lords, 31 January 1996: see col. 1536 of Hansard). Those statutory requirements would cover such secular matters as fire protection and health and safety legislation, as well as the general law as to ancient monuments, listed buildings, conservation areas, and the faculty jurisdiction.

13. Section 10 of the Act, having established the dispute resolution procedure outlined above, provides in subsections (16) and (17) as follows:

'(16) The award shall be conclusive and shall not except as provided by this section be questioned in any court.

(17) Either of the parties to the dispute may . . . appeal to the county court which may

(a) rescind the award or modify it in such manner as the court thinks fit; and

(b) make such order as to costs as the court thinks fit.'

14. Section 10(16) is general in its wording but must be read within the context both of the general law and the ambit of the Act itself. The award

is conclusive as to any matter which is connected with any work to which the Act relates (see s10(10) and (12)). The essence of the award is that it determines the nature of works and the manner of execution of works which a building owner may carry out on the property of the adjoining owner. The Act is concerned with the rights between neighbouring landowners (See, for a discussion of a not dissimilar issue under the former London Building Acts, *Gyle-Thompson v Wall Street (Properties)* [1974] 1 All ER 295.)

15. However, the exercise of any party wall right will be dependent upon obtaining all other requisite permissions, such as Listed Building Consent for the demolition of a listed wall, or a Home Office Licence in advance of exhuming human remains consequent upon the digging of foundations permitted by an award under section 10. As already explained above (para 5) a faculty should always be obtained. The faculty procedure is designed to protect church property against any undesirable work, and specifications are scrutinized during the process of obtaining a faculty.

16. If the need for a faculty is not drawn to the attention of the adjoining owner until after an award is concluded under the Act, then it will not only be likely to give rise to ill-feeling on the part of the adjoining owner but it will also create practical difficulties for the consistory court in seeking to alter or add to a specification of works already approved under the procedure provided for in the Act. It is therefore imperative that the incumbent does not purpose to give any consent and that because of the tight time limits in the Act any notice under the Act is immediately reported to the diocesan registry. The need for a faculty must also be drawn to the attention of the neighbouring landowner and the landowner's surveyor and legal advisers. (Similar action should be taken if it appears that works are contemplated by a neighbour who has *not* complied with the 1996 Act procedure.) The consistory court could take rapid action in cases of urgency, and it might be possible to secure the withdrawal of a notice under the Act pending the outcome of faculty proceedings. It may be necessary to serve a counter notice and to appoint a separate surveyor in the dispute-resolution procedure. If necessary, as a last resort, the archdeacon could obtain an injunction in the consistory court against the neighbour.

(January 2001)

Church building: private and proprietary chapels

Private chapels

1. Traditionally the expression 'private chapel' was applied to such chapels as noblemen and others had at their own private charge, built in or near their own houses, for them and their families to perform religious duties in (Burn, *Ecclesiastical Law*, 2nd edn, title 'Chapel'). The emphasis was upon the use of the chapel by the owner and the members of his household, as is evident from Canon 71 of 1603, substantially re-enacted as Canon B 41 para 1. Canon B 41 para 2 however, appears to include within the description of private chapel the chapel of any college, school, hospital, or public or charitable institution.

2. The general limitation placed upon the power of an ordained person to exercise his or her ministry is contained in Canon C 8, which provides in paragraph 2 that a duly ordained minister 'may officiate in any place only after he has received authority to do so from the bishop of the diocese or other Ordinary of the place'. The exercise of ministry by a person with the bishop's authority is further limited by paragraph 4 of the same Canon. No such person may minister 'in any place in which he has not the cure of souls' except in the following circumstances:

(a) with the permission of the minister having the cure of souls; or

(b) in the manner authorized by section 1 of the Extra-Parochial Ministry Measure 1967; or

(c) where the minister is authorized to do so in an educational, public, or charitable institution or a hospital by the 1967 Measure and Canon B 41; or

(d) in relation to funeral services, as provided by section 2 of the Church of England (Miscellaneous Provisions) Measure 1992 (as to which *see* **Burial and cremation**).

3. The effect of the above provisions is that a person exercising his or her ministry in a private chapel may only lawfully do so with the authority of the diocesan bishop or other Ordinary, together with the permission of the incumbent of the parish within which the chapel is situate. (For the purposes of Canon C 8 para 4 it is the incumbent of the parish and not the chaplain or other minister of the chapel who has the cure of souls.) There are only limited exceptions to the general rule. In the case of hospitals and other institutions within Canon B 41 para 2, the licence of the bishop but not the consent of the incumbent is required (see Canon B

41 para 3). A further exception might arise were the owner of a private chapel to be on the electoral roll of a parish other than that in which the chapel stands. In that event the minister of the parish on which electoral roll the owner's name appears would be entitled to officiate in the chapel without the need for any authority beyond section 1 of the Extra-Parochial Ministry Measure 1967. The offices and services should be attended only by the family and household of the non-resident elector.

Proprietary chapels

4. Proprietary chapels are provided and maintained by one or more proprietors for the purposes of Anglican worship. The proprietors generally admit members of the public to divine service, but are entitled as of right to exclude them (*Bosanquet v Heath* (1860) 3 LT 290). The distinction between a private and proprietary chapel, turning as it does upon the class of persons admitted to act of worship, is not always easy to draw. Sometimes proprietary chapels have been described as private chapels (for example, in *Hancock v Stephens* (1915) 31 TLR 434, CA). Furthermore, a private chapel may readily assume the characteristics of a proprietary chapel if the owner opens it to the public, or even a portion of the public, for worship.

5. In *Hodgson v Dillon* (1840) 2 Curt 388 at p. 392, Dr Lushington expressed the view that a bishop could not lawfully grant a licence to the minister of a proprietary chapel without the consent of the rector or vicar of the parish, because the cure of souls belonged exclusively to the rector or vicar. This Opinion is given legislative force by Canon C 8, which applies equally to proprietary chapels as it does to private chapels.

6. The exceptions referred to in paragraph 3 to the general restrictions set out in Canon C 8 cannot apply to a proprietary chapel. It is not a chapel attached to a hospital or other institution for the purposes of Canon B 41. Neither is the minister entitled to take advantage of section 1 of the Extra-Parochial Ministry Measure 1967, because those present at divine service are not limited to members of the proprietor's family and household. Thus in all cases both the authority of the bishop and the consent of the incumbent are a necessary prerequisite to the lawful exercise of an ordained person's ministry in a proprietary chapel.

Consecration

7. The law as stated above in relation to private and proprietary chapels is not displaced by the act of consecration. The instrument of consecration may, however, contain evidence of episcopal authority, and (if necessary)

the consent of the incumbent, upon which the chaplain or other minister is able to rely (*Moysey v Hillcoat* (1828) 2 Hag. Ecc. 30).

Use for funerals

8. The limitations imposed upon the use of private and proprietary chapels for worship generally extend to their use for funerals. Further legal constraints upon the conduct of funerals are set out in the Opinion **Burial and cremation: funerals in undertakers' private chapels**; the result is that there is no lawful authority for a funeral service to take place elsewhere than in a church, churchyard, crematorium or burial ground.

(*See also* **Church building: consecrated chapels and the faculty jurisdiction of the consistory court**)

(October 1990, revised 2006)

Church building: sanctuary lights

A faculty is required for installing a sanctuary light. In the Church of England red sanctuary lights are a call to prayer. White lamps indicate that the Blessed Sacrament is reserved. Blue lights are customarily hung in a Lady Chapel.

(1994)

Church building: seating of congregation

1. The churchwardens are entrusted with the duty of providing seats for the parishioners. In this capacity they act as the officers of the Ordinary. Their rights and duties may be limited by some overriding right of a private person, e.g. when a particular pew is attached to an estate by prescription or held under a faculty. Subject, however, to such private rights, the churchwardens may direct persons where to sit, and where not to sit, and may do this beforehand or for a particular service or for an indefinite period. But they cannot legally give the right to a particular seat for all time, because to do so would divest themselves or their successors of the liberty to re-arrange the seating accommodation at a future time.

2. Seats can legally only be assigned to parishioners, and before dispossessing a parishioner of a seat which has been so assigned, the churchwardens would be well advised to give the parishioner notice of their intention, so as to provide an opportunity to show cause why the churchwardens should not proceed with the dispossession.

3. This control of the seating accommodation belongs to the churchwardens in the interests of good order. They cannot exclude an orderly person on the ground that the church is full if that person can stand in such a part of the church as will not interfere with the conduct of the service. If a parishioner intrudes into a seat contrary to the directions of the churchwardens, they may remove the parishioner from the seat, provided that they do not use unnecessary force or cause a scandal by disturbing the worship of the church.

(1994)

Church building: tickets for services

Weddings in parish churches

1. It has been long recognized that parishioners have a right to attend weddings which take place in their parish church without an invitation or ticket. The basis for this is partly the right of access of a parishioner to the parish church during a divine service. A wedding is such a service. It is partly also to do with the public nature of marriage and the fact that within the service there is the solemnization of legal marriage in accordance with the Marriage Act 1949. For that reason, the service has to be conducted openly and publicly.

2. If parishioners have a right to be present do non-parishioners also have a right? If they do not have an absolute right, does that mean that steps can lawfully be taken to exclude them? It would be somewhat arbitrary to exclude someone who lived two miles outside the parish boundary but who had a genuine wish to attend. It is considered that an excluded non-parishioner would have a strong case for contending that exclusion would be unlawful if he or she could show a genuine wish to attend and take part.

(Revised 2003)

Elections: use of schools and churches

1. Candidates at parliamentary and local government elections are entitled to the use of a suitable room in a county, voluntary or grant-maintained school during the period of the election for public meetings in furtherance of their candidature. Although no charge may be made for the use of the room, the candidate may be asked to defray any expense incurred (e.g. for lighting, cleaning and attendance) and the cost of any damage done.

2. A candidate is not entitled to exercise the right of claiming the use of the room except upon reasonable notice, and in the case of a parliamentary election any question about this or the suitability of the room is to be determined by the Secretary of State for Education. In addition, the room may be used only at reasonable times, and there must be no interference with the use of the premises for educational purposes. There are various minor differences between the detailed provisions for the two kinds of election. (See the Representation of the People Act 1983, ss95 and 96 and Sch 5, as amended by the Representation of the People Act 1985, the Education Reform Act 1988, and the School Standards and Framework Act 1998.)

3. The returning officer at a parliamentary election is entitled to use free of charge for taking the poll a room in any school which is maintained or assisted by a local education authority or is in receipt of grants out of monies provided by Parliament. The same applies to local elections, but here the room may also be used for counting the votes. The returning officer must defray any expense incurred by reason of the room being used in this way, e.g. for heating and caretaking, and this is usually met by a flat rate payment. In addition he must make good any damage done. (See Representation of the People Act 1983, Sch 1 (Parliamentary Election Rules), r22, the Local Elections (Principal Areas) Rules 1986, SI 1986/2214, r17, and the Local Elections (Parishes and Communities) Rules 1986, SI 1986/2215, r17.)

4. The former prohibition in the Representation of the People Act 1949 that a local government election should not be held in a church, chapel or other place of public worship was repealed by the Representation of the People Act 1969, section 14.

(1997)

Part 8
Churchyards and Burial Grounds

Churchyards

Maintenance of churchyards and rights of herbage

1. The rector of an ancient parish church had originally the right to the herbage, but this right has generally devolved on the vicar. In either case the right is an absolute right subject to the user of the churchyard as a burial ground (see *Greenslade v Darby* (1868) LR 3 QB 421 at 429) and the jurisdiction of the Ordinary.

2. Canon F 13 para 2 states that the churchyard shall be kept 'in such an orderly and decent manner as becomes consecrated ground' and that it should be duly fenced.

3. It is somewhat significant that under section 18 of the Burial Act 1855 (now repealed by the Local Government Act 1972, s272, Sch 30, except in relation to the City of London) the churchwardens had to keep a closed churchyard (in which the rights to herbage of the vicar would be the same) 'in decent order'.

4. By section 4(1)(ii)(c) of the Parochial Church Councils (Powers) Measure 1956 the powers, duties and liabilities of the churchwardens relating to the care and maintenance of the churchyard were transferred to the PCC.

5. It would seem that at the least the duties of the PCC are to keep the churchyard properly fenced (see paras 12–14 below) and the paths in proper order, and therefore to clear away any grass on or overhanging paths. It also has a statutory responsibility for trees in churchyards which it is liable to maintain (see s6(1) of the Care of Churches and Ecclesiastical Jurisdiction Measure 1991, as amended by s13 of the Church of England (Miscellaneous Provisions) Measure 1995) and these should therefore be properly maintained in a safe condition.

6. The PCC would seem otherwise to have no duty or any general power to cut grass, though where the grass encroaches on a tombstone it may well be that the owner can abate the nuisance. On the other hand the owner of the herbage cannot turn the churchyard into a field and it would seem the owner of the herbage is bound to prevent the herbage from being an obstruction to parishioners making proper use of the churchyard. The right to turn in sheep is in no way inconsistent with this view. Long grass between the graves would not appear to be necessarily an obstruction, but long rank grass with weeds and brambles would be an obstruction. It is a question of degree.

7. If in the case of a dispute good sense does not prevail, the best course would appear to be for the churchwardens, as officers of the Ordinary, and the PCC, to apply by petition to the consistory court for liberty to put and keep the churchyard in order by cutting and keeping down the herbage so far as it encroaches on the paths or interferes with the proper use of the churchyard, or otherwise as may be directed.

Power to contribute towards the cost of providing and/or maintaining a churchyard

8. Section 214(6) and (8) of the Local Government Act 1972 enables district councils, parish councils, London borough councils and other authorities defined in the section as burial authorities to contribute towards the expenses of providing or maintaining a churchyard or other burial place, including a part set aside for the interment of cremated remains. (This replaces the former provision in the Parish Councils Act 1957, s10.) Contributions will normally be voted annually or preferably for an indefinite period, but where the PCC wishes to be certain that the contribution will continue for a number of years, e.g. because it is contemplating considerable expense in extending the churchyard, it might be appropriate to request the local authority to enter into an agreement to continue its contributions for a minimum number of years and thereafter indefinitely. (For precedents for such an agreement under the Act which could be adopted, see *Encyclopaedia of Forms and Precedents*, 5th edn, vol. 6, title 'Burial and Cremation'.)

9. The power would allow a contribution to be made towards the extension of a churchyard, which in rural areas at least may often be a more acceptable and also a less expensive method of securing additional burial space than providing a civil burial ground or cemetery.

Extension of churchyard

10. If an existing churchyard is disused, but not closed by Order in Council, an extension to it has the effect of making the whole churchyard open and used. For an extension to be an extension it must be contiguous and there should be no demarcation on the ground. So long as the extension is open the PCC will retain control over the whole churchyard.

11. The Home Office may declare part of a churchyard closed (leaving the remainder open), but in the absence of a Home Office order the whole churchyard must be considered as one. After an Order in Council closing a churchyard is made the local authority is obliged to maintain it if the PCC so requests (Local Government Act 1972, s215; *see also* **Churchyards: closed**).

Fencing of churchyards

12. The need for proper fencing of churchyards has been recognized from early times. By a constitution of Archbishop Winchelsey the parishioners were required to repair the fences at their own charge. By Canon 85 of 1603 the churchwardens were required to take care 'that the churchyards be well and sufficiently repaired, fences and maintained with walls, rails or pales, as have been in each place accustomed, at their charge unto whom by law the same appertaineth'. The powers and duties of the churchwardens in this respect have in modern times been transferred to the PCC (Parochial Church Councils (Powers) Measure 1956, s4(1)(ii)(c)).

13. The modern Canons provide that 'care shall be taken that the churchyards be duly fenced, and that the said fences be maintained at the charge of those to whom by law or custom the liability belongs' (Canon F 13 para 2). These obligations rest on the PCC (Canon F 14); but the council's liability is limited by the extent of the funds available for the purpose, and possibly in some cases by the legal obligations of adjoining landowners (see *Halsbury's Laws of England*, 4th edn, 1975, vol. 14, paras 581, 1097, 1109).

14. It is suggested that some latitude is permissible in determining the incidence and extent of the obligation in particular cases. Thus a PCC might properly exercise the discretion in the light of local circumstances; if, for instance, there appeared to be no risk of damage or undesirable intrusion into consecrated ground, the PCC might be justified in leaving one or more boundaries unfenced. It may be significant that words such as 'sufficiently' or 'properly' fenced have been used in the past; this may be thought to imply that it is a question of degree, depending on local circumstances and requirements. (*See also* **Churchyards: liability for personal injury accidents.**)

Consecrated land and adverse possession

15. Once land is consecrated it remains subject to the legal effects of consecration unless and until they are expressly removed by or under the authority of a statute or Measure (e.g. s22 of the Care of Churches and Ecclesiastical Jurisdiction Measure 1991) even though it is in private ownership. Other conveyancing rights may be acquired in respect of consecrated land, including adverse possession; section 15 of the Limitation Act 1980 refers to 'any land'.

Footpaths and rights of way over consecrated churchyards

16. A right in the nature of an easement over a churchyard may be granted by a faculty alone for a private footpath where the chancellor has ensured that all parties are petitioners. In most circumstances an agreement in writing would be desirable if not essential to set out all covenants and obligations, and to make clear the date on which it takes effect. Such an agreement in writing is capable of applying to private footpaths only because it is impossible for every member of the public to join in an agreement for a public footpath.

17. In the case of a public footpath the faculty gives the incumbent the authority to enter into an agreement and is not the agreement itself. An incumbent has no power to grant a legal estate: but in the common instance of part of the churchyard becoming part of the public highway, the incumbent as owner of the fee simple may with the authority of a faculty dedicate it in perpetuity as part of the highway.

18. Some footpaths through churchyards have been recorded by local authorities as rights of way under the National Parks and Access to the Countryside Act 1949, sections 32, 33 (now replaced by the Wildlife and Countryside Act 1981). Where members of the public are permitted to use footpaths through a churchyard as a matter of grace, it is therefore important to take adequate steps to prevent a presumption of dedication as a public right of way arising. This can be done by closing the footpath one day a year or exhibiting a notice in the churchyard or depositing a plan. If a plan is deposited, care must be taken to follow it up by a statutory declaration every six years.

Gift of land for churchyard subject to easement

19. The question whether a gift of land as an addition to a churchyard can be accepted if the gift is made subject to the reservation of an easement can only be answered after consideration of the nature of the easement. If it would interfere with the proper use of the land as a churchyard the gift could not be accepted, but if it would not the gift could be accepted, subject to the reservation of the easement.

Reservation of grave space by faculty

20. There cannot be a valid custom that a fee (other than an interment fee) should be payable to an incumbent upon the reservation of a grave space by faculty. The chancellor might allow a fee to the incumbent whether habitually or in a particular case and by way of interment fee or otherwise, and the incumbent could on the application for the faculty

ask for terms to be imposed on the petitioner in this respect. A further or alternative condition can be imposed that the petitioners make a contribution to a fund established for the maintenance of the church or churchyard.

Memorials in churchyards

21. A right of burial (*see* **Burial and cremation**) does not entitle the deceased's relatives or personal representatives to erect any memorial over the grave; for this a faculty or, where the chancellor's directions so permit, the incumbent's consent is needed.

22. The duty to keep the churchyard in decent order does not extend to the ordinary maintenance of monuments. The primary responsibility for their upkeep falls on the owners of the monuments, who are the heirs of the persons commemorated. However, where the heirs cannot be traced, because the responsibility for the maintenance of the churchyard in a safe state is prima facie on the PCC, it must bear the responsibility for the dangerous monuments. Where the churchyard has been handed over to the local authority under section 215 of the Local Government Act 1972, that responsibility passes to the local authority and a PCC can probably claim the indemnity of the local authority. (*See also* **Churchyards: closed.**)

Other types of burial ground

23. It may be helpful to mention two types of burial ground which are not legally churchyards, although at first sight some of them may seem indistinguishable from churchyards.

24. Section 10 of the Burial Act 1855 (repealed by the Burial Act 1900) provided that if the ratepayers in vestry resolved unanimously that a new burial ground should be held and used in like manner as the existing churchyard, it would not be necessary to leave part of the ground unconsecrated, though there was a contingent liability to provide a second burial ground within ten years if required, none of which would be consecrated. The Home Office knew of nearly 300 burial grounds wholly consecrated under this provision and thought there might be many more. As these are burial grounds provided under the Burial Acts the responsibility for their maintenance rests with the local authority.

25. There are also a number of church grounds provided by church people in the latter half of the nineteenth century subject to a condition that burials there should only take place with the Church of England service. As they are not churchyards the PCC would not appear to be legally responsible for their maintenance unless by agreement. If the

maintenance of such a burial ground now presents difficulty, then, in as much as its use will have saved grave spaces in a civil burial ground and in some cases may even have saved the local authority from having to provide a civil burial ground at all, the local authority might be prepared to undertake its maintenance as a burial ground under section 9(b) of the Open Spaces Act 1906, and any assets available for its general maintenance could be transferred to the local authority under section 1(2) of the Parish Councils and Burial Authorities (Miscellaneous Provisions) Act 1970.

(Revised 1997)

Churchyards: closed

Meaning of 'closed churchyard'

1. A 'closed churchyard' is generally taken to mean a churchyard which has been closed for burials by an Order in Council under the Burial Acts, and the term is used in that sense in this Opinion. A churchyard may have been entirely disused for many years but it would not on that account be described as a closed churchyard, nor would a churchyard where all further burials have been prohibited by a local Act of Parliament.

2. On the other hand the fact that a churchyard is a closed churchyard does not necessarily mean that no burials may legally take place there, as this will depend upon the exact terms of the Order (or Orders) in Council applicable to it. In some, all further burials are entirely prohibited; in others, the burial of relatives of those already buried in the churchyard may take place, subject to there being three, four or five feet of soil between the coffin lid and the surface of the ground: occasionally, with a tender regard for the individual, the Order provides that the burial of a named person shall be permitted. Burials in vaults are often excepted subject to special conditions. Sometimes part of a churchyard is closed.

3. The proviso to section 3(1) of the Church of England (Miscellaneous Provisions) Measure 1992 provides that a person shall not have a right of burial of his cremated remains in a closed churchyard in the absence of a particular or general faculty authorizing such interment.

4. The Ministry of Health (as it then was) expressed the view many years ago that a churchyard which is closed with exceptions is nevertheless a 'closed churchyard' for the purpose of recovery of expenses from a local authority.

Tracing Orders in Council

5. If a PCC or a local authority is not sure whether a particular churchyard has been closed or not, or wishes to find the exact terms of the Order in Council, the following are the lines of enquiry which are suggested:

(a)   there will probably be a copy of the Order in Council, or of the issue of the *London Gazette* in which it appeared, in the church chest, or with the local authority's records;

(b)   the Index to the *London Gazette* 1839–1883 (available in the bigger reference libraries) will mention the Order if made before 1884;

(c)   if made between 1884 and 1891 it could be traced through the quarterly indices to the *London Gazette*;

(d)   if made after 1891, the Order will be listed at the end of the annual volumes of Statutory Rules and Orders or Statutory Instruments, but this involves a tiresome search unless the approximate year is known; and

(e)   in the last resort enquiries may be made from the Home Office, ABC Unit, Room 972, 50 Queen Anne's Gate, London SW1H 9AT (telephone 0207 273 2883).

New Orders in Council

6. Most of the Orders in Council for the discontinuance of burials (with or without exceptions or qualifications) in churchyards were made in the middle of the nineteenth century for the protection of the public health at a time when open sewers and the absence of a piped water supply made it particularly important to prevent the seepage of offensive matter from decomposing bodies into wells or streams likely to be used for drinking water. But section 1 of the Burial Act 1853 does not in fact restrict the making of closing orders to cases where this is necessary for the protection of the public health. The legal advisers of the Ministry of Housing and Local Government (as it then was) agreed with this view of the law, but in practice the Minister will almost invariably only make representations to Her Majesty in Council for the making of a Closed Order where the Minister is satisfied that discontinuance of burials, with or without exceptions or qualifications, is necessary for reasons of public health, thus adhering to the practice of his predecessors, namely the Ministry of Health, the Local Government Board and the Home Secretary.

7. This does not mean that no Closing Orders are made today, but orders never have been made for the sole purpose of relieving the ecclesiastical authorities of the burden of maintaining a churchyard.

8. Notice of the representation which the Secretary of State proposes to make and of the date when it will be considered by the Privy Council must be given in the *London Gazette* and by notices affixed to the doors of the churches affected, and notice is also given to the incumbent and to the local authority. This does not mean that the relevant Department seeks the consent of the local authority; the notice is sent to it because it has succeeded to the civil powers of the vestry to whose clerk notice had to be sent under section 1 of the Burial Act 1853. The Department often arranges for the churchyard to be visited by one of its civil engineering inspectors.

Restriction on the making of Closing Orders

9. The former prohibition on making an Order in Council closing a burial ground which had been opened with the approval of the Secretary of State has been abolished for Greater London, but still applies to churchyards outside Greater London (Local Government Act 1972, Sch 26 para 15). Where an Order in Council provided that the opening of a new burial ground required the Secretary of State's approval it must be presumed in the absence of evidence to the contrary that the law was complied with and that the required approval was sought and granted. But if there is any evidence to prove that approval to the opening of the churchyard extension or a new churchyard was not given, the relevant Department may consider the possibility of a closing order being made.

Revocation and variation of Closing Orders

10. The Secretary of State has received advice from the Law Officers of the Crown to the effect that it is not possible to revoke an Order in Council closing a churchyard. The Law Officers' reasons are that there is no express statutory power to do so, and that the power under section 1 of the Burial Act 1855 to 'vary' a previous Order in Council does not extend to revoking the Order altogether, although it can be used, for example, to redefine the boundaries of the churchyard where they have been inaccurately described, or to change the categories of burial which are still allowed.

11. In reliance on that Opinion, the relevant Department is not willing to entertain applications to re-open a closed churchyard by revoking the Closing Order. In view of this, a parish thinking of applying for such an Order should be advised to consider carefully whether the churchyard or part of it may be needed for burials at some stage in the future. However, the Department has on occasion been willing to vary an Order to permit specific new burials or categories of burials.

Responsibility of local authorities for closed churchyards

12. The justification for the provision of section 18 of the Burial Act 1855 and the way in which it has led to the transfer of the responsibility for closed churchyards to local authorities was not intended to confer any privilege upon the Church of England but was a recognition of the fact that until the Burial Acts of 1852 and 1853 churchyards or additional churchyards were the only burial places available, apart from commercial cemeteries and a few denominational burial grounds belonging to trustees. More important, churchyards were (as they still are) the common burial places of the parishioners of any denomination and none. As the

churchyard was available for the whole community, and in the first half of the nineteenth century had sometimes been provided, or extended, by means of a compulsory church rate, it was considered reasonable that when it was closed in the interest of the community, the expense of keeping it in decent order should be reimbursed to the churchwardens from what was then the poor rate.

13. Section 18 of the Burial Act 1855, which was slightly amended for Greater London, and which was repealed by the Local Government Act 1972, section 272, Schedule 30, except as to the City of London, provided as follows:

> 'In every case in which any Order in Council has been or shall hereafter be issued for the discontinuance of burials in any churchyard or burial ground, the burial board or churchwardens, as the case may be, shall maintain such churchyard or burial ground of any parish in decent order, and also do the necessary repair of the walls and other fences thereof; and the costs and expenses shall be repaid by the overseers, upon the certificate of the burial board or churchwardens, as the case may be, out of the rate made for the relief of the poor of the parish or place in which such churchyard or burial ground is situate, unless there shall be some other fund legally chargeable with such costs and expenses.'

14. On that basis it was for the local authority, which succeeded to the functions of the overseers, to reimburse the PCC, which succeeded the churchwardens in this regard.

Transferring responsibility for closed churchyards to a local authority

15. From 1 April 1974 section 215 of the Local Government Act 1972 has provided a much simpler procedure for a PCC to request a local authority at three months' notice to take over the maintenance of a closed churchyard, and section 18 of the Burial Act 1855 (except in its application to the City of London) has been repealed from that date.

16. Where extensive repairs are required to the churchyard three months' notice is too short and can cause difficulties for the local authority's budget. It has been agreed with the Local Authorities Association that, in future, the practice should be to give twelve months' informal notice to the local authority of an intention to serve the three months' statutory notice under section 215 of the 1972 Act.

17. The effect of acting under section 215 is to transfer the functions and liabilities of the PCC with respect to the maintenance and repair of the

churchyard to the local authority. This does not mean that the churchyard itself is transferred to the local authority nor are any functions or liabilities transferred except those of the PCC with respect to maintenance and repair. Other rights and powers remain unaffected and the churchyard remains under the control of the incumbent subject to the overriding control of the bishop's consistory court, and the incumbent with the concurrence of the PCC has as free a hand as was the case before the transfer except where questions of maintenance and repair are involved. For example, the local authority cannot restrict the parishioners' access to the churchyard at all reasonable times, this being a matter for the incumbent to decide.

18. A disused churchyard can only become an open space under the Open Spaces Act 1906 by mutual agreement between the incumbent and the PCC and the local authority and usually with the sanction of a faculty from the consistory court (see ss6, 9, 11). But the obtaining of a Closing Order and transfer of responsibility for maintenance to a local authority may well be the prelude to a subsequent agreement and faculty for its conversion into an open space.

19. Quite apart from conversion into an open space, neither the incumbent, nor the lay rector (if there is one, as happens in some ancient parishes), nor the PCC nor the local authority may alter the layout of a churchyard, whether it is closed or not, without a faculty. Where the responsibility for maintenance has been transferred to the local authority and the incumbent and churchwardens seek a faculty for some alteration to the churchyard which might result in an increase of expenditure to the local authority, the Legal Board (the predecessor of the Legal Advisory Commission) advised many years ago that the local authority should be given notice of the petition in accordance with current faculty procedure.

20. A local authority's responsibility for the maintenance and repair of a closed churchyard is unaffected by the grant of a faculty for the interment of cremated remains within part of the churchyard. The local authority cannot be relieved of its obligation for any part of the churchyard. The interment of ashes in a closed churchyard does not itself make the churchyard or that part of it open again for burials (see also Church of England (Miscellaneous Provisions) Measure 1992, s3).

21. The practical effect of the transfer of the functions and liabilities of the PCC with respect to the maintenance and repair of a closed churchyard to the local authority is that it is for the local authority to decide how and when and by whom the work shall be done. This of course does not preclude a mutual arrangement between the local authority and the PCC whereby the latter voluntarily undertakes some 'extra' work in

the churchyard such as the planting of bulbs or flowers, care of particular memorials etc.

What is involved in the maintenance and repair of a closed churchyard by a local authority?

22. From the preceding paragraph it will be appreciated that when the responsibility for a closed churchyard is transferred to a local authority it succeeds to the functions and liabilities of the PCC. Section 18 of the Burial Act 1855 (see para 13 above) laid down that the churchwardens (now the PCC) 'shall maintain such churchyard . . . in decent order, and also do the necessary repair of the walls and other fences thereof'. It is generally relatively easy to determine what is involved in the necessary repair of walls and other fences, but it is sometimes hard to determine what is involved in maintaining the churchyard 'in decent order'. According to Prideaux's *Churchwardens Guide*, 16th edn, 1895, p. 99, the duty of churchwardens (which would seem to apply to a PCC and a local authority) is:

> '. . . to see that [the churchyard] be kept in a decent and fitting manner, that it be cleared of all rubbish, muck, thorns, briers, shrubs and anything else that may annoy parishioners when they come into it . . .'

23. Sometimes an incumbent and PCC feel that the local authority ought to devote more labour or spend more money on a particular closed churchyard than it does, or, on the other hand, a local authority sometimes feels that the incumbent and PCC are expecting too much and assuming that maintenance in decent order necessarily involves the same standard which it would adopt where a churchyard has been transferred for use as an open space under the Open Spaces Act 1906. Also sometimes a local authority takes refuge in the fact that a neighbouring churchyard, whether closed or not, for which another PCC is responsible is in a worse state than the one about which complaint is made. But although many questions reach the Legal Advisory Commission about closed churchyards, it is significant that relatively few relate to serious disputes about the practical questions of maintenance, and tribute should be paid to the understanding way in which most local authorities see that this task is carried out, especially as it is often difficult and unrewarding.

24. The Legal Advisory Commission appreciates the difficulty of making any general application of Opinions given on particular facts, but it may be of assistance to mention that in its view the duty of a local authority to maintain a churchyard in decent order includes the maintenance and repair of the paths and gates, and also the renewal of a gate when,

according to the ordinary rules of good management, it should be replaced. On the other hand, if drains which run under the churchyard and whose sole function is to carry off water from the downspouts and gutterings of the church itself become obstructed, the removal of the obstruction is not, in the Legal Advisory Commission's view, part of the duty of maintaining the churchyard in decent order and, therefore, is the responsibility of the PCC and not of the local authority.

25. Trees and herbage sometimes give rise to peculiar difficulties inherent in the freehold of a churchyard being vested in the incumbent (or lay rector if any). But generally speaking keeping the churchyard in decent order will involve dealing with saplings and bushes as coming within the 'thorns and shrubs' mentioned in the quotation from Prideaux above, especially if their continued growth may cause damage to a memorial; it also involves dealing with long rank grass and weeds and brambles, particularly of course any grass overhanging the paths. Exceptionally in rural areas it may occasionally happen that the incumbent (or the lay rector if any) may wish to exercise his rights to have the herbage, and therefore there should be consultation before the grass is cut, to allow the owner of the herbage the opportunity to exercise that right. No licence is required under the Forestry Act 1967 for felling trees in a churchyard (s9(2)(b)), and consent to felling etc. by the Diocesan Parsonages Board is no longer required (Care of Churches and Ecclesiastical Jurisdiction Measure 1991, s6(4)); a faculty will, however, be required. If a tree has fallen by act of nature in a closed churchyard for which a local authority is responsible, the authority should remove it unless the owner of the tree (normally the incumbent or the lay rector, if there is one) wishes to do so. As regards trees, see also section 13 of the Church of England (Miscellaneous Provisions) Measure 1995.

26. The Legal Advisory Commission is of the Opinion that the local authority's responsibility to keep a churchyard in decent, and therefore safe, order can be no greater than that of the PCC. The obligation to maintain the churchyard extends to all things attached to the realty, which includes tombs, monuments, war memorials, churchyard crosses and walls and fences. Decent order will be a matter for the local authority to decide, but if the PCC considers that the authority's standard is too low, the incumbent and PCC may seek to enforce the local authority's duty by proceedings in the county court.

Petition for faculty for removal of dangerous item

27. The PCC may petition for a faculty for the removal of a dangerous item from the churchyard. (This procedure is probably also available if the churchyard is closed.)

For tombs, monuments and churchyard crosses *see also* **Churchyards** and **Churchyards: ownership of monuments and trees.**

(Revised 2003)

Churchyards: Consecration of Churchyards Act 1867

1. The Commission was asked whether the general provision of section 8 of the Faculty Jurisdiction Measure 1964 amends the special provisions of section 9 of the Consecration of Churchyards Act 1867.

2. The material words of section 9 of the Act of 1867, as amended by the Consecration of Churchyards Act 1868, are:

> 'Where any land shall be . . . added [by way of gift] to a consecrated churchyard . . . it shall be lawful for the giver of such land to reserve the exclusive right in perpetuity of burial . . . in a part of the land so added, not exceeding one sixth part of the whole of the said land . . .'.

3. The material words of section 8 of the Measure of 1964 are:

> 'Any right to the exclusive use of any particular part of a churchyard, burial ground or other consecrated land for the purpose of sepulture, whether absolute or limited and however granted or acquired, shall cease one hundred years after the passing of this Measure, unless granted enlarged or continued by a faculty granted after the passing of this Measure.

> Provided that the court shall not issue a faculty granting enlarging or continuing any such right for a period longer than 100 years from the date of the faculty.'

4. The long title of the Measure of 1964 states, *inter alia*, that it is a Measure 'to limit the duration of rights of sepulture'. Other provisions in the Measure of 1964, which may be described as a 'miscellaneous provisions' Measure, show that it was intended to define and regulate some aspects of ecclesiastical law and practice where there was a lack of certainty. For example the other sections of the Measure gave powers to vest privately owned parts of churches in the incumbent as owner of the whole, defined the jurisdiction to grant faculties for the demolition of churches, declared that curtilages of churches were within the jurisdiction of the consistory court. The long title and the terms of section 8 suggest that it was the intention of the Church Assembly to bring certainty to the many existing and doubtful rights of sepulture, whether claimed through prescription, lost grant, faculty or otherwise by providing that all should cease in 2064 unless before that date a faculty was granted continuing any particular right, with a limit of 100 years upon any such continuation.

5. The effect of section 8 of the Act of 1867 is that a donor who seeks it is entitled as of right to the reservation of grave spaces in perpetuity, which reservation might, when the Act was passed, have been obtained by the grant of a faculty. Thus the ambit of the section concerns a private right over consecrated land and a right analogous with rights which may be granted in the exercise of the consistory court's faculty jurisdiction. The sections in question of the two statutes are therefore concerned with cognate subject matter and the latter must prevail and amend the former. The consequence is that any exclusive right of sepulture existing at the date of the passing of the 1964 Measure, or created after that date under section 9 of the 1867 Act without a faculty will expire in the year 2064. Any fresh grant of extension of such a right by faculty after the passing of the 1964 Measure may not be for a period of more than 100 years from the date of the faculty.

(May 1997)

Churchyards: liability for personal injury accidents

General

1. Liability for personal injury accidents in churchyards can arise both in negligence and under the Occupiers' Liability Acts 1957 and 1984. Except as regards 'trespassers' the duty of care owed is similar.

Who is liable?

2. Liability rests on the 'occupier' of the churchyard. 'Occupier' denotes the person or authority that has a sufficient degree of control over the churchyard to give rise to a duty of care towards those who come lawfully into the churchyard. Depending upon the precise situation any of the following could be held to be an 'occupier':

(a)   the PCC (as successor to the churchwardens – section 4(1)(ii)(c) of the Parochial Church Councils (Powers) Measure 1956);

(b)   the incumbent (as owner of the freehold);

(c)   in relation to a particular gravestone, the person who authorized the erection of the stone or after his death the heir at law of the person commemorated;

(d)   in a closed churchyard where liability for maintenance has passed to the local authority, the local authority.

To whom is a duty of care owed?

Visitors

3. The term 'visitors' includes all who formerly under common law were invitees or licensees (Occupiers' Liability Act 1957, s1(2)).

Others (persons other than visitors)

4. Persons other than visitors embrace not only trespassers, but also persons using private rights of way and entrants under the Countryside and Rights of Way Act 2000.

What is the duty of care?

Visitors

5. The duty is to take such care as in all the circumstances of the case is reasonable to see that the visitor will be reasonably safe in using the

premises for the purposes for which the visitor is invited or permitted to be there (1957 Act, s2(1), (2)). Interpreting this for churchyards, it seems that the three most likely hazards are:

(a)   the condition of the paths;

(b)   the condition of the gravestones/monuments;

(c)   stonework falling from the church building on to people in the churchyard.

The following guidelines might be helpful:

Paths
6. The PCC is, under Canon F 13 and the Parochial Church Councils (Powers) Measure 1956, responsible to see that churchyards are fenced and kept in an orderly and decent manner. However, its liability to visitors under the Occupiers' Liability Acts and at common law for the state of the paths to and from the church is greater, in that it must ensure the paths are in a reasonably good condition. What this will mean will depend on the nature of the path. For instance, if there is a paved path, undue projections or holes must be avoided by regular inspection and maintenance. If it is a gravel path, it will need to be kept reasonably level so that it is safe to walk on.

Fences
7. The PCC is responsible for maintenance of fences and walls (1956 Measure; Canon F 13 para 2, and Canon F 14); thus if a boundary wall were to collapse and injure someone there would be a prima facie liability on the PCC.

Trees
8. The duty of an occupier with regard to trees is to act as a prudent landowner to prevent his or her trees from being a danger to persons. The occupier is not bound to call an expert to examine the trees unless the occupier has reason to believe that they may be unsafe. (As to trees in churchyard, see the Care of Churches and Ecclesiastical Jurisdiction Measure 1991, s6, as amended by the Church of England (Miscellaneous Provisions) Measure 1995, s13.)

Gravestones / monuments
9. The PCC is responsible for keeping a churchyard in decent order. Decent order might well mean safe order, and it could well be that the duty extends to all things attached to the realty, which clearly includes tombs, war memorials and churchyard crosses, but the primary

responsibility for the upkeep of a monument falls on the owners, who are the heirs of the people commemorated. This will be of little help where they no longer exist or cannot be traced.

10. The PCC or local authority (in the case of a closed churchyard) could be in breach of this duty of care and therefore negligent if it failed to make safe tombs or memorials which it knew required attention or were in an unsafe condition.

11. In the event that a PCC finds that there are monuments that are dangerous it should act immediately to make them safe and then, if necessary, petition for a confirmatory faculty, but in some dioceses where gravestones are leaning dangerously the chancellor permits them to be laid flat without the authority of a faculty.

Church building
12. If part of a church building falls and injures someone a prima facie case against the 'occupier' will have been made for, in the normal course of events, pieces should not fall off buildings if they are properly maintained.

Others (persons other than visitors)
13. For persons other than visitors, the 'occupier' owes a duty in respect of any injury if the occupier:

(a)   is aware of the danger or has reasonable grounds to believe it exists;

(b)   knows or has reasonable grounds to believe that the other is in the vicinity of the danger or that that other may come into the vicinity of danger; and

(c)   the risk is one against which the occupier may reasonably be expected to offer the other some protection (Occupiers' Liability Act 1984, s1(3)).

14. One needs to bear in mind that a churchyard is a public place and whilst some people may be put off by the nature of the place from visiting it, others will be attracted to it – albeit in some cases for the wrong purposes.

Warning notices

15. Warning notices are of doubtful effectiveness at law, are aesthetically undesirable and would doubtless be subject to vandalism.

Insurance

16. The standard 'Churchyard' policy from the Ecclesiastical Insurance Group indemnifies (normally incumbent, churchwardens and PCC) against any claim for public liability. This would include claims under the Occupiers' Liability Acts 1957 and 1984 or for negligence, but, of course, breach of duty of care must be proved. The policy, however, lays a duty on the insured to take all reasonable precautions, and in the event that any defect in the churchyard is discovered the insured must take immediate steps to remedy the same and cause such temporary precautions to be taken as the circumstances may require. It is important for those insured to make sure that the policy covers the churchyard. The Ecclesiastical Insurance Group states that it would automatically cover a churchyard surrounding a church, but not necessarily a detached churchyard.

(Revised 2000)

Churchyards: ownership of monuments and trees

Monuments

1. At common law property in a tombstone is vested in the person who erected it and after that person's death in the heir or heirs at law of the deceased. Thus the party having title to the monument was able to maintain an action against the incumbent or churchwardens for interfering with it, even though the monument had been annexed to the freehold. Professor J. H. Baker (1970) 5 Irish Jurist N.S. 391) has traced the formulation of this principle in its present form to Sir Edward Coke (see *Corven's Case* (1612) 12 Co. Rep. 105, 1 Co. Litt. 18 and 3 Co. Inst. 202) who based himself upon less explicit case law. Coke's statement of the law has been repeated in the textbooks (summarized in Baker (op. cit.). See in particular Phillimore *Ecclesiastical Law*, 2nd edn, p. 691 and *Halsbury's Laws of England*, 4th edn, 1975, vol. 14, para 1085). In modern times the common law rule has been restated by the ecclesiastical courts; for example in *Re St Andrew's Thornhaugh* [1976] Fam 230, *Re St John the Baptist, Bishop's Castle* (1999, Hereford Consistory Court; unreported) and *Re Keynsham Cemetery* [2003] 1 WLR 66.

2. Under section 45(1)(a) of the Administration of Estates Act 1925 the descent of property to heirs was abolished. The operative words of the statute are as follows:

> 'With regard to the real estate and personal inheritance of every person dying after the commencement of this Act, there shall be abolished –
>
> (a)   All existing modes rules and canons of descent, and of devolution by special occupancy or otherwise, of real estate, or of personal inheritance . . .'

3. The impact of section 45 upon the transmission of title to monuments has never been satisfactorily determined. The title of the person who erected the monument is, of course, unaffected. As regards descent after that person's death the following possibilities arise:

(i)   At common law there is a transmission to the heir of the deceased, and on his death to the next heir, notwithstanding section 45. This is the outcome favoured in *Re St Andrew's Thornhaugh* and, probably, in *Re St John the Baptist, Bishop's Castle* (see above). Presumably on this analysis devolution operates outside the scope of section 45 because the rights in relation to the monument are neither 'real estate' nor 'personal inheritance'.

(ii)   The common law rule is restricted to cases in which the person commemorated died before 1 January 1926 or died after that date but (as is usual) had no title to the monument; and is further limited to effect a single transmission after that date from the person who set up the monument to the heir at law of the deceased, the descent from heir to heir being doubtful given the impact of section 45. This is the solution postulated by Baker (op. cit.).

(iii)   The shifting interest passes from the person erecting the monument to the personal representatives of the deceased by virtue of the Administration of Estates Act 1925, further devolution being governed by the provisions of that Act.

4. Despite the modifications to the rules of inheritance made by the Administration of Estates Act 1925, section 3 of the Faculty Jurisdiction Measure 1964 reiterated the common law by enacting that

'(4) For the purposes of this section . . . "owner" means the person who erected the monument in question and, after his death, the heir or heirs at law of the person or persons in whose memory the monument was erected . . .'

Since, however, section 3 concerned only faculties for the execution of works to monuments, including their removal, the definition of owner for that limited purpose does not necessarily reflect the general law on the subject. Moreover, as was pointed out in Newsom, *Faculty Jurisdiction of the Church of England*, 2nd edn, at p. 155,

'Until 1926, real estate devolved (in the absence of other testamentary provision) upon the heir at law of the owner, that being his nearest surviving relation under a system of primogeniture with males taking priority over females. This system of devolution ceased to have any practical application in the law of real property as a result of the Administration of Estates Act 1925, and at the present time it would in most cases be difficult, once the person who erected the monument is dead, to say who in fact is the "owner" within subsection (4).'

It would be equally difficult to ascertain how title might have passed through a succession of personal representatives.

5. In relation to a municipal cemetery where by Act of Parliament rights of interment were created by contractual licence, Chancellor Gray QC concluded that the associated monuments, like the land, became vested in the freeholders (originally the cemetery company) subject to the rights of the licensees: *Re West Norwood Cemetery* [1994] Fam 210 at p. 218. The chancellor held that under the statutory framework peculiar to West Norwood Cemetery the monument became annexed to the freehold upon installation so that even the person who had the licence to install it lost title in the monument, which passed to the freeholder as soon as it was affixed to the ground. Since at common law title to a churchyard monument is at the very least retained for his life by the person who set it up, *Re West Norwood Cemetery* is inapplicable in that context. Neither is any principle to be deduced from *Re West Norwood Cemetery* concerning the vesting of title to a monument in a churchyard where there was no, or no ascertainable, heir or other representative of the deceased.

6. Commonly the devolution of title to a monument is in doubt for one of the following reasons:

(a)   the inscription is defaced and there is no record of the interment beneath it; or

(b)   the family is without known heirs; or

(c)   the transmission of title cannot be proved, because of legal uncertainty or otherwise.

In each of these situations the problem, on analysis, is one of proof. Although the owner is unidentifiable, the monument cannot be treated as *res nullius*; the absence of an owner is itself incapable of being proved. The resultant uncertainties create a powerful argument for departing from previous practice by licensing new monuments for a term of 100 years or less, so as to facilitate their eventual removal. Where the owner is unknown but presumed to exist, the issue of title has been circumvented by the creation of legal responsibilities and powers, summarized in the following paragraph, which arise independently of ownership. It is for this reason that the law concerning transmission of title to monuments remains undeveloped.

7. In summary the responsibilities and powers affecting monuments (with or without an identified owner) in churchyards are as follows. They are variously applicable to churchyards which remain open for burials, closed churchyards, and those subject to redundancy.

Responsibilities

(i) The occupier of a churchyard owes the common duty of care to visitors pursuant to the Occupiers' Liability Act 1957; this duty extends to the safe condition of monuments. Where the churchyard remains open for burials the occupier is the Parochial Church Council (*see* **Churchyards: liability for personal injury acccidents**). In the case of a closed churchyard which is maintained by a local authority under section 215(2) of the Local Government Act 1972, the local authority exercises sufficient control over the churchyard to be an occupier, at least in relation to the safety of monuments therein. Both the local authority and the Parochial Church Council might simultaneously be liable as occupiers depending on the precise circumstances. (See generally *Wheat v Lacon* [1966] A.C. 552.) The identity of the occupier or occupiers of a churchyard which is subject to a redundancy scheme will depend upon the terms of the scheme itself.

(ii) A local authority which has taken over the maintenance of a churchyard thereby has provided a workplace for its employees to which the Workplace (Health, Safety and Welfare) Regulations 1992 apply. Duties are cast upon employers under the Regulations as to the general safety of the workplace (Reg 5) and protection from falling objects (Reg 13). Regulations 5 and 13 are of relevance where the local authority's employees work in a churchyard containing potentially dangerous monuments.

Powers

(i) Section 3 of the Faculty Jurisdiction Measure 1964 provides a procedure whereby a faculty may be granted for the moving, demolition, alteration or execution of other work to a monument where the owner withholds consent to the work or cannot be found. Where a monument is dangerous it is envisaged that this procedure will commonly be invoked whether a churchyard is open or closed.

(ii) Where a monument is listed under the Planning (Listed Buildings and Conservation Areas) Act 1990 the local authority may authorize its demolition (s8) or execute works urgently necessary for its preservation (s54) and has a right of recovery against the owner (if ascertainable) in respect of the expense of repairs. As an alternative to the exercise of its section 8 and section 54 powers the local authority may set in motion the statutory procedure applicable to dangerous structures under which demolition may take place. (See s56 of the 1990 Act and the legislation there referred to.)

(iii)   Where a redundancy scheme under the Pastoral Measure 1983 has been made in respect of a church or churchyard, paragraph 3 of Schedule 6 to that Measure gives 'the personal representatives or relatives of any deceased person' the right to dispose of any relevant tombstone, monument or other memorial there. The class of interested persons under paragraph 3 will in practice often include any identifiable owner. In the absence of a disposal under paragraph 3, Schedule 6 makes further provision for the retention, relocation or removal of monuments.

8. It remains an open question who is to pay for works to be carried out in relation to a monument lacking any identifiable owner. Funding is an issue separate from the availability of the legal processes outlined above.

Trees in churchyards

9. Under pre-Reformation canon law (summarized in Phillimore's *Ecclesiastical Law*, 2nd edn, para 1406) timber growing in churchyards was owned by the incumbent, who was enjoined not to fell it save for the purpose of repairing the chancel or the buildings of the benefice. The law currently applicable to trees in churchyards is contained in section 6 of the Care of Churches and Ecclesiastical Jurisdiction Measure 1991, as amended by section 13 of the Church of England (Miscellaneous Provisions) Measure 1995, the relevant part of which provides as follows:

'(1) The powers, duties and liabilities of a Parochial Church Council with respect to the care and maintenance of a Churchyard which the Council is liable to maintain shall extend to the trees therein, including those proposed to be planted.

(2) Where a tree in a Churchyard which a Parochial Church Council is liable to maintain is felled, lopped or topped the Council may sell or otherwise dispose of the timber and the net proceeds of any sale thereof shall be paid to the Council and applied for the maintenance of any Church or Churchyard which the Council is liable to maintain . . .'

10. It will be noted that the obligations for care and maintenance relate to 'a Churchyard which the Council is liable to maintain'. This definition

introduced by the 1995 Measure reflects the wording of section 215(1) of the Local Government Act 1972 which states '. . . Where . . . a Churchyard has been closed by an Order in Council, the Parochial Church Council shall maintain it by keeping it in decent order and its walls and fences in good repair.'

11. The remaining part of section 215 deals with the modern mechanism by which the PCC can pass responsibility of the maintenance of a closed churchyard over to the local authority. In fact it continues a mechanism originally contained in section 18 of the Burial Act 1855 which provided for the maintenance of a closed churchyard to be paid out of the rates, on the basis that it was treated as a community asset.

12. Thus, modern legislation has made it clear that the PCC has not retained any statutory powers or responsibilities in respect of the trees in a churchyard maintained by the local authority. The incumbent has retained ownership of the timber, but the proceeds of sale can only be used for maintenance of the church or the churchyard. In practice, most of the proceeds are absorbed by the cost of felling.

(July 2001, revised 2003)

Churchyards: war memorials

1. Any memorial in a church, a churchyard or other property which is subject to the faculty jurisdiction remains the property of the body, person or group of people who erected it, or the heirs or successors of such a person, group or body. This applies whether it be a free-standing memorial in a churchyard or cemetery, or a wooden, stone or marble plaque fixed to the wall of the church building itself. The fact that a faculty is required for the erection of the memorial in the first place has no bearing on its actual ownership. The memorial does not become part of the freehold of the church. Nor does it vest in the ownership of the churchwardens.

2. This general principle applies to war memorials. Although there are many private memorials to individuals killed in war, most war memorials are likely to have been erected by, and at the expense of, civic or parish communities, or, perhaps, the Commonwealth War Graves Commission, the British Legion or a particular regiment. Whether private or public, however, a war memorial remains in the ownership of the person, community, association, regiment or other body that erected it, or the heirs or successors of that person or body.

3. Under section 1 of the War Memorials (Local Authorities Powers) Act 1923, as amended by section 133(1) of the Local Government Act 1948, county, district, parish and community councils, and parish meetings of parishes without a parish council, have power to incur reasonable expenditure on the maintenance, repair and protection of war memorials, whether vested in them or not. This power extends to incurring expenditure in altering a war memorial so as to make it serve as a memorial in connection with any later war, see section 133(2) of the 1948 Act. However, a faculty is needed for any work carried out to a memorial which is subject to the faculty jurisdiction. Many war memorials were erected by local authorities or local residents after World War I to commemorate members of local families killed in that war, had names added after World War II, and continue to be maintained by a local authority under the powers in the 1923 Act. It is thought likely that in many such cases the local authority would acknowledge ownership of the memorial.

4. Where a war memorial is situated within a church, the PCC normally arranges in practice for it to be kept clean and for minor routine maintenance work to be carried out – for example, oiling a wooden plaque – in the same way as for other parts of the church. For practical purposes, the best course for a PCC may well be to invite a local authority to exercise its statutory power under the 1923 Act in the case of a public war

memorial, within the church or churchyard precincts, which requires work to maintain it or which is otherwise falling into disrepair. If a private war memorial requires maintenance or repair, the request for assistance would clearly go, in the first place, to the heir or heirs (if known) of the family who erected it. A similar position arises if the Commonwealth War Graves Commission the British Legion or a regimental association erected the memorial, or has at some stage assumed responsibility for it.

5. A local authority may exercise its power under the 1923 Act, as amended, whether or not a particular war memorial is in a closed churchyard. Under section 215 of the Local Government Act 1972, however, many closed churchyards are maintained by local authorities in any event. So the maintenance of a war memorial within the churchyard would effectively be carried out in the exercise of dual statutory functions.

6. The removal of a war memorial from a church, a churchyard or the consecrated part of a local authority cemetery requires a faculty. The same applies to the movement of a war memorial from one part of a churchyard to another. Unless there are compelling reasons to justify such a scheme, it unlikely that a faculty would be granted: see *In re St Peter and St Paul, Upper Teddington, and St Michael and St George, Fulwell* [1993] 1 WLR 852.

7. Before the grant of such a faculty can be considered, it is vital that the proposers of the scheme contact the body, person or persons in whom ownership of the memorial vests, or who is or are responsible for its upkeep. This situation may arise where, for example, a PCC proposes a scheme for the rearrangement of headstones in its churchyard, perhaps in connection with a desire to re-use part of the churchyard or possibly to extend the church itself. If, for example, a Commonwealth war grave or headstone or a memorial in which the Commonwealth War Graves Commission has an interest may be involved, and the Commission has not already been consulted, it should be informed at once through the diocesan registrar.

8. If a faculty is granted for the removal of a war memorial from a church, a churchyard or the consecrated part of a local authority cemetery, then if the new site for the memorial is outside the jurisdiction of the church (for instance, within the precincts of a local authority building), it will no longer be subject to the faculty jurisdiction. However, the disturbance of the status quo is more likely to be acceptable to the consistory court if the memorial is moved from one area of consecrated ground to another, as apart from the symbolic and pastoral considerations this has the advantage of continued control within the faculty jurisdiction: see *Re All Saints, Stanton on the Wolds*, 5 Ecc LJ 304,

where the chancellor granted a faculty to move a war memorial from a churchyard on condition that the new site was to be consecrated (which the bishop was willing to do) and a scheme agreed for the maintenance of the memorial and its landscaped surroundings.

9. Recently (December 2002) the Home Office has published a helpful guide entitled *WAR MEMORIALS – A Code of Practice for Custodians.* The booklet is available from HMSO. It contains some useful practical advice with regard to, inter alia:

(a)   the identification and recording of memorials;

(b)   the proper monitoring of memorials;

(c)   their removal and disposal (in the event of the land on which a memorial is positioned experiencing a change of use or ownership, or undergoing major structural change);

(d)   the possible availability of grants to assist with maintenance or repair costs;

(e)   and the effect on a memorial of a declaration of redundancy under the Pastoral Measure 1983.

In this last context it is worth noting the observation in the Home Office booklet:

'Where monuments and memorials remain in a redundant church following disposal, the new owner will be prohibited by covenant from removing or disturbing them without the prior approval of the relevant Church authorities. Removal of a war memorial from a listed church will also require secular listed building consent in addition to any discussions with the Church authorities under the terms of a covenant placed on the building.'

(May 2000, revised August 2003)

Consecration of burial grounds

1. There is no positive legal requirement for consecration of ground prior to interment in it; though it is presumed that such land *should* be consecrated, interments may lawfully take place in unconsecrated ground. Moreover, the bishop has no legal duty to consecrate ground for interments. Rather, the bishop has a formal legal right to consecrate new burial grounds for interment (Canon C 18(4)), and to consecrate areas for the interment of cremated remains (Church of England (Miscellaneous Provisions) Measure 1992, s3(2)). The exercise of the bishop's right to consecrate has been understood judicially as one cast in wide discretionary terms, and the secular courts are reluctant to interfere with its exercise (*R v Tiverton Burial Board* (1858) 6 WR 662). Nor would the courts be likely to question the validity of a consecration effected in exercise of that discretionary right (*Segwick v Bourne* [1920] 2 KB 267 at p. 275).

2. As a matter of ecclesiastical practice, the norm is for consecration of ground *prior* to interments in it. In petitions by a burial authority to a bishop to consecrate an area for burials, it has been assumed that there should have been no previous burials in the land to be so consecrated; the *Encyclopaedia of Forms and Precedents*, vol. 13(2), *Ecclesiastical Law*, 5th edn, London, 2000, p. 169, Form 67, provides that the petition should indicate that: 'No interments have as yet taken place within the [designated] land'. However, this assumption does not appear to be found in the substantive law governing such petitions (i.e. the Local Authorities' Cemeteries Order 1977, SI 1977/204, art. 5). Indeed, in the past, a parliamentary statute has assumed that consecration of land may lawfully *follow* interments in that land (Burial Act 1857, s13). A survey of a very extensive range of authorities, old and new, seems to disclose no legal evidence of a general rule forbidding the consecration of ground in which interments have previously taken place; previous interments are not listed amongst the impediments to consecration. For these reasons, the assumption that there should be no previous burials in land prior to consecration would seem to be based on no clear legal authority. In the light of the apparent silence of the law, therefore, there would seem to be a legal liberty for a bishop to consecrate ground in which interments have previously taken place.

3. However, whilst there may be no legal impediment to such a consecration, there may be pastoral or policy considerations in consecrating land in which burials have previously taken place. In the exercise of the episcopal discretion, thought will need to be given to the relatives of those whose burial pre-dates the proposed consecration of the burial ground. Although the deceased have no human rights, their

loved ones do. Article 8 (respect for private and family life) and Article 9 (freedom of religion) of the European Convention on Human Rights are likely to be engaged. Since both of these are 'qualified' rights and the provision of burial grounds is a legitimate social aim, it is unlikely that the Human Rights Act 1998 would preclude the later setting aside of land to be consecrated as a burial ground. However, those whose sensibilities are likely to be offended by such *ex post facto* consecration would have a powerful case for exhumation (see *Re Durrington Cemetery* [2001] Fam 33 and *Re Crawley Green Road Cemetery, Luton* [2001] 2 WLR 1175). Two specimen sentences of consecration (for a churchyard extension and for a further section of a local authority cemetery) are attached as Appendix A and B.

(April 2002)

Appendix A

IN THE NAME OF GOD <u>AMEN</u>

<u>WHEREAS</u> We have received the Petition of the Incumbent, Churchwardens and certain Inhabitants of the Parish of . . . . who have represented to Us . . . . by Divine Permission **<u>LORD BISHOP OF</u>** . . . . **THAT** it has become necessary to provide further space for interments according to the rites of the Church of England within the said Parish **THAT** a parcel of land has been acquired by a Transfer dated . . . . which said land is to be used as a burial ground for the said Parish **THAT** the piece of land delineated on the plan hereto annexed and thereon coloured pink is the parcel of the land so acquired **THAT** the said piece of land coloured pink has been properly prepared and is in a fit and proper state for the interments and is identified on the ground by boundary stones **THAT** no burials have as yet taken place within the said piece of land proposed to be consecrated and there are no easements or rights of way affecting the same

<u>AND WHEREAS</u> We have been requested to consecrate the said piece of land

<u>THEREFORE WE</u>. . . . . by Divine Permission **<u>LORD</u> <u>BISHOP OF</u>** . . . . acting through Our Commissary appointed for this purpose the Right Reverend . . . . **<u>DO HEREBY</u>** in Exercise of Our authority as Bishop set apart the said piece of land proposed to be consecrated and delineated and coloured pink on the plan hereto annexed from all profane common uses and for use as a burial ground according to the rites and ceremonies of the Church of England **<u>AND</u>** do assign the same as a consecration portion of the said burial ground to be known as . . . . Churchyard Extension and do dedicate and consecrate the same for that purpose **<u>AND</u>** by this Our Definitive Sentence and Final Decree (which we cause to be read and promulged by these presents) **<u>WE DO</u>** publicly pronounce that the same ought to remain so set apart dedicated and consecrated forever

<u>DATED</u> this . . . . day of . . . . in the year of Our Lord Two thousand and . . . . year of Our Translation

. . . .
<u>Bishop (or Commissary)</u>

I HEREBY CERTIFY that the above Sentence was read by me at
.... Churchyard on the .... day of
.... Two thousand and .... in the presence
of the Right Reverend ....

....
Registrar

Witnesses: (Two clergy to sign)

....   }
                                                   }
....   }

Appendix B

IN THE NAME OF GOD AMEN

WHEREAS We have received the Petition of ....
Borough Council (hereinafter called the 'Council') who have represented
to us .... by Divine Permission **BISHOP OF**
.... **THAT** it has become necessary to provide further
space for interments of remains according to the rites of the Church of
England **THAT** the said Council own a parcel of land which is situate in
the Diocese of .... which said land is used as a burial
ground for the said Council and is known as ....
THAT the piece of land coloured pink on the plan hereto annexed is a
portion of the land so acquired **THAT** the said piece of land has been
properly prepared and is in a fit and proper state for the interments and is
identified on the ground by boundary stones **THAT** no interments have as
yet taken place within the said piece of land proposed to be consecrated
and there are no easements or rights of way affecting the same

AND WHEREAS the Council have requested unto Us to consecrate the
said piece of land

THEREFORE WE................. by Divine Permission **BISHOP**
OF .... acting through Our Commissary appointed for this
purpose......................... **(ASSISTANT BISHOP within**
the diocese of ....**) DO HEREBY** in Exercise of
Our authority as Bishop set apart the said piece of land proposed to be
consecrated and coloured pink on the plan hereto annexed from all
profane common uses **AND** do assign the same as a consecrated portion
of the said burial ground to be known as ....
and do dedicate and consecrate the same for that purpose **AND** by this
Our Definitive Sentence and Final Decree (which we cause to be read and
promulged by these presents) **WE DO** publicly pronounce that the same
ought to remain so set apart dedicated and consecrated forever

DATED this .... day of .... Two
thousand and ....

.... **(Commissary)**

I HEREBY CERTIFY that the above Sentence was read by me at ....
.... Burial Ground on the .... day of ....
Two thousand and .... in the presence of the said Right
Reverend ....

.... **Registrar**

05/07

Part 9
Burial and Cremation

Burial and cremation

Right to burial in the churchyard

1. Subject to any public health regulations at common law every parishioner has the right of burial of his or her body in the burial place of the parish (unless closed by Order in Council), that is, the parish where the deceased resided or (by virtue of s6 of the Church of England (Miscellaneous Provisions) Measure 1976) was on the church electoral roll at the time of death. Moreover, any person whose death takes place within the area of a parish is by law entitled to be buried in that parish as a parishioner, irrespective of the length of time he or she has lived there – e.g. the victim of an air crash or motor accident who may have entered the parish only a few minutes before death occurred. In addition, personal representatives are entitled to remove the body to the parish of residence and demand its burial there.

2. Inhabitants of a new parish created (otherwise than by a union of parishes) under the Pastoral Measure 1983 retain their original rights of burial until they obtain rights of burial as parishioners of the new parish (Pastoral Measure 1983, Sch 3 para 15(2)).

3. Burial where no other arrangements can be made is regulated by the Public Health (Control of Disease) Act 1984, section 46.

4. A person who has a right of burial in a churchyard or other burial ground has a right of burial therein of his or her cremated remains (Church of England (Miscellaneous Provisions) Measure 1992, s3(1)).

5. Parishioners (including persons who for this purpose are regarded as parishioners) are entitled to Christian burial according to the ordinary rites of the Church of England except those who die unbaptized, or excommunicate, or have taken their own lives while of sound mind. In those cases the form of service is to be that prescribed or approved by the Ordinary (*see* **Burial and cremation: suicides**).

6. Apart from these special cases the minister is bound to say the Burial Service in its entirety over every parishioner. But the minister is entitled to due notice of the funeral (Canon B 38 para 2). The Burial Laws Amendment Act 1880, sections 1, 6, allows parishioners to be buried in the churchyard without any religious service or with such Christian and orderly religious service as the person responsible for the burial may think fit.

7. It should be noted that, although parishioners have the right of burial in the churchyard, they have no right to be buried in any particular spot,

nor have they any right to the exclusive property in a grave. The selection of the particular grave is a matter which is within the discretion of the incumbent, who cannot give any person exclusive rights in it. This can only be done by faculty. Grave spaces may be reserved by faculty for the benefit of the persons referred to therein for a maximum period of one hundred years from the date of the faculty or until AD 2064 in the case of a faculty granted before 15 April 1964 (Faculty Jurisdiction Measure 1964 s8). Part of a churchyard may be reserved to the donor of the land under the Consecration of Churchyards Acts 1867 and 1868.

8. Burial fees are contained in Parochial Fees Orders made under the Ecclesiastical Fees Measure 1986 and approved from time to time by the General Synod.

9. The responsibility for digging a grave is upon the executors or other persons responsible for the funeral arrangements. The incumbent's duty is merely to indicate the place at which the grave is to be dug, and its depth; the incumbent is not obliged to provide a grave-digger.

10. Although a parishioner normally has a right to have his or her ashes buried in a churchyard, this is not so when the churchyard has been closed by Order in Council except pursuant to a faculty.

11. Faculties are often granted to permit part of the churchyard (including a closed churchyard) to be set aside for the interment of cremated remains.

Burial in consecrated ground

12. There is a presumption that an area used for burials in a churchyard belonging to a parish, whether contiguous within the parish church or not, should be consecrated, and where no documentary evidence is available there is a presumption that it has been consecrated. Although the Canons do not expressly require that the burial of a corpse should be in consecrated ground, they assume that a churchyard will be consecrated, and paragraph 5 of Canon B 38 makes specific provision for burial in unconsecrated ground by requiring that 'the officiating minister, on coming to the grave, shall first bless the same'.

13. In the case of a burial ground other than a churchyard, such as a local authority or private cemetery company burial ground, there is no obligation on the local authority or cemetery company to provide a consecrated area within the burial ground for the burial of the dead according to the rites of the Church of England. Where an officiating minister conducts a burial according to the rites of the Church of

England in an unconsecrated burial ground or cemetery the minister is not subject to proceedings for a breach of ecclesiastical law for having done so (Burial Laws Amendment Act 1880, s12) but Canon B 38 again applies.

Reservation of grave space

14. A grave space may be reserved by faculty (*see also* **Churchyards**).

Births and Deaths Registration Act 1926

15. Before an ordinary Church of England burial takes place in a churchyard the incumbent of the parish must be satisfied that a 'certificate of disposal' of the body has been issued by the registrar of births and deaths, or a corresponding order made by the coroner.

16. The registrar's certificate (or coroner's order) should be produced to the incumbent, but if the incumbent is satisfied by a written declaration that the certificate or order has been issued, but has been left behind or mislaid, the burial may proceed, providing the incumbent gets an undertaking that the missing certificate or order will be produced as soon as possible. A duplicate of the certificate can if necessary be obtained from the registrar.

17. If there are several burials at the same time the certificates must not be mixed, because the particulars of each burial must be filled in by the incumbent on the detachable portion of the certificate or order authorizing that particular burial and no other. The detachable portion must then be torn off and delivered by messenger or in ordinary course of post to reach the registrar of births and deaths of the sub-district within 96 hours of the burial. The incumbent is responsible for all this.

18. The burial of stillborn children must be authorized by a certificate or order in the same way as in the case of an ordinary body; but in that case (a) the burial may in no case proceed without production of the actual certificate or order, and (b) the burial need not be notified, and the certificate or order has no detachable portion for that purpose.

19. In the case of a non-Anglican burial in a churchyard when the service is conducted under the Burial Laws Amendment Act 1880 the above duties do not fall on the incumbent but on the relative, friend or legal representative of the deceased having the charge of or being responsible for the burial.

Cremation

20. An application for cremation will normally be made by an executor or the nearest relative of the deceased, but the cremation authority may accept an application made for good reason by some other person. The application has to be countersigned by a householder to whom the applicant is known.

21. An earlier provision prohibiting the cremation of a person who has left a written direction to the contrary was revoked in 1965, so the decision whether or not to honour the wishes of the deceased, whether expressed in written or oral form, is a matter for the relatives.

Rights of incumbent in respect of cemetery or crematorium

22. An incumbent is not normally entitled to conduct funeral services at a cemetery or crematorium outside his or her own benefice without the leave of the incumbent of the place where the cemetery or crematorium is situated. If the incumbent who is to conduct the service is beneficed in a different diocese, the consent of the bishop of the diocese in which the cemetery or crematorium lies must also be obtained.

23. However, under section 2(1) and (2) of the Church of England (Miscellaneous Provisions) Measure 1992 and paragraph 2(d) of Canon C 8, this does not apply in the case of an incumbent taking the funeral service of a person who died in a parish in the incumbent's own benefice, or who was resident or on the church electoral roll there at the time of death. Under section 2(4) of the 1992 Measure, the incumbent is required to take or arrange for the funeral service (and does not merely have the right to do so) if the parish is within the area legally chargeable with the expenses of the cemetery in question, or if it lies within the area for the use of which the cemetery or crematorium in question has been designated by the bishop. (These provisions of s2 are not confined to incumbents, but apply to the 'minister' of the parish; 'minister' is defined by s2(6) as the incumbent or a team vicar with a special cure of souls, any priest-in-charge appointed during a suspension of presentation and the rural dean in the case of other vacancies.)

24. Similarly, under section 2(1) and (3) of the 1992 Measure and paragraph 2(d) of Canon C 8, a chaplain licensed to an institution under section 2 of the Extra-Parochial Ministry Measure 1967 may perform a funeral service at any cemetery or crematorium, without the consent of the incumbent of the place where the cemetery or crematorium is situated or the bishop of the diocese, if the deceased person was an employee or student of the institution at the time of death.

Conduct of services by unordained person

25. Unordained persons can conduct funerals in a churchyard or in the consecrated part of a cemetery in accordance with the provisions of section 6 of the Burial Laws Amendment Act 1880, but before the funeral takes place a notice as required by section 1 of that Act (as amended by s8 of the Burial Act 1900) must be given at such time and to such person as the burial authority directs. If the unordained person is going to read the Church of England service that person must be authorized to do so by the incumbent of the parish in which the burial ground is situated. Deaconesses, readers, evangelists and other persons admitted under the Canons as lay workers may be authorized by the bishop to read the Church of England service and bury the dead (Canons D 1, E 4 and E 7).

Exhumation, removal and reinterment of human remains

26. A faculty is required for the exhumation of human remains for reburial elsewhere. The law and practice in relation to this is set out in the judgement of the Chancery Court York in the case of *Re Christ Church Alsager* [1999] Fam 142 and in the judgement of the Court of Arches in *Re Blagdon Churchyard* [2002] Fam 299.

27. The removal of remains from one consecrated place to another such place, whether or not in the same churchyard or cemetery, does not require a licence under section 25 of the Burial Act 1857. All such removals may be undertaken solely on the authority of a faculty. This interpretation of section 25 was agreed by the Home Office in 1985.

(Revised 2003)

Burial and cremation: further burials in existing graves and in land already used for burials

1. This Opinion sets out the law as opposed to the culture regarding the reuse of old graves and the reopening of closed churchyards. For the public's attitude to reusing old graves in religious and secular settings reference should be made to such surveys as that carried out by Professor Douglas Davies and Alastair Shaw (*Reusing Old Graves: a Report on Popular British Attitudes*, Shaw & Sons, 1995). For a recent survey into the availability of burial space in the churchyards of six dioceses see a paper by the Church Commissioners dated 7 October 1998 for the Churches Group on Funeral Services at Cemeteries and Crematoria (CGF(98)34).

Summary of the law relating to burial in churchyards and parish burial grounds

2. At common law parishioners and those dying in a parish have a right of burial (through their personal representatives) in the churchyard or parish burial ground. This right now extends to those whose names were on the church electoral roll on the day of death (Church of England (Miscellaneous Provisions) Measure 1976 s6(1)). A person who has a right of burial in a churchyard or other burial ground in a parish also has a right of burial there of cremated remains (Church of England (Miscellaneous Provisions) Measure 1992 s3(1)) (*see* **Burial and cremation**). In all other cases the consent of the minister is required who should seek general guidance from the PCC (Church of England (Miscellaneous Provisions) Measure 1976 s6(2)). In any event it is for the minister to decide on the precise place of burial.

3. Apart from grave spaces reserved by faculty or under statute (*see* **Burial and cremation**), a person's right to burial is subject to there being room in the churchyard or parish burial ground at the time of the proposed burial. No problem need arise in the case of the burial of cremated remains if a small area is set aside by faculty for this purpose, as is usual.

4. If a churchyard or other burial ground has been wholly closed by Order in Council, no further burials of bodies may take place there unless the Order contains exceptions, for example for the burial of relations in existing vaults or graves (Burial Act 1853 s1). An Order in Council does not however prevent a faculty being granted for the burial of cremated remains either in a particular case or by means of a general faculty which would include provision setting aside an area for that purpose (*Halsbury's Laws of England*, 4th edn, 1975, vol. 14, para 1315).

Further burials in existing graves

5. Assuming the churchyard or burial ground has not been closed by Order in Council, further burials may take place in existing graves on the authority of the minister and without a faculty, save in the circumstances set out in paragraph 13 below. The minister should be satisfied that a further burial would be acceptable before granting permission.

6. In the case of a closed churchyard further burials may only take place in existing graves (or elsewhere) if the Order in Council makes specific provision for them, e.g. the burial of further family members. In such cases no faculty is required.

Depth of graves and distance between burials

7. There is no uniform provision throughout the country covering the depth of graves. Most old churchyards and burial grounds are subject to no restrictions at all, although local Acts of Parliament, planning conditions and diocesan churchyard regulations often specify that there should be a gap of at least 3ft (900 mm) between the coffin lid and the surface of the ground. Legislation now repealed specified either such a gap (the Local Authorities' Cemeteries Order 1974) or a gap of at least 30 inches (750 mm) (the Town Improvement Clauses Act 1847). In the case of a new churchyard, an extension to an existing one and a new separated burial ground, planning permission is required which might include requirements as to depth. Where further burials are permitted in churchyards and burial grounds closed by Order in Council, it is usual for the Order to provide for gaps of up to 4ft (1,200 mm) or 5ft (1,500 mm).

8. Some graves will have been dug in the first instance to double or treble depth to allow for future burials but there is no general provision regarding the distance that should be allowed between each coffin. Clearly care must be taken not to disturb a coffin or human remains that lie below unless a faculty has been granted for that purpose. The same applies where an existing coffin is to be deliberately lifted and lowered to make more room (see also para 12 below). In such cases rodding is often carried out to ascertain the position and state of any earlier burial.

Monuments

9. Burial does not confer a right to erect a tombstone or other monument and, subject to diocesan churchyard regulations giving the minister authority to permit the erection of monuments falling within certain categories as to size, shape and nature, a faculty is required. Once lawfully

erected a monument may not be removed permanently without a faculty although it would seem that a further interment which merely requires the lifting and replacement of the monument and the addition of a further name on it might not be regarded as requiring formal faculty authorization, especially if the grave is subject to a reservation by faculty.

Reuse of land already used for burials

10. Subject to the consent of the minister, the existence of any reservation or Order in Council and any health and safety legislation, there is nothing to prevent land which has been used for burials in the past being used again for that purpose. Indeed this was often the case prior to the late eighteenth century when monuments began to be introduced generally and the identity of graves was preserved. Furthermore today there is an urgent need to provide space for further burials as churchyards and burial grounds become full.

11. In the case of an individual burial where there may have been burials in the past, no further authority is required although it would clearly be wise to proceed with caution lest human remains are disturbed in which event a faculty should be sought for the new burial and the appropriate reburial of any disturbed remains. Any existing monument which will have to be removed and sited elsewhere would likewise have to be the subject of faculty proceedings.

12. In the case of a large area being prepared for reuse, where grave mounds may have to be levelled, monuments removed and resited, and human remains are likely to be disturbed and reinterred elsewhere, a faculty is clearly required and careful planning and preparation including publicity is essential. Provided the human remains are reinterred in the same churchyard or in other consecrated ground a Home Office licence would not be required (Burial Act 1857 s25). The Home Office considers that a licence is required in the case of removing a coffin so that it can then be reburied deeper in the same grave. Such a licence should be sought as well as a faculty (see para 8 above).

13. There are no prescribed periods before which such reuse should not take place but it would seem to be generally accepted that a period of 50–100 years should elapse since the last known burial, the precise period depending on all the circumstances of the case. Clearly the existence of monuments and the need to move them can cause delay because relatives may continue to visit the site and could be distressed by re-use. The problem is a pastoral one not a legal one.

Reopening of closed churchyards

14. While the Burial Act 1855 provides for the variation of an Order in Council made under the Burial Act 1853 section 1, the principal Act contains no provision for revocation of an Order in Council. Large scale reuse of land already closed for burials would not seem to come within the power (that is the view of the Secretary of State on advice from the Law Officers (*see* **Churchyards: closed churchyards**)) to vary although fresh legislation could authorize such a course.

Conclusion

15. Despite the popularity of cremation, it is clear that PCCs, whose churchyards and burial grounds are getting full, need to plan and to prepare well thought out schemes for re-ordering the churchyards or burial grounds so as to provide for burial in the foreseeable future if they wish burials to continue in a church setting. Otherwise, it is the responsibility of the local authority to provide space in a cemetery. The reuse of land in churchyards and burial grounds closed by Order in Council is under consideration in 2006 by the Department of Constitutional Affairs as part of a general review of burial law.

(May 2000, revised 2006)

Burial and cremation: 'American Caskets'

1. Concern has been expressed regarding the use of 'American Caskets' for interments in churchyards. The caskets are larger than their English counterparts and are fitted with a folding top. The increased space occupied by such caskets is thought to have serious implications for already crowded churchyards.

2. The legal issue arising from the use of the caskets is whether the personal representatives of the deceased have the right to insist upon the pattern of coffin or casket to be used for the interment; or whether this is a matter capable of regulation under ecclesiastical law.

3. The so-called right of a parishioner at common law to be buried in a particular churchyard:

> 'is no more than the right to be returned to his parent earth for dissolution, and does not carry with it the right to be interred in any special manner or in any particular spot or part of the churchyard'

(*Cripps on Church and Clergy*, 8th edn, p. 571). This statement of the law is consistent with the leading case of *Gilbert v Buzzard* (1820) 3 Phillimore 335; 2 Haggard 333. The judgement of Sir William Scott concerned the use of an iron coffin of no greater size than a wooden coffin. The issue of undue congestion of the churchyard did not, therefore, arise, and the only dispute was whether the churchwardens were entitled to require payment of a greater fee for an iron coffin than for a coffin of wood. It was held that the consistory court had jurisdiction to approve a higher fee for an iron coffin.

4. Parochial fees no longer fall within the jurisdiction of the consistory court but instead are regulated by Parochial Fees Orders made under the Ecclesiastical Fees Measure 1986. The practice has been to include in the Table of Parochial Fees authorized by such Orders a single composite fee for burial of a body in a churchyard. In principle a future Parochial Fees Order might provide for a higher fee payable for a burial in a container which exceeds certain specified dimensions. This would provide some disincentive to the use of large caskets.

5. Apart from the incidence of fees, the consistory court retains jurisdiction over the mode of burial. The existence of the jurisdiction is confirmed by *R v Coleridge* (1819) 2 B & A 806 and by *Gilbert v Buzzard* itself. In modern times it has been exercised in relation to the mode of interment of cremated remains. Both Churchyard Regulations made at

diocesan level, and provisions included in faculties for setting aside areas for cremated remains, regulate the materials and dimensions of caskets containing ashes. Just as a chancellor may by means of Churchyard Regulations delegate the power to approve monuments of certain types and dimensions, likewise the size of coffins is capable of control under such Regulations. The chancellor would have an overriding jurisdiction to allow by faculty a casket larger than that permitted under the Churchyard Regulations.

6. The framework outlined in paragraph 5 is not inconsistent with the right of burial at common law, since that right does not extend to the manner of burial. Where, therefore, the use of American Caskets is expected to cause inconvenience the chancellor should be invited to consider making appropriate provision in the Churchyard Regulations or (if a particular churchyard is involved) by way of a faculty.

(July 2001)

Burial and cremation: cemetery chapels

1. On the question of a local authority's obligation to maintain a cemetery chapel on consecrated ground, the Legal Advisory Commission's Opinion is that a distinction can be drawn between chapels built before 1900 and those built since 1900. In support of this proposition the following points are made:

(a) the functions of burial boards etc. which ceased to exist by virtue of section 214(1)(b) of the Local Government Act 1972 became exercisable by various local authorities as 'burial authorities' (see Sch 26)

(b) article 4(1) of the Local Authorities' Cemeteries Order 1977, SI 1977/204 (made pursuant to s214(3) of the 1972 Act) provides that:

> 'A burial authority may enclose, lay out and embellish a cemetery in such manner as they think fit, and from time to time improve it, and shall keep the cemetery in good order and repair, together with all buildings, walls and fences thereon and other buildings provided for use therewith.

> Nothing in this paragraph shall be construed as requiring any action in relation to any chapel provided as mentioned in article 6(1)(b).'

There is thus a general obligation to repair except in relation to an article 6(1)(b) chapel, which is a chapel erected at the request of members of the Church of England 'out of funds provided for the purpose otherwise than by the [burial] authority' (art 6(3)). The burial authority is expressly exempted from liability to maintain 'any chapel so provided except so far as funds provided otherwise than by them are available for that purpose'. Any chapel erected after 10 March 1977, when the Order came into effect, is obviously governed by these provisions.

2. The 1977 Order applies to some pre-1977 chapels because article 2(3) provides that:

> 'Any reference in this order to a chapel provided as mentioned in article 6(1)(b) includes a reference to any chapel provided under section 2(2) or (3) of the Burial Act 1900 or article 6(1)(b) of the order of 1974.'

The exception from liability to maintain contained in article 4(1) thus applies to these earlier chapels. The Local Authorities' Cemeteries Order 1974, SI 1974/628, contained an article 6 in the same terms as the new article 6 in the 1977 Order. Section 2(2) of the Burial Act 1900 empowered the burial authority at the request and cost of residents to erect and maintain a chapel, and section 2(3) empowered the Secretary of State to require a burial authority to erect and maintain such a chapel if the necessary funds were made available by local residents. The common feature of all these post-1900 chapels is that from the outset the cost of erection and maintenance is not to be borne by the burial authority.

3. It is not surprising to find a distinction drawn between pre- and post-1900 chapels because the responsibility for erecting and maintaining chapels appears to have rested entirely upon the appropriate burial authority (certainly under the public statutes). Thus section 30 of the Burial Act 1852 (repealed) empowered the burial board to erect a chapel and the board was empowered to pay for it by borrowing money and charging the debt upon future poor rates (s20). It was also provided that all expenses incurred under the Act should be chargeable upon and paid out of the poor rates (s19). Section 16 of the Cemeteries Clauses Act 1847 (which was incorporated with the Public Health (Interments) Act 1879) provided that the cemetery company 'shall keep the cemetery and the buildings and fences thereof in complete repair, and in good order and condition, out of the monies to be received by them by virtue of this and the special Act'.

4. Although the obligation to erect a chapel within the consecrated part of a burial ground provided under the Public Health (Interments) Act 1879 ceased in 1900 (see s2(4) of the Burial Act 1900) the obligation to maintain existing chapels continued, and section 16 of the Cemeteries Clauses Act 1847 was incorporated with the Local Government Act 1972 and continued to apply to cemeteries provided by local authorities until it was replaced by the maintenance provisions of article 4 of the Local Authorities' Cemeteries Order 1974, now article 4 of the 1977 Order (see para 14 of Sch 26 to the Local Government Act 1972).

(July 1979)

Burial and cremation: the consecration of private burial grounds and sites for 'green burials'

1. Where a request is made to a bishop to consecrate the whole or part of a burial ground or of a 'green burial' area, he will need to be advised on the principle of canon and ecclesiastical local law to be applied.

2. Whether or not to consecrate the whole or part of a cemetery or burial ground is a matter for the discretion of a bishop in the exercise of his episcopal jurisdiction, Canon C 18(4). In exercising that discretion the bishop should be guided by the following principles.

3. Consecration of a plot of land for the purposes of burial is the dedication of it for the sacred purpose of the burial in it of bodies and cremated remains with Christian rites and ceremonies. Christian burial is the committal to the ground of the body or cremated remains of the deceased for ever or, rather, for a period extending indefinitely into the unknown future. The legal consequences of consecration flow from these propositions. The land consecrated is deemed to be set aside for sacred uses and is brought within the jurisdiction of the Ordinary. Once the land is consecrated it cannot be divested of its sacred character by consent or surrender or abandonment but only by a lawful order. Such an order may be the removal of the effects of consecration by the bishop of the diocese under section 22 of the Care of Churches and Ecclesiastical Jurisdiction Measure 1991, a pastoral or other scheme under the Pastoral Measure 1983, or an order made under some other statutory provision. While these powers to remove the legal effects of consecration exist, unless and until an order in the exercise of one or more of them is made, an obligation rests upon all concerned with the consecration of the land in question and its subsequent care and upkeep to ensure that it is given and retains its sacred character. The mortal remains of those buried in it are in the custody of the Church; they may not be disturbed without the permission of the Ordinary and the ground in which they lie should be maintained in a decent and orderly state.

4. Many private burial grounds have been established by private Acts of Parliament, e.g. Kensal Green Cemetery, and the whole or parts of them have been consecrated. Where there is no Act of Parliament giving authority to an individual, corporation or limited company to establish a private burial ground such a person or body may, nevertheless, in law set aside land for the purpose of burial. If such a person were to petition the bishop to consecrate the whole or part of the land so set aside the bishop should, through his registrar, require answers to the questions in the following paragraph. Unless answers meeting the points mentioned below and satisfactory to the bishop are given then the jurisdiction to pronounce

a sentence of consecration of the land, or the part of the land being the subject of the petition, should not be exercised.

5. The questions are:

    (i)   Have all necessary planning consents for the use of the land in question as a burial ground for the indefinite future been granted?

    (ii)   Has the petitioner an unencumbered freehold interest in the land or will the petitioner have such an interest by the time of the proposed consecration?

    (iii)   What safeguards are there, or will there be, by the time of the proposed consecration, to ensure that if the freehold interest of the petitioner is alienated or charged, the identity of the holder of the freehold title changes or a lease is granted over the land, the fact of consecration will be known and its legal effects duly respected?

    (iv)   What security will there be for the upkeep of the land to be consecrated?

    (v)   If part only of the burial ground is to be consecrated how is it to be marked and identified as consecrated?

    (vi)   What arrangements will be in place to comply with the law relating to registration of burials and disposal of ashes?

    (vii)   Will the petitioner pay the costs of the registrar in investigating title, perusing and settling all documents and taking all necessary steps to carry the whole transaction through?

6. The reasons for questions (i) and (ii) are self-evident. With regard to question (vii) consecration of private burial grounds is not covered by the annual Ecclesiastical Judges and Legal Officers (Fees) Orders, and therefore the position of the registrar, who will be required to undertake considerable legal and conveyancing work, must be protected.

7. As for question (iii), the land may in the future be alienated. The legal effects of consecration will bind future owners and lessees, but on a practical level it is essential that they should be aware of the fact of consecration and the consequences which follow from it. Otherwise inappropriate and unauthorized acts may be done on the land before it is discovered to be consecrated, to the distress of the families of those buried here and the general public.

8. Parish priests and PCCs are under an obligation to take care that churchyards are duly fenced and kept in such an orderly and decent manner as becomes consecrated ground, Canon F 13(2). Local authorities and burial authorities maintaining cemeteries and burial grounds are under a similar obligation, viz. to keep the cemetery or burial ground in good order and repair (Local Authorities' Cemeteries Order 1977, SI 1977 No. 204, art 4). It may be safely assumed that the many private Acts of Parliament establishing private burial grounds require the corporations with statutory authority under those Acts to maintain such grounds in decent order, either by the terms of the private Act itself or under the terms of the Cemeteries Clauses Act 1847. These obligations under the canon law, or imposed by statute, do not extend to the private owners of the burial ground. Hence question (iv).

9. It is therefore recommended that where consecration is sought by a private owner, whether a commercial undertaking or a charity, the petitioners for themselves and their successors should be required to enter into a deed of covenant with the bishop and his successors covering the following matters:

(i)   The maintenance and upkeep of the consecrated land including its separation on the ground from any unconsecrated parts (and it may be appropriate to obtain a guarantor for the petitioner's obligations).

(ii)   A covenant by the petitioner not to use the consecrated land in any way which is inconsistent with its status as consecrated land.

(iii)   A requirement that on any disposition of the land, the purchaser, lessee or donee enter into a similar direct covenant with the bishop and his successors. In some cases it may be desirable to prohibit any disposition without the bishop's consent. In that way the bishop could block a disposition to an individual or organization which lacked the resources to comply with the maintenance obligations.

The deed of covenant should be protected by registration of an appropriate entry against the land owner's title. If that title is registered at the Land Registry a restriction should be registered to the effect either that no disposition is to be registered without the consent of the bishop or, perhaps, without a certificate by the diocesan registrar that the requirements of (ii) above have been complied with. If the title is unregistered, a land charge does not afford equivalent protection and consideration should be given to requiring the land owner to obtain voluntary first registration of his title to the land as a condition of the bishop's agreement to consecrate it. A specimen draft deed of covenant follows this Opinion.

10. 'Green burials' are burials in nature reserves, woodland and meadows. The graves have no memorials and there is no marking of burial plots. The ground set aside for burial is left in its natural, wild state. There is therefore no question of maintaining the ground as a churchyard (even a rambling, country churchyard) or cemetery has, traditionally, been maintained as the intention underlying the 'green burial' movement is that such a site should in no way appear to be a burial ground. Whether it is thought appropriate that ground consecrated for burials should so appear is, ultimately, a matter of policy and taste. Each case will have to be decided on its own merits and, no doubt, a factor in reaching a decision whether to consecrate will be the answer to question (v). The answer should show how, if part only of the burial ground is to be consecrated, it is to be marked off and plainly identified as consecrated.

11. The obligation to register burials and the disposal of ashes must be borne in mind. The Registration of Burials Act 1864, requires registers of burials to be maintained for all burials in all burial grounds 'according to the laws by which registers are required to be kept by rectors, vicars or curates of parishes or ecclesiastical districts in England'. The law presently applicable to the clergy of the Church of England is to be found in the Parochial Registers and Records Measure 1978, as amended by the Church of England (Miscellaneous Provisions) Measure 1992. The effect of these statutory provisions is that a book, corresponding with that now required to be kept by a parish priest, should be maintained, certainly for so much of the ground as may be consecrated, at the burial ground. A petitioner might be well advised to adopt and undertake to follow the provisions of Article 11 of the Local Authorities' Cemeteries Order 1977, which is a complete code for the registration of burials and disinterments. Both burials of bodies and interments of ashes should be registered. Before consecrating the whole or part of a private burial ground the bishop should, in so far as he can, make sure that there will be due compliance with the law relating to the registration of burials and disposals of ashes.

Specimen Deed of Covenant

THIS DEED is made the   day of   20

BETWEEN

(1) [N] BY DIVINE PERMISSION LORD BISHOP OF [D] ('the Bishop' which expression shall include the Bishop for the time being of the Diocese ('the Diocese') in which the Burial Site hereinafter defined is for the time being situate)

(2) [Petitioner] ('the Petitioner')

WHEREAS

(i) The Petitioner is the freehold owner of the piece of land ('the Burial Site') situate at . . . . in the Diocese and the Petitioner's title thereto is registered at H.M. Land Registry with title absolute under title number [No]

(ii) The Petitioner has petitioned the Bishop to consecrate a portion of[1] that part of the Burial Site ('the Consecrated Area') identified by red edging on the plan annexed hereto ('the Plan') for the purpose of burial according to the rites and ceremonies of the Church of England and the Bishop has agreed to grant the petition on condition that the Petitioner enters into covenants with the Bishop and his successors in the terms of this Deed

NOW THIS DEED WITNESSES AS FOLLOWS:

The Petitioner for himself and his successors covenants with the Bishop and his successors as follows:

1   Prior to its being consecrated to mark the Consecrated Area and separate it from the remainder of the Burial Site in the manner described in the First Schedule to this Deed and thereafter to maintain such demarcation in good condition and replace it as necessary

---

[1] The area edged red should include not only the portion to be consecrated but also its immediate curtilage and the pathways and means of access to it so that its ownership may be severed from the remainder of the Burial Ground if the Petitioner so wishes.

2   To maintain the Consecrated Area in accordance with the scheme of maintenance set out in the Second Schedule to this Deed or such other scheme as the Bishop may from time to time approve in writing and not to use the Consecrated Area in any way which is inconsistent with its status as consecrated land

3   Not to transfer lease charge share or part with possession or occupation of the Burial Site or any part of it which includes the Consecrated Area without obtaining the prior consent in writing of the Bishop

4   To pay the professional fees (including VAT thereon) of the Bishop in connection with the negotiation preparation and execution of this Deed and the registration of its provisions at H.M. Land Registry and of any application for consent or for a certificate pursuant to the provisions of this Deed

5   Not to transfer lease or charge the Burial Site or any part of it which includes the Consecrated Area unless the lessee or chargee enters into a deed of covenant with the Bishop in the terms of this Deed (with such modifications as may be necessary to fit the circumstances)

6   The Petitioner hereby applies to the Chief Land Registrar to enter a restriction on the register of title number [No] in the following terms:

> 'Except by order of the Registrar no disposition by the proprietor of the land is to be registered unless accompanied by a certificate given by the Registrar of the Diocese of [D] that the provisions of a deed made the [date of this Deed] between the Lord Bishop of [D] and [Petitioner] have been complied with'

IN WITNESS WHEREOF the Bishop has caused his Episcopal Seal and the Petitioner has caused its Common Seal to be hereunto affixed on the date first written above

THE FIRST SCHEDULE

[Details of the manner in which the consecrated land is to be marked on the ground]

THE SECOND SCHEDULE

[Scheme of maintenance]

Episcopal and common seals

(September 1998)

Burial and cremation: funerals in undertakers' private chapels

1. Canon law seldom prohibits the use of services in particular places. Canon B 40 ('Of Holy Communion elsewhere than in Consecrated Buildings') is an exception; most Canons on this subject are designed to secure that certain services *will* be held in prescribed places (cathedrals, parish churches).

2. The rubrics of the BCP (which is of course not a statute) envisage that the burial office will take place in the church or at the grave. This does not necessarily mean a consecrated church (it clearly includes parish centres of worship, for example); nor does it apply only to consecrated ground: see Canon B 38 para 5 on the duty of the minister to bless the grave when a body is to be buried in any unconsecrated ground according to the rites of the Church of England.

3. So far as services outside the church or the churchyard are concerned, there are a number of statutory provisions. In certain circumstances an incumbent is under an obligation to perform funeral services in the consecrated part of a public cemetery (see article 17(1) of the Local Authorities' Cemeteries Order 1977, SI 1977/204). There is no corresponding provision in respect of local authority crematoria, but see the Church of England (Miscellaneous Provisions) Measure 1992, section 2, regarding an incumbent's rights and obligations to conduct funeral services there (*see* **Burial and cremation**). So far as the unconsecrated parts of cemeteries are concerned, section 12 of the Burial Laws Amendment Act 1880 provides that a clergyman of the Church of England shall not be liable to any censure for officiating at a burial service according to the rites of the Church of England 'in any unconsecrated burial ground or cemetery . . . or in any building thereon, in any case in which he might have lawfully used the same service, if such burial ground . . . had been consecrated'. In proprietary cemeteries with consecrated ground the company may appoint an Anglican chaplain (Cemeteries Clauses Act 1847, s27, as amended by the Church of England (Miscellaneous Provisions) Measure 1992, Sch 3, para 1), but there may no longer be any cemeteries to which this provision applies.

4. None of these provisions relate to the case of an undertaker's chapel, which is essentially a place provided as a resting-place for the corpse and its 'viewing' by relatives and friends, and which is neither a church nor a building on the burial ground or within the boundaries of a crematorium.

5. Many of the Acts and other instruments referred to in paragraph 3 also deal with the relative duties and rights of the various clergy who may

be involved, e.g. the incumbent in whose parish the deceased died as against that of the parish whose burial ground is to be used. As an undertaker's chapel is not within any of the relevant provisions, nor is it an institution to which a minister may be licensed under section 2 of the Extra-Parochial Ministry Measure 1967 and Canon B 41, any exercise of ministry in such a chapel requires the consent of the local incumbent under Canon C 8 para 4. In practice, of course, this point would not be taken were a priest merely to accompany a mourning relative to view the body, and to pray with the relative, in the undertaker's chapel; but a burial service would be another matter.

6. Although the practice has been reported of the entire burial service including the committal being said in church (no further words being said at the crematorium), it is clear that both the BCP and *Common Worship* envisage the committal as being said at the burial or crematorium site. To that extent at least, the (whole) service could not be said in an undertaker's chapel. The question remains whether the earlier part of the office, either in the briefer BCP office or the slightly more elaborate order in *Common Worship*, may be said in such a chapel, always assuming the local incumbent either officiated or consented to another minister so doing.

7. Section 12 of the Burial Laws Amendment Act 1880, quoted in paragraph 3, certainly suggests that the use of the burial service outside the cases here mentioned (e.g. in a building not on a burial ground or cemetery) would attract ecclesiastical censure. It is arguable that the provision does not envisage services divided between different sites (much more common since crematoria became prevalent), but the language is plain in speaking of using the burial service and not merely of burying.

8. Canon B 38 para 1 specifically enjoins every minister to observe the law from time to time in force in relation to the burial of the dead. The effect of this provision is to exclude any argument that what is not expressly forbidden is lawful; the burden of proof, or of persuasion, is the other way.

9. The Legal Advisory Commission concludes that there is no lawful authority for a funeral service in an undertaker's chapel. Were it to be desired to permit such services, or services in other places, express statutory exemption from censure parallel to that given in section 12 of the 1880 Act would be required.

(October 1987, revised 2003)

Burial and cremation: suicides

The burial of those who have taken their own lives may take place in consecrated ground. Those who were not responsible for their own action are usually allowed one of the normal authorized forms of funeral service. The form of burial service used for those who have died by their own hand while of sound mind should be prescribed or approved by the diocesan bishop. Although the proviso to paragraph 2 of Canon B 38 refers to the possibility of a special form of service being approved by the General Synod for this purpose, none has yet been approved by the Synod.

(February 1994)

Part 10

Diocese

Diocese: access to meetings and minutes of diocesan advisory committees

Introductory

1. The faculty jurisdiction of the Church of England regulates the construction, alteration, adornment and furnishing of places of worship. The jurisdiction is that of the diocesan bishop exercised by his chancellor in the consistory court. Over time, this system of regulation has become systematic and sophisticated and its processes are governed by both primary and secondary legislation together with a substantial corpus of ecclesiastical common law and quasi-legislation in the form of directions and codes of practice.[1] The effective operation of the jurisdiction is central to the continuance of the ecclesiastical exemption by which the church buildings of the Church of England, and of certain other religious organizations, are exempted from listed building control, though not planning permission.[2] Whilst there are striking similarities between the faculty jurisdiction and the system of listed building control for secular buildings, since both concern the nation's built heritage, there are important differences both of principle and practicality.

2. The Diocesan Advisory Committee (DAC) in its current form is a creature of statute, established under section 2(1) of the Care of Churches and Ecclesiastical Jurisdiction Measure 1991 (CCEJM). It is required to have a written constitution containing the provisions set out in Schedule 1 of the CCEJM. The functions of the DAC are set out in Schedule 2 of the CCEJM. They include acting as an advisory body on matters affecting places of worship in the diocese and, in particular, to give advice when requested on matters relating to:

    (i)   the grant of faculties;

    (ii)   the architecture, archaeology, art and history of places of worship;

---

[1] See generally the Care of Churches and Ecclesiastical and Jurisdiction Measure 1991, the Faculty Jurisdiction Rules 2000 (SI 2000/2047), the *Care of Churches and Ecclesiastical Jurisdiction Measure Code of Practice* (Church House Publishing, 1993), *Making Changes to a Listed Church: Guidelines for Clergy, Churchwardens and Parochial Church Councils* (January 1999), and various diocesan regulations or guidance notes.

[2] See the Department for Culture, Media and Sport, *The Future of the Ecclesiastical Exemption: A Discussion Paper for England* (February 2004).

(iii)   the use, care, planning, design and redundancy of places of worship;

(iv)   the use and care of the contents of such places;

(v)   the use and care of churchyards and burial grounds.

The persons to whom the DAC is required to give advice when requested are the bishop, the chancellor, the archdeacons, PCCs, intending applicants for faculties, the pastoral committee, persons engaged in the planning, design or building of new places of worship in the diocese, not being places within the jurisdiction of the consistory court, and such other persons as the committee may consider appropriate.

3. It is important to note that, as its name suggests, the DAC's function is not in respect of these matters a decision making body and has no judicial or quasi-judicial function. Its membership comprises those with expertise and experience concerning the subject matter of likely faculties. The bishop's council is expressly enjoined by paragraph 5 of Schedule 1 of the CCEJM to ensure that the vast majority of the persons appointed to the DAC have between them knowledge of the history, development and use of church buildings; of Church of England liturgy and worship; of architecture, archaeology, art and history; and experience of the care of historic buildings and their contents. Advice is given not to the public as a whole but to specific and limited classes of persons. The categories are clearly defined and do not include potential objectors, parishioners, those on the electoral roll, nor local planning authorities. The residual discretionary category ought to be narrowly interpreted and, experience dictates, generally is.

4. Beyond this general advisory role, one particular function of the DAC is set out with greater specificity in the legislation. Section 15(1) of the CCEJM requires the chancellor to seek the advice of the DAC before making a final determination of any faculty,[3] and rule 3 of the Faculty Jurisdiction Rules 2000 provides that an intending applicant should seek the advice of the DAC before submitting a petition. The DAC may recommend the works, raise no objection, or decide not to recommend them. Whichever it decides it is required to issue a certificate in the prescribed form. See rule 3(5) and (6).

---

[3] The mandatory requirement of consultation does not apply in cases concerning exhumation or the reservation of a grave space, nor where the chancellor is satisfied that the matter is sufficiently urgent to justify the grant of a faculty or issue of an injunction without obtaining the DAC's advice.

Access to DAC meetings

5. The Local Government Act 1972 (as amended by the Local Government (Access to Information Act) 1985) deals with public access to meetings and documents of certain authorities, committees, and sub-committees. Meetings of a principal council and of committees and sub-committees must be open to the public and, in consequence, agenda and connected reports must be open to public inspection. Minutes must also be open for inspection for a period of six years. See sections 100A to 100E. These provisions of the Local Government Act 1972 relate to meetings of elected members exercising a function which is either original or delegated. Such members are answerable to their electorate. Theirs is a public function in the true sense of the word.

6. The foregoing provisions have no application to the DAC whose members are appointed for their knowledge, experience and expertise.[4] They are not elected by popular mandate or otherwise, nor are they delegates or representatives. Any analogy should properly be between the DAC and the officers of the council, be they dedicated conservation officers or members of the planning department. It is they who bring to bear their professional experience in forming advice for the council or committee. The public does not attend upon the discussions and deliberations of such officers. The summary and recommendations of the officers are available for scrutiny in advance of the relevant meeting of the council or committee. Likewise the DAC certificate is disseminated prior to any determination by the chancellor and a fuller statement of reasons may be sought and obtained from the DAC in the event that proceedings prove contentious, at which stage petitioners, objectors, amenity societies, the CCC and others are invited to make comments and representations.

7. Put shortly, a local authority council or committee is predominantly a decision making body. A DAC is not. It is a widely held misconception that the DAC is the primary decision maker with the consistory court acting as a rubber stamp or appellate body as appropriate.

Human Rights Act 1998

8. On balance, it is not considered that a DAC is a 'public authority' for the purposes of the Human Rights Act 1998. It is not a court or tribunal.

---

[4] Notwithstanding the *obiter dicta* in *Re Holy Cross, Pershore* [2002] Fam 1 at paragraphs 60–62 suggesting that the principle embodied by these provisions ought to apply to the DAC.

The mere fact that it is a creature of statute, and exercises statutory duties is not determinative; nor is it a natural consequence of the established status of the Church of England. See *Parochial Church Council of Aston Cantlow v Wallbank* [2004] 1 AC 546 HL. In issuing certificates and in offering advice to the limited category of persons to whom it is obliged so to do, it is considered that for the purposes of section 6 of the Act, the nature of the DAC's acts is private rather than public, albeit that its certificate and advice will be taken into account in the consistory court, which, by virtue of its status as a court, is a public authority. The actions of a PCC in maintaining the fabric of the parish church are not actions of a public nature. See *Aston Cantlow*.

9. Adopting the contrary opinion, however, and regarding the DAC as a public authority in the 'hybrid' category, some of whose functions are of a public nature, one must consider which, if any, Convention rights are engaged. The only conceivable right is Article 6, being the right to a fair trial. To the extent that it is material, the article reads:

'In the determination of his civil rights and obligations . . . everyone is entitled to a fair and public hearing within a reasonable time by an independent and impartial tribunal established by law.'

10. The procuring of advice from the DAC and the receipt of a certificate does not amount to the determination of civil rights and obligations. Such determination does not occur until resolution by the consistory court, which is a fully compliant independent, and impartial tribunal which sits in public unless the parties agree to a determination on written representations. Further there is no discrimination in the enjoyment of Convention rights and accordingly Article 14 is not engaged. Therefore the exclusion of the public from DAC meetings is not in breach of the Human Rights Act 1998.

Freedom of Information Act 2000

11. The Freedom of Information Act 2000 provides a general right of access to information held by public authorities. The relevant provisions of the Act came into force on 30 November 2005. In direct contrast to the Human Rights Act 1998 which contains only a conceptually circular definition of 'public authority',[5] leaving the matter for interpretation by

---

[5] 'In this section "public authority" includes (a) a court or tribunal, and (b) any person certain of whose functions are functions of a public nature . . .': see section 6(3).

the courts,[6] the Freedom of Information Act 2000 provides a statutory definition at section 3, describing public authority as any office holder or body listed in Schedule 1 to the Act or designated by order under section 5. The list is compendious but there is no mention of the DAC. To date neither DACs nor any other boards or committees of the Church of England have been designated under section 5, nor has there been any intimation that a consultation exercise may be embarked upon to consider so doing. Even if a DAC is considered to be a hybrid 'public authority' for the purposes of the Human Rights Act 1998, this will have no effect on its designation under the Freedom of Information Act 2000, because of its separate self-contained regime.

12. Further, even if the Act were to have application, it is concerned solely with giving individuals access to information held about them. It does not require prior notification of discussions, nor does it give an individual any right to attend meetings. At best it would entitle them to copies of the relevant part of any minutes.

Pragmatic considerations

13. There are a number of practical and pragmatic reasons why meetings of the DAC should not be open to the public:

(i) Dioceses lack the staff and financial resources to police public access and maintain order. It would be disproportionate to compel them to make such provision.

(ii) DACs do not need to hear from individuals nor balance competing views. Their role is solely to advise upon an application put forward by an intending petitioner. If they consider there is an insufficiency of information, they may (and frequently do) request more or, in some DACs, may invite an intending petitioner to attend that part of the meeting where the proposal is considered and speak to the proposal.[7]

(iii) People of distinction with particular knowledge and expertise will be discouraged from serving on DACs were they to be subjected to the presence of the public in a lobbying capacity.

---

[6] See the Seventh Report of Session 2003–04 of the Parliamentary Committee of Human Rights, *The Meaning of Public Authority under the Human Rights Act*, HL paper 39, HC 382, particularly the memorandum of N Doe, M Hill, F Cranmer, J Oliva, and C Cianitto of the Centre for Law and Religion at Cardiff Law School at pp. Ev 57–70.

[7] Other DACs adopt the practice of site visits and informal meetings with intending petitioners separate from the formal DAC meeting itself.

This would compromise the effectiveness of the working of the DAC, adversely affect the quality and independence of the advice given, and impede the mission of the Church in the functioning of the faculty jurisdiction.

(iv) The advisory role of the DAC would be further confused with the adjudicatory role of the consistory court.

Nonetheless, the Church of England must be astute to avoid the perception of a climate of secrecy permeating its activities. Fostering a fuller and wider understanding of the role and function of the DAC would achieve this objective, without compromising the effectiveness and value of its work.

Conclusions

14. The following conclusions may be drawn:

(1) The public do not have a right of access to meetings of the DAC.

(2) Intending petitioners do not have a right of access to meetings of a DAC, although there might be particular circumstances when a DAC would wish them to attend that part of a meeting where their proposal is to be considered.

(3) Would-be objectors do not have a right of access to meetings of a DAC.

(4) The advice which the DAC gives to any specified persons is personal to them and its wider dissemination is a matter between the DAC and the individual recipient.

(5) In most cases it would be beneficial for those who have sought the advice of the DAC to be informed of the substance of such part of the relevant minutes as relate to their application, or to receive a copy of the relevant extract, as soon after the meeting as is practicable. It is also good practice for the diocesan chancellor to be sent a copy of the minutes in their entirety.

(6) A DAC certificate is a matter of legal record which any person with a legitimate interest is entitled to inspect at the diocesan office or wherever else they may be kept.

(7)   There is no legal requirement for the agenda and minutes concerning DAC meetings to be disseminated beyond the membership of the committee.

(8)   It is however good practice for agenda and minutes to be disseminated on a voluntary basis to the Council for the Care of Churches, amenity societies and local planning authorities.

(2004)

Diocese: diocesan synod

Statement of doctrine

1. In accordance with the proviso to section 4(2) of the Synodical Government Measure 1969, it is out of order for a diocesan synod to consider a motion which would involve issuing a statement purporting to declare the doctrine of the Church of England, whether or not the motion involves only the reaffirmation of the statement of doctrine. However, a diocesan synod's functions include considering and expressing its Opinion on matters referred to it by the General Synod, and in particular approving or disapproving matters referred to it under Article 8 of the Constitution of the General Synod (Sch 2 to the 1969 Measure), even though these have doctrinal implications.

Casual vacancies

2. Rule 48(3) of the CRR provides that casual vacancies among persons elected under the Rules 'shall be filled and elections to fill such vacancies shall be conducted in the same manner as ordinary elections'; but in the case of a diocesan synod this is subject to rule 48(2), which provides that a casual vacancy may be filled by election by the appropriate House of the deanery synod concerned 'and a meeting of the members of that house who are electors may be held for that purpose'. In the opinion of the Legal Advisory Commission, the effect of these provisions is to authorize an optional alternative to the full procedure under rule 32. The provisions as to the holding of a meeting should thus be regarded as permissive, the word 'may' in the extract quoted from rule 48(2) being construed in its normal sense. While the full procedure under rule 32 is still available, there are obvious practical advantages in the use, for purposes of filling casual vacancies, of a simpler procedure and which allows the election to be conducted on the analogy of the procedure prescribed by rule 11 for elections at an APCM. It is evidently contemplated that the meeting of the House would be held on an occasion when the members would in any case be present for the deanery synod.

(Revised 2003)

Diocese: liability of members of diocesan advisory committee

1. In considering whether members of a Diocesan Advisory Committee ('DAC') may be held liable in damages to a person who suffers loss through negligent advice given by the Committee, it is necessary to begin by examining the DAC's constitution and functions.

2. The DAC of each diocese is required to have a written constitution drawn in accordance with Schedule 1 to the Care of Churches and Ecclesiastical Jurisdiction Measure 1991 (s2(2)). Every DAC has as its members a chairman appointed by the bishop, the archdeacons of the diocese, at least twelve other members appointed in accordance with the provisions of Schedule 1 and any members co-opted in accordance with those provisions.

3. The duties and functions of DACs have been enlarged and increased by the 1991 Measure and are set out in Schedule 2 to that Measure. A DAC is, under the Measure, required to act as an advisory body on matters affecting places of worship in the diocese (s2(5), Sch 2, para 1(a)). It is expressly required to give advice to four broad categories of persons or bodies:

(a)   office holders, individual and corporate, viz. the bishop, chancellor, archdeacons and pastoral committee of, and PCCs in, the diocese;

(b)   intending applicants for faculties in the diocese;

(c)   persons engaged in the planning, design or building of new places of worship in the diocese, *not* being places within the jurisdiction of the consistory court; and

(d)   such other persons as the DAC may consider appropriate (Sch 2, para 2).

4. The topics on which the DAC is required to give advice, when requested to do so, to the above persons or bodies, are expressed in the 1991 Measure to be:

(a)   the grant of faculties;

(b)   the architecture, archaeology, art and history of places of worship;

(c)   the use, care, planning, design and redundancy of places of worship;

(d)   the use and care of the contents of such places; and

(e)   the use and care of churchyards and burial grounds (Sch 2, para 1(a)).

5. The following duties placed on a DAC may involve the giving of advice on matters other than those mentioned:

(f)   to review and assess the risks to materials or of loss to archaeological or historic remains or records arising from petitions for faculties;

(g)   to issue guidance for the storage of records relating to works to places of worship;

(h)   to publicise [*sic*] methods of repair, construction, adaptation and redevelopment of places of worship and their contents; and

(i)   to perform such functions as may be requested by the bishop, chancellor or diocesan synod of the diocese (Sch 1, para 1(b), (d) (f) and (g)).

6. The advisory duties of a DAC under the 1991 Measure fall into three categories:

(a)   Those directly connected with the judicial functions of the chancellor and the archdeacons of the diocese when exercising the jurisdiction of the consistory court, i.e. those within a 'judicial process'. In this category the duties are to advise the chancellor and the archdeacons when any of them is considering a petition for a faculty. The only exceptions to this duty are cases before the chancellor of extreme urgency or cases involving exhumation or the reservation of grave spaces. The category also extends to advising application for faculties who, having filed their petitions and so becoming parties to proceedings, are within the 'judicial process'.

(b)   Those connected with the special jurisdiction given to archdeacons by section 21 of the 1991 Measure, to order that articles, appertaining to a church, of artistic and other value should be removed to a place of safety. In this category a DAC has the power to make representations, no doubt couched in the form of advice, to the archdeacon who, in exercising this jurisdiction, may be said to be exercising it as an officer of the court and quasi-judicially.

(c)   All other occasions on which advise is tendered pursuant to the duties mentioned in paragraphs 3 to 5.

7. The provisions relating to the functions and duties of DACs are drawn so widely in Schedule 2 to the 1991 Measure that it is difficult to envisage any advice which a DAC might give as a body which could not fairly be described as being given in pursuance of its statutory obligations under the Measure.

8. The general rule applied by law is that anyone holding himself or herself out as possessing reasonable competence in his or her avocation and undertaking to give advice owes a duty to advise with reasonable competence and care. The duty is owned to anyone the adviser should foresee may suffer loss if the duty is breached. If, in breach of that duty, the adviser fails to exercise reasonable competence or care and as a result the person to whom the duty is owed suffers damage, the adviser is liable to compensate that person for the damage suffered: per Lord Salmon, *Saif Ali v Sydney Mitchell & Co* [1980] AC 198 at 230, HL. The person advised will be able to recover damages only where the claimant relied upon the advice and took some action, or refrained from taking action, in consequence of the advice. There must also be a relationship between the claimant and the DAC of sufficient 'proximity' that it imposes upon the DAC a duty to take care to avoid or prevent that loss which has in fact been sustained. The question briefly stated, in each case, will be – was the claimant entitled to rely on the impugned advice and was it within the reasonable contemplation of the DAC that the claimant would rely upon it? See the speech of Lord Oliver in *Murphy v Brentwood District Council* [1991] 1 AC 398, HL.

9. So far as is known no DAC has as yet been sued for damages on the ground that a claimant suffered loss through negligent advice given by the Committee. Until such a case has been heard and decided it is impossible to give confident advice on the question whether a DAC would be held to be liable in law. It is important to remember that if the advice turns out to be wrong it does not necessarily follow that the Committee which gave it is liable for the loss caused by its imperfection. A DAC is not under any absolute duty to be right though it *is* under a duty to exercise reasonable care and competence. Nevertheless there may be those who, applying the modern law of negligence to advice given to them by a DAC, will claim that they have suffered loss through that advice because the DAC was

neither competent nor careful in giving it. For example, a PCC may allege that a new heating system commended to it by the DAC is thoroughly unsuitable and that the DAC failed to make the reasonable enquiries which would have shown it to be so. Or petitioners for a faculty may contend that costs have been wasted because the DAC did not advise them at an early juncture that their proposal has no realistic chance of success.

10. A DAC cannot qualify its advice by stating that it is given without accepting liability. It is implicit in the statutory obligation that advice must be the best advice, that the members of the DAC, pooling their skill and knowledge, can give and that the members giving it accept responsibility for their advice. By the same token the responsibility cannot be avoided or reduced because the advice is given gratuitously and not for valuable consideration or in discharge of a contractual duty. The statutory obligation is to give gratuitous advice.

11. It follows that no DAC can be assured, as the law stands, that if it is sued for damages on the ground that the claimant has suffered loss through its advice, the claim will fail because it is not sustainable. It has to be accepted that a risk of a DAC being found liable does exist in law. The degree of risk will vary as between the categories of business referred to in paragraph 6.

12. As regards the duties under the first two categories in paragraph 6:

(a)   In discharging these duties DACs are exercising a function which is by statute an integral part of the judicial process of the consistory court and of the exercise of the new statutory jurisdiction of the archdeacon. In exercising the faculty jurisdiction of the consistory court the chancellor and the archdeacons are bound by section 15 of the Care of Churches and Ecclesiastical Jurisdiction Measure 1991 to seek the advice of the DAC upon every petition, except in the limited classes of cases mentioned, viz. those relating to exhumation and reservation of graves and, so far as the chancellor is concerned, cases of extreme urgency.

(b)   There is a general principle that immunity from civil liability attaches to many persons who take part in proceedings before a court of justice: judges, court officials and witnesses (but not now the parties' counsel and solicitors (*Arthur J S Hall & Co v Simons* [2002] AC 615). The immunity of witnesses exists for the benefit of the public since justice would be greatly impeded if witnesses were to be in fear of disgruntled persons against whom they had given evidence subsequently involving them in litigation (*Darker v Chief Constable of the West Midlands Police* [2001] 1 AC 435). An instance of its application occurred in a case in 1981 when Drake J struck out a claim for negligence against a pathologist who was alleged to have been careless in giving advice to the police in relation to a possible prosecution against the claimant (*Evans v London Hospital Medical College (University of London)* [1981] 1 WLR 184). Another example is *Stanton v Callaghan* [2000] 1 QB 75 where an expert witness was held to be immune from an action for negligence arising from the preparation of a joint report with the opposing expert. The joint report was prepared for the purposes of litigation.

(c)   The immunity of those involved in the administration of justice for actions and words done and said in the execution of judicial office is established. The underlying principles of public policy are:

(i)   that those concerned must be free from the anxiety of possible action in discharging their office; and

(ii) that another court with a co-ordinate level of jurisdiction should not be asked to review previous decisions by means of an allegation of negligence against the previous court.

(d)   In exercising its statutory duty to advise the chancellor or an archdeacon, a DAC is assisting in a judicial function even though the decision is that of the chancellor or archdeacon and not the DAC. In this field the DAC has an obligation to give advice, and there is here an analogy with compellability of witnesses, where on the authorities the obligation to give evidence is one of the factors in granting immunity to witnesses. Also the chancellor may require the DAC to nominate a member to give evidence in court in support of any advice tendered.

(e)   It is considered therefore that the principle of immunity from suit of those concerned with the administration of justice will in principle afford a defence to a DAC alleged to have given negligent advice in the discharge of duties in the first two categories mentioned in paragraph 6.

13. As regards duties under the third category in paragraph 6, the defence arising from participation in the judicial process will not be available if no proceedings in the consistory court have been commenced or are immediately contemplated. However, in cases where an intending

applicant for a faculty is required by rule or practice to seek and obtain the advice of the DAC before commencing proceedings the defence may be available. In any claim for a breach of duty under this category the other defences mentioned in paragraph 15 should be considered.

14. The limits of the defence of participation in the judicial process must be borne in mind. The defence will be available to a DAC or any member of it when advising or giving evidence with a judicial process as mentioned above. But advice given to a person, e.g. to a PCC, before proceedings are begun or actually proposed will not be given retrospective immunity simply because it is repeated to the chancellor, archdeacon or, by way of evidence, in court. Claims that such, earlier, advice has given rise to loss must be met in the light of the points mentioned in the following paragraph.

15. In order to succeed in recovering damages a claimant alleging loss through reliance upon the negligent advice of a DAC would have to prove not only that in the particular case a duty of care was owed but that the duty had been broken. The fact that the advice in question was given pursuant to a statutory duty would be material in deciding the scope of the duty, what, in the circumstances, is the reasonable care required and whether or not on the facts there had been a failure to discharge the duty. Until the facts proved in court in relation to any individual case are established it cannot be foreseen what weight any argument or factor would carry. It might be open to the DAC to argue that the loss occasioned to the claimant was due to 'inevitable accident' or to some cause other than the negligence of the DAC. Again, the DAC might be able to establish that the effective cause of the loss was some act or omission by the claimant or that the claimant materially contributed to the loss by an act or omission (partial defence of contributory negligence). In a small category of cases the defence of voluntarily accepting the risk (*volenti non fit injuria*) might be available.

16. For convenience the previous paragraphs have discussed the liability of DACs as though there might be liability in a DAC as such. It must be borne in mind, however, that DACs are not bodies corporate; their members are appointed for limited terms. Members of a DAC are not agents for one another, as are partners in a firm. The individual members of a DAC therefore cannot be liable for negligence arising from a decision of the DAC unless the decision was that of the Committee formally arrived at and expressed in its recommendation or report. Even so, members not present when the decision was taken, or members voting against the proposal, cannot be liable. It is therefore not strictly accurate to speak of the liability of a DAC in negligence, but individual members, shown to be responsible for a decision, would be jointly and severally

liable for it. Any action would have to be against the individual members and not the DAC as a body, and each member sued would only be liable if it were proved that that member failed to exercise the care which was to be expected, having regard to the member's own particular skill, knowledge and experience, or that the member formally adopted the negligence of another member of the DAC, e.g. by voting to support a negligent decision when a responsible member of a DAC of ordinary competence ought to have realized that it was unsafe to do so. This principle might protect non-specialist members of a DAC, if the negligent advice given was in a specialist field (such as organs or bells) and the advice given by the specialist was of such a nature that a non-specialist could not be expected to take part in giving it. However it is considered that this argument would not assist in the majority of cases where the advice given is in areas in which all members of the DAC have competence and all members present at a meeting of the DAC concur in the advice.

17. In summary, it must be repeated that the circumstances certainly exist in which it is possible for members of a DAC to be held liable for negligence, but that in individual cases particular members may well be able to show that no liability is established against them either because of the facts of the particular case or because of the legal principles.

(Revised 2003)

Diocese: vacancy in see committees

1. Rule 47 of the CRR, under which a person is not to be disqualified from being elected or chosen as a member of any body under those rules by the fact that he is also a member ex officio, does not apply to a vacancy in see committee constituted under the Vacancy in See Committees Regulation 1993 (as amended by the Vacancy in See Committees (Amendment) Regulations 2003). The committee is not a body to which the CRR apply; it is not listed in those rules, and regulation 3(a), in relation to casual vacancies, was made despite rule 48 of the CRR, which also covers casual vacancies, albeit in a different fashion.

2. However, an ex officio member of a vacancy in see committee is not disqualified from being a candidate for election under regulation 1(a)(vii) or (viii) of the 1993 Regulation. Regulation 1 is clear and unambiguous as to the candidates who may stand for election; under regulation 1(a)(vii) not fewer than two clerks in Holy Orders beneficed in the diocese or licensed under seal by the bishop of the diocese are to be elected by the House of Clergy of the diocesan synod, and under regulation 1(a)(viii) not fewer than two actual communicant lay persons whose names are on the electoral roll of a parish in the diocese are to be elected by the House of Laity of the diocesan synod. There is no provision in regulation 1 or elsewhere in the Regulation disqualifying ex officio members from standing for election, and there is therefore no reason why the Regulation should be construed so as to take away their rights. (See *Halsbury's Laws of England*, 4th edn, 1975, vol. 44, paras 857 and 905; *R v Wimbledon Local Board* (1882) 8 QBD 459 and *R v Bishop of Salisbury* [1901] 1 KB 573 at 579.)

3. Regulation 1(b) of the 1993 Regulation requires the number of clerical and lay members who are to be elected to the committee under regulation 1(a)(vii) and (viii) to be such as to ensure, inter alia, that every archdeaconry in the diocese will be adequately represented. The manner in which this is to be achieved is left to the discretion of the diocesan synod. The Regulation requires it to take account of the place of residence of the ex officio members of the committee, but apart from that and the other provisions of regulation 1(b), no test or procedure is laid down.

(Revised 2003)

Part 11
Faculties

Faculties

Generally

1. The procedure in faculty cases is by way of petition and public notice. The practice varies slightly in the different dioceses but is now governed by the Care of Churches and Ecclesiastical Jurisdiction Measure 1991, sections 11–19, and the Faculty Jurisdiction Rules 2000, SI 2000 SI 2000/ 2047. In the majority of cases the incumbent and churchwardens are not only eligible, but also the most suitable petitioners. The views of the PCC on any proposals submitted to the court are usually required. Reference should also be made to the Faculty Jurisdiction (Appeals) Rules 1998, SI 1998/1713, and the Faculty Jurisdiction (Injunctions and Restoration Orders) Rules 1992, SI 1992/2884 and the Faculty Jurisdiction (Care of Places of Worship) Rules 2000, SI 2000/2048.

Requirement of faculty for dealing with land under section 17 of the New Parishes Measure 1943

2. The present section 17 of the New Parishes Measure 1943 was substituted by the Church Property (Miscellaneous Provisions) Measure 1960, section 6(2), and replaced section 16 of the original Measure. Subsection (5) of the original section stated that:

> 'Nothing in this section shall authorise the sale or disposal by the Commissioners of any consecrated land'

whereas subsection (5) of the present section states that:

> 'Nothing in this section shall authorise the sale or disposal of any consecrated land or affect the jurisdiction of the Consistory Court'

3. It is undisputed that land to which section 17 (or its predecessor) applied, and which is consecrated, cannot be disposed of under that section without a faculty (see *Halsbury's Laws of England*, 3rd edn, vol. 13, para 875 and *Halsbury's Laws of England*, 4th edn, 1975, vol. 14, para 1110). Clearly the words 'or affect the jurisdiction of the Consistory Court' must have been added in 1960 in order to protect the faculty jurisdiction of the court in relation to the authorization of sale or disposal of land under the 1943 Measure, and the question arises in what way that jurisdiction could have been considered at risk without the words, bearing in mind that the position as to consecrated land was already protected.

4. It is permissible when construing ecclesiastical legislation to refer to its legislative history (see *Hebbert v Purchas* (1871) LR 3 PC 605; *Ridsdale v*

Clifton (1877) 2 PD 276, PC). In the original draft of the 1960 Measure clause 6 provided for the re-enactment of subsection (5) in its original form. However, another clause declared, for the avoidance of doubt, that the jurisdiction of the consistory court applied to consecrated land annexed or belonging to a church (other than a cathedral church) as it did to consecrated land. It was explained in the Church Assembly debates on the Measure that for a number of years it had been the practice of a number of chancellors to exercise this jurisdiction. The declaratory clause was removed during the passage of the Measure through the Church Assembly, but subsection (5) was amended to its present form, and the legislative history makes it plain that the words added to the subsection were intended to embrace the unconsecrated portion of the curtilage of a consecrated church. The infelicitous language by which this was expressed (see *Re St Mary Magdalene's, Paddington* [1980] Fam 99 at 101H) seems to be due to the problem over the proposed declaratory clause and the then uncertainty of the jurisdiction (which was finally confirmed by section 7(1) of the Faculty Jurisdiction Measure 1964).

5. In *Re St Mary Magdalene's, Paddington* [1980] Fam 99 Chancellor Newsom reviewed the authorities in relation to the conveyance of unconsecrated curtilage and concluded (at 103 F–H) that there are two alternative modes of sale of such lane, namely:

(a)   under the consistory court's powers at common law; and

(b)   under the provisions of the New Parishes Measure 1943.

The chancellor's comments as to the latter are strictly *obiter dicta*, but he made his view plain that in relation to (b) a faculty is still necessary; there is, however, no absolute authority on the point (see also *Re Christ Church, Chiselhurst* [1974] 1 All ER 146; but compare in *Re St George's, Oakdale* [1976] Fam 210). A similar view is expressed in *Encyclopaedia of Forms and Precedents*, 5th edn, vol. 13, at para 44, note 2, and especially at precedent 43, as well as in Rees, *Ecclesiastical Conveyancing* (1989) at p. 137.

6. In the Legal Advisory Commission's opinion, when section 17 of the New Parishes Measure 1943 (as substituted) applies, a faculty is necessary whenever the land to be sold or disposed of falls within the jurisdiction of the consistory court, including any unconsecrated land which forms part of the curtilage of a consecrated church within the faculty jurisdiction. (As regards 'curtilage' *see also* **Church building: ecclesiastical exemption**).

Fixture, disposal: Faculty Jurisdiction Rules 2000

7. In the Legal Advisory Commission's opinion the term 'disposal' in 'disposal of any fixture' in rule 9(1)(b) the Faculty Jurisdiction Rules 2000, SI 2000/2047, has its ordinary English meaning and means 'getting rid of'. It therefore involves some element of alienation, and would not cover a case where a fixture is removed from the fabric of the church but ownership of the attached object is retained and the object is kept in the church or elsewhere.

(Revised 2003)

Part 12
Cathedrals

Cathedrals: disturbances during services and admission to episcopal enthronements and other services

Ecclesiastical Courts Jurisdiction Act 1860

1. By section 2 of the Ecclesiastical Courts Jurisdiction Act 1860 it is an offence for any person to be 'guilty of riotous, violent or indecent behaviour . . . in any cathedral church, parish or district church or chapel of the Church of England'. It is also an offence to 'molest, let, disturb, vex, trouble or by any other unlawful means disquiet or misuse any preacher . . . or any clergyman in holy orders ministering or celebrating any sacrament, or any divine service, rite or office in any cathedral, church or chapel'. Thus there is no difficulty in establishing that a disturbance caused in a cathedral service would be unlawful. The difficulty arises over the practical steps which can lawfully be taken to prevent or put an end to the disturbance. Section 3 as originally enacted provided that any offender 'may be apprehended and taken by any constable or churchwarden of the parish or place where the . . . offence shall be committed and taken before a justice of the peace'. However, the words 'constable or' were repealed by section 199 of and Schedule 7 to the Police and Criminal Evidence Act 1984.

2. By Canon F 15 paragraph 2 it is the duty of churchwardens to maintain good order at divine service and they have power under paragraph 3 'to restrain the offender and if necessary proceed against him according to the law'. In most cases the right course would be to call a police officer to attend.

3. The Deans and Provosts Conference asked in 1996 whether the power to arrest under the Act or the power to restrain under the Canon is available to an officer appointed by a dean and Chapter such as a cathedral verger. In an Opinion of the Legal Advisory Commission given in that year it was stated that 'No difficulty arises in the case of parish church cathedrals since these are parish churches as well as cathedrals and the Act and Canon both apply to such cathedrals, provided the removal is carried out by the properly appointed churchwarden.'

Cathedrals Measure 1999

4. However since that date the Cathedrals Measure 1999 may have altered the position. For most purposes the distinctions between a parish church cathedral and an ordinary (or ancient) cathedral have gone. All cathedrals except Christ Church Oxford now have constitutions, Councils and Chapters. The Chapter is responsible for directing and overseeing the

administration of the affairs of the cathedral and is accountable to the Council; no cathedral now has a PCC. The Chapter takes the place of the PCC. However, the former parish church cathedrals have parishes and the cathedral doubles as the parish church as well as the cathedral church of the diocese. Where there is a parish there must be churchwardens. But they are officers of the parish and not of the cathedral. In some former parish church cathedrals the churchwardens of the parish may serve as members of the Chapter but it is submitted that that does not alter their status and that they can still only act as churchwardens of the parish. See the 1999 Measure sections 9(3), 11(c) and 12 and Mark Hill, *Ecclesiastical Law*, 2nd edn, p. 224.

5. It is probable that if a disturbance were to occur in a cathedral which is also the parish church and the service taking place were an ordinary service for the normal cathedral congregation (i.e. the parishioners) the churchwardens would have the special powers given by section 3 of the 1860 Act. On the other hand, if a disturbance were to take place in a non-parish service, i.e. any service for the diocese or Province (such as an induction, enthronement, consecration or special diocesan service) the churchwardens may not have 1860 Act powers.

6. It is clear that a person appointed by a cathedral Council or by the Chapter of a cathedral would not come within the required category of 'churchwarden of the parish or place (of offence)' for the purposes of the Act and such a person would not be a churchwarden for the purpose of Canon F 15. It would not be lawful for a cathedral Council or Chapter to appoint a churchwarden. A purported appointment would be ineffective. Historically the office of churchwarden has always been associated with a parish whereas the ancient cathedrals did not have a parish. Formerly the functions of the churchwarden extended into the sphere of civil administration (see *Halsbury's Laws of England*, 4th edn, 1975, vol. 14, para 542). Some vestige of the churchwarden's role as a representative of the general body of parishioners is to be found in the provision that persons resident in the parish who are local government electors are entitled to take part in the choosing of a churchwarden (Churchwardens Measure 2001 ss4(2) and 5(6)). In short if there is no parish there can be no churchwarden.

7. The wording of section 3 of the 1860 Act – 'churchwarden of the parish or place where the offence shall be committed' – may at first sight seem to support a case that a churchwarden may belong to some place other than the parish and therefore may belong to a cathedral. But this is considered to be too wide a construction of the wording. The whole of the wording as originally enacted was 'any constable or churchwarden of the parish or place where the offence shall be committed'. The footnote

to *Halsbury's Laws of England*, 4th edn, 1975, vol. 14 at page 274 says that 'constable' here meant any person holding the office of constable and not just a member of the police force holding the rank of constable. The reference was to the ancient office of constable which would give jurisdiction to its holder within a certain area or 'place' not necessarily contiguous with a parish. It is therefore considered that the use of the word 'place' in this context does not imply that there can be a category of churchwarden who is not a parish churchwarden.

Other powers of arrest

8. The next question which arises for consideration is whether there are any other powers which might authorize the arrest of a trouble-maker by an appropriate person (e.g. a cathedral steward). Under section 24A of the Police and Criminal Evidence Act 1984 as substituted by the Serious Organised Crime and Police Act 2005, a person other than a constable may arrest without a warrant anyone who is in the act of committing an indictable offence, anyone whom the arresting person has reasonable grounds for suspecting to be committing an indictable offence and anyone whom the arresting person has reasonable grounds for suspecting to be guilty of an indictable offence. However these powers are exercisable only if the person making the arrest has reasonable grounds for believing that it is necessary to arrest the person in question to prevent that person causing physical injury to himself or any other person; suffering physical injury; causing loss of or damage to property; or making off before a constable can assume responsibility for him; and it appears to the person making the arrest that it is not reasonably practicable for a constable to make it instead.

9. In addition there may be a citizen's arrest if a breach of the peace has occurred or is threatened. An ordinary citizen (as well as a constable) may at common law arrest without warrant:

(a) a person committing a breach of the peace in the citizen's presence;

(b) a person whom the citizen reasonably believes will commit such a breach of the peace in the immediate future;

(c) a person who has committed a breach of the peace where it is reasonably believed that a renewal of the breach is threatened; and

(d) a person conducting himself or herself in such a fashion, by words or actions, that the natural consequence of his conduct, if persisted in, would be to provoke others to commit a breach of the peace.

10. A breach of the peace is committed where an act is done or threatened to be done which:

(a)   actually harms a person or, in that person's presence, his or her property;

(b)   is likely to cause such harm; or

(c)   puts someone in fear of such harm.

11. The propositions of law in paragraphs 8 and 9 above are to be deduced from *Halsbury's Laws of England*, 4th edn, 1989 re-issue, vol. 11(1), para 709 and *Percy v DPP* [1995] 1 WLR 1382 and from the authorities cited in both. A trouble-maker threatening violence, inside or outside a cathedral, to a minister or member of the laity or using language which may cause a violent reaction from members of the congregation, may therefore be arrested by a cathedral steward. Similarly if someone were to harm some ornament in the cathedral that person could, it is submitted, be properly arrested by a cathedral steward. Again if a protester carried a banner into a cathedral of a nature likely to cause a member of the congregation to pull it down and damage it the protester could be arrested. It should not be forgotten that no arrest is lawful unless the person arrested is informed of the ground for the arrest at the time of, or as soon as is practicable after, the arrest (Police and Criminal Evidence Act 1984, s28(3)) and is handed into the custody of a police constable or taken to a police station as soon as practicable (ibid., s30(1)).

12. A cathedral steward or other person authorized by the Chapter to deal with an anticipated disturbance would need to be carefully instructed. If a demonstrator or other trouble-maker were to be manhandled in circumstances which fell on the wrong side of citizen's arrest powers the person carrying out the manhandling (and that person's employers) could be sued for assault and false imprisonment in respect of the period of the detention. The most likely circumstances for an arrest to arise would be a demonstration, e.g. a person entering the cathedral and processing with a banner (or perhaps a loud-hailer). Such conduct is not itself a breach of the peace because it does not harm either person or property. The only legal basis for arrest would therefore be ground (d) in paragraph 9 above, viz. that the conduct might provoke someone else to breach the peace (e.g. to attack the banner-carrier). It would have to be shown that a breach of the peace would be the natural consequence of the conduct of the demonstrator. It would be a matter of evidence in each

case whether this was so. In practice a person authorized to make an arrest would have to act rapidly to prevent a demonstration turning into a breach of the peace, but in law also refrain from action until it became clear that there was a risk of a violent reaction from those in the cathedral against a demonstrator. If proceedings were brought for assault or false imprisonment the arresting person might be in difficulty without independent evidence to support his or her own assessment that a breach of the peace was likely to occur. It follows that the person concerned should have an excellent knowledge of the legal requirements and should also have considered the various practical situations which might arise. A Chapter faced with the possibility of a demonstration inside a cathedral which might require forcible removal of demonstrators should consider the need for a senior person to supervise the steward (or authorized person) and to give final advice to the steward whether he or she should arrest or not. It is suggested that the sort of senior person who would be suitable would be an experienced police officer or retired police officer. Thus in practice a cathedral body might have to use such a police officer, at least for supervisory purposes, and not rely only upon a steward.

13. The consequence of the foregoing paragraphs is that if the authorities of a cathedral should fear trouble at a particular service they would be well-advised to ask for a police officer to be present to exercise if necessary his powers of arrest without warrant. Under section 25 of the 1984 Act a police officer may arrest a person causing a disturbance if an offence is being committed or attempted (or if he suspects that there has been an offence or that an offence is being attempted) and if it is not practicable for a summons to be served. That would apply in the case of a breach of the peace being committed or attempted in a cathedral service. The offence does not have to be an arrestable offence. A police officer does not have to look for further evidence or probe every possible explanation before exercising his power of arrest (see *Ward v Chief Constable of Avon etc, The Times*, 26 June 1986 (CA) and *Archbold on Criminal Pleading*, (2006) paras 19–343). But there must be a reasonable apprehension (objectively judged) that violence might take place (see *Redmond-Bate v DPP* [1999] Crim L. R. 998).

Application for injunction

14. It may also be appropriate to consider whether an injunction could be obtained to prevent a person from causing a disturbance. An application could only be made if the intended perpetrator had already been identified and if there were enough evidence of what was intended to be able to justify an application. Up to the present time there has been only one known case where an application has been successfully made. This was

in the diocese of Liverpool and related to proposed disturbances by members of the Orange Order during a visit by the Pope.

Admission to episcopal enthronements and other services

15. The Deans and Provosts Conference also asked in 1996 whether there were any services in cathedrals from which the public at large might be excluded. It suggested that this might be so in the case of an episcopal enthronement service. Where there is no public right to attend services Chapters would like to be able to issue tickets for services and admit only persons having tickets. It was stated in previous editions of the *Opinions of the Legal Advisory Commission* that an enthronement is not a service at which members of the public have an 'absolute right' to attend and that the proper authority may issue tickets and decide who shall be present. But it was not clear from the Opinion whether the position as set out there was thought to arise from the nature of the service (i.e. that it was not a public service) or from the fact that the cathedral was not a parish church. Members of the public have a right of access to parish churches during divine service. In *Cole v Police Constable 443A* [1937] 1 KB 316 it was held that a parishioner had a right to attend his parish church during any divine service, provided that he did not cause a disorder and that this was a common law right as well as a right which is complementary to the duty of parishioners to attend church on Sundays and holy days imposed by the Act of Uniformity 1551 and the Act of Uniformity 1559. Today there is no statutory duty to attend church, but see Canon B 15 para 1 concerning the duty of those who are confirmed to attend Holy Communion.

16. It is submitted that the same rule applies to the right of a member of the public to attend a service in a cathedral as to that right to attend a parish church, if the service is a public one. It is considered that an enthronement is not a private service. This is partly for a general reason and partly for specific reasons. The general reason is that this service is to signify the admission of a new diocesan bishop into his episcopal authority within the area of the diocese. The process is of concern to people residing throughout that area. It is of concern not only to churchgoing people but also to the public at large because of the relationship which the bishop has with secular authorities and organizations in the diocese. He may also have (or later come to have) a seat in the House of Lords. He is a person with secular as well as ecclesiastical status. This conjuncture of roles is derived from the position of the Church of England as 'by law established'. The specific reasons are that there are certain public aspects of the service. For example if during the service the bishop makes the declaration of assent this by its nature should be done publicly and if the enthronement is followed by a Eucharist this is a public service.

17. It might be argued that, since the right to attend a service in a parish church is limited to parishioners, so the right to attend a service in a cathedral should be limited to residents of the diocese. But cathedrals have a national as well as diocesan role, so this argument may be too limited. Thus the statement in the earlier editions of the *Opinions* referred to above seems too wide.

18. In looking for a justification for having all-ticket services on special occasions in cathedrals the nature of the service should not be regarded as a useful factor. In the *Cole* case (see above) which related to Westminster Abbey (a royal peculiar but not a cathedral) du Parcq J said that there was no authority for the proposition that there is a right in any member of the public to enter the Abbey for divine service and that he considered that it would be most difficult to maintain such a proposition. Lord Goddard (then Goddard J) agreed and said that there is no authority to support the view that any member of the public (other than a parishioner) may enter any church where divine service is in progress. However he reserved the position where the service was one which had a more public aspect. He referred to marriages and ordinations where the celebrant may call on 'the people' to state whether there is any impediment, and he left open the question whether a member of the public (being a non-parishioner) could be excluded. All three members of the court in the *Cole* case were satisfied that the Dean of Westminster had the right to exclude the plaintiff who was not a parishioner (the Abbey has a small parish consisting of its precinct).

19. But with regard to ancient cathedrals Lord Goddard said (*obiter*) (at 334–5) that if the Abbey had been a cathedral then 'according to the opinion of many learned civilians and also according to a case in Ireland directly on the point (*in Re St Columb, Londonderry* (1863) 8 LT 861) it would be the parish church of the diocese and (that) possibly any inhabitant of the diocese would have a right to enter it'. This is an interesting statement. If an ancient cathedral is the 'parish church' of a diocese it would not be proper to exclude a resident of the 'parish'. Thus the answer to the question asked by the Conference may be that because an ancient cathedral is not a parish church there is no obligation to admit the public at large and services by ticket only may be arranged but that this is subject to an important exception that a resident of the diocese cannot be excluded. To put the proposition in more homely terms a potential trouble-maker could be refused admission but not one who resided in the diocese. A resident would have to be admitted and could not thereafter be removed unless he could be arrested. A service could be an all-ticket service but a person attending and producing reasonable evidence of residence in the diocese would have to be admitted. Such a person would not be entitled to insist on a seat because the right to be

present does not include the right to sit on a seat, but could not be excluded. In practice it would be difficult to tell non-residents of the diocese from residents, so the right to refuse admission to non-residents might be of little value.

20. In *Re St Columb* Dr Todd, the Vicar-General of the diocese of Londonderry, said (at 864) 'The cathedral is the parish church of the whole diocese, because it is the church of the bishop, who has the cure of souls of the whole diocese; and, though all of the diocese may receive the sacrament there, or be married there, yet they are not bound to do so.' Dr Todd also said: 'It would appear to be the case . . . that the nave of a cathedral should be free for all persons of the diocese'.

21. In support of the view expressed in *Re St Columb* there is the following statement in *Cripps on Church and Clergy*, 8th edn, at p. 121: 'An ancient cathedral church is the parish church of the whole diocese; which diocese was, in fact, anciently called *parochia*, until the application of this name to the lesser branches, into which it was divided, made it, for distinction's sake, to be called only by the name of the diocese; and it has been affirmed, therefore, that if one resort to the cathedral church for the purpose of hearing divine service, it is a resorting to the parish church within the sense of the meaning of the statutes.' The authority quoted is '*Gibs Cod* 171'. On this basis it seems right to accept that every person resident in a diocese has the right to resort to the cathedral of that diocese for the purpose of hearing divine service as though the cathedral were his parish church.

22. As a modification of that principle the general powers of the Chapter to manage the affairs of the cathedral must entitle them to put in place arrangements to refuse admission once the cathedral is genuinely full (i.e. when no further standing room is available) or if to admit any further people would create risk due to overcrowding or if there were security or health and safety grounds. Where members of the Royal Family are to attend, special security arrangements may have to include the restriction of access to those with tickets.

23. The right of residents of the diocese to enter cathedrals (of their own diocese) are relevant only when a service is due to take place. There is no general common law or other right to enter at any time. This is the situation which makes it lawful for cathedrals to charge an admission fee to visitors (other than those attending services).

24. With regard to the scope of the phrase 'divine service' and the question whether an enthronement is such a service it is relevant to quote the definition of divine service in section 5(2) of the Church of England

(Worship and Doctrine) Measure 1974: 'any act, service, prayer, rite or ceremony whatsoever, including the services for the ordination of priests and deacons and the consecration of bishops and the catechism or form of instruction before confirmation'.

25. Under Canon B 4 paras 2 and 3 an Archbishop may approve a form of service for use in any cathedral in his Province and a diocesan bishop may approve forms of service for use in any cathedral in his diocese for occasions for which no provision is made in the BCP or by General Synod under Canon B 2. Canon B 1 describes such a form of service as an authorized form of service for use in the Church of England. Therefore there can be no doubt that services such as Enthronements and Consecrations are authorized 'divine services' of the Church of England, so that questions of admissions of persons are the same for these large and special services in cathedrals as for ordinary services in parish churches. It is submitted that the major cathedral services should be regarded as public services to which the public at large have a right of admission. If so, the conclusion arrived at by the Legal Advisory Commission in 1984 that a non-diocesan member of the public does not have a right to attend an enthronement and that admission may lawfully be controlled by issuing tickets might not now be accepted as correct if the question of admission had to be tested in court. The dictum of Lord Goddard referred to in paragraph 17 above might not now be followed.

26. It is known that there have been certain occasions when all-ticket services have been held in cathedrals. An example is the first service of ordination of women clergy in Bristol cathedral on 12 March 1994. One person who could not gain admission was the Reverend P. Williamson. He sought to bring proceedings for judicial review of the decision to ordain. His application was refused by Macpherson J who did not rule on the issue whether an all-ticket service was lawful. *R v Bishop of Bristol ex parte Williamson* 1994 CO/764/94.

27. With regard specifically to an episcopal enthronement it is significant that *Halsbury's Laws of England*, 4th edn, 1975, vol. 14, para 468 describes a new bishop's installation as follows:

'Pursuant to the archbishop's mandate the bishop is introduced into the cathedral church in the presence of a public notary, and is placed in the episcopal seat with the customary formula. After the divine service proper to the occasion the bishop is conducted into the chapter house . . .'

A footnote states: 'Special forms of service are now drawn up for an installation or enthronement.'

28. There are two further arguments pointing in the direction of an absence of a right to exclude:

(a) A cathedral may have a legal status and role which are national as well as local (diocesan). If that is the case it would be wrong to refuse entry to any person resident in England unless it could be shown that he had some unlawful purpose for being present. Possibly even overseas visitors could assert an interest in being admitted on the basis that cathedrals (e.g. Canterbury and St Paul's cathedrals) have a place in international Christendom.

(b) The Human Rights Act 1998. A person wishing to express religious faith (being lawfully in the United Kingdom but not being resident in the diocese) by attending an ecclesiastical service might be able to rely on the right to freedom to manifest his religion and belief as granted in Article 9 of the European Convention of Human Rights. Such a person might assert a personal experience that religious faith could best be expressed in large cathedral services where the music is excellent, the ceremonial is at its most colourful and the most senior dignitaries of the church are present. It would not necessarily be a good reason for exclusion to say that such a person did not come within the *Cole* and *Re St Columb* categories of a resident of the diocese. An individual might be a person who regularly attended consecrations and enthronements in any diocese in the Church of England as often as possible. It is suggested that there is a real possibility that excluding such a person would be a breach of human rights. If so it would not be lawful to have an 'all-ticket' service until a satisfactory procedure were in place to make tickets available to all. On this understanding of the position of a cathedral it is not only a diocesan mother-church but also has national status and should be open to all.

(October 1996, revised 2006)

Cathedrals: the role of churchwardens in parish church cathedrals

1. The Commission has been asked to advise on the role, powers and duties of churchwardens where the parish church is, or forms part of, a cathedral. It is convenient to refer in this Opinion to 'parish church cathedrals' despite the abandonment of that term in recent legislation.

2. The functions of churchwardens are to be found in the Canons, statute law (including Measures) and the ecclesiastical common law. In a few cases there are express provisions as to the position in parish church cathedrals.

3. Canon E 1 ('Of Churchwardens'), especially paragraphs 4 and 5, is of especial importance. As amended by Amending Canon No. 20, those paragraphs read as follows:

> '4. The churchwardens when admitted are officers of the bishop. They shall discharge such duties as are by law and custom assigned to them; they shall be foremost in representing the laity and in co-operating with the incumbent; they shall use their best endeavours by example and precept to encourage the parishioners in the practice of true religion and to promote unity and peace among them. They shall also maintain order and decency in the church and churchyard, especially during the time of divine service.
>
> 5. In the churchwardens is vested the property in the plate, ornaments, and other movable goods of the church, and they shall keep an inventory thereof which they shall revise from time to time as occasion may require. On going out of office they shall duly deliver to their successors any goods of the church remaining in their hands together with the said inventory, which shall be checked by their successors.'

4. Churchwardens are given specific statutory functions in relation to the consecration of churchyards (Consecration of Churchyards Act 1867, s1 as amended by the Church of England (Miscellaneous Provisions) Measure 2000, s13), the recover of compensation after damage to a church by riotous behaviour (Riot (Damages) Act 1886, s7), and the institution of disciplinary proceedings (Clergy Discipline Measure 2003, s10). The powers and duties of churchwardens under the Inspection of Churches Measure 1955, the Incumbents and Churchwardens (Trusts) Measure 1964, and the Care of Churches and Ecclesiastical Jurisdiction

Measure 1991 (as to terriers and inventories) are excluded in the case of parish church cathedrals, as the relevant provisions of those Measures do not apply to such cathedrals. The duties of churchwardens under section 11 of the Parochial Registers and Records Measure 1978 are limited to material 'in parochial custody' and for that reason would seem inapplicable in parish church cathedrals.

5. The common law functions of churchwardens derive largely from the law as to visitations, but the archdeacon's jurisdiction over cathedrals was abolished by the Cathedrals Measure 1963 (repealed, but not so as to revive the jurisdiction) and the churchwardens have no specific responsibilities in the case of the visitation of a cathedral by the bishop under section 6 of the Cathedrals Measure 1999.

6. The constitutions and statutes of cathedrals made under the 1999 Measure may give additional functions to the churchwardens of a cathedral parish (for example in relation to a Cathedral Community Committee under s10 or a similar body) but may not remove powers or duties given to the churchwardens by canon or statute law.

7. Apart from the statutory functions mentioned in paragraph 4 of this Opinion, the principal functions of churchwardens in parish church cathedrals are derived primarily from Canon E 1. The question on which the Commission has to advise is whether these functions are affected by any other relevant legal provisions.

(a) to act as an officer of the bishop

8. Canon E 1 formerly described the churchwardens as officers 'of the Ordinary' and it was possible to argue that the Ordinary in a cathedral was someone, or some body, other than the bishop. The idea that churchwardens of parish church cathedrals were in a special category was reinforced by the practice of admitting churchwardens to office during the archdeacon's visitation, given the exclusion of cathedrals from the archdeacon's jurisdiction (though churchwardens may also be admitted during a special visitation of the cathedral). The current text of Canon E 1 describes the churchwardens as officers 'of the bishop' and paragraph 2 of that Canon and section 6(1) of the Churchwardens Measure 2001 require the admission of churchwardens to be at their appearance before 'the bishop or his substitute duly appointed'. This may well be the archdeacon, but he or she will be acting under Canon E 1 and the 2001 Measure, and not Canon C 22 which deals with visitations. As such an officer a churchwarden has a *locus standi* to communicate with the bishop on matters of concern to the parish.

(b) to represent the laity and encourage the parishioners in their religious duties

9. These duties seem as relevant in parish church cathedrals as they are in other parishes.

(c) to maintain order and decency in the church and churchyard

10. That this function applies in the case of parish church cathedrals seems clear, and this view is reflected in the Opinion of the Commission on **Cathedrals: disturbances during services and admission to episcopal enthronements and other services**.

11. It will be for the Chapter of a cathedral, as part of their general duty under section 4(8) of the Cathedrals Measure 1999 to direct and oversee the administration of the affairs of the cathedral, to decide what meetings may appropriately be held in the cathedral, but this applies to organized meetings. The reference in paragraph 1 of Canon F 15 to 'meetings' would include, for example, a gathering of men to play poker in a quiet corner of the cathedral; the churchwardens would have power to close the poker game.

12. Under section 7(2)(*c*) of the 1999 Measure, the duties of the dean include the maintenance of good order and proper reverence in the cathedral. The dean will exercise this power through vergers and other members of the cathedral staff, but this seems in no way inconsistent with the continuation of the churchwardens' independent functions in respect of good order and decency.

(d) to hold the plate, ornaments and other movable goods of the church

13. Paragraph 5 of Canon E 1 is clear in its terms: the plate, ornaments and other movable goods of the church vest in the churchwardens. It is often assumed that in parish church cathedrals all property is vested in the cathedral itself, but there is no provision to that effect. Under the Cathedrals Measure 1999 the cathedral holds all property formerly vested in the cathedral Chapter of a parish church cathedral (s13); the effect of section 12(6) of the 1999 Measure and its predecessor provisions in the Cathedrals Measure 1963 is to vest in the cathedral all property formerly held by the PCC (or vested in the Diocesan Authority on its behalf). Nothing is said about the property vested in the churchwardens.

14. Section 4(8)(*g*) of the 1999 Measure gives the Chapter the duty of managing 'all property vested in the cathedral'; but that does not extend to property vested in the churchwardens. The duty under the same

provision to ensure that necessary repairs and maintenance are carried out to 'the contents' of the cathedral is a particularization of the more general duty, and does not extend it.

15. Section 2 of the Care of Cathedrals Measure 1990 deals with works which require approval under the Measure. As originally enacted, it spoke of 'objects the property in which is vested in the corporate body [of the cathedral]'. The Care of Cathedrals (Amendment) Measure 2005, section 1, adds the words 'or which is in the possession or custody of the corporate body . . .'.

16. There seems little doubt that the Chapter has possession and custody of the plate, ornaments and movables of the cathedral church. But that is not inconsistent with the continued vesting of legal title in the churchwardens. The positions is analogous to that in other parishes, where the legal title is vested in the churchwardens but the PCC accepts responsibility for insurance, repairs and general safekeeping.

17. Paragraph 5 of Canon E 1 requires the churchwardens to keep an inventory of this property. Section 4 of the Care of Churches and Ecclesiastical Jurisdiction Measure 1991 amplifies this requirement, but does not apply to parish church cathedrals. The exclusion of parish church cathedrals from the statutory provision suggests, but does not strictly require, that the Canon be interpreted as limited in the same way. In the case of all cathedrals the Chapter has a duty under section 13(1) of the Care of Cathedrals Measure 1990 to compile and maintain an inventory, but this is limited to objects identified as of architectural, archaeological, artistic or historic interest and does not cover all the movables (for example service books) which would be in a full parish inventory. For that reason, section 13(1) cannot be regarded as strictly inconsistent with the duty in respect of an inventory imposed on churchwardens under Canon E 1. There is no duty on Chapters to compile and maintain full inventories, and it would be anomalous were the churchwardens of parish church cathedrals to be required to keep them.

Duties assigned 'by law and custom'

18. There remains the reference in paragraph 4 of Canon E 1 to 'such duties as are by law and custom assigned to [churchwardens]'. This language is a convenient way of referring to matters which may well change over time. For example, the churchwardens formerly had a role *ex officio* in the process of appointing to a vacant benefice, but now do so only if appointed as the parish representatives. Currently the reference will include the legal duties referred to in paragraph 4 of this Opinion though,

for the reasons there given, many are inapplicable in the case of parish church cathedrals. More generally, churchwardens may well be trustees of local trusts.

Summary

19. Some legislation dealing with the functions of churchwardens excludes parish church cathedrals from its scope; to that extent, the powers and duties of churchwardens in cathedral parishes are more limited than in other parishes. However, the provisions of Canon E 1 and Canon F 15 remain applicable to churchwardens in cathedral parishes save that, for the reasons given in paragraph 17 of this Opinion, the duty to keep an inventory may be regarded as inapplicable.

(2005)

Part 13
Worship

Worship

1. The Church of England (Worship and Doctrine) Measure 1974 makes provision for the incumbent and the PCC to make joint decisions about the forms of service to be used within those authorized by law (s1(3)(a)). For the purposes of the Measure, incumbent includes a priest-in-charge (s5).

If they cannot agree, the forms of service contained in the BCP are to be used unless during at least two of the preceding four years other authorized forms of service were regularly in use; in the latter case the PCC may require those other forms (as long as still authorized) to be used to the exclusion of, or in addition to, the BCP forms of service (s1(3)(b)).

2. In principle, each of the forms of service authorized by Canon B 1 must be regarded as separate and distinct from the others. As a general rule, an incumbent is not entitled to use – albeit with the approval of the PCC – a form of service which is in effect an amalgam of more than one authorized rite. Thus the BCP and *Common Worship* rites may all be available for use but on any given occasion one particular rite must be used, not a form of service combining elements from two or more. This general rule is subject to two qualifications:

(a)   express provision may be made in one form of service for borrowing material from another (although it should be noted that there is no such provision where the BCP rite is concerned); and

(b)   Canon B 5 para 1 gives the minister a discretion to 'make and use variations which are not of substantial importance in any form of service authorized by Canon B 1 according to particular circumstances' (see para 4 below).

3. The officiating minister may decide between any options authorized within any form of service and may make appropriate minor variations, but if the officiant is not the incumbent, the incumbent can give the officiant directions. The PCC has a right to comment upon the choice of such options and the incumbent will presumably endeavour as far as possible to meet its views and those of the congregation, if they are made known.

4. According to particular circumstances an officiating minister may within any authorized service use variations which are not of substantial importance (see Canon B 5 para 1). Any such variation must be reverent and seemly and must not be contrary to, nor indicative of any departure

from, the doctrine of the Church of England in any essential matter; a question may be referred to the bishop for his pastoral guidance or advice on such matters under Canon B 5 para 4.

(Revised September 2003)

Part 14

Baptism

Baptism

Fees

1. No fee or reward may be demanded for administering this sacrament or for the registering thereof, but the Parochial Fees Orders made under the Ecclesiastical Fees Measure 1986 provide for a fee payable to the incumbent for a certificate of baptism and searches of the baptismal register.

2. The Baptismal Registers Measure 1961 provided for the issue of a shortened certificate of baptism (s2, Sch, Pt II), now in general use.

Surnames and illegitimate children

3. Where a person's name appears on a birth certificate as that of the father of a child, the baptismal register should follow the birth certificate. The baptismal certificate is an extract from the baptismal register. If the birth certificate shows who the father is, his name can properly be inserted as that of the father in the baptismal register and consequently in the certificate which follows it. If no birth certificate is produced or if the birth certificate does not show who the father is, no person's name should be entered as father of an illegitimate child on the baptismal register without his consent in person and in writing (or by statutory declaration).

4. In a case where a married woman leaves her husband, goes to live with another man whose surname she assumes and has a child by him whom she desires to be baptized in church, declaring the child's intended Christian name and the surname of its natural father, the principle set out in paragraph 3 above should be followed. The surname is not required in the course of the ceremony.

5. The register cannot be altered in a case where a second husband accepts the child of his wife's first marriage and desires the entry to be amended to save the child from knowledge later that he is not in fact his father.

Children of persons in the Diplomatic Service and the Armed Forces baptized abroad

6. There is no power to enter the name of a child born to parents serving in embassies, High Commissions or consulates or in the Armed Forces and baptized abroad in the register of a parish in England in which the parents normally reside.

Baptisms in conventional districts

7. Although a conventional district possesses many of the attributes of a parish, including churchwardens, a PCC and a certain degree of independence from those parts of the parish which do not form part of the conventional district, there is no statutory (or other) provision which would remove conventional districts from the scope of the Parochial Registers and Records Measure 1978. Section 2(2) of that Measure applies as much to a baptism in the licensed place of worship of a conventional district as to a baptism in a place in a parish other than the parish church. Accordingly, where a ceremony of baptism according to the rites of the Church of England is performed in the place of worship of a conventional district, the person by whom the ceremony was performed should, as soon as possible thereafter, send to the incumbent or priest-in-charge of the parish a certificate signed by him certifying when and where the ceremony was performed (see also Sch 1 to the 1978 Measure).

8. It is understandable that a minister of the conventional district might wish to keep some form of record of baptisms which take place in his conventional district. Any such register should clearly include the following statement:

> 'The statutory register required by the Parochial Registers and Records Measure 1978 is held at the parish church. All baptisms must be recorded in that register. The entries herein are copies of the entries in that register only.'

(*See also* **Baptism: consent of parent**)

(Revised January 1988)

Baptism: change of baptismal name

Ecclesiastical law

1. Canon B 27 para 6 provides:

> 'If it is desired for sufficient reason that a Christian name be changed, the bishop may, under the laws of this realm, confirm a person by a new Christian name, which shall be thereafter deemed the lawful Christian name of such person.'

See *Halsbury's Laws of England*, 4th edn, 1975, vol. 14, at para 1000, pointing out that a certificate ought to be signed by the confirming bishop as well as a note being made in the register of the person's baptism.

2. Accordingly, at confirmation a bishop may for good reason add to, or alter, the Christian name of a person who is to be confirmed. The candidate is confirmed under the new name which is then deemed to be the lawful Christian name of that person. The Christian name may be in more than one part: for example, a person whose Christian name is 'Joseph George Peter' has a Christian name in three parts. The change of name may be either the addition of extra parts or its deletion and substitution by an entirely new name in one or more parts. No accidental change of name is possible as the intention of the bishop and the candidate is required before a change of name can occur.

Historical background

3. It is often assumed – see *In re Parrott's Will Trusts, Cox v Parrott* [1946] Ch 183 at 187 per Vaisey J – that the legal basis for the changing of a baptismal name at confirmation begins with a constitution of Johannes Peccham in 1281 *Circa Sacramentum*, sub tit. *De Baptismo*:

> 'Attendant etiam sacerdotes, ne lasciva nomina, quae scilicet mox prolata, sonent in lasciviam, imponi permittant parvulis baptizatis, sexus paecipue foeminini: Et si contrarium fiat, per confirmantes episcopos corrigatur.'

4. As appears in Linnell, *The Law of Names* (1938) at p. 9, the power of a bishop unilaterally to impose a change of name is different from a change at the request of the actual candidate for confirmation. However, it may be surmised that Peccham's constitution was made necessary by the imposition of 'improper' names by the laity during emergency baptisms; on such occasions, of course, the priest would not be present in order to insist upon a 'proper' name.

5. In fact the pre-Reformation canon law is set out in Lyndwood in his *Provinciale Angliae* (Oxford, at p. 246, gloss on *corrigatur* in Peccham's constitution) and from this it seems that the canonist's view was that an alteration of any name, 'improper' or not, was legally permissible. In part he bases his argument on Scripture (Abram/Abraham; Simon/Peter) and on the taking of a papal name.

6. At the Reformation the canon law was confirmed as part of the general law of England unless a particular part was 'repugnant, contrariant or derogatory' to the laws or statutes of the realm or to the prerogatives of the Crown (see *Halsbury's Laws of England*, 4th edn, 1975, vol. 14, at para 306). That the canon law as to changes of name was not regarded as being repugnant, etc. was the opinion of 'all the judges' in the 36th regnal year of Henry VIII, and is confirmed by Coke (*Institutes*, I, 3a) and by Holt, CJ (quoted in Linnell at p. 8). It would be difficult to find better authorities to prove recognition.

7. A change of name, although it might affect matters appertaining to the general common law of the land, was a matter for the church courts.

8. In order to show that any part of the pre-Reformation law is still binding it is now necessary not only to plead it in any particular case but also to prove that it has been recognized, continued and acted upon since the Reformation (see *Halsbury's Laws of England*, vol. 14, at para 307). Prima facie and save, perhaps, as to a unilateral change of name by the bishop, the various references given by Linnell themselves show that the pre-Reformation canon law has continued and has been acted upon.

9. Further confirmation of this view is to be found in Watson, *The Clergyman's Law or the Complete Incumbent*, 1st edn, 1701, at p. 377; 2nd edn, 1725, at p. 475:

'Note that any man that alters his Name at Confirmation may purchase by his new Name, 1 *Inst.f.3. a.* 1 *Brownloe* 147. *Lit. Rep. 182.* And it is said that the Name of a Corporation is as the Name of Baptism which cannot be changed, 2 *Bendlow.*'

10. Moreover, Gibson's *Codex Iuris Ecclesiastici Anglicani*, 1st edn, 1713, at p. 440; 2nd edn, 1761, at p. 363, sets out Peccham's constitution as representing the law, whilst citing both Coke and Lyndwood.

11. Nonetheless, Burn, *Ecclesiastical Law*, 1st edn, at p. 110; 9th edn, 1842 (?), vol. II at p. 10, having referred to Coke's opinion stated:

'But this seemeth to be altered by the form of the present liturgy. In the offices of old, the bishop pronounced the name of the child or person confirmed by him, and if he did not approve the name, or the person himself or his friends desired it to be altered, it might be done by the bishop's pronouncing a new name upon his administering the rite, and the common law allowed the alteration; but upon review of the liturgy at King Charles the Second's restoration, the office of confirmation is altered at this point, for now the bishop doth not pronounce the name of the person confirmed, and therefore cannot alter it.'

12. This passage is quoted in Stephens, *Laws Relating to the Clergy*, 1848, vol. I, at p. 372, with the additional comment (at p. 97):

'It may, however, be observed, that as there is no rubric which expressly takes away the authority of the bishop to comply with the foregoing constitution [of Peccham], he can, if he think proper, prevent a child from being baptized in an improper name.'

Presumably this comment refers to a child brought for both baptism and confirmation at the same time.

13. Rogers, *A Practical Arrangement of Ecclesiastical Law*, 2nd edn, 1849, at pp. 68–9, having referred to Peccham's constitution, stated:

'Which being so changed, Lord *Coke* says shall be deemed to be the lawful name. *Co. Litt 3a; 2 Roll. Abrid. 135a.* But, as now the bishop does not pronounce the name of the child at confirmation, something beyond the ordinary ceremony must be introduced. *Burn's E. L. 111.*'

In a footnote the author adds:

'Not withstanding the authority of Lord *Coke*, and the case of Sir *Francis Gawdie*, cited by him, it may be doubtful, whether a name given at baptism can be legally changed at confirmation. Nothing is more certain than that the "one" baptism once sufficiently performed is final and complete, can then that holy covenant be safely varied even in non-essentials?'

However, this argument seems to muddle the giving of a name at baptism with the theological (and legal) view that there can be only one baptism.

14. In *A Hand-book of Ecclesiastical Law and Duty for the use of the Irish Clergy*, 1861, at p. 211, Archdeacon Stopford says:

'Up to the last review [*scilicet* of the liturgy], A.D. 1661, the confirmation service required the Bishop to address each person confirmed by his or her Christian name; and it was then held that if the Bishop addressed the person by a name other than the baptismal name, the name so used by the Bishop became the legal name. But since the service was altered so that the Bishop no longer addresses the person by name, it has been held that a Christian name cannot now be altered at confirmation. (Stephens, Laws of the Clergy, 372.)'

15. However, Robert Phillimore in *The Ecclesiastical Law of the Church of England*, 1873, at pp. 673–4, having set out both Coke's and Burn's opinions, says:

'But Lord Coke's authority cannot be set aside in this way. He had before him at the time when he thus laid down the law the confirmation services of Edward and Elizabeth, which are *not*, as might be inferred from the remark of Dr. Burn, different in this respect from that of Charles the Second. There seems to be no reason to impugn the authority of the precedent cited by Lord Coke.'

He then goes on to cite instances in 1707 and 1761 before adding: 'and the practice is occasionally continued to the present day'. The passage is not altered in the second edition by Walter Phillimore in 1895 at pp. 517–18.

16. It is therefore not surprising that in Blunt, *The Book of Church Law*, 2nd edn, 1876, at pp. 59–61, Walter Phillimore, having set out the ancient constitution and instances of changes of name at confirmation had previously stated:

'It is believed that cases still occur in which this is done. The ancient *canon* law certainly only referred to such a change when the baptismal name was of an improper kind, yet this may only represent a portion of the *common* law of the Church on this subject.'

17. Kenneth MacMorran in Cripps, *A Practical Treatise on the Law relating to the Church and Clergy*, 8th edn, 1937, at p. 520, having summarized Peccham's constitution, cites Coke on Littleton in a footnote. He then continues:

'By the form of the present rite, the bishop does not pronounce the name of the person to be confirmed, as used to be done in ancient offices of confirmation, and therefore it has been said he cannot alter it; but although he does not ordinarily pronounce the same, there is no rubric which forbids it; and there seems no reason why he might not do so, if he should think fit, for the purposes of complying with the constitution above mentioned, if an improper name has been given at baptism.'

18. In 1946 Vaisey J in *In re Parrott's Will Trusts, Cox v Parrott* [1946] Ch 182 decided in favour of the view expressed by Phillimore. He stated (at p. 186) in relation to Dr Burns's view: 'This, however, was a mistake, as is pointed out by Phillimore . . .'. He also pointed out that he knew that a number of bishops in recent years had exercised the power 'on quite a few occasions' (ibid.). In addition he drew attention to the fact that the Adoption of Children (High Court) Rules 1926 gave recognition of this position (at pp. 186–7).

19. Bursell *Liturgy, Order and the Law* (1996, at p. 156) took the same view citing Canon B 27 and *In re Parrott's Will Trusts*. He also points out (at p. 39) that the addition, although not sanctioned by the wording of the 1662 rite, was permitted in the same way as the singing of psalms and hymns during divine service; this was recognized as legal in *Hutchins v Denziloe and Loveland* (1792) 1 Hag. Con. 170 at pp. 175–80 because of liturgical practice both ancient and at the Reformation (see also *Read v Bishop of Lincoln* [1892] AC 644 at pp. 659–61). (In fact there are other examples of additions, such as the taking of collections at morning and evening prayer – see *Marson v Unmack* [1923] P 163 at pp. 167–8.)

20. Both Leeder, *Ecclesiastical Law Handbook*, 1997, at para 10.30, and Hill, *Ecclesiastical Law*, 2nd edn, 2001 at para 5.19, take the same view as to legality.

21. As can be seen the preponderance of authority is therefore in favour of the law as currently expressed in Canon B 27 para 6. The opposing view stems from Burn's argument as to the wording of the rite in the BCP. Although not expressed in precisely these terms his argument must be on the basis that no addition might lawfully have been made to the rite because the use of the 1662 Prayer Book was enjoined by Act of Parliament (see *Martin v Mackonochie* (1868) LR 2PC 365 at 382–3). That being so, the contrary argument in Phillimore perhaps requires a little amplification.

22. The Act of Uniformity 1548 required that 'any manner of parson, vicar or other whatsoever minister' should use the Edwardian Prayer Book 'in such order and form as they be mentioned and set forth in the said book' and the Act of Uniformity 1558 used almost identical wording. The Act of Uniformity 1662, section 2, stated

'. . . all and singular ministers in any cathedral, collegiate or parish church or chapel, or other place of public worship . . . shall be bound to say and use [the Book of Common Prayer] in such order and form as is mentioned in the said book annexed and joined to this present act . . .'

23. In the light of the wording of these Acts it is difficult to see how the 1662 Prayer Book should be treated differently from the previous Prayer Books as Phillimore points out. The pronunciation of the candidate's name must be legal or illegal whichever Prayer Book was being used. In fact, as the unchallenged views of the lay judges and of the ecclesiastical writers attested, such pronunciation for the purpose of changing a name was always regarded as legal and therefore an exception to too rigorous an interpretation of the Acts of Uniformity. Similar exceptions have already been pointed out (see para 21 above).

24. In law, therefore, a Christian name given at baptism can only *formally* be altered by Act of Parliament, at confirmation or upon adoption (see *In re Parrott's Will Trusts* at pp. 186–7); to this list must be added authorization by royal licence (see *Halsbury's Laws of England*, 4th edn, 1975, vol. 35, at para 1273). Such a Christian name – at least for an Anglican – remains his or her first, or formal, name. That, however, does not mean that a Christian may not be known by some other name or nickname. Such a usage is clearly lawful (see *Halsbury's Laws of England*, vol. 35, para 1273) as long as it is not used to defraud (or perhaps in some cases to mislead, intentionally or otherwise – for example, an application for a passport should presumably disclose the applicant's formal name). Indeed, such a change of name occurs in relation to the religious upon taking their vows. In the case of any such informal change of name the use of a deed poll is clearly to be recommended (see *Halsbury's Laws of England*, vol. 35, para 1279)

Treatment under secular law

25. An individual may be known by whatever name he chooses. Forenames may therefore be 'changed' in the same way as surnames. More formal methods, such as a deed poll (regulated by The Enrolment of Deeds (Change of Name) Regulations 1994, SI 1994 No. 604) or a statutory declaration, are no more than evidence of a change. 'There is no magic in a deed poll' (per Buckley J in *Re T (otherwise H) (An Infant)* [1963] Ch 238). There is no restriction on changing forenames save that they must not be changed for any fraudulent purpose and the change must not be 'calculated to deceive and inflict financial loss on another' (*Burgess v Burgess* (1853) 3 De G M & G 896).

26. In *Re H (Child's Name: First Name)* [2002] EWCA Civ 190; [2002] 1 FLR 973, Thorpe L J indicated that it was easier to change a child's forename (or given name) than his surname:

> '[N]one of the authorities that guide the courts in determining disputes as to the surname by which a child should be known seems to be of any application to a dispute of this sort. The surname by which a child is registered and known is of particular significance insofar as it denotes the family to which the child belongs.
>
> Given names have a much less concrete character. It is commonplace for a child to receive statutory registration with one or more given names and, subsequently, to receive different given names, maybe at baptism, or maybe, by custom and adoption. During the course of family life as a child develops personality and individuality, parents or other members of the family, may be attracted to some nickname or some alternative given name which will then adhere, possibly for the rest of the child's life, or possibly only until the child's individuality and maturity allow it to make a choice for itself as to the name by which he or she wishes to be known.'

27. The secular case law in this regard thus reflects Church of England canon law; this is not surprising since the latter is part of the law of the land. It does not, however, permit Christians to change their names with the level of ease enjoyed by non-Christians. As has been seen, in *Re Parrott's Will Trusts*, Vaisey J refused to recognize the validity of any method of changing a Christian name other than those recognized by canon law and described above. However, Helen Mead in *Change of Name*, 15th edn, Sweet & Maxwell, at pp. 10–11, notes that as a matter of practice deeds poll purporting to change baptismal names are frequently executed. She points out that the Central Office of the Supreme Court will accept a deed poll purporting to change a Christian name provided the householder's declaration is endorsed with the appropriate certificate to the effect that 'notwithstanding the decision of Mr Justice Vaisey in *Re Parrott's Will Trusts*, the applicant desires the enrolment to proceed'. (Thus the applicant takes the risk of the deed subsequently being declared ineffective so far as the change of Christian name is concerned.) Further, *The Encyclopaedia of Forms and Precedents* notes the need for a certificate as described by Helen Mead, but adds, 'However this is probably no longer necessary' (vol. 29, 2001 Re-issue, para 11 note 9). Interestingly, the College of Arms will *not* enrol a deed purporting to change a person's Christian name.

The effect of Article 14 of the European Convention on Human Rights

28. There exists a freedom to change one's name enjoyed by all save *formally* for those baptized in accordance with the rites and, *ex hypothesi*, the laws of the Church of England. However, this distinction is not discriminatory on the part of the state as it would appear that strict rigour of the rule enunciated by Vaisey J is not enforced in practice, save by the College of Arms. Thus there is no *de facto* discrimination between members of the Church of England and members of other faiths or of no faith in the manner in which a change in name may be effected and formally registered. All are treated equally and Article 14 (Discrimination) is not therefore engaged.

The effect of Article 8 of the European Convention on Human Rights

29. Is the Church of England acting contrary to Article 8 in that its canon law does not permit a change of baptismal name save in the circumstances mentioned above? That Article 8 (Private and Family Life) applies to names was ascertained in *Burghartz* (1994) 18 ECHR 101. The court in its judgement stated:

> 'Unlike some other international instruments, such as the *International Covenant on Civil and Political Rights* (Article 24 para 2), the *Convention on the Rights of the Child* of 20 November 1989 (Articles 7 and 8) or the *American Convention on Human Rights* (Article 18), Article 8 (art. 8) of the convention does not contain any explicit provisions on names. As a means of personal identification and of linking to a family, a person's name nonetheless concerns his or her private and family life. The fact that society and the State have an interest in regulating the use of names does not exclude this, since these public-law aspects are compatible with private life conceived of as including, to a certain degree, the right to establish and develop relationships with other human beings, in professional or business contexts as in others (see, *mutatis mutandis*, the *Niemietz v. Germany* judgement of 16 December 1992, Series A no. 251-B, p. 33, para 29). In the instant case, the applicant's retention of the surname by which, according to him, he has become known in academic circles may significantly affect his career. Article 8 (art. 8) therefore applies.'

30. However, it is clear from the admissibility decision in *KB v The Netherlands* (Application 18806/91) that not all restrictions on any change of name would be in breach of Article 8:

'The Commission further notes that the Netherlands' policy concerning changes in family names is based on the necessity to prevent arbitrariness, to maintain the required stability in the rules governing family names and to prevent double family names.

The Commission accepts that there may be exceptional cases where the carrying of a particular name creates such suffering or practical difficulties that the right under Article 8 (Art. 8) of the Convention is affected. There are, however, good reasons for restrictions in this area, and a right to change one's surname cannot, in principle, be considered to be included in the right to respect for private life, as protected by Article 8 (Art. 8).'

31. The Strasbourg jurisprudence recognizes that restrictions may be placed by the State upon the freedom of an individual to change his or her name. A useful summary of the restrictions which may be imposed were given by the European Court of Justice in *Stjerna v Finland* (1994) 24 ECHR 195:

'Under the legislation on names in the twelve member States of the International Commission on Civil Status, all members of the Council of Europe, the possibility of a person to change his or her name is subject to certain conditions. In Belgium, Portugal and Turkey, any reason may be invoked in support of a request for a change of name. In France, Germany, Luxembourg and Switzerland the reasons must be convincing ones. In some countries specific reasons are required: for instance that the current name gives rise to pronunciation and spelling difficulties (Austria) or causes legal or social difficulties (Austria and Greece) or is contrary to decency (the Netherlands and Spain), or is ridiculous (Austria, Italy and the Netherlands) or is otherwise contrary to the dignity of the person concerned (Spain) (see the International Commission's Guide pratique international de l'état civil, Paris). Name changes are noted in population records, at the request of the interested person (Belgium and France) or of a public authority (France), or are done so automatically (the other ten members of the International Commission).

Under English law a person is entitled to adopt a surname of his own choosing and to use this name without any restrictions or formalities, except in connection with the practice of some professions (*Halsbury's Laws of England*, 4th edn, 1975, vol. 35, paras 1173–76). The new name is valid for purposes of legal identification, may be used in public documents and is entered

on the electoral roll (*Cossey v the United Kingdom* judgement of
27 September 1990, Series A no. 184 p. 9, para 16). The United
Kingdom has no civil status certificates or equivalent current
identity documents (ibid., para 17). The near absence in English
law of formalities governing changes of name has not resulted in a
large number of changes.'

32. *Stjerna* therefore recognizes that restrictions may be justified and went
on to state that:

'There is little common ground between the domestic systems of
the Convention countries as to the conditions on which a change
of name may be legally effected. The Court deduces that in the
particular sphere under consideration the Contracting States enjoy
a wide margin of appreciation.'

33. In *Rees v The United Kingdom* [1987] 2 FLR 111 the case of a
transsexual, it was expressly recognized that, 'an entry in a birth register
and the certificate derived therefrom are records of facts at the time of
the birth'. Despite the recent revisiting of the law concerning gender
re-assignment, it is still arguable that a baptism certificate does no more
than record the name used at the time. [This Opinion was settled before
the Gender Recognition Act 2004, which however makes no reference to
baptism certificates.]

34. In *Guillot v France* (52/1995/558/644) the European Court of Human
Rights, when deciding whether Article 8 was breached, considered the
effect of the refusal to change name:

'The Court can understand that Mr and Mrs Guillot were upset
by the refusal to register the forename they had chosen for their
daughter. It notes that this forename consequently cannot appear
on official documents and deeds. In addition, it finds it probable
that the difference between the child's forename in law and the
forename which she actually uses – she is called "Fleur de Marie"
by her family and is known by that name socially – entails certain
complications for the applicants when acting as her statutory
representatives. However, the Court notes that it is not disputed
that the child regularly uses the forename in issue without
hindrance and that the French courts – which considered the
child's interest – allowed the application made in the alternative
by the applicants for registration of the forename "Fleur-Marie".
In the light of the foregoing, the Court does not find that the
inconvenience complained of by the applicants is sufficient to raise
an issue of failure to respect their private and family life under

Article 8 para. 1 (art. 8–1). Consequently, there has not been a violation of Article 8 (art. 8).'

35. This situation is very similar to the position of members of the Church of England. They can use whatever name they choose, although their baptismal name, as registered at the time, cannot be changed save in limited and specific circumstances. It is therefore unlikely that this will be considered to be a breach of Article 8. This point was taken further in *Salonen v Finland* (27868/95):

'In the Commission's opinion, it is in the interests of society to regulate the choice of forenames in order to protect the child from the possible inconveniences caused by a forename which may be considered inappropriate by others. Restrictions on the choice of forenames can therefore be justified in the interests of the child and of society . . .

In the view of the Commission, the refusal of the Finnish authorities to allow the applicants to name their daughter Ainut Vain Marjaana cannot be considered unreasonable, having regard to the aim of the restrictions placed on the use of names to protect a person from inconveniences caused by his or her name and the margin of appreciation the States enjoy. Furthermore, the refusal to register the forename does not prevent its use by family and acquaintances (see the *Guillot v. France* judgement, op. cit., para. 27).'

36. It is therefore highly unlikely that the relevant canon law of the Church of England will be considered to be in violation of Article 8 of the European Convention on Human Rights because:

- States enjoy a wide margin of appreciation.

- No inconvenience or distress can be demonstrated by the Church's refusal to change a baptismal name.

- The State itself does not prevent the recognition of a *de facto* change in forename irrespective of the law of the Church.

- In any event under section 13 of the Human Rights Act 1998, particular regard is to be given to the right to freedom of religion and the UK domestic courts are unlikely to interfere with the ecclesiology of the Church and its law and teaching on baptismal names.

37. It should be noted however that the relevant organs of the Church of England are almost certainly not public authorities for the purposes of

the Human Rights Act 1998: see *Aston Cantlow Parochial Church Council v Wallbank* [2003] UKHL 37; [2004] 1 AC 546.

Conclusion

38. Although the ecclesiastical and secular law does not permit a baptized member of the Church of England *formally* to alter his or her Christian (or forenames) other than in the circumstances set out in paragraph 26 above, nevertheless a member of the Church of England may quite legally be known by, and use, different names from those given at baptism or confirmation as long as this does not flow from any fraudulent or similar motive. It is highly unlikely that the *formal* position could constitute discrimination on grounds of religion in the enjoyment of a convention right under Article 14 of the European Convention of Human Rights.

(May 2003)

Baptism: consent of parent

Introduction

1. The pre-Reformation canon law provided that women at their confinement should have water ready for baptizing the child in case of necessity and that the clergy should instruct the laity in the proper form of baptism. There is no explicit legal duty upon a parent to bring a child for baptism, although such a duty may perhaps be inferred from the above provisions and from the services relating to emergency baptism in both the BCP and *Common Worship: Initiation Services*.

2. There is little doubt that those who were Christian would (at least since 1662) have made every endeavour to have their children baptized. Those who were unbaptized could not be buried in consecrated ground and were regarded as not being members of the Christian Church. Indeed, it seems that baptism was regarded as a prerequisite to salvation.

3. Fortunately, the rigour of the law has now been mitigated as in these circumstances Canon B 38 para 2 provides for a form of service other than that set out in the BCP. Moreover, it seems that the doctrine of the Church of England may also have been ameliorated as *Common Worship: Initiation Services*: Emergency Baptism (Note 2 at p. 94) states:

> '[The parents] should be assured that questions of ultimate salvation or of the provision of a Christian funeral for an infant who dies do not depend upon whether or not he has been baptised.'

4. This is particularly important as a refusal, or postponement, or baptism is no longer to be seen as endangering a child's ultimate salvation. This is also relevant to the duty of a minister under Canon B 22 para 6 (see para 12 below).

Involvement of parents or guardians

5. The canon law has never required the consent of a parent before a child is baptized. Indeed, had that been so, emergency baptism would often have proved impossible. Although the *Common Worship: Initiation Services*: Emergency Baptism provides that it is the parents' responsibility to request emergency baptism, it also recognizes that the parents may be absent and that they may not even have named the child (see Note 3 at p. 94). The Ministration of Private Baptism of Children in Houses in the BCP also seems to envisage the possibility of the absence of the parents. In relation to a healthy infant, however, Canon B 22 envisages the

involvement of the child's parents or guardians as the minister is required to instruct them in their responsibilities.

6. However, Canon B 22 must be construed in relation to the general law of the land and the word 'parent' must therefore be construed as referring to a person having parental responsibility for the child. The Children Act 1989 provides that where a child's father and mother are married to each other at the time of the birth each parent has parental responsibility (s2(1)). If they are not married at that time the natural father can only gain parental responsibility under the provisions of the Act (ss4 and 12); this must be by order of the civil court, or by a parental responsibility agreement with the mother which has been made and recorded in the prescribed manner, or by the registration of the father as such under the Births and Deaths Registration Act 1953, sections 10 and 10A. An adoption order gives parental responsibility to the adopters (Adoption and Children Act 2002, s46(1) as does the placement of a child with prospective adopters (2002 Act, s25(2)) and the rights, powers and obligations of the natural parents or any guardian are extinguished by an adoption order (Adoption and Children Act 2002, s46(2)). A guardian can be appointed either by the civil courts, by a person having parental responsibility or by a guardian (Children Act 1989, s5). Where there is only one such parent or guardian the Canon only applies to that one person.

7. Usually a child will be brought for baptism by the parents or the guardian or guardians. However, circumstances may vary widely and it may happen that only one parent may bring a child to baptism: the other parent may have died; the natural parents may never have married or may now be divorced; the other parent may have a different religion or be an atheist or agnostic; the other parent may object to the baptism or merely be uninterested. The minister can only discover the true state of affairs by making enquiries; in the first instance this will be from the parent who requests the baptism.

8. Even though section 2(7) of the Children Act 1989 permits one parent to act without the authority of the other, if a child is brought by one parent alone the minister remains under a duty (save in an emergency) to instruct both parents or guardians in the responsibilities that rest upon them (Canon B 22 para 4). He should therefore enquire as to the reason for the absence of the other parent or guardian and, if there is another parent and that other can be located, he must endeavour to instruct them both. In order to do so he may postpone the baptism (save in an emergency) (Canon B 22 para 3).

9. If the other parent cannot be found, the minister is entitled then to baptize the child. On the other hand, if the other parent or guardian does

not agree to a baptism, or refuses to be prepared or instructed, the minister should apply to the diocesan bishop for guidance and directions under Canon C 18. If the minister learns that a court order to prohibit baptism has been made or is being sought (for example, until leave of the court has been obtained), he should refuse baptism until the matter has been resolved by the court; in the meantime he should inform the bishop as to the reason for his refusal.

10. If the child is brought for baptism by persons other than the parents or guardians, the minister's obligation nevertheless remains the same.

11. If the minister refuses to baptize the child, or unduly delays in so doing, the parent or guardian who brought the child for baptism may also apply to the bishop under Canon B 22 para 2, and after consultation with the minister the bishop must give such directions as he thinks fit.

Emergency baptism

12. Canon B 22 para 6 provides:

'No minister being informed of the weakness or danger of death of any infant within his cure and therefore desired to go to baptise the same shall either refuse or delay to do so.'

There is no exception to the duty upon a minister having the cure of souls to attend upon an emergency under Canon B 22 para 6, for example, to await the presence of parents, guardians or godparents or to give instruction; indeed, the summons may come from someone entirely unconnected with the family. However, if upon attendance the minister were to find that the child was perfectly healthy, he would not be under any obligation to administer baptism then and there, as private baptism should only occur 'in case of great danger' (see the rubric at the end of The Ministration of Public Baptism to such as are of Riper Years in the BCP) or 'emergency' (see Note 1 of *Common Worship: Initiation Services*: Emergency Baptism). Canon B 22 para 6 obliges the minister to attend without refusal or delay rather than expressly to administer the Sacrament.

13. Nevertheless, if the child is indeed in danger of death, or will remain at risk (which would seem to be the purport of the word 'weakness' in Canon B 22 para 6), there is a clearly implied duty to administer the Sacrament (see Canon B 22 para 7) unless there is an order in existence from the civil courts forbidding such a baptism. In this regard the minister should be guided by any available medical opinion. The minister should not claim medical expertise unless actually qualified to make such a claim.

If there is any doubt as to the emergency, the child should still be baptized. The decision as to whether the child should be baptized, however, is in no way dependent upon whether it is 'within his cure'; these words only delimitate upon whom the duty of attendance falls.

14. If told of the existence of an order of the courts forbidding the baptism, a minister who nevertheless administered baptism would be in danger of having to answer to the civil court.

15. Does the duty to baptize in an emergency exist in relation to every child irrespective of the views or religion of one or both parents? The duty to attend under Canon B 22 para 6 is absolute and only when present will the minister be able to appraise the situation. Hospital admission records or other information may reveal that the parents are not Christian and in those circumstances the minister's duty to baptize has to be considered within the context of the significance of baptism in the universal Church. Baptism is the Sacrament instituted by Christ for those who wish to become members of his Church (see the Welcome and Peace in *Common Worship: Initiation Services*: Holy Baptism) and, as such, the congregation '. . . shall receive him as one of the flock of true Christian people' (rubric after the questions to those who bring a child to church after emergency baptism in the Ministration of Private Baptism of Children in Houses in the BCP). This being so, and especially as baptism is not a prerequisite of ultimate salvation, it can no longer be argued that baptism ought to be administered against the wishes or beliefs of the child's parents on the ground that the salvation of the child must be of paramount concern. Therefore, although there is no exception expressly mentioned in Canon B 22 para 6, it can nevertheless be implied that a minister should not baptize a child where it is evident that, if the child lives, it is unlikely that he or she will be brought up in the Christian faith.

16. In an emergency anyone may lawfully baptize (see e.g. Note 1 at p. 94 in *Common Worship: Initiation Services*), although the duty under Canon B 22 para 6 only falls upon a minister having the cure of souls. Subject to the general cure of the bishop, it is usually only the incumbent who has an exclusive cure of souls within a parish (*Halsbury's Laws of England*, 4th edn, 1975, vol. 14, at para 690), although the minister of a conventional district has a cure of souls, as does a vicar in a team ministry where a special cure of souls in respect of the parish has been assigned to that team vicar by a scheme under the Pastoral Measure 1983 or by a licence from the bishop. A priest-in-charge licensed to a parish during a vacancy has the cure of souls in that parish (*see also* **Clergy: priest-in-charge**). On the other hand, an assistant curate has no cure of souls except as the minister in charge of the parish by reason of a vacancy. Moreover, hospital chaplains who are licensed under the

Extra-Parochial Ministry Measure 1967 are to be regarded as having a cure of souls within the meaning of Canon B 22.

(September 1995, revised 2003)

Baptism: the presence of godparents at baptism

1. The Commission has considered whether it is legal for a godparent: (i) to assume his or her responsibilities by affidavit; (ii) to participate via mobile phone or electronic mail; or (iii) to participate by an internet video link. Indeed, according to the *Daily Telegraph* for the 29 May 2001, a yachtsman participated as a godfather in a baptism service held in Portsmouth Cathedral via video equipment installed beside the cathedral font.

2. In addressing this question it is necessary to bear in mind that possible 'participation' in the manner contemplated in (ii) and (iii) above is a modern and recent phenomenon arising out of advances in technology. The BCP pre-dates such technology, and its rapid development means that the same can be said of modern liturgical texts including the ASB and *Common Worship* certainly as to the degree of sophistication now available. It is, therefore, necessary to note how the question of presence at a baptism has been addressed in the past but also to consider what, if any, change in approach is legally possible at the present day and for the future.

3. The BCP is on its face entirely clear. The final rubric that precedes the Ministration of Public Baptism of Infants categorically states:

> 'At the time appointed, the godfathers and godmothers and the parents or guardians with the child must be ready at the Font . . .'

Moreover, according to the rubric at the Naming of the Child, the godparents are to certify if the child is too weak to be dipped into the water, a matter of some importance in the seventeenth century. This requirement and the words 'ready at the Font' presuppose physical presence.[1]

4. However, although the presence of both godparents and parents are equally required by the rubric, Canon 29 of the 1603 Canons stated:

> '*No parent shall be urged to be present,*[2] *nor admitted to answer as*

---

[1] The rubrics in the ASB followed the BCP: the rubric to paragraph 12 in Baptism, Confirmation and Holy Communion stated: 'Those who are to be baptized, the parents and godparents of the children to be baptized . . . stand before the Bishop' and the rubric at paragraph 55 of the Baptism of Children stated: 'The parents and godparents being present with each child. . .'.

[2] In Victorian times the mother would often still be confined to bed. Moreover, one or both of the parents may not be alive or the whereabouts of the mother and/or father unknown.

Godfather for his own Child; nor any[3] Godfather or Godmother shall be suffered to make any other answer or speech, than by the Book of Common Prayer is prescribed in that behalf . . .' (Emphasis supplied)

Despite the requirement for presence, at least by 1850 the use of proxy godparents was by no means uncommon although contrary to the rubric.[4] Indeed, Cripps on *Church and Clergy* (Sweet and Maxwell, 1937) at p. 519 stated:

'Rubric before the Public Baptism of Infants. The above directive is positive, but custom[5] appears to have sanctioned a very frequent departure from the strict rubrical directions in this respect.'

A proxy was a means of providing a physical presence (albeit as a substitute or agent). It seems that there was a general recognition of a need for presence but also that a baptism should not be delayed by reason of the absence of the chosen godparent by reason of illness or some other reason. It is not a sound precedent for unauthorized activity in the future but it points to a need for flexibility if it can be lawfully achieved.

5. On a strict reading the rite of Initiation in *Common Worship* does not specifically require the physical presence of the godparents or sponsors.[6] The rubric at the commencement of the Presentation of the Candidates only states:

---

[3] A new Canon omitting the words in italics was made and published by the Convocation of Canterbury in 1865 but was not confirmed by Royal Letters Patent.

[4] Stephens, *The Book of Common Prayer* (London, 1850) states at p. 1423: 'It may be here remarked, that there is no authority in the Baptismal Offices for a practice by no means uncommon, of "Godfathers and Godmothers" being represented by proxy.'

[5] The word 'custom' when used in the context of ecclesiastical law is often ambiguous. It may refer to a custom as established according to the common law, a custom established under canon law or, merely, a practice without the authority of law. Bearing in mind that the Book of Common Prayer was annexed to the Act of Uniformity, it is difficult to see how either of the first two possibilities could 'sanction' departure from the strict rule. This being so, the 'custom' should probably be understood as a mere 'practice'. If so, the word 'sanctioned' in the passage from Cripps should not be read in its strict legal sense.

[6] Note 6 to the Initiation Services, entitled Godparents and Sponsors, states: 'The term "godparent" is used for those asked to present children for baptism and to continue to support them. The term "sponsor" is used for those who agree to support in the journey of faith candidates (of any age) for baptism, confirmation or affirmation of baptismal faith . . .'.

'The candidates are presented to the congregation. Where appropriate, they are presented by their godparents or sponsors.'

Nevertheless, as the president addressed the parents and godparents, the implication is that the parents and the requisite number of godparents are to be present. In this respect there is no good reason for differentiating between child and adult baptism because the rite applies to both, as does Canon B 23. Indeed, Canon B 23 para 3 requires an adult to –

'choose three, or at least two, to be his sponsors, who shall be ready to present him at the font'.

This clearly involves physical presence. Similarly, it is implicit that in order for godparents to present a child to the congregation during the service they have to be participants in the service either by being physically present or otherwise being visible and audible to the congregation.

6. The question before the Commission relates to the legality of a single godparent being absent during the baptism. It is therefore necessary to note that Canon B 23 para 1 requires three godparents for a child –

'save that, when three cannot conveniently be had, one godfather and godmother[7] shall suffice'.

A baptism will, therefore, be canonically valid with only two godparents although in order to comply with the rubrics in the BCP and the ASB both must be present. The fact that a third or fourth godparent cannot be present on the appointed day would not be a reason for delaying the baptism if the other provisions[8] relating to godparents in the Canons are observed. If, however, such additional godparents can participate in an appropriate manner using modern technology then the practical difficulty in relation to physical presence can be overcome. Moreover, in this way the norm of three godparents (see Canon B 23 para 1) may also be observed.

7. However, as long as two godparents are physically present in the church there seems to be no reason why the participation of other godparents should not be fulfilled through the use of modern technology as long as at the baptism the congregation is able to see all those who take on the responsibilities of godparents and can clearly hear their responses. Nevertheless, the actual use of such technology should not be contrary to good order by reason of its location, size or distraction.

---

[7] Moreover, by Canon B 23 para 1: 'Parents may be godparents for their own children provided that the child have at least one other godparent.'
[8] See Canon B 23 para 4.

8. The only technology that presently fulfils the necessary requirements of both visibility and audibility, however, is the video link. Use of a mobile phone cannot fulfil the requirement of visibility. Moreover, while the use of electronic mail has the merit of involving an exchange between the minister and godparent with a written record of the making of vows, it lacks the elements of visibility (unless also electronically displayed to the congregation) and audibility. An affidavit, being a unilateral act, lacks the element of dialogue with the minister and would not suffice.[9]

(1997)

---

[9] However, any of these means might be used to create an informal arrangement of quasi-godparent additional to the required legal godparents: *see* **Baptism: godparents: removal and replacement**.

Baptism: godparents: removal and replacement

There is no procedure to enable the parents of a child to remove a person as godparent of their child and substitute another person in his or her stead. Godparents have no obligations in substantive law and there is no legal significance in a particular person being godparent. There is no reason why parents should not make an informal arrangement with other persons to act as additional 'godparents'.

(December 1983)

Part 15

Holy Communion

Holy Communion: administration of the Sacrament

1. In considering whether it is lawful in the Holy Communion for the priest to consecrate wine in a lipped chalice or flagon and then to administer the wine so consecrated to communicants by pouring the same into a cup held by each communicant, in order that the communicant may drink the wine from his or her own cup, the following are relevant passages from Scripture:

Matthew 26.27
'Then [Jesus] took a cup and having offered thanks to God he gave it to [the disciples] with the words: "Drink from it, all of you . . .".'

Mark 14.23
'Then [Jesus] took a cup, and having offered thanks to God he gave it to them; and they all drank from it . . .'

Luke 22.17
'Then [Jesus] took a cup, and after giving thanks he said: "Take this and share it among yourselves . . ." '

Paul: 1 Corinthians 11.26–29
'. . . For every time you eat this bread and drink the cup, you proclaim the death of the Lord, till he comes. It follows that anyone who eats the bread or drinks the cup of the Lord unworthily will be guilty of desecrating the body and blood of the Lord. A man must test himself before eating his share of the bread and drinking from the cup . . .'

(All texts taken from the *New English Bible*.)

2. It is well settled that the canon law of the Church of England requires the priest to deliver the Sacrament to communicants in both kinds. The rubric in the BCP requires the priest to deliver it 'into their hands' and refers specifically to delivering both the bread and the cup; the rubric relating to the words to be said by the priest on delivering the cup is as follows:

'And the Minister that delivereth the Cup to any one shall say . . .'

3. This reflected the wording of Canon 21 of the 1603 Canons, which provided that:

'. . . the Minister shall deliver both the Bread and the Wine to each Communicant severally'.

That Canon has now been repealed, but the present Canon B 12 para 3 speaks of distributing the Holy Sacrament to the people.

4. Moreover, section 8 of the Sacrament Act 1547, which is still in force, provides that:

> '. . . the . . . most blessed Sacrament be hereafter commonly delivered and ministered unto the people . . . under both the kinds, that is to say of bread and wine, except necessity otherwise require . . .' [spelling modernized].

As regards the exception for necessity, see paragraph 10 below.

5. All the authors of commentaries on the BCP whose works are available to the Legal Advisory Commission emphasize the importance to be attached to the requirement that the priest should deliver the cup into the hands of each communicant. A. J. Stephens in his *Notes, Legal and Historical, on the Book of Common Prayer*, 1850, asserts, at p. 1098, that it was the practice of the primitive Church that the holy elements should be delivered into the hands of the communicants, and cites much authority in proof. C. Wheatly, *Book of Common Prayer*, 1858 edn, p. 354 makes the same assertion. Percy Dearmer, in *The Parson's Handbook*, 1903 edn, p. 274, gives practical directions on the reception of the cup by communicants. Prebendary Reynolds in his *Handbook to the BCP*, 2nd edn, 1907 at p. 297 says:

> 'The people are directed to take the cup into their hands: those who from a mistaken idea of reverence avoid doing so are breaking the rule of the Church and ancient custom.'

Wheatly (op. cit. p. 355) gives an account of a practice which grew up after St Cyril's time:

> 'And in some few ages afterwards some indiscreet persons pretending greater reverence to the Elements, as if they were defiled with their hand, put themselves to the charges of providing little saucers or plates of gold to receive the bread, until they were forbidden by the Sixth General Council.'

6. Thus the well-established practice of the Church of England, enjoined by the rubrics in the BCP following ancient custom and reflected in canon law and statute, is that the Holy Sacrament, in both kinds, should be delivered into the hands of the communicants. This custom of the Church of England was recognized in the ASB. Rite B provided for alternative ways of administration; in the second way, at section 39, there is a rubric as follows:

'One of the ministers then delivers the cup to each communicant saying . . . The blood of Christ.'

7. The rubrics of the BCP clearly contemplate that there is to be administration to each communicant in a common cup. (This was also true of the wording of the ASB; *Common Worship* is silent on the matter.) This mode of distribution is important, as it ensures that all communicants are treated without distinction and is an outward and visible sign of unity. However, the rubrics in the BCP require that all parishioners shall communicate at Easter, and the use of a single chalice would not normally be sufficient to ensure a seemly and orderly service on that occasion. It is therefore considered that the use of more than one chalice, for administration by more than one minister and with a number of communicants receiving from each chalice, is lawful where the number of communicants warrants it. On that basis, there is also no objection to one or more chalices being replenished by a flagon in which wine has been consecrated.

8. The Legal Advisory Commission's answer to the question posed in paragraph 1 is in the negative, whether the Holy Communion is celebrated in accordance with the rite in the BCP or *Common Worship*. To administer the consecrated wine in the manner indicated in the question would be unlawful in that the priest would be departing from establishing liturgical custom, which custom is enjoined by, or conformable to, the forms of service authorized for use (see Canon B 1). In the Legal Advisory Commission's view Canon B 5 para 1, which permits the minister in his discretion to 'make and use variations which are not of substantial importance' in any authorized form of service, does not authorize a variation such as is envisaged in the question. However, the Commission's answer is not to be taken as suggesting that the practice in some cathedral and parish churches of consecrating the wine in a flagon, to be poured into chalices for administration by more than one minister, is canonically irregular.

9. Some further points may be made:

(a)   If the priest drinks from the chalice or flagon in which the wine is consecrated, as presumably is proposed, the priest would be thereby making a difference between priest and other communicants which itself would be contrary to the tradition of the Church of England.

(b)   The suggested practice would raise a serious difficulty over the ablution of the vessels into which the consecrated wine was poured. Are these to be washed by the priest – and if so how and when? Or taken away to be washed by each communicant? If the latter is proposed such a practice would be contrary to well settled liturgical custom.

(c) Who provides the individual cups? If the communicants, how can a seemly uniformity be ensured? If it is not, some will be of gold, others silver, glass, pottery and plastic; again mischievous distinctions will occur. If the parish provides the cups many practical difficulties may occur which the present simple custom of the Church avoids.

10. The particular congregation in respect of which the question posed in paragraph 1 was raised was said to find the practice of intinction unacceptable. The practice of intinction may be regarded as lawful where a communicant or the congregation as a whole is fearful of contracting or communicating a contagious disease through drinking from the cup. Such a departure, viz. by the practice of intinction, from the general custom of the Church of England may be justified by the doctrine of necessity. This is expressly recognized by section 8 of the Sacrament Act 1547 (see para 4 above) because, it is thought, communicants were unwilling to drink from a common cup in times of plague.

11. There is a way of administering the elements by intinction which is consistent with the custom and law mentioned above. The priest delivers the bread into the hand of the communicant who then dips the bread into the cup, which is so held by the priest or another priest or deacon or any other person duly authorized to do so, immediately following the priest, that the communicant may lay his or her other hand upon it while dipping the bread.

(January 1991, revised September 2003)

Holy Communion: administration of the reserved Sacrament

1. Any deacon or lay person can be authorized by the bishop to distribute the Sacrament under Canon B 12 para 3, including distribution to sick people. This is so even though they cannot give absolution.

2. With regard to the ancient tradition of penitence followed by absolution before receiving communion, it is suggested that the bishop's authorization should provide that when the Sacrament is distributed by someone other than a priest and a BCP form of words is used, the communicant should make an act of penitence and the person administering the Sacrament should say some such prayer as the collect for Trinity XXI or XXIV in the BCP. Where the form of words used is taken from *Common Worship: Pastoral Services* the word 'us' rather than 'you' should be used in the absolution.

3. This advice does not apply to *Public Worship with Communion by Extension.*

(Revised September 2003)

Part 16

Marriage

Marriage

1. Incumbents and others concerned with the conduct of marriage services are advised to obtain a copy of the booklets *Suggestions for the Guidance of the Clergy with reference to the Marriage and Registration Acts &c* issued by the Registrar General, St Catherine's House, 10 Kingsway, London WC2B 6JP, and *Anglican Marriage in England and Wales – A Guide to the Law for the Clergy* issued by The Faculty Office, 1 The Sanctuary, Westminster, London SW1P 3JT.

Right to marry

2. Speaking generally, a person of the age of sixteen or above (Marriage Act 1949 ('MA'), s2; for those aged between 16 and 18, see para 11 below) has a legal right to be married after banns in his or her parish church or parish centre of worship or in the church on the electoral roll of which his or her name is entered (MA, s72(1)). A corresponding legal duty rests upon the clergy concerned to perform the marriage. This right and duty also applies to a person residing within the district of a public chapel licensed by the bishop for the marriage of persons residing within a certain district (MA, s20). It is the Commission's opinion that this right and duty arise under the common law and, in the absence of any remedy in the ecclesiastical courts, can be enforced by judicial review in the secular courts, if need be. However, it is subject to exceptions: *see* **Marriage: right of parishioner to marry in parish church.**

3. Where a parish has more then one parish church the bishop can give a direction under paragraph 14(4) of Schedule 3 to the Pastoral Measure 1983 as to the publication of banns or where marriages may be solemnized. If the bishop does not give such a direction, parishioners can specify in which parish church they wish their banns to be published and the marriage solemnized. If they do not do so, then in the opinion of the Legal Advisory Commission it is within the incumbent's discretion to decide in which of the several parish churches the banns should be published and the marriage later solemnized. Subject to any direction by the bishop under paragraph 14(4) of Schedule 3 to the Pastoral Measure 1983, the marriage must be solemnized in the parish church where the banns were published.

4. The marriage may be after publication of banns or by special or common licence (MA, s5(1)–(c)). Banns and common licences alike hold good for three months only (MA, ss12(2) and 16(3)). Marriage after banns or by common licence must be celebrated between 8.00 a.m. and 6.00 p.m. (MA, s4) (see paras 47–8 below). Marriage by special licence may be 'at any convenient time or place' (MA, s79(6)) subject to the terms

of the special licence itself. In the case of persons under eighteen (MA, s78(1) as amended by the Family Law Reform Act 1987) a marriage may not take place under the authority of a common licence or superintendent registrar's certificate without the consent of that person's parent or guardian (or permission of the court) (MA, s3(2)). Further, if a parent or guardian of a person under eighteen publicly declares his or her dissent from an intended marriage at the time of publication of banns of marriage, such publication is void and the marriage must not take place (MA, s3(3)).

Registration

5. After the marriage the officiating clergyman must register the marriage in duplicate register books provided by the Registrar General (MA, ss53–5). Copies of the registers are to be certified and sent to the Registrar General quarterly (MA, s57), and when the books are full, one must be sent to the Registrar General and the other kept by the incumbent with the registers of baptisms and burials (MA, s60).

Application for marriage

6. Under MA, section 8, notice of the intended marriage after banns must be given to the incumbent of the parish in which each party resides, and, if the marriage is to be solemnized outside the parish, in the usual place of worship of either of them, also to the incumbent of the parish on the electoral roll of which his or her name is entered. An incumbent may claim seven days' notice in writing by the parties, who have to give their Christian names and surnames, their respective abodes, and the time during which they have dwelt there. The particulars must be entered in a book provided for this purpose by the PCC, and the banns must be published from this book on three Sundays (MA, s7(1)). These need not be three successive Sundays, but the incumbent should give careful consideration to the desirability of publishing banns where there has been a very long interval between publications. If the incumbent considers the interval to be excessive, the incumbent should insist on starting the process again.

Publication of banns

7. The time for publication is during the morning service, but, if there is no morning service on a Sunday on which banns are to be published, publication may take place during evening service (MA, 27(1)). The form of words for publication in the BCP should be followed, but in cases of a marriage in a church which is the usual place of worship of one or both of the parties, it is permissible to substitute for the words 'of this parish', the

words 'on the electoral roll of this parish'. Certificates of publication must be produced to the incumbent of the church where the marriage is to take place before the marriage can be solemnized (MA, s11).

8. Under MA, section 9, where a clergyman does not officiate at the service at which it is usual in that church to publish banns, the publication may be made either:

(a)   by a clergyman at some other service at which the clergyman is present and at which banns may be published; or

(b)   by a lay person at the service at which it is usual to publish banns, subject to the following conditions:

    (i)   the publication must be made during a public reading authorized by the bishop of portions of Morning or Evening Prayer, such public reading being at the hour when the service at which banns are usually published is commonly held, unless the bishop authorizes otherwise; and

    (ii)   the incumbent or minister in charge or some other clerk in Holy Orders nominated by the bishop must, before the first publication, have made or authorized the making of the requisite entry in the register of banns.

9. Problems sometimes arise in relation to churches that are the subject of a sharing agreement under the Sharing of Church Buildings Act 1969, or churches in local ecumenical projects where the main morning service may not be a Church of England service, or may be a joint service. The view of the Legal Advisory Commission is that banns should, if possible, be published by a clergyman, and the publication will only be lawful if it is at a service performed according to the rites of the Church of England, or duly authorized by Canon. If banns are being published by a lay person the Legal Advisory Commission's view is that this may only be in the course of a service of Morning or Evening Prayer according to the rites of the Church of England.

10. A lay person or licensed church worker publishing banns must sign the register of banns, and for that purpose is deemed to be the officiating clergyman (MA, s9(3)). A certificate of due publication signed by the incumbent or minister in charge, or by some other clerk in Holy Orders nominated by the bishop, is equivalent to a like certificate given by a clerk in Holy Orders who has published banns (MA, s11(4)).

11. If an objection is made by a qualified parent or guardian when the banns of a minor are published, then the publication is void, and the incumbent should proceed no further with the calling of those banns. In all other cases where objection is made when banns are published the certificate of calling banns must be issued subject to endorsement or amendment clearly stating that an objection has been made, and the circumstances alleged must be fully investigated before a marriage ceremony takes place.

12. There is no need to state the parties' marital status when calling banns.

13. It is lawful for persons to marry in their parish church on the authority of a superintendent registrar's certificate rather than following the publication of banns. However, unlike marriages pursuant to banns, common licences and special licences, the member of the clergy is under no legal obligation to conduct such a marriage if he or she does not consent to do so (MA, s17).

Publication of banns of a divorced person

14. The publication of banns may not be refused on the grounds that one or both parties are divorced and have a former spouse still living. The statutory duty to publish banns set out in MA section 6 is not subject to the Matrimonial Causes Act 1965 section 8(2) which enables a member of the clergy to refuse to solemnize a marriage in such circumstances.

15. If at the time of calling of banns a person has not yet had his existing marriage dissolved by decree absolute, then at that time an impediment to marriage exists. Nevertheless, the publication of banns in such circumstances is both valid and obligatory. However it is also essential to ensure that the existing marriage has been dissolved by decree absolute before any further marriage takes place. The Legal Advisory Commission's advice to clergy who are given notice to publish banns by a divorced or divorcing person is to request production of the original sealed decree absolute before publishing banns, if the person requesting agrees to provide it. If the decree is not produced, or has not yet been pronounced, this fact should be recorded on the certificate of banns, to put the clergyman due to celebrate the marriage on notice of a potential difficulty.

Marriage by licence

16. Marriage may also take place upon a licence obtained from the Ordinary; in practice this licence is obtained by application to the

diocesan registrar or a Surrogate. Such a licence is, in fact, a dispensation from the necessity of publishing banns. The procedure is laid down by MA, sections 15 and 16. In some cases a special licence can be obtained from the Archbishop of Canterbury enabling a marriage to be solemnized at any convenient time and place in either Province (see MA, s79(6)).

17. In cases where the superintendent registrar's certificate takes the place of publication of banns or the marriage is by licence, regard must be had to the consents required by MA, section 3, and to the various dispensing powers thereby given which enable the court to override refusals to consent. It is obvious that difficulties may easily arise in ascertaining whether the proper consents have been given, and in any such case the minister should act with caution, and consult the diocesan registrar in case of doubt.

One party a foreigner

18. (a)   Where one of the parties is a foreign national or has his or her permanent home outside the UK there is a possibility that the marriage may not be recognized in his or her home country. In practice this problem has not been encountered in the case of nationals of EU countries, or of Australia, Canada, New Zealand, South Africa and the United States. In all other cases, however, the parties should be told that the Church recommends that enquiries should be made, to ascertain whether a marriage in accordance with the rites and ceremonies of the Church of England will be recognized as a valid marriage in the foreign national's home country.

(b)   It is also recommended that all marriages involving foreign nationals (except the citizens of the countries specifically mentioned above) should be by licence, even if banns are legally possible. In the case of a common licence this will enable the diocesan registrar to ascertain whether sufficient enquiries have been made, and their result, before authorizing the marriage to proceed. It is understood that a Special Licence will not normally be issued unless the application is accompanied by a letter from the relevant embassy or consulate confirming that a marriage of one of its citizens in accordance with the rites and ceremonies of the Church of England, will be recognized in the country in question.

(c)   The parties can also obtain a superintendent registrar's certificate. It should be noted, however, that since 1 January

2001 a person who is visiting England for the purpose of marriage by superintendent registrar's certificate will need to satisfy the residential qualification of 7 days, and then wait a further 15 clear days before he or she will be eligible to marry. However, section 19 of the Asylum and Immigration (Treatment of Claimants etc) Act 2004 prevents a certificate being issued where one party is subject to immigration control unless certain additional requirements are met, including in the usual case written permission from the Secretary of State to marry in the United Kingdom. [This Opinion was settled before the decision in *R (on the application of Baiai and others) v Secretary of State for the Home Department* [2006] EWHC 1035 (Admin).]

(d)   The 2004 Act does not apply where the preliminaries to marriage are in the forms of banns or a common or special licence. The Commission recommends that all cases which would fall within section 19 were a superintendent registrar's certificate sought should be referred to the diocesan registrar and (where the chancellor has so directed) be considered by the chancellor. The grant of a licence is discretionary and it would be proper to take into account whether the parties were baptized or had some other church connection; whether they genuinely intended to live together as a married couple; and whether there was evidence that they genuinely desired marriage according to the rites of the Church of England and were not simply seeking to avoid the need to comply with section 19.

One or both parties divorced

19. No member of the clergy of the Church of England may be compelled to solemnize the marriage of a divorced person whose former spouse is still living, nor may he or she be compelled to permit the use of the church or chapel of which he or she is the minister for the solemnization of such a marriage (Matrimonial Causes Act 1965, s8(2)). The effect of the 1965 Act is to leave the decision as to whether or not to exercise the conscientious right of objection under section 8(2) in a particular case to the relevant member of the clergy alone, thus the Church cannot require him or her to act in a particular way, either in an individual case by imposing a requirement to apply certain criteria or follow certain procedures.

20. The Marriage Resolutions embodied in an Act of the Convocation of Canterbury dating from 1957 and the Marriage Resolutions adopted by

the Convocation of York in 1938 both stated that the Church should not allow the use of the Marriage Service in the case of a person whose previous marriage had ended in divorce and the former partner was still living. Those provisions were rescinded as from 14 November 2003. The House of Bishops has issued advice to the Clergy to assist them in reaching decisions on such cases.

Marriage of persons residing in a parish with a parish centre of worship

21. If a building is designated as a parish centre of worship under section 29(1) of the Pastoral Measure 1983 it is deemed to be a parish church for the purpose of the MA. Banns of persons resident in the parish will normally be called, and marriages solemnized in that building. However, section 29(3) of the Measure provides that:

> 'Where . . . a building . . . has been so designated [i.e. as a parish centre of worship] and the parish has no parish church, then, if the parties to be married so elect, they may proceed . . . as if the . . . building . . . had not been so designated; and this subsection shall have effect notwithstanding that there is in the parish . . . a church or chapel in which divine service is usually solemnized every Sunday.'

22. The effect of this is that, if the election is made, the parish with the parish centre of worship is treated as being a parish without a parish church. The fact that there may be a 'church or chapel in which divine service is usually solemnized every Sunday' (the parish centre of worship) is disregarded for the purpose of MA, section 6(3), with the result that the parish with the parish centre of worship is 'deemed to belong to any adjoining parish or chapelry'. If an election is made, therefore, the parish with the parish centre of worship is treated as if it were part of the adjoining parish for the purpose of both banns and the solemnization of marriage.

23. It follows from this that persons residing in a parish that has a parish centre of worship and no parish church, may be married either in the parish centre of worship or, if they so elect, in the parish church of an adjoining parish. It is the couple being married who have the right to make the election, i.e. to choose, and not their incumbent, or the incumbent of the adjoining parish.

Residential qualifications

24. The qualification to marry in a particular place, and requirements as to the calling of banns, depend very much upon where a person lives. This

is not always easy to determine. The wording of the statute depends on the type of preliminary being used:

> '[the] parish in which one of [the parties] resides' (banns: MA, s6(1));

> 'the parish . . . in which one of the persons to be married has had his or her usual place of residence for fifteen days immediately before the grant of the licence' (common licence: MA, s15(1)(a));

> 'a registration district in which one of the persons to be married has resided . . . for the period of seven days immediately before the giving of the notice of marriage' (superintendent registrar's certificate: MA, s34).

25. Two questions commonly arise in considering whether the statutory requirement of residence is satisfied: these concern:

(a)   the person who claims an address at his or her 'home' even though, in physical terms, living somewhere else; and

(b)   the person who arrives in a parish expressly in order to marry there, and so is physically resident at the relevant date or dates but may have no intention to make a permanent base in the parish.

Common licence

26. So far as situation (a) is concerned, the words 'usual place of residence' in the common licence test suggest that a generous approach should be taken to temporary absences; a person may usually live in a place even though not physically living there at present. Students who live in college or hall during term time, or people away on holiday or on an employment-related tour of duty abroad, may still be usually resident in a parish to which they intend to return. The person in situation (b) would lose out by this approach, since stress laid on the word 'usual' might lead to the conclusion that although living in the parish in question, this was not the usual situation and the 'usual' residence remained elsewhere.

27. Against this, however, there is the fifteen-day period; on one view this suggests that one must focus solely on this period and ask what was 'usual' for the person during that time. This would operate against the person in situation (a), because during the fifteen days it might be usual for him or her to be in college or on board ship. It would favour the person in

situation (b) because during the fifteen days it would be 'usual' for him or her to be in bed-and-breakfast accommodation in the parish.

28. What is clear is that howsoever the test is to be expressed, it must be satisfied at the start of the fifteen days, and at the end, and throughout the intervening period.

29. It is also clear that on either view of the test, it is not satisfied by someone who is physically absent from the parish (i.e. not in situation (b)) if that person, although having lived there some time previously, has established a permanent base elsewhere to such an extent that a return to the parish is in the nature of a 'visit' (e.g. to parents) rather than 'going home'. A member of the Armed Forces, a sailor, an oil rig worker, or a diplomat, for example, may have nowhere else to go on leave than the parental home, and will still be 'going home' when going there on leave. So will a student who is turned out of a hall of residence during vacations. A room in the parental home regarded as his or her room, containing the student's possessions and unoccupied during terms, would support this view, though it would not be conclusive on its own.

30. A student who shares a house in the university town and lives there all the year round may, by contrast, be just a visitor when going to stay with his or her parents, in which case the usual residence is in the university town. The same reasoning applies *a fortiori* to people who have embarked upon a career away from the parental home or who have cohabited elsewhere for some time before having the marriage solemnized.

Superintendent registrar's certificate

31. The superintendent registrar's certificate requirement, like the common licence requirement, has a specified period during which it must be satisfied. However, during that period the person is required to 'reside' not to 'have a usual place of residence'. The person in situation (b) above would almost certainly satisfy this test. The person in situation (a) would be in more difficulty; but guidelines issued to civil registrars instruct them to treat as 'resident' persons who are temporarily absent from a home within the district, but who retain a room there for their use and their belongings, and return there when opportunity offers.

Banns

32. Uniquely, the residence requirement for banns does not have to be satisfied over a stated period, but simply at one instant in time (that is, the moment when the prescribed application for the calling of banns is given to the minister of the parish or to someone acting for the minister). The considerations mentioned above under 'common licences' apply here in

reverse: the absence of the word 'usual' may suggest that actual physical residence is enough; but if this is wrong and 'residence' has to have an element of performance, looking at a status at one moment in time defeats any argument that such permanence need only last over a defined period.

Conclusion

33. Although it has been possible to give some clear guidelines in this section, the law on residence is clearly susceptible of more than one interpretation. The view of the Legal Advisory Commission is that the word 'resides' for banns and superintendent registrar's certificate requires a physical presence and occupation of premises as a home. This need not be a permanent arrangement, but it must subsist at the relevant time. For common licences, the Legal Advisory Commission's view is that 'usual place of residence' does not require a physical presence but there must throughout the fifteen day period be a place within the parish which can properly be regarded as the home of the person in question. In the final analysis, clergy will have to form their own conclusions on whether a genuine local residence has been shown, based on common sense and (in the case of common licences) directions and guidelines given by the bishop and/or vicar-general of each diocese.

Note: Paragraphs 24 to 33 are adapted from the corresponding section, with which the Legal Advisory Commission agrees, in *Anglican Marriage in England and Wales – A Guide to the Law for the Clergy* (1992) (see para 1 above).

Marriages of retired clerks in Holy Orders

34. A clerk in Holy Orders cannot have his or her name entered on the electoral roll of a parish. As entry on the electoral roll is a requirement of MA, section 72(1), a retired clerk in Holy Orders who wishes to be married in a church which is his or her usual place of worship and which is not the parish church of either party, and where the other party is not on the electoral roll of that church, can do so only under the authority of a special licence.

Marriage in cathedrals

35. Although the Cathedrals Measure 1999 removed many of the distinctions between 'parish church cathedrals' and 'dean and Chapter cathedrals', it is relevant for present purposes whether or not the cathedral has a parish. If it has, the cathedral, as far as civil and canon law concerning the solemnization of marriages is concerned, is in the same position as any other parish church. People living within the parish or

whose names are on the electoral roll may be married in the cathedral either by common licence or by banns.

36. A cathedral without a parish is an extra-parochial place, together with its precincts, and may be authorized by the bishop as an authorized church or chapel where marriages may be solemnized according to the rites of the Church of England (MA, s21).

37. In exercising his authority under section 21, the bishop should authorize the publication of banns and solemnization of marriages by banns or licence in the cathedral church between parties both or either of whom reside in the close or precincts. Marriages may also be solemnized in the cathedral, if it is authorized under section 21, on the authority of a superintendent registrar's certificate, provided the consent of the dean and Chapter is given (MA, s17). If the cathedral has not been authorized under section 21, then a marriage may only be solemnized in it on the authority of a special licence obtained from the Archbishop of Canterbury.

38. Although the point is not beyond doubt, the opinion of the Legal Advisory Commission is that a list of persons who are habitual worshippers at a cathedral church, prepared for the purposes of a scheme under rule 27 of the CRR, is not an electoral roll for the purposes of the law of marriage, and consequently persons (unless they reside in the close or precincts) whose names are on such a list may not be married in the cathedral after banns even if it is an authorized church or chapel. The same appears to be true of a roll of members of the cathedral community maintained under section 9 of the Cathedrals Measure 1999.

Service in a foreign language

39. Where an English person is marrying a foreigner who is not resident in England and does not speak English, or where the first language of the two people to be married and/or of the congregation is not English, then:

(a)   The whole service must be in accordance with the rites and ceremonies of the Church of England and must therefore be conducted in English (Canon B 42 'Of the Language of Divine Service' generally requires all services prescribed in and by the BCP to be said or sung 'in the vulgar tongue'): a regular marriage would not be solemnized if the whole service were to be conducted in a foreign language only.

(b)   The officiating clergyman is obliged to endeavour to ensure that the persons to be married understand the service. Therefore, where one or both persons to be married do not understand English the minister he must ensure that the essential parts which include the charge, promises and vows are translated by an interpreter into a language which he, she or they do understand. The Legal Advisory Commission strongly advises that the clergyman chooses the interpreter independently, that the interpreter is not a relative or friend of the couple, and that the interpreter should sign the marriage register as one of the witnesses.

(c)   Where the majority of a worshipping congregation of a parish do not understand English, and have a common tongue, then the calling of banns should be announced in both English and the common tongue.

(d)   There is one statutory exception to the whole service being conducted in English. In any place in which the Welsh language is commonly used, the authorized translation into Welsh of the declaratory and contracting words (which may be found in the Registration of Marriages (Welsh Language) Regulations 1986, SI 1986/1445) may be used if the parties wish.

(e)   Latin may be used in the Convocations, colleges and halls in the universities, university churches, the colleges of Westminster, Winchester, and Eton, and in 'such other places of religious and sound learning as custom allows or the bishop or other the Ordinary may permit'; other foreign languages or the British Sign Language with written permission of the bishop (Canon B 42 paras 2, 3 and 4).

Marriage in Anglican churches according to the rites of the Roman Catholic Church and other Non-Anglican Churches

40. A question that is often asked is whether it is possible for an Anglican church that is not the subject of a sharing agreement under the Sharing of Church Buildings Act 1969 to be used for the solemnization of marriages according to the rites of the Roman Catholic Church or some other non-Anglican Church.

41. A Roman Catholic marriage in this country must be preceded by civil preliminaries and take place in a registered building. Under MA, section 41(1), a building cannot be registered for the solemnization of marriages unless it has been certified as a place of religious worship, i.e. certified to the Registrar General through the appropriate superintendent registrar pursuant to the Places of Worship Registration Act 1855, and section 10

of the 1855 Act precludes the certification of churches or chapels of the Church of England, except where there is a sharing agreement under the 1969 Act. Consequently, a Church of England church is not, and cannot be, a registered building in which Roman Catholic or other non-Anglican marriages can take place.

42. There are further difficulties with regard to registration; for example, MA, section 53 (which prescribed the persons by whom marriages are to be registered) makes no provision for a registrar or an authorized person to register marriages solemnized in Anglican churches. This reflects the fact that the law makes no provision for a marriage to take place in an Anglican church otherwise than in accordance with the rites of the Church of England, and a marriage according to the rites of the Roman Catholic Church, or any other Church, can only take place in an Anglican church that is the subject of a sharing agreement under the 1969 Act.

Non-Anglican minister assisting at marriage according to the rites and ceremonies of the Church of England

43. Another question that is often asked is what parts of the marriage service must be taken by a clerk in Holy Orders of the Church of England in order for a legally valid marriage, as provided for in the MA, to be contracted.

(a) Section 3(b) of the Church of England (Ecumenical Relations) Measure 1988 states that:

'No person shall, unless he is a clerk in Holy Orders of the Church of England, solemnize a marriage according to the rites of the Church of England.'

(b) Canon B 43 para 1(1)(e) provides that:

'A minister or lay person who is a member in good standing of a Church to which this Canon applies and is a baptised person may, subject to the provisions of this Canon, be invited . . . to assist at . . . the Solemnization of Matrimony . . . if the minister or lay person is authorised to perform a similar duty in his or her own Church.'

(c) 'Solemnize' means 'to perform the ceremony of marriage' (see *Shorter Oxford Dictionary*), in a canonically regular way.

(d) In the notes to the *Common Worship* service, note 13 on 'ecumenical considerations' provides as follows:

'Where a minister of another Christian Church is invited to assist at the Solemnization of Matrimony, the permissions and procedures set out in Canon B 43 are to be followed. The Church of England minister who solemnizes the marriage must establish the absence of impediment, direct the exchange of vows, declare the existence of the marriage, say the final blessing, and sign the registers. A minister invited to assist may say all or part of the opening address, lead the declarations of intent, supervise the exchange of rings, and join in the blessing of the marriage. He or she may also read a lesson and lead all or part of the prayers. Where the couple come from different Christian communions the bishop may authorize such variations to the marriage service as are set out in *An Order for the Marriage of Christians from Different Churches*, which is published separately.'

Solemnization by clergy of the Scottish Episcopal Church or Church of Ireland

44. The Episcopal Church (Scotland) Act 1964, section 1(1), makes it lawful for a clergyman of the Scottish Episcopal Church '. . . to officiate . . . in a church or chapel belonging to the Church of England . . . subject to the same conditions as would be applicable to him if he had been admitted into Holy Orders by the Bishop of a Diocese in the Church of England'. In *Halsbury's Laws of England*, 4th edn, 2003 re-issue, p. 628, the editorial comment on the section states '. . . this section puts Scots Episcopal Ministers into the same position, within the provinces of Canterbury and York, as clergymen of the Church of England'. Relying on this provision, the Legal Advisory Commission's opinion is that it is lawful for a priest of the Scottish Episcopal Church to solemnize a marriage in England, according to the rites and ceremonies of the Church of England, and to sign the marriage register to that effect: such a clergyman does not require any permission from either the Archbishop of the Province or the bishop of the diocese but can simply rely on the terms of the 1964 Act.

45. Under section 1 of the Church of England (Miscellaneous Provisions) Measure 1995, clergy of the Church of Ireland are now in the same position.

Fees for marriages in schools, hospitals and other institutions

46. As has been noted, the incumbent may direct that the fee due to the incumbent is to be payable to whoever actually solemnizes the marriage, provided, of course, that the incumbent has not assigned fees to the DBF.

If the incumbent does not make this direction then the chaplain may request an additional non-statutory fee for solemnizing the wedding.

Timing of services

47. Both civil and ecclesiastical law (MA, s4 and Canon B 35 para 3) require a marriage service (excepting where the authority to marry is a special licence) to be solemnized – i.e. completed – before 6.00 p.m. The clergyman must say the whole rite and perform the whole ceremony (one of the authorized marriage services) by 6.00 p.m. The registration of the marriage is required by MA, section 55(1), to be made immediately after the solemnization of the marriage: this may, therefore, take place after 6.00 pm.

48. It is unlikely that an offence would be committed as to time unless there is a conscious and deliberate breach of the requirements. If circumstances warrant, all hymns, psalms, and the sermon or homily might be omitted, but it is advisable that a service is not arranged to begin later than 5.00 p.m. The fact that a marriage was solemnized outside the permitted hours would not affect its validity, but it would be legally irregular, and a member of the clergy should not celebrate a marriage in breach of the statutory requirement.

(Revised 2003)

Marriage: definition of 'the minister' for the purposes of the Matrimonial Causes Act 1965 section 8(2)(b)

1. Section 8(2) of the Matrimonial Causes Act 1965 reads as follows:

'No clergyman of the Church of England or the Church in Wales shall be compelled –

(a)   to solemnise the marriage of any person whose former marriage has been dissolved and whose former spouse is still living; or

(b)   to permit the marriage of such a person to be solemnised in the church or chapel of which he is *the minister.*'

2. The protection given by section 8(2)(b) is protection from being 'compelled to permit' the solemnization of a marriage. Therefore only someone who has the authority to permit a marriage to take place can be protected from such compulsion. Those with no authority to permit a marriage to take place in a particular church cannot be compelled to permit it as any such 'permission' given would be invalid.

3. In the Canons of the Church of England it is clearly established that it is the minister having the cure of souls in any place who has the authority to permit or refuse others to officiate in the place where he has such cure. Canon C 8 para 4 provides:

'No minister who has such authority to exercise his ministry in any diocese [i.e. authority conferred by the bishop by institution or admission under licence] shall do so therein in any place in which he has not the cure of souls *without the permission of the minister having such cure,* except at the homes of persons whose names are entered on the electoral roll of the parish which he serves and to the extent authorised by the Extra-Parochial Ministry Measure 1967, or in a university, college, school, hospital, or public or charitable institution in which he is licensed to officiate as provided by the said Measure and Canon B 41 or, in relation to funeral services, as provided by section 2 of the Church of England (Miscellaneous Provisions) Measure 1992.'

4. Canon C 24 para 1 also presumes that 'the minister of a church' is the person with the cure of souls. It reads:

'Every priest having a cure of souls shall provide that, in the absence of reasonable hindrance, Morning and Evening Prayer daily and on appointed days the Litany shall be said in the church, or one of the churches, of which he is *the minister.*'

Canon C 24 para 3 also makes a similar link between 'the minister' and the priest having cure of souls.

5. This understanding is supported by the language used in the Marriage Act 1949 (as amended). Section 5A of that statute is as follows:

'No clergyman [defined as a clerk in Holy Orders in the Church of England] shall be obliged:

(a)   . . . to solemnise a marriage which, apart from the Marriage (Prohibited Degrees of Relationship) Act 1986, would have been void by reason of the relationship of the persons to be married; or

(b)   to permit such marriage to be solemnised in the church or chapel of which he is *the minister.*'

6. Unless there are good reasons to suggest otherwise, where the same phrase is used in related legislation it should be understood as having the same meaning. (See for example *Effort Shipping Co Ltd v Linden Management SA* [1998] 1 All ER 495 at 512 and *Wellcome Trust Ltd v Hamad* [1998] 1 All ER 657 at 669.) Elsewhere in the 1949 Act reference is made to the 'officiating clergyman' with regard to duties regarding the publication of banns. There is therefore a distinction contained within this statute between the person who is conducting the service, the 'officiating clergyman', and the person with authority to permit services to take place, that is, the 'minister' of the church or chapel. This is underlined by section 17 under which marriage on the authority of a superintendent registrar's certificate 'shall not be solemnised in any church or chapel without the consent of *the minister* thereof'.

Incumbents

7. Save during a vacancy, the cure of souls in a parish is held by the incumbent or, where there is a team ministry, by the team rector and team vicars together (subject to any specific responsibility in certain areas as provided for by the scheme creating the team ministry).

8. Therefore, subject to the position of a team ministry (see below), where an incumbent gives permission to a third party to officiate whether at a wedding or any other service no other person, whether assistant curate, PCC member, churchwarden, etc. has the authority to veto that permission.

Interregnum

9. The question then arises: who exercises the authority to permit other clergy to officiate during an interregnum?

10. With regard to ministry generally Canon C 8 para 2(a) provides:

> 'The minister having cure of souls of a church or chapel or the sequestrator when the cure is vacant . . . may allow any minister concerning whom they are satisfied either by actual personal knowledge or by good and sufficient evidence that he is of good life and standing and otherwise qualified under this Canon, to minister within their church or chapel for a period of not more than seven days within three months without reference to the bishop . . .'

11. Therefore in an interregnum it is the sequestrator that has authority to permit other clergy to officiate, and by implication to conduct weddings of divorcees. The sequestrators are the churchwardens, the rural dean and such other persons as may be appointed by the bishop: Church of England (Miscellaneous Provisions) Measure 1992 section 1. However, it is only a 'clergyman' who is referred to in the 1965 Act. Unlike the rural dean and any other clergyman appointed by the bishop, therefore, any lay sequestrators are not protected by the 1965 legislation because they are not clergymen. It is only the conscience of the ordained person that is protected by the statute, not that of lay persons.

12. This reflects the fact that it was 'the minister' of any church or chapel who was compelled to permit another clergyman to officiate at the remarriage of divorcees under the earlier legislation; namely the Matrimonial Causes Act 1857 and the Supreme Court of Judicature (Consolidation) Act 1925. For example section 182(3) of the 1925 Act provided:

> 'If any minister of any church or chapel of the Church of England refuses to perform the marriage service between any persons who but for his refusal would be entitled to have the service performed in that church or chapel, he shall permit any other minister of the Church of England entitled to officiate within the diocese in which the church or chapel is situate to perform the marriage service in that church or chapel.'

13. It was this compulsion that was repealed by the enactment of the terms of the Matrimonial Causes Act 1937 which now appear in the 1965 Act. There has never been legislation which *compelled* sequestrators to permit clergy to conduct particular services.

14. During an interregnum the bishop may also appoint a priest-in-charge. This may be a short appointment pending the induction of a new incumbent, or it may be a long term post where the freehold has been suspended (e.g. under the Pastoral Measure 1983).

15. A priest-in-charge has the same rights and duties in respect of the services in the church and the cure of souls as the incumbent. *Pinder v Barr* (1854) E & B 105. (See also Leeder, *Ecclesiastical Law Handbook*, para 7.22.) In determining the extent of the duties of a priest-in-charge under Canon 91 of the 1603 Canons (which referred to 'the minister of the church for the time being') Coleridge J said,

> 'It appears to us that, by the words "parson" "vicar" "minister" the canon intends to describe the functionary, whatever title he may bear, who for the time being has the cure of the parish as principal. In some senses a mere stipendiary or assistant curate might be described as the minister; but, being so only as representing another person who is the real incumbent, he is not properly the minister of the parish.'

16. On the basis of this case, a priest-in-charge may be properly regarded as 'the minister' of a church or chapel and therefore fall within the ambit of section 8(2)(b) of the 1965 Act.

Assistant clergy

17. Assistant clergy, who have neither the office of incumbent nor are licensed as a priest-in-charge with authority equivalent to an incumbent, cannot be regarded as 'the minister' of the relevant church or chapel within the meaning of section 8(2)(b) because they do not have the authority to permit others to minister there. Rather, they minister there themselves with the permission of the incumbent, priest-in-charge or the sequestrators. Moreover, it is appropriate to interpret the exemption contained in section 8(2)(b) as narrowly as is properly consonant with the plain and natural meaning of the words of the section, as it contains a clergy privilege the exercise of which restricts the legal rights of people to have their marriage solemnized in their parish church.

Group ministries

18. Section 21 of the Pastoral Measure 1983 states:

> '(1) A pastoral scheme may provide for establishing for a group of benefices specified in the scheme a group ministry to which the following provisions shall apply:–

(a) each of the incumbents of the benefices in the group shall have authority to perform in the area of every such benefice all such offices and services as may be performed by the incumbent of that benefice;

(b) the incumbent of any such benefice shall, in performing such offices and services in the area of another benefice, act in accordance with the directions of the incumbent of that other benefice;

(c) it shall be the duty of all the incumbents to assist each other so far as to make the best possible provision for the cure of souls throughout the area of the group ministry.'

Thus, although each incumbent has the duty to assist each other to make the best possible provision for the cure of souls throughout the area of the group ministry and each incumbent has authority to perform all such offices and services as may be performed by the incumbent of that benefice, it is expressly provided that in performing such offices and services in the area of another benefice the incumbent from the neighbouring benefice shall 'act in accordance with the directions of the incumbent' of the benefice in which he is operating.

19. It follows that in a group ministry an incumbent can direct whether in his own benefice another incumbent (or, indeed, any other clergyman) may celebrate a marriage of a divorced person; similarly, he can direct whether one of the other incumbents in the group ministry may permit other ministers to solemnize such a marriage. In effect he has a veto over fellow incumbents within the group.

Team ministries

20. However the position is different in relation to team ministries.

21. The key statutory provisions are sections 20(1), (7) and (8) of the Pastoral Measure. These provide:

'(1) A pastoral scheme may make provision for the establishment of a team ministry for the area of any benefice, and such a scheme shall provide –

(a) for the sharing of the cure of souls in that area by the incumbent of the benefice . . . and one or more ministers who shall have the title of vicar and a status equal to that of an incumbent of a benefice; and

(b) for the pastoral care of persons in that area by those who are to share the cure of souls therein together with all other persons who are for time to time authorised . . . to serve in that area as members of the team . . .

(7) The rector in a team ministry shall have a general responsibility for the cure of souls in the area of the benefice, which may be subject to any special cure of special responsibility given to a vicar as hereinafter provided, and shall be responsible for the leadership of the team; and the scheme may make further provision as to the relationship of the rector and other members of the team ministry.

(8) A vicar in a team ministry shall by virtue of his office, but subject to his licence, have authority to perform in the area of the benefice all such offices and services as may be performed by an incumbent, and the scheme or, subject to the scheme, the bishop's licence may –

(a) assign to a vicar a special cure of souls in respect of a part of the said area and, if appropriate, the name of vicar of a church in that part;

(b) assign to a vicar a special responsibility for a particular pastoral function;

(c) provide that any such special cure or responsibility shall be independent of the rector's general responsibility;

(d) assign to a vicar a general responsibility to be shared with the rector for a cure of souls in the area as a whole . . .'

22. To determine the respective rights and responsibilities within a team ministry, the first point of reference must be provisions of the scheme itself together with any bishop's licence issued under it, as under section 20(8) of the Pastoral Measure the licence may designate specific responsibilities for part of the benefice or a particular pastoral function.[1]

---

[1] A special cure of souls or other similar responsibilities can also be assigned to a team vicar under a pastoral order: Pastoral Measure 1983, section 37(e).

If the scheme gives a team vicar[2] a special cure of souls of the relevant church or chapel independent of the rector's general responsibility under section 20(7)(8)(c), then only that team vicar may give permission for a marriage to be solemnized there. In addition, the scheme may provide under section 20(8)(b) that one team vicar has 'a special responsibility' for permitting marriages to take place. In both of these circumstances section 8(2)(b) of the 1965 Act can only apply to the team vicar given that special responsibility.

23. Section 20(1) states that the scheme 'shall provide . . . for the sharing of the cure of souls' in the area of the team ministry. Therefore, subject to any specific designation of responsibilities under section 20(8) of the Pastoral Measure,[3] the cure of souls is in the team rector and the team vicars together. This being so, in the absence of any such specific determination, the team rector or any of the team vicars may give permission for the marriage of divorced persons. Section 8(2)(b) of the Matrimonial Causes Act 1965 applies to each of them. However, the team rector is under a duty to convene regular meetings 'for the purpose of discussing and reaching a common mind on all matters of general concern or special interest to the team ministry': see section 20(10). If the team members cannot reach a common mind on the question of the remarriage of divorcees,[4] it seems that it may be permitted by any one of them. Subject to any specific designation of responsibilities, no team member has the right of veto.

Summary

1. The provisions of section 8(2)(a) of the Matrimonial Causes Act 1965 apply to all the clergy.

2. The provisions of section 8(2)(b) apply to sole incumbents and clergy sequestrators but not to assistant clergy or to lay sequestrators.

3. Within a group ministry the provisions of section 8(2)(b) apply to an incumbent within his own benefice.

---

[2] Although the Interpretation Act 1978 section 6 provides that 'words in the singular include the plural' unless 'the contrary intention appears', it seems likely that section 20(8)(a)(c) can only apply to one team vicar because of the words 'and, if appropriate, the name of vicar of a church in that part'.

[3] Or section 37(e).

[4] Some of the issues over the application of section 8(2)(b) to team ministries arise from the fact that the origins of both section 8(2) and the relevant canon law provisions referred to in this Opinion predate the origins of the law on team ministries.

4. Within a team ministry, a pastoral scheme (or order) or, subject to the scheme, the bishop's licence, may make special provision as to who may permit the remarriage of divorced persons (Pastoral Measure 1983 s20(8)(b) and (c) and s37(e)). If such provision is made, it is definitive as to the application of section 8(2)(b) of the 1965 Act. Otherwise section 8(2)(b) of the Matrimonial Causes Act 1965 applies to the team rector and each of the team vicars individually.

(2005)

Marriage: right of parishioner to marry in parish church

Introduction

1. The parishioner's right to marry, and the corresponding duty on the minister to solemnize the marriage, derive from the common law. The authorities, beginning with *Argar v Holdsworth* (1758) 2 Lee 515, are usefully brought together in Bursell, *Liturgy, Order and the Law*, 1996, at pp. 181–3. So far as the textbook-writers are concerned, Phillimore, *Ecclesiastical Law*, 2nd edn, 1895, at p. 605, acknowledges the right and duty, and Cripps, *The Law relating to Church and Clergy*, 8th edn, 1937, at p. 558, states robustly that 'it is the duty of the proper clergyman to marry persons who apply to him to perform the ceremony, all the necessary preliminaries and conditions being complied with'.

2. According to *Halsbury's Laws of England*, 4th edn, 1975, vol. 14, at para 1003, the right of the parishioner is:

'. . . in general . . . to be married according to the rites of the Church of England in an authorised place if one of [the parties] possesses the legal qualifications of residence'.

The corresponding duty of the clergy derives from the fact that:

'In *Argar v Holdsworth*, it was held that a minister who without just cause refuses to marry persons entitled to be married in his church commits an ecclesiastical offence for which he is punishable in the ecclesiastical courts.'

This latter statement is taken from an Appendix to the Report *An Honourable Estate* (Church House Publishing, 1988) at p. 82; the Appendix was prepared by the then Legal Adviser to the General Synod, commenting on a Question and Answer that had been dealt with in Synod sessions in February 1986.

3. The understanding set out in the previous paragraph underlay the Commission's Opinion on Marriage as published in the 1994 edition of *Legal Opinions concerning the Church of England*.

4. However, the extent of the right and duty have been called into question from time to time, notably in relation to the unbaptized. That issue was widely debated in the early 1950s, when the 1603 Canons were in process of reformulation, and a new draft canon was proposed which would forbid the marriage of unbaptized persons. Its importance to the whole issue of the established nature of the Church of England is reflected

in the careful treatment accorded to it in paragraphs 200–210 of the 1970 *Church and State* Report. The application of the right and duty to divorcees has been the subject of perennial discussion with a view to legislative change: notable examples of the examination of this subject in the last 40 years are *Putting Asunder* (SPCK, 1966); *Marriage, Divorce and the Church* (SPCK, 1971); *Marriage and the Church's Task* (CIO, 1978); *Marriage and the Standing Committee's Task* (CIO, 1983); *Marriage in Church after Divorce* (1993, 2 Ecc LJ 359); and *Marriage and Remarriage* (Archbishops' Council, 2000).

5. Recently, academic commentators have analysed the case of *Argar v Holdsworth*: see the articles by the Revd Michael Smith in 1998 on *An Interpretation of Argar v Holdsworth* (5 Ecc LJ 34 and 140) and Professor Norman Doe's book *The Legal Framework of the Church of England* (OUP, 1996) at pp. 357 et seq. Professor Doe has concluded that the right and duty are based upon a legal fiction. However, this does not, of course, mean that as a matter of law they are fictitious or non-existent.

Relevant law

6. As indicated above, *Argar v Holdsworth* and the cases flowing from it are taken as the authority for the propositions set out above. The civil legislation (the Marriage Act 1949, as amended, and for example, the Sharing of Church Buildings Act 1969), Measures and the Canons on marriage (Canons B 30 to B 36) nowhere grant an explicit right, or impose an explicit duty.

7. The Marriage Act 1949 ('MA'), for example, confines itself to setting out the four means by which marriages according to the rites and ceremonies of the Church of England may be authorized (namely by banns, special licence, common licence or superintendent registrar's certificate: see s5). It is mandatory as to the process of publication of banns and the place(s) where a marriage may then be solemnized (see ss6(1) and 12(1)). However, the right to marry in the church or chapel and the duty to solemnize the marriage are taken for granted. They are dealt with in *Halsbury's Laws of England* in lengthy footnotes to both sections 6 (banns) and 12 (solemnization), each of which ultimately refers back to *Argar v Holdsworth*.

8. The Canons lay duties on a minister to explain the nature of Christian marriage (Canon B 30 para 3), to investigate impediments (Canon B 33), and to observe the preliminary requirements to solemnizing the marriage (Canons B 34 and 35). So far as solemnization is concerned, however, the minister is merely enjoined to 'observe the law relating [to marriage], including, so far as they are applicable, the rules prescribed by the rubric

prefixed to the office of Solemnization of Matrimony in the Book of Common Prayer' (Canon B 35 para 2). These rubrics do not help a great deal, and primarily relate to the calling of banns. However, there is a reference in the rubrics to 'the day and time appointed for the solemnization of Matrimony', which suggests a degree of prior arrangement between the couple and the minister. As regards this, the guidance given to clergy by the Faculty Office comments that 'The incumbent is entitled to appoint the date and time of the marriage, provided that he/she acts reasonably', but goes on to point out that 'arrangements for marriage are almost always made by mutual agreement, rather than in reliance on the letter of the law' (*Anglican Marriage in England and Wales*, Faculty Office, 1999, para 6.3) Chancellor Bursell, in *Liturgy, Order and the Law*, at p. 182, note 260, comments that 'the minister cannot escape his duty by failing to agree a day or time'.

Can the common law be relied on?

9. Part of the challenge to the traditional understanding of the position by the Revd Michael Smith and Professor Doe (see para 5 above) seems to be that the comments of the court in *Argar v Holdsworth* are technically *obiter*. It is suggested that the decision of Sir George Lee, the Dean of the Arches, concerned only procedural not substantive points, that in any event the case related to marriages solemnized under licence, rather than banns, and that it could have authority only in the Southern Province. It is also argued that the judge himself had misunderstood the articles set before him for decision, and introduced an unnecessary summary, which has then been relied on as a general formulation of the law.

10. Further, Professor Doe (at p. 361) notes that Sir George Lee, though deciding *Argar v Holdsworth* only five years after Lord Hardwicke's Marriage Act 1753, makes no reference to it. He considers this significant, in that 'the 1753 Act never conferred a right but rather imposed a duty. If the 1753 statute is (as is commonly understood) the origin of the parishioner's "right" (and the ministerial duty), it existed only until 1836. At that date Parliament abolished the duty, and it has survived since as a legal fiction.' (However, as already indicated in para 6 above, that does not mean that either the right or the duty are fictitious or non-existent as a matter of law.)

11. These are interesting arguments, but by no means convincing. From the Reformation onwards, Anglican jurisprudence had been developing differently from that of the Roman Catholic Church (where the clergy have long had a right to refuse to marry). The Council of Trent, for example, had introduced clerical participation as an essential element in the solemnization of marriage some two hundred years before Lord

Hardwicke's Marriage Act (even though its decrees on marriage were not implemented immediately or at the same speed in all places, and have to be understood against the background of a general parochial obligation for marriage before the Reformation, even if parents or guardians objected.) Until Lord Hardwicke's Act required (with only very few exceptions) that the validity of all marriages should depend on their having been solemnized *in facie ecclesia*, the Church of England had merely encouraged couples to have their marriages solemnized in the church; it had been content to recognize the validity of marriages contracted in the traditional manner (based on Roman Law origins) by consent of the parties followed by consummation, without involvement of the clergy.

12. The Commission respectfully disagrees with Professor Doe's view: Lord Hardwicke's Act had been introduced in response to the particular scandal of clandestine marriages, and did not, in the Commission's view, either introduce a new right for the benefit of parishioners, or impose a general duty upon the clergy that had not existed previously. The duty to marry parishioners, and their right to be married, had existed long before the Act. The Act simply restricted the parishioners' freedom of action, by removing one of the traditional means of marrying (by publicly acknowledged consent, and consummation); it limited the Church of England's recognition of marriages to those marriages that had been solemnized *in facie ecclesiae*; and it laid down certain further conditions (for example, as to length of residence of the parties) upon the way in which the clergy should perform their existing duties.

13. That being the case, it is not surprising that Sir George Lee made no specific reference to the Act in his judgement. His notes (as quoted in Smith's article at p. 140) read that 'By the Canons, etc, every minister is to obey his Ordinary's licence . . . [and] every minister by law is obliged to marry such of his parishioners as have resided a month in his parish . . .'. His judgement (2 Lee 515 at 517) states that 'I was of opinion a licence was a legal authority for marriage, and that a minister was guilty of a breach of duty who should refuse to marry pursuant to a proper licence from his ordinary.' In the Commission's view, although Sir George Lee may have made a passing mention of the new timetable introduced by the Act, his general statement was merely declaratory of the law which had been in place before 1753.

14. The Commission considers that Sir George did not need to make reference to any authority for the general duty, as it was well understood (even if it had not necessarily been invariably welcomed or observed. Thus Cressy, in *Birth, Marriage and Death* (1997) at p. 315 refers to Edmund Grindal, the reforming Archbishop of York, instructing his clergy in 1571

not to marry any persons or call their banns unless they could say the catechism; Cressy observes that 'Godly ministers may sometimes have attempted to impose such a test, but it could not be sustained in law.'). Sir George Lee's statements may, in strict terms, be *obiter*, but this does not deprive them of their importance as an indication of the common law that had developed up to that time; nor should it diminish the authority of the statements of law that have subsequently been made in reliance upon them.

15. Nevertheless, the origin of the right and duty is obscure. It is probably now impossible to identify the point in time at which the rule became established, but if Cressy's assessment of the historical position shortly after the Reformation can be relied upon, and bishops and clergy were already by then looking to restrict the extent of their obligation towards their parishioners, the position must have been well understood at an early stage in the establishment of the Elizabethan Settlement. This would suggest that, even without primary legislation, a right and duty had arisen by custom and usage. (Chancellor Mark Hill, in his *Ecclesiastical Law* (Butterworths, 1995, at p. 305 note 2), while appearing to accept Professor Doe's thesis, concludes that, even after 1836, 'the passage of time and unqualified acceptance of such a right (and corresponding duty on the priest) makes it highly likely that a custom right (and duty) has now evolved'.)

16. The lack of any statutory obligation upon the clergy to solemnize marriages in the MA (and its predecessors from 1836) then becomes understandable: the obligation is one laid upon the clergy by their general duty of obedience to the bishop in carrying out the ministry which they share with him. This point is made explicitly by Kindersley V-C in the licence case of *Davis v Black* (1841) 1 QB 900 at 906, where he says that '. . . if a licence is produced to a clergyman from his ordinary . . . directing him, or in terms authorizing him, to marry two persons . . . his canonical obedience requires him, as well as the rights of the parties require him, to perform the marriage . . .'. The reference to intention in 'where a marriage is intended to be solemnised after the publication of banns of matrimony' in section 6(1) of the MA also becomes understandable as a reference to the intention of the couple, and survival of the traditional understanding of marriage as a contract willingly entered into between the parties *per verba de praesenti*, merely witnessed by clergy or others. (The same phrase occurs in the MA in relation to marriages in registry offices and in registered buildings in sections 45 and 44 respectively, with a similar lack of express formal obligation upon the ministers or other persons authorized to solemnize, presumably because they are subject to internal disciplines within their denominations or by their terms of employment.)

17. It follows, therefore, that the Commission considers that the assumptions reflected in all current legislation are correct. An acid test would seem to be the perceived need for specific legislation in the Matrimonial Causes Act 1965, without which the clergy of the Church of England would have no choice but to remarry divorcees whose partners were still alive. Thus section 8(2) provides that: 'No clergyman . . . shall be compelled . . . to solemnise the marriage of any person whose former marriage has been dissolved and whose former spouse is still living . . .'. Similar wording is also found in other matrimonial statutes (e.g. MA s5A, concerning marriages within certain prohibited degrees), all suggesting that but for the excepting provision, the duty would be enforceable.

18. It also must be remembered that the present 'conscience clause' arrangements for clergy have been in place for only a little over sixty years, since the A. P. Herbert Marriage Act of 1938; for the previous eighty years, Anglican clergy were obliged to allow the use of their buildings for such marriages, though not obliged to officiate personally; The debates prior to the A. P. Herbert Act, and sections in that and subsequent Acts relieving incumbents of the duty to perform marriages (or to allow marriages in their churches) of persons one or both of whom have been divorced and have a former spouse still living, have little meaning unless there is a general duty to marry. The Commission considers that there is no pressing need for the present understanding of the right and duty, based on the common law, to be reviewed.

How wide is the right / duty?

19. There seems no reason to question the traditional understanding that the right and duty extend to all parishioners. During the period 1753 to 1836, no special provision was made for Dissenters or Recusants, with the implication that the right and duty extended to them (a cause of great offence, leading eventually to the Reform Acts of the early 1830s – see *James v Robinson* (1815) 2 Phillimore 285). It is not clear that the exception of Jews and members of the Society of Friends from the obligation to marry *in facie ecclesiae* under the Hardwicke Act itself excluded them from the right to marry or duty to be married by the parochial clergy, in the unlikely event of any so choosing. The conclusion to be drawn, however, is that the right and duty would seem to be no less extensive in modern conditions, though the range of choice under current legislation makes it highly unlikely that any members of one of the other faith communities in England would wish to avail themselves of the right, or insist on the duty.

20. Finally, it should be noted that the right has been specifically extended by section 72(2) of the MA, which provides that 'Persons intending to be

married shall have the like right but no greater right of having their banns published and marriage solemnized . . . in a parish church or authorized chapel which is the usual place of worship of one or both of them as they have of having their banns published and marriage solemnized in the parish church or public chapel of the parish or chapelry in which they or one of them resides'. (Under s72(1), the necessary evidence for this qualification is inclusion on the church electoral roll of the parish prepared under the CRR.) By implication, there will be a corresponding duty on the clergy, ultimately enforceable as a matter of due canonical obedience, on the lines discussed above.

(October 2000, revised 2004)

Part 17
Miscellaneous

Control of Asbestos at Work Regulations 2002

1. The purpose of this Opinion is to indicate whether, and if so to what extent, the requirements of Regulation 4 of the Control of Asbestos at Work Regulations impose duties in relation to certain classes of building used by the Church of England.

2. Regulation 4, which in essence requires assessments to be carried out in relation to the potential presence of asbestos in the premises to which it applies, is framed in terms unfamiliar to ecclesiastical law. Critical to an understanding of the Regulation are the expressions 'non-domestic premises' and 'dutyholders'.

Non-domestic premises

3. Although this term is not defined in the Regulations themselves, an aid to construction is to be found in section 53 of the Health and Safety at Work etc Act 1974. The Regulations were made under section 15 of the Act; this section falls within Part 1 to which the definitions in section 53 apply. There being no express intention to the contrary, the Act and the Regulations should be construed consistently with each other in accordance with section 11 of the Interpretation Act 1978, which applies to earlier legislation by virtue of section 22(1).

4. Section 53 gives a very wide meaning to 'premises' including 'any place' as well as a vehicle, vessel, tent or movable structure. For this purpose all buildings are premises. Section 53 also provides that:

> '. . . "domestic premises" means premises occupied as a private dwelling (including any garden, yard, garage, outhouse or other appurtenance of such premises which is not used in common by the occupants of more than one such dwelling), and "non-domestic premises" shall be construed accordingly . . .'

Thus any building not occupied as a private dwelling is within the definition of non-domestic premises.

5. No specific provision is made for a building put to more than one use; for example a dwelling also serving as an office. Where, however, a sensible division can be drawn between parts of a building (such as the common parts of a block of flats and the individual flats themselves) the court will treat the appropriate part as coming within the definition of domestic or non-domestic (*Westminster City Council v Select Management Ltd* [1985] 1 WLR 576). The status of a single unit used for both domestic and other purposes remains open to doubt. There is,

however, a compelling argument that providing premises satisfy the test in section 53 of being occupied as a private dwelling no ancillary user (such as for an office or venue for meetings) will deprive them of their 'domestic' character.

The dutyholder

6. The dutyholder is a person required to discharge the duties imposed by Regulation 4, which itself gives a definition of this term:

'Duty to manage asbestos in non-domestic premises

4.—(1) In this regulation "the dutyholder" means –

(a)   every person who has, by virtue of a contract or tenancy, an obligation of any extent in relation to the maintenance or repair of non-domestic premises or any means of access thereto or egress therefrom; or

(b)   in relation to any part of non-domestic premises where there is no such contract or tenancy, every person who has, to any extent, control of that part of those non-domestic premises or any means of access thereto or egress therefrom,

and where there is more than one dutyholder, the relative contribution to be made by each such person in complying with the requirements of this regulation will be determined by the nature and extent of the maintenance and repair obligation owed by that person.

(2) Every person shall co-operate with the dutyholder so far as is necessary to enable the dutyholder to comply with his duties under this regulation.'

7. Among the persons falling within the concept of the dutyholder are:

(i)   landlords or licensors subject to a repairing obligation in a tenancy agreement or licence;

(ii)   tenants or licensees subject to a similar obligation;

(iii)   occupiers (as under the Occupiers' Liability Act 1957) upon whom the duty devolves in the absence of the kind of contract or tenancy envisaged by paragraph 4(1).

Although Regulation 4(1) contemplates that there may be more than one dutyholder, it appears also to permit an occupier to divest himself of the duty by contracting out an obligation of maintenance or repair to another. This consequence flows from the fact that sub-paragraph (b) is expressed as an alternative to (a).

Parsonage houses

8. In so far as parsonage houses and other clergy houses of residence are occupied as private dwellings Regulation 4 does not apply to them. The question whether premises are so occupied is one of fact in each case. Since circumstances may vary from case to case the following principles will assist in answering that question.

(i)   If the house is a single unit used exclusively for residential purposes it will be classified as domestic.

(ii)   Where a building contains separate domestic and other elements (for instance a flat over a meeting room) the parts will be characterized separately as domestic or non-domestic for the purposes of the Regulations.

(iii)   A dwelling house subject to mixed uses, such as a parsonage with a study also used as an office, or a place for meetings, will not lose its character as domestic premises.

(iv)   Some parsonage houses are designed with integral purpose-built offices or meeting rooms. Such a building is likely to be viewed as a single unit containing a material non-domestic element and therefore characterized as non-domestic.

The dutyholder in respect of churches

9. Where the test of control is applied under Regulation 4(1)(b) in the case of a parish church, the dutyholders will be the members of the PCC including the minister and churchwardens. A licence or (where lawful) a lease of part of a church may by the inclusion of an appropriate repairing obligation transfer to the licensee or lessee the function of dutyholder in respect of that part.

10. The wording of Regulation 4(1) is not, however, apt to cover an archdeacon exercising his or her functions under the Care of Churches and Ecclesiastical Jurisdiction Measure 1991. These functions amount to a jurisdiction created by law; they do not arise 'by virtue of a contract or tenancy' under paragraph (1)(a), neither are they the 'control of premises' under paragraph (1)(b).

Diocesan authorities

11. Similar reasoning excludes Diocesan Boards of Finance, or other bodies or persons functioning at diocesan level, from responsibility under Regulation 4 in the event of its contravention by a PCC. There is no relevant contract or tenancy, and the PCC members, as occupiers, are in control of the church building for the purposes of paragraph 1(b). There being no dutyholder in the form of a diocesan institution, such an institution will not bear legal responsibility for the default of the PCC.

(April 2005)

Copyright and performance protection

Introduction

Warning

1. The law of copyright and performance protection is complex and may be far-reaching. Copyright considerations arise on reproduction of a work by copying (duplicating, photocopying, printing etc.) or by recording (on record, film or video or audio tape), or by a public performance or broadcast of a work (at a concert, recital or discotheque). Care must be taken not to infringe copyright, e.g. by reproducing, recording or by public performance, or by authorizing an infringement of copyright without the licence of the owner of the copyright. Almost all modern literary, dramatic and musical works are copyright. Modern hymns, psalms, carols and songs together with their music and pointing are protected by copyright. Modern versions and arrangements of old literature, including the Bible, and music are also protected by copyright. Similarly records and the typographical arrangements of published editions of copyright works are protected.

2. This Opinion does not purport to give general legal advice. In cases of doubt clergy, especially incumbents, and PCCs are strongly advised to seek legal advice and/or the assistance of the publishers of the copyright work and/or the advice of an appropriate organization (see below). Unless they are satisfied that all necessary copyright permissions or licences have been obtained they should not allow the reproduction, recording or performance of the work or other act which would infringe the copyright. Clergy and others who unwittingly allow an infringement of copyright by third parties are themselves at risk of being sued for the infringement if they have authorized it. Clergy and others are also at risk of legal action if the rights of performers are infringed.

3. Monetary sanctions imposed by courts for infringement of copyright may be substantial. For example, in 1983 the Music Publishers' Association (MPA) sued both the County Council and the director of music at Queen Elizabeth High School, Hexham, for infringement of copyright by photocopying sheet music for use by the choir of the school. Damages of £5,000 inclusive of the plaintiff's costs were ordered to be paid and injunctions were granted against both the County Council and the school's director of music. A year or two earlier the Trustees of Oakham School and a member of staff were also sued by the MPA because a booklet of photocopied sheet music had been produced: the school was obliged to pay damages of a similarly substantial amount and costs. Thus photocopying sheet music or the words of modern hymns or

songs, for example, constitutes a serious infringement of both the originator's and publisher's copyrights unless the licence of the copyright owners has been obtained. Infringement can prove expensive and the infringing copies will usually be confiscated or destroyed.

What is protected by copyright?

4. Part I of the Copyright, Designs and Patents Act 1988 provides that copyright subsists in original literary, dramatic and musical works. The term 'work' has been liberally interpreted by the courts. In addition to the original work itself copyright can also subsist in:

an arrangement or adaptation of a work;

a recording of a work;

the typographical arrangement of the published edition of a work;

an artistic work (see below).

Where there is doubt whether material is copyright – for instance whether material is original, an arrangement or an adaptation – the publisher will usually be able to assist, since the publisher normally handles copyright on behalf of the copyright owner. It is advisable to make application, giving full details, in good time before the permission is required.

5. In general, copyright in a work expires at the end of the period of 70 years from the end of the calendar year in which the originator (author or composer) dies. The period of protection for a new arrangement of music is 70 years from the end of the calendar year in which the musical arranger dies. The law protects not only works whose author is a British citizen or a British resident, but also works whose authors are citizens or residents of many foreign countries.

Sound recordings, published editions and films

6. Part I of the 1988 Act also deals with copyright in sound recordings, films (which includes videotapes), television broadcasts, sound broadcasts, and published editions. No comment on these works is included in this Opinion other than brief comments on copyright in sound recordings (see paras 7 and 14 below) and in published editions (see para 8).

7. Copyright in a sound recording expires at the end of the period of 50 years from the end of the calendar year in which the recording is made or, if it is released before the end of that period, 50 years from the end of the calendar year in which it is released. The acts restricted by the copyright in a sound recording include doing or authorizing the following:

(a)   copying the recording and issuing copies of it to the public;

(b)   playing it in public;

(c)   broadcasting the recording.

An occupier of premises may be liable for infringing the copyright in the recording if the occupier gives permission for record-playing apparatus to be brought onto premises, and knows or has reason to believe that the apparatus is likely to be used so as to infringe copyright. If a sound recording which is copyright is to be played in public then a licence is usually required (see para 28).

8. The publisher's permission must be obtained before copying, usually by photocopying of, or authorizing the coping of, any substantial part of the typographical arrangement of a published edition of a work. Typographical arrangement is the design, layout and typeface on a printed page. Copyright in the published edition expires at the end of the period of 25 years from the end of the calendar year in which the edition containing the arrangement was first published. The copyright is usually owned by the publisher and is independent of the copyright, if any, in the work reproduced in the edition.

Infringement of copyright: copying of substantial part

9. A person infringes copyright in a literary, dramatic or musical work by copying, or authorizing the copying of, the work or a substantial part of it without the copyright owner's licence. In the case of a literary, dramatic or musical work this includes reproducing in the form of photocopy, record or film. The expression 'film' includes videotape. Infringement of copyright by public performance includes signing or recitation or authorizing the public performance of a work or a substantial part of it; it must be distinguished from the protection given to performers by Part II of the 1988 Act.

10. What is a substantial part of a work is a question of fact; but for the part to be 'substantial' it does not have to be proportionately large. In the case of a musical work, for example, it may be as little as a few notes: if it is recognizable, that may be sufficient. Therefore quantity is not the sole consideration.

Rights in performances

11. The position of performers may also have to be given consideration. This is separate and distinct from the question of infringement of copyright in the work performed. Part II of the 1988 Act confers rights

on performers, by requiring their consent to the exploitation of their performances. It also confers rights on a person having recording rights in relation to a performance, in relation to recordings made without that person's consent or that of the performer. The performances protected include dramatic and musical performances and the reading or recitation of a literary work given live by one or more individuals. The performer's rights are infringed by a person who, without consent, makes a recording of the whole or a substantial part of the performance or includes the performance in a live broadcast or cable programme service. It is not an infringement, however, to make a recording for private and domestic use. A performer's rights are also infringed by a person who, without consent, shows or plays in public the whole or any substantial part of a performance by means of a recording which was, and which that person knows or has reason to believe was, made without the performer's consent. The rights of a person who has exclusive recording rights may also be infringed by the making of recordings of performances without appropriate consents. Criminal liability may also be incurred by dealing in illicit recordings.

12. Therefore Part II of the Act applies to organists, musicians, choristers, members of a church orchestra, and other singers and performers in churches and church halls. The prior consent of all these persons, if their performance is recorded or videotaped with the intention of making any public or commercial use of the tape, would have to be obtained. Obtaining such consents would not be the direct concern of the incumbent or PCC, unless they had given authority for the making of a record or tape and such authority envisaged its possible publication. In such circumstances they might, if no consents were obtained, be held to be liable along with the makers of the record or tape. The performers will usually have a right of action against the recordist, but it should not be assumed that the incumbent or PCC would escape liability if they were held to have permitted or caused the offence.

Public performance of a work

13. In addition to the reproduction or recording of a work the law of copyright also prohibits the public performance of a work without the necessary copyright licence.

14. Separate considerations arise for the public performance of literary, dramatic or musical works, but it is important to be aware of what constitutes a 'public performance'. The 1988 Act defines 'performance' as including oral delivery, and any mode of visual or acoustic presentation. The Act does not define the term 'public', which has been widely interpreted by the courts. The fact that the audience is restricted to a

certain category of persons, e.g. members of a private club or of an association, does not render the performance private. It has been held that the term only excludes those occasions of an essentially family nature within the domestic circle.

Artistic works in churches

(with particular reference to stained glass and photographs of artistic works in churches)

Ownership

15. Part I of the Copyright, Designs and Patents Act 1988 extends to artistic works. Copyright belongs to the author (i.e. the person who creates the work, whether engraver, artist or sculptor) of an artistic work. The copyright expires at the end of the period of 70 years from the end of the calendar year in which the author dies. If the author is commissioned, the person commissioning the work may be beneficially entitled to copyright. Copyright may be assigned, by writing signed by or on behalf of the assignor, as personal property. Assignment may be total or partial (s90). Special statutory provisions exist for a work made in the course of the author's employment, making the employer the first owner of the copyright, subject to any agreement to the contrary.

Works in public places

16. The copyright in certain works, which are permanently situated in public places or in premises open to the public, is not infringed by the making of a graphic work representing the work (e.g. painting or drawing) or a photograph or film of the work, nor by including it in a broadcast. The works in question are sculptures, models for buildings and works of artistic craftsmanship which are not paintings, drawings, engravings or photographs (s62). Stained glass windows and tapestries come within this description.

17. When an artistic work is introduced into a church by fixing it to the fabric, as in the case of a stained glass window and, frequently, in the case of sculpture, the copyright does not, by virtue of the attachment to the fabric, pass from the owner of the copyright to the incumbent owner of the freehold. Assignment of copyright must be in writing.

18. A church is undoubtedly 'premises open to the public' (s62(1)). It follows that once an artistic work, other than a picture, such as a piece of sculpture e.g. a memorial tablet, a tapestry or a window is introduced into a church on a permanent footing members of the public cannot be restrained from photographing or otherwise making graphic

representations of such a work on the ground that to do so is an infringement of copyright. But note that the incumbent has the right to refuse entry to the church. It follows that if a person takes a photograph of a window in a church the copyright in that photograph belongs to the photographer or the person commissioning the photograph. Pictures, however, continue to be protected, and the photographing or making of other copies of them would be an infringement of copyright, if copyright continues to exist.

19. A chancellor might properly enquire in whom the copyright of an artistic work will be vested before granting a faculty for the introduction of the work into a church. (In the light of the statutory provisions summarized above it would be sound practice to require that the copyright be assigned in writing to the PCC in the case of pictures, but such a requirement is unnecessary in the case of other artistic works.)

20. Where the PCC owns the copyright in an artistic work (e.g. a stained-glass window) in the church or obtains the consent of the copyright owner or the work is out of copyright, the incumbent could give permission for photographs of the work to be taken subject to any specified conditions. The copyright of any such photograph of the work, commissioned and paid for by the PCC, would, subject to the position about the work's copyright, vest in the PCC.

21. Copyright in buildings or models for buildings is also not infringed by the acts mentioned above (s62(1)).

Copyright in gravestones and other monuments in churchyards

22. Under the Copyright, Designs and Patents Act 1988, copyright subsists in a gravestone or similar monument either as a work of sculpture or as a work of artistic craftsmanship within the meaning of sections 1(1)(a) and 4(1)(a) or (c) and (2). A separate copyright may also subsist in the verbal inscription as a literary work within the meaning of sections 1(1)(a) and 3(1). In order to qualify as a literary work the inscription would need to be something rather more than the mere identification by reference to the name and lifespan of the deceased (see *Exxon Corporation v Exxon Insurance Consultants International Limited* [1982] Ch 199 at 143, CA). However, a short biography of the deceased, recording achievements, personal virtues and so on, could well qualify.

23. The owners of the artistic and literary copyrights are the respective authors, i.e. the persons who created the relevant works (ss9(1) and 11(1)). The sculptor would be the first owner of the copyright in the gravestone and the person who composed and arranged the verbal inscription would

be the first owner of the copyright in that literary work. If, however, the author was an employee who made the relevant work in the course of employment, the employer would be the first owner of any copyright in the work, subject to any agreement to the contrary (s11(2)). Further, the copyright may become vested in a legal or equitable assignee if it is the subject of a written assignment or of an express or implied agreement to assign (s90).

24. But for the special defences set out below, photographing the works and publishing those photographs would be infringements of the artistic and the literary copyrights. Copyright in artistic and literary works is infringed by copying them, i.e. reproducing them in any material form, without the licence of the relevant owner (ss16(1)(a), (2), 17(1), (2)).

25. However, under section 62(1)(b) and 2(b) of the 1988 Act, the copyright in a work of sculpture or artistic craftsmanship is not infringed by making a photograph of it if the work is 'permanently situated in a public place or in premises open to the public', and in that event, under section 62(3), it will not be an infringement of the copyright to issue copies of the photograph to the public. A churchyard will normally fall within the description of 'premises open to the public'. 'Premises' may include not only land on which buildings have been erected but also open land, particularly open land adjoining buildings. Further, although the public generally (as distinct from parishioners) may have no rights in the churchyard (see *Re St Clement, Eastcheap* [1964] P 20), churchyards are normally 'open to the public' in the relevant sense that members of the public enjoy de facto access to them for the purposes of looking at the gravestones and monuments.

26. Although the special statutory defence for photographs of artistic works on public display is not applicable to literary works, it would not be an infringement of copyright to photograph a literary work inscribed on a gravestone in circumstances where no infringement of the artistic copyright takes place by virtue of the provisions referred to in paragraph 58. It is highly probable that the court would, in such cases, imply a licence, on the part of the owner of the literary copyright, to photograph the inscription of that work on the gravestone permanently placed in premises open to the public. If there is a licence by the owner of the copyright to do the act in question, no infringement of his copyright will occur (s16(2)). The licence need not be in writing and need not be express; it can be implied from conduct and from all the relevant circumstances.

27. Thus the publication in a book of photographs of gravestones and other monuments in churchyards does not infringe any copyrights that

may subsist in the gravestones etc photographed, in the lettering or other stone carvings on them, or in the inscriptions.

Obtaining permission to use copyright material

28. Information and advice on the use of copyright material for church-related purposes may be obtained from the following sources:

(1)   *A Brief Guide to Liturgical Copyright*, published by Church House Publishing, which may be downloaded free of charge from the Church of England website (www.cofe.anglican.org/worship/liturgy/commonworship/copyright/index.html). This covers the copyright requirements for liturgical use of various material, including *Common Worship*, the BCP, the most frequently used translations of the Bible, hymns and musical settings. It also gives advice concerning the audio/video recording of services.

(2)   Christian Copyright Licensing International (www.ccli.co.uk). This body represents a number of publishers and copyright owners in granting licences for the use of copyright material by churches, including books, music and films. Where material is not covered by one of these licences, application will need to be made to the copyright owners and CCLI may be able to offer advice and assistance.

(1997)

Copyright in speeches made in the General Synod

1. The Commission was asked for an Opinion on the ownership of and rights in respect of the copyright in speeches made in the General Synod.

2. The making of a speech in the General Synod may involve or generate multiple copyright works in different ownership. The legal position is potentially complex and can only be stated in general terms. If a dispute arises about the use of a speech it will be necessary to examine and consider all the facts of the particular case.

The prepared speech

3. The majority of speakers read or speak from a prepared text or from notes. The text and the notes are protected as literary works irrespective of their literary merit or intellectual content. The copyright in them is vested in the author of them and remains with the author until the author executes an assignment of it to someone else. Except in special situations, such as employment, it is unusual to find provisions, statutory or otherwise, vesting the copyright by operation of law in someone other than the author of the work.

4. The copyright position is the same whether the speakers are elected members of the synod or are ex-officio members, such as the diocesan bishops, or are co-opted members.

5. The author of the speech controls the copyright in the text and notes by granting or withholding permission to copy them or substantial parts of them. Permission does not have to be given in writing. It may be given informally e.g. orally or implied from conduct.

The spontaneous speech

6. If the speech is delivered spontaneously without any prepared text or notes there is no copyright in it until it is reduced to a material form e.g. as a result of being recorded by the Communications Unit or of being taken down verbatim by a professional stenographer who produces an 'unedited transcript' of the proceedings of the Synod, which is then corrected and 'lightly' edited in collaboration with in-house staff. A speech reduced to a material form is protected as a literary work. The copyright vests in the speaker as the author of it. The position is the same in the case of the prepared speaker who departs from his or her notes or text to respond to points made in debate or in response to the imposition of a time-limit on speeches.

Report of a speech

7. The copyright position in the case of an edited or abbreviated report of a speech (e.g. produced by a journalist) is that a separate copyright subsists in the particular report. The reporter will be the owner of the copyright in the report of the speech, though not in the speech reported. The report of the speech is the product of the reporter's own labour and skill. If the reporter is employed to make the report the copyright in the report will belong to the employer.

Recording of a speech

8. If the speech is recorded on audio-tape as it is delivered a separate copyright exists in the sound recording of the speech. The copyright in the sound recording vests in the person who produces the sound recording.

Official Report of Proceedings

9. The compilation of speeches in the form of an official *Report of Proceeding* prepared by staff employed in-house in the course of their employment generates a separate copyright in that compilation, as a literary work. That copyright of those published since the National Institutions Measure 1998 vests in the Archbishops' Council as the entity which holds the copyright and other assets of the General Synod. The Synod has no corporate existence, whereas the Archbishops' Council, which acts as the financial executive of the Synod, is a body corporate established for charitable purposes and can hold copyright and other assets. The compilation copyright is then under the control of the Archbishops' Council who can grant and withhold permission to copy the compilation or parts of it.

10. The recording of the speeches and the inclusion of the speeches in the Official Report does not infringe the rights of the speakers in the underlying works provided that those who speak know and consent to this use. Consent to use their copyright material will readily be implied from their knowledge that a recording is to be made and that an Official Report is to be prepared and that this has been done in previous years. This knowledge could be reinforced, without the need to obtain individual signed forms of consent or assignment from each speaker, by including in Standing Orders and making available to speakers appropriate provisions stating the practice of taping speeches delivered in the General Synod, and the making of an Official Report of the proceedings and a compilation recording for sale and distribution.

11. The same considerations apply to the making of a compilation tape of the highlights from the speeches for sale and distribution to the public.

12. If the literary or audio compilation produced in-house is directly copied either in whole or as to a substantial part (e.g. by an unauthorized compilation of highlights of the Synod), proceedings for infringement of copyright in the Official Report could be taken by the Archbishops' Council by whom the Synod's rights are held. The Synod could not, however, object to use of less than a substantial part of the audio material or the Official Report or to various uses of copyright material allowed by law e.g. fair dealing for the purpose of reporting current events and for the purpose of criticism or review.

(September 1999)

Gas Safety (Installation and Use) Regulations 1998

1. This Opinion aims to give a general indication of the effect on buildings owned by the Church of the Gas Safety (Installation and Use) Regulations 1998, SI 1998/2451, as amended by the Quarries Regulations 1999, SI 1999/2024. It is not a comprehensive commentary on the Gas Safety Regulations, whose detailed provisions should be referred to in any particular case.

2. The Regulations apply in different ways to different parts of a gas installation (including flues) and the different persons responsible for them. This Opinion concentrates on the use of appliances rather than their installation, since it is assumed that installation would normally be left to gas engineers: among the general provision regulation 3(1) requires that 'work' (which is widely defined in regulation 2(1)) to gas fittings should be carried out only by a competent person, generally someone recognized as such by the Health and Safety Executive.

3. For present purposes there are three categories of person who are given duties under the Regulations:

(a) the 'responsible person' for any premises;

(b) an employer or self-employed person who has a place of work under his or her control or has control of work in relation to a gas fitting;

(c) the landlord (including a licensor) of residential premises containing or served by a gas appliance (including the pipework) connecting it to the main supply.

The 'responsible person' in relation to any premises

4. This expression is defined in regulation 2(1) as the occupier or, where there is no occupier or the occupier is away, the owner of the premises or any person with authority for the time being to take appropriate action in relation to any gas fitting there; for the purposes of regulation 34(1) mentioned below it means all of those persons. For a person to be an 'occupier' it is not necessary for that person to have a particular interest in the property concerned; rather it is a matter of physical presence there. In the case of domestic premises the identity of the occupier will usually be obvious. As regards other buildings in a parish the incumbent is likely to be the occupier of the church (or, where the benefice is vacant, any priest-in-charge); the PCC will probably also be an 'occupier' in view of its general responsibility for maintenance; the PCC will be the occupier

of a church hall or other building used for parochial purposes. The DBF will be the occupier of buildings used for diocesan purposes, and the Chapter in the case of property used for the purposes of a cathedral.

5. In the case of any given building, one or more persons or bodies other than the 'occupier' may have power or be subject to a duty under other legislation to carry out repairs or other work to the gas fittings. Under the definition in regulation 2(1) referred to in the previous paragraph, they will then be 'responsible persons' for the purpose of regulation 34(1) and, if there is no occupier or the occupier is away, for the purpose of the Regulations as a whole. Thus the existence of powers or duties under completely separate legislation will have the effect of imposing duties under the 1998 Regulations on the person or body concerned. In the case of a parsonage house this principle applies in relation to the Diocesan Parsonages Board, which will normally be 'authorised to take appropriate action' in relation to gas fittings under the Repair of Benefice Buildings Measure 1972. It will also apply to the sequestrators of a vacant benefice if they have the bishop's approval under section 2 of the Benefices (Sequestration) Measure 1933 to use the benefice income on work to the parsonage house, provided that approval extends to work to the gas fittings.

6. The 'responsible person' is referred to in a number of Regulations, under which the responsible person:

18(2) is to be informed by an installer that any necessary electrical cross-bonding should be carried out by a competent person.

23(2) is to ensure that gas pipework in any non-domestic premises remains readily recognizable as such.

26(9) is to be notified of any defect found in a gas appliance by any person performing work on it. The owner is also to be notified if different from the responsible person.

34(1) is not to use a gas appliance or permit one to be used if he or she knows or has reason to suspect that it cannot be used without constituting a danger to any person.

34(3) is to be informed where any person engaged in carrying out work to a gas installation knows or has reason to suspect that a gas appliance within the authority of the responsible person cannot be used without constituting a danger to any person. (The owner of the appliance, if different, is also to be informed.)

37(2) if he or she knows or has reason to suspect that gas is escaping, must take all reasonable steps to cause the supply to be shut off.

37(3) if the escape continues, must notify the supplier.

Most of these Regulations impose particular duties upon the responsible person. In some instances, however, the responsible person is to be the recipient of notice of a defect; in such circumstances regulation 34(1) will normally require the responsible person to withdraw the affected appliance from use.

An employer or self-employed person having a place of work under his or her control

7. This raises the question of what is a place of work. The Regulations are made under section 15 of the Health and Safety at Work etc Act 1974 for the general purposes of Part I of the Act, which are to secure the health, safety and welfare of persons at work, to protect others from risks arising out of the activities of those persons, and to control the handling of dangerous substances (s1(1)). A place of work is not defined, but evidently it can include domestic premises; section 4 imposes duties on those in control of non-domestic premises made available for use as a place of work by persons who are not their employees, and the inference is clear. By section 52(1) 'work' means work as an employee or as a self-employed person, and a person is 'at work' when in the course of employment or (as a self-employed person) is devoting time to work. The definitions may be extended in Regulations, and the Regulations under consideration contain a definition of 'work' in relation to a gas fitting but no more general extension. A person is self-employed (under s53(1)) if working for gain or reward otherwise than under a contract of employment: a self-employed person may employ others. The employment of domestic servants is excluded (s51).

8. Diocesan offices, and buildings used for the many purposes of a cathedral, are clearly places of work, and will normally be under the control of the DBF and the Chapter respectively. At parochial level, the place of work of an employee (such as a paid verger or a secretary) will depend on the nature of the work and will be subject to regulation 35 mentioned below; if in accordance with usual practice the PCC is the employer it will be bound to comply with the Regulations. A consecrated or licensed place of worship in the parish is to be regarded as an incumbent's place of work under his or her control, and so also is the study contained in the parsonage, at least while the incumbent is working there: the question arises, however, whether an incumbent is working for gain or reward. As a matter of ecclesiastical law the Legal Advisory Commission accepts the description of a stipend contained in a statement by the House of Bishops in 1943:

'. . . The stipends of the clergy have always, we imagine, been rightly regarded not as pay in the sense in which that word is understood in the world of industry today, not as a reward for services rendered, so that the more valuable the service in somebody's judgement or the more hours worked the more should be the pay, but rather as a maintenance allowance to enable the priest to live without undue financial worry, to do his work effectively in the sphere to which he is called and if married to maintain his wife and bring up his family in accordance with a standard which might be described as that neither of poverty nor riches . . .'

'Gain or reward' in the definition of self-employment in the Regulations must primarily, it is thought, be understood in material or commercial terms, and for that reason it is arguable that they are not apt to apply to the self-employment of a clergyman. In the context of health and safety, however, the Commission considers that it is appropriate to take a broader view, so that a clergyman who is paid a stipend should be regarded as working for 'gain or reward' for the purpose of the Regulations.

9. An *employer* or *self-employed person* having a place of work under his or her control or having control of work in relation to a gas fitting is referred to in the following Regulations, under which the person concerned:

4   is to take reasonable steps to ensure that any person undertaking work in relation to a gas fitting is, or is employed by, someone approved by the Health and Safety Executive.

8   so far as is reasonably practicable, is to ensure that there is no alteration of premises containing a gas fitting that would adversely affect the safety of the fitting and that nothing is done to the fitting or any flue which would make the subsequent use of the fitting dangerous.

35   has a duty to ensure that any gas appliance or pipework connecting it to the main supply or flue is maintained in a safe condition so as to prevent risk of personal injury.

The landlord of residential premises containing or served by a gas appliance (including the pipework connecting it to the main supply)

10. Regulation 36 (text on p. 425) places duties on a 'landlord', an expression which as defined for the purposes of the regulation can include a licensor. Paragraph (1) also contains detailed definitions of other words given a special meaning in the regulation and for convenience it is set out at the end of this Opinion.

11. Where the regulation applies, the landlord, like the employer under regulation 35, must ensure that the appliance or pipework and any flue serving the appliance is maintained in a safe condition by a competent person so as to prevent risk of personal injury, but must also ensure that a safety check is made by such a person at not more than twelve monthly intervals. (In the case of a lease granted on or after the 1 November 1998 the check must have been made within twelve months before the grant or twelve months after the installation, whichever is the later.) There are restrictions on the type of fire or water heater which can be installed in premises used as sleeping accommodation.

The landlord must ensure that a record is made and kept for a period of two years after the check, to include the following information:

(i)   the date of the check;

(ii)   the address of the installation;

(iii)   the name of the landlord or his agent;

(iv)   a description and the location of the appliance or flue checked;

(v)   any defect identified;

(vi)   any remedial action taken;

(vii)   confirmation that the check included examination of particular features mentioned in regulation 26(9);

(viii) the name and signature of the person carrying out the check;

(ix)   the registration number of that person, or of his employer, with a body approved by the Health and Safety Executive for the purposes of regulation 3(3) (competent persons).

A copy of the record must be given to each existing tenant (or prominently displayed if the appliance or flue is outside the tenant's premises) within 28 days of the check, and to any new tenant (unless displayed as mentioned above); it must also be made available upon request to any person in lawful occupation of the premises.

12. Regulation 30 contains general requirements for the room-sealing of gas appliances installed in bathrooms or shower rooms, and imposes limitations on gas heaters in rooms intended for use as sleeping accommodation. Regulation 36(11) places a particular responsibility on

landlords in this respect, but there is no contravention of the requirements in relation to sleeping accommodation in the case of a room which has been, or been intended to be, so used since before 31 October 1998.

13. As appears from regulation 36(1), the landlord's duty does not extend to a gas appliance which the tenant is entitled to remove, but it does extend to an appliance or pipework serving the premises which is installed in other premises of the landlord, or which is owned by the landlord or is under his or her control.

Contravention

14. Contravention of the Regulations constitutes an offence under the 1974 Act (s33(1)(c)), triable summarily or on indictment, but regulation 39 affords a defence to anyone who can show that he or she took all reasonable steps to prevent a contravention of (inter alia) regulations 30 (to a limited extent), 35 and 36, the only regulations mentioned in regulation 39 which are also mentioned in this Opinion.

Conclusion

15. To sum up, therefore, the Gas Safety (Installation and Use) Regulations 1998 affect church property in the following ways:

(a)   A 'responsible person' could be: (i) the incumbent or priest-in-charge and the PCC in the case of a church; (ii) the PCC in the case of a church hall or other property under the control of the PCC; (iii) the incumbent or priest-in-charge, the Diocesan Parsonages Board or, possibly, the sequestrators in the case of a parsonage house; (iv) the DBF in the case of property used for diocesan purposes; or (v) the Chapter in the case of property used for the purposes of a cathedral.

(b)   An employer or a self-employed person having a place of work under his or her control or having control of work in relation to a gas fitting could have a duty in respect of (i) diocesan offices; (ii) buildings used for the purposes of a cathedral, including the cathedral itself; (iii) churches; and (iv) parsonage houses, including the incumbent or priest-in-charge on the basis that the clergy work for reward.

(c)   In the case of residential property liability for a gas appliance as a 'landlord' could fall on a DBF, a PCC, an incumbent in relation to part of the vicarage, or any other ecclesiastical body executing a lease or a licence.

Duties of landlords

36.(1) In this Regulation –

'landlord' means –

(a) in England and Wales –

    (i) where the relevant premises are occupied under a lease, the person for the time being entitled to the reversion expectant on that lease or who, apart from any statutory tenancy, would be entitled to possession of the premises; and

    (ii) where the relevant premises are occupied under a licence, the licensor, save that where the licensor is himself a tenant in respect of those premises, it means the person referred to in paragraph (i) above;

(b) in Scotland, the person for the time being entitled to the landlord's interest under a lease.

'lease' means –

(a) a lease for a term of less than 7 years; and

(b) a tenancy for a periodic term; and

(c) any statutory tenancy arising out of a lease or tenancy referred to in sub-paragraphs (a) or (b) above

and in determining whether a lease is one which falls within sub-paragraph (a) above –

    (i) in England and Wales, any part of the term which falls before the grant shall be left out of account and the lease shall be treated as a lease for a term commencing with the grant;

    (ii) a lease which is determinable at the option of the lessor before the expiration of 7 years from the commencement of the term shall be treated as a lease for a term of less than 7 years;

    (iii) a lease (other than a lease to which sub-paragraph (b) above applies shall not be treated as a lease for a term of less than 7 years if it confers on the lessee an option for renewal for a term which, together with the original term, amounts to 7 years or more; and

(iv) a 'lease' does not include a mortgage term;

'relevant gas fitting' means –

(a) any gas appliance (other than an appliance which the tenant is entitled to remove from the relevant premises) or any installation pipework installed in any relevant premises; and

(b) any gas appliance or installation pipework which, directly or indirectly, serves the relevant premises and which either –

(i) is installed in any part of premises in which the landlord has an estate or interest; or

(ii) is owned by the landlord or is under his control;

except that it shall not include any gas appliance or installation pipework exclusively used in a part of premises occupied for non-residential purposes.

'relevant premises' means premises or any part of premises occupied, whether exclusively or not, for residential purposes (such occupation being in consideration of money or money's worth) under –

(a) a lease; or

(b) a licence;

'statutory tenancy' means –

(a) in England and Wales, a statutory tenancy within the meaning of the Rent Act 1977 and the Rent (Agriculture) Act 1976; and

(b) in Scotland, a statutory tenancy within the meaning of the Rent (Scotland) Act 1984, a statutory assured tenancy within the meaning of the Housing (Scotland) Act 1988 or a secure tenancy within the meaning of the Housing (Scotland) Act 1987;

'tenant' means a person who occupies relevant premises being –

(a) in England and Wales –

   (i) where the relevant premises are so occupied under a lease, the person for the time being entitled to the term of that lease; and

   (ii) where the relevant premises are so occupied under a licence, the licensee;

(b) in Scotland, the person for the time being entitled to the tenant's interest under a lease.

(October 1996, revised 2003)

Index

Note: the following abbreviations are used in subentries in the index:
APCM   annual parochial church meeting
DBF   diocesan board of finance
PCC   parochial church council